The Wandering Princess

The Wandering Princess

PRINCESS HÉLÈNE *of* FRANCE,
DUCHESS *of* AOSTA
(1871-1951)

EDWARD HANSON

FONTHILL

Dedicated, with much appreciation for their assistance with this project, to:

The Duchess's three grandchildren,
Archduchess Margherita
Princess Maria Cristina
and
Prince Amedeo

and also to
Silvana Casale,
long-time curator of the Fondo Aosta in Naples

Fonthill Media Language Policy

Fonthill Media publishes in the international English language market. One language edition is published worldwide. As there are minor differences in spelling and presentation, especially with regard to American English and British English, a policy is necessary to define which form of English to use. The Fonthill Policy is to use the form of English native to the author. Edward Hanson was born and educated in the United States but prefers to write in British English; therefore British English has been adopted in this publication.

Fonthill Media Limited
Fonthill Media LLC
www.fonthillmedia.com
office@fonthillmedia.com

First published in the United Kingdom and the United States of America 2017

British Library Cataloguing in Publication Data:
A catalogue record for this book is available from the British Library

Preface

Standing over six foot tall (1.85 m) in her prime, Princess Hélène de France, the Duchess of Aosta, was easily recognizable in any group, particularly in the days when the average Italian woman measured about a foot shorter. Most men, indeed, likewise had to look up to her—Mussolini himself was just 1.69 m, while King Victor Emanuel was a mere 1.54 m. Hélène's height was accentuated by her slender figure and such a tiny waist as to draw comment. Neapolitans would affectionately refer to her as *La girafe reale*—the royal giraffe. In her youth, she was renowned as a beauty; when she chose to drape herself with royal jewels for special occasions or official photographs, there was no disputing her regal dignity and poise, which some chose to interpret as pride and haughtiness. However, Hélène was actually more comfortable in simpler garments, most especially the travelling clothes she wore during her many trips to Africa.

In old age, Hélène sat in her small suite of rented rooms in a hotel at Castellamare di Stabia, a far cry from the elegance of the Capodimonte Palace overlooking the fabled Bay of Naples where she had spent much of her life. She described herself as a 'putrification' of her former self, and even her favourite sister Isabelle had to admit that Hélène was now 'very, very diminished, weakened.' Just as her looks had faded, so had the grand international world of royalty in which she had started her life. Although born while her family was in English exile, they had been allowed to return to France within weeks of her birth, and for a time they lived an affluent lifestyle wandering from one of their *châteaux* to another, or to relatives in Spain and their *palacios*. That comfortable lifestyle briefly took on an increased glow when her older sister married the Crown Prince of Portugal, but was immediately crushed when the family was sent into English exile again.

Welcomed back into the court of their cousin Queen Victoria, yet retaining hopes for an eventual restoration of the French monarchy, the family resumed the seasonal moves of the affluent. They continued to winter in Spain and now Portugal as well, but instead of the seasonal migrations to Normandy, Paris, and

Cannes, they now went to London, Worcestershire, and Scotland. Within these new circles, especially the Marlborough Set which surrounded the Prince and Princess of Wales (later King Edward VII and Queen Alexandra), the French cousins held a surprisingly high profile. It was through these connections that young Hélène met and fell in love with Queen Victoria's eldest English grandson. Prince Albert Victor, Duke of Clarence and Avondale, or Eddy as he was known to family and friends, fell in and out of love regularly. At one point, Hélène was the centre of his attention, and he became her first true love. However, problems over religion could not be surmounted; after nearly a year of negotiations, their unofficial engagement was ended.

Later, she married Emanuele Filiberto di Savoia, Duke of Aosta, an Italian prince and second in line to that throne. Especially following their move to Naples, Hélène became known in her new homeland as an indefatigable charity worker, including with the Red Cross during wartime and following volcanic eruptions, earthquakes, and other natural disasters. However, by some, she was also considered an intriguer, ambitious, and scheming on behalf of her husband and sons—who were at some time each suggested for thrones or viceroy positions in Spain, Greece, Hungary, Poland, Croatia, Ethiopia, Trieste, and, most importantly of all, Italy itself. These ambitious thoughts were sometimes supported by her indeed, although never to the extent that public opinion credited, and were generally situations created by others.

As part of the great international royal family tree, Hélène was intimately involved in the tremendous changes from the stability of Victorian times, through two world wars, the end of the Italian monarchy, her nephew's overthrow from the throne of Portugal and her cousin's from the throne of Spain, as well as the downfall of the empires of Russia, Germany and Austria. In and among all these events, Hélène was also a great traveller and big game hunter circling the globe and frequently returning to Africa, originally for reasons of health and escape from the tedium of court life and later for the love of the land. She wrote about and photographed these adventures extensively. In 1921, Hélène published her third major travel book—*La Vie Errante* (*The Wandering Life*). Hélène dedicated that book to what might be considered her motive in life—'To the ideal always pursued, never attained'—which through life leads us from dream to dream to the tomb.

Hélène's life was one of broken expectations. Her one great romance, with Queen Victoria's grandson, was not allowed to flourish because of the difference in religion. When she did marry, it was with the hope of large inheritance from her great-uncle and godfather, the Duc d'Aumale, and the possibility that she and her husband might eventually succeed to the throne of Italy; neither happened. She was an early and ardent supporter of Fascism in Italy, but her hopes for that movement to restore Italy to glory ended in a devastating war. Her marriage was not successful. Even with her two sons, hopeful expectations ended abruptly with their premature deaths. At the end, even the desire to spend her final days in a monarchy was not to be after the 1946 referendum turned Italy into a republic. The only part of her life that never let down her expectations was that which she created for herself—a life travelling, hunting, and photographing in Africa—and a second, secret, marriage.

The starting point for this biography came when I purchased a small collection of postcards at the Olympia Book Fair in London. The dozen or so notes were mainly written by Hélène to her childhood friend Renée Saint Maur, daughter to Camille Dupuy, her parents' private secretary. The cards were sent from France, Italy, and Switzerland, from Egypt and Ethiopia, and even from a hospital ship off the coast of Libya, a first indication to me of the widespread travels and interests of this woman. However, my first awareness of the historical existence of Hélène de France had come years earlier while reading James Pope-Hennessy's impressive biography of Britain's Queen Mary. Mary had shared—although not simultaneously—a fiancé with Hélène: Prince Albert Victor, the Duke of Clarence and Avondale. Hélène ended her unofficial engagement with 'Eddy' and he later became officially engaged to a cousin, Princess Mary of Teck, but died of typhoid shortly afterwards. Pope-Hennessy's striking description of the deathbed scene records the prince's lips turning purple, his hands cold, while his last uttered words included a single name—Hélène. At the time Pope-Hennessy was writing, more than fifty years after the event, there was still a wreath of *immortels* laying on his tomb bearing the name Hélène.

One of the poets whose works stood on her library shelves at Capodimonte was the American John Greenleaf Whittier. His poem 'The Brewing of Soma' took some of its inspiration from the story of the prophet Elijah in the First Book of Kings in the Bible and some from Indian mysticism. Part of it reads:

> *Breathe through the hearts of our desire*
> *Thy coolness and Thy balm;*
> *Let sense be numb, let flesh retire;*
> *Speak through the earthquake, wind, and fire,*
> *O still, small voice of calm!*

While the 'still, small voice of calm' was something that Hélène craved and found in Africa, it was the 'earthquake, wind, and fire' along with warfare that energized her and gave her a purpose. She filled her life with elements from both ends of this spectrum, and still found 'it is so short, life, and one wastes so many days!'[1]

A Note on Names and Titles

Reading a book on royalty of this period can be rather like negotiating one's way through a Russian novel, where characters are known by various names, nicknames and titles. One example is Hélène's younger son—his given name was Aimone, but he was known in the family as 'Bob'; however, his title was Duke of Spoleto from childhood until the death of his older brother, when he became the Duke of Aosta, and he was also briefly known as King Tomislav of Croatia, when the Fascists unsuccessfully placed him upon that puppet throne.

Throughout this book, the main protagonist is named as Hélène, the style that she herself used almost universally. In the early days, she was usually known as Princess Hélène d'Orléans, but she herself later adopted the usage of Hélène de France, indicating rank as the daughter of the head of the House of France (although, technically, this was an incorrect usage as her father was never a reigning sovereign). Nonetheless, it is the one which she usually chose to use for herself and so is employed here. Always proud of her French origins, she sometimes even chose to sign herself as 'France-Savoia-Aosta' without any given name.

Otherwise, the names and titles are usually given in the language of the individual concerned. Hélène's parents are generally called the Comte and Comtesse de Paris, as was the custom of contemporary English newspapers as well. Her husband is called variously Emanuele Filiberto, Emanuele (as she sometimes called him), and very occasionally Manolo (which she also used from time to time), or Nolo (which he would use himself). More formally, and particularly after the breakdown of their marriage, he is called the Duke of Aosta, or simply Aosta. An exception is made in the case of the King of Italy who is usually called Victor Emmanuel, as he was known in the west, while his wife is referred to as Elena, the name she generally used in Italy to differentiate her from Hélène. When the name Vittorio Emanuele is used, it usually refers to Aosta's brother the Count of Turin, known in the family as Toio.

The titles reflect the time period in which particular individuals are mentioned, and that too can be confusing. At one point, from 1942 until her death in 1951, there were three Duchesses of Aosta—Hélène herself (who was called the Duchessa Madre), her daughter-in-law Anne (la Duchessa vedova), and her other daughter-in-law Irene.

A Note on Sources

When Hélène moved out of Capodimonte in 1947, her possessions were divided into two lots—the first and larger portion went to the National Library as the Fondo Aosta, and consists mainly of her library, hunting trophies, and her photographs. These now fill five rooms in the library, which is located in the Royal Palace in Naples. A smaller section—approximately 3,500 books, half belonging to Hélène and half to her second husband Otto Campini—followed them to Hélène's final residence at Castellemare. After her death, Campini took them north, and eventually, they were purchased in 2003 by the Province of Turin and now form the Fondo Campini, housed in the Biblioteca storico in the former family home, the Palazzo Cisterna in Turin. For the purposes of this biography, the most useful parts of that collection are Hélène's unpublished travel journals. Other important documentation utilised here has been retained by her family.

The fate of her incoming correspondence is unknown, but it is known that much of it was burned both before and after her death. Other important potential primary sources—such as the personal correspondence of her father to her mother, that of her brother Philippe and that of Queen Alexandra—were also ordered to be destroyed upon the deaths of the individuals—although numerous letters from Hélène to Philippe and some to other family members survive in the Fonds de la Maison de France in Paris. Many other scattered references can be found, but they are indeed scattered rather than comprehensive.

The digitalization of contemporary newspapers and their availability online has been a great boon for studying this period, and I have made generous use of many of them, especially *The Times* from England; *Le Figaro* from France; and *La Stampa* from Italy. Particularly during the pre-Second World War period, the daily comings and goings of royalty was a staple for these papers and that has helped immensely with developing a chronology of events, while I also recognise the shortcomings of such sources.

Acknowledgements

To Her Majesty The Queen for her gracious permission to use and quote from the Royal Archives at Windsor Castle.

To the Duke of Aosta, grandson of Hélène, who has maintained a constant interest in this project since I first contacted him, as well as my thanks to Duchess Silvia; to Princess Maria Cristina of the Two Sicilies, whose help, hospitality, and interest in this project has been very generous, as well as Prince Casimiro and their children Padre Alessandro and Princess Elena; to Archduchess Margherita of Austria-Este, whose memories and insights have helped tremendously, as well as her son Archduke Martin for his interest in the project; to Prince Michael of Greece, especially for his assistance in obtaining access to the archives of the House of France in Paris.

To Dottoressa Silvana Casale of the Fondo Aosta at the Biblioteca Nazionale, Naples, whose infectious interest in the life of the Duchess has enriched the telling of Hélène's tale and encouraged me along the way; also to her colleagues, especially Lucia Marinelli and Anurak Viradecha for enthusiastically translating for us. To Luigi Magaria of the Fondo Campini, Torino, for allowing me to use uncatalogued material in that collection. To Colonel Maurizio Napoletano, commandant of the Nunziatella in Naples for his warm welcome to the Aosta Museum at the military academy and the use of material there, as well as to his staff, especially Giovanni Calemma and Filomena Colella for their assistance. To Andrea Beretta of the Parco Naturale de la Mandria for the private tour of the Castello de La Mandria where Hélène and Emanuele Filiberto had their first married home.

To the archivists and librarians of the Royal Archives, Windsor, especially Miss Allison Derrett; the Archives nationales, Paris; the Massachusetts Historical Society, Boston; the Biblioteca nationale di Firenze; the Biblioteca nationale di Napoli; Les Archives du Château de Chantilly; The London Library; The British Library; the National Archives (Kew), formerly the Public Record Office; the Parliamentary Archives, Westminster; the Archivio Contemporaneo 'Alessandro

Bonsanti,' Florence; the British Institute library in Florence; the Surrey History Centre, Woking; and the Gloucestershire Record Office.

To the digitalisation projects which have made historical newspapers so widely available, especially *The Times Digital Archives*, *La Stampa: Archivio Storico dal 1867*, and *Gallica: bibliothèque numérique* from the Bibliothèque nationale de France.

To my friends who have helped through practical and moral support over the years, especially the Venerable Vickie Sims and her husband David Tabbat of Milan for help with translations and early readings of the manuscript, and Flora Capostagno of Genova for additional translation assistance. To those other friends who have been also been readers of the early drafts: The Reverend Canon Glyndwr and Anita Jones, Betty Jo Kaveney, Dr Erik Goldstein, Donald M. Nielsen, Richard Page, Ronald Porter, Ted Rosvall, David Tweddle, Victoria Wallop, and Sir David Williams.

Finally to the publishers at Fonthill, especially Alan Sutton, Jay Slater, and Jamie Hardwick, for their appreciated assistance in achieving this publication after a very long research project.

CONTENTS

1

1871–1886

la chère petite Hélène[1]

The people of Paris were starving; their city lay in ruins. The French capital was devastated at the beginning of 1871. While Baron Haussmann had recently and intentionally destroyed many of the streets and buildings of medieval Paris to create the elegant boulevards of Napoléon III's glamourous capital of the Third Empire, the Prussian siege and the subsequent ravages of the Commune ruined much of that new glory. The relatively new medium of photography caught the pathos of the architectural ruin, while reports in the newspapers caught the anguish of the people.

Emperor Napoléon III had surrendered after the Battle of Sedan on 1 September 1870 at the conclusion of the Franco-Prussian War, and the Third Republic was declared. Rejoicing in the streets, however, was brief as Paris was encircled by German troops in a siege that got progressively worse during its four-month duration. Once Versailles surrendered and Paris was completely encircled, the only outgoing communications with the rest of France was through the 'Balloon Post,' an adventurous series of balloon flights including one which airlifted Léon Gambetta, the minister of the interior, out of the city. These were counterbalanced with incoming communications brought by a flight of pigeons carrying microphotographed dispatches into the city. By early October, traditional sources of fresh meat had been exhausted, and Parisian butchers turned to horsemeat, previously the diet of only the poorest citizens.

By mid-November, when the stables and racetracks were empty, signs for 'Feline and Canine Butchers' were seen in the streets of Paris, and later rats joined the diet of the people. Eventually even the zoos opened their cages to provide food for the populace. Apparently, lions and tigers were considered too dangerous to kill and the monkeys were saved by Darwin's explanation of their kinship to mankind, but all other animals were doomed to the cooking pots. One Englishman caught in the Siege reported that he had eaten camel, antelope, dog, donkey, mule, and elephant in that order. However, the supply of red wine in the city seemed inexhaustible and 'never ran out, even when Paris was down to her last rat.'[2]

On 5 January 1871, as the siege deepened with increasing hunger and cold, the Prussian army began a systematic bombardment of central Paris, with three to four hundred shells falling every day. Just three days later, King Wilhelm I of Prussia proclaimed himself Emperor of Germany in the Hall of Mirrors of the Palace of Versailles, where Napoléon III had danced with Queen Victoria only a few years earlier.

By the last week of January, the French Republican Army had been defeated; on the 28th, an armistice was signed. The siege had finally broken the city, and food—most of it from England—was finally able to pour into Paris. On 2 February, *The Times* reported:

> The next fortnight will witness the course and disclose the results of a most awful struggle—a struggle in which the energies of humanity will contend for the mastery with the powers of Famine. Nothing in recent history furnishes any parallel to the possible starvation of Paris. The Irish Famine—to take the example most familiar to ourselves—was long foreseen; it approached slowly, was chronic rather than acute, and never culminated in any great or definite crisis. The Famine of Paris is all crisis. The need is desperate and immediate, though in a certain sense transitory. We have to enable a population of two millions to tide over, say, fourteen days—that is the problem. After that there may but too certainly be suffering, but there will not be danger. All now depends upon despatch.

Meanwhile, the new French president Adolphe Thiers moved both the government and the army to Versailles, but a revolutionary group of insurgents set up the Commune de Paris inside the Hôtel de Ville. It now became a matter of Frenchman against Frenchman, and bombardment of Paris from Versailles began anew. In late May, Republican troops poured into the city through five great holes in the city wall between the Portes de Passy and Saint-Cloud. Savage street battles between the army and the Communards in the *semaine sanglante* took between 20,000 and 25,000 lives, mostly through wholesale executions by the Versailles army—far more deaths than the Reign of Terror in 1793. Atrocities were committed on both side, and the Archbishop of Paris was among those executed by the Commune during that bloody week. The city and its people ended up in tatters. The Tuileries Palace and the medieval Hôtel de Ville were razed to the ground, and much of the city was burned and in ruins. The last of the Communards held out among the gravestones of Père Lachaise Cemetery until 28 May, when the army marched 147 captives out of the graveyard and shot them against the cemetery wall.[3]

Beyond Paris, the parliamentary elections of 8 February 1871 voted 400 royalists into the 645 seats of the National Assembly, including the royal princes the

Duc d'Aumale and the Prince de Joinville who were elected to the Chamber of Deputies. On 8 June, the National Assembly voted to validate those elections by a vote of 448 to 113; and on the same day, the Assembly voted 472 to 97 to revoke the 1832 and 1848 laws of exile against the royal family. The Duc d'Aumale was elected as deputy from l'Oise with the platform: 'I do not oppose the Republic if there is a majority which accepts it.'[4]

Among the very few who benefited from the turmoil in Paris was the extended family of the Comte de Paris, the many descendants of King Louis Philippe, when the Law of Exile against them was lifted. Four days later, President Adolphe Thiers gave a dinner at Versailles in honour of the Prince de Joinville, the Duc d'Aumale and the Duc de Chartres, the sons and grandson of the late king. The *Soir* reported that the Prince de Joinville would proceed to the Château de Randan, while the Duc d'Aumale would shortly leave for Twickenham to be present at the accouchement of the Countess of Paris.[5]

There was also a great divide among royalists, between the Legitimists—who supported the Comte de Chambord—and the Orléanists—who supported the Comte de Paris. Fifty-year-old Henri, Comte de Chambord, was the grandson of King Charles X, who had been forced to abdicate in 1830 to be succeeded only momentarily by his son Louis, the Duc d'Angoulême (who was married to his cousin Marie Thérèse, the only surviving child of Louis XVI and Marie Antoinette). Angoulême in turn renounced his rights in favour of his nine-year-old nephew, the Comte de Chambord, who had to flee the country within the month. Instead, Louis Philippe of the younger Orléans line was elected 'King of the French.' The new king was the son of the previous Louis Philippe, Duc d'Orléans, who had taken the name Philippe Egalité during the Revolution which he supported. He had been a delegate from Paris in the National Convention and voted for the execution of his cousin the King, but, as a member of the House of Bourbon, was himself guillotined in 1793. 'There had been various attempts at "fusion" between the two lines of the dynasty since Louis-Philippe's death in 1850; but they had repeatedly failed due to personal animosities and the inability to compose ideological differences.' If the two royalist parties had been able to join together at this time by having the childless Chambord come to the throne with the younger Paris waiting in the wings as heir, the monarchy might well have been re-established at this time. However, it would be two years before Paris formally acknowledged Chambord as head of the house with a visit to his Château de Frohsdorf in Austria; by that time, the opportunity was lost. 'A royal house divided against itself, a national defeat and the prospects of a humiliating peace, a restless urban population and the absence of an effective police force to back up the decisions of the Assembly: these were the portents which the royalists had to consider in February 1871. They were after all Frenchmen first and royalists second, and they came to the conclusion that a restoration was impossible under the circumstances.'[6] On 18 February, the National Assembly voted Adolphe Thiers as

'Chief of the Executive Power of the French Republic.' Originally intended as a transitional government, the Third Republic would indeed become the permanent form of governance.

In early February 1871, in London, relief work for the benefit of the people of Paris had been planned and was to be initiated at a large public meeting in the Egyptian Hall of the Mansion House. The Lord Mayor gathered together the Governor of the Bank of England, the bishops of London, Winchester and Gloucester, Cardinal Manning, the Dean of St Paul's Cathedral, Alfred de Rothschild, the head of Barings Bank, and many others of influence. The Comtesse de Paris, as head of the Ladies' Committee, intended to be present but was prevented by family mourning due to the recent death of a cousin.

Isabelle, the Comtesse de Paris, at age twenty-two, was already in the second trimester of her third pregnancy. Born in Spain of a French father and Spanish mother, married to a first cousin, who was half French and half German, and now living in exile in England, Isabelle epitomised the peripatetic life style of nineteenth-century royals, particularly those from deposed dynasties. She was now living in the London suburb of Twickenham, where her first two children had been born—a daughter Amélie in 1865 and a son Philippe in 1869.

Princess Hélène Louise Henriette d'Orléans was born at York House, Twickenham, on Tuesday, 13 June at 6 p.m.[7] She was baptised the next day with her great-uncle Henri, the Duc d'Aumale, and her aunt, Françoise, the Duchesse de Chartres, serving as godparents.[8] Among the first telegrams which the Comte de Paris sent to announce the birth was one to Queen Victoria at Balmoral. He wrote to her at greater length a few days later, appreciating the Queen's interest in the news—not only of the child's birth, but more so for the dramatic changes in Paris, especially the lifting of the law of exile. Paris wrote that he would soon go to France himself and return a few days later to take the Comtesse and the children, and he also acknowledged the debt that he owed England and the Queen for '*toutes les bontés*' shown to the family during their long exile in Great Britain.[9] Queen Victoria responded that she was delighted that '*la chère petite* Hélène' was given the name of the Comte's mother, the late Duchesse d'Orléans, who was a cousin of Prince Albert. She also well understood his emotions caused by all the events in Paris, 'but I fear that the state will be very uncertain for a long time.' Before closing, Queen Victoria also mentioned her regrets in learning of the death of the Comte's '*excellente Grand-Mère*' the Hereditary Grand Duchess of Mecklenburg.[10]

The French and British royal families were very different—both in style and in substance—yet they were drawn together by family ties unusual between the Protestant and Catholic houses of Europe. Among these connections, the French King Louis Philippe's eldest son and heir, the Duc d'Orléans, was married to Prince Albert's cousin Hélène of Mecklenburg-Schwerin. This latter relationship was close enough for Queen Victoria to name their third daughter after the

Duchesse d'Orléans, who stood as young Helena's godmother, and Victoria never tired of reminding the Comte that it was through his German Protestant mother that they were connected.[11] However, his identity was dominated by the Roman Catholic Orléans dynasty of France. These were the descendants of Louis Philippe and Marie Amélie, who were grandparents to both the Comte and Comtesse de Paris and who had reigned as King and Queen of the French from 1830 to 1848 before going into a final exile in England.

Louis Philippe and Marie Amélie had six sons—Ferdinand, duc d'Orléans (father of the Comte de Paris); Louis, duc de Nemours (who married Victoria of Saxe-Coburg, a favourite cousin of Queen Victoria); François, Prince de Joinville (who married a daughter of the Emperor of Brazil); Charles, duc de Penthièvre (who died in childhood); Henri, duc d'Aumale (who was to become the most prominent member of the family); and Antoine, duc de Montpensier (husband of the Infanta Luisa Fernanda of Spain and father of the Comtesse de Paris). The daughters of the family included Louise Marie (married to Queen Victoria's uncle and mentor King Leopold of the Belgians); Marie (who married Duke Alexander of Württemberg, who was also a cousin of Queen Victoria through the Coburgs); Françoise (who died at the age of two); and Clémentine (who had her own intriguing role in the family and was the wife of yet another Coburg, Duke August, and mother of the future King Ferdinand of Bulgaria).

Hélène's father—Philippe, the Comte de Paris—was thirty-two years old at this time and had spent most of his life in exile from France. He was only nine years old in 1848 when his grandfather, King Louis Philippe, abdicated. As his own father had died in a carriage accident in 1842, young Philippe, as the elder son of the eldest son, was theoretically king momentarily from the abdication until the declaration of the Second Republic. In a dramatic move, his mother brought him before the *Chambre des Deputés* in a valiant but vain attempt to continue the monarchy. When the family went into exile, his mother returned to live primarily in Germany and with long stays in England, but died at Richmond in 1857 following an attack of influenza at the age of forty-four. Although his main identity was as an Orléans, the Comte de Paris physically favoured the German side of his family. There is an unkind remark about the Comte attributed to President Thiers of France in 1871 that 'from a distance he is a German, from close up a zero.' An even less kind version, attributed to General Blowitz, goes 'from a distance, one would say a Prussian; from close up, an imbecile.' Along the same vein, the French statesman Léon Say wrote: 'He has the qualities of a German professor; not those of a French prince.[12]

After his mother's death, Paris was raised by his paternal grandparents at Claremont, their British home in exile. This Palladian mansion near Esher in Surrey had been built for his own use by Sir John Vanbrugh—the architect of Castle Howard and Blenheim Palace. In 1816 the British nation had purchased it as a wedding gift for Princess Charlotte, the only daughter of the Prince Regent, and her husband, Prince Leopold of Saxe-Coburg-Gotha. After Charlotte died in childbirth, Leopold retained the house as his home until he was elected as King of the Belgians and married Princess Louise, the eldest daughter of King Louis Philippe, and he was able to loan it to his in-laws when they needed a new residence in England.

The Law of Exile that had expelled the Orléans dynasty from France also barred the young princes from serving in the French military. To follow the family's traditions within the armed forces, they had to look elsewhere, and so Paris and his brother, Robert, Duc de Chartres, volunteered to fight with the Union Army during the American Civil War. In 1861, they went to America with their uncle the Prince de Joinville, entered the Federal Army, and served as aides-de-camp to General McClellan during the Peninsular campaign, and were present at the siege and capture of Yorktown, and saw action at Williamsburg and Gaine's Hill. Paris returned to England in 1863, and throughout Hélène's childhood, he worked on a massive six-volume *History of the War of Secession*. When the final two volumes were published in Paris in 1883, the London *Times* announced that 'it is well known with what scrupulous care the illustrious historian of this formidable conflict has collated documents and facts, and with what insight he has judged men and events. His work has met in America with a very warm welcome, and there, as everywhere else, has been pronounced to be of lasting merit.'[13]

When the two brothers reached marriageable age, they discovered that as dispossessed and exiled royalty—especially from what some considered to be a usurper dynasty—they were not considered suitable partners for princesses of any of the reigning houses. Their solution was to marry within the family, and each married a first cousin. Chartres married Françoise, daughter of their uncle the Prince de Joinville, in 1863; the next year, Paris married Isabelle, the eldest daughter of another uncle the Duc de Montpensier. Although the Orléans gene pool has widened through Paris's German mother, it now seriously contracted through this intermarriage on top of those of earlier generations. As a result, their children were descendants of King Carlos III of Spain (1716-1788)—just five generations back—in eight different ways. The family tree was both complicated and very repetitive.

Hélène's mother—Isabelle, the Comtesse de Paris—was only fifteen when she married the Comte, while her own mother, the Spanish Infanta Luisa had herself been a fourteen-year-old bride. About five weeks after their wedding, the new Comte and Comtesse de Paris went to Windsor Castle to visit Queen Victoria, who wrote in her journal that she found Isabelle 'very nice, excessively reasonable & sensible, like a girl of eighteen or nineteen, instead of not quite sixteen!' and declared that she was 'much pleased with the young couple, who seem very happy.'[14]

Hélène's maternal grandparents, Antoine, the Duc de Montpensier, and his wife the Infanta Luisa Fernanda, sister of Queen Isabel of Spain, were part of the great diplomatic game following the War of the Spanish Succession known as the question of the 'Spanish Marriages,' with the great powers of Britain, France, and Austria deciding who the queen and her sister might marry. The only compromise acceptable to them all was that the queen would marry her first cousin Don Francisco de Asis, while the Infanta Luisa Fernanda was married to Montpensier. There were a great many problems in the resultant family. Queen Isabel had an unsatisfactory marriage and turned to a series of lovers who are thought to have fathered most of her children. Although kind-hearted and generous by nature, she was no more responsible in politics than she was in the marital bed; in 1866, a military plot planned to overthrow her. The attempted coup by General Juan Prim failed, and he was sent into exile in France, where he was financially assisted in his continuing machinations by the Duc de Montpensier, who hoped to gain the throne for himself and his wife. When this was discovered, the Montpensiers were likewise sent into exile, for them to Portugal. A further military uprising in September 1868 did indeed topple Isabel from the throne, and she and her children also became exiles in France, although the Montpensiers at this point were allowed to return from Portugal. However, Queen Isabel's brother-in-law, Enrique, the Duke of Seville, in an open letter to the Regent Francesco Serrano which was widely reported in the press, warned that he would gladly shed his last drop to blood to prevent Montpensier from ever becoming king or regent and referred to him as simply 'a puffed-up French pastrycook.' Montpensier challenged him to a duel, and killed the Duke on an artillery ground near Madrid on 12 March 1871, for which he was court-martialled and banished from Madrid for a month.[15]

The vacant Spanish throne was filled not by Montpensier, but by an elected king, twenty-five-year-old Amedeo, Duke of Aosta, the second son of King Victor Emmanuel of Italy. He arrived in Madrid in January 1871 with his wife Maria Victoria and their two young sons Emanuele Filiberto and Vittorio Emanuele. However, military and political struggles continued in Spain and distanced the new king from any kind of real role, so in February 1873, he abdicated and the family—which now included baby Luigi, just a fortnight old—returned to Italy. A year later, Queen Isabel's son was declared King Alfonso XII, and the Bourbon monarchy was restored.

Although this would all change very quickly after Hélène's birth, at the beginning of 1871 most of her family lived in the western suburbs of London, in a series of houses on or near the Thames. Ever since King Louis Philippe had arrived in England during one of his early exiles and settled at High Shot House in Twickenham, 'dear quiet Twick'—as he called the town—had been a centre for the Orléans family and would remain so for generations. York House, where Hélène was born, is on the banks of the Thames near the parish church of St Mary, and its oldest parts date back to the 1630s. Originally the home of a courtier of King Charles I, the house passed through a number of hands including Henry Hyde, 2nd Earl of Clarendon (uncle to Queen Mary II and Queen Anne), Prince

Starhemberg (the Austrian ambassador), and the linguist Sir Alexander Johnstone (a founder of the Royal Asiatic Society). In 1864, it was acquired for the Comte de Paris and would remain in the family off and on until 1906.[16] The 1871 census provides a snapshot of the household just before Hélène's birth. It consisted of the Comte and Comtesse and their two older children, plus a lady-in-waiting, the administrator of the Paris household, and a visiting French Army captain. The servants included the French cook and under-cook (both men), two French lady's maids, and one French nursery maid, although the rest of the servants were all English—two more nursery maids, a footman, under-footman-cum-post boy, three housemaids, and a kitchen maid; two grooms lived in the stables and the gardener and his family lived in the lodge.

Further along the river was Orleans House, which King Louis Philippe had leased from 1815 to 1817 and where his son the Duc d'Aumale later lived. Also in Twickenham, the Prince de Joinville, the king's third son, lived at Mount Lebanon House. Across the river, the Duc de Chartres and his family lived in Morgan House on Ham Common, while the Duc de Nemours lived not far away in Bushey House. Despite all the excitement and confusion about returning to France permanently, the French princes planned to keep their English homes available.

When the men of the French royal family did return to France, the Comte de Paris was received in the capital by Adolphe Thiers, president of the Republic, on 1 July, and the next day, the Comte de Chambord arrived in Paris under an assumed name. A few days later, Chambord foolishly issued the 'White Flag Manifesto' declaring that his own banner of the golden lily on a white field—'the banner of Henri IV, Francis I, and Joan of Arc' as he called it—must replace the tricolour as the national flag before he would accept the crown. This manifesto was published in the newspapers on the 7th, just as Chambord was leaving the country again. The flag was not accepted, the crown was not offered, and the Comte returned to his exile in Austria. Due to the fundamental lack of understanding on Chambord's part of the new sense of nationhood, it was in essence the end of his role as a viable pretender to the throne although he steadfastly refused to abdicate his claims which would have opened a real opportunity for the Comte de Paris at the time.[17]

The Comte de Paris returned to Twickenham and found the Comtesse 'as well as possible' although, because of the fatigue of childbirth, her doctors recommended ten days or so at the seaside at Folkestone. Philippe and Isabelle returned from the coast to Twickenham a few days earlier than anticipated, leaving the children at Folkestone while they made their final preparations to leave for France. Then, on 4 August, the Comte and Comtesse made the crossing to France together with their children. The ruins of the Tuileries Palace would become the first Parisian memory of five-year-old Amélie. The family spent the first few days at the home of the Comte de Ségur, and then many months at the *hôtel particulier* of Monsieur de Villeneuve, which was one of the great private mansions on the rue de Messine in the eighth arrondissement.[18]

At the end of this eventful year, on 9 December, the Confiscation Act was overturned, and former royal properties were returned to fifty-two descendants of Louis Philippe. In the division, the Comte de Paris received the Châteaux d'Eu, d'Amboise, and de Randan. The family spent the winter of 1872 in Paris at the home of the duc d'Aumale, who had purchased the hôtel Fould on the rue du Faubourg-Saint-Honoré and turned over the first floor to the Paris family.[19] Between the capital, Eu, and Dinard in Brittany for summer holidays, a new pattern for the family's life quickly developed.

For centuries, Eu, a small town on the northern coast of Normandy, was best remembered as the place where Duke William (the Conqueror, the Bastard) married Matilda of Flanders in 1050. The original fortress there was destroyed four hundred years later upon orders of Louis IX, fearing its capture by the English. The current château was started in 1578 after the marriage of Henri, duc de Guise, with Catherine de Clèves, the comtesse d'Eu. A later owner, 'La Grande Mademoiselle,' Anne-Marie d'Orléans, the Duchess of Montpensier, one of the wealthiest people in France and a niece of Louis XIII, purchased the comté d'Eu, including the château in 1660. When Louis Philippe inherited the estate from his mother, he began extensive renovations to the buildings. Over the years of his reign, it became the scene of some notable events, none more memorable than the two visits of Queen Victoria and Prince Albert in 1843 (her first trip abroad) and 1845.

In 1874, the Comte de Paris began his own renovations of the château under the direction of the architect Eugène Viollet-le-Duc, who had established his reputation as restorer of the town of Carcassonne as well as the Cathedral of Notre Dame in Paris. Gas lighting was installed along with central heating and new bathrooms, while the kitchens were returned to the palace from the outbuildings where they had previously been re-located. Viollet-le-Duc was also responsible for restoring the Collegial Church of St Laurence O'Toole, just steps away from the château. O'Toole had been archbishop of Dublin but was remembered locally because he died at Eu in 1180.

After their return to France, the Comte and his family continued to maintain their connections with the British royal family. Bertie and Alix, the Prince and Princess of Wales, visited Paris in March 1872, and they lunched with the Comte and Comtesse, together with the Prince and Princess de Joinville, the Duc d'Aumale, and the Duc de Nemours.

On 24 May 1873, Marshal Patrice de MacMahon became president of the Third Republic. He was the hero of the Battle of Magenta in Lombardy, in honour of which he was created a duke with that title, a descendant of an old Irish family which had taken refuge in France with the exiled King James II, and most importantly for the Comte de Paris, a devoted royalist. However, the monarchist peak of power had already been reached, and republicans and

Bonapartists increasingly gained strength in the Assembly. With Thiers's power waning with the strengthening of the left, the Duc d'Aumale had briefly been promoted as a possible president, but when Thiers resigned, he was replaced by Marshal MacMahon.

As a reaction to the weakening royalist majority and in a final bid to achieve fusion between the two branches of the royal family, on 5 August 1873, the Comte de Paris went to Austria to visit the Comte de Chambord at his home in Frohsdorf and acknowledge him as the head of the House of France. After some initial disagreement about the real purpose of this visit, the Comte de Paris issued a statement:

> I make this visit, long one of my wishes, in my name and in the name of all the members of my family; I present my respectful homage, not only to the Head of our Family, but to the representative of the monarchical principle in France. I hope the day shall come when France understands that her salvation lies in this principle; and if she ever expresses her will to restore the monarchy, there will be no competitors to the throne in my family.[20]

Paris's statement caused some dissent among his own Orléanist supporters but in general brought some new vigour to the royalist cause in France. However, Chambord's intransigence on keeping his white flag killed any new initiative.

The Comte and Comtesse were in England in February 1874 and visited Queen Victoria at Windsor. She recorded in her journal that 'Paris & Isabelle (who came over a week ago from Paris) & Robert Chartres came to luncheon, as did also Lenchen & Christian [her daughter Princess Helena and her husband]. They looked well & were very amiable but did not talk much of politics. They remained till past three & then left. They have come to pack up their things. Eu (strange to say) now belongs to Paris. It was to have been Nemours.'[21] Later in the year, the Prince of Wales, accompanied by the Comte de Paris, the Duc de Montpensier, and the Duc de Chartres, left Paris for Chantilly. Marshal MacMahon also spent the day at Chantilly and took part in the *battue*. The Duc d'Aumale gave a grand dinner, followed the next day by a stag hunt.

On 21 January 1875, the Comtesse de Paris gave birth in the capital to her first French-born child, young Prince Charles. The little boy suffered what they thought was a mild case of measles in May, but his mother was worried about an adverse reaction to vaccination and some continuing stomach trouble.[22] The family had been staying at Chantilly, but the Comte and Comtesse took Charles to Paris where it was hoped that a change of air would benefit him and at first that proved the case. However, one evening when they took him for a carriage ride toward the Bois de Boulogne, little Charles was taken by a convulsion and was no longer breathing by the time they got back to the faubourg Saint-Honoré where they were staying. After a funeral mass at Neuilly, they took the tiny body to the family chapel at Dreux.

The chapelle royale de St Louis at Dreux had become a royal burial chapel in 1783, when the Duc de Penthièvre received the comté de Dreux from his cousin Louis XVI in exchange for Rambouillet. At that time, Penthièvre had the coffins of his family members moved from Rambouillet to Dreux, but those graves had all been violated and destroyed during the Revolution. Dreux and its chapel later passed into the Orléans branch of the family; upon the death of Louis Philippe's young daughter Françoise in 1818, it became the primary burial place for the dynasty.

The year after little Prince Charles was buried at Dreux, other members of the family were moved from their burial place in England to join him there. For about three years, the Comte de Paris and other members of the family had discussed the possibility of moving the coffins of his grandparents King Louis Philippe and Queen Amélie; his mother, the Duchesse d'Orléans; his aunt, the Duchesse d'Aumale; his cousin, the Prince de Condé; and a number of small infants from their tombs in the little church at Weybridge in Surrey back to France. Only the Duc de Nemours asked that the remains of his wife, Victoria of Saxe-Coburg, stay in England.

The Comte de Paris accompanied the coffins across the Channel to Honfleur and then by train to Paris, where he was joined by the Comtesse and a number of family members for the final leg of the journey, arriving at Dreux at 7 a.m. of 9 June. An hour later, six hearses, each drawn by four horses, took the coffins to the chapel through persistent rain, which rendered 'gloomier than ever the already gloomy aspect of the whole place.' An English reporter from *The Times* wrote of the long service, with its 'monotonous chanting and the grating of the bass viol in the responses being occasionally broken by very sweet music from the organ' before the coffins were taken down into the vault.[23]

The coffin of the Duchesse d'Orléans, as a Protestant, had been placed separately in the tower. Although the reporter from *The Times* assumed that this was awaiting a second religious service, the Comte de Paris wrote to Queen Victoria about the event he said that it was not the custom of those of the Augsburg confession to have any religious service attached to the moving of bodies. The body of his mother, he wrote to the Queen, was temporarily placed in a special room in the chapel awaiting the preparation of a vault where she would be placed 'as close as possible to my father respecting the conditions imposed by their difference in worship.'[24] The eventual result of this separation is perhaps the most poignant funeral monument in the chapel today, a full-length effigy of the Duchess in a separate chapel with her right arm extending towards her husband's effigy nearby, almost but not quite touching his hand.

Although the Comte was indeed half-German through his mother, he marginalized this connection as much as possible. Even when he sought to 'reknit family relations' with the Prussian royal family following the Franco-Prussian War, he did this through Queen Victoria and her eldest daughter.[25] The British connection was far more important to the Orléans family, even after they returned to live in France. In the summer of 1877, for example, the Comte and Comtesse went to stay at Strawberry Hill, the Gothic-revival house built by Horace Walpole at Twickenham and now the home of Lord Carlington and his wife, Frances, Countess Waldegrave, who was a long-time supporter of the Comte. They were at Windsor Park to attend Queen Victoria's review of the Army Corps, at the State Ball at Buckingham Palace, and a garden party at Marlborough House.

To the delight—yet surprise—of all, Mercedes, the youngest sister of the Comtesse, became engaged to their first cousin, King Alfonso XII of Spain. The family discord of previous years was forgiven if not forgotten by all except Queen Isabel who boycotted the wedding. The Comte and Comtesse de Paris travelled to Madrid to join the rest of the family for the wedding on 23 January 1878, but less than six months later, the joy had turned to ashes when Mercedes died suddenly on 26 June—two days after her eighteenth birthday—from complications following a miscarriage and resultant blood poisoning, although the cause was officially given as typhoid. 'What a contrast to our last visit here! Can one ever again be gay?' wrote the King's sister, the Infanta Maria de la Paz. She recorded in her diary when the Duke and Duchess of Montpensier arrived with their daughter the Comtesse of Paris and their son Antonio. 'One could see how very hard on our poor Aunt Luisa was this visit to Aranjuez, the place where she had been with Mercedes such a short time before the wedding.'[26]

In the months between her sister's wedding and funeral, the Comtesse had given birth to another daughter, Isabelle, at the Château d'Eu on 7 May 1878. The nature of life in France for the Comte and Comtesse and their children was remembered by Mrs Ella Priestley, wife of Dr (later Sir) William Priestley, a well-known obstetrician who had been physician-accoucheur for the Comtesse when Amélie was born and had also performed the same duties for two of Queen Victoria's daughters. The Priestleys first visited the Paris family at the Villa Julie in Cannes, where the Comtesse asked Mrs Priestley about the English attitude towards French politics. Later, after luncheon, they strolled in the garden, 'where the Comte gathered a bouquet of camellias and anemones for me while I hunted about with the two young princesses for trap-door spiders' nests, which they had not heard of before.' The Priestleys returned at 4 p.m. for a tea party, where the chief guest was the composer Charles Gounod. The Comtesse sang a duet with another young guest, accompanied by Gounod on the piano, after which he continued to play the accompaniment while his daughter sang.

At Easter in 1880, the Priestleys visited the family again, this time at the Château d'Eu, and Mrs Priestley was charmed by the simple domesticity there alongside the pervasive mourning for Queen Mercedes, including in the children's bedrooms where the visitors 'noticed over every bed a portrait of the unfortunate Queen Mercedes, with a bit of her wedding cake and orange blossom enclosed under the glass.' After dinner, the Comtesse de Paris would take her daughters to her own bedroom for quiet reading and prayers, after which they returned to the sitting room where Mrs Priestley would teach Amélie and Hélène how to make tam o'shanters for their dolls until bedtime.[27]

The death of their baby brother Charles in 1875 left a gap in the family which consolidated the oldest three children—Amélie, Philippe, and Hélène—into their own close cohort of siblings, the older children. Years later, Hélène would remember their little pranks together at Eu, reminding Amélie of 'the toilet where you hid the *foie gras* that you and Philippe, after emptying the terrine, generously offered me the remains which had turned green!' When visiting their grandparents in Spain, one day the girls decided to ride a white donkey around the farm without either bridle or saddle. The resultant tumble left Amélie bruised but amused. Hélène then turned towards the coast, of which she wrote: 'I have always loved ports. While still a child, in Normandy, at Tréport, I would go on the quays among the seafaring people. And I would stay there, fascinated, near the boats, intoxicated by the heady scents of the rope, the smell of old fish, of tar. When they arrived, these wonderful fishermen, I would want to climb aboard these rustic barques, to leave with them for distant countries which I imagined were dangerous and beautiful....A port always gave me hope, the hope of something new and something better. It is a door opened upon a dream.'[28]

The girls shared a study room and received some of their tuition from the Sisters of Providence, who awarded Hélène prizes in religious instruction and handwriting in 1880. Hélène had not previously excelled in the classroom; when she was seven, her father wrote a chastising little note saying he had heard she had been lazy and worked very little. He hoped that she would change and that he would receive a more satisfying account of her work. She must have made the effort as her father soon complemented her upon receiving a letter that was 'clean and well written,' although in the future there would be more complaints about both her handwriting and spelling.[29]

The Comtesse de Paris gave birth to her sixth child, Jacques, at the Château d'Eu in April 1880, but he died suddenly at Eu when he was only nine months old. The Duchesse de Chartres, her sister-in-law, wrote to a family friend in England that 'the Comtesse de Paris has lost through convulsion in teething her youngest child a beautiful little boy of ten months; she had nursed him herself and was passionately fond of him.'[30] The little prince was buried with his brother Charles and the other family members in the family chapel.

After the death of Prince Jacques in 1881, the Comtesse went to stay with the Duc de Chartres and his family in Cannes. She liked the environment so much that the Comte purchased the Villa St Jean, which was formerly owned by the Comtesse de Chapponnay and was where Mérimée wrote *Lettres à une inconnue*. The house was described as 'a modest dwelling, differing in no way from the other houses in Cannes, standing in a pretty green enclosure, wherein grew some fine palm trees and mimosas, and roses flowered in great abundance.' There, they lived a family life, frequently seeing the Duc and Duchesse de Chartres, and their cousins the Comte and Comtesse de Caserta, or receiving visiting foreign princes who regularly passed through the Riviera. The Duc de Vallombrosa, who was called 'the King of Cannes,' his wife, and their daughters were also frequent visitors, and Amélie, Philippe and Hélène were said to be particularly fond of visiting the Duchesse de Luynes and her children at the Villa Luynes.[31] The Comte greatly enlarged the place by building a second house next to the first. However, when it came time for Princess Louise to be born on 24 February 1882, the birth took place at the Grand Hotel, where they had moved on doctors' advice that the Villa was too recently built.

While they wintered at Cannes, they had visits from the Prince of Wales, as well as Aunt Clémentine and her sons. Before long, the family returned to Normandy, where Hélène made her first Communion at Eu, as her sister Amélie and brother Philippe had done before her.[32]

In 1877, the Comte and Comtesse had visited the Alsatian settlements in Algiers, and there is a story that in 1883 the Comte de Paris planned to move his family to Africa—to the south of the conquered zone. There was indeed real concern within the family and among their supporters that year that legislation then before the Chamber of Deputies and the Senate would once again force the Orléans princes into exile. From their Villa St Jean at Cannes, the Comtesse lamented to her friend Marthe, Vicomtesse Vigier: 'Where and when will we see each other again? God only knows … It would be very hard to leave France again! where we returned with such great happiness and hope for the future and to take up again the sad life of exile.'[33]

In the event, the legislation failed, and matters changed completely when the Comte de Chambord died at Frohsdorf, and Paris became head of the house and unchallenged head of the family. Although only sixty-two years old, the Comte de Chambord had been in increasingly poor health for some time. He had injured his leg earlier in the year, and his obesity limited his movement so that he spent more time in bed or on a chaise longue. During the spring, he regained some mobility, but by mid-June, stomach and digestive problems began to plague him to the point of his declaring 'I am lost.'[34]

In early July—almost exactly ten years after his earlier visit to Frohsdorf—the Comte de Paris, along with his uncle the Duc de Nemours and Nemours's son the Duc d'Alençon, again journeyed to Austria. They stopped in Vienna, visiting with Aunt Clémentine's family at the Coburg Palace, while they sent an emissary to Frohsdorf to see if a visit would be acceptable. Despite his doctor's advice to the contrary, the Comte de Chambord did decide to receive the Orléans princes.

The Comtesse de Chambord met the princes with great friendliness in the Red Salon at Frohsdorf, which was filled with the portraits of kings and princes of the Bourbon dynasty and was near the Grey Salon which had been transformed into the bedroom of the ailing Chambord. When they entered that room, Chambord stood and embraced the Comte de Paris, Nemours, and Alençon in turn, before sitting down again, tightly holding Paris's hand in his own. For ten minutes Chambord asked about news of the family and the visiting princes are said to have been moved nearly to tears. When the Comtesse de Chambord saw that her husband was tiring, she made a sign for the visitors to rise. Chambord embraced them once again before they left.[35]

It was no surprise to hear a few weeks later that Chambord had died. The Comte de Paris, Nemours, and Alençon returned to Frohsdorf once again, this time dressed in deep mourning. The Portrait Salon was now transformed into a mortuary chapel, and the princes prayed at the side of the coffin, above which stood Chambord's precious white flag. The Comtesse was said to be suffering from 'severe indisposition' and did not meet with them before they returned to Vienna for the evening. While they were waiting in the city, the Emperor Franz Josef paid a visit to the Comte de Paris at his hotel; when the Comte returned the visit, he received military honours at the palace which indicated a change in his rank. However, then word came from Frohsdorf that the Comtesse de Chambord had decided that precedence at the funeral would be given to the Comte's closest relatives rather than to the new head of the House of France. According to the official explanation, by giving the role of chief mourner to her nephew Don Carlos, the Duke of Madrid (who was married to Chambord's own niece), the Comtesse would keep this as a private family affair, rather than creating a state occasion.

The Comte de Paris then decided neither he nor any of his family would attend the funeral. The Legitimist newspapers endorsed the decision not to attend, publicly stating that it was generous of him not to claim precedence at this time over the nearer relatives and the ex-Duke of Parma and ex-Grand Duke of Tuscany, who were also to attend. The Archduke Louis Victor, who was to have represented his brother the Emperor at the funeral, also withdrew his intention to attend. However, the Orléanist newspapers were more accurate in reporting that the Comte de Paris and his relatives would boycott the funeral as he could not, should not, and would not yield precedence to Spanish or Italian princes at the funeral of the head of the House of France. Meanwhile, the Comtesse de Paris with her daughters Amélie and Hélène, along with her parents and brother, attended a quiet memorial service for Chambord at Eu, and the Comte returned to Paris, where he met the King of Spain who was himself a Bourbon from yet a different line of descent. Despite the brouhaha of the funeral, the Comte de Paris was now generally accepted as the Head of the House of France.

Perhaps the best comment on the situation came from London at the end of the year. Visitors at Madame Tussaud's exhibition hall were particularly attracted to two new displays—that of Hicks Pasha, Baker Pasha, and General Sir Evelyn Wood, 'the commander of the ill-fated Soudan expedition', and nearby, the Comte de Chambord, the Comte de Paris, and the Duc de Nemours, all in lifeless wax.

In January 1884, the Comtesse went south to spend part of the winter with her father at Sanlúcar de Barrameda in Andalusia. By the end of the month, the children went on ahead to Cannes before their parents. However, even for deposed royalty, political tensions continued, including the threat of violence; before the Comte himself left Paris, a suspicious package addressed to him and disguised as a commission of silks, ironmongery, and samples was discovered to be a box of dynamite.

During the previous few years, Cannes had become a popular winter resort for royalty and nobility from across Europe. Among them this winter was Queen Victoria's youngest son, Prince Leopold, the Duke of Albany, who suffered from hemophilia and was sent to Cannes to escape the rigours of an English winter. However, the thirty-year-old prince slipped on a staircase which brought about a brain hemorrhage from which he died on 28 March. The Comte and Comtesse were among the few who were invited to attend the memorial service at the Villa Nevada before the Prince of Wales took his brother's coffin home to England. The Paris family remained at Cannes until early May when they returned to Eu.

One day in September 1884, the Comtesse set off from the Château d'Eu with the Comte at 9 a.m. for a day of shooting—one of her greatest pleasures in life. 'After beating hills and valleys, they did not get back till four, and the same day at half-past six Prince Ferdinand was born.' 'Mamma goes hunting three days out of four,' said the young Princess Amélie. Ferdinand, the youngest child in the Paris family, was christened at Eu the next month with thirteen-year-old Hélène holding him as proxy for the godmother, the Infanta Isabella.[36]

The French, Danish, British, Russian, and Belgian royal families, as well as various German houses, gathered at the Château d'Eu for the October 1885 wedding of Hélène's cousin Princess Marie d'Orléans, daughter of the Duc and Duchesse de Chartres, with Prince Valdemar of Denmark, the youngest brother of the Princess of Wales and the Empress of Russia.

On the evening before the religious services, the Comte de Paris—wearing the Danish Order of the Elephant, which he received that morning—hosted a grand reception for the forty princes and princesses along with 170 other guests in the Galerie des Guises: the mosaic-floored, oak-and-gold-paneled gallery lined with portraits of the original owners of the château. The correspondent for *The Times* reported back to London on the 'imposing spectacle to see the children of the great crowned heads of Europe received by the head of the House of Orléans, now the head of the House of Bourbon' and hearing the Comtesse *tutoyer* the Princess of Wales as a dear and intimate friend.

An earlier civil wedding in Paris was now followed by a Roman Catholic service and then a Protestant service by a Danish clergyman under Pope Leo XIII's special dispensation, by which sons of this union would be raised as Lutherans while any daughters would be Catholic. The Prince of Wales attended the festivities (although not the actual wedding itself), accompanied by his wife, their three daughters, and younger son, Prince George. Various Danish and German relations of the bridegroom, and French relatives of the bride, along with Russia's Grand Duke Alexis and Belgium's Count of Flanders, joined in the procession through the ground floor gallery and into the small chapel of the château. At the very end of the wedding procession came the bride's fourteen-year-old cousin Princess Hélène d'Orléans, escorted by her uncle Prince Antonio d'Orléans. The newlyweds left for Paris that evening, but the rest of the party—some seventy-eight people went in twenty-five carriages—to a wild boar hunt meet. Even though it was pouring rain the whole day, the party mounted their horses, flushed a boar at once, had a beautiful run, and then accomplished the kill in the open before returning to the Château d'Eu.[37]

From celebrating, the family had to turn to mourning in November when King Alfonso of Spain died suddenly, just two days before his twenty-eighth birthday. His marriage to the Comtesse's sister Mercedes had ended upon her sudden death just six months after their wedding in 1878, but in order to secure the succession, the King had married again the next year to the Archduchess Maria Cristina of Austria. They had two daughters, and now the Queen was expecting a third child at the King's death; the country waited until April 1886 to discover that the infant was a boy who became King Alfonso XIII immediately upon his birth.

During this period of waiting, and with the Spanish court still in mourning, the Comtesse de Paris travelled to Madrid with her brother-in-law, the Duc de Chartres, for the wedding of her brother Antonio to their cousin, the Infanta Eulalia, sister of the recently dead king. The Comte with his daughters—along with the Crown Prince of Portugal—remained at Cannes, where they entertained, among others, the Prince of Wales and his son George.[38]

Princess Clémentine, the youngest daughter of King Louis Philippe and wife of Duke August of Saxe-Coburg, lived in the grand Coburg Palace in Vienna. Throughout her long lifetime, she enjoyed the role of manipulator so often associated with the Orléans clan, so much so that a recent biography dubbed her *La Médicis des Cobourg*. However, throughout the nineteenth century, a regular occupation for royal ladies was to find suitable husbands for the younger women in the family. So, it was in the role of matchmaker that Clémentine invited her twenty-one-year-old great niece Amélie to Vienna to introduce her to Emperor Franz Joseph and some of the marriageable archdukes. However, each of them was considered either too distant from the throne, too poor, or not inclined towards marriage. The only possible one, Franz Ferdinand, second in line to the throne, was travelling in Egypt. The entourage of the Comte de Paris proposed the Russian Grand Duke Nicolas Mikhailovich, but he did not yet want to marry. Then. Amélie met the Portuguese crown prince during the course of a hunting party at Chantilly. On 7 February, they became engaged.[39]

The engagement of Dom Carlos, Duke of Braganza and Crown Prince of Portugal, to Princess Amélie was an occasion for rejoicing among France's royalists, a recognition of their standing equal to a reigning dynasty, a marriage with a future monarch. In fact, there was perhaps too much rejoicing. The Comte and Comtesse de Paris held a great farewell reception for Amélie on 16 May 1886 at the Rue de Varennes mansion in Paris of the Duchesse de Galliera. Some three thousand attended—including the Grand Duke and Grand Duchess Vladimir of Russia, the Duc de Nemours, the Duc d'Aumale, the Prince and Princess de Joinville, Princess Marguerite de Chartres and her brother Henri, the Princess Clémentine and her son Prince Ferdinand of Saxe-Coburg—and the *Times* reporter particularly commented that the Comtesse de Paris 'graciously welcomed the guests, beamed with maternal satisfaction, and with her princely toilette somewhat surprised those accustomed to see her riding, driving, or hunting at Eu, or simply dressed, shopping, almost in incognito, in Paris.'[40] Unfortunately, the exuberant display of interest in the Orléans family caused so much concern for the republican government that within a few days the cabinet met to discuss expelling the Orléans princes from France once again.

However, in the meantime the Orléans family went to Lisbon to celebrate the wedding in the presence of special representatives of all the crowned heads of Europe, the Emperors of Brazil and Japan, and the republics of France and Guatemala. Among the special guests was a family friend, twenty-year-old Prince George of Wales, then serving in the Royal Navy. Prince George was lodged in the Necessidades Palace along with the Orléans clan, and that first afternoon, he joined them for tea—the Count and Countess of Paris and their children Philippe and Hélène together with Aunt Clémentine and her son Ferdinand. The bride, the Duc d'Aumale, the Duc de Chartres, and the Princesse de Joinville were also staying at the Necessidades, and together they all went to the Ajuda Palace for dinner with the King and Queen. Also joining them was the Queen's brother, Amedeo, the Duke of Aosta, who was staying at the Ajuda. It was, as Prince George phrased it in his diary, 'only a family dinner.' The *Times* correspondent noted that while Prince George and the Duke of Aosta were greeted by full military honours and cannon salutes upon their arrivals, the Orléans family were all received as private individuals. Likewise, the decorations on the streets of Lisbon represented the Portuguese colours and the French tricolour, rather than the fleur-de-lys or the white flag of the Bourbons, so as not to upset the Republic, which had authorised its minister to be an official representative at the upcoming wedding.

On the day of the wedding itself, the close family and principal guests drove through the streets of Lisbon in state carriages, each drawn by eight horses. For the ceremony, the Comtesse de Paris wore a dress *de velours frappé d'un rose très doux et doré*. The Queen Maria Pia, more flamboyant than ever, chose a costume based upon 'The Triumph of Marie de Medicis' by Rubens, a dress in sky-blue velvet, *manteau bleu de roi*. Hélène herself wore a pink gown trimmed with pearls and adorned with the pink-and-white Portuguese Order of Isabella. While Prince George of Wales was able to wear the uniform of a commodore of the British navy along with the red cordon of the Order of Christ, the French princes again had to content themselves with civilian clothes, dressed up with various orders. The Duc d'Aumale and Prince of Joinville with the insignia of the Order of the Tower and of the Sword, the highest Portuguese military distinction. The young Duc d'Orléans wore the family order of the Immaculate Conception of Vilavicosa. The chest of the Comte de Paris was covered with the red and green cordon of three Portuguese orders.[41]

The bridal procession arrived at the Church of São Domingos at 2 p.m., and the service lasted nearly three hours. After the wedding Mass the guests went in procession to the Belem Palace, Hélène riding in a coach with Prince George, her great-aunt, the Princesse de Joinville, and the Duke of Aosta. At their new home, the guests and the crowds wished them well and the royals then returned to the Ajuda Palace to dine again '*en famille.*'

On the Sunday, there was a grand reception at Belem Palace with the newly-weds greeting between four and five thousand people. That evening, again in full uniform or dress clothes, they attended a gala night at the opera, which included two acts from Aida and two acts from other operas. Then, on the Monday, it was time to relax. Prince George recorded in his diary that they left in the morning in five mule-drawn carriages for the palace at Sintra, where they lunched before riding on donkeys up to Pena, where 'the view was finer than ever as it was a lovely hot day.' The Duc de Chartres photographed them on their donkeys, and Prince George pronounced that 'It was great fun, Hélène, Phillip & I had a capital gallop.'

The next day, it was back to formal business and time for the official review of the Lisbon garrison. The King, Duke of Braganza, and the Duke of Aosta came in a carriage to collect Prince George at the Necessidades Palace before going on to the Arsenal. There they mounted horses and rode through the streets to Liberty Avenue where the review of some 6,000 troops took place. 'It was a beautiful sight, a very hot day, the place was crowded, about 600,000 people in the streets.' They returned to Liberty Avenue in the evening for 'some excellent fire works' which Prince George proudly noted were from England.

The family party went to lunch with Amélie and Carlos at their new home, Belem Palace, on the Wednesday. 'They gave us a most excellent lunch & showed us all over their house which is lovely.' Then, in the afternoon, it was off to the races with the King and Queen, but even though 'there were a great many people there, & we got a very pretty view of the Tagus'; the races themselves 'were not particularly good.' In the evening, it was time for the grand wedding ball at the Ajuda Palace. Prince George complained that 'We had to wait till 11.30 before we went in to ball room. There were 3,000 people the heat was fearful, there were only three dances, two quadrilles (which I danced) & a valise' and ending up with supper at 2 a.m.

Late nights required late mornings the next day, and it was noon when Amélie and Carlos came to the Necessidades for lunch with her family before they all left for a bull fight. As the Comtesse de Paris was a Spanish infanta and the family often visited in Spain, bull fighting was not the novelty that it was for Prince George, although the Portuguese sport was different from the Spanish. 'It was a very pretty sight about 3,000 people there. We saw about five bulls used in the ring, it was most exciting, & they never kill the bull or any horses like in Spain but they catch the bull, it was intresting.'[42]

The various members of the extended Orléans family had been slowly trickling away from Lisbon after the wedding, most of them returning to Paris via Madrid where they stopped off to congratulate Queen Maria Cristina on the birth of King Alfonso earlier in the month. After the bullfight, it was the turn of the Comte and Comtesse de Paris and their children to go to the rail station.

Buoyed by all the celebrations surrounding the fact that their eldest daughter had married into a reigning dynasty and indeed could expect to become queen, the Comte and Comtesse could not have anticipated the next twist that fate would deal them. However, throughout their stay in Lisbon, the Orléans family had received reports of concerns over the exuberance of the recent royalist demonstrations in Paris surrounding Amélie's wedding. These republican concerns quickly coalesced and resulted in a new Law of Exile. The family had only recently returned to the Château d'Eu when, on 23 June, they learned their future. That same day, the *Journal officiel* published the decree:

Article I: The territory of the Republic is and remains forbidden to the Heads of former ruling families and their direct heirs.

Article II: The Government is authorized to forbid the territory of the Republic to the members of these families.

Article III: Anyone, who in violation of this interdict, shall be found in France, Algeria, or the colonies, will be punished with two to five years of imprisonment. He will be brought back to the border upon completion of his sentence.

Article IV: Members of former ruling families will not be allowed to enlist in land or sea forces, or to exercise any public function or electoral mandate.[43]

1886–1889

Obliged to leave France I come to reclaim the hospitality that free England gives the honour to accord to prescripts.[1]

The chalk cliffs of Le Tréport in Normandy mirror those of Dover on the other side of the English Channel, yet when the Comte de Paris exchanged one set of cliffs for the other, his new life became less a mirror image than simply a dull echo of the former one—at times, a rumbling echo, yet still always simply an echo.

At 6 a.m. on 25 June 1886, the family and household gathered together for Mass which was said at the Château d'Eu. They then went to the parish church to pray before returning to the château where the gates were opened to the public for a final farewell. For nearly two hours, the Comte and Comtesse with their children Philippe and Hélène shook hands and responded 'with sad smiles' to the words of sympathy and affection that they received. While watching the Comte take leave of this faithful few at Eu, his uncle the Duc d'Aumale commented: 'Can you imagine a greater torture than receiving condolences on one's own death and assisting at one's own funeral.'[2]

At Tréport, the Comte and Comtesse—along with the Duc d'Orléans, the Duc de Chartres, and his son Henri—boarded the British steamer *Victoria* with some thirty or forty friends and supporters and a number of Paris journalists. The trans-Manche journey took four and a half hours, and they arrived at Dover alongside the Ostend mail packet shortly after 7 a.m.. As they approached England, the party was standing on the bridge of the boat and was greeted by a 'hearty cheer' from a small crowd gathered there, headed by the Mayor of Dover. They disembarked, but shortly afterwards, there was another farewell scene aboard the Calais-bound boat at Admiralty Pier, when the Comtesse returned to France to care for Princess Louise, who was ill, and the Duc de Chartres returned to his family. As only the head of the house and his direct heir were proscribed by the act of exile, the rest of the family was legally allowed to stay, although the Comtesse and the rest of the children would also move to England shortly.

At Dover, the Comte stayed at the Lord Warden Hotel, the same establishment where Napoléon III met Eugénie when they began their exile together in 1871. From the hotel, the Comte sent a telegram to Queen Victoria:

> Obliged to leave France I come to reclaim the hospitality that free England gives the honour to accord to proscripts; I have had proof of it during the long years, the King, my grandmother, the Queen Marie Amélie and all my family were welcomed by Your Majesty and by Your people in a manner which left in my heart an enduring memory.

Paris goes on to say that his first thought was to offer the Queen his respectful homage and to express the hope that he would soon be able to address her in person. While he was not yet in a position to look for a fixed residence, he was indeed counting on sojourning in England for the moment. The Queen responded from Windsor:

> I received your touching telegram, which moved me greatly. I am happy and proud that my free and hospitable country, where you have lived so long, is once again ready to receive you and to give you the same hospitality. You will understand the sympathy that I feel for my dear Cousins.[3]

Four-year-old Louise was soon restored to health, and the British papers announced that the Comtesse would arrive in England in early July accompanied by her father, the Duc de Montpensier. Meanwhile, the Duc de Chartres, who had returned to England, joined his brother Paris going to London to have lunch with the Prince and Princess of Wales at Marlborough House. Chartres shuttled back to Normandy, and was there on the morning of 5 July to escort the Comtesse and her children to Calais.

At first, the family stayed at Tunbridge Wells; it was from that spa town that the Comte de Paris wrote to Queen Victoria about his son Philippe, who was approaching his eighteenth birthday. The Comte had hoped to send Philippe to Saint Cyr for a military education and then on to service in the French army, which had been denied him. Now in exile, he hoped that his son might enter Sandhurst.

> Our current situation does not permit him to enter a foreign army, to serve as an officer. But I would consider it a great happiness for him to do a turn in a military school, this would be equally useful for his instruction, his education and his situation in the middle of young people of his age.[4]

Both the Prince of Wales and Duke of Cambridge supported the idea, and Philippe was accepted as a supernumerary cadet at Sandhurst.

Indeed, it is amazing how quickly the whole family adapted to their new life in England. The peripatetic life of moving from home to home that many of the royal families already followed provided an easy pattern to replicate in new surroundings. Instead of moving between Normandy, Cannes, and Spain, it now became London for the 'social season,' Scotland for the hunting season, and Portugal or Spain for the winter. Exactly one month after arriving in England as an exile, the Comtesse, along with her daughters Hélène and Isabelle, plus the Duc and Duchesse de Chartres and their children Henri, Marguerite, and Jean, arrived at the Balmoral Hotel in Edinburgh to visit the International Exhibition before going on to the Highlands for the hunting.

Once the Paris family was re-established in England, they very quickly became integrated into society at the highest levels, especially as part of the Marlborough House set around the Prince and Princess of Wales. They settled at Sheen House, near Richmond in London's western suburbs, which became the family's new home. Philippe dismissed it as 'my parents' shack', and other visitors were not much more complementary. A cousin of the Comte, Duke Paul of Mecklenburg, commented on the 'dull, sad look of the place.' He said 'it does look gloomy, enclosed in high walls, such a contrast to Eu and the beautiful, bright sunny homes where the Orléans Princes spent their childish years.' However, the Comte and Comtesse saw it as a temporary stopping place only. The courtiers, who accompanied the family to England, were so certain of an early and triumphant return to France as soon as the public changed its mind again that they convinced the Comtesse de Paris not to unpack her largest trunks—which she didn't do until they moved again in 1890.[5]

One of the staff who joined the household in the kitchens at Sheen was young Rosa Oveden—later better known as Rosa Lewis, 'the Duchess of Jermyn Street', one of the most famous cooks and hoteliers in London of the Edwardian age. She left a portrait of the family from that period remembering the Comtesse:

[She was] the most interesting woman in the world. There never was a better brought up family anywhere than her. Every child had its two nurses, and every child was made to learn something—something useful—to make a boot, cook a cake and so on. The comtesse was the best shot, and the best rider imaginable. She was very masculine. She used to smoke big cigars. She was very methodical, too. Why, she even put her chemise on the same hour every day of her life, and all her family were never even a minute late for Mass; and they knew this time this year exactly what they were going to do at the same time next year. The comtesse de Paris … was very particular about one's appearance. The Queen of Portugal and Princess Hélène, who were her children, and all the rest of them, would come into the kitchen to see me; and if you had a round back, when the Comtesse passed through, she would give you a whack and tell you to stand up straight. She told me to keep my back straight just as she told her daughters—with a whip! The Comte de Paris was a marvellous man. If he could save even a handkerchief to give to the poor he would do so....The marriage of the Comte de Paris and his wife was the most perfect match in the world.[6]

Within months of their arrival in England, fifteen-year-old Hélène was confirmed at the recently restored Chapel of St Louis of France, Portman Square. Officiating at the service was Henry Cardinal Manning, the Archbishop of Westminster. At the age of seventy-eight, Cardinal Manning was—along with his colleague John Henry Cardinal Newman, now in failing health—among the most famous English converts to Roman Catholicism in the 1850s. He had quickly risen through the hierarchy to become archbishop in 1865 and cardinal ten years later. With a red skull cap on his balding head and sharp aquiline features, Manning more resembled a medieval monk than a Victorian prelate. His conservative theology was a good match with that of Popes Pius IX and Leo XIII, and Manning was a strong advocate of the Doctrine of Papal Infallibility, which was only formally defined at the First Vatican Council in 1870.

Hélène was dressed and veiled in white as she entered the chapel with her parents, brother Philippe, sister Isabelle, and various members of the household to the music of the 'Veni Creator', 'Come, Holy Spirit.' The chapel was already full of visitors including an array of French, German, and English clergymen; the service began with the Cardinal directly addressing Hélène:

> The blessing which had been conferred upon her in Holy Baptism, when the Holy Ghost had entered into the sanctuary of her soul and from that hour to this had been her guardian and guide, and had led her step by step through the innocence of childhood until the time came, when the second great Sacrament of the Church she was to be confirmed and strengthened to obtain the grace of perseverance though her later years.

At the end of the address, Hélène entered the sanctuary and the sacrament of Confirmation was administered, and her life as a full member of the Catholic Church began.[7]

In November, Hélène went to Sandringham with her parents and uncle Aumale to visit the Prince and Princess of Wales. Shooting was an important part of any visit to Norfolk, and the Comtesse made an impression upon the British royal private secretaries. 'You should see the Countess de Paris go out shooting here, with two guns and in a short dress. She shoots tolerably well and enjoys it immensely.'[8]

The Comtesse cut an unusual figure in court circles. The Marquis de Breteuil provides a sketch of her at the time:

When one judges Madame the Comtesse de Paris on her appearance, when one sees her dressed almost like a man, smoking constantly, drinking glasses of brandy like an officer of the hussars, using expressions which are out of place in the mouth of a woman, leaving for the hunt wearing swamp boots and a rifle slung over her shoulder, the impression she makes is not a favourable one. When, after that, one hears that she pushes her children around, moreover when one hears that she mistreats her adorable daughter Madame Amélie, when she cuts with disagreeable words of authority one is hardly disposed to indulge her. But, under this appearance of brusqueness, under this difficult exterior, under these airs of independence, there is a great heart and the most noble sentiments. This woman who loses her temper and who slaps her children, it is necessary to see her when one of them is sick or when it has to do with their interests or their future! However, the Comtesse de Paris surprises people when she puts down her Havana cigar to sit at the piano and to sing fashionable songs, many of them English, and it was really a touching sight to see this simple life.[9]

Although Hélène and the other children had spent virtually their whole lives in France up until this point, exile was better known to the Comte who had spent most of his life in that situation. Even if some of his courtiers bemoaned the fact that at dinners at Windsor the Comte would be seated below the Coburgs rather than as the head of the Bourbons, the oldest royal house in Europe, Paris knew the importance of being welcomed at the British court and treated as family. His situation, however, was complicated by the fact that Napoléon III and Eugénie had also been welcomed to England in their own exile, and Queen Victoria maintained a close friendship with them. One particular incident occurred when some members of the Orléans family wrote for permission to visit the Queen at Windsor. The Empress Eugénie had already been invited but wrote to say that her presence might prove awkward to all parties in such a case. The Queen responded that 'No, by no means put off the visit. If anyone postpones it, it had better be they. The Orleanists are my relations, but the Empress is my friend and that is much more sacred to me.'[10]

Following the death of Eugénie's only child, the Prince Imperial, while serving in the British Army during the Zulu Wars, Lord Granville, the Secretary of State for Foreign Affairs, asked Queen Victoria for her opinion of the Comte de Paris and the Bonapartist party. As usual, she was quite forthright. The Queen wrote that 'she believes him to be a good, steady, well-informed man, but not brilliant, and—like all the Orleans Princes—thoroughly imbued with Chauvinisme & not friendly to the English.' She felt:

Orleans Princes have lowered themselves by their lives and total want of dignity in living in Paris under a Republic. It is a strange circumstance, but nearly connected with the Orleans family as the Queen is, knowing them all intimately, and very fond of them as she is—they *never* liked England or even accepted willingly any marks of friendship or of respect, or any assistance offered to them.

Whereas the Emperor Napoléon was 'devoted to England' and the young Prince Imperial had been 'deeply attached to the English and the British Army' and would have been faithful allies to Britain and Germany, Victoria felt the Orléans princes would have encouraged a 'war of revenge' against Prussia. She felt now that there was no chance of the Orléans regaining the throne and France's future now lay between the Republic or the Empire. As for the Bonaparte party, 'Unfortunately Prince Napoléon, though very clever, is a very bad man. But his two sons are very promising' and thus the death of the Prince Imperial in battle was a European misfortune.[11]

Nonetheless, the relations between the Queen and her French cousins were very close. She recorded in her journal a two-night visit they made to her at Osborne on the Isle of Wight for January 1887. The Comte, Comtesse, and Hélène arrived an hour and a half late due to dense fog in the passage to the harbour. Princess Beatrice took them to their suite—formerly the rooms of Prince Leopold. The next day, when the Queen saw the Comte, she thought he was 'wonderfully enlightened & sensible.' After lunch, the Queen went for a drive through the woods with the Comtesse, Hélène, and Princess Beatrice, before they had tea together back at Osborne. This visit may be the first time that Queen Victoria had met Hélène—or, at least, the first time that she took particular notice of her. At tea that night, she commented that Hélène 'looked so pretty in white.' When the family left the next day, Queen Victoria recorded in her journal that 'Isabelle is tremendously lively, & good humoured, & so full of good spirits. Paris is also very pleasant, & Hélène is a very sweet, charming girl. She speaks English perfectly.'[12]

A few days later, on 14 January, Hélène accompanied her mother to Boulogne as they travelled through France en route for Spain and eventually on to Portugal where her sister Amélie was expecting her first child. The Comte—because of the Law of Exile—was not able to make that part of the journey and went to Portugal by sea. Before reaching Lisbon, the Comtesse and Hélène stopped in Madrid where Crista, the Queen Regent, met them at the station. They spent a few days at the Royal Palace before continuing on to Sanlúcar in Andalusia. On 21 March Amélie gave birth to a son whom they named Luís Filipe and who was given the title of Prince of Beira. His christening took place in the Ajuda chapel on 14 April with the Patriarch of the Indies officiating. With troops lining the streets, the Orléans family processed through the streets in Court carriages from the Central Hotel. Inside the chapel the new father, the Duke of Braganza, the grandparents, the King and Queen of Portugal and the Comte and Comtesse de Paris, the infant's great-grandparents the Duc and Duchesse of Montpensier, plus the Duc d'Orléans, and Princess Hélène joined the diplomatic corps to witness the ceremony. The King and the Comtesse de Paris stood as godparents. The next day, the Comtesse wrote to Queen Victoria to thank her for allowing her son to wear the Portuguese Order of the Tower and Sword on his Sandhurst uniform and reported that the child behaved quite well during the service that they all found rather long but he also proved that he had a good voice.[13]

When they returned to London, the social season was underway, and less than a year into their exile, the Orléans family was already fully integrated into that society. Among the first events was the arrival of Buffalo Bill and his Wild West Show in London; the Comtesse de Paris sat in the Royal Box along with her cousin, the Comte d'Eu, and his wife, the Princess Imperial of Brazil. Queen Victoria herself ordered a private performance for the next day. The Comtesse enjoyed it so much that she and her sister-in-law Chichita (Françoise, Duchesse de Chartres) took their children there to celebrate the Fourth of July.[14]

Also in May was the society wedding of Viscount Cranborne, the eldest son of the Prime Minister Lord Salisbury. The wedding guests at St Margaret's Westminster included the Prince and Princess of Wales with their three daughters, the Duke and Duchess of Teck with their daughter Princess May, as well as the Comte and Comtesse with Hélène. Also attending was the Crown Prince of Denmark, one of the early arrivals for the main event of the summer, the Queen's Golden Jubilee. The celebration of fifty years on the throne was to be marked with a great international gathering—not only from the far-flung reaches of the Empire, but also from the equally far-flung royal families of the world, including many of Queen Victoria's own descendants.

As the number of international guests increased, so did the special lunches and dinners. On 17 June, Hélène (who had celebrated her sixteenth birthday a few days before) and Amélie were at a dinner hosted by the Duc d'Aumale, where they were joined by Prince George of Wales. Shortly after this, Hélène received a delayed birthday gift and note from George's older brother, Prince Albert Victor, known in the family as Eddy. After offering the gift, Eddy wrote: 'I hope you will forget all the nonsense I told you that evening at White Lodge for I feel I had no right to say what I did, although I felt it at the time, and was rather too outspoken I fear.'[15]

The main event was on 21 June, Jubilee Day itself, which included a procession from Buckingham Palace to a service in Westminster Abbey with all the Queen's sons, sons-in-law, and grandsons on horseback preceding her carriage. Another of the grand events to celebrate the Jubilee was the great garden party given at Buckingham Palace on the 29th. Most of the queen's immediate family was there, plus the kings of Denmark, Greece, Belgium and Saxony, along with more exotic royalties like the Queen of Hawaii and princes from Japan, Siam, and Persia. Hélène was included among the guests along with her parents and Philippe, her uncle Chartres with his children Henri and Marguerite, and the Duc d'Aumale while Amélie and Carlos represented Portugal.

There was plenty of activity within the French community in London too. On 27 June, the Comtesse presided at the opening of the French Charity bazaar at Willis' Rooms. Organised for the poor of Paris, the French chapel in Little George Street, Portman Square, and the French Hospital in London, the bazaar featured a 'large number of beautiful and valuable objects, artistic or useful' donated by artists, commercial houses in France, and private individuals. Sketches and paintings in watercolour and oils by the Prince de Joinville, the Duchesse de Chartres, Carlos and Amélie of Portugal, the Infanta Eulalia, the Princess d'Aremberg, and the Duchesses of Luynes and d'Uzès were for sale at stalls which Hélène and her cousin Marguerite de Chartres staffed along with the Countess of Denbigh and the Duchesse de Luynes.

The festivities continued into July; on the 13th, Queen Victoria travelled to Hatfield House, the home of the Marquess of Salisbury, for a great garden party in her honour. Special trains out of London brought the guests, among whom were most of the Queen's relatives and guests who had come for the Jubilee and were still in town. Among the French party were the Comte and Comtesse de Paris with Hélène and Philippe, as well as Amélie and Carlos, the Duc and Duchesse de Chartres, and the Comtesse's brother Antonio and his wife the Infanta Eulalia. Thousands lined the avenue to the house to catch a glimpse of the arriving royals in one of the rare appearances of the Queen outside of her own royal residences.

Prince George noted in his diary that he joined his father at a Grand Levée at St James's Palace on the 16th, when individuals were formally introduced to the monarch, or in this case the Prince of Wales—'Presentations to his Royal Highness at this Court are by the Queen's pleasure are considered as equivalent to presentations to Her Majesty'—although those being presented might not have thought so. Later, when they returned to Marlborough House, George went to sit with his sisters, and Hélène and Eulalia came to see them. A few days later, the Comte and Comtesse de Paris with their three older children and son-in-law had lunch at Marlborough House with the Waleses; later in the afternoon Prince Eddy, Prince George, and their cousin Crown Prince Constantine of Greece went riding in the park and 'met all the Orléans family & Duc d'Aumale & rode with them & also Lady Randolph [Churchill].'[16]

The Comte and Comtesse adopted a new routine and would now spend the social season at their home, Sheen House, outside London, the hunting season at Loch Kennard Lodge in Aberfeldy, Perthshire, whence they were frequent visitors of the Waleses at Abergeldie Castle, itself two miles from Balmoral, and spending much of the winter combining visits to the Comtesse's parents at Villamanrique near Seville and to Amélie in Lisbon.

That first summer, the Comtesse ventured into the Highlands to investigate Loch Kennard Lodge, which has been described as 'a lovely place in a fir wood high up on the moors. The house is a wooden one without any kind of pretension. The inside of varnished deal, no upper story, no garden, and no attempt at beautifying inside or out.' When they returned to the Breadalbane Arms Hotel in Aberfeldy that night, she wrote enthusiastically to the Comte about their new home; the moors reminded her of the plains of Normandy, the bright sun that of Andalusia, and the heather was in bloom. Inside the Lodge, she made several rearrangements of the rooms which she and the Comte had previously agreed, hoping he would approve. The new salon was a veritable ballroom, and the Comtesse wrote 'tell Hélène that on entering the house I played the Marseillaise on the excellent piano which awaits her charming fingers to charm my ears, tired out by the noises of the civilized world.' Best of all for the Countess was the hunting. 'It seems that we have to kill at least 2,000 Braces!!! what a massacre, but how much fun it will be!' She was indeed a good shot and cut quite a figure in the field. As one companion reported, 'She marches over the heather like a grenadier, shouts at the beaters, and jokes in rough country fashion with those near her.'[17]

Hélène and the whole family were there for the autumn that year with a great family house party and grouse shoot at Loch Kennard Lodge, where the Comte and Comtesse entertained Carlos and Amélie, who were extending their visit for the Jubilee, along with the Duc and Duchesse de Chartres and their children Jean and Marguerite. At the end of November, the Comte and Comtesse went to Sandringham for a week with Hélène as guests of the Prince and Princess of Wales, and were there to attend the Princess's birthday ball on the evening of 2 December and visit the Smithfield Show with the Prince. On the Sunday morning, they drove to King's Lynn to attend Mass there, and returned to London the next day. Later in the month the three of them went to stay at Windsor, and on the 17th went to Sandhurst, where the Duke of Cambridge was making his half-yearly inspection of the Royal Military College. The Duke and Duchess of Teck were also there with their daughter May as they watched the inspections of the cadets who included Prince Adolphus of Teck, Prince Christian Victor of Schleswig-Holstein, the Duc d'Orléans, and Prince Victor Duleep Singh. Still later in the month, the Comte and Comtesse along with Hélène and Philippe lunched with the Prince and Princess of Wales at Marlborough House.

Early in the New Year, Philippe having passed from Sandhurst left for Bombay with his regiment, the King's Royal Rifles, for a tour of duty as a staff officer attached to Lord Roberts, then Commander-in-Chief in India. The Comte went to Gibraltar to see him off. Later in the year, Philippe wrote to Hélène in secret saying that he wanted to bring two elephants with two Indian attendants to care for them back to Villamanrique. His mother—ever the huntswoman—was horrified to think that they would scare away every bird in the Marimma. Hélène wrote him an eight-page 'sermon' to dissuade him from the idea.

In mid-May 1888, the Comte and Comtesse with Hélène went to Windsor Castle to spend an overnight visit with Queen Victoria who once again proclaimed Hélène 'charming.' In June, the Comtesse and Hélène went to Aix-les-Bains in France for their 'water cure,' while the Comte returned to Ems in

Germany for his, and the three younger children were sent to Eastbourne. The Comtesse wrote from the Grand Hotel de l'Europe, Bernascon, Aix-les-Bains that Hélène was not too tired from her baths, but enjoyed the twenty-five minute swims in the pool, although she then had to rest at least an hour to recover; she is said to 'adore the showers.'[18]

Hélène wrote to thank her father for remembering her seventeenth birthday, but also that she was always thinking of him and considered the stay in France very painful considering the circumstance of his enforced exile. Nonetheless, the 'doctor seems enchanted to see us so overworked and consoles us by promising that it will remain the same for some time.' Each afternoon, they went out for a carriage ride 'because the doctor recommended oxygenating ourselves as much as possible, it is so agreeable to breathe a bit of pure air; and the rides are delightful.'[19]

The rest break, however, was saddened by news of the death of the German Emperor Frederick after a reign of just ninety-nine days. The Comtesse wrote that both she and Hélène would wear mourning. For the Comtesse, it was also melancholy to remember that it was the second anniversary of their departure from their dear Château d'Eu, and she longed to be with her husband, 'when will it be? God alone knows that but you know that even finding the time long and life sometimes very hard, I am always happy near you whatever might be!' When they left Aix, Hélène and her mother went to Geneva, where they took a tour of the lake, and then to Brussels, Ostend, and finally back to England.[20]

The family was back together for the summer, and in July, the Comte received a delegation of Parisian workers at Sheen House, and addressed them in a short speech which was published by the French newspapers. After making his address, he invited them into the dining room, where luncheon was being served, and Hélène and the Comtesse both spoke with them as well. Later in the week, the Prince and Princess of Wales with their three daughters were the guests at luncheon.

During the autumn, the Comte and Comtesse and Hélène went for a great house party at Sandringham, where one of the highlights was always the shooting. Prince George noted in his diary that 'the comtesse de Paris shot very well.' They were there to join in the celebration of the birthday of the Princess of Wales on the 1 December. On the Sunday, the Orleans drove to nearby King's Lynn to attend Mass at the Catholic church of St Mary. The party dispersed the next day about noon, and once again the Paris family headed to Spain. On Christmas Eve, the Comtesse wrote to Prince George from Villamanrique:

Here I am out all day shooting and riding, it is such a treat to me to find myself again in my little home and my native country, I am sure you and the Babies would enjoy the wild life we have here, no dressing, nobody about, only fresh air, sun and Liberty! I hope Hélène and her Father will not have a too bad crossing they where [*sic*] delayed at Dartmouth by bad weather. Hélène was so happy to see you all it, was so very kind of your mother to ask her.[21]

In January 1889, Amélie and Carlos came from Portugal to visit the Duc and Duchesse de Montpensier at Villamanrique, and when they returned to Lisbon they took Hélène with them. She stayed with them there until the end of April and returned to London the same day that their brother Philippe returned from his tour of duty in India. From Portugal, Hélène wrote to her father that she was trying hard—but unfruitfully—to better her spelling. 'I assure you,' she wrote, 'that I do everything I possibly can. I read a lot and I copy pages and pages from Pascal and others!!!' Two weeks later, she was still worried. Although she had brought a number of books with her to read—including a military history on the 1870 war recommended by Camille Dupuy, her parents' private secretary—her spelling was not improving. Hélène admitted to her father: 'This saddens me terribly because I am ashamed of my ignorance.' Her sister Amélie lauded her efforts to better her spelling, but wrote to their father that 'if when she was ten years old there had been more severity on your part it might have spared her the *ennui* that she was undergoing now.'[22]

However, the main reason that Hélène was staying in Portugal was not because of her spelling problems, but rather because of her health. Amélie wrote to her father of anemia and rheumatic pains which had weakened and undermined Hélène's physical condition, but that she was making good progress. It was felt that the air at Belem would benefit her. Hélène, for her part, was enjoying her time in Portugal and found it 'very consoling and very touching' to see how much the royal family was loved in Portugal. She was impressed to hear Carlos and Amélie acclaimed by the crowds, and also to find herself receiving her share of 'vivats' along with repeated cries of '*Vive le comte de Paris.*'[23]

Hélène was back in London in time for 'the Season,' which ran from April until the opening of the grouse hunting season in August. Along with her parents and brother Philippe, Hélène visited Queen Victoria at Windsor, and a few days later lunched with the Edinburghs at Clarence House along with Prince George.[24] She was a regular at Ascot and at the Buckingham Palace garden parties, very much part of the London social scene.

At the end of May 1889, the Comte and Comtesse celebrated their Silver Wedding anniversary by sending 10,000 francs to the Archbishop of Paris for the poor of the city and with a Mass at St Raphael's Church at Kingston-on-Thames, where they had married. This was followed by luncheon for the family, and then a reception for some 500 guests—about 150 of whom had attended the wedding in 1864. At 4 p.m., the band of the Coldstream Guards struck up the opening bars of the National Anthem to announce the arrival of the Prince and Princess of Wales along with their three daughters. The British royal family was also represented by the Duchess of Edinburgh, Princess Christian and her daughters, and the young Duke of Albany with his mother. The Prince of Wales had earlier tele-graphed his sister the Crown Princess of Prussia about the celebrations '& I think if you may send them a telegram congratulating them on the "auspicious" occa-sion they would be much gratified.' The Duchess of Manchester, the Countess of Dudley, Lady Burdett-Coutts, Sir Henry Ponsonby, and Leopold de Rothschild were among the other British guests, while it was also remarked that 'some of the most noted of the agents of the Boulangist alliance, the Duchesse d'Uzès and M. Arthur Meyer, of the *Gaulois* newspaper, were also prominent in the group of French people.'[25]

General Boulanger became the lion of the 1889 social season in London, and the Duchesse d'Uzès introduced him to the Comte de Paris. As French Minister of War, Georges Ernest Boulanger had managed to quickly move from being a republican Radical to becoming spokesman for the anti-parliamentary movement. Aged forty-nine years old, the general had had a respectable career, 'including a fair share of battle-wounds, decorations, and quick promotions. He was handsome, in a vulgar sort of way, sat a horse well, and above all possessed a keen sense of publicity.' He made a meteoric rise to prominence and at least ver-bally assured followers that, if triumphant, he would give power to the Comte de Paris. Backed by Arthur Meyer of *Le Gaulois* and by funds generously provided by the Duchesse d'Uzès, Boulanger seemed set to achieve a spectacular victory with the elections of 27 January 1889. Excitement reigned in Paris with shouts of '*Vive Boulanger, à l'Elysée, à l'Elysée.*'

> Paris that night was ready to throw herself in the victor's arms. But so was his mistress, Madame de Bonnemains. Disregarding the urgent pleas of his advi-sors, Boulanger scorned the advances of the former for the familiar embrace of the latter.

By the next day, the excitement of election night had died down, the opportu-nity for major change was once again lost, and the sitting government 'spread broad hints that it was preparing to prosecute the general himself for conspir-acy against the state.' Boulanger fled to Belgium on 1 April. By the time of the September general elections, the tide had well and truly turned. 366 Republicans were returned as compared with 140 Royalists, Bonapartists, and Conservatives, and only forty Boulganists.[26]

In July, Hélène went to St Mortiz for another water cure with daily baths ordered. In August, she was in France, staying with her aunt (and godmother) the Duchesse de Chartres and cousin Marguerite, known in the family as 'Puss', who was Philippe d'Orléan's unofficial fiancée. One day, Uncle Joinville took them to see a bull fight, and on another day they went to visit Uncle Aumale at his chateau where he was entertaining young Prince Baudoin of Belgium, a meeting which would later give rise to a rumour that the Belgian heir might become a suitor for Hélène.[27]

The Comte and Comtesse with Hélène were once again visiting the queen at Windsor in late November, and then at Sandringham with the Prince and Princess of Wales in early December. They arrived in Norfolk along with the Duc de Chartres and the Duchess of Edinburgh on the evening train of the 2nd. Prince George made a point of recording in his diary that he sat between Hélène and his Aunt Marie, the Duchess of Edinburgh, that night at dinner, and two days later after tea, spent time with Hélène and Lady Mandeville looking through photographs. There were the usual rounds of shooting. On the 5th, Prince George again recorded that they had many good partridge drives and killed 260 birds in the showery but not too cold weather, after which 'The Ladies came to lunch & walked with us afterwards.' The ladies' routine followed the same pattern the next day after the men had slain '948 head, seventeen woodcocks & 203 duck' before they all returned for tea in the hall and a bit of a rest before the County Ball which began at 10.30 p.m., with supper at 12.30 a.m., and dancing which continued until 3 a.m. It was snowing heavily the next morning when Hélène, the Prince and Princess of Wales, Chartres, Prince George, and others piled into three sledges for a drive to Hillington where the Prince of Wales made some presentations to the hunting party.[28] The Comte, Comtesse, Hélène, and Chartres left early the next morning.

Prince Eddy was not part of the house party at Sandringham, for he and his father, the Prince of Wales, had left for a traditional family gathering in Denmark on 1 October 1889, then on to Athens for the wedding of two cousins, after which Eddy continued on a cruise which took him to Cairo, Aden, Bombay, and around India. Eddy would not return to London until seven months later, on 2 May 1890, but Hélène did write to him at least once while he was in India.[29]

Less than a week after returning from Sandringham, the Paris family headed to Portugal, where Carlos and Amelie had become king and queen upon the death of his father on 19 October. However, the main occasion on this visit was the christening of the latest Portuguese grandson—Manoel, who had been born on 15 November. The Comte stood as godparent to the child along with Queen Maria Pia, and among those attending the ceremony was the Emperor Pedro of Brazil, who had been toppled from his throne on the day of the infant's birth. Then, the Comtesse and the younger children went on to Villamanrique for Christmas.

At some point during these years, Hélène sat for the Richmond photographer W. J. Byrne who took a series of studio portraits of the young princess. The white dress showed off her tiny waist, the half-sleeves were drawn in by bows, and she was shown holding an ostrich-feather fan or draped with a white boa in a number of positions in the various photographs. Hélène—blonde and blue-eyed like her father and his German antecedents—wore her hair up but in a style which Queen Victoria decried in her own granddaughters claiming it made them look 'like little *poodles!*'[30] Style and substance would both soon change in her life.

1890–1892

The year 1890 began badly for the Orléans family. The Duc de Montpensier, father of the Comtesse de Paris, suddenly collapsed and died in the arms of his *aide-de-camp* while riding in his carriage at their hunting estate of Coto de Torre Breve at Sanlúcar de Barramedain on 4 February. The Comte de Paris was away on a tour of the Grand Antilles, Puerto Rico, and Cuba at the time; the Comtesse and the children were already in Spain where they had gone for Christmas. Hélène wrote to her father that 'You already know the great sadness which struck us like a clap of lightning. Your poor dear *Bon Papa* who we had left so gay, seeming so well on Saturday night,' and so this 'death so sudden makes us reflect on human fraility.' While Hélène felt her mother was 'courageous' through these troubles, she worried about her grandmother who 'has not spilled a tear, and does not seem able to understand the frightful sadness.'[2]

There was an imposing funeral procession through the streets of Madrid on 7 February to transport the coffin from the southern railway station to the northern one. The procession began with a detachment of the Civil Guard, followed by half a battery of artillery and then by two riderless black horses, their saddles draped in crêpe. The hearse itself was drawn by six black horses and escorted by a group of clergy flanked by court servants in full livery and bearing lighted tapers. Once at the northern station, the funeral party set out *en route* to the Monastery of El Escorial, where he was buried in the first chapel of the Pantheon of the Infantes, where two of his young daughters Amelia and Christina were already buried. Of the ten Montpensier children, only the Comtesse of Paris (the eldest) and Antonio (the next to youngest) survived their father.

Also on 7 February, the very day of his grandfather's funeral and the day after his own twenty-first birthday, Hélène's brother Philippe, the Duc d'Orléans, was arrested in France following his abortive attempt to enlist in the French army in contradiction of the Law of Exile. He had taken the train from Geneva, where he was studying military theory, and arrived at the Gare de Lyons in Paris about 7 a.m. He then presented himself at the recruiting office on rue Saint-Dominique about two in the afternoon, accompanied by an old family friend, the Duc de Luynes. When he was sent away by the recruiting officer, Philippe went to the mairie of the 7th arrondisement, rue de Grenelle, then to the Ministry of War where one of the *sous-directeurs*, General Gallimard, rebuffed him again. Philippe went back to the Hôtel de Luynes and wrote to the minister of war. A number of royalists had gathered there to congratulate Orléans, but the prefect of police sent men to arrest him. They took him to the Conciergerie, the Parisian prison best known as the final holding place of Queen Marie Antoinette before she went to the guillotine.

As the Law of Exile applied only to the pretender and his direct heir (the Comte de Paris and the Duc d'Orléans), the other members of the family were free to visit and live in France. So, while his great-uncles, the Duc d'Aumale and Duc de Nemours attended a memorial service for their brother Montpensier at Dreux on 8 February, Philippe's fiancée Marguerite and her mother, the Duchesse de Chartres, visited him in prison which they continued to do regularly. On the 13th, the Duc d'Aumale went to visit him in prison too, and demanded to know 'Who gave you the idea of this? (Orléans remained silent). Did you reflect on the consequences of this absurdity? Did you do this with the consent of the count of Paris?'[3]

Hélène, however, was firmly on Philippe's side and wrote to their still absent father that 'I completely admired the courage of my brother, and most of all the sudden revealing of this truly French heart.' On the 24th, Philippe was shifted to another prison at Clairvaux, so Marguerite and her mother moved to the nearby Château de Arc-en-Barrois so that they could continue their visits.[4]

The Comtesse de Paris and Hélène arrived in Paris from Villamanrique, staying with the Duc and Duchesse de Chartres. They went to visit Philippe on 25 March, and Hélène reported to her father that night that 'I wish to transmit to you, while they are still fresh, the news and impressions that I brought away from Claireveaux.' She found 'Philippe in a perfect state of health and of spirit. He had only the best to say about everyone and everything. I don't need to tell you how much your letter touched him.' Although Hélène entered Clairvaux in 'great emotion', her brother's 'gaity was so contagious that there was no way to resist it. In this prison one laughs a lot, more so than in the salons. Philippe is admirable, he goes to everyone and very simply tells his whole story.'[5]

Hélène and the Comtesse left Paris for Madrid just two days later, on the 27th, and returned to Villamanrique. The Comte had arrived there from Havana on the 17th but was legally forbidden to join his wife and daughter in their prison visit. They had not planned to leave Spain until after Easter, and so on 22 April, the Comte left Gibraltar for Plymouth, with the Comtesse staying on until 5 May.[6] It is not clear with which parent Hélène herself returned to England, but it was probably on the earlier date.

Eventually, Philippe was released from prison on the night of 3–4 June and deported to Basel, from where he made his way across Germany, Belgium, and the North Sea to England. It was not a secret flight; in fact, he was treated like a hero. At Brussels, he was received by the Grand Marshal of the Belgian Court at the rail station, breakfasted with King Leopold, exchanged visits with the Count of Flanders, and later visited the Queen at Laeken before visiting the Théâtre Molière that night and continuing his journey to Ostend the next morning. His father met him at Dover on 6 June with open arms saying 'you are a brave one, you have done your duty; I am happy, I am proud of you.' They went on to the Grosvenor Hotel in London where the Comtesse and Hélène were awaiting them, and after dinner, they all returned to Sheen House.

On 11 June, the Comte and Comtesse held a reception at Sheen House with the double intention of celebrating Philippe's release from prison and return to the family as well as to officially announce his engagement to his cousin, the faithful Marguerite de Chartres. However, according to his secretary Marcel Barrière, having his mind much more on actresses and singers Philippe was repulsed by the idea of marrying his cousin although he didn't have the fortitude to resist the official engagement, but instead wrote to the Pope on 19 June asking him to intercede. The Pope decided that discretion was the best route and kept silent until the engagement died its own death.

It was not long afterwards that Philippe leased the London home of Lord Minto at 2 Portman Square for the social season. It was at Portman Square that Philippe held a grand dinner where Hélène accompanied her parents. Barrière wrote of the astonishment of the Comte when he saw the sumptuous livery in which Philippe was dressing his many servants, compared with the soberly black-suited few servants at Sheen House—rather like a country gentleman going to visit a sovereign, he claimed.[7] The hero's welcome that he had received from certain quarters after leaving Clairvaux had gone to his head, and he was now acting like the Dauphin of France.

Meanwhile, Prince Eddy returned to England from his cruise to India in early May; shortly after that, he received formal word that his infatuation with his cousin, Princess Alix of Hesse, was not reciprocated, thereby rejecting 'the greatest position there is' in Queen Victoria's opinion. However, within days, a new relationship was revealed. Eddy's sisters let him know that Hélène had been harbouring feelings for him 'for years.' On 27 May, he wrote to Hélène from Sandringham, saying how pleased he was that she had returned to England 'after being away for so many months' and hoping that she forgave him for not thanking her for the letter she sent to him in India, knowing 'that you had not quite forgotten me, although I was so far away.'[8]

Later, Eddy wrote to his brother George, then abroad on naval duty:

You probably know through the girls, who told me that dear Hélène had been fond of me for some time. I did not realise this at first although the girls constantly told me she liked me, for she never showed it in any way. Well, soon after you left and as I knew my chances with Alicky were all over, which I think I told you of when I came back from abroad, I saw Hélène several times at Sheen, and naturally thought her everything that is nice in a girl and she had become very pretty which I saw at once, and also gradually perceived that she really like me. Well this went on until one day, when she came to lunch, and came up to the girls room afterward. I then told her I liked her very much etc., and she also said the same thing to me. But then the unfortunate point of religion came in, and she said although she was very fond of me, she feared it was quite impossible to think of marrying or any thing of the sort.[9]

By mid-month, there were rumours flying between Marlborough House and Windsor of a romance between Hélène and Eddy. The private secretaries of the Queen and the Prince of Wales—Sir Henry Ponsonby and Sir Francis Knollys— were sharing their gossip and opinions, compounding the problem when Knollys wrote the name of the princess in question as 'Marguerite' instead of 'Hélène.'[10] Then, Queen Victoria herself entered the conversation, writing to Eddy on 19 May, and making Knollys' unintentional shift of names intentional:

I wish to say a few words about the subject of your future marriage. I quite agree with you that you should not be hurried and I feel sure that you will resist all the wiles and attempts of intriguers and bad women to catch you. But I wish to say that I have heard it rumoured that <u>you</u> had been thinking and talking of Princess Hélène d'Orléans! I cannot believe this for you know that I told you (as I did your Parents who agreed with me) that such a marriage is utterly <u>impossible</u>. None of our family can marry a Catholic without losing all their rights and I am sure that she would never change her religion and to change her religion merely to marry is a thing much to be deprecated and which would have the very worst effect possible and be most unpopular, besides which <u>you</u> could not marry the daughter of the Pretender to the French Throne. Politically in this way it would also be impossible. That being the case you should avoid meeting her as much as possible as it would only lead to make you unhappy if you formed an attachment for her.[11]

The Queen then goes on to suggest another grandchild, Princess Margarethe of Prussia, as a possible bride, admitting 'she is not regularly pretty but she has a very pretty figure, is very amiable and half English with great love for England which you will find in few if any others.' Not surprisingly, such a recommendation did not go far with the young prince. Ponsonby wrote to Knollys:

Queen suspected that Marlborough House was encouraging Hélène so she wrote to an Orléans friend—I think the Pss [Clémentine] of Coburg to say that if these two met much they would inevitably fall in love and as from religious reasons a union was impossible it was cruel to encourage it and that she ought to warn the Paris' against it.[12]

Surprisingly, Hélène's father, the Comte de Paris, was keen on exploring the possibility of a marriage with Prince Eddy at this point; on 17 June, he went to consult with Cardinal Manning. Paris held the dream of a Catholic queen who might bring England back to the Catholic Church, but once the cardinal had an opportunity to seriously consider the matter he wrote to the Comte to deflate that idea. Cardinal Manning wrote that the practice of the church was to insist that any children of a mixed marriage be raised in the Catholic Church without exception. He enclosed a copy of instructions from Pope Pius IX on this subject but also pointed out that it was 'founded upon the Catholic tradition of all times.' As for the Comte's hope of bringing England back to the time of the Stuarts when the last Catholic queen sat on the throne, Manning wisely commented that 'the mind of Great Britain towards the Catholic Religion as the religion of individuals is tolerant and passive.' However, even 'the slightest contact of the Catholic Church with the public and political life of the country would arouse on the spot an active and all but universal reaction of the kind, if less in degree, which we saw and suffered in the years 1850 and 1851', when the Catholic hierarchy was reinstated in England by Pius IX.[13]

Undeterred, the Comte wrote to a friend, probably General de Charette, asking him to make an approach to the Pope himself to see if some moderation might be possible. 'Due to particular circumstances which one can truly call providential, the heir to the throne of Henry VIII and William of Orange wants to be able to seek the hand of a Catholic princess of the highest lineage.' If England did have a Catholic queen, 'will not all Europe see this as a great event, a new manifestation of the expansion of the Church under the bold leadership of the great Pope who is its ruler?' The Comte recognized that there would have to be compromises in both directions—only if the Queen and Prince Eddy led a change in the British constitution could an heir marry a Catholic, and only if the Pope put no restrictions on the religion of any children from that marriage would the British public possibly accept such a situation. Paris himself did not feel in a position to approach the Pope directly, but if his friend should 'find it favourable, I will hurry to the Vatican to reap what you sow, to reaffirm formally what you have already arranged on an informal basis.'[14]

Despite the Queen's deprecation, the young couple probably met again at the races at Ascot for Cup Day in June when they both spent part of the day in the Queen's stand, and a more auspicious meeting was in the offing. In early August, the Comte de Paris arrived in Scotland, staying at Loch Kennard Lodge for the shooting season. Then, Prince Eddy passed through Aberdeen on 15 August on his way to Mar Lodge, the home of his sister and brother-in-law, the Duchess and Duke of Fife. The occasion was the upcoming birthday of the Princess of Wales. The house party at Mar Lodge included Princess of Wales and Princess Victoria of Wales, the Comte and Comtesse de Paris and Hélène, Prince Eddy, his uncle Prince Valdemar of Denmark, the Russian ambassador Baron de Staal, the Hon. Julia Stonor, Sir Dighton Probyn, Sir Charles Hall, MP, and Mr Horace Farquhar. Of these guests, Prince Valdemar was the same one who had received dispensation from the Pope to marry Hélène's cousin in 1885, and Julie Stonor, orphaned daughter of a lady-in-waiting to the Princess of Wales and grand-daughter of Sir Robert Peel, was a Roman Catholic with whom Eddy's brother George had been romantically involved earlier.[15]

On Friday, 29 August, a small party travelled from Mar Lodge to visit the Queen at Balmoral. The *Court Circular* published an innocuous little notice reporting that 'The Princess of Wales, Princess Louise, Duchess of Fife, Princess Victoria of Wales, Princess Hélène d'Orléans, and the Duke of Clarence and Avondale visited Her Majesty this afternoon.'[16] Prince Eddy related the events to his brother:

I had a long talk to Motherdear about the dear girl and she said if I really wished to win her, it was to show her how fond I was of her, and then try and persuade her to change to my sake. I naturally got to like, or rather love her by the manner she showed her affection for me, which I very soon found out. I put the question to her several times before she would think of such a step as changing which after all is a great thing for anybody to do and especially a Catholic, who consider it a terrible thing and about a crime: I had a hard job of it as you may imagine and Motherdear also talked to her about it. Poor girl I felt very much for her, for she was pulled as it were both ways, and not knowing what to do. I could see as I know well now that she was really fond of me, and told me she would do any thing for me. So at last with a great effort she said she would do this great thing for my sake, which I considered a noble act as it was, for any woman to do for the sake of the man she loved. After this was settled, Motherdear hit upon a capital idea which however rather took me aback at first, but was the last thing we could possibly have done. It was to go off at once to Balmoral and tell Grandmama everything and apeal to her feelings and ask for her help and support. Well we did so, and arrived just after their lunch, having had ours in the carriage on the way down. You can imagine what a thing to go through and I did not at all relish the idea of going into Grandmama and telling her that this sweet girl, which indeed she is, had promised to change her religion to become my wife. I naturally expected Grandmama would be furious at the idea, and say it was quite impossible etc. But instead of that she was very nice about it and promised to help us as much as possible, which she is now doing, and I have been over to see her several times since and have had long talks about it all. I believe what pleased her most was my taking Hélène into her, and saying we had arranged it entirely between ourselves without consulting our parents first. This expression was not quite true but she believed it all and was quite pleased.[17]

The Queen, who was a terrible romantic, was entirely taken in by the usually guileless Eddy, who told her that 'I thought I would come straight to you, I have not told Mama even' which she took as a proof of his confidence. He arrived with Hélène, announced their devotion to each other, and asked for the Queen's help. When the Queen protested that they both knew it was impossible, Eddy responded by saying that Hélène agreed to change her religion for his sake. Although the Queen recognized that this would be 'very difficult and painful for her to do,' Hélène herself answered 'For him only for him. Oh! do help pray do.' The Queen 'assured them I would do what I could to help them but it might be difficult.' Eddy took Hélène to the door, but then returned and told his grandmother that 'I was very fond of Alicky but she never returned my affection' whereas Hélène 'had loved him for some years' and that 'he never could marry anyone else. That she had grown quite thin from anxiety and worry.' He recognized that 'her father would be very angry' but assumed that 'would wear off,' while 'her mother winked at it.' Even when the Queen said that she must tell the government and that there might be political difficulties, Eddy naively responded that he thought there wouldn't be, especially as 'she knows that her father will never succeed there,' and that he thought Lord Salisbury would not object, 'to which I replied I was afraid he would think it difficult.'[18]

That night—as if nothing had happened—the Duke and Duchess of Fife hosted a dinner followed by a torch-light dance in which some sixty of the duke's clansmen took part, and then a ball which was opened by the Duke of Fife and his mother-in-law, the Princess of Wales.[19]

After returning from Balmoral, Eddy broke the news to the Comtesse de Paris, who 'was very nice about it when I told her for I knew she guessed what was going on, and really wished it were possible that we two would be brought together. But of course on the religious part of it she had nothing to say.'[20] Balfour's analysis was that he suspected 'the Ctsse. de Paris, in the intervals of deer stalking, to be favourable to it also. She is more certain that it is good to be Queen of England than she is that it is bad to marry a Protestant.' That evening, there was a ghillie's dance at Abergeldie, and Eddy used the opportunity to speak at length with both mother and daughter, before they left the next day for their home in Perthshire. This may have been the last time that Eddy and Hélène ever met in person, but at some point, he presented her with an engagement ring:

[He had brought it] all the way from India, and always intended it for an engagement ring for whomever I should be fortunate enough to find, willing to marry me. and I have indeed found one, and one in a thousand, as I consider you are my Sweetest. As I have said before, you are far too good for me, but I will do my utmost to prove myself worthy of you some day, if I only have the chance.[21]

That same night, the Queen met with Arthur James Balfour, at this time Chief Secretary for Ireland—who was at Balmoral as Minister in attendance upon the Queen—and he pointed out 'the extremely awkward position every one would be placed in if, after an abortive attempt on the French throne, the D. d'Orléans were to take refuge at the court of his sister the Queen of England.' The next day, Balfour received a letter succinctly making virtually all the points which would be argued throughout the coming year from his uncle Lord Salisbury, the prime minister. First of all, Balfour was to 'urge the Comte de Paris should be immediately communicated with.' It should be pointed out that 'marriage with a French woman will be very unpopular, still more with one who was a Roman Catholic and has changed her religion to obtain the English throne.' As some people would not believe it a sincere conversion and that the princess would continue to act in Catholic interests, 'all will despise her for it.' Moreover, such a union would 'produce great and general offence abroad. Germans will be angry because she is French; Republicans in France and because of her Orléans family French Royalists on account of change of religion.' Balfour was to do his best to prevent any royal assent and allow time 'to work on the Princess.' Salisbury concluded with his doubts about the 'perseverance of the young Prince.' Balfour responded 'now that I have your full instructions I will develope to the best of my ability the whole case agt. the marriage.'[22]

Balfour met with the Queen that afternoon and reiterated all the prime minister's arguments, and the Queen 'admitted the full force of all of them.' She feared that her conversation with Prince Eddy 'implied a policy more favourable to his wishes than she will be able to carry out.' But, likewise, she said that the Prince must marry, and the options were very limited with just 'three marriageable protestant princesses at this moment in Europe, besides the Teck girl and the Hesse girl.' Princess May of Teck was ruled out 'because they hate Teck' and because the thought of the Duchess of Teck 'haunting Marlborough House makes the Prince of Wales ill.' Princess Alix of Hesse had already rejected him, and 'there remain a Mecklenburgh and two Anhalt princesses (I am not sure that I have the names right). According to Her Majesty, they are all three ugly, unhealthy, and idiotic: and if that be not enough, they are also penniless and narrow minded! or as she put it German of the Germans!' So, the Queen continued: 'Here we have a charming and clever young lady—against whom no legal objection can be urged, who has loved Prince Eddy for three years to whom he is devoted, and who will fill her position splendidly—how can it be stopped?' She continued saying that 'The Prince will never marry any one else—his health will break down: & so on!!'[23]

The same day, the Princess of Wales wrote to Queen Victoria pronouncing that 'Nothing on earth could have given me greater pleasure than to see those two dear children united ... so suited to each other in every way ... I hardly dared allow myself to dwell on so blessed a prospect.' What Alexandra does dwell upon in this letter is underlining the Queen's promised help in the matter, that Hélène has promised to 'sacrifice all that she holds most dear (i.e. I suppose the religion in which she still believes) for his sake,' and the assurance that the Prince of Wales will be 'as much pleased as we are when he hears as he ... often expressed a wish that she might be our daughter-in-law.' The shadow, however, remained the anticipated 'great opposition' from the Comte de Paris in light of Hélène's offer to convert to Anglicanism.[24] However, the Queen voiced the concerns of the government as her own thoughts when she wrote back to Princess Alexandra:

> I fear you greatly understate the difficulties and obstacles which are manifold. By changing her religion only to be able to marry him, she will be furiously attacked and may be tormented by the Roman Catholics and may be mistrusted by the protestants, for the English and the Scotch think roman Catholics (foolishly I admit) quite wicked and I fear they will be very angry. Then politically it might become very serious and involve the country in quarrels with France. If that foolish brother of hers were to make some attempt again and fail, and came here and she were possibly Princess of Wales or even Queen and he went to her, it might involve England in war.[25]

The expected support of the Prince of Wales was apparently strong and forthcoming, because his mother wrote to him from Balmoral on 7 September responding to a letter of the previous day:

> I do all in my power to promote the realization of poor dear Eddy's & sweet Hélène's ardent wishes! The <u>great</u> difficulty is Paris! I am longing & trembling to hear what Hélène will write. Nothing is come yet, & it will be a week tomorrow since they left ... I agree with you also that it is too late to go back.[26]

When Balfour was shown the letter, he had to admit that 'my opinion of the Princess of Wales' diplomacy is raised to the highest power. She is determined on the match. She contrived (nothing will persuade me to the contrary) the visit of yesterday. She has pinned the Queen to the half promises of aid given in the heat of a dramatic situation: and those half promises she has turned into whole ones.'[27]

The next day brought a response by the Queen and a return response from the Princess of Wales, but Balfour reported to his uncle that 'this reply she has <u>not</u> shewn me—(as I believe) because it is too hot!—She said with a laugh that when she has done <u>her</u> best to stop the marriage, she will leave you to fight it out with the Princess.—I wish you joy!' Prince Eddy wrote to the Queen too, again saying that he could not understand any problem if Hélène were to convert and that he was 'rather distressed' by Lord Salisbury's answer. 'But forgive me Grandmamma for saying that I believe that in this case it is quite sufficient to have the Sovereign's consent and that the Prime Minister need only be told of her decision.'[28]

Eddy also wrote to Hélène cherishing the 'lovely and sweet few minutes we had together' before she left Mar Lodge. 'I can't tell you how much happier I am now, since things have turned out so much better than I had even dreamt of,' yet he was also fully aware of the imminent problem of confronting the Comte de Paris with the possibility of conversion. 'I hope you won't worry yourself too much, you darling, although I know you have a terribly hard task before you. But sooner it is done the better I think, and get the worst over, for it must come. What would I not do to help you in this.' The same day, Hélène did indeed tell her father of her intention to convert in order to marry Eddy, and it was 'a serious and painful conversation.' The Comte made it very clear that he would never give his consent, and that under French law, Hélène would not be free to marry without his permission before she reached the age of twenty-five. Although the Comtesse wrote to the Princess of Wales of 'how often both of us have talked about the future of our children and you also know what is the only obstacle to their happiness, the question of religion,' she now felt that 'Our children must be patient, they must wait for the circumstances that time alone can bring about, that may perhaps make possible the realisation of their dream and ours.'[29] Eddy wrote to his brother George:

> [Hélène] had a terrible scene with her Father ... and he said he would never give his consent to such a thing ... I can understand in some ways his refusing to give his consent for he is a very strict Catholic, and the idea of such a thing to a man like him must have been rather a shock, if not a surprise, but he did not expect anything until Hélène told him, or he would have perhaps been less excited and angry.

Paris then wrote an angry and 'unfortunate' letter to the Prince of Wales, which does not survive, but apparently was strong enough to make the Prince very angry himself.[30]

Despite all the problems, the young couple remained confident that things would work out if they had enough patience. Eddy assured Hélène that 'what ever happens even if I had to wait fifty years or more. After the true and beautiful devotion you have shown me, and the great sacrifice you have made, which I believe there is hardly a woman living who would do the same for a man, could I possibly change my mind for an instant?' Even the mothers continued under the same illusion, and the Princess of Wales wrote to the Comtesse:

> I hope that one day her father's heart will soften and will have pity on these two who are so much in love and who seem to be made for one another.

In the meantime, our poor children must be patient and wait for a change
in circumstances to come in time which might permit the revival of their
hopes and ours.[31]

The Queen hoped to limit knowledge of the affair and requested that Lord
Cadogan, serving as Lord Privy Seal, not be told when he succeeded Balfour
as minister in attendance at the end of the month, and that it not be considered
in full cabinet. Lord Salisbury, however, thought that this was impractical and
urged a consultation with the Cabinet as soon as it met. He also drew up another
memorandum outlining his reasons for opposition: principally the lacking permission of the Comte de Paris, as the intended bride was only nineteen years
old and could not marry under English law without her father's consent until
she was twenty-one; and under French law, between the ages of twenty-one and
twenty-five she could marry without his consent but only after a series of legal
sommations respectueuses. Salisbury then says that if the permission of the Comte is
actually obtained, then the Cabinet should be consulted.

> Of course, as the Duke of Clarence observes, the Queen is not bound by the
> opinion of her ministers. But they ought to have the opportunity of submitting
> it to her. For her consent to this marriage is a State Act of the greatest gravity.
> It may profoundly affect the feelings of the people towards the throne, and of
> foreign countries towards England; and therefore the opinions of her constitu-
> tional advisers ought to be before the Queen, before her mind is made up.

Salisbury reminded the Queen of the traditional enmity towards the French,
and that Henrietta Maria had been the only French queen since the War of the
Roses. The next issue was that of the conversion itself, which Salisbury predicted
British Catholics would view 'with extreme repugnance' and that Protestants
would suspect its soundness and always be fearful of a 'fall back under the spiritual
influences under which she has been brought up.' He also argued the adverse
reaction of the French Republic, which Hélène's father had so recently—and so
unsuccessfully—tried to overthrow through his support for General Boulanger.
Finally, for the first time, the issue of the Act of Settlement was formally raised.
Salisbury admitted to responding solely as a layman and to the need of thorough legal advice, but he propounded that the 1689 Parliament, in drafting the
Act, considered that 'the stain of Popery could not, in the case of the heir to
the throne, be washed out by a subsequent conversion to Protestantism.' Even if
Hélène did convert, the Roman Catholic Church would still consider her one of
theirs, as 'the Roman Catholic laity, once members of the Church of Rome, can
only cease to be so by the action of the Church of Rome itself. She would be a
very bad Roman Catholic if she came to our Church, but a Roman Catholic, for
all formal purposes she would remain.'[32]

Hélène's aunt, the Infanta Eulalia, was staying with the Paris family at Loch Kennard Lodge; her letters at the time seem oblivious of the storm around her. On 5 September, she wrote to her sister:

> Yesterday quite a number of gentlemen arrived here, amongst them Alfonso Rothschild. They went off early to shoot, Hélène and I rode out to join them at luncheon. We remained for two drives and then came home. This present country life is very diversified and suits me very well. Tomorrow the Prince de Wagram gives a shooting party. I shall go again with Hélène to lunch at the Castle. I am enjoying myself enormously.

However, less than a week letter, Eulalia's tone had changed. 'My mother-in-law has sciatica; Antonio is therefore leaving for San Lucar,' and 'if my mother-in-law does not get well soon I can only stay a short time with you. My sister-in-law [the Comtesse de Paris] will also go to Andalusia. I think I shall go mad between all my relations. There is no doubt the happiest people are the foundlings.'[33]

Paris had left Loch Kennard Lodge by 17 September, when the Comtesse wrote to him that 'Hélène is always very tired but very kind. She has been walking a bit, which is progress.' Eddy had misplaced hopes that Hélène's brother Philippe, the Duc d'Orléans, might be able to intercede on their behalf, especially as he and his father were preparing for a long trip together.[34] They were to visit the United States—where the Comte had served with the Union Army during the Civil War and wanted to revisit the sites with his son—and Canada—where they would appeal to the French inhabitants in Montréal and Québec. However, Philippe's own engagement to his faithful cousin Marguerite de Chartres was on the point of collapse itself, a fact that Philippe was eager to hide from his father as long as possible.

By 7 September, newspaper reports began to appear claiming that Orléans's marriage with Marguerite would not proceed, when he was grouse hunting at the Duc d'Aumale's Worcestershire estate, Wood Norton—the house which Aumale built in 1897 upon the 3,600 acre estate near Evesham. Philippe was there at the invitation of Aumale along with Chartres. The plan was for a letter to be addressed to Princess Marguerite asking her to renounce the engagement, dated on 24 September (the day Philippe and Paris were leaving for America), so that an answer would be determined by his return. The letter was never written, and Orléans wrote to his secretary Barrière from two days outside of New York that he did not want to harm his relations with his father during the trip.[35] Father and son sailed from Liverpool on 23 September and would not return until 8 November.

It seems that Hélène consciously decided that it was time to make changes in her life, and in her letters to her father beginning in September 1890, she begins a new style of very angular handwriting which would mark her writing thereafter. The normal schoolgirl cursive writing was distinctly replaced with a new style characterised by sharp oblique strokes of the pens. The letters 'n' and 'm,' for example, became simply a series of parallel lines without any connective.[36]

This was an important letter for Hélène as she set out plans to change the one impediment that might change all else:

> My dear Papa, I was very happy to receive your letter from Queenstown, and I thank you for it with all my heart. I don't know how to tell you how much I was touched by the goodness that you have shown me recently. I am still very troubled by all that has taken place. I am going to undertake with the grace of God, a trip which I hope will succeed even if it accomplishes nothing for the moment. General deCharette is very much ready and has spoken to me about the magnitude of this project, etc. I must admit, my dear Papa, that I thought it more honest to tell him everything, and I have been ashamed to have to tell him what I wanted to do. Our plans are nearly fixed. Madame deCharette will come to get me and we will leave on the 27th.
>
> I hope that your crossing will end as well as it started. You will be very busy upon your arrival there, that will perhaps change the course of Philippe's ideas—who I pity with all my heart.
>
> Adieu, my dear Papa, I embrace you with all my heart, praying that you always believe me, Your obedient and very affectionate daughter, Hélène.[37]

The evening before, Hélène had drafted a letter to Eddy laying out the plan:

> Everything must yield to our love, everything except our honour. You know how important this sentiment is. As a daughter of France I owe it to myself. I owe it to my conscience to remain Catholic, the affection I feel for my father demands nothing less than a perfect submission. I want our love to be eternal! But if it can only be won by a gesture which I consider to be without honour, I will not do it.
>
> You, whose sentiments are so noble, you will understand me. Only one person in the world can lower the barrier, the obstacles, and that is the Pope. With my father's blessing, I am going to throw myself at the feet of the one who at all times has been ready to listen and who alone has the right to advise me, to absolve me.
>
> When you receive this letter I will already have left. Pray to God, let us both pray, that I will return to say to you, in the full honour of my heart, 'I put my hand in yours.' Whatever happens, etc.[38]

Although in the letter Hélène claims that she is acting with her father's blessing, the Comte later said that 'Hélène decided spontaneously to go to Rome' once it was decided that she could not—and would not—convert.

The Comte de Paris later had a long conversation with Queen Victoria about the depth of Hélène's devotion to the church and recounted part of an in-depth discussion he had with his daughter on the subject; he asked her:

Suppose you have become Protestant, you have married Eddy. You find that you are seriously ill, you feel close to death. What will you do? I will send for a Catholic priest, she replied, without hesitation. So you see, I then told her, your conversion would not be sincere and in consequence you would be sorry until the day you disowned it. If, after having seen the Catholic priest, you were restored to health, ask yourself then what would be your position and that of your husband. Having professed your Catholic faith, you would then have forced him to choose, either to renounce his rights to the throne or to announce your divorce. This thought made her consider the question in its true light. She understood that not even for this man whom she loved could she make the sacrifice of her religion, and that this sacrifice, made only in words, would be the cause of remorse which would be a threat to the happiness of the marriage.[39]

Meanwhile, both Lord Cadogan, as Lord Privy Seal, and the Lord Chancellor, Lord Halsbury, became involved. Cadogan, who was still duty minister at Balmoral, was brought into the loop on 11 September when the Queen instructed Ponsonby to share the relevant correspondence with Cadogan and then she met with him in the afternoon. Although recognizing the 'gravity of the difficulties,' the Queen dwelt on the personal aspect of the relationship, 'enlarging upon the graces & virtues of the Princess Hélène, and the promise of happiness which a union with such a Princess might be expected to realize for the D. of Clarence.'[40] Cadogan, for his part, emphasized that the personal aspect had to remain secondary to affairs of state.

The Queen stressed her hope that the prime minister and Cabinet keep that their prime object, and they 'ought to be—to try & overcome the gt. difficulties if possible—not to strengthen their opposition & objections by not trying to overcome them, but rather to confirm them. wch. the Queen cd. not sanction.'[41]

In mid-September, Salisbury took the opportunity to raise the fear of republicanism:

> The really serious consideration—after the legal questions have been disposed of—is whether such a marriage would greatly diminish the affection which the people now feel for the Monarchy. It is a very difficult problem to judge of—whether the feelings which once actuated the English people so intensely have, or have not, lost their force.[42]

The next day, it was Ponsonby's turn to report back to the Prince of Wales upon a meeting which the Prince had requested about the prospective marriage with Lord Rosebery, the future prime minister. Rosebery was perhaps the most positive among the politicians on this subject. 'He said that her religion made this impossible but that if she were to become a Protestant, in a manner which left no doubt as to the sincerity of her conversion he thought it possible that a marriage with a Frenchwoman might not be unpopular in England.' Ponsonby went on that 'I think on the whole he was rather favourable to the idea, but of course governed by the assumption that the Princess would be a thorough Protestant and entirely dissociated from the Orleanist attempt on the throne of France.'[43]

Prince Eddy upped the stakes when he declared that 'he will marry his Princess at all costs even if he is dispossessed of the succession,' believing that the crown would then go to his eldest son.[44] The Queen had already queried the Lord Chancellor about these aspects.

Question I
If the heir apparent or next in succession to the Throne of Great Britain marries a roman Catholic, is he for ever excluded from the succession, or if his wife becomes Protestant can he then resume his rights to the Crown?
Answer: I entertain no doubt that the Statute excludes him from the succession and that the subsequent change of religion by the wife would not operate to reinvest him with a right to inherit the Crown.

Question II
If he is excluded from the throne who comes next in succession? His children if they are Protestants?
Answer: Yes certainly.

Question III
If a Prince or Princess of a Foreign Princely family is born in England, does he come under the laws of England? Does he become of age at 21 according to English law—or does he come of age according to the laws of the country of his father?
Answer: According to English law he would be a natural born subject and subject in all respects to the laws of England but this is one of the subjects upon which the laws of all civilized countries are not uniform and there is in some respects a conflict of laws.[45]

Hélène, however, was already regretting the impetuousness of her agreement to convert. The Comtesse received a telegram from the Princess of Wales on the evening of 13 October inviting the Comtesse and Hélène to join her and her daughters for a private luncheon at Marlborough House. Hélène at once said that it was better if they did not go, but the Comtesse said that she would go alone. She went with a message from Hélène for the Princess to say that while she still had the same feelings about Eddy, her statements at Balmoral had been made in a state of exultation, but now she felt she could not live a continual lie as she knew it was impossible for Eddy to marry a Catholic. Alexandra, 'who was nicer than ever,' said that she had expected this as it showed how honest she was, and now they must wait for a miracle from God. She even made a copy of the relevant passage from the Act of Succession to confirm their thoughts. The Comtesse believed that Eddy was truly in love with Hélène, but the idea that he would renounce his succession rights and live as a simple duke to marry her would make nobody happy, nor would it be popular in England. She left Marlborough House that day saddened but resigned—'it is hard to not be able to unite two children who seem made for each other and on the other hand to marry them to someone they don't love. That's life, I know, but it is always so sad.'[46]

Meanwhile, Ponsonby and Knollys continued to bat their own ideas back and forth. Ponsonby felt particular pity for the Princess of Wales 'because I think she is in earnest and that she feels how serious a rebuff may be to her son.' He also felt that the Chancellor's opinion about the succession rights skipping a generation and vesting in a future eldest son of Eddy and Hélène was both 'illogical and absurd' not least of all because if he did, 'it would be necessary to declare in Parliament how the succession should go which would raise a debate as to whether there should be any succession at all.'

> Now all I have spoke to on the subject say it will never do for her to [con]vert and at the same moment be engaged to the Duke of Clarence. Everyone will say that she remains at heart a R.C. but verts for the sake of the British Crown. They say that if she is going to Vert, she should vert now & let the engagement come out later—will she vert now?

Finally, on the political aspect abroad:

> Waddington [the French ambassador in London] has already protested against the supposition of such a marriage and if it were declared the French Govt. would publicly protest and English republicans would ally themselves with the French nation against the Combined Royal families. All this will make a minister think.

Two unnamed ministers with whom Ponsonby did speak both said that a repeal of the religion clause of the Act of Settlement would be impossible and 'you might as well propose to restore the Stuarts.'[47]

In a desperate bid to save her engagement, Hélène travelled to Rome to put her case before the Pope personally and beg for a dispensation in regard to the upbringing of her future children. Undoubtedly with her mother's support and with Baron de Charette and his wife, as chaperones, Hélène arrived in Paris on 31 October, the day before the Comte de Paris was scheduled to leave America for the return to Europe. The Baron, who was considered a hero in Rome for his service with the papal Zouaves and was made a general in the French army, was a nephew of the Comte de Chambord, the grandson of the Duc de Berry by his English mistress Amy Brown. The Baroness was Antoinette Polk, an American from Tennessee.[48] Together, they travelled quickly and incognito across France to Rome; once they arrived, Hélène drafted a letter to the Pope:

> [I] very humbly prostrate at the feet of His Holiness. I come as a Daughter of France to ask his blessing, on myself, first of all—on all my family—and on my sister Isabelle, who is about to make her first communion. I come also to open my heart to him, to whom God has given the power to bind and to set free. I submit in advance to everything that His Holiness instructs me to do concerning the matter which I am going to set before him. I have given my heart to the Hereditary Prince to the throne of England he promised his faith to me. But a religious question remains which only Your Holiness can resolve. I must confess to him that I have acted imprudently, carried along by circumstances we went, the Prince and I, without my Father's knowledge, to ask the Queen for her permission! I was so confused I do not know what I said. but what I do know is that I do not wish to remain under any misunderstanding and that I am before the feet of S. P. [Sainte Père, the Holy Father] because my approach to the Queen is known by no one outside the royal family, and if need be I want the whole world to know that I have come to S. P., that I will never renounce my faith. For the rest, I can read the letters I have written to the Pope. I have made my confession and I await the Pope's decision in confidence and humility.[49]

On 3 November, Hélène attended Mass in the Pope's private chapel in the Vatican and then joined him for luncheon. Eighty-year-old Leo XIII had been pope since 1878 and was a member of the Roman noble family Pecci. Presumably, Hélène put forth the precedence of her cousin Marie d'Orléans marrying into a Protestant royal house with a papal dispensation from Leo. However, she presumably also remembered that the Act of Settlement required a conversion by her in order to secure the succession, and that was a different matter altogether. She threatened to never marry anyone if she was not allowed to marry Eddy, but to no one's surprise, the Pope said no.[50]

General Charette and his wife joined Hélène in the first part of her audience with the Pope and then left for fifteen minutes, after which Charette returned:

> [Charette] found Princess Hélène in tears by the Holy Father's knee. I put myself on the other side. 'You know the issue?' 'Yes, Holy Father.' 'Understand, poor Elena, that the Holy Father is the guardian of principles from which he cannot depart; that even if I were to agree—which is impossible—what guarantee would there be for the education of the children? And the Queen cannot want this marriage'.... This elderly man, in his white cassock, reaching out with both his hands to the Princess who pressed them over her heart, adorable in her grief; he looked on with great compassion at this beautiful, weeping girl, this Daughter of France at his feet, imploring forgiveness and mercy for her first and only love!... 'Poor Elena!' he repeated constantly as he lay his hands upon her.[51]

On the surface, Leo's refusal seems straightforward. As Pope, he could not sanction the conversion of any Catholic to another faith, essentially an apostasy. However, many other factors were at work as well. The relationship between the Popes and the French was mixed, to say the least. France had invaded the Papal States in 1798, forcing Pius VI into exile. Although the Pope was restored to his lands in 1800, the Papal States were again invaded by France in 1808 and occupied until the downfall of Napoléon. Following upon revolutions that broke out across Europe in 1848, a Roman Republic was declared the following year and Pope Pius IX fled. The French Second Republic—under the presidency of Louis Napoléon Bonaparte (later Emperor Napoléon III)—sent troops to restore the Pope. Again in 1871, the city of Rome was occupied by the new Italian government, and the Pope became restricted to the limits of the Vatican itself. After that, not until the signing of the Lateran Pact in 1929 would any reigning Pope leave the confines of the Vatican. Pope Leo could not afford to antagonize the French Republic by helping to put an Orléans princess on the British throne when he might soon need that same Republic's help in either securing Rome for the Papacy again or providing a place of refuge if everything went wrong.[52]

In any event, the answer was no, and Hélène got back to England via Calais, the night before her father and brother returned from their American tour. Hélène, 'poor child who should be in despair but is very courageous,' told her mother that she would never marry since she could not marry Eddy.[53] Eddy's reaction to the news was one of misery:

Now it appears as if my last ray of hope was gone. But I never will give up hope as long as I have life in my wretched body. In spite of all this unhappiness, and apparently hopeless state of things, you become far more dear to me now, although it seems hardly possible that you could be dearer to me, than you have already been. I can do nothing but think of you my darling from morning till night, and know how unhappy you must be, and what would I not give to be able to comfort you now, and tell you that you are beloved by me more than any woman in the world. It is quite impossible I could ever love another woman again, or in the same way after what has happened, even if I should live to be a hundred and not near you. You have become so truly dear to me that nothing can alter my feelings now, even if you ere to give me up in despair, which however I believe you never will, after what you have already said.

Less than a week later, Eddy passed through Calais in the other direction en route to attend the Berlin wedding of his cousin Princess Victoria of Prussia, the Kaiser's sister. When he returned, he continued writing to Hélène as 'my beloved one', assuring her that he still wore the St George medal with her picture on the reverse which she had given him and that the photograph she gave him at Mar was always on his table. He added that 'I had a talk to my Grandmama about our affairs on my return from Berlin, and she was as nice about it as possible and said so many kind things about us both. I know no one who desires to see us united more than she does, and I know she will do all she can do help us.'[54]

Early in the year, the Comte leased Stowe House in Buckinghamshire; in May, he went with his wife and their uncle, the Prince de Joinville, to inspect the property and grounds. It was a huge stately country house, which has been described as 'the largest and most completely realised private neo-classical building in the world.' With its enfilade of ten interconnecting state rooms looking out over extensive landscaped gardens and a total of four-hundred rooms, it was the grandest house where the family ever lived, with its Marble Saloon, Egyptian Hall, State Dining Room, the Grenville Drawing Room (which the Comte de Paris converted into a chapel), and the Garter Room. The house at Stowe was originally built in 1677 for Sir Richard Temple, the third Baronet, but vastly expanded during the next two generations with John Vanbrugh, Robert Adam, and many others having a hand in the design and decoration. In 1809, on the occasion of visits from many members of the French royal family, the owner, the first Duke of Buckingham and Chandos, is said to have witnessed the future King Louis Philippe begging pardon from King Louis XVIII for ever having worn the republican *tricolour*. However, by the early nineteenth century, the Duke was so heavily in debt that the house was closed and was frequently on the sales market. The third Duke died without a male heir, and Stowe was inherited by his eldest daughter, Lady Kinloss, who attempted to sell the property but failing that leased it to the Comte de Paris.[55]

On 10 November, the Comte and Comtesse with Philippe and Hélène made an official entry in the town of Buckingham, which was decorated in their honour and where, in response to a welcome address from the mayor and corporation, the Comte responded with an address of his own, thanking the people and looking forward to the 'charm and resources of English country life' there.[56]

Barrière, secretary to the Duc d'Orléans, described a typical day of their new life at Stowe. The Comte would rise between 5 and 6 a.m., read some of his newspapers, breakfast, do his correspondence—which he seldom dictated—and then, after his toilette, would receive his chamberlain de service and his secretary between nine and ten, when he did not meet with his private Council. The Comtesse, having taken care of the various household duties—something she excelled in—would ordinarily attend meetings of the Council where she did not fail to give her opinion on the matters of the day. The Duc d'Orléans, living with the family as an economic move in order to finance a trip to the Far East, was tremendously bored with life at Stowe, always rising late, and sneaking off to London for two or three days. A quarter of an hour before lunch, the family gathered in the hall or the grand salon to meet with any guests, then at the second sound of the dinner gong went in to eat. After lunch, they returned to the salon to drink coffee or liqueurs, to smoke, and chat. In the evening, a servant went around to light all the lamps before dinner at seven. Afterwards, evenings were spent in the hall where the Comte would read and sometimes comment on news from *The Times*, and the Comtesse and Hélène would provide music. By ten or ten thirty, everyone retired for the evening.[57]

Stowe also provided grand hunting country, and the Comtesse became Master of the Wood Norton Hounds. The pack of harriers was kept by the Comte at Stowe, and it was the only instance in England, where a lady acted as master. At the opening meet at Stowe the following year, some two hundred invitations were issued to a champagne luncheon at which the Comtesse was presented with a silver horn inscribed 'by the farmers in Buckingham and neighbourhood hunting with the Wood Norton Hounds.'[58] Hélène joined in the hunts at both Stowe and Wood Norton, and many commented upon her daring in the field.

The front page of *Le Figaro* of 17 November published a small notice of a gift of 20,000 francs which the Comte de Paris gave to the Pope for the 'denier de Saint-Pierre'—St Peter's Pence—in appreciation of the welcome that His Holiness had given to Princess Hélène, although General de Charette had said it was 7,000 francs on telegraphed instructions from the Comte in Montréal 'that he did not wish to leave his daughter alone to give her savings.'[59] However, on the same page, they ran a larger story questioning why young Princess Hélène was allowed to make such a trip to Rome while her father was out of the country, and was not in the company of her mother. The article commented on the many suppositions behind the trip but said the most likely reason was a projected marriage which would have religious implications. Most importantly, they named Prince Albert Victor as the potential bridegroom. Furthermore, they suggested that whereas her grandmother, Hélène, Duchesse d'Orléans, could have been Protestant queen of a Catholic France, Princess Hélène could likewise be a Catholic queen of a Protestant England.[60]

The next day, *Le Figaro* published a denial of the story with a statement from the Comte de Paris stating that Princess Hélène had done nothing more than any other Catholic was able to do in greeting the Holy Father and asking for his blessing for herself and her family. However, the story would not go away. On the 19th, another report told that the trip to Rome had been made in company with General de Charette and his wife—travelling as the Comte and Comtesse de Polk (the baronne's maiden name). It also said that Hélène herself had given a large sum of money to the Pope for the '*denier de Saint-Pierre*' using money that her father had given her to buy an English horse.

Le Gaulois in Paris published a story entitled *Pour sa foi* (For her faith) as its lead article on page one of the 2 December edition. This piece picked up the report originally used by *Le Soleil du Midi*, a provincial royalist newspaper, which denied—but fully repeated—the story that Hélène had been to Rome to seek a papal dispensation. Instead, *Le Gaulois* insisted that she had 'sacrificed her heart to her religious faith' and travelled to Rome 'to assure the Pope of her unshakeable attachment to the Roman Catholic religion.' The next day, *Le Figaro* printed 'Broken Hearts,' yet another story which said it marked the definitive end of the romance because of the religious differences, and likewise wrote of the end of the engagement of the Duc d'Orléans with his cousin Marguerite de Chartres. The same day, *The Standard* printed it in London, and from there it spread to the provincial newspapers. The Comte immediately wrote to complain to the Prince of Wales, who responded:

> In these days of free Press it is impossible to control the newspapers & the best plan is to take no notice of what is said however annoying to ones feelings it must be. However I cannot help observing that those paragraphs would probably not have appeared if more discretion had been shown by your friends![61]

Normally, a letter from the Pope would be a great joy to the Comte, but that was undoubtedly not the case when Leo XIII's letter of 14 December arrived.

> Highness, During the visit that We had recently with Princess Hélène, your daughter, We received from her the confidential information about her inclination for a prince born outside the catholic religion. It would have been agreeable to consent to her desires and grant her that which she came to ask Us, but the duty of Our charge absolutely forbids that and requires Us to turn away from any union which the Holy Church could not bless.
>
> Today a similar duty inspires Us to write to Your Highness to speak about the projected marriage of you elder son, the duc d'Orléans, with the Princess Marguerite, daughter of the duc de Chartres.
>
> By a letter, dated 19 June past, the young duke told Us of the troubles and the anguishes that this project was causing him.
>
> In reading it Your Highness will see the noble sentiments which are stated there. The duke there accuses himself and no one else. He had given his word very lightly, and he repents that because since then he learned the graves dangers of consanguinous unions, dangers that he was no longer able to doubt after the unhappiness which occured to his uncle. He loves his family and the principle that it represents and this is why he cannot resign himself to a marriage, which opens itself up to a similar unhappiness and would jeopardize both parties. But he also know how much this union is valued by his Father and that a refusal on his part would bring great unhappiness. His filial piety moves him to address himself to Us....
>
> From the Vatican, 14 December 1890. Leo PP XII[62]

The year ended with the Comte de Paris writing from Stowe House to Queen Victoria, detailing his respects and good wishes from the Comtesse and Hélène, and remembering his very early childhood memories of England and especially the Queen's 'cordiale affection' for his mother. There was neither mention of, nor allusion to, the ruptured romance. Prince Eddy, for his part, wrote a long chatty letter to his brother George on New Year's Day talking about their sisters, hunting, and naval activities. Only at the end did he add: 'I have not time to write more now, but when I write again I will tell you all about dear Hélène and how things are going, which at present are not in a very happy state for me or her either. You have no idea how I love this sweet girl now, and feel I could never be happy without her.' The Queen herself kept the link alive by sending two signed photographs to Hélène, who at the end of January replied to '*Madame et bien chère Tante*' from San Lucar in Spain of her gratitude for this sign of the Queen's affection.[63]

The Comtesse and Hélène left Stowe House on 12 January, arriving the next day in Paris, where they stayed at the Hotel Bristol; they spent the evening with the Duchesse de Chartres and her sons Henri and Jean *en route* to Spain. The Comte and Philippe left Southampton for Portugal and then to Andalusia where they met up with the rest of the family.

When Eddy did write to George again, it was 'about how my affairs are proceeding; not well I can assure you.' Now, it was not so much the Comte de Paris's continuing dissent, but rather Hélène herself:

She now thinks it so wrong to change after having been to see the Pope. That was the most fatal step possible, and I deplore it more than anything for it now makes it doubly hard for me to combat against. But I mean to remain firm, in fact there is nothing else to be done, if I ever can expect and hope to marry Hélène, which you may be sure I do. If I had only had the chance of seeing her some times, which however I have not I feel certain I should have prevented her going to Rome, for I would have pointed out to her that no good could possibly come of it, and that she must stick to what she had said at the first, that she would change for my sake, and then all would have been well so far. But now I have all this to fight over again for she thinks there is some way out of the difficulty without being obliged to change. I know it will be no easy matter to make her again promise me that she will change for my sake after this visit to the Pope, for he could have only told her one thing. But still I believe I have now her love so thoroughly, and that she is really so fond of me now, that she will eventually give in. But it will take time that I am certain of, and there is still the other question, whether her Father seeing her determination to stick to me in spite of everything will still withould his consent to her marrying. But I can hardly believe he will, bigotted Catholic that he is, and that he will give in sooner or later. This is how things stand at present, and I fear I cannot get any one to help me now, but must do the whole business myself. They are all abroad now in Spain, and I fear will not be back much before the beginning of April, so that I shall have to wait till then before I can do any more. You may rest assured that I shall never give in now that things have gone so far, for it would be weakness in the extreme were I to give it up now. I know she told the Pope that she would never marry at all if she were unable to marry me, that I believe knowing as much of her as I do now. I write to her every week, and she also writes, and very dear affectionate letters too, so that we up our feelings that way which is the only thing to be done when you are absent from the object of your affections. I think I shall feel the happiest now in England, if it only comes right some day, for I feel certain we should live the happiest and most devoted of couples. I have spent a good deal of time writing all this but as I had not told you before how things really were, I thought it best to do so. Grandmama has been really most kind about it all and has done all she can for us. She promised me to see Hélène on her return home, and have a good talk to her about it all. But I fear she will not be able to do much good although she thinks she can. Since I wrote to you last a great deal has been going on in one way and another, and on the whole I have had a good time of it.[64]

'All we can do now is to wait and see what time can do for us and trust to God to help us,' the Princess of Wales wrote to Prince George, 'in the meantime they go on corresponding and loving one another from a distance and strange to say her Parents have not yet put a stop to it—which looks as if they also hope for the best.' The corresponding did indeed continue, although only Eddy's letters have survived. In January 1891, he wrote from the cavalry barracks to thank her for the lovers' knot ring that she sent him for his birthday along with a diamond pin in the shape of a heart and a copy of *The Imitation of Christ*, which he claimed he always thought 'such an excellent book.'[65]

Family hopes, however, remained alive. In March, Queen Victoria's eldest daughter, Vicky, the Empress Frederick, was visiting at Sandringham and wondered whether her mother would see Hélène again about their hopes for an accepted engagement. The Empress had spoken about the situation to the Princess of Wales, who 'was so distressed about the visit to the Pope, & the pressure that would be put on the poor girl by her family!!' Vicky still hoped that 'it may come right' because 'it would be extremely sad & hard if it did not.' The two young people continued to write:

There is no question about it, that you would make the most perfect wife and companion any man could dream of ever having. And to think that I might be that fortunate man is certainly a dream to be felt very often and slept on, and gives great comfort to the mind I can assure you. You won't doubt for an instant my fidelity, will you darling.

Even the Comte de Paris wrote to Hélène that 'I ask God every day to intervene, that he will work a miracle, as he knows how to do in our times, to make possible an honourable union with the young prince who has conquered your heart and has given you his own.' However, he recognised that Hélène could not and would not commit apostacy by renouncing her faith; their union must remain an 'unrealisable dream' and Hélène must not prolong the current situation but release Eddy from his promises.[66]

Hélène had been away from England since early January and would not return until early July. The whole family had gathered for several months in Andalusia, where her mother had inherited the great palace at Villamanrique from her father. Philippe was the first to return to England at the end of January, and then the Comte de Paris towards the end of April after a brief visit to Lisbon. The Comtesse did not return to England until mid-May with the three younger children, but Hélène remained in Lisbon until 1 July. The Comtesse carried with her a letter for Eddy dated 1 May:

> My dear Eddy,
>
> It is with deep sorrow that I write to you, for what I have to tell you costs me a great deal and I need all my courage.
>
> I have always flattered myself with the illusion that what is not possible today will one day perhaps become possible—and you know how much I have longed for this. Alas, I see clearly that I was wrong; a marriage will always be impossible, the political obstacles are unsurmountable and as for those raised by my religion, I cannot dishonour you and I will not cast them aside. In spite of all the suffering it costs me, I am forced to renounce the happiness I have dreamed of and with this letter I bid you farewell.
>
> I owe it to you, to your parents, to the Queen, who has been so kind to me, not to stand in the way of what England expects from you. I must ask you to release me from my word; I return to you that which, in my illusion, I truly felt able to accept, and, at the same time, I send back the things which were so precious to me, but which I have no right to keep.
>
> I ask you to show this letter to your parents. I beg you, do not try to fight against my decision, it is irrevocable, we must not see one another again.
>
> Do your duty as an English Prince without hesitation and forget me.
>
> Hélène[67]

The Comtesse wrote to Hélène that when her father had read the letter, 'he simply said, "There is a brave heart that deserves to be happy and I am proud of Hélène!" This should be enough to show you that he approves absolutely.' When he wrote to Hélène directly, the Comte spoke of the 'profound emotion with which I read the letter—so noble, so touching, so simple.' He made a copy for himself and the more he re-read the letter, the more he came to the conclusion that this was the only possible outcome:

> I would add that I admire more than I know how to say the manner in which you express sentiments which at the same time are so noble and so painful to

formulate. You knew how to link closure with delicacy in a way that a professional writer would no doubt not have found.[68]

Eventually, on 29 May, the Comtesse was finally able to deliver the letter to Prince Eddy in his mother's presence. The Comtesse wrote to Hélène:

> You know without my telling you what a terrible time I have had. Two and a half hours of conversation, sometimes with the mother, sometimes the son, she very reasonable though in tears, he less reasonable and at first violent, then in despair; finally I was promised that on Wednesday I will be sent the response you desire.[69]

That response came:

> My dearest Hélène,
>   No words can possibly describe the misery I felt on reading your letter given me by your dear Mama, and I can hardly bring myself to believe that you or your own free will have decided that all should be over between us two, and that your decision is irrevocable, and that it is an utter impossibility for you ever to change your religion, even for my sake. You well know how deeply rooted my devotion for you is, and it almost breaks my heart to think that our lives must be spent apart. Of course, I suppose I ought to try and submit to your parents and your own decision, but it seems to me impossible to realise that such is to be our fate. God bless you and may He help us both to do what is right. Though the cross is laid upon us, it is indeed a heavy one to bear.
>   Yours, Eddy.[70]

Princess Alexandra wrote to her absent son George about the end of the prospective engagement, saying 'to me too it is a horrible grief, I own, as she would have made the most perfect wife for Eddy in every way & they were so fond of each other. He still declares he will see here again & won't give her up but I fear it is all of no use.'[71]

The Comte and Comtesse de Paris lunched with Queen Victoria at Windsor on 30 June, and they had a long discussion about the recent events. The Comte said that he had received a communication through his Aunt Clémentine that earlier in the previous year, Queen Victoria had said that all meetings between Eddy and Hélène should be avoided considering where they might lead. However, he said he received this only after he had arrived at Mar Lodge where the fateful meeting took place. Otherwise, he claimed he would not have gone there.[72]

However, Queen Victoria had already recognized the futility of continuing the situation of an engagement in limbo and told Lord Salisbury so. He replied that he 'entirely concurs in the wisdom of Your Majesty's decision—not to encourage any further meeting between the Prince & Princess Hélène. It is evident that the obstacles are quite insuperable & though the Prince deserves every sympathy, there is no course open to him but to try & forget this episode in his life.'[73]

Around this ongoing crisis, family life for the Paris clan continued with its regular travel patterns as well as another crisis caused by the Duc d'Orléans. The Comtesse returned briefly to Paris in June to attend the consecration of the Basilica of Sacre Coeur on Montmartre, which would become one of the city's emblematic symbols. The Comte in July went to spend time with his younger children at the seaside at Westgate-on-Sea before heading to Scotland for the shooting. That autumn, Philippe was cited in a London Divorce Court case, and the Duc d'Aumale held a conference with royalist leaders in France seeking the Comte's censure of his son's conduct.

In addition to the family troubles, the Comte de Paris suffered another blow when it was learned that General Boulanger had commited suicide on his lover's grave in Brussels on 30 September; the next day, *The Times* published a damning article clearly implicating the Comte de Paris in the greater scandal. The Comte had 'lost his money—two or three millions of francs—but he lost much more besides. Perhaps, in the long run, that will be the most serious result of Boulangerism—the final disappearance of the present generation of Orleanists from the list of possible claimants of supreme power in France.' The report from *The Times* concluded that 'Boulanger had killed himself; but before he died he killed the Orleanists and he killed the *plébiscite*.'[74]

Within just a few weeks, Prince Eddy took the first step and proposed to his cousin Princess May of Teck, an English-born Protestant princess, whom Hélène knew well. The proposal came on 3 December; before it was publicly announced, Queen Victoria wrote to both the Comtesse de Paris and the Princess of Wales. She informed the Comtesse that Eddy's first thought had been for '*la pauvre* Hélène and the pain that this news will cause her' and that he had become engaged because of the great desire of his family and the English people in general to see him married. 'You know, dear Isabelle,' the Queen wrote, 'all my feelings towards you, and all the regrets that I have had that other plans were not able to be achieved.' She wrote to the Princess of Wales of her joy and thankfulness for the engagement and told her that she had written to the Comtesse de Paris to 'save Eddy & also you the pain of announcing it to them. Dear Eddy is so nice about poor Hélène.' Both the Comte and Comtesse wrote back to thank the Queen for her thoughtfulness, and both told of Hélène's strength despite the pain that the news brought to her on the day as well as renewing the sad memories, which both the Comtesse and Hélène share over the end of the romance. Despite her sadness, Hélène was 'courageous and knew her duty.'[75]

The timing was in one sense fortunate, as the Paris family had already arranged to go to Portugal for Christmas, leaving on 16 December—the Comte with Philippe and Isabelle sailing there directly from Southampton, the Comtesse with Hélène and the other children going via Paris, where they were met at the Gare du Nord by Queen Isabel, the Duc and Duchesse de Chartres, and their children Jean and Marguerite—then on to Madrid and eventually to Lisbon.

Eddy's prospective happiness with May, Princess Victoria Mary, however, would not have time to take root and flourish. The family of the Prince and Princess of Wales gathered at Sandringham for the New Year and to celebrate Eddy's birthday. His brother George had suffered a severe bout of typhoid fever in early November, and was still weak and recovering when he made his first walk outside in nearly eight weeks on New Year's Day. Then, their sister Victoria came down with influenza, and Eddy himself began to feel 'seedy with influenza.' He was not well enough to put in an appearance at the family dinner in honour of his twenty-eighth birthday on the 8th, and so George took his place sitting between 'Motherdear' and May, while the Duke of Teck proposed the health of his future son-in-law. By the next day, however, inflammation of the lungs had set it, and over the next few days the symptoms peaked and troughed. Then, in the early morning hours of 14 January, the Prince of Wales called George to the room where Eddy had gotten much worse. The Prince and Princess of Wales had been with their son all night, and now George summoned the rest of the family, who waited and watched and prayed with the chaplain. Princess Maud later wrote to Hélène that 'the whole time he was delirious he kept talking in French. I am sure he was thinking of you.' Princess Victoria made is more explicit—'Your name was on his dying lips more than once.' Then, as Prince George recorded in his diary:

> At 9.35 my beloved darling Eddy passed away quite quietly & peacefully. Oh! how shall I ever forget that too awful moment, it will haunt me for ever; how shall I ever forget that dreadful scene all of us sobbing round him as if our hearts would break. Our grief & sorrow was too terrible.[76]

Princess Maud wrote to Hélène that 'later on we arranged flowers all around his bed & he looked so beautiful with a most heavenly expression on his beloved face, just as if he was asleep with his dear hands folded in front of him, like a saint or some knight of old. So tall & so thin he looked, if only you could have seen him like that.'

Although his mother hoped for a completely private funeral, something more formal was required. Six days after that terrible morning, the extended family and a few foreign representatives gathered together at Windsor along Eddy's regiment to bury him in St George's Chapel. In the days after the funeral, Eddy's three sisters all wrote to Hélène, and she learned that Eddy was buried with the little coin medallion she had given him—with St George on one side and her picture on the other. His mother and sisters Victoria and Maud had placed it around his neck 'and nobody knew it.' Victoria wrote:

> My first thought during our overwhelming grief was of you, who I felt must be suffering. Oh! That I could but be near you now, my darling. What a comfort

we could be to each other. For you knew and understood him better than anyone. He is yours now!! The Lord is merciful you see & as you could not have him in life he is yours in death.[77]

Quite amazingly, writing just the day after the funeral, Princess Victoria wrote in the same letter saying:

Do you know that as I watched them carrying him into the very same Church where a month later he was to be married I felt I could bear this indeed ten thousand times more than that he should belong to another but you! Wicked indeed you must think me for saying this but it is sacred [*word unreadable*]. He was meant for you only even God wished it to be so. His holy will be done.

Princess Louise compounded the sentiment:

My heart has bled all along for you, knowing so well how you loved him, (& which you confided to me, the first of all) & I can feel for you, & know how much you have had to bear & what yo must have gone through! Now that all is over, we can speak of it. God had been merciful and done all for the best instead of him belonging to another, He is keeping him above in heaven [*line missing*] yours in life, he is yours in death & waiting above for us all to come & join him there.

At some point, the Princess of Wales sent along a note enclosing a memento: 'For my dear angel Hélène, a memorial ring of our darling Eddy. From his broken-hearted, desolate, miserable Mother dear.'[78]

Hélène herself had longed to have flowers on Eddy's coffin in her name, but did not dare to ask. However, she was later able to thank Queen Victoria that 'you anticipated my wishes and kindly took charge of my loving memorial.' Eventually, Hélène was able to visit the tomb herself along with Princess Beatrice, who later returned with a wreath which she laid there on Hélène's behalf. For years afterwards, there lay a wreath of immortelles on his tomb with the single word 'HÉLÈNE'.[79]

4

1892–1895

Where will her lot be cast some day poor dear girl?

After Eddy's death, his family continued to worry about 'poor sweet young Hélène' and wonder 'Where will her lot be cast some day poor dear girl?' Within the year, Hélène was again visiting Marlborough House and Sandringham, and she remained very closely attached to the Princess of Wales throughout the latter's lifetime, while various rumours about possible husbands began to abound. The Empress of Russia briefly suggested Hélène as a bride for her son, the future Tsar Nicholas II; a French count thought that she should be introduced to the heir to the Austrian throne; the German Empress Augusta Victoria was scandalized when her brother announced his intention to marry her; and King Leopold II of the Belgians is said to have had the Constitution changed when he thought his nephew and heir Baudouin wanted to marry Hélène. Aunt Clémentine of Saxe-Coburg had approached the Comte de Paris in 1891 about the possibility of a match with her son Ferdinand (later King of Bulgaria), but he wrote that was 'an approach which naturally I did not welcome, Hélène having entirely different ideas and myself not believing that Ferdinand is destined to make a good husband.' Hélène's cousin Marie of Denmark felt obliged to report to the French *chargé d'affaires* in Copenhagen that newspaper rumours of Hélène's '*projets de mariage*' were unfounded. However, the speculation continued.[1]

Through an intermediary, the Comte de St Priest, one of the entourage of the Comte de Paris, wrote to Queen Victoria from Bayonne to suggest that she might promote a marriage with the Archduke Franz Ferdinand, nephew and heir to the Emperor Franz Joseph since the suicide of Crown Prince Rudolph in 1889. As there were newspaper reports that the Archduke would soon be visiting London, St Priest thought that the timing might be appropriate because he had heard that Hélène had decided not to marry and that the Queen was the only one who might be able to help her change her mind. As for the Archduke, the Comte felt sure that once he saw Hélène 'the physical and spiritual qualities of the Princess could perhaps touch his heart.' The intermediary sent a note to Victoria stating the proposal: 'Le Comte de St Priest asks The Queen to favor a marriage between the Crown Prince of Austria and Princess Helen of Orléans. He thinks the Crown Prince is coming here soon.' The note was quickly annotated by the royal hand 'The Queen will do no such thing,' that it would be cruel to suggest such a thing 'except out of affection' and furthermore he was not Crown Prince, but rather the heir presumptive.[2]

Other rumours were circulating as well. As early as 1888, there had been a newspaper rumour that the Grand Duke Alexis of Russia had been given permission to marry Hélène. Then, on the back of the Franco-Russian fêtes in October 1893, which portended a growing alliance between the two countries, a German diplomatic report came out of St Petersburg at the end of November reporting an imminent engagement between Hélène and the Tsarevich. However, the concerned parties do not seem to have been consulted because it was not until 29 January 1894 that Tsarevich Nicholas, who had already fallen in love with Princess Alix of Hesse—the same princess who had earlier rejected Prince Eddy—recorded in his diary:

> While I was talking to Mama this morning she made several hints about Hélène, the daughter of the Comte de Paris, which puts me in an awkward position. I am at the crossing of two paths; I myself want to go in the other direction, while Mama obviously wants me to take this one! What will happen? [3]

This was a critical period in Franco-Russian relations, as France was hoping for an alliance with Russia to break its German-constructed diplomatic isolation, and Russia needed to raise investment capital in Paris. However, while some have suggested that Tsar Alexander wanted this match to strengthen the alliance with France, it is unlikely that a marriage with an Orléans princess would have favourably impressed the French republic. Just three years earlier, the Tsar had rejected an application by Hélène's brother Philippe for admission into a Russian cavalry unit on the grounds that 'the French Government, with which he had excellent relations, might construe this as favouring the royalist party in France,' while 'Russia meant to hold aloof from party disputes as long as France had so respected a Chief Magistrate as M. Carnot.' Prince Valdemar of Denmark—the Tsar's brother-in-law who was married to Philippe's cousin Marie—had made the original application, and pointed out that Prince Louis Napoléon Bonaparte had been admitted into the Russian army; the Tsar pointed out that that prince was not a pretender to the French throne and 'had never come into collision with the Republican government.'[4] Therefore, it seems unlikely that there was ever much more than the Empress Marie picking up on the interest that her sister, the Princess of Wales, had shown in Hélène.

Still, as early as 1894, *Le Matin* wrote that a romance with Nicholas of Russia failed only due to the Pope's refusal to allow her to change her religion, and the next year, her father's confessor publicly wrote that the Russian crown might have been Hélène's had she been less attached to her faith and willing to convert to Orthodoxy.[5] However, since she had in the end not converted to marry someone she loved, it was unlikely that she would have considered something similar for another prince she barely knew. These plans, if they really existed, seem to have circulated around Hélène and Nicholas, with them being barely consulted; ultimately, it came to nothing.

Even before Eddy's illness, Hélène's father decided that she should make another extended visit to Amélie and Carlos in Portugal. Amélie wrote that they would be happy as soon as she could be sent, and Carlos himself wrote that it would be a great pleasure to have Hélène with them and that he was sure that it would do her a great deal of good to spend some time with them. However, when it was suggested that Philippe should join her, Carlos made it clear that his visit must be a short one. 'This is for many reasons; you know very well that, unfortunately, during his stay at Cascais, his "allures" and his manner of being and of speaking produced a very bad effect (pardon my habitual frankness).'[6]

A month later, the dangerous illness of his grandmother, the Duchesse de Montpensier (which developed into pleurisy and continued to be serious through early April 1892), gave a good reason for the Comtesse de Paris to visit her mother in Seville and take both Hélène and the Duc d'Orléans with her. It was important to keep Hélène away from an England grieving for Eddy. It was just as important to get Philippe away, as he had just been named as co-respondent in another divorce case; this time, the proceedings were brought by a baronet's son, Charles Nesbitt Armstrong, against his wife, the increasingly celebrated singer Nellie Melba. Philippe had already fathered a son by an actress in the casino at Lausanne, but that had been kept quiet.[7] His affair with Madame Melba was not so easy to cover up. It had begun in 1890, but gossip grew into scandal when Philippe followed her to Brussels, Vienna, and finally St Petersburg, where she was to sing before the Tsar. Although Armstrong quietly dropped the suit, the damage was done and Philippe left for a two-year tour of Africa.

Their sometime-cook Rosa Lewis considered Philippe 'a most charming person, but he would fall in love with anybody. The most extraordinary thing' about the Orléans family was that 'both their sons always fell in love with old women.' It was probably the Melba affair that she was referring to when she wrote that 'I had to go once to the Crystal Palace with the Comtesse de Paris just to have a look at her and see what she was really like, because the Comtesse always found, much to her annoyance, that her sons were always falling in love with the ugliest old women they could find. Some men are like that.'[8]

Later, in November 1892, the Paris family visited Queen Victoria at Balmoral, who reported to her own daughter the Empress Frederick about 'poor dear sweet Hélène':

She is vy. touching in her gt. love & grief for our poor dear Eddy. She was with me for a few minutes alone & was so sweet & touching. 'I loved him so much; & I may have been imprudent but I could not do otherwise, I loved him so much—he was so good.' Poor dear Child she has no one who understands what she feels & shuts it up within herself.—I told her how I felt for her & that I shld. always love her as she might have been my Gd. Child!—tho'—the difficulties never cld. have been applanies [*sic*], that I know.[9]

Queen Victoria kept up a strong connection with Hélène and encouraged the young woman to call her 'Grandmama.' Hélène wrote to her:

I was profoundly moved when you were so gracious as to tell me to call You by this name that at one time I dreamed of having the right to give You. This is how, in our conversations together, we spoke of the Queen. He who is no more taught me to know You, and above all, to love You as a mother. These hopes had flown even before the heart that brought them into being, but my feelings have always remained the same. And those which I have for You, my dear Grandmama, have grown, if that is possible, with the cruel grief which has so tested us both.

Although Hélène signs this letter as 'the Queen's very humble and very devoted granddaughter', the two surviving letters from Hélène to Queen Victoria written in the year after Eddy's death are signed, as usual, from 'your very respectful and very affectionate niece.'[10] After her engagement to the Duke of Aosta, Hélène reverted to calling the Queen *Ma chère Tante*.

The romance between Eddy and Hélène never reached the stage of governmental crisis, but it certainly did create governmental concern. Queen Victoria's passion for matchmaking came to naught, as it often did. However, her role as constitutional monarch reigned supreme, relying upon advice from her ministers rather than upon her personal family feelings.

Back in 1879, Queen Victoria had been in favour of Prince Eddy and Prince George both going on an eight-month cruise as part of their education. The First Lord of the Admiralty, W. H. Smith, expressed doubts about risking the lives of the second and third in line to the throne in such a way, but the Queen 'rebuked him indignantly in a letter to Disraeli. The Prince of Wales, she told him, was extremely annoyed at Smith raising in cabinet a matter which had been settled within the family.'[11] Thirteen years later, the Queen's perspective had changed, and she recognized the interests of the government in the affairs of the Royal Family.

Hélène's physical health—as well as her emotional state—was a great concern to the family. Her brother-in-law King Carlos took charge and admitted that he loved Hélène as if she were his own daughter and that the affection was reciprocated and indeed she 'obeys me absolutely in everything (a rare thing).' Carlos wrote to the Comte de Paris that 'she is, perhaps, a bit better since she has been here, but not yet well. She continues to have rather strong suffocations and a disagreeable cough.' The King's own physician, Dr Feijão, examined Hélène and found nothing that indicated a chest illness but did find a marked difference between the strength of the left and right lung, the right one breathing badly. He felt this was probably the result of a rather rare nervous disease but wanted to observe her more carefully before proceeding further. Some circulation problem in her extremities was attributed to anaemia, but none of this was considered dangerous 'for the moment.' In the meantime, Dr Feijão recommended a fairly even climate, avoiding cold air and the moisture from the sea during the hot season. Heat and hot climates could only do her good, as long as it were not a moist heat. She needed exercise, but with moderation, and most essentially, must be continually distracted so that she didn't think too much about herself and her condition. Hélène's father was relieved to know that Dr Feijão concurred with their own doctor, M. de Mussy, in saying that there was no lung disease, no doubt fearing the consumption which had already claimed so many young members of the family. The Comte felt that it 'is a sort of asthma, due to an emphysema whose earliest origins one could trace to whooping cough which she had when eight or nine years old. This was certainly aggravated by a hereditary arthritic disposition and by anaemia.' Combined with the nervous stress of recent months, a return visit for a 'serious cure' in the waters at Marienbad with her mother was planned for July.[12]

On 24 March, Amélie wrote that 'Hélène is truly better emotionally, and I believe physically, even though she coughs easily after an effort like climbing stairs too quickly. She has decided to return to riding horseback and finds it good.' However, it was apparently only on Amélie's insistence that Hélène took to the saddle again. 'Amélie forced me to go out on horseback yesterday, which seemed very funny to me, to find myself on the back of a horse, and in starting I felt very ill at ease—this morning I am doing much better.' Over the coming weeks, Hélène's equestrian talents returned, and she spoke of riding a great deal in her letters to her father. Other interests also resurfaced. She wrote to her father that she had read the entire encyclical recently issued by the Pope on the church and state in France—'even if it is very long'—which her mother had kindly sent.[13]

At the end of April, Amélie received news that the Pope would be awarding her the Golden Rose—one the highest awards that the Catholic church could give to a woman—and Amélie also began preparations to move into the Necessidades Palace. The Comtesse de Paris with the three younger children arrived at the Necessidades in early May after two months apart from Hélène, the longest separation they had ever experienced.[14] That month the family returned to England—the Comte de Paris and Philippe d'Orléans, as usual, going by steamer from Cadiz to Gibraltar and then on to England. The Comtesse, still in Seville, went to Lisbon for Hélène and then proceeded overland to Paris and from there to England.

Years later, Hélène would write of her wandering life, her *vie errante*, speaking about her travelling life in Africa. At this point in her life, she and all her family were also wandering, from one rented property to another, from one relative's home to another, from one country to another, from hotel to spa. In July, she and her mother went to France to visit Uncle Aumale at Chantilly, and Hélène admitted to feeling flattered by the good words and compliments which she received there. Then the two of them went to the German spas at Marienbad, which included a side trip to Bayreuth to hear 'Parsifal' and where they met Prince Henry and Princess Beatrice of Battenberg, Queen Victoria's youngest daughter. Next, it was on to Vienna, where Princess Metternich took Hélène to the ballet, and where she was to lunch with the Archduchess Elisabeth. A week later, she was back in France with her mother at the Château de Randan, where she was pleased to hear the old women say 'She has not changed, Madame the Comtesse, not in fourteen years.' Then it was back to England, but even then not to Stowe, but rather to the Royal Pavilion Hotel in Folkestone, where there was another brief meeting with Uncle Aumale. She did eventually return to Stowe and was there when Cousin Marie and her husband Valdemar of Denmark visited in November, and Hélène joined her parents when they went to lunch with Queen Victoria at Windsor.[15] By the end of that month, the family was again preparing to go to Spain for Christmas and the winter holidays, with the Comte sailing from Southampton to Lisbon, while the Comtesse and her three daughters travelled by way of Paris and Madrid.

The Comtesse with the girls and her younger son returned to England from Spain in early May, spending a short time in Paris with the Duc de Chartres as well as making a visit to Dreux and the family burial chapel there, where they attended Sunday Mass. Back in England, the Comte and Comtesse de Paris and Hélène left Stowe House to stay at the Bristol Hotel in London to join in a number of celebrations in anticipation of the wedding of Prince George with Princess May of Teck, Eddy's former fiancée having become engaged to his brother sixteen months after Eddy's death.

First, there was a family lunch at Marlborough House, which the Comte and Comtesse attended with Hélène and Philippe. Further matchmaking may have been on the mind of the Princess of Wales when she organized another luncheon party at Marlborough House on 4 July 1893. Hélène was there with her parents and brother, along with Alexandra's parents, the King and Queen of Denmark, and their son Valdemar (who was married to Marie d'Orléans), their grandson Tsarevich Nicholas of Russia, and the unmarried Catholic heir to the Belgian throne, Prince Albert, although he was four years younger than Hélène. Earlier, Albert's father, the Count of Flanders, had written to Queen Victoria that his brother King Leopold wanted to change the Belgian constitution to require princes to get the monarch's permission before marrying because he had 'taken it into his head' that his heir, Albert's elder brother the young Prince Baudoin, wanted to marry Hélène. There had indeed been a suggestion back in March 1890 that a match might be arranged between the two of them, but apparently, King Leopold had forbidden it, as he had with a proposal that her brother Philippe marry Leopold's daughter Clémentine, or indeed later that her sister Isabelle might be a possible match for Prince Albert. In any event, that was no longer an option, as Baudouin had died in early 1891 when he was just twenty-one.[16]

The next evening, Queen Victoria attended the 'gigantic Garden-party' at Marlborough House where some 5,000 people had been invited. Of those thousands, the queen noted her immediate family, four Indian princes, the diplomatic corps, and British politicians, plus the Comte and Comtesse de Paris but singled out a special mention in her journal that Hélène was there 'in great beauty.' The Queen stayed only for about an hour, complaining about the 'quite awful' heat, before returning to Buckingham Palace to prepare for another event in the evening.[17]

Again the following evening, Hélène and her parents were among the guests for a dinner party at Marlborough House in honour of the approaching wedding as the band of the Grenadier Guards played. However, they were not at the wedding itself, as the Chapel Royal accomodates only about 150 people.

Later in the autumn, the Prince of Wales celebrated his fifty-second birthday with a house party at Sandringham. Along with his wife Princess Alexandra, the newly married Duke and Duchess of York, his two unmarried daughters Victoria and Maud, and his brother Alfred (who had recently succeeded their uncle as the Duke of Saxe-Coburg), Prince Bertie welcomed the Comte and Comtesse de Paris with Hélène. Also included among the guests were the minister for Brazil, the Portuguese minister, Count Albert Mensdorff (who was both the Austrian minister and a Coburg relation), the Earl of Rosebery (the future Prime Minister), the Earl and Countess Cadogan, and other members of the household. On the birthday itself, 9 November they enjoyed a day of shooting in the Norfolk fields. Then, on the Saturday, two days later, the Paris family left for London aboard the same train as Lord Rosebery, and Hélène in particular seems to have made an impression on him. A friend bumped into Rosebery later at Euston station and they spoke about Hélène, and 'Rosebery, as it happens, was loud in her praises, rather remarkable in him, who seldom shows any interest in women, least of all a friendly and winning one.'[18]

On 30 November, the Comtesse travelled to Paris with Hélène, Isabelle, Louise and Ferdinand, and they were all greeted by the Duc de Chartres at the Gare du Nord. The Comtesse then transferred to the Gare d'Orléans and continued her journey to Madrid with the younger children. However, Hélène went to the *Gare de l'Est* with the Comtesse Françoise Costa de Beauregard for a train to Brindisi in Italy to meet Hélène's brother Philippe and the Countess's husband

Gonzague who was accompanying him. This was the beginning of an extended trip that the four of them would make together to Egypt and the Holy Land. *Le Figaro* announced this journey on the same day as it produced an explosive front-page story 'Idylle Royale,' which exposed the whole story of Hélène's failed engagement with Eddy. It was a good time to be away.

On 19 December, from the banks of the Nile, where they had been for several days and would remain for some time longer, Hélène wrote one of her '*Ma chère Grand'Maman*' letters to Queen Victoria to wish her joy, health, and happiness for the New Year and to ensure the queen that Hélène would remember her in prayer when they got to Jerusalem.

Early in their trip, Hélène met with the poet and writer Wilfred Scawen Blunt and his wife and daughter at Shepherd's Hotel in Cairo. Hélène knew Blunt from shooting parties in Scotland as well as for having taught her lawn tennis. With his wife, Anne—the daughter of Ada Lovelace, now renowned as one of the earliest computer programmers, and granddaughter of the poet Byron—the Blunts were founders of the Crabbet Arabian Stud, based at Sheykh Obeyd outside of Cairo; Hélène and Philippe promised to meet them there after their journey up the Nile. It was also during these days of their trip that they travelled out to Giza and climbed the Great Pyramid.[19]

At the end of December, Hélène and Philippe left Cairo and went down the Nile to visit Thebes and Karnak, then aboard a *dahabieh*, through the first cataract at Aswan, mooring at Elephantine Island. She was enchanted by Aswan and the delicate temple at Philae. Years later, Hélène would remember the imagery of one night when she went to the end of the island and sat by herself watching the waves splashing against the black rocks, the moon reflecting on the Nile. It was at moments like this when Hélène felt all these new sights were not new to her but perhaps remembered from having lived there a long time ago. Her 'new modern spirit,' she thought, was unable to precisely call to mind the mysteries and beautiful pictures of earlier days, but the sense of *déjà vu* was very strong.[20]

Hélène's letters home gave her father the opportunity to read them aloud in the salon and relive his own desert adventures. The photographs she sent—one of herself alone and one with Françoise de Costa—'disguised as peasant women were appalling,' he wrote approvingly.[21]

The party continued as far as the second cataract in the Sudan, with the plan of returning to Cairo about 15 February and then continued on to vist Palestine. While they were in Cairo, they met the thirty-year-old Duke Ernst Günther of Schleswig-Holstein, brother-in-law of the German Kaiser. German diplomatic reports considered that something 'very intimate' developed between Hélène and Ernst Günther and that an engagement was in prospect. Philippe and Hélène left Cairo on 3 March bound for Palestine. Hélène was mounted on an Arabian horse, presented to her by the *Khedive*, and the whole party—which included the Comte and Comtesse Costa de Beauregard—spent the night in a tent in the desert.[22]

Philippe, Hélène, and Ernst Günther—along with Félix Faure, vice president of the Chambre des Députés (who would become President of the Republic the following January)—were in Jerusalem for the celebration of Holy Week and Easter, which fell on 25 March that year. Philippe and Hélène later returned to Egypt, which they left on 2 April, headed for Villamanrique via Brindisi and Gibraltar. Their sisters Isabelle and Louise went to meet them at Malaga, when they arrived on the afternoon of the 12th. The Comte and his son Philippe left Villamanrique at the beginning of May, returning to England and Stowe House via Gibraltar, while the Comtesse, Hélène, and the younger children went to Paris for a couple of days, staying at the Hôtel Campbell, Avenue Friedland. There, they visited friends and family—including the exiled Queen Isabel.

While the family had been in Spain, a royal furore broke out when Duke Ernst Günther announced his intention to marry Hélène. The previous year, Ernst Günther had proposed to the widowed Duchess of Aosta, Princess Laetitia Bonaparte, but Count Münster, the German ambassador to Paris, was able to put an end to that. Philipp Eulenburg, the German ambassador to Austria-Hungary, was now given the job of thwarting this latest romance. He reported that Ernst Günther was 'like a rutting stag in spring. Perhaps even stupider.' His sister, the Empress, was in despair. His brother-in-law, the Kaiser, was furious and refused to approve the match seeing it as an intrigue by the Orléans family, who 'want to make themselves a good name through the House of Hohenzollern.' Diplomats acknowledged Hélène to be beautiful and very smart, but also branded her as ambitious and 'perfidious,' declaring the whole Orléans family to be zealous Catholics, 'passionately French.' Bernhard von Bülow, the Ambassador in Rome, declared that 'we can not allow' the marriage 'under any circumstances.' Using the code name of Heloise for Hélène, he worried that 'there is so much that she could find out, betray, prevent, stir up! What an opening she would give to our worst enemies! With her the Trojan horse would come within our walls.'[23]

Kaiser Wilhelm asked his mother, the Empress Frederick, to solicit the assistance of her mother—Queen Victoria—to use her influence and end any possible romance.

William was almost exclusively preoccupied with an affair wch. seems to me very strange! He says that Ernest Günther wants to marry Hélène of Orléans. W. thinks this quite dreadful and wishes to prevent it by all means in their power! A french woman in the family would not do—he says—nor a catholic—in an old protestant House. He says Dona cannot sleep & sends him Letters and telegrams without end to see whether such a calamity could not be prevented. William asked me whether I knew no means of stopping such a project! I could only answer that all I could do would be to put the matter before you, that you were very fond of Hélène of Orléans & had perhaps means of ascertaining whether such a report were true. I thought it unlikely that the Parents would allow a marriage with a protestant and a German & I also added that I hardly thought it probable that so charming & beautiful a princess would accept Ernest Gunther who is not especially attractive or prepossessing... . I think that Hélène would not entertain the idea for a moment. I think Dona's excitement and agitation & religious prejudices quite exaggerated and ridiculous! I am always very sorry when a Catholic branch is started in an old Protestant family, but it often cannot be avoided. William hopes you would be able to induce the Parents & young Lady to refuse Gunther and close the matter, I said that it was quite possible & even probable that this would happen. W. says on political and religious grounds he would never allow it. I fancy that Gunter is in no way bound except as an official of the Army to ask William's permission at all, but can do as he likes being head of his own family & not a prussian Prince. It seems Gunther tried to marry the Duchesse d'Aosta—wch. W. says—he also would not have allowed.

The Empress Frederick, instead, suggested an alternative. 'If sweet lovely Hélène of Orléans does marry into a family of another religion why not Georgie of Greece—who is so charming—& such a splendid young man!'[24]

Queen Victoria, who had a low opinion of Dona's brother, was able to write back that 'I think I can positively say that there is not a word of truth in the report about Hélène's engagment to horrid Ernst Günther.'[25] Nothing more was said about this putative romance, but a few years later, Ernst Günther did indeed marry a Catholic princess—albeit a German one, the Princess Dorothea of Saxe-Coburg, a granddaughter of Hélène's great-aunt Princess Clémentine.

Within a few days of their return to London, Hélène and her mother went to visit the Princess of Wales at Marlborough House. Then, less than a month later, Hélène was back in Paris on 6 June, this time accompanied by General de Charette, on a visit to her Uncle Aumale at Chantilly. Ten days later, Hélène returned to London with Aumale who made a visit of about three weeks.

The London social season of 1894 was brightened by the presence of the heirs to the thrones of Russia and Austria-Hungary, the young men who had earlier been targeted as prospective husbands for Hélène. In July, the Comte and Comtesse, along with Hélène, were invited to a large family luncheon at Marlborough House, hosted by the Prince and Princess of Wales. A host of the extended royal family was there, along with Archduke Franz Ferdinand of Austria, the Tsarevich Nicholas of Russia, and Aunt Eulalia of Spain. Nicholas was in England to receive Queen Victoria's stamp of approval upon his engagement to her granddaughter Princess Alix of Hesse. Franz Ferdinand was still looking for a bride, and it was not until the next year that he would meet Countess Sophie Chotek at a ball in Prague. There was obviously some hope that Hélène would become his bride, but Queen Victoria wrote to her daughter 'I fear that the young Archduke has no intention of marrying poor Hélène'; at the same time, she wrote the worrying news that 'I hear poor Paris looks awfully ill & seems as tho' he had some mortal illness! It is vy. sad.'[26]

Although the French royalist press reported that the Comte merely suffered from neuraglia, he was indeed suffering from what would prove to be a mortal illness. The Comtesse returned early from a visit she had made with Hélène to the health spas at Marienbad, while Hélène remained there a few days more. Philippe accompanied his mother to the French border, but then went on to Ostend until he too was summoned home, while Amélie set out from Lisbon, and Chartres from the Isle of Skye. Hélène was back at Stowe shortly afterwards.

Queen Victoria was kept in regular contact by telegram, and on 22 August, sent General Gardiner to Stowe to get first-hand information. Although he could not see the Comte, who was resting, nor the Comtesse or Hélène who were out walking, Gardiner did learn from Camille Dupuy 'that the Comte de Paris is still appearing daily at the déjeuner & dinner and drives out every afternoon weather permitting. There has been severe inflammation of the stomach requiring much morphine but this has now subsided & they hope the inflammation may not return.' The Comte was 'fearfully weak', and had 'a distaste for food & what he takes fails to nourish him or keep up his strength.' Dupuy, however, was somewhat encouraging saying 'The situation is serious, because of weakness, but there is still hope that the appetite will come back when the effects of the morphine that he had to be given comes into effect.'

Amélie arrived from Portugal on the morning of 26 August. Philippe had arrived the night before from the continent, and he joined his mother, Hélène, and Uncle Chartres at the station to meet Amélie. From thence, they travelled through torrential rain to reach Stowe House. The wider family gathered too—the aunts, uncles, and cousins. Queen Victoria continued sending messages of concern from Balmoral, including a 'special message to Hélène who is very much affected.'[27] So many telegrams were flying to and from Stowe that the post office commandeered the local schoolroom as an adjunct office with a special staff of telegraphers.

The Comte de Paris died at Stowe House, 8 September 1894 at 7.40 a.m., surrounded by his family. When she heard the news, Queen Victoria remembered Paris as 'a good, honourable, sensible man, and his life had been one of bitter disappointment. For five years he had been suffering from a malignant internal complaint, the fact of which had been denied, as well as the danger of his condition, till the last few weeks. But all those who had seen him this summer saw he was in a dying state.' Within a week of his death, the cause of death was revealed in a medical journal as stomach cancer, which had been diagnosed 'by the electric illumination of that organ.' Although the doctors discussed 'the desperate expedient of the excision of the entire stomach and the substitution of the same organ from a lamb, an operation which has been successful in one case in French surgery,' the risk was deemed too great, 'and the patient was not informed of the real nature of the disease until recently.'[28]

After the Prince of Wales went to make a condolence visit, he reported to Queen Victoria that he found the Comtesse 'wonderfully resigned.' However, others in the family worried more about Hélène, who had shared with the Comtesse all the care of the patient—'she seems to be hit the hardest. She is pale and very changed. Poor girl.' Years later, Hélène would recall her feelings at her father's death:

> Hardly had I guessed the tenderness hidden in my father's heart, hardly had the flame of this beautiful soul shone for me, that the flame was extinguished. With it went all this secret treasure, all of the unknown things that my father carried in himself and which I had only insufficiently penetrated.

Hélène remembered her youth when her only goal was to please her father: how many books she read so that she could interject a single word into his conversations; the memoirs that she read at night as soon as they were published, so that she could speak to him of them, even if she were always a bit trembling in the act; and the pride when he asked my advice or expressed the desire to know the work himself. 'I keep as a relic the last book that his dying hands held.' She remembered the days in Scotland, where they would spend two months each year, and when everyone else was on the hunt, she would read the newspapers to tell him what they contained when he returned. She spent a week with him in a little inn hidden in a corner of Scotland. They would leave in the morning and not return until the evening, fishing all day long in a black and wild lake. 'He loved to play chess, so I learned in order to become his partner of an evening.'[29]

The British Court went into full mourning for the 'Cousin to Her Majesty the Queen' on the day before the funeral, 11 September by order of the Lord Chamberlain's Office, changing to half mourning on the 18th, which allowed white or grey dresses with black ribbons for the ladies in addition to black with coloured ribbons. Mourning was to end after ten days on the 21st.

The Comte was laid in state in the Marble Saloon of Stowe House, the great entrance hall inspired by the Pantheon in Rome. His body was enclosed in four coffins, the outer one being of mahogany, covered with black velvet, and adorned with white ornamental handles and nails, all covered by a violet velvet pall and the Tricolour atop it all, surrounded by floral tributes which would eventually fill two railway vans when the mourners made their way by special train to the little church at Weybridge, where his grandparents King Louise Philippe and Queen Amélie had been buried until their return to Dreux in 1876.

On Wednesday, 12 September, the interior of the small church was draped in black with white bows. Only about 150 could be accommodated inside the church, with the ladies sitting on the left-hand side and the men on the right. The Comtesse was supported by her daughters Amélie and Hélène. Her youngest child, ten-year-old Ferdinand, Duc de Montpensier, walked with the men of the family. Lord Carrington, who attended with the Duke of York, reported that the Duc d'Orléans 'walked in a theatrical way with his arms folded' and that the Duc d'Aumale and the Prince de Joinville both 'seemed terribly worn and aged.'[30] The

Duke of York represented his grandmother Queen Victoria; the Duke of Oporto was there to represent the King of Portugal; and to represent the King of Italy, the young Duke of Aosta came to England.

The Comte's confessor (and some say his half-brother, for it was rumoured that the priest was the son of the late Duc d'Orléans by Madame d'Hulst, a friend of his sister Louise, Queen of the Belgians), Monseigneur d'Hulst, said the low requiem Mass; at the end of this, Cardinal Vaughan, the Archbishop of Westminster, together with the Bishop of Southwark and the priests from the French churches in London, circled around the coffin with incense, saying the absolution before the coffin was taken into the vault by the men of the family and the visiting princes. There, the coffin would be placed inside the stone sarcophagus which had previously held the remains of his grandfather King Louis Philippe.[31] The words of the Latin funeral Mass expressed a hope for something which the Comte never found in life, a new and permanent home:

> *Requiem aeternam dona eis, Domine:*
> *et lux perpetua luceat eis.*
> Grant him eternal rest, O Lord,
> and may light eternal shine upon him.

The rest of the year passed quietly as the family began to come to terms with its new order, with the unpredictable twenty-five-year-old Philippe as the head of the family. The downsizing of the Comtesse de Paris's household would eventually include giving up the lease at Stowe House after Hélène's wedding; in October 1894, it was announced that the Wood Norton pack of harriers, which had formerly belonged to the Duc d'Aumale but which the Comtesse de Paris had used during the past three hunting seasons, was sold after the Comte's death, 'much to the regret of the residents in the neighbourhood of Buckingham.'[32]

Then, the family gathered together at Weybridge on All Souls' Day to pray at the tomb of the Comte de Paris—the Comtesse was with all her children, except for Amélie who was in Portugal. Later in the month, the Duc de Chartres accompanied Hélène and Isabelle to Paris for about a week for some medical treatment for Isabelle.

Newspaper rumours that Hélène might marry the Archduke Franz Ferdinand reappeared in September. Those rumors continued into October, fuelled by a visit by Hélène to Princess Clémentine in Vienna. When Philippe d'Orléans went to Vienna in November, his friend and companion Alfred de Gramont was surprised to hear the Duc d'Alençon and his son Prince Emmanuel speaking so negatively about all the Austrian princes who might be available to marry Hélène. Later, it transpired that this was perhaps because Emmanuel himself hoped to marry her. However, Philippe had a bigger matrimonial prize in mind for his sister than another Orléans cousin and had set his sights once again on Franz Ferdinand, the heir presumptive to the throne of the Austro-Hungarian Empire. According to Gramont again, Emperor Franz Joseph was not favourable towards such a match but would not oppose it either, while Franz Ferdinand himself did not say no but wanted to defer a decision until the following spring. The next step in the plan was to visit the Emperor again in February in Vienna and then to take Hélène to visit Princess Marguerite of Wurttemberg, sister of Franz Ferdinand, at Gmunden in the summer. Philippe, however, seems to have been unaware that other members of the family were also busy matchmaking, for meanwhile, the Duc d'Aumale had come up with another candidate, the Italian Duke of Aosta.[33]

It was toward the end of October that the Italian ambassador to France, Costantino Ressmann, made an initial approach to the Duc d'Aumale on behalf of the young Aosta who, it was said, had 'the greatest desire to marry the Princess Hélène' and that King Umberto approved of the match in the strongest terms. At this point, Ressmann's role was to gather information, particularly on Hélène's 'fortune.' Before making any kind of response, Aumale wanted to be assured that Hélène was not opposed to the idea from the start and that both mother and daughter would authorise him to take the request further without giving the young man any encouragement. On the matter of the 'fortune', Aumale noted that he couldn't say anything directly or indirectly because he knew nothing of the circumstances, and in any event, that level of discussion should not take place before the affair advances further 'if it does advance.' Aumale was also not the first—and would not be the last—to note that 'if the Prince of Naples is called to a better world the Duke of A. will be heir to the throne of Italy.'[34]

Emanuele Filiberto was the twenty-six-year-old nephew of King Umberto of Italy, the son of his deceased brother Amedeo, the previous Duke of Aosta, and sometime king of Spain. The young Duke had attended the Comte de Paris's funeral in September, and had visited England several other times in recent years. He first arrived in June 1892 for what was planned as a three-week incognito visit travelling as the 'Count della Cisterna,' a title that the family would often use while abroad. As obvious from such newspaper accounts, travelling incognito did not mean travelling in secret, but rather travelling privately and not requiring the elaborate formalities of a formal visit which necessitated a strict system of calls on palaces and embassies. For example, in later years, when the 'Countess of Cisterna' visited the 'Countess of Balmoral' at Nice, everyone knew that it was Hélène visiting Queen Victoria but that it was a private rather than official event.

Eventually, this first trip was extended until the end of August. The papers noted his interest in horses, particularly breeding stock, his attendance at a state concert at Buckingham Palace, a visit to the Prince and Princess of Wales at Sandringham, and a lunch with the Kaiser, who was also visiting England at the time.

Emanuele Filiberto was back in England for a fortnight beginning in February 1893, once again maintaining a 'strict incognito' with 'only an *aide-de-camp* and two servants with him.' He visited the Queen at Windsor, and dined with her and the extended Royal Family—including the Empress Frederick, Prince and Princess Henry of Battenberg, the Duke and Duchess of Teck and their daughter Princess Mary. The next month, he was able to visit the Queen again, this time when she was staying at the Villa Palmieri in Florence, where he was posted with his regiment and where he lived in the Pitti Palace.[35] He was back in England again in September 1894 as the official Italian representative at the funeral of Comte de Paris.

Queen Victoria—who always had an eye for a handsome man—declared that 'the Duc d'Aosta is pleasing & good looking.' In fact, she thought the whole Savoy family were 'all handsome' except for the heir to the throne, Prince Victor Emmanuel, who 'is unfortunately not only so small but so *chétif* looking. It almost amounts to a deformity—for his arms are vy. long & he sits high—but from the knees downwards his legs appear not to have grown.' The Queen felt that it would be very difficult to find him a wife, 'tho' he is clever, pleasing & has a nice face.' In 1893, Victor Emmanuel was said to be 'pining' after one of Queen Victoria's granddaughters, Princess Victoria Melita of Saxe-Coburg, but her mother dismissed him then as 'the little monster the Prince of Naples' and four years later declared him even 'more monstrous than ever.'[36]

There had already been rumours in Italy that the Duke of Aosta had decided to find an Orléans heiress—specifically Hélène—as a bride, but that the King had refused to consider any match at this time in deference to the still unmarried heir, Victor Emmanuel, the Prince of Naples.[37] Those rumors, at least the latter one, seemed to have been unfounded, and negotiations continued.

Aumale saw the Italian ambassador on 4 November, and the next day wrote to the Comtesse de Paris about the prospective proposal, saying that the information he had received about financial matters seemed satisfactory. By mid-December, everyone agreed on a meeting of the young people at Chantilly in the spring. Before that meeting, there was one more concern about Hélène's financial prospects. Auguste Laugel, the secretary and confidant to the Duc d'Aumale, wrote to him of a visit from Ressmann, who had spoken to the King who was 'most favorable' and then he stopped at Turin to see Aosta and 'found him very *monté* on the subject, very desirous, if ... you know what this means.' However, the Ambassador 'heard that the Queen of Portugal has 100 a year, I dont know, but he knows, and when I made to him the announcement of 90.' Ressmann 'seemed perplexed and grieved. He would so much prefer the round sum even this round sum falls much under his hopes. As for hopes, I told him also the number you mentioned (70).'[38]

Before leaving for Chantilly, the Comtesse de Paris and Hélène went to see the Queen and let her know about the plans. Queen Victoria noted in her journal that after luncheon, the Comtesse told her about the upcoming trip and that the Duc d'Aosta was coming, and he 'much wished to marry Hélène.' The Comtesse was unsure of the result of the meeting, but 'she thought there was a possibility of the marriage coming off, which would be a very suitable one.' For her part, Queen Victoria said 'we know the Duc d'Aosta very well & liked him.' The Comtesse promised to telegraph as soon as anything was settled and also 'talked a great deal & very sadly about poor Paris & his illness.'[39]

The Duke of Aosta arrived at Chantilly on 16 March. Aumale noted in his diary the next day: 'It is done. The young man spoke to Hélène—she is happy, so am I—everyone embraced.' Nearly the whole Orléans family had gathered at Chantilly for the occasion, and the Duc d'Aumale in particular never seemed happier. One night before dinner, he started marching before his guests, marking his step, and shaking his cane like a drum major. When they entered the dining room, he turned to Hélène and Emanuele Filiberto and said 'Perhaps you would like me to be the verger at your wedding?'[40]

Telegrams and letters flew across Europe, and everyone seemed to be pleased with the match. The Comtesse de Paris telegraphed Queen Victoria from Chantilly to say that '*Hélène est trés heureuse*' and the engagement was no longer secret. The Empress Frederick was surprised by the news but pleased. As she wrote to her mother, Queen Victoria: 'Hélène of Orléans is engaged to be married to the Duc d'Aosta! Has it not come rather suddenly?' The Empress then went on to suggest something radical for another marriage: 'I think Philippe had better marry the young Duchesse d'Aosta—& bring about a fusion of the 2 monarchial parties in France? It would not be a bad idea perhaps both these young people would steady down a little and be less giddy. You will laugh at this idea of mine.' Queen Victoria, who was holidaying at Nice, wrote back that she too rejoiced at the engagement. 'I am very glad of it as I know and like him. He is so very English in his tastes which she is also.' However, the suggestion that Hélène's future step-mother-in-law Laetitia Bonaparte marry her brother was less likely, although the Queen humoured her daughter's thoughts. 'Your idea about Philippe d'Orléans and the Duchesse d'Aosta is not at all a bad one, but I fear is not like[ly] to succeed. However anything is possible.' Empress Frederick wrote to her daughter Sophie in Athens that 'Lovely Princess Hélène of Orléans is engaged to the Duc d'Aosta, it is a very good marriage for both, and I hope they will be happy.'[41]

Aside from the hope for happiness, there was also a hope for a grand inheritance someday from the Duc d'Aumale, who played a role in the engagement and who was Hélène's godfather as well as great-uncle. Henri, the duc d'Aumale, was the fifth and next youngest son of King Louis Philippe and Queen Marie Amélie. When he was born in 1822, Aumale's father pinpointed the sixty-five-year-old Duc de Bourbon as godfather. Bourbon—who was also inheritor of the vast Condé fortune—had married Philippe Égalité's sister Bathilde and was thus an uncle to Louis Philippe. Bourbon had lost his only child, the Duc d'Enghien, when Napoléon had him shot in 1804. As a result, there was considerable negotiation about keeping the Bourbon inheritance within the family—some courtiers suggested that Charles X should authorize Condé to adopt one of the brothers of the Duchesse de Berry, but the King preferred that the inheritance of the Condés remain with the French Bourbons rather than go to the Neapolitan branch. This inheritance was a fabulous one by any measure and included châteaux, extensive forests, and other lands throughout France, the crown jewel being the *domaine de* Chantilly.[42] When the old duke died in 1830, young Aumale inherited the vast bulk of his estate.

Aumale would eventually find himself without a direct heir for this great inheritance. Two sons died in infancy; then his eldest, Louis Philippe, the Prince of Condé, died in Australia in 1866 at the age of twenty. The youngest, François, Duc de Guise, survived to return to France with his father but died in Paris, 25 July 1872 at the age of eighteen. It was a hopeful expectation that Hélène would become a beneficiary one day.

However pleased the various royal families may have been with this match, at least some politicians in Italy were aggressively opposed. Domenico Farini, president of the Senate, wrote in his diary that if the marriage did take place it would be a great error. 'Legitimists, Catholics, Orleanists, the French will have a foot in our house, at our Court.'[43] He saw it as contrary to everything that Cavour and Garibaldi had fought for, everything that was represented by the occupation of Rome. These were sentiments that would shadow Hélène for years.

When the Comtesse de Paris and Hélène returned to London, they visited Marlborough House to share the news personally with the Prince and Princess of Wales. Hélène had already written to Queen Victoria but now reverted to her earlier form of address as '*Ma chère Tante*' rather than '*Grand'Maman*', although her attachment was still very strong.

> On this occasion, so important in my life, one of my first thoughts was for You, whose almost maternal goodness has been such a help to me. A new life opens before me today—I am confident that I will be happy; but my happiness will not be complete if I do not feel it accompanied by the kindness that you have already accorded me and that The Queen wishes it to continue, I ask it of her immediately. She may be assured from my side, I will never forget that which she had for me and which I will keep always, for Her the sentiments of a respectful affection and a profound attachment.[44]

On the night of 4 April, the Comtesse and Hélène went to Sandringham for a couple of days with the Princess of Wales and her daughters. The next day, the Duke and Duchess of York showed them around their new home at York Cottage, and walked them back to the big house. The following day, the Yorks went back to the big house to bid farewell to Hélène and 'Granny,' as the Comtesse was affectionately known to George.[45]

Emanuele Filiberto arrived at Stowe House on the 8th along with his brother the Count of Turin and Count Bertarelli; they were met by Hélène at

Buckingham Station. After a few days, they all went to stay in London at the Hotel Bristol, along with the Comtesse de Paris and the younger children. On the Sunday, they attended services at Notre Dame de France in Leicester Square and in the afternoon drove to visit the other Catholic churches in London. It was pertinent that the same newspaper which reported these activities also noted that, according to the *Univers*, Pope Leo XIII, in reply to the telegram from the Duc d'Orléans announcing his sister's betrothal to the Duke of Aosta, 'sent a courteous and paternal letter, but made the reservations incumbent upon him as to the position of the Savoy dynasty at Rome.' On the 12th, they held a reception at the Bristol to congratulate Hélène and Emanuele Filiberto. Guests included the Russian and Austrian ambassadors and their wives, the Spanish ambassador, the Counsellor of the Italian Embassy, the Duke of Alba, nephew of the Empress Eugenie, and Charles Spencer, a Member of Parliament and later Earl Spencer.

The party returned to Stowe House on the 15th, and *The Times* confidently announced that the wedding would take place at Twickenham on 8 June. Although they got the date right, the place was wrong as the Comtesse had already telegraphed Queen Victoria that Hélène would be married at Kingston, '*où je suis mariée*.'[46] Within days, though, the wedding was indefinitely postponed due to a hunting accident in Spain.

Philippe, the Duc d'Orléans, had gone to Lisbon to visit Amélie on 5 April and then went on to Seville, where the twenty-six-year-old prince was very popular. During the season of fiestas and bullfights, Philippe played his role as the son of a Spanish infanta, donned Andalusian dress including its great spreading sombrero, and took great interest in the *corridas*. 'His youth, smart bearing, and his general liveliness, have everywhere aroused sincere sympathy.' Then, on the 26th, Philippe was hunting at Lebrija outside Seville when his horse slipped and fell on top of him, fracturing his leg. There was no particular concern, but still Hélène and Emanuele Filiberto announced the postponement of their wedding. Hélène and her mother decided to go to London for two days and then proceed to Seville via Lisbon while Emanuele returned to Italy. While in Spain, the Queen Mother gave a dinner in honour of the bride-to-be Hélène at the Royal Palace in Madrid.

Despite a brief bout of pneumonia during his convalescence, Philippe progressed well at the Palace of Sant Elmo, and at the end of the month was carried to the Portuguese royal yacht *Amelia* to bring him to England. The Comtesse and her daughters Hélène and Isabelle went to Paris for a few days before returning to England on 3 June.

In May, Hélène went to see Margot Asquith—herself married just the year before to the future prime minister. Margot recorded in her diary:

> She looked tall, black and distinguished. She spoke of Prince Eddy to me with great frankness. I told her I had sometimes wondered at her devotion to one less clever than herself. At this her eyes filled with tears and she explained to me

how much she had been in love and the sweetness and nobility of his character. I had reason to know the truth of what she said when one day Queen Alexandra, after talking to me in moving terms of her dead son, wrote in my Prayer Book: 'Man looketh upon the countenance, but God upon the heart.' Hélène adores the Princess of Wales but not the Prince! and says the latter's rudeness to her brother, the Duc d'Orléans, is terrible. I said nothing, as I am devoted to the Prince and think her brother deserves any ill-treatment he gets. I asked her if she was afraid of the future: a new country and the prospect of babies, etc. She answered that d'Aosta was so genuinely devoted that it would make everything easy for her. 'What would you do if he were unfaithful to you?' I asked. Princess Hélène: 'Oh! I told Emanuel. ... I said, "You see? I leave you ... If you are not true to me, I instantly leave you," and I should do so at once.' 'She begged me never to forget her, but always to pray for her.' 'I love you,' she said, 'as every one else does'; and with a warm embrace she left the room.[47]

Emanuele and his suite arrived back in London during the second week of June, staying at the Bristol Hotel. Later, he would journey out to Stowe to stay before the wedding, and there are photos of him and Hélène there on horseback and also in a carriage driven by Emanuele on the estate. On her birthday, Hélène wrote to 'My beloved little husband'—opening and closing (as 'Kiss me my love—Ever and for ever—Your loving and devoted little wife') the letter in English and writing the body of the text in French; Hélène thanked Emanuele Filiberto for 'in opening my eyes, my thoughts always fly to you—my eyes meet the flowers and presents of all kinds.' She was delighted to spend the day with him. 'It's a new year which begins, and a new life—all love and happiness.' However, mixed with the bride's hopes were her fears. 'I might wound you without wanting to do so—I can sometimes be awkward in saying things—but despite that—despite appearances which may be against me—think and never doubt that my sole goal is to please you, to love you and to make you happy.'[48] It was one of the very few personal letters that Emanuele Filiberto would keep for the rest of his life.

The wedding ceremony itself was re-scheduled for 25 June. It was announced that the Comtesse and her family would take up residence at Orléans House, Twickenham, a few days before the wedding, and that a grand reception would take place there after the wedding with a display of the bride's presents. At the same time, it was also announced that after the wedding, the Comtesse and her younger children would move to the Château de Randan, about ten miles from Vichy. Randan had fallen to the Comte de Paris during the redistribution of property when the royal family was allowed to return from exile. The Château was built in the sixteenth century upon the site of an early medieval Benedictine convent, and heavily restored in the nineteenth century by Madame Adelaïde, the sister of King Louis Philippe. In the future, the Comtesse would divide her time between this French residence, and the Andalusian palace at Villamanrique which she had inherited from her father.

Two days before the wedding, Hélène and Emanuele Filiberto went for luncheon with Queen Victoria, along with the Comtesse de Paris and the Prince of Naples. The Queen thought that Aosta 'seemed very bright & happy' and afterwards, when she saw Isabelle and Hélène alone, the bride-to-be 'said she was happy & contented, & that the Duke of Aosta was very kind.'[49] As a wedding gift, the Queen gave her a diamond bracelet set with a shamrock in rubies.

The day before the wedding, Hélène wrote to thank Queen Victoria for her gift. Hélène said that she had planned to depart after the wedding in black as she still considered herself in mourning for her father, but accepted the Queen's advice asking her 'not to appear at your wedding in a black dress,' because in England 'this would be seen as a bad omen, and I know that it would make a painful impression here, where you have lived so long, and I am sure you would not wish to alarm the prejudices of the people where the marriage takes place.' In the event, her going-away dress would be white silk with a black and white hat. Most of the bride's trousseau was made in France, except for her riding outfits which were all English. As it was still within a year of her father's death, half-mourning colours of white, mauve, and grey predominated among her clothes, although it was noted that the court dress that she would wear for her presentation in Italy was white satin and turquoise blue.[50]

The wedding day was blessed with 'a brilliant blue sky with a light north wind to freshen the sun's heat.' The streets were decorated with flags and flowers, and several triumphant arches. Crowds, which filled the route from Orléans House to Kingston—a distance of about four miles—were enthusiastic. Special trains were run out of London for the occasion, and some 400 extra police were allocated for the 'maintenance of order,' although no special effort was needed on the day. It had the feel of a public holiday. In the church, the altar was surrounded with palm fronds and white lilies, while the columns were wound with garlands of roses and linked together with other garlands.[51]

Much of the French family was there, most particularly the Comtesse de Paris with her daughters Isabelle and Louise, and the bride's godfather the Duc d'Aumale. Philippe d'Orléans was not yet fully recovered from his accident and was carried into the church in an invalid chair by four blue-uniformed *gardes de chasse* from Château d'Eu. The British royal family was also present in full force—all of Queen Victoria's children (except for the Empress Frederick) were there with their spouses and many of their children. The Duke and Duchess of Fife, and Princesses Victoria and Maud—the sisters of Prince Eddy—were all there, along with the Duke and Duchess of Teck, the parents of Princess May. Indeed, George and May (the new Duke and Duchess of York) were among the only absentees, having 'a previous engagement.' The Italian royal family was represented by the

Prince of Naples, and Emanuele Filiberto's brother Vittorio Emanuele and his step-mother Laetitia and half-brother Umberto. Laetitia's brother Prince Louis Napoléon was also there, which was probably the first time a Bonaparte took part in an Orléans celebration. Much of the diplomatic corps—including the ambassadors of Austria-Hungary, Russia, Spain, and Turkey—and many from the old French nobility were also in attendance.[52]

Emanuele Filiberto, in uniform as colonel of the Fifth Regiment of Italian Artillery, was supported by his brother the Count of Turin and the Prince of Naples. While the French princes all wore evening dress, the Italian and British princes were all in full uniform. The Prince of Wales and the Duke of Cambridge, both appeared in their uniforms as Field Marshals.

The bridal party arrived about quarter to eleven. Hélène, escorted by her mother, was dressed in 'soft white satin, perfectly plain' trimmed with orange blossom and with orange blossom in her hair. At the entrance of the chapel, Hélène gave her arm to her uncle, the Duc de Chartres, taking the place of her brother.[53] Dr Butt, the Bishop of Southwark, celebrated the wedding service, which was conducted in English as required by English law, and after the vows Father Morley, the local priest, said the Low Mass '*Pro Sponso et Pro Sponsa*.' Mozart and Gounod highlighted the music from the choir, organ and accompanying harp, while a selection from Rossini's *Moïse* represented Italy. The official witnesses were the Prince of Wales, the Prince of Naples, the Duc d'Orléans, and the Duc de Chartres.

Afterwards, the wedding party and guests returned through Kingston to Twickenham, and according to one guest it was 'a really pretty sight, with multitudes of flags and large crowds cheering and every window filled in the old-fashioned houses. There was something Hogarthian in it all.'

The wedding breakfast took place in the Octagon Room of Orléans House, lent to them for the day by the current owner, William Cunard. The Blue Hungarian Band provided the music, while in the library of the house, the wedding gifts were on display. They included a diamond tiara with upright stars and high sprays of diamonds from the King and Queen of Italy; a gold-and-sapphire bracelet from Queen Margherita; a diamond-and-emerald tiara from the Duc d'Orléans; and a 'novel and tasteful' caduceus set in diamonds, pearls and rubies from the Prince and Princess of Wales and their children. From the bridegroom came an entire set of pearls and diamonds, a string of thirty-five 'exquisite' pearls, a necklace of eleven rows of pearls, plus a diamond-and-emerald necklace. The Comtesse de Paris gave her daughter a collection of precious stones, two black pearls, a diamond crescent, a carriage rug in white fox skin, an English pony carriage and pony, a modern cashmere shawl, and a cashmere shawl formerly belonging to the Duchess d'Orléans as well as another from the trousseau of the Duchesse de Montpensier. From her godfather, the Duc d'Aumale came a magnificent necklace of emeralds and diamonds set in gold and silver.[54] Following the wedding breakfast, the Duke of Aosta and the new Duchess greeted their guests in the garden before they left for a honeymoon at Wood Norton, the Worcestershire home of the Duc d'Aumale, while the Duc d'Orléans hosted an evening dinner for the guests at the Hotel Métropole in London.

1895–1900

Fatta l'Italia, dobbiamo fare gli italiani
'Having made Italy, we must now make Italians'[1]

After a heat wave when temperatures in Rome hovered between 35 and 36°C, the morning of 6 July brought beautiful weather as a special train carried the Duke and the new Duchess of Aosta into the capital. Their arrival was announced by a salvo of cannon fired from the fort of Monte Mario. Emanuele Filiberto and Hélène were met by the two Vittorio Emanueles in the family—his cousin, the Prince of Naples and his brother, the Count of Turin—as well as Prince Ruspoli, the Mayor of Rome, who presented Hélène with a bouquet and made an address on behalf of the city. A large group of generals, high officials, and court dignitaries were at the station, and crowds of Romans lined the streets in anticipation of the procession.

Hélène wore a white dress covered with lace, while Emanuele had on his uniform as a colonel of the artillery. Even the six horses pulling the main carriage were dressed in white trappings in honour of the newlyweds. The royal party then entered the state carriages and proceeded to the Quirinale Palace, the seat of the monarchy. Escorted by the officers of the garrison of Rome and a detachment of the king's cuirassiers with their silver breastplates glistening, the carriages moved at walking pace through the Via Nazionale, Via del Quirinale to the Piazza del Quirinale. Throughout the route, the Aostas were greeted by the cheering crowds amid buildings decorated with flags, banners, and flowers. Hats and handkerchiefs were waved in the air by the crowds, who broke through the police lines, cheering the couple on their way.

At the palace, the newlyweds were received first by Count Giannotti, the grand master of ceremony, while King Umberto ignoring protocol came down the grand staircase himself to personally greet his nephew and new niece, embracing each of them. The King then offered Hélène his arm and escorted them to the Royal apartments, where Queen Margherita was awaiting them. The reporter from *The Times* recorded that the Queen 'kissed the young couple several times with much warmth.' There were formal presentations of some of the leading officials, including the Prime Minister Francesco Crispi. Meanwhile the noise of the crowds in the piazza Quirinale grew louder until Hélène and Emanuele went onto the balcony of the palace from which they 'bowed their acknowledgments of the hearty cheers of the crowds.' Later in the afternoon, the Aostas drove to the Villa Borghese in an open carriage, and all along the Corso, the crowds again gave them a warm ovation. In the evening, they enjoyed a quiet family dinner.

The signing of the formal marriage contract took place the next day at the Quirinale Palace. Among those invited were all the holders of the Order of the Annunziata—who in Italy held rank as 'cousins of the King'—the ministers, the presidents of the Senate and of the Chamber, as well as the high dignitaries of the Court. Domenico Farini, the president of the Senate, noted in his diary that Queen Margherita remarked that the bride was going to be a beautiful woman, while the Prince of Naples commented that she was too tall, but also added 'Of course, I am too small.' It is said that in his later years, Vittorio Emanuele would continue to joke about his height; he is said to have quipped to one courtier: 'I hear that people are whispering that I dislike my cousins the Aostas. Of course I do. They are so tall!'[2]

What seemed to rankle most was that the bride signed the registers as 'Hélène' rather than 'Elena.' Farini complained, at least to his diary, that she failed to comprehend the honour and urgency of transforming herself into an Italian princess. Victor Emmanuel told her directly that she must quickly learn to speak Italian, the language of their great homeland, a country which she would love more each time she returned from abroad.[3]

Hélène later began language studies with Professoressa Teresa Quattrino but, in fact, never completely mastered Italian. Although, to be fair, it was said later in her life that while she spoke four languages—English, French, Italian, and Arabic—plus a smattering of various African dialects, she spoke all of them imperfectly, and Emanuele Filiberto was also faulted for his improper Italian grammar.[4] However, the question of her own name was more telling. 'Hélène de France, Duchessa d'Aosta' was how she generally signed herself and considered herself throughout the remainder of her life. Although she adopted it to testify that her father was the legitimate head of the House of France, the 'de France' rather than 'd'Orléans' was seen by many as both pretentious and not fully accepting her status within Italy. There was, in fact, a strange period in the 1920s when she signed herself simply as 'France Savoia-Aosta' as if she had taken 'France' as her given name.

When Hélène and Emanuele reached Turin on 13 July, their reception was equally enthusiastic. They were met at the station by his step-mother Princess Laetitia, his cousin the Duchess of Genoa, and his brother the Count of Turin along with members of many popular associations. Troops lined that streets, and bands played the 'Marcia Reale' while the crowds cheered *Viva gli sposi!*—Long

Live the Newlyweds!—and flowers rained into the royal carriage from the windows of many houses they passed.

The Italy into which Hélène arrived was barely a generation old. In fact, Emanuele Filiberto—named for the warrior ancestor of the Savoy dynasty— was the first prince born after the *risorgimento*. Although Rome was one of the most ancient cities in Europe, it was capital to one of the newest countries. Emanuele Filiberto's grandfather, King Victor Emmanuel II, was King of Sardinia from 1849, but was only declared King of Italy on 17 March 1861. It was a decade later, after the French removed their protective troops that Victor Emmanuel entered Rome as king on 2 July 1871. 'For a millennium and a half, from the fall of Rome until the middle of the nineteenth century, Italy was, in the dismissive words of the Austrian statesman Metternich, merely "a geographical expression," a congerie of many small city-states and semi-colonial dominions of foreign empires.' During the reign of Victor Emmanuel, the country was directed by a clique of Piedmontese officials and generals, acting directly under the king who made it clear that his native land and his native dialect was where he was most comfortable. When the Italian state was proclaimed in 1860, linguistic variation was so pronounced that no more than 10 per cent of all 'Italians' (and perhaps as few as 2.5 per cent) spoke the national language, and the court language was French. 'For the Piedmontese monarchists who unified Italy, regional differentiation was the principal obstacle to national development. *Fatta l'Italia, dobbiamo fare gli italiani* was their slogan: Having made Italy, we must now make Italians.'[5]

The King had direct control over foreign affairs and finance, and most importantly the military and its budget. The massive civil list that was granted to the king included maintenance for the 343 royal palaces and hunting establishments, most of which had been obtained from the deposed dynasties in Lombardy, Tuscany, Naples, and Lucca.[6]

In January 1878, Victor Emmanuel died and was succeeded by his elder son, King Umberto, who has been characterized as 'a colourless and timid character, with little desire to take time away from his mistresses, horses, and hunting by assuming an active political role.' So, day-to-day control of the running of the country increasingly fell to the prime minister. Francesco Crispi first became prime minister in August 1887 and held the post for three and a half years, but returned in December 1893 and remained until March 1896. It was during this latter term that Italy became essentially a dictatorship under his premiership. Corruption in the banking system implicated not only politicians but the king himself. An alleged Russian-backed uprising in Sicily allowed heavy-handed repression throughout the country by royal decree. Parliament was prorogued on 11 July 1894 and was only allowed to meet on 3 December for just ten days until 10 June 1895. Although voting privileges were still restricted to a small minority of the population, this was made even smaller by the papal edict that forbade all

Catholics from participating in the political life of the country following the seizure of Rome. To be Catholic was seen to be anti-Italian, and for generations, the
'black aristocracy' of Rome were firm supporters of the Pope against the King.
The introduction of a French princess from an ultra-Catholic family into this
mix was highly controversial.[7]

One of the major symbols of the church-state conflict was the Quirinale
Palace itself. Originally constructed by Pope Gregory XIII in 1583 as a new summer palace, it housed some thirty popes until the Papal States were overthrown in
1870 and it became the home of the new king in 1871. From this time forward—
until 1929—the reigning pope never left the confines of the Vatican City enclave.

The family into which Hélène had married was unusual even by
nineteenth-century royal standards. Although he was a first cousin to the King
of Portugal, Amélie's husband, Emanuele Filiberto, was about as distantly related
to Hélène as any of their contemporaries in European royal circles. They were
fourth cousins as descendants of King Carlos III of Spain, from whom Emanuele
descended once, while Hélène came down in five different lines because of the
heavy Orléans intermarrying. Emanuele's Savoy line brought in some Hapsburg,
Saxon, and Bourbon blood, and further back through the Sardinian kings he
was descended from Eleanor Oglethorpe, the sister of the eighteenth-century
founder of the English colony of Georgia in America.[8]

Due to the conflicts of the Risorgimento, the depositions of monarchs from
minor thrones on the Italian peninsula, and the later seizure of Rome and virtual
imprisonment of the Pope in the Vatican, the Savoys were boycotted as marriage
partners by most Catholic dynasties and as a result royal unions within the wider
circles of reigning families were generally not an option. So, King Umberto
married to his first cousin, Princess Margherita of Savoy-Genoa, and his brother
Amedeo, the Duke of Aosta married into the Italian nobility.[9] His heiress bride,
Princess Maria Vittoria dal Pozzo della Cisterna, was part Italian and part Belgian.
Her father—Carlo Emanuele dal Pozzo, Principe della Cisterna—had been created a Baron of the French Empire in 1810 and a Senator of the new Italian
Kingdom in 1848, and her mother was the Belgian countess Louise de Mérode,
some thirty years her husband's junior. Louise's sister Antoinette married Prince
Charles III of Monaco and became ancestor to the subsequent Grimaldi rulers
of that tiny principality. Over the years, Emanuele Filiberto would visit Belgium,
the homeland of his grandmother, so often that newspapers speculated on his
engagement to Princess Clémentine, the daughter of Belgian King Leopold, in
1894. The Pozzo della Cisterna-Mérode connection was seen as just as danger-
ously clerical as were the Orléans, at least to Farini—'clerical blood mixed with
clerical blood cannot bring good luck.'[10]

After Hélène's great-aunt Queen Isabel was deposed from the throne of
Spain, Emanuele had briefly been the Crown Prince there during his father's

reign there from 16 November 1870 until 11 February 1873 (when he abdicated and returned to Italy). During that time the family, which included a younger brother Vittorio Emanuele (later Count of Turin), lived in Madrid where a third son, Luigi (later the great explorer, the Duke of the Abruzzi) was born shortly before they left the country. Maria Vittoria died at San Remo in 1876, aged just twenty-nine, leaving behind her husband and three young sons. Emanuele Filiberto, the eldest, was only seven years old. Her body was taken to the Savoy family tomb in the Basilica of Superga at Turin, and a floral tribute sent by the women of Madrid to their sometime queen is still preserved behind glass next to her tomb. Twelve years later, Amedeo had scandalized Europe by taking his own niece as his second wife, the Princess Laetitia Bonaparte, the daughter of his sister, the deeply religious Princess Clothilde and Prince Napoléon, the next in line to the Bonaparte succession. Laetitia's frequent visits to the Aosta family home suggested to some a possible union with her first cousin Emanuele Filiberto, but it was her uncle who was the centre of her attention. Although such a union would be considered incestuous and illegal in most European countries, the marriage took place with a dispensation granted by Pope Leo XIII.[11] Amedeo died only sixteen months later, having fathered a fourth son, Umberto (Count of Salemi).

Laetitia, as a young widow, enjoyed shocking the staid Savoy court. One American newspaper described her as 'handsome, tall, athletic, and her 175 pounds avoirdupois is judiciously distributed over her fine figure. She does not mind exhibiting her beautiful neck and arms.' On the day of the Grand Prix in Turin in 1894, the Duchess of Genoa made her appearance with scarlet-liveried outriders for a gala coach and six. Laetitia, on the other hand, and her entire suite arrived on bicycles. King Umberto was not amused and telegraphed 'Keep to your apartments until further notice. If disobedient, allowance stopped.'[12]

Shortly after moving to Turin in 1888, Nietzsche wrote to a friend extolling the city:

> What a dignified and serious city it is! It has nothing of the capital city, and nothing modern, as I feared: it is rather more a residence from the seventeenth century, which had the court and the nobility, and a single prevailing taste in everything. Aristocratic tranquillity is what has been preserved here in everything: there are no squalid suburbs.[13]

Turin had been the capital for the Dukes of Savoy and Kings of Sardinia and then for the whole country of Italy for the first years of its unification until the centre of government was transferred to Florence in 1865 and afterwards to Rome in 1871. The long reign of King Carlo Emanuele III of Sardinia and Duke of Savoy transformed Turin into one of the grand cities of Europe, emulating some of the style of his cousins (the Kings of France), particularly in the architectural embellishments which dominated both the city and countryside.

Although the Aosta family home in Turin was the great Palazzo Cisterna, which had been the home of Emanuele's mother's family since 1685, Hélène and Emanuele Filiberto first went to live at Castello della Mandria, north of the city and near Venaria Reale, where the Duke's 5ᵉ *artiglieria da campagna reggimento* was stationed. The grand palace of Venaria Reale had been commissioned by Duke Carlo Emanuele II in 1675 and served as a favourite hunting residence for the royal family for two further generations after which it was seldom used. During the Napoleonic occupation of the province, the palace was turned into a barracks and the famous gardens destroyed to create training grounds. Nearby was the much less grand La Mandria, the former home of King Victor Emmanuel II and his mistress (and later morganatic wife) Rosa Vercellana, *la bella Rosina*. Hélène described La Mandria as 'completely in the countryside, an hour from Turin.' The life there was 'tranquil, soft, exactly that which I love.' Emanuele Filiberto kept busy with his regiment, and 'then, the rest of the day we are generally on horseback. The country is beautiful; the climate a bit rough; cold in the winter, very hot in the summer.'[14]

Once established in Turin, Hélène had her own household with the Marchese and Marchesa Torrigiani and Count and Countess Bianconcini as her ladies and gentlemen of the palace. The Torrigianis, in particular, would be with Hélène for years and share many adventures, especially during the First World War. Carlo Torrigiani was from an old Florentine family and had been taught by the Jesuits in England at Stonyhurst college in Lancashire, where a younger classmate was the future author Arthur Conan Doyle.[15] Anna, who had married Carlo Torrigiani in Florence in 1884, was an American, born in 1861, the daughter of Horace Fry, a Wall Street stockbroker, whose wife Emilie had started a very public suit for divorce on the grounds of ill treatment in 1859, a year after their marriage. Eventually, the couple reconciled, although Emilie died in 1875 when their daughter and son were still young.

At the end of the year, Hélène wrote to Queen Victoria to say that she and Emanuele would spend Christmas Day with the King and Queen in Rome—'Your Majesty cannot imagine with what truly parental affection they treat me'—before returning to their home in La Mandria for the New Year. Hélène assured Queen Victoria that 'the great and true happiness that I have found in my marriage has not made me forget how good you have been to me. It is always with heartfelt gratitude that I think upon this point, The Queen was indulgent towards me.'[16]

Hélène's brother Philippe came to visit at La Mandria, but one day in mid-January 1896 while riding with Emanuele Filiberto, Philippe's horse stumbled and fell. He ended up with a dislocated shoulder and a factured ankle, and it was late February before he was able to leave for Milan. The fanciful idea of the Empress Frederick from two years earlier of a potential bride for the Duc d'Orléans resurfaced when Princess Laetitia became a frequent—almost daily—visitor to Philippe at La Mandria. As one newspaper viewed the situation:

She is just the kind of Juno-like woman that he admires, and with her insatiate ambition and restlessness is likely to act as a powerful incentive to him in his role as a pretender... while there is no doubt that a union of the Bonapartist and royalist factions into one united party would vastly strengthen the monarchical cause and give it a chance of success which at present it does not enjoy.[17]

On a broader international scale, about the same time, in early 1896, Italy organized in Ethiopia the strongest expeditionary force that Africa had ever seen—some 16,000 men and fifty-two guns strong. This foothold was gained, as one author put it, 'by the grace of God, the weakness of Egypt, and the tolerance of England.' A new empire for Italy was their goal. Emanuele Filberto made formal—but unsuccessful—application on 16 February to join the two batteries of his regiment preparing to join the army under Gen. Oreste Baratieri. On 1 March, the Italian army attacked the native force at Adowa, but was soundly defeated with the loss of 262 officers and 4,000 soldiers, plus some 1,900 taken prisoner. In a single day, more Italians were killed than in all of the wars of the Risorgimento put together.[18]

It was the greatest European colonial defeat ever, and the deepest humiliation that the new nation of Italy had yet faced. Although many of the captured Eritrean mercenaries were killed or mutilated by the victorious Ethiopians, Italian prisoners were well treated, the worst humiliation said to be one soldier taken before the Empress Taitu and forced to sing '*Funiculi, Funicula*' and '*Dolce Napoli.*' At home, it meant a fall of the government, which brought an end to the dictatorial rule of Crispi, but also resulted in street demonstrations with people shouting 'death to the king' and 'long live the republic.' This was the worst position that the throne had been in since 1860, and King Umberto at least briefly considered abdication during this crisis. Eventually, a peace was established with the Ethiopian emperor Menelik, a new government installed in Rome, and that brought about major reforms both in the army and in parliament.[19]

Hélène made the crossing from Calais to England on 7 September 1896 along with Emanuele Filiberto and her mother and the younger children—Isabelle, Louise, and Ferdinand. Joining them on the channel trip was Princess Mary, the Duchess of York, on her return from a family visit to Germany. Mary later wrote to her mother, the Duchess of Teck, that Hélène 'looks so well, but I think he has a disagreeable expression & I am glad I am not his wife!'[20]

The family was on their pilgrimage to the church at Weybridge for a memorial Mass for the Comte de Paris on the second anniversary of his death. The church itself was draped in white and purple in mourning for the low Mass celebrated by Father Thomas from Leicester Place. They were joined by the dukes of Orléans, Chartres, and Aumale. After the service, the family descended into the vault itself for some private prayers and thoughts, and later returned for a second quiet period. The Duc d'Orléans remained in England to join his great-uncle the Duc d'Aumale at Wood Norton, but the rest of the family returned to the Continent the same day.

As the visit was so short, Hélène did not have the opportunity to visit Queen Victoria, who was at Balmoral, but did write to her to *offrir nos hommages* and to reassure the Queen of her happiness in Italy. 'I am very attached to my new country, it's true that when one is as happy as I am in my home, everything is agreeable, moreover Italy is a beautiful country,' and the welcome she received from the Royal Family 'as well as the sympathy shown to me, has won my heart.' Now, she found it 'a true joy that I find myself again in England where, despite the sad events, I have spent so many good sweet years. I replay them often in my mind.' And most of all she would never forget 'the indulgence that the Queen has always had for me, and the goodness that she has always shown me, and which are written upon my heart.'[21]

While briefly at Wood Norton with the family, they also got an opportunity to see her brother Philippe and his new fiancée, the Archduchess Maria Dorothea of Austria. The Duc d'Aumale had taken a paternal interest in the Duc d'Orléans, especially after the death of the Comte de Paris, and it was definitely time to get Philippe married as he had been named as co-respondent in yet another divorce case the previous autumn. Now, Aumale again played a role as match-maker, when he and his sister, the ubiquitous Princess Clémentine, met together at Chantilly and decided to promote a marriage between the Duc d'Orléans and Clémentine's granddaughter, the Archduchess Maria Dorothea, known in the family as Mariska. The young people, it is said, were delighted with the idea. Philippe proposed, and on 15 July, the engagement was officially announced with a wedding planned for the autumn. Although Hélène hoped to be able to attend her brother's wedding in Vienna, she was not able to commit to that until another wedding date had been settled.[22]

On 18 August in Rome and in Cettinje, the capital of Montenegro, the engagement was announced between Victor Emmanuel, the diminutive heir to the Italian throne, and Elena, a younger daughter from the tiny principality. The choice of the Balkan princess for the heir to the crown of Italy was surprising on a number of levels. First of all, many people had assumed that Victor Emmanuel would never marry simply because of his physical deformity. He was only just over five feet tall (1.54 metres) while the intended bride was some eight inches taller (1.74 metres). The obvious lack of height brought about other—usually unspoken—questions about other physical lacks which might prohibit marriage or at least procreation of a future heir. However, while Victor Emmanuel was an only child, Elena was from an abundantly fertile family, one of twelve children.

Montenegro had been ruled by hereditary prince-bishops (*vladikas*) from the late seventeenth century until 1852. Then, Danilo II declined being ordained so that he might marry, and declared himself prince instead. His nephew, Elena's father, Nikola, had been reigning since 1860. Due to a shared Orthodox religion, there were close ties with the Russian imperial court, and most of Nikola's daughters were sent to study at the Smolny Institute in St Petersburg under the protection of the empress. Elena herself was goddaughter of Tsar Alexander II and the Tsaritsa Marie Alexandrovna; she also spent her formative years in Russia, where Victor Emmanuel met her when he went to attend the coronation of Nicholas II. He is said to have declared 'I will marry her or no other.'[23]

Despite there being so many Montenegrin princelings and princesses, there was a question of their royal standing, and their suitability as marriage partners. The general requirement of equal birth, often expressed by the German term *Ebenbürtigkeit*, became formalized about the time of the Congress of Vienna, with some dynasties placing more importance in the concept than others. A few countries, like Great Britain, chose to ignore the continental rules, and so Queen Victoria allowed her daughter Louise to marry a subject, and daughter Beatrice to marry a member of the Battenberg family which was a morganatic branch of the Hessian grand ducal family, while Princess May of Teck—whose father was the child of a marriage between a prince of Württemberg and a Hungarian countess—was not considered an eligible bride for German princes but ended up with the heir to the British throne. It was in 1889 that Emperor Alexander III of Russia allowed the marriage of Elena's sister Militza with his cousin, Grand Duke Peter Nikolaievich, thus establishing a precedence which one British diplomat charmingly called 'connubial equality', and paving the way for Elena's eventual marriage to Victor Emmanuel.[24]

The other consideration was, of course, that of religion. Once she arrived on Italian soil in preparation for the wedding, Elena was required to sign an abjuration of her own faith, declaring that she 'believed and professed all that taught by the Holy Mother Church, catholic, apostolic, Roman', that she declared 'all other religions false', and promised to raise her children in the Roman Catholic Church.[25]

Their wedding in Rome took place on 24 October and was a grand state occasion, the first time that the Savoys celebrated so publicly in Rome since the annexation of the papal states.[26] Still, due to the ongoing antipathy with the Vatican, the religious service at the Church of Santa Maria degli Angeli was conducted by a mere monsignore, and there were no foreign royalties attending beyond close family members. Emanuele Filiberto and his brother Turin were the witnesses for the groom, while Elena's brother Mirko and brother-in-law Prince Peter Karageorgevich did the honours for the bride. Their duties included holding a veil of silver thread over the couple as Monsignore Piscicelli celebrated the nuptials.

Hélène processed into the church on the arm of Prince Victor Napoléon, preceded by Princess Laetitia and her escort, the Duke of Oporto; they were followed by Emanuele Filiberto with the Dowager Duchess of Genoa, the mother of Queen Margherita. The knights of the Order of the Annunziata were there in their special role as official 'cousins' of the king. The diplomatic corps appeared in full uniform and decorations, along with the civil authorities and the civil and military households of the king. After the service, the couple left the church to the cheers of the crowd, the military bands playing Italian and Montenegrin hymns along the route, and the cannons of the Castel San Angelo firing honorary salutes.[27]

The wedding in Vienna on 5 November must have seemed rather anticlimatic by comparison to the Roman festivities. Philippe and Mariska were married in the chapel of the Hofburg Palace. In the procession into the chapel, Emperor Franz Joseph escorted Queen Amélie; then came the Duke of Connaught with Hélène on his arm, the correspondent from *The Times* noting that 'in both instances the lady was the taller of the two.' Then came Emanuele Filiberto with the bride's mother, the Archduchess Maria Josepha; and the Duc d'Alençon escorting the bride's grandmother, Princess Clémentine. *Vogue* Magazine also sent a correspondent to cover fashions at the wedding, and amid all the glitter, Hélène was highlighted:

> The Duchess of Aosta, lovelier than ever in spite of her recent sorrows, had donned a strikingly original gown of Ophelia-tinted satin, brocaded with green-gold and with steel. Around her slender waist, and reaching up to the armpits, was a corselet made entirely of huge diamonds, which sparkled and shone dazzlingly as she moved. A tiny coiffe of the same gems sat quaintly on the young Duchess's bright tresses, and flat bands of rubies and diamonds encircled her wrists and throat.[28]

Clémentine hosted the reception at the Coburg Palace, and the festivities also included a night at the opera, where Hélène sat with her three sisters in the Imperial box, and according to one witness they 'formed a bevy of beauty which did not fail to attract the experienced eye of the old Emperor.'[29] After the wedding, the Comtesse de Paris and her younger daughters went to visit Hélène's new home at La Mandria.

At the end of the year, Hélène once again wrote New Year's greetings and best wishes to Queen Victoria, wishing that she had the chance to kiss her hand 'and to tell her again in person that neither time, no distance, could erase from my heart, the marks of interest which I have received.' The Aostas spent Christmas again in Rome with the King and Queen, joined this year by the Prince of Naples and his new wife, who Hélène said was 'quite nice and pretty. She wins the sympathy of all who approach her.'[30]

Despite this outward show of good cheer, there were already signs of cracks within the Aosta marriage that would continue and develop over the years. The

Duc d'Orléans and his new Duchess went to visit the Aostas at La Mandria in February 1897, and the possibility of separation and a divorce was mentioned for the first time. The Comte de Gramont, Orléans's aide, recorded that one evening the Duke of Aosta 'who almost never talks' came over to him while the others were dancing and, indicating Hélène, said 'Isn't it impossible to have a more beautiful princess?' De Gramont felt certain that this was a comment prepared in advance and one that he was supposed to repeat to the interested parties, but he had a practice of never repeating things except to his journal, so the plan fell flat. However, the next day at lunch, Aosta leaned over to de Gramont and said in a low voice:

> You know what they're saying? They say that we are going to separate. You can see how true that is; you can tell the truth when you return to France. Besides, I know who put this rumour about, it's the Marquis Costa de Beauregard. He passed through Turin, asked for an audience with me, and was very vexed because I could not receive him right away.[31]

This marital crisis—the first of several—may have resulted from the fact that Hélène was still not pregnant some twenty months after their wedding or from Emanuele Filiberto's roving eye, but it seems to have passed, perhaps after some encouragement from Hélène's uncle.

On 15 April, Hélène and Emanuele Filiberto went to Sicily to visit Uncle Henri, the Duc d'Aumale, who showed them around his gardens at the Palais d'Orléans in Palermo, which he had inherited from his mother, Queen Marie Amélie:

> … just a jumble of old buildings bought at odd moments and thrown together anyhow … the whole effect is strangely harmonious, with a charm that only old places like that in Italy can acquire. There are acres and acres of land at the back, all planted with orange and lemon trees, and in spring when they are all in bloom the air is heavy with the sharp, sweet perfume.

On the Sunday, Uncle Aumale took the Aostas to the park of La Favorita, and then on the next day, they all went to the Duke's agricultural estate of Zucco, which he had purchased in 1853. However, that night, Aumale and the Aostas returned to Palermo where the local population gave them such a warm welcome as to astonish the local authorities.[32] The Aostas left the next day, and Aumale returned to Zucco.

A few days later, on 22 April, Pietro Acciarito, a young unemployed ironsmith, attempted to stab King Umberto while he was in an open carriage on his way to the Capannelle Racecourse. The King warded off the dagger blow by rising from his seat and was unhurt, but memories of a previous attempt on his life in 1878 resurfaced, and the fragility of the senior branch of the family became apparent again.

The next month, many members of the Orléans family had gathered in Sicily to plan for Aunt Clémentine's eightieth birthday when news came from Paris that on 4 May there had been a ghastly fire at a charity bazaar and Sophie, the Duchesse d'Alençon, was among the many burned to death. The bazaar was located on two empty lots, numbers 15–17 rue Jean Goujon, near the Champs Elysées, a short walk from the Seine, and just doors away from where the Duc and Duchesse de Chartres lived at number 27. The bazaar had opened only the day before, and it was shortly after 4 p.m., when the greatest crowds had gathered for the event, that the fire broke out. It is said to have started in the cinema at the back of the bazaar, through an electrical surge too close to a petrol container. Within minutes, the whole fair was enveloped in flames, and about 130 people, mostly women, were burned to death. Among the many victims were the sister of the late Duc d'Uzès, an old friend of the Orléans family; two young daughters of the comte de Chevilly, an intimate friend of the Duc d'Orléans; and Sister Ginoux, mother superior of the Order of St Vincent de Paul, whose body was found kneeling with her hands clasped in prayer. Within moments, that *quartier* of Paris had turned from a fairground into a morgue. Sophie herself was soon declared a heroine by the newspapers when *Le Figaro* published eyewitness accounts which told that she insisted that the others be evacuated first: 'No, first save the guests. The presidents must leave last.' Then, a minute later, already suffocating, Sophie cried out: 'No, not yet, later... the last. Duty before all!' Then, it was over.[33]

Fifty-year-old Sophie was the youngest sister of Empress Elizabeth of Austria and of Queen Marie of the Two Sicilies as well as daughter-in-law of Louis, Duc de Nemours. When younger, she had been the *enfant terrible* of the family. At just nineteen, she became engaged to her cousin, King Ludwig of Bavaria, but later the same year, he broke the engagement. After that, Sophie refused to consider the various German, Austrian, and Portuguese princes who were offered as candidates for her hand in marriage, but two years later, in 1868, she married Hélène's cousin, Ferdinand, the Duc d'Alençon. They had two children, but Sophie suffered from bouts of depression, and she began an affair with her gynaecologist, Dr Glaser. The lovers fled to Switzerland but were apprehended, and Sophie was forcibly detained near Graz in a sanatorium which specialised in treating 'sexual abnormalities.' After five months of 'shock treatment involving the use of ice-cold water, blistering ointment and pistol shots her will was broken and she returned to her husband, ostensibly "cured."'[34]

The Duc d'Aumale was severely shaken by the death of his niece and many friends, and wrote in his journal: 'News of the horrifying catastrophe of the Charity Bazaar, burned in Paris. The dreadful death of Sophie! Messages to the unhappy Alençon, to his son, to the parents.' A memorial Mass was held at Zucco on 6 May, and immediately after that, the Duc d'Aumale accompanied the Duc de Chartres and Comte d'Eu to the station whence they went to Paris for the funeral. The Duc d'Aumale himself went back to Zucco and, early the next morning, died in his sleep. The shocked family arranged for a funeral Mass for him to be said in Palermo, and then Aumale's coffin was loaded onto a funeral train, which Hélène and Emanuele Filiberto joined in Turin. Queen Victoria received the news through a telegram from Clémentine and in her journal, she remembered Aumale as 'a most charming, very well informed, clever, large minded & agreeable man. He wrote very well & was so kind & generous to his whole family, by whom he was greatly beloved.'[35]

The funeral train arrived in Paris during the evening of the 14th, the same day that Sophie Alençon's funeral had taken place in the Church of St Philippe du Roule. Aumale's body lay in state in the Church of the Madeleine, and some 20,000 members of the public were said to have filed past to pay their respects, while Hélène, Emanuele Filiberto, the Comtesse de Paris, her daughter Isabelle, and most of the rest of the family and foreign dignitaries went to Dreux for Sophie's burial. On the 17th, they all attended Aumale's funeral at the Madeleine in Paris, and then the following day went back to Dreux for his burial service.

The Times in London and *Le Figaro* in Paris both reported the rumour that Aumale had bequeathed all his Sicilian estates to Hélène, and the *Echo de Paris* said not only the Sicilian estates, but also 100,000 livres in rents. However, in fact, she probably received nothing, at least no property. Aumale left all the Italian lands to her brother Orléans along with the French domains of Aumale and Eu, all of which he had inherited from his father, King Louis Philippe. Hélène's cousin Jean de Chartres was named Duc de Guise, an historic title that had previously been held by Aumale's three younger sons before the untimely deaths of each of them. Jean was also given the mansion at Le Nouvion with his parents having a life tenancy, while the hôtel on the rue Montalivet in Paris went to the Duc de Penthièvre. However, the jewel in the crown—the extensive domain at Chantilly with its magnificent château and stables along with his personal library and other art collections—was left to the Institute de France, a legacy that had been made at the time of his return from exile but not made public until later. Aumale had made a secret will dated 3 June 1884 (made public 29 September 1886) to leave to the Institute de France the domain of Chantilly. When the presidential administration changed, Aumale—who had been exiled to Brussels—was allowed to return by a decree on 10 March 1889, he returned to Paris the following day and on the 12th was back at Chantilly.[36]

Among the other properties that Philippe inherited from Uncle Aumale was the Wood Norton estate in Worcestershire overlooking the River Avon. During the coming year, he would demolish the old shooting box and erect a large country house, which would become the centre of many family gatherings in the coming years. At the entrance of the property were iron-wrought gates surmounted by three golden lilies, the emblem of the House of France. The gates had originally stood at Versailles and then at York House, Twickenham, until its sale by the family.

Philippe, the Duc d'Orléans, sold Zucco in 1923 while the Palais d'Orléans in Palermo was eventually inherited by Isabelle's husband, the Duc de Guise, as the new dynastic head; it remained in the family until 1940.

The Aostas were back in France in August, visiting the Comtesse de Paris at Randan with side trips to Vichy for the waters and the races. Also visiting Randan that month was exiled Queen Isabel of Spain, who came to see her sister, Hélène's grandmother, the Duchesse de Montpensier. It was while they were all staying at Randan that a family feud reached its crescendo.

While disputes exist in every family, few go as far as a formal duel, even though there was already the example of Hélène's grandfather, the Duc de Montpensier, having killed the Duke of Seville in 1870. Now, the potential of a repeat scenario occurred when Hélène's brother-in-law, Vittorio Emanuele, the Count of Turin, challenged her cousin, Prince Henri d'Orléans, to a duel in Paris to defend the honour of Italy over some published remarks about Abyssinia in *Le Figaro*.

Henri d'Orléans was four years older than Hélène, the son of her uncle and aunt, the Duc and Duchesse de Chartres, and a great favourite in the family. From an early age, he was an explorer and adventurer. In 1888, Henri had invited the 19-year-old Duc d'Orléans to join him on a shooting expedition in Nepal before Philippe was to rejoin his regiment in the Punjab. In 1892, he travelled into Abyssinia west of Harar, mapping the land as he went. He journeyed to the Gulf of Aden and Madagascar, then into south-east Asia, where he explored Cochinchina, Cambodia, and Annam. His explorations of the Mekong won him a gold medal from the Geographical Society. French and foreign newspapers, especially *Le Figaro*, welcomed Henri's stories. In that particular paper, he criticized the Italian military actions in Abyssinia, and Vittorio Emanuele felt that he had impugned the honour of the Italian army.[37]

The duel with swords took place in the Bois des Maréchaux at Vaucresson outside Paris at 5 a.m. of 15 August, lasted for twenty-six minutes and consisted of five assaults. In the first assault, Henri was lightly hit in the chest; on the third, Turin was struck in the hand; and then on the fifth, Henri was wounded in the abdomen seriously enough for the duel to be ended. After his wounds were dressed, Henri rose, and the two men shook hands. The King sent Vittorio Emanuele a telegram to welcome him back to Italy and congratulate him on his courage and bravery. Turin was treated like a hero throughout Italy with provincial towns setting up books of congratulation and piles of telegrams arrived in his honour. Among these was one sent by Hélène from Randan where she was visiting with her mother. Although she must have had divided loyalties, she wrote 'Receive most sincere and tender congratulations from a sister who approves and admires you.'[38] Sadly, this duel seems to have been the major accomplishment of Turin's life.

Several months after the duel, Henri went back to Djibouti and formed a sixty-camel caravan to take him to Addis Ababa, where he was received by Menelik II and reminded the Negus of the French connection in which his great-grandfather Louis Philippe had signed an alliance with Abyssinia.[39]

In July and August, Hélène spent three weeks in France with her sister Isabelle at the thermal springs at Mont-Dore, where they stayed at the Hôtel Bellon amid rumours of Isabelle's engagement to Prince Albert of Belgium. Then, in September, while Emanuele visited Prince Napoléon in Brussels, Hélène went to London accompanied by the Torrigianis. The Comtesse de Paris and the younger children joined them, the Duc and Duchesse d'Orléans, and other family members for the pilgrimage to Weybridge for the anniversary Mass in honour of the Comte de Paris. Hélène and the Torrigianis then returned to Paris on 12 September to be met by Emanuele Filiberto at the Gare du Nord. It was only a brief meeting for a dinner at the Italian embassy, because when Hélène returned to Turin and La Mandria, Aosta headed north to represent the King in Stockholm at the twenty-fifth anniversary of the reign of King Oscar II.

In the autumn, foreign newspapers began to publicly speculate on the Aosta marriage, picking up some of the private concerns of earlier in the year

> The relations between the duke and Duchess of Aosta, the former being the eldest nephew of the King of Italy and the latter being Princess Helena of Orleans, daughter of the late count of Paris, are once more reported to be strained, and it is further stated that their separation is only a question of a short time. Although they were only married about two years ago, in June 1895, *Figaro* announced recently that the marriage had turned out to be very unhappy for both parties and that a judicial separation had been prevented only by the intervention of the Duke of Aumale. The duchess, *Figaro* added, refused to be reconciled to her husband and kept separate apartments. In December last there was held a family council of the members of the houses of Savoy and Orleans, at the end of which it was announced that the Duke and Duchess of Aosta had been induced to abandon their intention of an immediate separation. When the duchess was here [in London] last week she declared she would never live in Italy again. Her mother, the Countess of Paris, has done all she can to soothe the ruffled feelings of the duchess; but all her efforts to make her change her mind seem to have been unavailing, and it is generally admitted that her separation from the duke is again looked on as being almost inevitable.[40]

However, within a few months of this newspaper report Hélène would be pregnant with the long-awaited heir, and questions about the durability of the marriage receded again.

In September 1898, the world was shocked when an Italian anarchist, Luigi Luchini, assassinated the glamourous yet elusive Empress Elisabeth of Austria while she was visiting Geneva. This came only sixteen months after the death of her sister Sophie in the Parisian charity fire and the assassination attempt on King Umberto by yet another Italian anarchist. It is said that Elisabeth was only a substitute victim after the original target—Hélène's cousin, Prince Henri d'Orléans—cancelled his visit to the city at short notice. The anarchist movement had developed a political theory of the 'propaganda of the deed,' by which the act of violent attention-getting was more important than the intended victim.

That same month, Hélène and Emanuele Filiberto moved from La Mandria into central Turin upon Emanuele's promotion to Brigadier General and to prepare for the birth of their first child. It was at the Palazzo Cisterna on 21 October that Amedeo was born. The Comtesse de Paris was able to telegraph Queen Victoria at Balmoral that she found Hélène doing admirably well and declared the baby 'superb.'[41] Celebrations took place across Italy; in Rome, royal salutes were fired, the national flag was raised on public buildings and many private homes, and it was noted—not for the first, nor the last time—that should the Prince of Naples have no male issue, this infant would be in direct line of succession to the throne of Italy.

Domenico Farini, as President of the Senate, arrived to officially record the birth of the new prince at the Palazzo Cisterna and noticed how shabby it was. The walls were painted a uniform brown, the white paint was peeling, the floors were worn and not clean, and most of the furniture had been stripped out by Laetitia. The Duke apologized for the condition of the place; he said that everything had been turned upside down recently and that it would take at least a year and a half to get everything in good order. However, even two years later, Hélène complained that work on the Palazzo was not advancing, and they were reduced to living in three rooms. By 1901, there was still no dining room, so they ate their meals in Hélène's salon.[42]

The little prince's christening took place on 3 November in the Chapel of the Holy Shroud in Turin Cathedral with King Umberto and the Comtesse de Paris standing as godparents. The principino was given the names Amedeo Umberto Isabella Luigi Filippo Maria Giuseppe Giovanni. To Hélène, he became simply 'Bouby'; the nickname is said to originated with his Alsatian nurse, Frau Zimmermann, who called him 'Bübchen,' meaning little boy. It was an affectionate name that Hélène and the whole family retained for the rest of his life.

The Empress Frederick wrote to her daughter, the Crown Princess Sophie of Greece, that 'Helen Aosta (Orléans) has a son, how pleased they will be, there seemed no chance for a long while.'[43] Indeed, there would be some public discussion as early as 1900, when their second son was born, that Hélène had needed the medical assistance of Professor Leopold Schenk. Schenk was professor at the Imperial and Royal University and director of the Embryological Institute of Vienna, and internationally known for *Schenk's Theory: The Determination of Sex*, which was published Austria and Germany and in English translation in 1898. As early as 1878, Schenk had experimented with *in vitro* fertilization with the sperm and ova of rabbits, but he was best known for his controversial claim that the diet of the mother could determine the gender of a child. He held that mothers desiring sons should abstain from the use of sweets and other rich foods. He said that the sex of a child was dependent upon the number of red corpuscles in the mother's blood, as men's bodies generally have about 5 million red corpuscles as opposed to 4 million in women.

Schenk is said to have also assisted the Countess of Warwick to produce a male heir, and most notably, the Archduchess Frederick of Austria who finally gave birth to a son and heir in 1897 after eight daughters. However, Schenk's self-seeking publicity became his downfall, when his colleagues in Vienna forced his retirement on the grounds of perverting the truth for the sake of notoriety.

When the young family returned to stay at La Mandria, one observer remarked on the Comtesse de Paris as a '*bonne bourgeoise*, smoking cigars and going out deer stalking' while her daughter Hélène was 'infinitely more regal.'[44]

As they would over the course of the next several years, in February 1899, Emanuele Filiberto and Hélène gave their patronage and attended a grand ball at the Hotel Europa in Turin in aid of the Red Cross work with wounded and sick soldiers in Africa. Laetitia was also there to lend her support, along with the Duke and Duchess of Genoa, the Dowager Duchess of Genoa, and the visiting Duke and Duchess d'Orléans. Hélène's brother Philippe suggested meeting again in Venice in March; although she would have liked to see both him and the city of Venice again, she had to decline because little Amedeo was ill at the time, and even though he was starting to recover 'I wouldn't feel right if I left him even for twenty-four hours. When you have children (come on, get on with it) you will see that you can't do what you want.'[45]

However, later in the month, travelling incognito as the Countess della Cisterna, Hélène did go to Genoa to visit Alexandra, the Princess of Wales aboard the royal yacht *Osborne*, and then the next month went to Nice to visit Queen Victoria—herself travelling incognito as the Countess of Balmoral. The Queen thought Hélène was 'in great good looks.'[46]

In 1899, the engagement was announced between Hélène's next younger sister Isabelle and their first cousin, Jean, youngest son of the Duc and Duchesse de Chartres. The relationship was even closer as their parents were first cousins to each other as well. Whereas in unconnected families, there would have been sixteen sets of great-grandparents, here there were only eight. Queen Victoria, for one, was appalled:

> I think that marriage of Isabelle Paris's very pretty third daughter to her cousin Jean d'Orléans, whose eldest brother was an idiot and the other is a shocking lump, is very sad, for the fathers were brothers and the mothers are first cousins.

What will the children be like? The only exception to this rule is the Jews, who do not become stupid by perpetual intermarriage.'[47]

Unless it was his duel in 1897 or his constant travelling overseas, it is not clear what the explorer Prince Henri did to deserve Queen Victoria's opprobrium as a 'shocking lump.'

Jean also had two sisters: the Princess Marguerite, who had been jilted by Hélène's brother the Duc d'Orléans and later married the Duc de Magenta; and also Princess Marie, who was married to Prince Valdemar of Denmark. It was this last connection that was particularly significant in Jean's early life. As the law of 22 June 1886 forbade members of the former French royal families from serving in the military forces of France or holding any public or elected office, the sons of the family in particular needed to find surrogate countries if they were going gain any military experience. His connection with the Danish royal family enabled Jean to go to Copenhagen, where he arrived in December 1891. It took him two years to learn Danish and to prepare for the admission examinations, and an exotic companion in all of this was Prince Chira, son of the King of Siam. Together, the two student princes dined with the Danish Royal Court every Sunday. On 1 March 1894, Jean entered the officers' school at the Castle of Frederiksborg, and altogether served eight years in the Danish army.[48]

Hélène and her mother travelled from Paris to London together on the 26th. On the Saturday night before the wedding, The Duke of Orléans gave a large dinner on Saturday evening at York House, Twickenham, for the members of both families and friends assembled in London for the wedding of his sister and their cousin. On the Monday, the weather was wretched even by English standards, but the little Church of St Raphael in Kingston-on-Thames was full to overflowing with guests and well-wishers from France. Unlike Hélène's own wedding four years earlier when most of the British royal family and much of the Italian royal family attended, this time the royal guests were only from the extended Orléans family, not even Queen Amélie was able to be present. Hélène and her cousin Marie of Denmark were the only guests from currently reigning sovereign families. But Princess Clémentine was there was her son Philip, along with other cousins. Jean, the bridegroom, in his scarlet uniform as a captain of the Danish army, arrived with his parents, brother Henri, and sister Marie. The bride arrived on the arm of her brother, the Duc d'Orléans. The Bishop of Southwark, the Curé of the Madeleine ('who delivered an eloquent and pathetic address'), and the priests in charge of the Kingston and Twickenham Catholic churches officiated at the wedding. Then, after the service, the wedding party returned to York House in Twickenham, where the streets had been hung with bunting and the bells of the next-door parish Church of St Mary rang out to celebrate another royal wedding.

In the New Year and the eighth month of her second pregnancy, Hélène suffered from a light attack of influenza in February but recovered quickly. Her
Aunt Eulalia of Spain was visiting the Duke and Duchess of Genoa in Turin
for a few days in early March, and Hélène and Emanuele, as well as Laetitia,
were among those to see her off at the station. A couple of days later Hélène,
assisted by Professor Vicarelli, gave birth to a second son at Turin on 9 March
1900. Aimone Roberto Margherita Maria Giuseppe Torino would be known in
the family as 'Bob.' The birth was greeted with a twenty-one gun salute from the
cannon atop the monte dei Cappuccini and was seen as a national event just as
the birth of Amedeo two years earlier. When the news became known in Rome,
public buildings and many private houses were decorated. As soon as she was able,
Hélène had a telegram sent to Pope Leo XIII announcing the birth of her son,
and the news was also communicated about the same time by Cardinal Richelmi,
the archbishop of Turin. The Pope responded to the cardinal almost immediately, charging him to present the pontiff's congratulations and best wishes to the
Duchess—although because of the ongoing strain between the Papacy and the
House of Savoy, the congratulations were extended to Hélène alone.

The day after his birth Aimone was anointed at the ducal palace by l'abbe Bosio,
the court chaplain, and that was followed by the civil registration of the birth.
Queen Margherita and the Prince de Joinville were announced as his godparents
at his anointing. At age eighty-one, Joinville was the last surviving son of King
Louis Philippe; before the end of the year, he would join his ancestors in the burial crypt at Dreux. Aimone's formal baptism did not take place until 3 December
in the private chapel of the Castello Stupinigi with the Duc de Chartres now
filling the role of godfather in place of his late uncle. Immediately after the baptism, Cardinal Richelmy administered the sacrament of Confirmation upon little
Aimone's uncle, the Count of Salemi. Then, Chartres dashed back to France,
where—two days later—he again stood as godfather, this time to his own granddaughter, little Princess Isabelle, Hélène's niece, the firstborn child of the Duc and
Duchesse de Guise.

6

1900–1907

Come è bella la vita quando non soffia vento!
'How beautiful life is when no wind is blowing'[1]

Sunday, 29 July 1900, was a hot day—too hot, King Umberto decided, for his usual morning ride on horseback at Monza where he and Queen Margherita were staying in the Villa Reale, the neo-classical Royal Villa which had been built in the eighteenth century by the Empress Maria Theresa for her son, the Archduke Ferdinand, when he was governor of Milan. It was one of the hundreds of palaces that the Savoys inherited from the various deposed dynasties upon the unification of Italy. Instead of his morning ride, the King had his hair cut and his tremendous trademark white mustaches tended by his personal barber. In the afternoon, he attended Mass in the private chapel of the villa and lunched with the Queen, went into the gardens and then had a solitary carriage ride in the park. The King and Queen sat down to dinner punctually at 8.00 p.m., and at 9.20 p.m., the King Umberto drove to the grounds of the Provincial Athletic Club in Monza, where he had agreed to attend the distribution of prizes for a recent gymnastic competition. The ceremony took about an hour, and then the King and his *aide-de-camp* got into his carriage surrounded by a cheering crowd. Three revolvers shots rang out in quick succession, and the king fell back into the carriage, while the crowd seized the assassin. Although the carriage reached the royal villa in just three minutes, the King died as he was being carried inside.[2]

The thirty-year-old assassin, Gaetano Bresci, was originally from near Prato in Tuscany, but had for six years lived and worked in Paterson, New Jersey, a hub of anarchist activity. Bresci immediately admitted the crime, saying that it was in retribution for King Umberto having decorated General Fiorenzo Bava-Beccaris following the Milan bread riots of 1898, when Bava-Beccaris ordered his troops to fire upon a crowd when it failed to respond to the warning to disperse. More than ninety were killed by musket and cannon fire that day, yet the general was awarded with the Great Cross of the Military Order of Savoy, commended by the king for his 'brave defense' of the royal house, and a few days later appointed to the Senate. The newspapers quickly noted that Italian anarchists had also been responsible for the deaths of President Carnot of France in 1894; the Spanish prime minister in 1897; and the Empress Elizabeth of Austria in 1898.[3] Umberto himself had survived earlier attempts in 1878 and 1898.

With his brother Turin and their cousin the Portuguese Duke of Oporto, Emanuele Filiberto rushed to Monza and took turns standing in full-dress uniform as a guard of honour by the king's coffin at the royal villa while Queen Margherita and the princesses prayed and priests from Monza and Milan celebrated regular Masses in the adjacent room. The new King Victor Emmanuel and Queen Elena, who were on an Aegean cruise at the time of the assassination, returned quickly to Rome, then immediately went on to Monza to be with the newly widowed Queen Mother. Victor Emmanuel and Elena returned to Rome at 10 a.m. of the 8th, and were met by all the ministers dressed in mourning, the senators, undersecretaries of state, and monarchist delegations. When they reached the palace, Prince Nikola of Montenegro was waiting at the foot of the grand staircase, and his daughter ran weeping into his arms. That afternoon in Monza, Aosta, his brother Turin, and Prince Victor Napoléon were joined by the presidents of the Senate and the Chamber, as well as the ministers of War, Justice, and Agriculture, to accompany the coffin along the black-draped streets to the station *en route* for Rome. Queen Margherita, accompanied by her mother the Dowager Duchess of Genoa, Queen Maria Pia, Hélène, and Laetitia, arrived in Rome at 8 p.m. Strict instructions for privacy sealed the station so that not even ministers were there to meet them, yet immense silent crowds surrounded the station and the entire route to the Quirinale as the six landaus passed through the streets.

The male mourners gathered at the station in Rome as the early morning fog lifted into a light haze. The new King, his closest relatives—including Emanuele Filiberto who was now heir presumptive to the throne—along with the foreign representatives, and ministers of state stood at attention as the coffin was removed from the train. 300 clergy carrying tapers preceded the gun carriage bearing the late king. Immediately following came a general bearing the great medieval symbol, the Iron Crown of Lombardy, said to contain a piece of one of the nails from Christ's cross and to have been used by Charlemagne at his coronation as king of the Lombards as well as by subsequent kings of Italy. The king's riderless charger then preceded the new king and other mourners on foot. The lengthy procession—the front of which reached the church before the final marchers had left the station—stretched through vast crowds lining the streets of Rome where the electric lights remained lit under black fabric coverings giving an eerie effect to the already sombre occasion. Meanwhile, the female mourners—including the new Queen, the Queen Mother, Hélène and Laetitia—gathered inside the Pantheon where the Archbishop of Genoa conducted the funeral Mass before King Umberto was laid to rest next to his father.

The new king, Victor Emmanuel III, ascended the throne dutifully but reluctantly. 'By his own account,' he 'had half-convinced his father to let him renounce the throne in favour of his far more glamorous cousin the Duke of Aosta.'[4]

Adding to the verve of the Aosta branch of the royal family, Emanuele Filiberto's twenty-seven-year-old younger brother Luigi arrived home in Turin in September from his polar expedition. The Duke of the Abruzzi—affectionately known in the family as Luigino—had missed Hélène's wedding as he was then in the middle of a circumnavigation of the world with the Navy. He was also absent from King Umberto's funeral as he was then on an Arctic exploration.

Luigi had developed an interest in mountain climbing while still a boy, and as a teenager, he progressed on to scaling the Alps. When he was only twenty-one, after climbing the Matterhorn across the Zmutt Ridge as part of a team with Albert Mummery, Luigi was made honorary president of the Club Alpino Italiano and a member of London's prestigious Alpine Club. During his twenty-six month voyage around the world as first lieutenant aboard the royal naval battle cruiser *Cristoforo Colombo*, he first had sight of the Himalayas as well as Mount Saint Elias in Alaska, both of which became scaling goals of his. In 1897, Luigi headed an Alaskan wilderness expedition that became the first to conquer Mount Saint Elias at 18,008 feet (5,489 metres). Luigi was pushed on by his sense of adventure and challenge, although the expedition's photographer, Vittorio Sella, who would accompany Luigi on other journeys in the future, sadly noted that the 'prince has not an artistic temperament at all and the beauty of a view does not interest him.'[5]

In 1899, Abruzzi mounted an even more ambitious expedition—the conquest of the North Pole. Hélène was the only one to accompany Luigi from the Palazzo Cisterna to the station at Porta Susa where he began the initial rail journey to Christiania in Norway. The party, which included Umberto Cagni from the Alaskan adventure, sailed aboard the *Polar Star*, the ship which was originally named the *Jason* and which had carried Fridtjof Nansen on his 1893–1896 Greenland expeditions. From the beginning, it was a difficult journey, and Luigi wrote in his journal 'We ceaselessly pass from hopes to delusions and from delusions to hopes.' They planned to winter aboard the ship in a small bay on the northernmost point of Prince Rudolph Island, but the *Polar Star* was severely damaged by a pressure ridge of ice, and the crew was forced to set up winter camp on land. Small gifts to the crew from Queen Margherita, Hélène, and Laetitia were opened in honour of the queen's birthday in late November, but instead of making them happy, this made the men realize their isolation and despair, and nearly destroyed their morale. Eventually temporary repairs to the ship finished and explorations resumed, but the brutally severe weather resulted in Luigi losing parts of three fingers on his left hand to frostbite. One detachment from the expedition achieved a latitude of 86°34', a new record, some twenty-three miles (37 kilometres) further than Nansen's mark, but that was the closest they were able to achieve. After great trials, the expedition returned to Norway, where Luigi learned of the assassination of his uncle, the king. He presided over a solemn torchlight parade in Christiania in honour of King Umberto, and remained there for a month. During that time, he was visited by Robert F. Scott, who was preparing his own polar expedition. Hoping to learn details that would help his own trek, Scott later reported that while the Duke had 'nice manners', there 'was not much to be learned' from him.[6]

Although he didn't achieve his goal, Luigi was feted as a hero upon his return to Italy in September with cheering crowds at each city he passed through. Hélène and Laetitia were at the station in Turin to greet him along with local authorities and crowds of cheering spectators. Once they reached the palace, the demonstrations were renewed and Abruzzi went out twice to acknowledge the cheers. In January, Hélène, Emanuele Filiberto, and most of the royal family went to Rome for a conference of the Italian Geographic Society where Luigi and Dr Cagni reported on the expedition.

Following the assassination of King Umberto, Emanuele Filiberto became the heir presumptive to the throne and would remain so while the new king and queen had no son. Aosta's public role now included more ceremonial events, and in mid-January, he went to Berlin to represent Italy at the Bicentenary of Prussian Monarchy. At the grand banquet in the Royal Palace on the 17 January, Aosta and Grand Duke Vladimir (brother of Tsar Alexander III) were seated at either side of the Kaiser, while Archduke Franz Ferdinand and the Duke of Connaught were seated opposite, on either side of the Empress. However, within a few days, the Kaiser and his Uncle Connaught were aboard the Prussian royal yacht headed for the Isle of Wight, where Queen Victoria lay seriously ill.

On the 22nd, the most iconic royal figure of the age, Queen Victoria, died surrounded by many of her descendants at Osborne House after the longest reign in British history to that point. The woman, whom Hélène was once allowed to call *Ma chère Grand'Maman* when she was getting over the death of Prince Eddy, was eighty-one years old. Emanuele was named as Italy's official representative to the Queen's funeral, and it was announced that Hélène would join him on this sad journey.

While England was mourning their queen, Italy was mourning its best-loved composer, as Giuseppe Verdi died on 27 January. Originally, it was announced that Emanuele would represent the Crown at Verdi's funeral in Milan on the 30th, but Verdi had requested a simple funeral—no flowers, no bands, no troops—and in the end, there was no royal representative at the service. Instead of bands, the music along the funeral route in Milan was provided by the thousands of mourners who lined the streets and spontaneously sang '*Va, pensiero*' (the 'Chorus of the Hebrew Slaves') from Verdi's opera *Nabucco*. This magnificent chorus had special meaning in Italy as it had been the unofficial anthem of the *Risorgimento* during the country's unification process.

Hélène had expected to leave Turin for London and Queen Victoria's funeral on the 30th, as she told her brother.[7] However, it was later publicly announced that she was unable to join her husband due to illness. Another version of the story relates that the King—'ceding to the intrigues of Princess Laetitia and the Duchess of Genoa'—telegraphed Hélène at the border to proceed no further. Whatever the real story, Emanuele Filiberto went to England alone, carrying with him a wreath from Hélène with the message '*Éternelle reconnaissance.*'

Hélène's brother Philippe also had intended to attend the funeral but had been advised by a telegram from the Princess of Wales—now Queen Alexandra—that her husband felt Philippe's return to England at this time would be premature and not understood by the British public. In March 1900, Philippe's tactlessness had landed him in trouble when he wrote a letter of congratulations to the French cartoonist Adolphe Willette for his caricature of 'Oom Paul' spanking Queen Victoria. With the Boer War raging in South Africa, British feelings were particularly outraged by this act of discourtesy by someone who had been sheltered in England during his exile. Philippe's London clubs demanded his resignation, while he complained that they were 'requiring of him, as the price for the hospitality of England, the abdication of his French sentiments.' Philippe and his wife Mariska then found it prudent to take an extended tour of the Mediterranean, visiting Hélène before going on to Venice.

While he was in Turin, Hélène hosted a family dinner which also included their uncle, the Duc de Chartres, and the Duke of the Abruzzi. During the meal, Chartres told how on the morning of Queen Victoria's death, he had telegraphed London and knowing that she was not yet dead, went out hunting with the hounds. Hélène leaned to her dinner partner, the Comte de Gramont, and whispered '*Quelle famille!*' De Gramont wrote in his journal that he wanted to say 'But, Madame, it's your family!' although he decided that discretion was more appropriate than words at the time.[8]

Queen Elena gave birth to her first child on 1 June after nearly five years of marriage. The child was a girl, and so Emanuele Filiberto and the boys were still secure in their place in the succession. The baby princess was christened a fortnight later in the ballroom of the Quirinale and given the name Jolanda. The procession of the Italian and Montenegrin royal families showed the Italian princes in military uniform, the princesses in white, while the Montenegrins wore national costume. King Victor Emmanuel led the procession with his aunt, Queen Maria Pia of Portugal; then came the baby's grandfather, Prince Nikola of Montenegro, with Queen Margherita; the Duke of Aosta with the grandmother Princess Milena; the Duke of Oporto with the Dowager Duchess of Genoa; Prince Mirko with Princess Laetitia; and finally the Duke of the Abruzzi with Hélène.

In France, anti-Semitism was on the rise again following the re-trial of Alfred Dreyfus. Hélène's brother Philippe supported the cause by subsidizing—and at one point seeking to buy—the *Libre Parole*, the leading anti-Semitic newspaper, as well as giving subventions to the Anti-Semitic League. These and other traits were lauded by Charles Maurras, editor of the right-wing *Action Française:* 'All the acts of this prince, his nationalism, his anti-Semitism, his politics at once popular and military-like, his taste for authority, his declarations in favor of decentralization, permit me to conclude that Philippe VIII will regenerate the French State.' Hélène, on the other hand, was reported to be a supporter of the Dreyfus cause and insisted upon his innocence. Likewise, her close connection with Prince Victor Napoléon (Emanuele's first cousin and brother to Princess Laetitia) caused some to call her a Bonapartist.[9]

In April, Hélène and Emanuele Filiberto joined Jean and Isabelle de Guise for a stay at the Hotel Alexandre in Mentone. Later in the month, Hélène and Emanuele went to Florence, where the Count of Turin presented them with a review of the 'Lancieri Novara,' the company earlier commanded by their father, Duke Amedeo. The Aostas attended on horseback; in the evening, they went to a garden party in the Boboli Gardens.

However, throughout Italy, there were widespread agricultural strikes from April through June, followed by tramway strikes in Rome, Naples, and Milan in August.

George von Lengerke Meyer was appointed American ambassador to Rome in 1900 by President William McKinley. He was a Harvard classmate and friend of Theodore Roosevelt, who succeeded to the presidency when McKinley was assassinated in 1901. Drawn together by a love of riding, Meyer quickly became a friend of the Aostas, particularly to Hélène. Meyer's wife Alice was very much star-struck by royalty, and she wrote up every encounter fulsomely, such as when they went to Turin for the 7 May for the opening of the First International Exposition of Modern Decorative Art, which highlighted the developing Art Nouveau movement. Mrs Meyer recorded that the morning began with the unveiling of a statue to Emanuele Filiberto's father. The King and Queen were there along with Emanuele Filiberto and Hélène, as well as Princess Laetitia and her son, and the Duke and Duchess of Genoa all of them 'driving up in beautiful carriages, red liveries, and surrounded with the cuirassiers.' 'Speeches were made, long and dull after which there was the unveiling of the statue a beautiful piece of work full of life. The Artist was called to the Royal box, and complimented, then a signing of names in the royal stand.'[10]

In the evening, they all went to the Teatro Regio for a 'carousel,' a pageant on horseback with costumed riders acting out parts of historical characters. In the theatre, 'the stage seats were banked, and in the pit, arranged like a circus. The theatre all hung with brocades, and the effect most artistic.' Emanuele Filiberto rode dressed as Amedeo II, Prince of Savoy, while his brother Vittorio Emanuele acted in the role of the son, Vittorio Amedeo. Their role was to receive a delegation of

Sicilian horsemen, paying homage on behalf of the King of Sicily. Mrs Meyer declared the whole pageant 'most interesting and beautifully done.'[11]

The date for the coronation of Edward VII and Queen Alexandra in London was set for 26 June. The King was himself keenly interested in all aspects of ceremonials, and since there had not been a coronation for such a long time, he sought the advice of the oldest member of the royal family, Princess May's aunt, the seventy-nine-year-old Grand Duchess of Mecklenburg-Strelitz. Aunt Augusta could remember back to the 1831 coronation of her uncle, King William IV and was delighted to be asked, although less delighted when most of her memories were ignored in order to create a new protocol.[12] As early as January, the procession route was published along with other details, and invitations were soon sent out to guests. One of the customs that had developed over the centuries was that no other crowned monarchs should attend the ceremony. Instead, literally the next best choice was sent—the heir. It seems likely that Hélène would have received a personal invitation from Queen Alexandra in any event, but only when the government was assured that the Duke of Aosta would succeed to the Italian throne if the King should die without male issue was he officially invited to represent his country.

As usual, the Aostas began their journey through France. Emanuele arrived at the Hotel d'Albe in Paris on 20 June in order to thank the President of the Republic for the award of the Grand Cross of the Legion d'Honneur. Hélène arrived the next evening having left her sons with the Comtesse de Paris at the Château de Randan. Accompanied by the Torrigianis and their military suite, the Aostas arrived at Victoria Station from Dover in the evening of the 22nd. There, they were met by officials from the British royal household, the Italian ambassador and consul general plus a large number of Italian war veterans now living in London, 'with each one of whom the Duke d'Aosta shook hands.' Then, it was on to Dorchester House, Park Lane, the home of Sir George Holford, where they stayed during their visit.

Royalty gathered in London from around the world. From the royal families of Europe, many came who were nephews, nieces, or cousins to the King and Queen. From further afield came exotic Queen Lilioukalani of Hawaii, princes from Egypt, Japan, Persia, Korea, Ethiopia, Zanzibar, and Siam, as well as several Indian maharajahs. On 24 June, the Aostas and Hélène's nephew Luis Filipe, the Crown Prince of Portugal, visited with Prince and Princess of Wales during the afternoon, and were at Buckingham Palace for a dinner for about eighty royal guests, followed by a reception for all the accompanying suites. Although the published *Court Circular* announced that both Their Majesties entertained the guests, it was in fact Queen Alexandra who acted as hostess alone, as the King was seriously ill.

King Edward had been suffering while he and the Queen were at Aldershot for a major military review the previous week. He was in such pain that he could not attend the review, and Queen Alexandra had to deputise for him, taking the salute of 31,000 troops in a march past that lasted two-and-a-half hours. It was first given out that the king was simply suffering from lumbago, but when they got back to Buckingham Palace, the doctors diagnosed appendicitis and insisted on an immediate operation. However necessary, this type of surgery was still very risky, but it proved completely successful.[13]

Public sympathy outweighed disappointment caused by the postponed coronation, and a great many social functions still continued. On the day after the operation, Hélène and Emanuele were invited to luncheon privately at the palace with the royal family. The next day, they joined Hélène's nephew Luis Filipe of Portugal at a 'little dinner party' that the Prince and Princess of Wales gave at York House; it was also attended by the Crown Prince Ferdinand and Crown Princess Marie of Romania, as well as Marie's sister Beatrice, Prince Nicholas of Greece, the young Duke of Saxe-Coburg, and the Duke and Duchess of Teck, as well as two favourites of the diplomatic corps—Count Mensdorff, the Austrian minister who was a cousin to the Coburgs, and Soveral, the Portuguese minister, friend of the new king and member of the 'Marlborough Set.'[14]

On the morning of 1 July, Hélène was the only one from outside the British royal family to join Queen Alexandra in the carriage procession from Buckingham Palace to Horse Guards Parade for the grand parade of the British and colonial troops, an event marred only by the absence of the King. Emanuele Fililberto joined the Prince of Wales and Duke of Connaught and other visiting royalties as troops from around the world paraded and then were inspected by the Queen and Prince of Wales. The special correspondent for *The Times* declared it 'undoubtedly one of the most brilliant and significant displays ever held in this country.' When they returned to Buckingham Palace, Hélène and Emanuele Filiberto were the only ones invited to lunch with Queen Alexandra and her daughter and son-in-law, the Fifes. That evening, the Secretary of State for Foreign Affairs and Lady Lansdowne gave a lavish late-night reception for the visiting delegations. The Aostas were among the first of the royal guests to arrive shortly after 11 a.m., and they joined a great crowd from the diplomatic corps and the special delegations from overseas. The Aga Khan, the maharajahs of Gwalior, Jaipur, Kolhapur, Bikaner, and Cooch Behar joined those enjoying music played at the garden entrance by the band of the Irish Guards and by Gottlieb's Viennese Orchestra in the ballroom. One of the other guests, the Duchess of Sermoneta, was particularly impressed with the Indians princes with their 'brocade coats of exquisite colours, their sunset-like turbans, jewelled brooches and enormous pearl necklaces,' while she also remembered Hélène being there 'in the full splendour of her stately good looks.'[15]

The recuperating King Edward personally presented the Order of the Garter to Emanuele Filiberto at Buckingham Palace on 2 July on the night that he was leaving London.[16] Over the years, Emanuele Filiberto would become perhaps the most decorated individual in Europe, receiving virtually all the royal orders of his time.

Hélène stayed on in London for a few days and was at yet another gala reception, this one at the India Office on 4 July. The correspondent, tripping over his superlatives, declared that 'never has a more magnificent or impressive reception been given in London.' On the day before she left, Hélène went out for a ride in the park along with the Prince of Wales, his sister Victoria, his brother-in-law, Prince Carl of Denmark, and the Crown Prince of Greece. George also went to the station to see Hélène off to Turin.[17] Hélène, accompanied by Carlo and Anna Torrigiani, stopped first at the Château de Randan, where the Comtesse de Paris had been caring for Amedeo and Aimone. Before taking the children home, Hélène went to Mont Dore, near Vichy and not far from Randan, for a cure. The postponed British coronation finally took place on 9 August, attended by some of the extended British and continental royal families, but far fewer than the originally intended numbers.

Toward the end of the year, on 11 November, the Château d'Eu, an old family home where Hélène had spent her happy youth between the two exiles, was severely damaged by fire. It would lay empty for several years until the Duc d'Orléans sold it in 1905 to the branch of the Orléans family which had then recently been exiled from Brazil. They began the restoration which returned the château to a family residence, which it remained until 1945.

On 27 April, Hélène went to Livorno to meet her sister Amélie for the first time since their brother Philippe's wedding in 1896. Amélie and her sons had left Portugal in February aboard the royal yacht *Amélia* for an extended trip around the Mediterranean—Algeria, Tunisia, Egypt, Malta, and finally Italy. When Amélie continued her journey into France, her two sons would go to stay with Hélène at Capodimonte before they returned to Portugal.[18]

In June, the Aostas invited the American ambassador and his wife for a visit to Turin. Arriving at mid-morning, the Meyers were met by Carlo Torrigiani who offered them the option of going to see the Duke review his troops or to go directly to the Palazzo Cisterna. Alice thought they were 'all too dusty to present ourselves before Royalty,' so they opted for their rooms first, but watched the Duchess leave with the two little boys for the review. Afterwards, Hélène came to greet them. 'She is most charming in manner, and charming to look at also with her tall and slim figure.' The Ambassador and the Duchess indulged their mutual love of horses and had several early rides together, while Mrs Meyer 'got several charming drives with the Duke in his American buggy. He is far more talkative alone than in a crowd when he generally remains quite silent.' One evening, they went to a dance 'at a sort of club.' Mrs Meyer found that 'Princess L[a]etitia sent for me to join her at supper. Her Royal Highness is full of fun, and must have

been very handsome a few years ago.' Mrs Meyer was also able to provide a rare
view of the inside of the Palazzo Cisterna.

> We were shown over the palace which is very fine, and luxurious in the private
> rooms. The duchess has a charming suite of bedroom, dressing room, dress clos-
> ets, and boudoir. The wardrobe for Her Royal Highness shoes was as much
> like a well stocked shop with all its varieties! The reception rooms are very
> handsome, but formal but the duke has collected beautiful pieces of furniture.[19]

When the Aostas were in Rome in January 1904, Hélène wrote to the diplomat
to see if she could accept his earlier offer of a mount— if 'you still that kind
intention if so could i go tomorrow to the hunt? Or is it "indiscret" to ask you?'
Riding was an important part of Hélène's routine throughout her life, and while
in Turin, a key figure in equestrian circles was Captain Federico Caprilli. The
dashing young cavalry officer developed a new technique for jumping horses in
a more naturalistic way. His 'forward seat' soon became the international standard
and brought him to the attention of Hélène's brother-in-law, the Count of Turin,
who was the Italian Army's General Inspector of Cavalry and commander of the
cavalry school at Pinerolo near Turin. Caprilli was appointed as chief instructor
at Pinerolo, and became well known to the whole Aosta family. Capprilli's success with horses was on a par with his success with women. Hélène herself was
a regular riding partner, although later rumours that their relationship went any
further were almost certainly fabrications.[20] Another visitor to Turin was Wilfred
Blunt, who commented on the Palazzo della Cisterna:

> [It has been] thoroughly furbished up since I was here three or four years ago,
> but it is still a somewhat gloomy house, as few of the windows look out on
> open spaces, and many are filled with opaque or coloured glass. We have been
> given, however, a cheerful apartment of half-a-dozen small rooms looking out
> on some chestnut trees in their first leafage filling the square acre plot which is
> the Palace Garden.

He was much more impressed by the ducal stables with some forty horses, 'most
of them English weight-carrying hunters in the prime of life, and obtained at
high prices, with as many men in livery to look after them', and even more
impressed with Hélène herself:

> The Princess is looking her best with her two boys, Amadeo and Aymon,
> charming children, with pretty manners, and talking already three languages,
> Italian, English, and German. French they have not been taught as they are
> expected to pick it up naturally later from their parents who talk it *en intimité*.

Over luncheon, Hélène discussed Buddhist philosophy with Blunt, particularly that reflected in the writings of Lafcadio Hearn and afterwards gave Blunt a Buddhist catechism to study.[21]

A new member of the household arrived at the Palazzo Cisterna in October 1903 in the person of Erminia Piano as governess to the two little princes. Although the *principini* were just five and four years old, they now began their formal education with three hours of lessons a week in the presence of their mother in her salon. Soon, this progressed to daily lessons taken in the school-room in their rooms on the top floor of the palace.[22]

Ever since her marriage to Emanuele Filiberto, the leitmotif that followed both of them was the very real possibility that they could eventually become King and Queen of Italy. At first, Victor Emmanuel was thought to be incapable of fathering a child, and then when he did, it was as a father to daughters only. Court gossip criticized Hélène for referring to Amedeo as *mon petit roi* (my little king), but in Italy, the first-born son was and still is always treated as, and often referred to as, the prince. Since Amedeo was already a prince, the elevation to 'king' was a natural one.

However, on 15 September 1904 at Racconigi, after nearly eight years of marriage, Queen Elena gave birth to a son and heir to the Italian throne. Named Umberto in honour of his late grandfather, the child pushed the Aosta branch out of the immediate rights of succession and further down the line. As compensation, a week later, the King by Royal decree, created Amedeo as Duke of Apulia, and Aimone as Duke of Spoleto. When their governess showed them on the map where these territories were, little Aimone was annoyed because his brother's territory was larger and therefore felt his own title must be worth less.[23]

The American ambassador Meyer continued a great favourite of the Aostas, and was back in Turin for a visit in October. He stayed with the family at the Palazzo Cisterna along with the Comtesse de Paris and her youngest daughter Louise. After a ride in the park with the Duke, he joined the family for tea, dinner and then the opera for a performance of 'Adrienne Lecouvreur', which Meyer pronounced 'not very good.' Returning to the palace about midnight, they 'had some "grog" in H. R. H. the Duchess' private salon, where the duke joined us, he having been studying an oration that he had to make next day' and Hélène invited the ambassador to join her for a ride the next morning. At 8.30 a.m. the next day, Meyer wrote:

[He] was in the courtyard of the Palace where the horses were already standing, two greys, and a bay for the groom. In about five minutes the Duke and Duchess of Aosta walked in, having attended mass together. In less than five minutes she was down again, all dressed for the saddle. It was a beautiful morning a slight mist which the sun was rapidly driving away, which gave a sort of Corot effect to the fields and trees. We went straight across the country, fording streams and jumping ditches and having long canters down some of the alleys of Stupinigi, where the Queen Mother was coming later, and in which palace we had breakfast just a year ago. The Duchess was in great spirits and most charming. She said she envied me and my family travelling so much, and that now that her husband was no longer heir presumptive, she hoped that they would travel about more, adding that it was a delicate matter before, as it would look as though they were trying to give themselves special prominence. This was the only reference made to the Prince of Piedmont, born to the Queen a month ago. We never got back until nearly 11.30, after a charming ride. It is such a pleasure to see her in the saddle and handling her horse—so graceful and such wonderful hands with a horse.[24]

Hélène's comment about being under less pressure and more able to travel now that the King had a male heir covers a disappointment that the whole Aosta family undoubtedly felt at being displaced in the succession.

Shortly after this visit, though, Hélène fell seriously ill with combined bronchitis, pneumonia, and pleurisy, blamed on a long horseback ride she took one cold morning. The weather in Turin could be severe during the winter, beautiful with the snow-covered Alps in the near background, but with temperatures well below freezing and heavy snows, along with cold, damp, and foggy mornings. None of this benefited Hélène's weak chest. Emanuele remained in Turin to be with her and missed the opening of parliament in Rome on 30 November. Her condition grew more serious, and on Saturday, 3 December, a Reuters telegram reported that she had taken a turn for the worse that afternoon with moments of coma and difficulty breathing. The doctors diagnosed pleurisy of the left lung with pneumonia in the right lung. Cardinal Richelmy, the Archbishop of Turin, ordered that public prayers be offered up in all the city's churches. Every day, Emanuele Filiberto took the boys to pray for the recovery of their mother at the Sanctuario della Consolata. One day, following the Sunday Mass at the nearby parish church of San Filippo, young Amedeo appeared in the classroom and told his governess that during the prayers he had seen his father cry—and in front of Colonel Elia. 'Is it possible for soldiers to cry?' he asked. Rina Piano explained to the little boy that it was indeed possible for soldiers to cry, especially when a great sadness affected their families.[25]

Queen Amélie cut a visit to England short to go to be with Hélène at Turin, arriving on 5 December and staying for five days. Manolo remained with her day and night, except for meals, although she was so weak that no other visitors were allowed. It was three days before Amélie could see her, and then, their mother arrived with her youngest daughter Louise along with Monsieur Dupuy. However, it was not until the 10th that the doctors allowed the Comtesse to see Hélène for a few moments. Reuters reported that 'the meeting was most touching. The duchess, who had tears in her eyes, was overjoyed at seeing her mother, but said nothing. After the meeting, however, she remarked that she felt better and was sure to recover. The doctors are now chiefly concerned with the renal symptoms.' Not until the end of January was Hélène declared 'cured.'[26] Hélène's recovery was slow, and in May she was able to continue her convalescence at the thermal baths at Aqui, where she had spent some time the previous year.

While Hélène was still desperately ill in Turin, most of the family had gathered together in Rome for the baptism of little Umberto, the heir to the throne, on 4 December. The ballroom of the Quirinale Palace was transformed into a chapel, large enough to accommodate all the guests who included Prince Arthur of Connaught and Prince Albert of Prussia representing their monarchs, who were honorary godparents in addition to Queen Margherita and Prince Nikola of Montenegro, the grandparents. 'The spectacle was magnificent in the extreme. All the ladies present, including those of the royal party, were dressed in white, with creamy lace veils on their heads, and were glittering with jewels.' Countess Bruschi-Falgari carried the infant into the room on a lace pillow, and the Queen then carried him to the altar while the King had his small daughters Jolanda and Mafalda at his side. The infant prince 'behaved splendidly, his only outcry being when he felt the holy water upon his forehead.' A small reception followed, but that was shortened due to the 'grave illness' of the Duchess of Aosta.

It may have been a result of Amedeo's question about whether it was possible for a soldier to cry that Hélène wrote out in 1904 some 'commandments' for her sons to follow in their royal lives:

My sons, repeat the princes' commandments
Always remember that
A prince—is never tired
—never hungry
—never thirsty
—never says he is suffering
—never says that he is ill
—is never bored
—never cries in public
—is never angry
—never shouts
—never tells a lie
—a lie is cowardice—a defense of the weak
—never talks about yourself, what you know or do
—does not affect the public—no concerns him
—respond to superiors simply
—smile and give thanks
—be cheerful and grateful to those who support you
your dear Mamma.[27]

Hélène also established a new schedule for the boys that would include time for study, riding lessons, walking and various recreational activities, and so much rest that Amedeo complained to his governess that he was expected to go to bed not only at night but also for a half hour after riding lessons and another half hour after lunch each day. 'If we sleep too much, we will become stupid.'[28]

Queen Alexandra was on a Mediterranean tour in March 1905 and visited Lisbon and then went on to spend a night with the Comtesse de Paris. Queen Alexandra was delighted to write home about her visit to 'dear Granny Isabel' at Villamanrique, the palace near Seville which came to her upon the death of the old Duchess of Montpensier in 1897 and 'where she leads the life of Buffalo Bill.'[29] The Queen Mother continued her journey aboard the British royal yacht the *Victoria and Albert*, which arrived on 3 April in Genoa, where Hélène was able to greet her. They took a drive through Genoa; the next morning, they sailed together for Villefranche.

On 1 April, Hélène had a farewell audience with her friend Meyer, the American Ambassador, who was going to the embassy in St Petersburg. Meyer recorded that at their meeting in the Quirinale Palace, she looked very well and 'was very outspoken about the Russians and the Grand Dukes, saying they were such terrible thieves.' She told him about going to live in Naples and that she hoped to get some riding there. Meyer assured her that would be easy if she were living at Capodimonte. The next year she was able to let Meyer know that they did indeed have 'capital fun' riding at Capodimonte with three excellent new horses and a magnificent terrain for gallops and that Emanuele Filiberto planned to have a pack of drag hounds for hunting there.[30]

The official announcement that Emanuele was designated as Commander of the Army Corps at Naples came on 5 April; it was also announced that the family was given the use of an apartment in the Reggia di Capodimonte. The Palace was designed in 1738 by the Sicilian architect Giovanni Medrano, who had also planned the San Carlo Theatre, and was set on top of a hill and inside a park with splendid views over the city. The gardens were open to the public on Sundays, although *Baedeker's Guide* specifically noted that 'One-horse carriages are not admitted to the park.' However, the museum at the palace was also open to the public on Sundays and Thursdays. Originally built to house the extraordinary Farnese collection of paintings which King Carlo III of the Two Sicilies had inherited from his mother, most of which were moved to the Museo Nazionale in 1806, the palace was not completed until 1839 in the reign of King Ferdinand II. He spent a vast amount of money on building at Capodimonte 'just because this hill was on the route of migrating *beccafiche*—warblers of all kinds—and having finished the palace, a road to Naples had to be built at the cost of another million or two.' It was estimated 'that every warbler eaten by the royal sportsmen cost the nation a thousand ducats.' When the Aostas arrived in Naples, the palace museum contained what Baedeker disdainfully described as 'a somewhat extensive but not very valuable collection of pictures, chiefly by modern Neapolitan masters, and of modern sculptures, distributed throughout the different apartments.'[31] Also in the museum was the outstanding collection of Capodimonte porcelain from the factory that had been established there in 1743 by Carlo III and continued until suppressed by the French in 1807, as well as the armour collection.

A guest who was visiting with the Aostas a few years later gave an even less enthusiastic impression of the palace:

It is a great big place of several stone courtyards & pillared sides, the walls washed buff with grey facings, it stands very well high up above the town, with beautiful views, & is surrounded by clumps of ilex cypress etc., untidily cut brown grass plots one or two beds of low roses, & a fine marble fountain one side, but no attempt at a flower garden—a gate on the S. E. corner, another to N. W., & blocks of servants rooms & big stables to the N., beyond which is the park which must be about 1 mile long but quite narrow with a high wall all round. I wandered up & down various paths for some time. There are no very big trees but some fair size ones Spanish chesnuts chiefly & planes & then was unwillingly allowed by the Carabinieri to return to my rooms. The public being allowed in the grounds on Sundays, & to the Museum with a permit.... By far the great part of the place is a museum; it being one of the King's palaces, T. R. H. [Their Royal Highnesses] are only here in a military capacity & it contains a big collection of armour, most of it very fine largely of the plain solid variety any number of arms both of former use & ornemented also some beautiful china, Sevres, Capodimonte & Tenagra figures, a few good modern statues, some pieces of good furniture, & a hideous collection of pictures, which the King has been obliged to buy at various times. One room is decorated entirely in china panels & candlesticks etc., with figures like a Chinese wall paper. There is a long banqueting hall with much looking glass & gold in French style & another big room with a huge mosaic dinner table. Most of the rooms ... & in the living rooms have would be marble linoleum on the floors a sort of brick red—very ugly. In a living room are one or two decent pictures, some crayons of Louis Philippe's family, but as a whole everything is very ugly...

The guest accommodations on the first floor consisted of 'sitting room & a bed room, not remarkable for beauty the walls painted in the style of a third rate hotel, imitation marble floors & hideous furniture, but big French windows with a side view between ilex trees over Naples.'[32] It was indeed the view out over the Bay of Naples that was the glory of Capodimonte and gave it a real sense of place.

It was on 22 June that the family left Turin for Naples, departing from the Porta Nuova station, where a crowd had gathered to cheer them on their way.

As the train drew away, the Duke saluted, the boys stood at attention, and the Duchess nodded her farewell, not hiding her emotions. After stops in Florence and Rome, they arrived in Naples. While their departure from Turin was marked with restrained affection from the crowds, in Naples they were greeted with an overwhelming enthusiasm with the waving of handkerchiefs, throwing of flowers and of kisses as the carriage procession moved off to the sounds of the Marcia Reale.[33] It was an exciting beginning to a connection that Hélène would have with Naples for the rest of her life.

Naples was a very different world from Turin. It was—and remains today—a city of contradictions. Modern Italy was represented by the Galleria Umberto I, a grand glass-roofed shopping and dining arcade opposite the San Carlo Theatre, which was opened to great fanfare in 1891 as part of a nation-wide building programme known as the *Risanamento*, 'making healthy again.' The country's first train ran as early as 1839 from Naples to Portici—a grand four-and-a-half miles—although Pope Gregory XVI denounced the railroad as the road to hell (punning the French *chemin de fer*, for railroad, with *chemin d'enfer*), but then he was also against gas lighting. The city was staunchly Catholic—in ways perhaps more superstitious than doctrinal—and staunchly royalist—although perhaps more devoted to the old Bourbons rather than the new Savoys. It was the poorest of Italy's large cities, and many of its dark, cavernous streets were more reminiscent of the souks of North Africa than the grand boulevards of Northern Europe. The people themselves embodied all these. Despite—or perhaps because of—all its contradictions, Naples became the city of Hélène's heart; she would live there or nearby for the rest of her life.

Kaiser Wilhelm II and the Empress Victoria Augusta, along with various members of their family, visited Italy in the spring of 1905; when they returned home, Hélène was at the station in Venice seeing them off along with a loudly cheering crowd. They would meet up again the following month when Hélène was in Berlin for the wedding of the Kaiser's eldest son, the Crown Prince, to Duchess Cecile of Mecklenburg-Schwerin. The bride was a cousin of Hélène's through her paternal grandmother; this was probably why Hélène attended as this was one of the few occasions that she participated in a state event outside of the Orléans and Savoy families, except with the British Royal Family of which she was considered an adjunct member. Unlike most royal processions where the guests marched two-by-two, they went in groups of three in Berlin; Hélène appeared with Prince Arisugawa of Japan on her right, and on her left, the Portuguese Duke of Oporto, who was both Emanuele Filiberto's first cousin as well as Amélie's brother-in-law. Of the jewels worn by the ladies in the wedding procession in Berlin, the newspapers singled out Hélène with her 'lovely tiara of diamonds and sapphires.' Another guest was also struck by Hélène's looks. English-born Princess Daisy of Pless wrote, quoting her diary first: 'The Silesian papers said that "among the beautiful of the beautiful" (if you could only have seen some of them!) the Duchess of Aosta and I were the best looking. It is not difficult to be good-looking in Germany.' She then goes on to say: 'Even now the Duchess of Aosta is easily the handsomest Royalty at any gathering at which she appears. Like her brother the late Duke of Orléans, she is tall; with characteristic good looks and a style of her own she combines much of the sweetness and inextinguishable charm of her sister Queen Amélie.'[34]

By the end of the summer, the Aostas were established at Capodimonte, where there was plenty of room to ride their horses; Hélène even had an automobile of her own, which she would drive around the park. Before long, they began to establish links throughout the Campagna region. They were at Castellamare in September for the launching of the new battleship *Napoli*. More importantly, the following week, Hélène and Emanuele Filiberto made a big impression on Naples when they attended the feast day of San Gennaro at the Cathedral to witness the ritual of the liquidification of the saint's blood. Gennaro was bishop of nearby Benevento but was martyred during the Diocletian persecutions and became the patron saint for the city of Naples. Ever since the 14th century, vials of his dried blood were annually brought into the San Gennaro Chapel and the contents mysteriously (or miraculously) returned to liquid form. This was always considered a sign of good luck among the people. When King Victor Emmanuel II came to kiss the relics in 1862 and they failed to change, it was an embarrassment for the man who considered himself an instrument of divine providence, no matter what the pope might have thought of the new Kingdom of Italy.[35] When Hélène and Emanuele attended the actual feast day, it was the first time that a member of the ruling dynasty had attended the festival since the overthrow of the Neapolitan Bourbons and caused great rejoicing among the local population.

The Marquise de Fontenoy (the nom de plume used jointly by Frederick Cunliffe-Owen and his wife Marguerite, comtesse du Planty de Sourdis) wrote in 'her' gossip column in the *Washington Post*:

> Although the political texture of the Present Italian Parliament is supposed to be strongly anti-Clerical, yet when Deputy Gaudenzi, of the Extreme Left, attacked the Royal Duke of Aosta in the Chamber of Deputies the other day for having been present in full uniform in the Neapolitan Church of St. Januarius [Gennaro], on the occasion of the festival of that popular saint, the legislator was promptly howled down, and it was pointed out to him that freedom of conscience is guaranteed to every Italian citizen, be he peasant or prince of the blood.[36]

Later in September, Hélène and Emanuele Filiberto made a trip abroad to Paris and London, including a visit to the Duc d'Orléans's estate at Wood Norton. While they were abroad, the boys stayed with the King, Queen, and their children at Racconigi. Apparently, Hélène had some concern about how little Aimone might act in the regal presence, as when he first met the King at the age of three he looked at Victor Emmanuel and simply said 'You are ... lllittle!' However, this time the boys were a bit older and walked into the room and stood silently at attention in front of the King and Queen. 'They hold themselves like posts,' the King joked, and then everyone relaxed into laughter.[37]

In the beginning of April 1906, Hélène had a visit at Capodimonte from the Princess Marie Louise of Schleswig-Holstein—one of Queen Victoria's innumerable granddaughters. About the same time, Aosta met Marie Louise's uncle, the Duke of Connaught at the military headquarters in Naples, in preparation for the upcoming visit of the British King and Queen later in the month. At first, it seemed like it would be a pleasant spring in Naples. That is, until the rumbles from Vesuvius grew increasingly more alarming and developed into what Hélène would call 'this wretched nightmare.' Clearly visible from Capodimonte, the volcano was simply a picturesque part of normal everyday life until it erupted, and it felt like an earthquake had shaken the palace. Hélène made plans to evacuate the boys, if necessary, to the safety of Rome with the King and Queen, but was clear that her place and that of Emanuele Filiberto was to be with the people in their need.[38]

Although its last full eruption had been in 1872, throughout the new year, Vesuvius had shown signs of increased activity. By February, lava was flowing and pooling, cutting the railway line in three different places. By March the lava was 'fountaining' and nearly reached the crater's rim. Then on 3 April, *The Times* correspondent reported that the 'central crater of Vesuvius is again vomiting forth enormous quantities of lava, and flames are shooting up to a height of 450 feet.'[39] Each day, the severity of the situation escalated. On the 4th, a new lava stream began to flow in the direction of Pompeii, and the telegraph line to the Observatory was disrupted. During the next night, 'great blocks of rock were hurled as far as the lower station of the funicular railway,' and a new crater began exuding more lava which streamed into the vineyards of Bosco-Trecaso and within three or four miles of the village. Eventually, Vesuvius threw out more lava during this eruption than at any other time recorded.

On the 7th, Emanuele Filiberto and Cardinal Prisco went to Bosco Reale, the cardinal's hometown. 'The cardinal gave away food, clothing, and even his own rings to the peasants. The Duke ordered soldiers and engineers to erect parapets and dig trenches to divert the lava, and he grabbed a shovel himself to help from time to time.'[40] Hélène and Princess Marie Louise visited the village in the afternoon, even though it was already surrounded by lava.

All the Vesuvian villages were now being evacuated. Earthquakes shook the ground, and lava flowed in enormous quantities. *The Times* correspondent reported that the 'utmost panic prevails, and the terrified people are fleeing wildly in all directions.' Naples itself became crowded with thousands of refugees. The military authorities ordered 10,000 emergency rations, and Emanuele Filiberto and Hélène personally pledged 25,000 lire (£1,000) to the sufferers. A fleet of sailing vessels brought more refugees into the harbor, and 'all the steamers in the harbour have steam up and are prepared for all eventualities.'[41]

The most serious loss of life came on Palm Sunday (8 April) in the village of San Giuseppe, where a great number of women and elderly people had gathered in the church to pray for protection. The protection didn't come, the roof collapsed under the weight of ash and volcanic debris, and eventually thirty-seven dead and many injured were pulled out of the ruin. British geologist H. J. Johnston-Lavis was particularly critical of the situation saying that the roof collapsed because the people had not taken care to clean the roof from the gathered debris. 'Even during the heaviest part of the fall, persons could have moved about if they covered their heads and shoulders with pillows, tables, and other such improvised shields.'[42]

By the 10th, the volcanic activity finally began to settle down. The intermittent rumbles could only be heard close to the volcano itself. The wind changed direction and carried the cloud of ash out to sea, a 'thick veil between Naples itself and the coastline of Castellammare and Sorrento.' And, mostly importantly, the lava flow stopped at Torre Annunziata and Torre del Greco, even though a new subsidiary stream started to move to Pompeii. Naples was able to resume its normal life, although as *The Times* correspondent reported, far from its normal aspect as the ash still lay inches deep in all the streets and coated every building. The weight of the ash caused the collapse of Naples' Monte Oliveto market, crushing twelve to death and injuring more than a hundred. Hélène and Emanuele Filiberto visited the collapsed market and then went to the Pilgrims' Hospital where many of the wounded were being tended. One story tells that as Hélène 'bent in the hospital to give a cooling drink to a badly bruised little girl she felt a kiss upon her hand. Looking down, she saw a woman kneeling at her feet, who gratefully said: "Your Excellency, she is all I have. I am a widow. May God reward you."'[43]

Despite the dangers and damage—or perhaps because of them—Naples soon became a tourist attraction again. Hélène's brother, the Duc d'Orléans, arrived on the 16th aboard the North German Lloyd steamer *Barbarossa*, the same ship that was carrying the American athletic team to the Olympic Games in Athens. Hélène and Emanuele Filiberto met Philippe at the pier, where a band played the Italian and French national anthems, and then she took him on a tour of the Vesuvius area.

Ten days later, even more illustrious guests arrived in Naples. King Edward, Queen Alexandra and their daughter Princess Victoria were returning from Athens, where they had attended the Olympic Games. Early in the morning, just as the royal yacht approached the Arsenal, the persistent rain and fog lifted briefly for a 'magnificent rainbow' which stretched from Vesuvius to the Castle of St Elmo. Hélène and Emanuele Filiberto were there to greet them at the dock in the afternoon and then accompanied them and their suites up the still-smoking Vesuvius, although the roads were not clear enough for them to reach the Observatory, so they turned off to Ottajano, which was heavily damaged during the eruption. Later in the day, they visited the ancient ruins of Pompeii before returning to the royal yacht, the *Victoria and Albert*. The next day, they were able to reach the Observatory for a better view of the damage caused by the eruption; then, King Edward—who had made himself very popular by personally donating £800 to the relief fund—left by train while Queen Alexandra and Princess Victoria remained a few more days in Naples before a short visit to Rome. Hélène sent them enough fragrant May roses from Capodimonte to fill the yacht's two breakfast rooms, and she was there to see them off on the afternoon of 4 May when the yacht sailed for Genoa and Marseilles.

At the beginning of July, Hélène and Emanuele returned to Vesuvius to lay the cornerstone of the new village of Ottajano, which had been so heavily damaged in the eruption that it was dubbed 'the new Pompeii.' Although the heat was oppressive that day and there was a heavy thunder storm, a large number of people from the surrounding villages came to mark this new beginning.

At the beginning of the summer, the Aostas made their first family visit abroad together. During their initial stay in Belgium—Emanuele Filiberto visited his cousin Prince Napoléon in Brussels while Hélène was at the beach in Ostend with the boys—the Duke and Duchess made a quick trip to Nouvion-en-Thiérache in Picardy for the baptism of Princess Anne, the baby daughter of the Duke and Duchess de Guise, for whom they stood as godparents. Immediately after the service, they returned to Brussels and from there went on to visit her brother Philippe at Wood Norton in England and then on to Ireland, while the boys stayed with the Guise family.[44]

While in Ireland on 29 August, Hélène and Emanuele Filiberto attended the opening day of the Dublin Horse Show which had been widely publicized among Italian cavalry regiments, and the Aostas bought several horses for themselves and many others also went to Italy from that sale. From Ireland, they went to England where they were able to spend time with Hélène's family—'all together, everyone in good humor, and everyone happy.' Hélène and Emanuele also visited the Queen at Buckingham Palace; that evening, on the 25 September, Hélène joined Queen Alexandra and Princess Victoria on the special royal train to Balmoral, where they arrived the next morning. On the 28th, the King and Prince of Wales went to the Birkhall Woods for a stag hunt; although the party bagged six stags, including one 'Royal', Prince George complained that neither he nor his father even got a shot all day, and somehow 'these drives never do seem to succeed.' However, 'it was another glorious day & quite hot' and Hélène joined Queen Alexandra, Princess Victoria, Princess May, and her children, when they gathered with the men for a lunch in the woods. According to the *Court Circular*, Hélène joined the King and Queen, the Prince and Princess of Wales and their children, Princess Victoria, as well as the Duke of Connaught, and his son Prince Arthur at the Crathie Parish Church on Sunday morning for worship there. In the afternoon, they visited the Duke and Duchess of Fife at Mar Lodge (except for the Wales family. who were staying nearby at Abergeldie Castle). This was probably Hélène's first visit there since that fateful dance during her romance with Prince Eddy in 1890. Queen Alexandra later sent Hélène a photograph album as a commemoration of this visit and signed it 'For Dearest Hélène' from 'Aunt "Motherdear"', 'Motherdear' being the name by which all Alexandra's children called her.[45] Hélène left Balmoral on 1 October and travelled back to London with the Princess of Wales. She and Emanuele Filiberto left Victoria Station for Paris the next day, and later in the month they were together in Milan.

However, the stay in Milan proved problematic. On the 21 October, Hélène wrote to '*Mon Manolo Chéri*' that 'I hope the air of the town of flowers which is dear to you and of which you have such sweet memories will end up destroying the little cloud which obscured our lovely stay in Milan. For my part, if I did something to displease you, I am sorry—and since I cannot make my apologies—you know that my sole goal in life is to please you and to make life easy for you. If I don't succeed in that, I assure you that it is not my fault. Love me, Manolo, that is all I ask of you. God bless you. Hélène.'[46]

Later the same day, Hélène took to the skies as she made a balloon ascent aboard the *Fides II*, piloted by Lieutenant Cianetti, an event which was considered striking enough to make its way into the international newspapers. The balloon descended close to the town; Hélène and her party returned to Milan by motor-car.

When the family returned to Capodimonte, the boys' lessons with Rina Piano were supplemented with a special mathematics teacher, increased gymnastic work, and the beginning of some military teaching about building forts, for which they built a small model in the park.[47]

In November, there was a report that police in Naples had made two arrests of anarchists, thus foiling plots to assassinate Emanuele and Hélène as well as King Victor Emmanuel. The conspiracies had been organized in Paterson, New Jersey, the same place where King Umberto's assassination in 1900 had been plotted.

In April 1907, King Edward, Queen Alexandra, and Princess Victoria returned to Naples for another visit following an official meeting with King Victor Emmanuel at Gaeta. Although the visit was technically informal, King Edward wore the uniform of an admiral as the royal yacht *Victoria and Albert* sailed into Naples harbour, with Queen Alexandra standing on deck to admire one of the great vistas in the world. Hélène and Emanuele Filiberto received them at the Arsenal and then went aboard the yacht, along with Prince Victor Napoléon, for dinner. The next afternoon, they all lunched aboard the royal yacht again—

this time joined by Queen Alexandra's brother-in-law and sister, the Duke and Duchess of Cumberland, before Hélène took Queen Alexandra and Princess Victoria driving 'through the principal streets, stopping at various shops, where they made purchases' of several water colour paintings, some cameos, and other mementoes in coral and tortoise-shell, until meeting the King at the Museum for a tour from the British consul. While the King continued at the museum, Hélène took Alexandra and Victoria for a quick visit to Capodimonte. On the Sunday, there was a luncheon for the British royal family at Capodimonte, where they were joined by Prince Napoléon, and in the afternoon they went to a horse show at the Campo di Marte, where the band played 'God Save the King.' When they were at Capodimonte, Queen Alexandra admired the purple orchids there, and the next day a bouquet of them was sent to her on the yacht. The papers reported that Hélène spent a long time aboard the yacht that day, before the *Victoria and Albert* sailed off to Sicily for a few days. When they returned to Naples on the morning of the 27th, Hélène went aboard again, this time carrying a series of views of Naples for Queen Alexandra along with a number of photographs that Alexandra had taken earlier and which were developed during her absence. Like Hélène, Queen Alexandra was an avid photographer; the following year, *The Daily Telegraph* published a volume of pictures from her trusty Kodak camera as a fund-raising effort for charity. Among the shots of family and friends were two of Hélène during a visit to Balmoral.[48]

On the 29th, Princess Victoria came to luncheon at Capodimonte on her own, and Hélène returned to the yacht later to take the King and Queen to tea on the terrace at Capodimonte. The next morning, the King left for Rome, and Hélène and Prince Victor Napoléon were among the crowd to see him off. That afternoon, Alexandra and Victoria joined Hélène at a concert conducted by Martucci at the Politeama, which was filled to overflowing and there was 'a great outburst of enthusiasm' when the Queen arrived and loud cheers for the British national anthem. They had planned a visit to Capri earlier but were deterred by rough seas; Hélène joined them there aboard the king's scout *Sentinel*, returning in the evening. Although they planned to leave for Corfu early on the morning of the 2nd, rough seas again changed their plans, and Hélène again went to the royal yacht to take Alexandra and Victoria on a motor drive through the city before they were finally able to sail at 7.00 p.m.

After visiting her brother, the King of the Hellenes, and his family at Corfu, Queen Alexandra returned to Naples on the 21st, and Hélène and Emanuele Filiberto again went on board to greet her and Princess Victoria. This time, they were also joined by Prince Louis of Battenberg, an officer serving in the British Navy and *en route* to Malta. He was doubly related to the royal family as the husband of one of Queen Victoria's granddaughters as well as the brother of Princess Beatrice's husband. Prince Louis and other British naval squadron officers visiting

Naples were feted both in the city and on the 29th, when Hélène and Emanuele gave a shooting party in Louis's honour at the royal estate at Licola, where many of the Neapolitan nobility joined them.

Hélène and Emanuele Filiberto left on 25 August on the train directly to London. One of the motives for this short trip was to find a travelling companion for Hélène. Earlier in the year Hélène had written to her brother Philippe to see if she could interest him in joining her on a trip to Africa. 'My old pal. You told me that you will leave in July for the North. Before that do you want to make a provision for sun and heat? Let's go, the two of us, for two months only, to go and return to Africa. Not an expedition but simply to travel together. Do you want to? ... I've been thinking about this project for thirteen years. Come with me—it will be so good. I await your answer.'[49] When that suggestion to her brother bore no fruit, Hélène decided on a different tack. She decided to interview for an English travelling companion.

Through an acquaintance in London, Ella Douglas Pennant, Hélène was introduced to Susan Hicks Beach. Susan was the twenty-nine-year-old daughter of Sir Michael Hicks Beach, who served as a Member of Parliament for over forty years and had been Chancellor of the Exchequer. For his services, Hicks Beach was raised from the status of a baronet to become first Viscount St. Aldwyn in 1906. Along with the political connections the family also had connections with the Royal Court, and Queen Victoria was godmother to Susan's younger sister, accordingly named Victoria Alexandrina. More importantly, Susan already had extensive experience travelling, especially in India. Susan also had a bit of notoriety herself, as she had been the model for the figure of Britannia which appeared on British coins during the reign of King Edward. Years later, Susan was remembered for 'her terse phrases and piercing blue eyes [which] gave her a masculine habit of command.' Indeed, Queen Amélie would later refer to Susan and Tora as '*les soeurs* Hicks Beech (Pitch-pine) *si masculine*.'[50]

Susan was delighted with the prospect and enjoyed her first meeting with Hélène, who she found 'a most charming lady, & not a bit stiff or difficult to get on with, though we were naturally very shy of each other.' Susan wrote to her mother:

> It does sound ripping, & she is obviously prepared to revel, & unless anything stops her between now & then, certainly means to go. She seems to be busy shopping for it now, has got lists of medicines clothes etc., supplied by the Italian, the latter chiefly khaki skirts & many pair of stockings. I think she would be great fun. She is going to see somebody else, but will let me know in a few days. She is very anxious nobody should know anything about it, for fear of her being stopped, as she would give out merely that she is spending the winter in Egypt.[51]

Hélène and Emanuele Filiberto returned to Turin from Belgium via Paris on 12 September. The big change in the family came later that month, when the two boys progressed from the charge of their governess to that of Major Emilio Montasini.[52] Then, on 7 November, Hélène was back in Paris with the Torrigianis on her way to England for the wedding of her sister Louise.

The youngest and least attractive of the Paris sisters, Louise was twenty-five when she married Prince Carlos of Bourbon-Sicily, twelve years her senior and widower of their cousin, Infanta Mercedes (elder sister of King Alfonso XIII). They were married on 16 November 1907 in two different services. First, a small party went to St Mary's Church in Evesham at 8 a.m. for the civil ceremony, where King Alfonso, the Duc d'Orléans, the Duc de Guise, and the Duke of Calabria served as witnesses. Then in the afternoon, the religious service took place on the Wood Norton estate in a specially built chapel as the existing chapel was only big enough to accommodate thirty people. The Comtesse de Paris was there with all her children to greet the guests, who included the King and Queen of Spain, and the Grand Duke and Grand Duchess Vladimir of Russia; the Grand Duchess was a second cousin of Hélène and her sisters through the Mecklenburg connection, although there never seems to have been much of a personal connection with her. Among the other guests were their cousin Princess Stephanie of Belgium, the widow of Austrian Crown Prince Rudolf, making one of her rare family appearances following her remarriage to a Hungarian count; Queen Victoria's youngest daughter Princess Beatrice; and an array of other Spanish, French, German, and Italian relatives.

The next day, Hélène and Amélie went to visit the King and Queen at Windsor Castle, along with King Alfonso and Queen Ena of Spain, and Vladimir and Marie of Russia. The Kaiser and Empress of Germany were on a week-long state visit to Britain, and the occasion became one of the greatest gatherings of royalty not directly connected with a wedding or funeral. They were joined by the Prince and Princess of Wales, Princess Royal, and Princess Victoria; and the Duke and Duchess of Connaught with their children Prince Arthur and Princess Patricia. A grand photo shoot was arranged in the castle; the resulting images were widely sold as postcards with the various royalties organized in two different seating arrangements. At the luncheon that day, 'Georgie,' the Prince of Wales, made a point of recording in his diary that he sat between Amélie and Hélène.[52]

This visit to her native land re-connected Helene with the grand web of pan-European royalty, but during her stay in England troubling rumours emerged from Italy which would seriously impact upon her own future happiness.

1907–1909

it's to Africa that one must go to breathe, to dream and
to stretch out the hours with an infinity of sensations[1]

Hélène had been seriously ill in late 1904 with what was reported as combined
bronchitis, pneumonia, and pleurisy, but a long convalescence and the move to a
milder climate in Naples seemed to have taken care of things. However, when the
problem recurred in late 1907, *La Stampa* called her condition an advanced case
of bronco-alveolite, an inflammation of the airways leading to the lungs which
can progress to bronco-pneumonia. It is said to have been aggravated by her
activities in England, and that doctors considered her condition so serious that
they insisted on an immediate trip to a warmer climate. She and Emanuele left
for Egypt in late November.

Although Hélène had been considering such a trip for a long time and began
actively planning it in London, reasons for her departure for Africa were compounded by both health and marital problems. There were again rumours, which
grew louder and louder, about serious trouble in the Aosta marriage. By early
December, American newspapers were writing that the King of Italy was 'incensed
by the behaviour of his cousin, the Duke of Aosta.' The *Chicago Daily Tribune*
reported based on an 'exclusive dispatch' from Rome that the king was considering
sending Emanuele Filiberto into exile because of his 'flagrant conduct in Naples
with a coterie of young girls and Duchesses and Marchionesses of high rank.' Victor
Emmanuel was 'highly incensed' that his cousin is 'lacking in all sense of pride and
decency,' and his actions have created one of the 'greatest scandals' in Italian society.
The paper further reported that Hélène had apparently 'denounced her husband to
the king and queen, and has left him.' According to this account:

The king demanded that the Duke of Aosta return home, where he 'read him
a lecture and demand that he mend his ways.' The Duke of Aosta returned to

Naples, however, where he 'resumed his notorious carousels, openly flaunt-ing his depravity.' The duke has been in the habit of inviting young women to Capodimonte, women who were introduced to the duke by women of the highest aristocracy in Naples. Several of these noble women associated with the Duchess of Aosta. At different balls and other events, the duchess would hear 'strange innuendos' about her husband's behaviour. In time, she was able to 'uncover everything,' after returning home early from a ball, where she confronted the duke about 'the stories she had heard about his conduct.' The Duchess left Naples and returned to Rome, where she met with the king and queen informing them of her husband's actions. She then went to England to attend the wedding of her sister, Princess Louise, and while she was in England, she 'learned additional and distressing facts' about her husband and his women.[2]

According to the French newspaper *Le Matin*, the socialists had begun a violent press campaign against the Duke, publishing in *La Propaganda* and *La Sentinella* scandalous accounts of his 'immoral acts' and they would send copies to Hélène marked in red pencil to draw her attention to the stories, and it was then that she went to Rome to ask for the king's intervention. *La Stampa* in Turin reported that the quick departure was caused by the grave illness of the Duchess, but even that paper had to allude to the 'hypothetical marital infidelity' and also reported another suggestion that the trip was a punishment for marital discord.[3]

There had certainly been suggestions of problems before this time. Emanuele Filiberto was said to have broken off a relationship with a divorced English woman in Florence just before their engagement.[4] Then, just before her wedding, an English friend asked Hélène 'What would you do if he were unfaithful to you?' to which she responded 'Oh! I told Emanuel ... I said, "You see? I leave you ... If you are not true to me, I instantly leave you," and I should do so at once.'[5]

A spirit of travel, adventure, and exploration ran deeply through both the Orléans and Savoy families, born of the fact that they were either underemployed in their own country or (in the case of Hélène's family) forceably alienated from their homeland. Hélène's father, the Comte de Paris, and his brother Robert, the Duc de Chartres, along with their Uncle Joinville had gone to the United States for a military adventure in the American Civil War in the 1860s, while others in the family—notably the Duc d'Aumale—had served in the North African cam-paigns. Hélène's cousin Henri d'Orléans travelled widely through Africa and Asia, however, at the beginning of 1901, Henri returned to south east Asia to further explore some of the lesser-known areas of Tonkin and Laos. He developed a high fever as the result of an abscess to the liver, and was taken to Saigon as a matter of urgency; he died there aged just thirty-four years.[6]

Hélène's own brothers were likewise great travellers. Philippe, duc d'Orléans, made three polar expeditions—to the coast of Greenland and the Barents and Kara seas (between 1905 and 1909), in addition to his other journeys to India and Nepal. The youngest in the family, Ferdinand, inherited the title of Duc de Montpensier when his grandfather died, and had joined the Spanish navy while still quite young due to the prohibition of French princes serving in the military in France. His first travel book was based upon his journey which started in Spain and took him to the Canary Islands, across the Atlantic to Argentina and Uruguay, then across to South Africa and back to Spain by way of Saint Helena, arriving home in 1904.[7] Three years later, he made a long journey to the Far East in his yacht, exploring Cochinchina, Cambodia, and Laos, spending many months in the interior of Annam with the Moi tribes, installing medical services, hospitals, and ambulances. Upon his return to Europe in 1912, he delivered many lectures and wrote two more books.

Emanuele Filiberto's brother, Vittorio Emanuele, the Count of Turin, also made at least one big game shooting trip to Africa. In November 1908, he left for Mombasa with the plan of making his way across Central Africa by way of the lakes and the Congo, and then from the west coast of Africa proceeding to the Cape and then beginning a second journey up through Africa to the Upper Nile and Egypt.[8] However, one newspaper account suggests that it was not a personal decision but rather that the king had become annoyed with the scandals associated with his name and ordered him out of the country. 'What,' he is reported to have said, 'do you think we live in the Middle Ages that the friendship of a royal Prince is a compliment? You had better go to Africa and think the matter over.' Therefore, to Africa the Count went.[9]

Undoubtedly the greatest explorer and adventurer of them all was Luigi, the Duke of the Abruzzi. A mountaineer and explorer, he made the first ascent of Mt St Elias in Alaska in 1897; two years later, he led an expedition toward the North Pole. He ascended Ruwenzori in Africa in 1906 and Mt Godwin-Austen in Kashmir, India. For his accomplishments, Abruzzi received the gold medal of the Geographical Society at a meeting in Rome in January 1907 which Hélène and the whole family attended.

Hélène herself had already tasted adventure in her travels to Egypt and Palestine with her brother Philippe; soon, it would become a way of life for her. However, the real motivating factor for her first major African trip appears to be the breakdown of her marriage combined with a breakdown of her health. From Capodimonte, Hélène found Africa nearer than ever as Naples is closer to Africa than much of Europe, and at certain times of the year, the wind blows the pink sands of the Sahara throughout southern Italy and into the streets of Naples. From Capodimonte, Tunis is closer than Genoa, and Tripoli closer than Lausanne. A generation later, the American writer Martha Gellhorn also fell in love with Africa, and made similar journeys there, particularly in East Africa. Whenever asked why she loved Africa, 'she would talk about the great wide sky; the sense of time to live and not live through; the weather and the emptiness.

She felt drunk there, she would say, on space and silence. And then there were the animals, when she sat at night listening to the coughing of the hyenas and the sounds of hooves in the dark.'[10] Gellhorn, a war correspondent during the Spanish Civil War and Second World War, would, like Hélène, find both the action of warfare and constant travelling the only satisfactory antidote to an otherwise crippling boredom.

Hélène and Emanuele left Naples together on 30 November and sailed for Alexandria aboard the *Hohenzollern*. When departing Naples, Hélène wrote of the sadness of leaving her children and of the boys' sadness—their sobs, their tears, the two handkerchiefs waving vigorously in their little hands until they disappeared from sight. 'My heart sank,' wrote Hélène, as the ship left the Bay of Naples, past Capri and the Amalfi coast. Despite the sadness of separation, she also felt the growing freedom from daily life—from the post, from the telegraph, from the telephone.[11] This was not to be a simple sojourn of the winter months in Cairo or Luxor, but rather a much more adventuresome trip well into Africa that would last for six months. It also marked the beginning of Hélène's extensive foreign travels during the next several decades. Over the next three years, Hélène would be away from Europe more often than not—six months in 1907–1908, ten months in 1909–1910, and eight months in 1910–1911. If she had remained in the hot and dry climate of Egypt and the Sudan for health reasons that would be understandable, but even on the first trip, she was venturing into tropical weather in the Congo and Uganda. The situation had all the hallmarks of a woman running away from an unhappy marriage and an entire way of life, except that her husband joined her for the first portion of the journey. Of course, as seen from her letter to her brother Philippe, she had been planning this for some time. Although there appear to be some efforts at reconciliation, Hélène and Emanuele Filiberto would lead increasingly separate lives and would eventually—particularly after the First World War—live separately, with Hélène continuing to be based at Capodimonte while Emanuele returned to the Palazzo Cisterna in Turin.

Hélène and Emanuele arrived in Alexandria on 2 December and were met by Captain the Marchese Maurizio Piscicelli, whom Emanuele had chosen as head of their caravan because of his knowledge of the countries they would visit. He had already spent several years in the Congo on government service, and was the type of man who could turn his hand to anything. They went on to Cairo to stay at the Savoy. When Emanuele and Piscicelli climbed up the Great Pyramid, Hélène remembered that she had done so fifteen years earlier on her first visit to Egypt with her brother Philippe.[12]

Their party was soon joined by Susan Hicks Beach, who was to be Hélène's travelling companion not only on this trip but eventually on a number of others over the years.[13] Susan remembered their first day together in Egypt.

After unpacking, in fear & trembling I drove off to the Savoy & was shown up to the Duchess. She is certainly one of the most attractive people I have ever met—6 foot or so, very good looking, fair haired, very thin with a beautiful figure, & very Royal. She was most nice to me, as was the duke—a tall good looking man not foreign looking, but he is a great stickler for ceremony, & his great politeness was frightening. Her '*chef-de-caravan*' was also there—their only attendant—a tall man of thirty-six seems nice & a gentleman, but very ugly, & looks as if he may have a temper. We had lunch in the Restaurant, & they talked English & French by turns, varied by a little Italian—after lunch we went up to open & inspect the two carteens I had brought for the Duchess & found them badly arranged, & most of the china things 'le capetaine' had wished for, smashed; these were promptly thrown at his feet, & he was much ragged about it, the Duchess most amusing.[14]

In a letter to her father, she reported: 'The Duke meantime looks on at all the preparations & laughs. All the officials both here & in the Sudan, Uganda & the Congo have been set on the run & the Duchess means to get all she can.'[15]

Among the scurrying officials were those in the British Foreign Office; their major concerns were for Hélène's plans in the Congo, through the Katanga, the Province Orientale, Kivu, and the Lakes, particularly in regard to Kivu which was considered 'too unsettled for Her Royal Highness to pass through it except with a strong military escort,' and there were no soldiers there to provide adequate protection.[16]

During their first few days in Cairo, Susan was trying to understand the dynamics of the little travelling party, as well as her own duties and the practicalities of their luggage. As she wrote to her sister: 'The Duke seems to take no interest in anything foreign, least of all in travelling ... They are here by way of being incognito & call themselves Count & Countess de la Cisterna & the doctor man is the only person with them. He looks decent & exceedingly ugly!' As for clothing, the Duchess 'seems really to be taking very little,' just 'one other long one [dress] & she takes a sort of 3-piece frock for evening, it seems she hardly ever wears a low one,' and 'It will be interesting to see what other things she considers necessities, she has got several more boxes than me anyhow.' As for personal relations, 'She is most awfully nice to me, & the Duke most polite. I am very glad he is not coming he frightens me much, she will be delightful to travel with.' As for duties, 'At present I write letters for her, & am to keep small change for her, & look after the table cloths, etc. I expect there will be plenty of small jobs.'[17]

Emanuele left them on 9 December for Suez to see the canal and then to continue home to Italy from Alexandria.[18] Meanwhile, still in Cairo, Hélène was beginning to throw off the constraints of court life. Susan reported:

Everybody is much agitated & amazed at the vagueness of the expedition, they all seem to be tearing their hair because the Duchess does not seem to realise what it means & make proper arrangements, but appears to imagine that everything can easily be done, & is bored at so much fuss, & they can get nothing out of Capt Piscicelli. Major Herbert [of the 'E.A.', English Embassy?] implored me to let him & the Sirdar know as soon as possible anything I could about future plans—the Sirdar seems much fussed because the Duchess says she wants to go by the ordinary post-boat to Gondobero on Jan 1ˢᵗ where there is no proper accomodation & it may not even go to Gondobero, & she won't have special carriages on the train.[19]

When they did begin to prepare to leave the following day, Susan took her 'luggage four tin boxes, two sacks, rifle case & suit case (temporary) to the Savoy, where everything was being despatched some to Asswan, & the rest to go on— the Duchess scandalising the Hotel by running down the back stairs & standing to watch in the street' and later when Susan arrived at the station 'we found the duchess in rather a loud plain check suit & sailor hat, the captain ditto, a tearful maid parting with her, but no one else. A sleeping compartment each to ourselves but no other luxury & off at 6.30 ... Dined on the train, the Duchess radiant at having got away from court clothes & ceremony.'[20]

They began their journey down the Nile aboard the *Ibis*, which Susan considered 'quite a good boat, very comfortable cabins, & decent food.' Although there were about sixteen other people onboard and 'we sit permanently within 3 foot of them we speak to nobody, the Duchess's one idea is to have no duty conversation to make.' Hélène, however, had plenty to say to Susan and especially to Piscicelli, 'their arguments & chaff together are most amusing, she is delightful to listen to, or to watch—he ended by being quite cross last night, she teased him so.' To occupy their days, they 'write elaborate diaries & stick in photographs, interspersed with much conversation, all day.' Susan admired the way that Hélène cared for herself: 'She is wonderful the way she turns herself out without a maid, always beautiful & most neat, & she declines to let me help her at all.'[21]

In the early days of this trip, while Susan was still getting to know Hélène, she was regularly amazed at the way the princess enjoyed being simply one of the crowd, waiting for trains, packing herself into a railway carriage with other people, and showing up at the Cataract Hotel in Aswan without reserved rooms. 'The Duchess is blissfully happy at being & doing like ordinary people; she is more & more fascinating, most amusing, & full of go, rags Capt Piscicelli all the time, who chaffs her back, & is more than nice to me.' While they were beginning to take their precautionary cocktail mix of quinine and arsenic against various tropical illnesses, Hélène 'doesn't seem so very tired, & has only coughed once since

Cairo.' When the three travellers rode camels out into the desert, the Duchess was 'blissfully happy, & thinking what shocks her court people would have.' Even the simple opportunity 'to shop by herself [was] also a joy to her.'[22]

Hélène and her party moved down the Nile and continued deeper into Egypt, visiting Luxor and Aswan, where they saw the new dam which promised renewed fertility for the Nile valley and where they found many Italian quarry-men working on the project, although Hélène regretted that the delicate temple of Philae had already nearly disappeared beneath the waters. They continued down the Nile for several days, passing the four great statues of Ramses II, before transferring at Wadi-Halfa to a train which took them onward to Khartoum passing through the desert which Hélène found deeply soothing—*le repos absolu*. However, Khartoum was a different story, and they found themselves helping move their baggage into the hotel 'because the natives were remarkable for doing things slowly or doing nothing at all.'[23] They were reminded of more energetic times the next day when they visited Omdurman, where the Mahdi had centred his movement, which attempted to roust the British presence from the Sudan; this resulte in the siege and capture of Khartoum and the death and beheading of General Gordon in 1885. Not until 1898 did the British regain the upper hand when Kitchener defeated the *Mahdi*'s successor, the *Khalifa*.

The travellers went on horseback through the bazaar of Omdurman and met Father Ovalda, an Austrian missionary, who had been prisoner of the Khalifa for ten years but upon his release stayed on to continue his missionary work. They also met with Sir Reginald Wingate, Sirdar of the Egyptian Army and Governor-General of the Sudan, and his wife. Hélène made the effort to find her best clothes, but admit-ted that 'my choice wasn't very great and my skirt terribly short!' They were invited to stay at the Governor's residence but declined, beginning a pattern of living in a tent which Hélène generally followed. From Khartoum, they headed out led by a camel-mounted soldier while Hélène and Susan followed on their donkeys; Hélène had tried about twenty before settling on hers. The procession ended with Mohamet '*mon* boy' on another donkey. When they reached 'camp', they found the three tents erected, the beds made, baggage delivered, the fire lit, and tea ready. Sitting on the veranda of her tent in a comfortable armchair, Hélène bathed in the delight of doing nothing, sitting between the river and the desert, watching the marvelous setting of the sun, followed almost immediately by the rising of the moon. The informality of travel arrangements continued to surprise Susan, and on the day before Christmas when she 'got up at 7 to the sound of the distant band of a review which I had meant to attend—the F. M. [Piscicelli] prancing round with coffee in pyjamas coat & camel boots... & had breakfast about 9—the Duchess in dressing gown pyjamas—fur coat, & a scarf tyed round her head—always looking nice.' Later in the day, Susan went into town on her own, attended by a camel man, and saw Winston Churchill walking the streets.[24]

Thirty-three-year-old Winston Churchill was Undersecretary of State for the

Colonies at this time and was in the process of journeying through Kenya and Uganda, then down the Nile to the Sudan to look at British progress—or lack thereof—in the various colonies, dependencies, and protectorates. In particular, he fell in love with Uganda and felt that this would be the best place for British to concentrate her efforts in the future.[25]

On Christmas morning, Susan was woken at 6.30 a.m. with a packet from Hélène 'with good wishes & a little gold twisted wire bracelet, so nice of her.' So, she 'put on dressing gown & coat, went to her tent, where [I] found the F. M. [Piscicelli] in pyjamas & coat—had coffee there together.' Later they enjoyed together 'a Xmas dinner of plum pudding—creme de menthe.' The next day, she wrote home to her mother

> Duchess is revelling in being out of civilisation at last, she has left off curling her hair, & the stuffing in it, & still does it quite nicely—her skirts are short, & her boots thick, & she will shortly leave off her stays. She is more than nice to me, quite delightful—apparently is not going to give me the sack at present!

However, Susan had to 'bully' her 'into going to her own Church on Sunday, so she dragged off the unwilling Capt P. at 6.30, & they returned, feeling very holy, & very sleepy & had to retire to their beds after luncheon—whence he got up, to try & buy donkeys in his pyjamas, imagining himself irresistable.' Hélène found herself at peace, thinking that only if her dear ones had not been so distant, it would be paradise. There would be little reminders of home throughout the trip, such as on Christmas Day the bread in camp reminded her of the Andalusian bread of her childhood at Villamanrique.[26]

Although she may have given up wearing corset stays and curling her hair, Hélène was not yet able to shed all her inhibitions and obligations, and asked Susan to put stamps on 'fifty picture postcards to all the crowned heads of Europe & others containing the Duchess's New Year greetings.' However, slowly, as they moved into their tents—'two tents about 10 feet (no bathroom) & the Duchess' bigger with a verandah put in front for dining room' with 'some good chairs & tables'—and recruited a native staff—'a servants cook, Bashiri the Zanzibar boy, Mahomet Ali (the Duchess' boy) & Mahomet Achmet (wait) & two coolies—all amiable' plus sheep, goats, fowls, 'two policemen'— Hélène became more and more relaxed.[27] While Susan grew fonder of Hélène, she initially grew less fond of Piscicelli and for a while referred to him as 'the F. M.' (Field Marshal) in her journal although before long he was 'Capt. P.' with only an occasional reference back to 'F. M.'

Susan reported home:

> We are glad to find our boat gets to Lado on the 15th instead of dawdling till

the 25th, & we are mortally afraid some tiresome Austrian Royalties will be on board too—the Duchess says "Damn." They look so boring & proper, which we are not—however even if they are, we shall not see more of them than absolutely necessary I expect.

The real reason, though, was that Hélène 'told hardly a soul even of her surroundings where & why she was really going, kept it absolutely dark, which was very clever, the result is oceans of letters containing the most anxious enquiries after her health.' The health considerations, Susan thought, were rather overstated: 'I think she is pretty tough, the way she stands long days shopping in the sun, rummaging at Khartoum, & returns without having had tea as smiling & amusing as ever.' As for the whole party: 'You should see the party setting out on its donkey rides, sitting well back, with a gun slung over each back, & large sun hat on head, we look killing. I am sure an illustrated paper would give large sums for a photo.'[28]

They remained in camp at Gordon-Tree for a week and then embarked on New Year's Day for a fortnight on the Nile. In his New Year's Day reception of Senators, Deputies, and Ministers in Rome, the King spoke about Hélène commenting that 'the Egyptian climate had improved her health, as was proved by her Royal Highness's long excursion to Khartum with Senator Blaserna.' Then, at the end of the month, Emanuele received 'most satisfactory news of the health of the duchess, who has found the climate of southern Egypt most beneficial, especially that of Khartum. Her Royal Highness expects to remain in Egypt for several weeks yet, after which she will go for a cruise in the Mediterranean.'[29]

However, it was not long before her travels became more adventuresome. This did not please everyone. The British military *attaché* reported:

> [King Victor Emmanuel] would so much like to go up the Nile to the region of the great lakes. He said that Her Royal Highness the Duchess of Aosta was about to undertake the journey. His Majesty said that the Duchess really ought to do nothing of the kind, as she ought to be resting and trying to get stronger, but that she could not keep quiet and must always be doing something active.[30]

Hélène and her travelling companions spent two weeks travelling down the Nile aboard the steamer *J. W. Dal*, having cut down their luggage to a bare minimum—some eighty parcels. As they progressed down the river, they saw their first crocodiles and then hippopotamuses, followed each day by a wider array of wildlife—water bucks, gazelles, eagles, black herons, purple herons, toucans, and ducks of all colours. On 7 January, they reached Fashoda—'this little corner of earth whose name had impassioned Europe!'[31] Just ten years earlier, French colonial aspirations to extend their control in a continuous line from Dakar in West Africa to Djibouti in the east collided with the British ambition to have a similar line of influence from Capetown in the south to Cairo in the north. The intersection of these two ambitions was at Fashoda. British and French forces collided there, but although the dispute inflamed Europe at the time, it was eventually resolved diplomatically with the source of the Congo and Nile rivers established as the respective spheres of influence between the two European powers.

When Hélène arrived at Fashoda, one of her fellow passengers on the *Dal*, Major Palmer of the British army, suggested a meeting with some of the 'savage tribes' of the area. For Hélène, this was an 'inexpressible pleasure.' They arrived in time to see a parade of Shilluk warriors, who Hélène described as 'magnificent men, taller than us, well presented, thin waists, good features' with panther or leopard skin clothing. With their weapons, tattoos, and bracelets of ivory and copper, they were a race of warriors and they were entrancing to Hélène. Then, during the dance they attended, all the men sang as a chorus—'The Shilluk songs have savage yet sweet rhythms, very melodic'—and Hélène truly felt she had entered a different world. When they returned to their boat that evening, the grasses along the river bank had caught fire and burned red for several kilometres, an image which struck Hélène as 'even more brilliant against the dusk' of the growing evening. Although Hélène gives the impression that the dances and ceremonial events were part of everyday ritual that she happily stumbled across, Winston Churchill, in his travels, recognized that the ceremonies were often 'merely a representation given to interest us.'[32]

As usual, Susan's unpublished account provides quite a different insight from Hélène's into the way they were really operating. From aboard the *Dal*, she wrote home:

> [The] thermometer went up to 100° one day, since then it has been lower, but damper, so it feels much the same, but we are getting quite accustomed to it, & the Duchess minds it no more than I do. You can't think what a disgusting sight Capt P. looks, he began by not shaving for 4 days, & [I] rashly remarked to the Duchess how horrid unshaven men looked, not thinking he would understand, but unfortunately he did... However Capt P's unshavenness is developing into an approach to a beard. I suppose we shall get used to dirty collars, & he is beginning to find it is possible to speak to me again. I have certainly seen no approach to a temper on the part of the Duchess, it must be a libel—she is as nice as she could be.... We stopped at a wooding station this morning, & the Duchess & I pursued naked people with cameras—she loves them, & they are lovely some of them so beautifully made, & hold themselves so well.[33]

As they progressed down the Nile, Hélène was continually struck by the new sights—the people, the animals, and the vegetation. They briefly touched the Belgian Congo at Lado and received a cannon salute and a guard of honour headed by the three officers of the Belgian Post Office. They spent several days at Lado, and Hélène was intoxicated by the wildlife around her—the elephants, buffalo, gazelles, wild boars, and birds of all descriptions—along with the dancing around campfires to the beat of the tom-toms.[34] She wrote to her brother Philippe:

> What a great beast you are for not coming with me. This is an ideal trip— good weather—nicely hot—and the game—in abundance—one only has to aim ... each time I see the 'big' game—or the extraordinary birds, I invoke your image—I say to your rifles—'good rifles which have been in such illustrious hands kill for me'. The shot leaves—but alas! not always with results. In going up the Nile every day we saw crocodiles—masses of hippos—elephants— giraffes—waterbucks, buffalo, gazelles of every kind, boars—birds of every sort, storks—eagles—geese—toucans—pelicans, great bustards (and the blues) down to hummingbirds—Oh! my big brother that you are not here. What carnage you would have done..... Health and spirits excellent.[35]

Susan commented that the natives 'seem to have very few children, but they are rather attractive, specially one little round baby, which the Duchess nurses at every opportunity.'[36]

As they continued, Hélène, Susan and Piscicelli travelled by ass or by foot, through muddy fords, through bamboo forests, towards the mountains, into native villages—in one of which a black child came forward to present Hélène with a welcoming bouquet of flowers but instead panicked and threw it at her in fear.[37]

When they reached Mont Watti, in mid-February, they stopped at a small military post, where they took advantage of a better quality of water than they had seen in some time to develop some of the rolls of Kodak films which had been accumulating since Lado. When a new group of porters arrived, they mounted their asses again and on the first day, they marched for five hours. On 26 February, Hélène and her party arrived at Mahagi, at 1,000 metres elevation. At this last stop before travelling into Lake Albert, there was a packet which arrived aboard a steamer from the English coast. The bag was full of condolence letters for Hélène, which spoke of mourning and of sudden death in Portugal, but gave no details, and she was left to helplessly worry about who had been killed; she feared for her sister Amélie. They sent a messenger to Koba, the nearest place from where a telegram could be sent.[38] On 2 March, the party finally arrived at Buti-Aba at midday and were met by a guide sent by the Governor of the Protectorate of Uganda, Frederick Henry Leakey from the Colonial Service, along with Gensémiti-Kago, the chief native of the region, who provided them with porters. Among the facilities at But-Aba was a telegraph office, and there were various dispatches awaiting Hélène. The worst news came from Portugal.

A month earlier, on 1 February her brother-in-law King Carlos and nephew

Crown Prince Luis Filipe were both assassinated while riding in a carriage with Amélie and the younger son Manoel. It was only Amélie beating off the attacker with her bouquet which probably saved her younger son. Hélène could react only through her journal:

> Carlos and Luiz assassinated! ... this frightful tragedy made me shudder ... It seems that I would go mad if I had to cowardly watch my husband and my son killed in front of my own eyes ... Poor Amélie! God help her! One son remains, a great task to accomplish; her moral strength and Providence will sustain her.[39]

As bad as the situation was, Susan was able to report that 'the Duchess' spirits have risen considerably' once she knew that her sister was safe.[40] Young Manoel, who was wounded in the attack, took the oath of office as the new King of Portugal with his arm in a sling. Amélie, who one cousin called 'the man of the family', would provide a certain element of stability for him during the coming years.[41]

A week later, African thoughts and actions had again submerged European ones. They went deep into a little side lagoon 'where there were said to be heaps of crocodiles, & we could see the paths trampled by them in the reeds,' but it was the wrong time of day to see them '& all we saw was a huge dead one—a monster that Mr Leakey had shot the day before, & which his companions had not yet eaten'and 'the Duchess insisted on going close up to photograph him.' Next, they turned their attention to the birds, and 'Capt. P. shot a paddy bird, an ibis, & a lily-stalker, amid not very complimentary remarks from the boatmen., translated by Mr Leakey; they said this couldn't be an Englishman—they always shot flying, not sitting!' The boatmen were encouraged to sing a canoe song, 'which became personal; they sang that "these Princesses are very tall, but they are tied so tight we don't know how they can eat food!" The Duchess was delighted, she is not tied tight, but she has got a very small waist.'[42]

The British Governor, Hesketh Bell, heard that Hélène and her party had arrived in Uganda and was concerned because Entebbe, where they were headed, was 'in rather an unsettled condition, on account of the dispute with the Belgians concerning the question of the boundary.' Therefore, Bell sent an escort, but 'in reply to my telegram of welcome the Duchess said that she is travelling quite privately and does not want any fuss to be made about her,' and she sent the escort away. The governor responded that 'This is all very well but I don't want a royal funeral here, so I am sending young [Arthur Clement] Knollys, the best-looking of the Asst. Secretaries, to look after her and to see that proper camps are provided for the lady and her party.'[43] That seems to have done the trick. Although at first they 'all thought, & said later, what a pretty little boy, he looked about eighteen, & he had such pretty curling eye lashes & hair & white complexion, & small feet, & we all thought we had much rather have kept Mr Leakey.' However, as Susan wrote, 'the pretty boy turned out older, & much more of a man that he looked, & quite as good a caretaker, besides being most amusing, & we all fell in love with him.'[44]

When Governor Bell finally met Hélène in person, he declared her a 'very charming and gracious lady and I should think, one of the tallest of Princesses with the smallest waist in the world.' He was concerned that as he was staying provisionally in a small house while a new Government House was being built, he was unable to provide accommodations. However, Hélène actually preferred being in tents on the old Government House grounds. Bell's particular concern at the time was the widespread disaster of sleeping sickness which he estimated had killed 200,000 of the 300,000 living on the shores of Lake Victoria during the previous ten years. Although there was yet no cure for the disease, they knew that the cause was the tsetse fly and were just beginning to take preventative steps to clearing the flies from their breeding ground near the rivers.[45] They went to visit the sleeping sickness camp of Buanuka, on the slope of a hill, 'a collection of big reed & mud huts composing the doctors house, dispensary, wards, kitchen etc., & lunatic asylum.' It was one of several government camps 'to which the infected people are collected away from the Lake & the particular species of tsetse fly, & there are about 500 patients, either in the wards or in the huts spotted round in the fields.' Inside the wards, there 'were very sad sights, limp figures, the worst ones very thin, half paralysed & doubled up, quite blind, & all semi or wholly asleep.'[46] Later, they would have another opportunity to learn about the dreaded sleeping sickness.

A few days afterwards, they went to Kampala to visit the local king, with Hélène riding a government mule, preceded by the king's drummer, 'a splendid person who beats his drum with all his force & loud shrieks from his enormous mouth.' In the audience hall inside the third enclosure, they were received by 'the little Kabaka Daudi Chura,' who was 'a nice little person dressed in a buff gold embroidered cloak, white gown patent leather shoes & gold embroidered cap.' The three regents with him were 'Sir Apolo Kagwa, a most evil looking big man, the Treasurer Stanislas Mugwanya & Zachariah Kisungiri all in buff or black cloaks.' Conversation proved labourious, 'the little Kabaka being shy & not very ready with his English, he is only eleven but tall for his age, & says he likes football & riding & mechanics, he seems a sharp little person, but he must have rather a deadly time.' They took some photographs of the young king, both with his advisors and with Hélène, before departing. From Kampala, they moved on to Entebbe, and Susan recorded that the 'boat started at dawn with much noise, passing islands beautiful in the sun-rise, & got to Maryonys the post of Kampala about 8 o'clock.' They went ashore, 'Mdme. & the F. M. resplendent in Khaki shirts & lower garments, provided with cartridge holders, much pleased with themselves.'[47]

As this trip was beginning to draw to an end, Hélène was already thinking about another expedition 'as soon as she can get away again', perhaps to Lake Rudolph through Abyssinia and down to Entebbe, Tanganyika, and across Africa.

'She is making a list out of the things we found necessary & of what were unnecessary, so that we shall have an even more perfectly supplied expeditions next time—Mexico is to be the alternative trip.' Meanwhile, Susan continued to be bemused by Maurizio Piscicelli, as she confided to her journal. 'Capt. P. shaved off his beard yesterday I hardly knew him, it gave me such a shock, & he looks so clean, & almost handsome. He is an odd specimen, as obstinate as six mules, & can be exceedingly rude at times, & most disobliging, especially to Englishmen'.[48]

After Kampala and Entebbe, they arrived at Nairobi, which was already changing out of all recognition. Just a few years before lions and leopards could still occasionally be seen in the streets at night and herds of antelope grazing within a few miles, but now the endemic grey galvanized iron buildings predominated the townscape.[49] Susan recorded that when the train arrived in Nairobi 'We backed into the station with difficulty, the platforms crowded with white & black people of all sorts, & a real hubbub. We got out our mis-cellaneous luggage, while others clamored for our places, & got outside to a jumble of traps & waggons & rickshaws, horses mules, oxen & men.' There was no official to meet Hélène, 'but a Eurasian lady belonging to the hotel appeared, & packed us into a victoria, & we left her to look after the rest.' They drove through the town '& turned into an attempt at a garden before a verandahed single storey house, the Norfolk Hotel.' The clientele did not impress. 'Some very weird looking people about, two or three with long hair & a Robinson Crusoe appearance besides other oddities, & a Jew or two.' In addition, there were 'lots of white people about of a not very attractive type on horses, in rickshaws, a good many shops & being Saturday, most of them shut. The whole place rather of the young Canadian town type, & rather its lack of manners & swarms of Indians.'[50]

While staying at their hotel in Nairobi, Hélène did have visits from Sir James Sadler, the governor of British East Africa, with Lady Sadler and their son. But she was more impressed when they went to the Boma Trading Company and met a 'man of the bush and of adventures,' the Marchese Ralph Gandolfi—the half-English, half Italian 'young, clean-shaven man dressed like Buffalo Bill, with his sleeves rolled up, an open-necked shirt, and a great hat.'[51] Susan thought him 'a strange specimen' who was 'an Englishman with a Papal title, not a very high class young man. He has apparently done a good deal of travelling but amuses us.'[52] Although the government would eventually close the company down because of its smuggling of ivory and other illicit activities, at this time, the Boma was one of the leading outfitters and they promised a grand hunt.[53]

They left Nairobi at 7 a.m. on 3 April, and Hélène was delighted to exchange her humble ass for one of the horses which Gandolfi provided. However, her pleasure was short-lived when she discovered that the horses needed to be constantly pushed and prodded and still would suddenly stop for no reason. She found it more tiring than walking and told Gandolfi so. He left camp the next morning. The hunt nonetheless continued inland, to the banks of the Simba River, some 150 kilometres from Nairobi. The hunt began in earnest. Susan killed an impala and Piscicelli a hartebeest one day; the next, Hélène bagged a water buck and Susan took many antelopes. However, Piscicelli shot a lion, and that night they dined on lion steak, which Hélène thought 'excellent and rather unusual.' The next day, their Somali hunter-guide took them deeper into the bush, and Piscicelli and Hélène each shot a rhinoceros, although the women were disappointed in not getting a lion.[54]

Back in Nairobi, they spent an amusing evening with Lord Cardross and Lord Delamere, with their wild beards and long hair, listening to their stories of the founding of the colony. Palm Sunday fell on 12 April in this year, and despite using thuai branches instead of palms, Hélène felt that the Catholic rites overcame any differences through its grace and beauty. Emanuele Filiberto and the boys were listening to Mass in the chapel at Capodimonte. 'They were thinking of me as I was thinking of them. Despite the distance, our prayers met before God and asked him to unite us, in this life and the next.' They moved on to Mombasa, where they stayed at the less-than-luxurious Grand Hotel, and where they were pushed through the streets by two boys propelling two-seater wagons over a course of rails. Although there were growing international tensions with agents of the East Africa Company over the German occupation of Heligoland Island, Hélène and her party touched briefly into German East Africa, when they took the cargo boat *Arnold Amsinck* to the seaport of Tanga. When they reached Zanzibar, the whole place smelling strongly of cloves, the Sultan sent a landau complete with a red-liveried coachman to take them to the Hotel Afrika. They dined with the governor, the Italian consul, and commanders of the two Italian ships in the harbour, as Hélène began her progress back into the European scene, although she found lunch with the Sultan in his palace and a visit to the leprosy hospital the next day more interesting.[55]

From Zanzibar, they moved on to Dijbouti in French Somaliland, whence Hélène wrote to her husband, '*Cher Manolo*'. Hélène said that she had given up ideas to visit Greece, Corfu or Constantinople, but hoped that Emanuele might meet her in Port Said or Alexandria. 'Above all, I wish to see you again as soon as possible, I hope that you will come to me where you wish—but to see you soon. Do you have this impatience to see me? I fear not.' She continued:

… be assured that you will find in me a good friend—disposed to leave you in peace, always ready to help you—and never to bother you. As for myself I ask only one thing—to be left in peace. I return to Naples in good health and I wish to be with you and the children quietly—as for the world, *Zut!* At the moment I have the pretext of mourning, after that I will release myself as I may.[56]

Hélène closed this letter in English with 'Love', yet it is full of contradictions. She wants to see Emanuele, the sooner, the better. However, she makes it clear that their relationship was broken. She will remain his friend, but wants to be left in peace herself. She addresses banalities, such as arranging for Susan's accommodations on the journey to Italy and to ensure that she will be able to ride horseback while there. She questions the news that her brother-in-law Luigi degli Abruzzi is engaged to marry. She covers any actions that she might undertake under the cloak of the ongoing mourning for her Portuguese brother-in-law and nephew.

In the event, Emanuele did travel to Alexandria to meet Hélène— but Susan felt that the 'duke makes the party much more formal at once though he is pleasant enough.' They travelled back to Naples aboard the steamship *Schleswig* arriving on 23 May. Hélène had been gone for nearly six months. Waiting at the quayside were the little princes standing stiffly at attention in sailor suits, but as soon as they were allowed, Amedeo and Aimone 'ran on board beaming all over.' They reached Capodimonte, as Susan wrote, 'stopping at a side door, where a lift took Madame up the rest of us going up stairs two floors.' The duke then took Susan to her rooms on the first floor, a bedroom and sitting room, but she was not impressed with 'the walls painted in the style of a third rate hotel, imitation marble floors & hideous furniture.' Later Hélène sent the boys down to take Susan around the park, where 'they showed me their guinea-pigs, rabbits & caracul sheep & gymnastic arrangements, & then left me at a gateway from which spread high cliffed alleys of ilex, very attractive.' At dinner that evening it was the young princes who kept up most of the conversation, 'after which they let off rockets from the window, & we were speedily sent to bed.' While Susan found the boys 'such jolly little people, eight & nine, with the most beautiful manners & talk excellent English,' to her the Duke was more enigmatic, 'very kind, & at times quite easy to get on with, at other times not.'[57]

Hélène slowly began her adjustment to European life again. One day, she, Susan, and the boys had dejeuner out under the trees, 'apparently an innovation & not generally approved of,' however natural it might have seemed to people who had been camping in the forests so recently. They made a day trip into Rome so that Hélène could visit her dentist, and she showed Susan her rooms at the Quirinale, 'such a huge prison-house & so airless.' Back at Capodimonte, Hélène, Emanuele Filiberto, and Susan went for a ride through the estate on some of the big hunters from the stables—'horribly wasted here on only their silly paper hunts'—and rode back through the woods to find the little princes 'trying to cook potatoes in a fire.'[58]

Within a few days of her return to Capodimonte, Hélène wrote to her brother Philippe to assure him that 'the cannibals did not eat me' and that 'my health is much better.' Although Hélène found her return to civilization 'very painful', she was very happy to see '*mon vieux Manolo*' and 'my two brats' (*mes deux mioches*).

She also wanted to know if Philippe wanted her to send his 303 carbine along or to hold it until his next visit. A month later, Hélène wrote to Philippe again, this time asking for some taxidermy advice for her 'precious beasts.' She knew that her brother's favourite was the Englishman Rowland Ward and that he was a 'great artist,' but Hélène felt he was also a 'great thief' and, in any event, her purse was too flat for the transport to Paris.[59]

Hélène's African adventure left her longing for more, as she explained in a letter to Wilfred Blunt:

> My trip did me enormous good, I have only one dream, to return to these countries. The more I see, the more horror I have about that which is called civilisation, which is nothing more than corruption and human maliciousness. If I did not have a husband and children, I go and establish myself there.[60]

'The Duchess of Aosta is dying' announced *Le Matin* on its front page in August 1908, but then asked 'Is it a physical illness? Is it an emotional illness?'[61] The article claimed that Hélène had not left Capodimonte since her return from Africa, and that during the trip, she had recovered physically but not emotionally from the public revelations of Emanuele's infidelities. It recapitulated the entire tale, but added nothing new.

Mid-September saw the arrival of two American battleships in Naples harbour. The USS *Alabama* and USS *Maine* had just gone through the Suez Canal before making this one stop in the Mediterranean before returning to the United States at the end of a circumnavigation of the world. Hélène and Emanuele visited the ships in harbour and entertained the officers at Capodimonte. The American ambassador Lloyd Griscom and his wife also came to greet the ships in Naples, and joined Hélène in 'the wild rides, which the Duchess habitually indulges in on horses that many women would hesitate to approach.'[62]

It was also in November that rumours began to crescendo among the international newspapers that Emanuele's younger brother, Luigi, the Duke of the Abruzzi, was about to go to America and propose marriage to Katherine Elkins, the daughter of Senator Stephen Benton Elkins of West Virginia, and a family meeting had been called at Superga to discuss the matter. There had been murmurs about the romance of Luigi and the young American woman as early as the previous year when he was sent to the United States to represent Italy at the tercentenary exhibition at Jamestown, Virginia. In February 1908, Luigi had travelled incognito to Florida, where he met Katherine and her mother, and the next month the *New York Times* published half-page photographs of them anticipating an announcement of the engagement.[63]

Two years earlier, in 1906, a British diplomat had met Luigi Abruzzi while he was en route to his ascent of Mount Ruwenzori on the border of Uganda and the Congo. Hesketh Bell described him as 'about thirty-five years old, slender and good-looking, and speaks English admirably.'When Abruzzi left about a week later, Bell wrote in his diary:'I shall miss him, as he is a charming companion.' He continued on about his explorations and his all-round sportsman interests and 'Also a great ladies' man and loves nothing more than to talk about the fair sex.'When Bell challenged him on the pursuits of beauties he assumed that 'as a Royal prince, he only had to throw his handkerchief anywhere to have it picked up at once.' Abruzzi replied:'Yes, but there is always one that won't, and that's the one I want!'[64]

For months, there were conflicting rumors—that there had already been a secret marriage, that an American cardinal assured the pope that there were no difficulties about Katherine converting, or that the Queen Mother and Hélène were opposed to having an American enter the royal family. At one point, it was even stated who was making the trousseau and who one of the bridesmaids would be. However, by the end of the year, it was certain that the marriage would not take place at all, and Luigi began preparations for another exploration, this time to the Himalayas. Although he was not able to achieve his goal of scaling K2, his 1909 climbs in the Karakarom mountain range in Kashmir would break altitude records there, and also disproved earlier theories that man was not able to spend the night at altitudes over 20,000 feet (6,096 metres).[65]

Three days after Christmas, a natural disaster took place which put Hélène's concerns into a different perspective and gave her a new purpose. On 28 December 1908, a terrible earthquake struck Messina and the coast of Calabria and was followed by a tidal wave. Estimates of the dead range from 80,000 to 150,000. British and Russian warships were on the spot within hours to give immediate help, but local authorities were much slower to react and it was two days before Italian ships left Naples to aid in the effort. The Russian battleship *Admiral Makaroff* arrived in Naples on the 31st with hundreds of refugees. The newspapers reported that many of the refugees were horribly mutilated, and ten of them died *en route* and had to be buried at sea. 'The landing of the refugees profoundly moved those present, and the duchess of Aosta was unable to restrain her tears.' Among these survivors was Miss Peirce, a member of a family of shipping merchants long established in Messina. Except for one male relative, all her family was killed in the quake. When she arrived in Naples, she was housed by Hélène. That same morning, Hélène visited the injured in the local hospital and took three orphans away with her to care for. A number of the Neapolitan noble women were also at the docks to assist with landing the injured, and many of them took the little ones home to nurse them personally. The Red Cross set up a hospital in a school on via Maddalena, fifteen volunteer nurses arrived from Milan, and Hélène is said to have arranged for five sisters of the Neapolitan Order of the Daughters of Charity to join them.[66] Queen Mother Margherita arrived in Naples the next day to join Hélène in her hospital visits; soon, the French Red Cross was active in the city and Emanuele led the Central Committee of Relief. Over the course of the following two months, Hélène visited hospitals almost every day or served soup to the victims of the quake, although the photographs of the time show top-hatted gentlemen surrounding Hélène, who is elegantly dressed and gloved while ladling out soup for a single lady to take away. It is an image that she would soon shed for more practical nursing.

In the spring of 1909, Hélène had a number of visitors, including her brother Ferdinand who arrived in early February, and a few days later Queen Victoria's younger son, the Duke of Connaught, and his wife. The Connaughts lunched with Hélène at Capodimonte, and when their daughter Princess Patricia arrived that evening, Hélène was at the station with the Duke and Duchess to greet her. The next day, Hélène toured them around Pompeii. Princess Beatrice of Battenberg, Queen Victoria's youngest daughter, came to Capodimonte at the end of March. The Duchesse de Guiche and Hélène went for a visit to Capri, incognito as the Princesse de Villiers and Countess della Cisterna. Then, the visit of the most well-known American of the day, Teddy Roosevelt, came in early April.

The former American president was quite an international hero and sportsman, and Hélène wanted to meet him. Roosevelt's own expectations of Naples itself were undoubtedly low, influenced from his old friend Henry Cabot Lodge who wrote to him about the scene:

Vesuvius, the Sorrento coast and Capri spread out before us. It is really one of the great views of the world ... And attached to this splendid landscape is Naples the most hopelessly ugly town in the world—not a decent building, the churches sunk in the most degraded 18th century rococo to be found in Europe. It is so bad that any new building is an improvement and even the new quarters are shabby and dirty. There is nothing so squalid as shabby newness.[67]

Hélène had made the new American ambassador Lloyd Griscom promise to bring Roosevelt out to Capodimonte as soon as he arrived. Roosevelt was, he admitted, somewhat 'shabbily clad' but went to meet the Aostas at the palace. He reported home that first 'I was ushered in to see the Duke alone—apparently he & she wished to see me separately. He is a tall, slim good looking man, but not of good character; I didn't really like him and should hate to have him know any young girl.' However, when he met the Duchess, she 'was a dear; so friendly and interested and interesting. With each of them I finally had to get up myself, as in each case it became evident that otherwise I should be kept until I could not possibly do the things I had to do.' Hélène is said to have told reporters that Mr Roosevelt was 'the most interesting American she had ever met—she might almost say, the most interesting man.'[68]

While Roosevelt's visit stirred up recent memories of Africa, another visit later in the month brought back older memories. King Edward and Queen Alexandra made a Mediterranean cruise, accompanied by their daughter Victoria and by Alexandra's sister the Dowager Empress Marie of Russia. They arrived at Baia near Naples in beautiful weather on 29 April aboard the royal yacht *Victoria and Albert*, escorted by cruisers. Both British and Italian warships exchanged salutes, and King Edward was greeted by King Victor Emmanuel aboard the Italian battleship *Re Umberto*. The quick formalities of a royal visit took about half an hour before the British king returned to his yacht, and then the Italian king came on board to greet the Queen, Empress, and princess. More salutes were fired, and then the British party went to the *Re Umberto* for luncheon, where Queen Elena was present along with Hélène and Emanuele.

Despite the formal visits and salutes, this was not a ceremonial visit, and Baia had been selected as the site to 'mark its intimate character.' It offered an opportunity for a personal and friendly meeting, as well as some business when Tommaso Tittoni, the Minister for Foreign affairs, had a long conversation with King Edward.[69]

After luncheon that first day, Hélène was unwell, fainted, and left the party for a rest. However, King Edward and Queen Alexandra and the rest of their party went to see Capodimonte, visiting the museum with the Aostas, and afterwards took tea in the gardens. *The Times* reported that on the morning of 2 May, the *Victoria and Albert* left for Capri; it was intended that they lunch on the island and visit the sights, but the sea was too rough for a landing, and therefore the yacht proceeded to Castellammare, where Queen Alexandra, the Empress Marie, and Princess Victoria landed and visited Hélène at the hotel to which she had been taken after being taken ill and where she was being nursed by her sister Isabelle. The Empress Marie wrote to her son the Tsar that 'She is terribly thin and feels very ill, poor thing. She is always coughing, always feels cold, does not even find Naples warm enough.'[70]

When the Duke of Aosta heard that the *Victoria and Albert* moored at Castellamare, he drove there in his motor car with his two sons. King Edward joined the ladies at the hotel and there was a pleasant meeting, which the Duchess seemed to enjoy. 'The young princes offered all the ladies little bouquets of flowers with so much charm that they were almost overwhelmed with kisses.' The royal party went on to Naples, and a few days later Queen Alexandra left her sister and daughter there shopping and sightseeing in order to visit Hélène at Castellamare again. The next day Hélène was well enough to return onboard the *Victoria and Albert* for lunch. Still later in the month, Sir Hesketh Ball, the British Governor of Uganda, was in Rome and had tea with Hélène at the Quirinale. 'The Duchess, who was charming and gracious as ever, gave me a very interesting account of her last shooting trip in Africa. Buffalo, lion and elephant all fell before her.'[71]

At the end of August, Hélène and Emanuele travelled by automobile via Paris, Brussels, and Holland to take the boys to school in England.[72] This was a brave innovation, as young princes of all nationalities were normally expected to be educated in their own countries, most usually in military school after their early years with private tutors at home. The choice of England for their education was undoubtedly influenced by Hélène's own experience there, but must have also received the approval of King Victor Emmanuel.

The Aostas made a brief stop in Paris en route, including lunch at the Ritz and some shopping in the Rue de la Paix, while Hélène visited the Marquise d'Harcourt and returned to dine with the Comte and Comtesse Gonzague Costa de Beauregard, companions on her first journey to Africa and the Holy Land. While in England, she took the boys for a nine-day visit in Gloucestershire to the family of her more recent travelling companion, Susan Hicks Beach.[73]

Hélène also attended the annual requiem Mass at Weybridge for the Comte de Paris in the company of her mother, her childhood friend Renée St Maur, Renée's father Camille Dupuy, and the Baron de Fonscolombe. Hélène whistfully wrote to her brother Philippe that of the Comtesse's children who could have been surrounding their mother, she was the only one present that year. Hélène used the same letter to ask Orléans if he would be willing to host the boys during their long Christmas break from their new school.[74] During the school year, which would begin on 17 September, the boys would be staying at the college, although on weekends, they were to go into London to attend Mass and to stay with Major Emilio Montasini, their tutor from Naples and Emanuele's staff officer.[75]

St David's in Reigate, Surrey, was the college chosen by the Aostas for their sons—Amedeo, a few weeks short of his eleventh birthday, while Aimone was just nine years old.[76] It was a small school, with only about thirty-five students and located 25 kilometres outside of London. The Rev. William Churchill and his wife Constance had established the college in 1883 to prepare the sons of the nobility for preparatory school and eventually university. By the time the Aosta boys arrived, the principal was forty-eight-year-old William Henry Joyce, MA, an Oxford graduate from Keble College, a cricketer and golfer, and the son of an Anglican clergyman, the vicar of Dorking. Guy Henry Fisher-Rowe was under-master. Fisher-Rowe in particular was remembered by boys of the school 'for his generous nature and his strict sense of right and wrong. His own straightforward mind never had to hesitate on moral issues and he was incapable of a mean thought or action.'[77] A contemporary student was Sacheverell Sitwell, who entered St David's in 1908; he remembered the Duchess coming to visit her boys there. Sitwell attended St David's (as did his brother Osbert) before going on to Eton, with other St David's boys, many of whom eventually progressed on to Oxford.[78] Although no school lists survive from the period when Amedeo and Aimone were at St David's, the 1911 census—taken shortly after they had left—included among the students the thirteen-year-old Earl of Shannon, Viscount Crowhurst (later the Earl of Cottenham), and the Russians, Prince André Bariatinsky and Prince Alexander Yourievsky (both morganatic grandsons of Tsar Alexander II).[79] The future dukes of Westminster and Northumberland were also students at Reigate.

Hélène felt that her leave-taking for her African journey in 1907 had been too abrupt and painful, so as she prepared for another expedition, she decided on a more transitional pattern. After she and Emanuele left the boys in England, Hélène planned to spend a month revisiting those close to her, but the whole expedition was placed in jeopardy when Emanuele dislocated his right leg in a riding accident at Licola in late October, and it was thought that he would have to remain in bed for about a month. As a result, they missed the state banquet at Racconigi in honour of the visiting Tsar of Russia. However, Emanuele was well enough to accompany Hélène to Rome whence she began her new adventure.

'Thus I would have left bit by bit on my route that which I hold most dear in the world. May God protect them all! May he equip my children for life and spare them from all peril!' Hélène then went to Biarritz to soak up the atmosphere of being beside the sea. 'Like the sphinx in the desert, the sea frightens me, fascinates me, calls me, routs me.'[80] Soon, it was time to join her old travelling companions again—Susan Hicks Beach and Maurizio Piscicelli—for the journey by train to Lisbon, where they were met by Queen Amélie, and then by boat to Funchal in Madeira. There they stayed at Reids Palace Hotel, and Susan wrote to her mother that 'the Duchess has been bathing, which takes a good deal of time, & she hasn't felt inclined for great exertions after. She is a beautiful swimmer, & loves it.' At Lisbon, there had been 'much too much hand-kissing, & polite conversation to please the Duchess, she hasn't much more use for that sort of thing than I have,' and they were glad to be more relaxed.[81]

After a few days of rest, they embarked aboard the *Walmer Castle* for the long sea journey around West Africa. The long days of travel were broken up by the young people playing cricket on the bridge, and by long conversations with fellow passenger Martinus Theunis Steyn, the last president of the independent Orange Free State in South Africa. Steyn and his wife had been in London, where he was trying to obtain rights for South Africa equivalent to those enjoyed by India, Australia, and Canada.[82]

They reached Capetown on 9 November, but re-embarked the next day for Port Elizabeth and then on to Durban. Then they transferred to the *Guelph* and went on to Lourenço-Marquès in the Portuguese territory of Mozambique, arriving five weeks after their departure from Europe. Hélène's eldest nephew, the late Crown Prince Luis Filipe of Portugal, had made an official visit to the Portuguese colonies in Africa two years earlier, in July 1907, visiting São Tome, Angola, Mozambique, and Cape Verde. That trip had been so successful that one writer commented that 'nobody in Africa could understand the existence of republicans in Portugal when they had a prince such as Dom Luis Filipe.'[83]

Alfredo Augusto Freire de Andrade, the governor of the colony, met Hélène and her party in a Fiat and took them on a tour of the city and lunch at the Residence. The next day, they weighed anchor again and sailed to Beira, where they stayed at the Hotel Savoy. There, they were met by the local governor, Nuño de Freitas Queiriol. Hélène told him of her desire to penetrate the interior, visit a bit of the country, and to hunt, but the governor offered all sorts of other options, trying to dissuade the Duchess and was worried about the lack of comfort. Eventually, he arranged a special train—complete with salon, cabins, and bathrooms—to take the party into the interior to visit some mines before heading onto their safari.[84]

8

1909–1911

How can one describe the beauty of the place,
the imposing grandeur of the falls,
the poetry of its surroundings? [1]

Three thousand warriors of the Varna tribe are assembled. On our arrival they are drawn up in a square, with a single line on either side; their ranks are as well dressed as a regiment. When I come before them, the oldest of their chiefs lifts his hand and cries, 'Bayete!' The cry is taken up by these thousands of men and echoed all along the line like a *feu de joie*. The Conseillier d'Almeida makes a fine speech to the kings and kinglets of the province, here united, explaining that I am the 'little mother' (aunt) of the king of all the white and all the black men of the country. A black Master of the Ceremonies then calls each chief in turn by name; he steps out of the ranks, and, bending low before me, strokes the bottom of my dress with the palms of his hands. One of the oldest even rubs my foot.

The ranks are broken; there are now only two lines, extending into the far distance. A song begins with a stamping and swaying of the body backward, forward. The warriors sing in tierce in different tones, producing a metallic sound like a silver bell; the result is perfect and without discord. The dance becomes furious; they grow more animated, and the bolder ones challenge one another; they come out of the ranks and run and spring, leaping and whirling with the agility of an acrobat. They leap around us, shaking their lances in our faces to see if we are afraid, and become more and more excited. The braves run and yell, and the chorus continues to accompany them with stamping feet and song. We hardly notice how the time passes, until the sinking sun reminds us that we must return to camp.

The long line of warriors quickly dissolves and forms into close battalions; dancing still, they approach slowly in order, bow and battle-axe in one hand and lance in the other; it is thus that they advance to battle.[2]

Hélène recorded this episode at Chindu in the Portuguese territory of Mozambique, 12 December 1909. She seemed to revel in her royal status among native Africans, while excoriating it while with colonial officials. She enjoyed the benefits but decried the obligations. In Africa, she found more of the former and fewer of the latter.

The travellers moved into the Mozambique bush, where Hélène felt quite at home inside her tent, with its open flaps forming a 'picturesque and shady' window into the world, her table and chair at the entrance, and the rifle rack close at hand. From there they walked in silence for half an hour before coming to a lake which Hélène described as a 'floating prairie.' It was at the lake that the native hunters went out in boats, moved toward a bathing hippopotamus, and dispatched it with their lances. 'His agony was pathetic... With effort he lifted the back part of his body out of the water. He sadly pressed his head against the boat from which he had been attacked, leaned further and further, closed his eyes... and died'[3] The hunters dragged the body to shore, formed a circle, and started dancing. They sang in full voice, glorifying the hunt, courage, skill, and the favourable spirits that had protected them.

While near the Buzi River in December 1909, Hélène admired the 'wide plain—high, yellow grass—trees scattered or in clumps as in a park, hillocks covered with flowers, insects of all colours, birds of every size and every variety, whose strange cries wake in us chords that have never before vibrated.' In places like this, she loved the separation from 'civilization' and the closeness of nature.

> One feels utterly at peace, far from civilization, far from the big centres, with their narrow ideas, where the air is as vitiated as the minds of the inhabitants. Here, though in the midst of men, one has a feeling of being far from man, but near to God. One sees His work just as He created it; the soul, like the lungs, breathes better in this pure, free atmosphere. Here one understands better the greatness of the Master, and one's whole being is lifted up to Him who has created all things and who has conferred on us the good gift of enjoying nature.

However, they were indeed there as hunters. Awakened from her 'reverie' by a whistle from one of the native guides, Hélène saw a water-buck 'with a fine head' passing. 'I take a good aim and pull the trigger. I felt certain of my shot, but—the rifle is at safe!' Although a number of animals now passed, the beaters (some 'thousand of them converging in a circle') were too close. Hélène found the 'half-naked black beaters, with their strange head-dresses, and bows, arrows, and spears, are wonderfully picturesque.' Then, 'Frightened gazelles, big antelopes, water-bucks—all the fauna of the plain is on the move; running, galloping, trying to escape at one side, meeting the line of beaters and turning back and stopping short; finally, taking a great resolve, charging the circle with lowered heads.' Then, the native hunters loosed their spears and arrow. 'The men have wonderful eyesight and dexterity, and seldom miss their mark.' Now on horseback, Hélène was able to overtake the hunters, 'in time to assist at the pursuit of a pointed-nosed hyena, surprised in the middle of a meal. An arrow strikes him and he rolls over, blotting out in blood the crimes he had committed.' That marked the end of the hunt, and they returned to camp 'followed by a line of blacks carrying the game: an endless line of men, one behind the other, a long black ribbon streaking the plain like a big snake gliding through the grass.'[4]

By the time these two days of hunting finished, they had seventy-three 'great beasts' laid out in front of their tents—antelopes of all sizes, gazelles, wild boar, and more—not counting the birds.[5]

They returned to Beira, from where they took the train into Rhodesia reaching Bulawayo on 23 December. The provincial administrator himself organized the group of porters which would take the party on to Broken Hill, and they found their own dealer for the horses, donkeys, mules and cattle for the journey. Then, having settled into the Grand Hotel—which left a lot to be desired with its dirty walls and holes in the ceiling, yet Hélène commented 'I've seen better inns but also worse!' That evening, a ball was held in the hotel, with the women in their low-cut gowns and the men in their white ties. Hélène and the horse dealer opened the ball with a waltz. The next day, Hélène spent the morning of Christmas Eve selecting donkeys for the next leg of their journey. 'It's an important operation and more delicate than one would think,' as few were generally used as draught animals and most were unaccustomed to saddles or packs. On Christmas morning, the church bells rang, and Hélène attended a low Mass in the local church. 'There were negroes of both sexes. Many went to receive Communion. The black mothers advanced with great meditation toward the Holy Table, carrying their youngest on their backs. One of the big children waved, then the other, from the bag where it was suspended, started to tug at the clothes of its mother (the blacks nurse their children until two or three years old). The poor woman, patient and resigned, got up, interrupted her action of grace, and without departing from the meditation with which she approached the Holy Table, led her child away.'[6]

Hélène had arranged for her two sons to spend the holidays with the Duc and Duchesse d'Orléans at Wood Norton; there, they became very fond of both 'Zio Philippo' and 'La Zia.' Charming little thank you notes survive, both dated 27 January 1910, the day before their return to college. Amedeo told of his last attempt at shooting clay pigeons, while little Aimone had found a toy deer in London which he sent in the hope that his aunt would like it as a souvenir of their visit.[7]

From Bulawayo, Hélène and her companions went inland to Victoria Falls on a rail line which had been established in 1905 and was providing increasingly popular tourist access to the 'Mosi-a-tunya' ('the Smoke that thunders'). 'What can one say?' Hélène asked. 'How can one describe the beauty of the place, the imposing grandeur of the falls, the poetry of its surroundings?' It was a sight that was particularly impressive when set in contrast with the rain forest into which they then entered. With trees so large that they blocked much of the sunlight, restricted air circulation aside the roiling waters of the Zambesi River. They continued over the extraordinary rail bridge, and in the late afternoon arrived at their hotel, where they met Mr Lawrence Wallace and his charming French wife Marguerite-Marie, who was originally from Le Havre. Wallace was a civil engineer by training, who was now administrator of North-Western Rhodesia, an area bigger than Germany. He was also an experienced hunter, and was the man who had organized two hundred porters for Hélène's party. The porters were gathered together and waiting for them at Broken Hill.[8]

Sometime during this trip, Hélène gained the services of Pedro, who she called '*mon* boy.' Since she called others the same earlier on the first voyage, it is not certain when Pedro joined the party, but it was probably in Mozambique in December 1909. He was a Zulu and probably about ten or eleven years old at this time.[9] Over the years, he became a servant in the household at Capodimonte and would accompany Hélène on a second safari to Africa in 1910, aboard the hospital ship during the Libyan war in 1911, and on her round-the-world journey which started in 1913 and finished days before the outbreak of the First World War. Along with the stuffed animal heads dotted around Capodimonte, Pedro was as much of a curiosity for the King's children to ogle when the Queen brought them for tea as were the palace art collections when they visited in 1913.[9] Pedro's later history is unknown.

The train took them to Broken Hill, which developed as a town when zinc and lead deposits were found there in 1902. They arrived on 2 January and spent a few days organizing the safari. The donkeys were proving particularly difficult— Susan had a bad fall from one, and another threw little Pedro, who fell directly on his nose—'fearful or hurt, he did not want to come with us and went to lie down under his cover crying.' The dark nights were noisy, filled with the sounds of frogs and other croaking animals and also filled with fears for their livestock as a lion circled the camp.[10]

After being delayed for several days by rain, the caravan finally started its march, 'having said adieu to civilization for months, I hope.' Moving off with their 200 porters, cases, and animals, they made slow but steady progress. After his previous experience, little Pedro preferred walking, but Hélène's '*autre* boy' told her 'Mrs ride very well donkey, me fall five times!' They injected the donkeys with arsenic twice a week to try to prevent trypoanasome, which could lead to a variety of diseases including sleeping sickness among humans. Hélène also casually commented that she used iodoform to treat the 'boys for whom a certain part of the body was damaged by the whip and who could only walk with difficulty. They were covered with it. One might think oneself in a hospital.'[11]

During this part of the trip, they also spent a great deal of time collecting natural history specimens. They would press the flowers that they found along their route, number them, and inscribe each one in the collections notebooks, indicating the nature of the terrain where they were found and their colour. Hélène would supervise Pedro and Pangamuchelo, their hunter, digging orchid bulbs, which would then also require cataloguing. Piscicelli made collections of minerals, butterflys, and insects, while they would all collect birds which had the double purpose of ornithological study and of food. All of this, plus the development of their photographs, filled many of their days.[12]

By the end of January, they passed into the Belgian Congo. Hélène seemed delighted by their anonymity when they came across an Englishman in a caravan from Lake Banguélo, and he was more interested in the whisky-soda that Hélène offered than in finding out who she might be. As they progressed towards white beaches and flower-edged Lake Banguélo, the donkeys began to weaken, and Susan and Piscicelli took to walking. Their monotonous diet was enriched by some spurred geese, and Hélène found the meat firm and savory, preferable to the mutton which they carried with them. It was late February when they reached the large village of Kasoma, where one of the local chiefs, Sultan Kasoma, arrived on the beach to greet them, draped in his Roman toga-style covering. However, he was dismissed with a silent nod of the head and sat down on the sand, while the travellers practiced their carbine shots on the three hippopotamuses as moving targets.[13]

As they progressed along the shoreline in their boats, Hélène shot a large monkey with her 303, but mostly, they watched the vast array of birds—small bitterns, white herons, Goliath herons, white egrets, the brown ibis, kingfishers, turtledoves, green pigeons, and flights of toucans—their colours and cries filling the sky. After an extended stay at Kasoma, they moved on; in the bobbing boats on the river, Hélène was perched on a small native stool struggling to keep her ammunition and camera dry. By early March, they were at a place free of the dreaded tsetse fly, the Mission of the White Fathers on Lake Kifumabuli. The official title of the order was the Missionaries of Our Lady of Africa of Algiers. It had been founded by the first Archbishop of Algiers in 1868, and in 1878, ten missionaries left Algiers to found posts in Lakes Victoria, Nyanza, and Tanganyika. This little mission station consisting of three priests and one brother had been established there for four and a half years and centred on a coffee plantation and the beginning of some new rice fields. The Fathers were able to lend their larger boats each rowed by eight men, and Hélène and Susan stretched out on their chaises longues while Captain Piscicelli directed the other boat and the porters took the land route. At the end of the lake, they reached Niambala, where they were greeted by the Sultana who reigned there. Hélène wrote that the Sultana had neither the timidity nor the darting look of the usual black woman. She came directly to them and engaged in a long conversation, punctuated with nods of her head and 'hiu heu'. 'Her gestures and her voice are full of authority; she is sensitive to the compliments which I give to her belt and her bead necklaces, but even more to the awful bright blue cotton cloth which I gave to her as a present.' The prince, her husband, seemed uncomfortable when the Sultana began to flirt with Piscicelli, and Susan felt that he must be a new acquisition of the Sultana. When she turned to one of their boys to ask how many husbands she had, the answer came back 'Oh! every body!'[14]

At Chilubula, they visited another mission of the White Fathers, and camped about a kilometre away from their enclosure. Hélène expressed her delight at the siting of the camp, and Piscicelli assured her 'Yes, yes, if it does not rain, it will be charming.' However, as they were enjoying a hot dinner sent to them by the sisters at the mission, a storm broke with thunder, lightning, and torrents of rain. The water level grew, the furniture began to float, and the porters began to cry out '*Mamma kati kati na mai!*' ('Mamma is in the middle of the water!'). Luckily, the water level dropped as quickly as it had developed.[15]

They spent a week at Kasama, the centre of the northern province of Rhodesia, and enjoyed the hospitality of the governor, his wife, and their two little daughters. The night before they planned to leave, the porters, cooks, and 'boys' all went into the village and overindulged in millet beer. The police were called, charges were pressed, and Charlie, Hélène's 'boy no. 1' in particular was sentenced to six months of forced labour for indecent assault and 'resisting the policemen in the execution of their duty.' In the event, his sentence was commuted, and the party moved on.[16]

As the hunting party now progressed further into the bush, they were led by a Mr Poingdestre, a hunter renowned for having killed fifty elephants in his career 'and I don't know how many buffalo.' Their goal this time was to find elephants. After days of missed opportunities, on 19 April a solitary elephant was spotted. Hélène wrote 'it turned its back on us. It was so big that its body rose over the grass. Its enormous ears were flapping. It is far away, but we must make a move.' They positioned themselves into a better spot, and then 'my shot hit it behind the ear and penetrated the head. The poor giant remained standing, but it stumbled. It could no longer see, the blood blinded it.' The great beast 'took a few more steps, then butted into a tree. It now presented us with a beautiful target.' Soon, it was on the ground, 'an imposing mass. From the shoulder, it measured 3.45 m; from the trunk to the tail, 6.86 m; around its waist 4.75 m and its ears were 1.40 m long.' The head was so large that it would require six porters to carry it along the journey.[17] Susan confided in a letter to her mother that 'Mdme. & the Capt. between them got 3 elephants & a buffalo, so Mdme. is much pleased in consequence. If she were an ordinary person she would certainly be fined for killing such small tuskers as two of them—the third is a beauty—but being her it doesn't matter.'[18]

In the middle of this ten-month trip, Hélène was gaining a certain notoriety both in Europe and in America. *The Washington Post* reported a print for sale across Europe—'A Woman Roosevelt'—which featured a photograph taken on her last hunting expedition while in Portuguese territory 'back of Delagoa Bay', showing Hélène holding her rifle at full cock and looking at the dead rhinoceros that she has just felled.[19] Hélène was also sending back reports of her journey, which were published serially in the widely popular American magazine *Harper's Weekly*. Casting her in the role of the goddess of the hunt, the articles appeared under the title 'Diana in Africa' and played on the same lines as the published photograph; they were precursors to her several travel books that would appear in the coming years. She had made an arrangement for five articles of 2,000–3,000 words apiece for a total payment of £300. Hélène and Piscicelli composed the articles in French, and then Susan translated them into English. Hélène told Susan that because of the articles 'There will be fearful rows with her relations, which she is rather looking forward to.'[20] Excerpts from these articles were also published in Paris by *Le Gaulois du Dimanche*, the Sunday literary supplement to the daily *Gaulois*, the influential journal owned by Arthur Meyer, a longtime friend and supporter of the Orléans family.

Next, the party continued along the Tanganyika Plateau on the route from Kassama to Abercorn in northern Rhodesia. On 29 April, they reached Abercorn, a small settlement with only three or four houses, but the surroundings reminded Hélène of the Scottish Highlands and the happy days of her youth. 'Abercorn is an enchanting place to stay. One could assert without exaggeration that this is one of the most completely beautiful places that one could see. It is also a perfectly healthy place, at least for those who don't dread the freshness of the morning or of the evening. The air is pure and invigorating.... Even the mosquitos are trivial.' The healthy aspects here belied the conditions further on. Mr Marshall, the District Commissioner, tried to dissuade Hélène and their party from continuing further into an area infected with sleeping sickness. Healthy natives who had not been exposed to that disease were not allowed into that territory, and so new porters were required but Mr Marshall could find only 128 of the 250 they required.[21]

Susan recorded in her journal:

> We are well, as usual, but it has been so horribly cold this last week or so, that Mdme. has been coughing a good deal also we have had another, & apparently unusual dose of rain... We parted with all our porters yesterday, & were quite sad, some of them had become great friends after 4 months, they are awfully good, cheerful, uncomplaining people too, though a little of the stick is necessary at time. The cook & one of the boys go too, the cook is a relief to be rid of, he is such a scoundrel, & has been most trying to the temper. The other is a good boy, but we shall probably replace them well enough for the short remaining time.[22]

While at Abercorn, 'to our great relief', they finished up and posted the last of Hélène's articles for *Harper's Weekly*.[23]

It was on 8 May when they were camped at Kalambo Falls that Hélène heard of the news of the death in London two days earlier of King Edward VII. 'My thoughts went out to this mourning family, which was a bit my own. The pain of those who are more than friends to me is my pain.' That brought to Hélène memories of her own father's death and the loss that she felt then. That evening, she dreamt of her father 'with a striking clarity, and this vision to me is dear.'[24]

Emanuele Filiberto went to London to represent the King of Italy at King Edward's funeral, arriving on the 14th, when he was met at Victoria Station by the late king's only surviving brother, the Duke of Connaught, who himself had just returned from a shooting trip in Africa. The boys—Amedeo and Aimone—had arrived in England only about a week before to continue their studies.

Meanwhile in Africa, Hélène and her travelling companions continued to document their trip. On 14 May, 'We had a party of Swahili ladies—wives of the Arabs—up to photograph.' The women were 'all dressed in their best & brightest cottons & turbans & many rows of big beads on silver chains.' Many of them also came with umbrellas, a sign of superiority among the Zulus. In the afternoon the travellers 'were treated to dances, the whole population assembling before the gates, a gaily coloured crowd in every shade & pattern of cotton.' The men were mostly dressed in 'the Arab white gown, with embroidered white skull caps,' while 'one or two chief Arabs in the gold embroidered black or brown cloak like the chiefs worn in Uganda. A Muscat Arab with rather an evil face wearing a tarboosh, is apparently the great man. We had native, Swahili & Arab dances.'[25]

Then, Hélène and her party moved to Lake Tanganyika and the town of Bismarkburg. They went on the little steamer *Edwing Wissman* along the eastern shore of the great lake and at Ugigi, among other sights, Hélène and Susan visited a hospital for those suffering from sleeping sickness. 'Those who have reached the last stage of the illness are greatly to be pitied. Reduced to skeletons, they are unmoving, stretched out on their beds. While we were still in the room, one poor woman all huddled up and covered with white spots, ceased to suffer; God called her back to Him.'[26]

A few days later, they felt that their time had almost been called too. While exploring the western banks of the lake, they went ashore at Uvira, but by the time that they were ready to reboard the steamer by means of a little barque, the wind had picked up and was rocking the boat fiercely. They went into the water and got into the boat, but Susan lost her balance and would have fallen overboard if Hélène had not been able to pull her back by her clothing. Piscicelli waded into the water up to his waist carrying young Pedro in his arms and then threw him into the boat. Once they all made it into the boat, they faced 'mountains of waves.' The storm grew worse and threatened to capsize the boat, so the men started to sing to encourage themselves and rowed harder until they finally reached the safety of the larger steamer. 'We are saved!'[27]

At Usumbura, Hélène was delighted to leave the rocking ship and return to the comfort of her own tent. From there, it was on to Mtara in German East Africa; once there, the porters, who had now reached 350 in number, were subjected to a medical exam and it was found that eighty-six were suffering from sleeping sickness. The rest of them pushed on, passing a swamp, through vast banana plantations, and eventually into a desert area. Throughout much of this trip, Hélène was carried by the porters in a *maschilla*, which has been described as a 'species of portable hammock' sometimes rigged up out of blankets, although the first time it was demonstrated, the 'man who kindly proceeded to show us how to get into them promptly fell out on his head, so we came to the conclusion that we preferred the donkeys.'[28] It was in a *maschilla* that Hélène was carried up the mountain at Chia, some 1,390 metres high. They continued to climb and camped at 2,000 metres, where Hélène found the sun blocked by the surrounding mountains resulting in very cold temperatures. At 2,400 metres, Hélène wrote:

> O virgin forest! tropical forest! How generous nature has been towards you. Today we penetrated into a forest which has remained intact and instinctively we were seized with respect and contemplation. Here the eternal Sower must have thrown seed upon a blessed land ... One feels small at the feet of this giant vegetation under which, aside from the beaten path, no human being has penetrated.

Here, Hélène encountered the Watusi for the first time, 'a race of African giants, a warrior and pastoral tribe.' They were subjects of Chief Kaslivani, who greeted them through an interpreter 'because he did not understand Swahili.' Kaslivani's men, dressed in their war costumes of leopard skins, performed a war dance for their guests. Hélène was impressed and surprised that they danced silently, without drums, without singing, unlike anywhere else in Africa. 'Perhaps the long generations accustomed to fighting without noise, hidden in the grass to surprise the enemy, would explain this rare characteristic.'[29]

At Isavi, they visited another mission of the White Fathers; when they left, they carried with them fruits, vegetables, and even roses as gifts from the Fathers. They moved into the territory of Mzinga, king of the Warundi. They were escorted through the forest to the beat of the *ngoma* drums until reaching the royal palisade, where the king himself was waiting for them, surrounded by his guard, all dressed in traditional costumes which they now wore only for gala occasions. 'Mzinga was a head taller than his subjects who were already much taller than us,' noted Hélène, who was herself taller than most Europeans. Covering the king's head was 'a monkey-fur mane surrounded by a crown of blue and white pearls from which pendants came down to his eyes. A fringe in front covered his nose. This apparel combined to blur the vision of the king, which was already bad since he had measles as a child.' Mzinga was impressed by Hélène's tent and bed, but even more interested in her rifles: 'My carbine with telescopic lens left him dreaming.' When Mzinga tried the rifle, his first shot knocked his headdress into the dust; after a second attempt, he had had enough. Then came the gifts. Hélène was presented with eggs, great earthen jars filled with fresh butter, honey, then a cow, a whole herd of goats, and bananas; the porters received sweet potatoes. Then, the supreme luxury: some wood, as they could pass many days without finding even a shrub for a fire. 'The black kings are great lords. This one knows how a practice a particularly generous hospitality.' They were then treated to a display of dancing, followed by yet more gifts. Presents of native objects—straw baskets of different colours, wooden cups, and sickles—but in exchange, Mzinga wanted a rifle. Instead, Hélène gave him her revolver with some cartridges, a belt, a knife, a blanket and other small items.[30]

Once they left Mzinga's territory, the party moved on to Kigali and from there to the papyrus covered banks of the River Kagera and out of the land of Rwanda. At Kanazi on 28 June, they were greeted by the prime minister of Kahigi, 'cross sultan von Kyanya,' as his calling card read. Hélène deplored the way that the native chieftains had become 'marionettes in the hands of the whites, decorated, dressed by them, intoxicated by their attention, wanting to resemble them at all costs, borrowing all their habits and never accomplishing more than aping their exterior signs!' He even had visiting cards 'when he didn't know how to read.'[31]

Soon, they reached Lake Victoria-Nyanza, which Hélène had last seen two years earlier, and by 6 July were back in Uganda at Entebbe and then to Nairobi in Kenya, Hélène admitting that she found six days in town more tiring than a month in the bush. From there, the travellers took the train to Mombasa, passing by herds of hartebeest, wildebeest, and Thomson gazelles. After eight months of travel, exploration, hunting, and adventure, Captain Piscicelli made certain that all the baggage was safely aboard the *Adolph Woermann* and then bade farewell to Hélène and Susan as he prepared to leave for an expedition to Kivu. For both of the women, Piscicelli was someone 'who knew how to take care of everything as if it were nothing, of treating the greatest difficulties like the easiest things.' During these eight months, they grew to 'appreciate the even humour, the quickness and strength of decision as well as the courage and the devotion of this amiable traveling companion.'[32] Although they parted at Mombasa at this time, before the end of the year, they would all be together again—along with Pedro— on another adventure.

Hélène and Susan sailed to Aden, thence to Suez, arriving at Port Saïd on 30 July and then onward to Europe. Emanuele Filiberto and the boys were there to greet Hélène, when she and Susan—whom *La Stampa* charmingly mis-identified as 'Miss Kirch Pears'—arrived back in Naples on 3 August. The newspapers carried front-page stories of their adventures but only two days later also reported that Hélène would return to Africa in October.

Le Figaro reported that the Duke and Duchess of Aosta, together with the Duke of the Abruzzi, arrived in France and after visiting the Château de Chantilly went to the hotel in Paris where Mrs Elkins and her daughter were staying. This was seen as particularly significant because, according to some press reports, Hélène was particularly against the match between her brother-in-law Luigi and the young American. However, no announcement was made, no engagement ensued, and Katherine Elkins eventually married someone else in 1913. When Luigi founded his agricultural colony in Somalia, Katherine would be one of his greatest financial supports contributing from her inherited wealth funds for road building, railroad equipment and modern medical facilities. Until the end of her life, she would continue to wear jewelry which Luigi had given her including a locket containing a snip of his hair. When Katherine died in 1936, it is said that her funeral was delayed until a particular bracelet could be located. She had specified in her will that she be buried wearing this bracelet which had been a gift from her prince.[33]

Hélène and Emanuele Filiberto were together in England in September for the annual Mass in Weybridge in memory of the Comte de Paris, along with Hélène's mother and aunt and uncle, the Duc and Duchesse de Chartres. It was to be the last such visit for Chartres, who died on 5 December at the age of seventy. As he was not the direct heir, Chartres had been allowed to live in France and was likewise allowed to be buried in the family chapel at Dreux. Hélène, however, was not there to attend her uncle's funeral as once again she was in Africa.

Before Hélène left Italy, there was a public health crisis in Naples with a cholera epidemic, centred in the poorest districts in the city—Vicaria and Mercato. Some 100,000 of the 'better classes' fled, but Hélène and Emanuele Filiberto returned to the city to organize some relief methods. Promoting better sanitary conditions, Hélène visited the hospitals of Naples in the company of Sister Carolina, who would become a companion in charitable work at least through the 1930s. For a long period, the public authorities censored news of the outbreak despite the fact that a number of people had died in the streets. Only when the press began to make the true facts known did officials begin to make arrangements, such as the establishment of a quarantine station in the island of Nisida in the Bay of Naples. By the time that the news became public knowledge, the outbreak had already begun to abate.

Between October 1909 and May 1911, Hélène was in Europe for only two months (August and September 1910), and part of that time was spent in England. Her family still did not understand her fascination with 'the dark Continent.' The Infanta Eulalia of Spain, Hélène's aunt and hardly the most conventional of royalty herself, thought:

[Hélène was] a somewhat masculine type of woman, and spends a great deal of her time in Abyssinia. She leaves her husband and two boys and, with no companion except an elderly Englishwoman, sets out on a hunting expedition. She is lost in the heart of Africa for months, and then suddenly reappears and settles down to the humdrum life of her palace. But soon she hears again the call of the wild, and is away once more. What she does in Abyssinia nobody knows, if one excepts the elderly Englishwoman. The country seems to have cast a spell on her, and she cannot resist its fascinations.[34]

At age thirty-two (seven years younger than Hélène herself), Susan Hicks Beach would probably not have been amused to be described as 'an elderly Englishwoman.'

There were the health issues that originally sent Hélène to Egypt for a warmer and drier climate than Italy could provide in the winter, but that could not explain the travels into tropical climates. There was the separation from Emanuele Filiberto during a difficult time in their marriage. There were the adventuresome examples of her brothers Orléans and Montpensier, her brother-in-law Abruzzi, and her cousin Henri d'Orléans. And, as her son Amedeo commented years later about himself: 'The one thing that really pains me and which I cannot endure is boredom. Like Mama, just the same.'[35] Whenever there were wars, earthquakes, or volcanic eruptions, Hélène was in her element and at her best, but it was the 'humdrum life of her palace,' as her Aunt Eulalia of Spain phrased it, that pushed her into other activities.

For Hélène, Africa represented freedom. She felt that 'it's to Africa that one must go to breathe, to dream and to stretch out the hours with an infinity of sensations. One's spirit itself expands there, magnificent, above the terrestial infirmity in a stupendous communion with the Supreme Being. Even the air is full of a divine serenity!' A British official, who met Hélène in 1913 in Ceylon perhaps captured the true rationale for her travels when he referred to 'her annual escapes from the West.'[36] She was escaping from her problems into a new identity that she had created for herself. In Africa especially, Hélène was still a princess but very much on her own terms.

For this trip, Hélène left from Marseilles on 1 October 1910, along with Pedro, '*mon boy noir*', Susan Hicks Beach, and her sister Tora. Maurizio Piscicelli was also once again organizing the trip. They sailed to Port Said aboard the German liner *Prinzessin*, but as soon as they arrived Hélène learned of a revolution in Portugal which deposed her nephew Manoel from his throne and drove the family into exile. The news was incomplete and contradictory—Manoel, a prisoner having been bombed at the Necessidades Palace, or safely at Mafra, Amélie at Gibraltar. 'Poor Amélie, she continues to climb her Calvary!' She wrote to their brother Philippe about 'how painful it is to see our own augment the painful list of those princes out of employment. Poor *Grande* [Amélie] who has already had so much pain in her life—and for Manoel, such a sad future.'[37] Queen Mother Maria Pia and her son the Duke of Oporto went into exile to Italy, while Amélie and King Manoel went to England where they stayed with Philippe at Wood Norton until they moved into more permanent homes in the London area.

While still despairing for her sister, Hélène was momentarily distracted by the expected arrival on board of the Sultan of Zanzibar for the passage through the Suez Canal. The distraction increased when a huge pile of packages of all shapes and sizes appeared on deck, followed by a lady hidden by a huge hat and thereafter by the Sultan himself. Apparently, the British Governor of Zanzibar and his wife who were also travelling on the same ship were none too pleased to be accompanied by the white 'lady' accompanying the Sultan, and he was able to convince the Sultan to return to Cairo and await another ship. The German captain had a different view and told Hélène that the 'lady' herself 'was a perfect darling.' The incident played to the advantage of Hélène's party as she moved into the large now-empty state room, while Susan and her sister each got their own cabin.[38]

Once they arrived at Mombassa, Hélène took leave of all the others, as Susan and her sister went on a tour of Zanzibar and Tanganyika while Captain Piscicelli went to visit the great lakes in the central region. By herself, Hélène took the train for Nairobi—'Alone! it's a rare situation for a princess.' At Nairobi, Hélène was met by Sir Percy Girouard, Governor of British East Africa. A Canadian, Girouard charmed Hélène with the echoes of old-style Norman French in his speech, but Girouard was horrified when he heard about her intended travel plans. 'He couldn't have jumped better if he had seen the devil in my place!' Girouard brought out a map to explain the difficulties of the journey but to no avail. 'How embarrassing for a governor to have on his territories such a turbulent princess!'[39]

Preparations became rather fraught. Susan wrote home to her mother that 'the Governor has been a nuisance' as he rejected their plan to go to Lake Rudolf suggesting instead a passage down the Guaso Nyero and across to the Juba. Hélène eventually agreed to this new itinerary and asked for a permit to get the camels at the Lorian, but a week later the governor delayed again to consult Lord Crewe, who had recently been appointed Secretary of State for India. 'As if Lord Crewe had anything to do with it, he probably doesn't even know where the Juba is.' So a new plan was established, that they would 'go just for 3 months up the Guaso Nyero & return here to go round to Kisnayu or somewhere & start afresh.' As Susan admitted, 'I expect very likely once we are really started, we shall find we can get the camels perfectly easily without the Governor, & shall go on as we meant.' While the others prepared for their trek into the interior, Tora Hicks Beach returned to Egypt from Nairobi.[40]

About 150 kilometres north of Nairobi, they reached the central highlands of Kenya at Nyeri, which had only been founded in 1902 after the King's Royal Rifles, a colonial regiment raised in the colonies of British East Africa and under the command of Richard Meinertzhagen, defeated the local Kikuyu. Coffee plantations, wheat farms, and cattle ranches developed quickly, and by the time that Hélène and her party arrived there was already a golf club established, as well as a mission of the fathers of the Consalata. All this development drove the game away from the Nyeri area, but there were still fresh tales of conditions only a few years earlier. The Fathers told of one long caravan of nuns which was charged by a rhinoceros. Unaware of the dangers, one of the sisters, instead of fleeing, opened her umbrella in the nose of the beast. The animal, surprised and frightened by this unknown thing, stopped, turned around, and ran back at a gallop. A less fortunate priest who was working on the plantation was attacked without warning, badly trampled and thrown into the air.[41] Four visits to various missions marked the end of official obligations, and the real journey began.[42]

From Nyeri, they set out into the forest on 17 November in an immense caravan composed of 205 Kikuyu porters, twenty-five more robust Swahili porters, three mule-drivers, three Somali gun bearers, two water boys, four boys attached to them individually, the cook, five mules, and a herd of sheep. Next, they were joined by fifty donkeys bearing sacks of wheat to feed them all. They abandoned their northerly direction and moved west. The search for game now began in earnest. At first, Susan spotted a leopard and a lion, and a few days later, Hélène got her first kills—two Grant's gazelles and then an impala. Over the coming weeks, as the hunting party moved deeper inland, more and more game was taken. In early December, rhino was the main target; Susan made the first kill. After first wounding the beast, she chased it on muleback, finally getting a shot through the heart at 70 yards. Later, the one which Piscicelli shot 'rose from the dead suddenly, & scattered him & Mdme. & gunbearers in all directions before he finally expired.' Piscicelli usually accompanied Hélène on the hunt now, Susan guessing 'I think he doesn't quite like to leave her alone after rhino.' As a result, Susan felt she 'got the best bag, specially as I don't trail about a white parasol.' However, Hélène did 'get' a giraffe and Piscicelli two rhinos, 'otherwise they have only got the antelope so far, none of my other beasts.' A few days later, the Duchess 'has got another giraffe, a hyaena, cow eland, rhino & baby, besides gerenuk & the Capt. two giraffes—both cows—they are breaking every rule & regulation—I can't quite see why he should even if she does, but he doesn't seem to see it in that light.'[43]

On 7 December, they reached Neuman Camp, northeast of Mount Kenya, which would become their base for the rest of the month. Neuman Camp was named after a sportsman and naturalist given the name 'Niama yango' by the locals—'my meat' or 'the one who gives me meat.' It was a nickname that could equally have been applied to the newcomers, as they arrived with more game than they could eat. Still, they continued with hunting, and among the photographs that later appeared in Hélène's travel book for this period, one shows her holding a rifle and sitting next to a fallen buffalo, captioned 'The daily victim,' while another poses her next to a rhinoceros she had shot. Sometimes, as they wandered further away from camp, they just enjoyed watching nature pass by. One day, 'We were suddenly stopped by the noise of a furious gallop, which seemed to be like a charging regiment. In the distance whirled a cloud of dust. Hundreds of zebras galloping in tight rows, then hundreds of oryx.' Then, they saw the oryx 'with their straight horns coming out like a moving forest under the clear sky. Behind them, stomach to the ground, attempting to join them and giving all the allure of which it was capable, was our provisions mule!' Hélène sympathised with the pack animal, 'the vision of liberty having no doubt struck the brain of the poor beast, it was making a desperate effort to join the fleeing hordes.'[44] Susan reported to her mother:

> We are enjoying ourselves enormously, it is delightful going out after game every day, whether one shoots or whether one doesn't, & much of it is delight-ful country, long rolling hill & valley, or open plain, with patches of thorn & bush … We have seen hundreds of head of game, & have got 14 or 15 different species… We are supposed to go each in a different direction, but Mdme. & the Capt. usually start together, & then each go after their own animal.

Hélène's prowess impressed her companion: 'She is certainly a very good shot, she killed a giraffe at 400 yards with only a 303 rifle—& all these animals can stand a great many bullets, one has to hit them in exactly the right place to kill or dis-able them.' The downside for her was that 'Storms of rain have rather spoilt their giraffe skins—they are beautiful, but a great deal too big for the average house.'[45]

On the day after Christmas, their Somali camel driver Hadji-Ali-Aden arrived with forty-seven camels, just three short of their hoped-for number. Then, shortly after New Year's Day, this newly configured caravan set out. Almost as soon as they left, while crossing the first river, one of the camels decided to shed itself of both driver and load and Hélène watching her hat box float away—'the hat I had specifically brought so as not to appear too much of a savage upon my return to Naples!' Another mutinous camel smashed a case of wine to the ground. When they finally reached a camping spot, water was in short supply—'Our washing allowance is 2 whiskey bottles each, but we have got enough to drink, & the men have about a pint apiece'—while the 'refractory' camels continued to do their damage—'several more pieces of the remaining china smashed, a box of Mdme's bent out of shape, & my hat box stove in in every direction.' The next day they continued their damage when the camels and sheep left before dawn, 'making a fearful noise about it, & breaking two bottles of whiskey in the course of loading.'[46]

One night at the end of January, a fight broke out in the camp between two of the porters, and one of them was cut so badly that his insides were spilling out. With the captain, Hélène first attempted to push the protuding organs back into place but failed, and then tried to administer laudanum but found that her whole supply was not sufficient to the task. Susan confided to her journal that 'It is a tragedy over a trifle—a good porter too, & very good at doing heads & skins, his job being to do mine. The only mercy is that it isn't a white man.' About the same time, the local governor felt that certain of the local tribes were rather 'out of hand' and decided that Hélène's party should not proceed beyond Moyale. Mr [Samuel Francis] Deck, the district commissioner, arrived with his orders 'to stop us buying camels etc., & to put guards over the wells & us, & various other little ways of annoyance.' Hélène 'laughs & says she will go where she pleases, & we want none of their protection or assistance. She is much annoyed, & it is very silly of Govr. & a great shame to put an underling in such an unpleasant position.' Publicly, they announced that they would be going instead to Addis Ababa, but Susan admitted that we 'mean to go direct to Bardera from here, instead of going to Moyale.'[47]

Although the journey started in water, lack of water would be their major concern over the coming days as they marched from Guasso Nyiro to Marsabit-Moyale. There would be travelling days lasting more than fourteen hours in temperatures that reached 46° in the shade of their tents as they progressed through the scrubland and then into the desert of southern Ethiopia and Somalia. They began to travel by night in order to avoid the heat of the day. 'We wandered on in the moonlight, the caravan getting on unusually well, fewer trees in the path than usual, but a comfortable camel making it even more difficult to keep awake, one lost a certain amount of skin even so.' When they got to the shoulder of the hill, they saw 'the earth & many quartz stones glimmering white in the moonlight.' When they reached their camping place, the King's African Rifles were already there on one side to guard them night and day now that they were now coming to the 'dangerous' country.

To save on cooking water, they decided that the usual 'bunga' (the wheat which formed the basis of their diet and which required cooking) would be replaced by hard beef for the Swahili men and camel meat for the Somalis. The wells that they passed were dry or nearly so. They arrived as 'El Wak, which has a large name on the maps, & is said to have 100 wells but only three of them are visible, unless some dry holes count as wells, & of course not even a hut!'[48]

Then, they had a 'long night of slow walking—stops—waiting—one sick man fell en route and it was necessary to use lanterns to find him—a camel carrying water escaped into the bush—five other beasts dead or abandoned behind us. Moreover, the thorns from the trees literally plough into our faces.' The camels began to drop, one after another as they passed four days without any new water supplies. Finally on 2 March, they reached the Djouba River and water. From Guasso Nyiro to Serenly, they had walked thirty-five days, eighteen of them without water, an average of eight hours of walking a day; often ten, twelve, or more than thirteen hours a day. Of the seventy camels that they started with, forty-eight died along the way.[49]

Once they reached Bardera, they were in Italian territory, and after the rigours of the journey, Hélène accepted accommodations in the house offered by Captain Cibelli, commander of the place. A return to civilization brought piles of post—'the news which it brings to us is mixed with joys and sadness.'[50] Susan was able to report to her mother back in England that the 'Duchess is very well (& so am I of course) & just as fat as she was on the Guaso Nyero, which does her credit; she is wonderful what she can stand,' but she 'says she will never go near a waterless country again.'

Hélène was 'extremely annoyed' with the Governor and felt 'it really was a pretty low thing to do, to offer us this way of coming, definitely saying we might, & then to send & say we must come back, when we had just crossed the worst bit of desert, & were only 20 days from our destination.' After all, 'what could they expect but that we should go on all the same!' Instead, the government 'merely put their poor junior officials in a most unpleasant position, which is a shame, & are now calling them names, whereas except by hand cuffing us & shooting all our animals they were powerless to stop us.' The Camel Corps escort during the last fortnight 'were supposed to defend us against marauding tribes, but except at the few & far between waterholes there was never a tribesman to be seen & there they looked most peaceable.' Susan then had to translate a letter from Hélène to King George 'telling of our troubles with the Govt. She says he won't read it if she sends it in French.'[51]

After six days of rest at Jumbo, they headed down to Mombasa, 'rather a relief, for there was nothing to do there & nowhere to go.' Hélène then 'had a letter from Newland & Tarlton, saying that the Govt. had confiscated all her extra heads & giraffe skins, as not being on her license. So of course she is much annoyed, & is going up to Nairobi for 2 nights to tell them what she thinks of them.' Although 'of course she does give the ones she doesn't want to museums, but as she didn't tell them so beforehand strictly speaking they are within their rights, though maybe a bit rude to a foreign Princess.' Susan admitted 'privately I don't quite see why they should have ever given us free license—although I profited by it.'[52]

They rested for nearly a fortnight before leaving Bardera and making the final push along the route of the Djouba, boarding the steamer *Erutria* for the last leg of the trip into Nairobi, then Mogadiscio, and finally across the Red Sea to Aden. It was at Aden that Hélène learned that she was to be invited to one of the grandest events, the coronation of the new king and queen in London on 22 June. The readjustment to royal life came crashing through. Hélène and Susan arrived back in Naples on 21 May, and there was less than a month to prepare for London.[53]

Before London, there was a grand reunion of all the Italian royal family in Rome on 4 June for the dedication of the Vittoriano, the huge neoclassical monument to King Victor Emmanuel II. Overshadowing the ruins of imperial Rome and often derided as looking more like a wedding cake than anything else, the monument was intended to inspire confidence in the stability and unifying power of the Savoy dynasty. The boys were given four days of leave from school for the coronation in London, but by 'order of the King', they returned to Rome for the family occasion. Hélène, Emanuele Filiberto, and their sons were in the carriage procession leading to the dedication service, which was all part of the International

Exhibition in Rome, commemorating the fiftieth anniversary of unification. For the occasion, Hélène—'always most elegant'—was swathed in a black foulard with a multi-colour design and a large black hat plumed with white feathers.[54]

Later in June, Hélène and Emanuele went to London to attend the coronation of King George and Queen Mary. It was one of the great royal occasions—especially memorable for those who were not able to attend the postponed coronation of King Edward and Queen Alexandra nine years earlier. The 5.15 boat train, which pulled into Victoria Station on 19 June and was met by the Duke of Connaught, was crammed with royal visitors. With so many royalties in town, accommodations were restricted, and Hélène and Emanuele Filiberto stayed at Forbes House in Belgravia, the home of the Earl of Granard and his American wife Beatrice Mills.

Over the course of the next nine days—until Coronation Day itself—Hélène and Emanuele were guests at luncheons, dinners, and balls all over London—dinner at Buckingham Palace, luncheon in Grosvenor Square, dinner with the King and Queen at the Foreign Office. This was a grand build up to the even grander Coronation itself which took place on 22 June in Westminster Abbey.

During the days which followed the ceremony, the celebrations continued, and one night foreign embassies and legations across London celebrated dinners in honour of the royal guests with the Aostas at a dinner in the Italian embassy. After that was a grand ball which the Duchess of Westminster gave at Grosvenor House attended by Hélène and Emanuele Filiberto as well as most of the royal guests in England. Then, from Italy, came the news that Emanuele Filiberto's aunt, the Princess Clothilde Bonaparte, had died at Moncalieri on 25 June; they were required to go into court mourning and had to cancel most of their remaining engagements.

Emanuele then returned home to Italy, but Hélène remained in England to join Queen Alexandra at Sandringham, where a large house party gathered. On the 28th, Hélène arrived at the Norfolk estate along with other royals and courtiers for a short visit of two nights, and left on the 30th before the next wave of guests arrived. Hélène returned to London and then left for the Continent on 3 July. Shortly after her return, she wrote back to Lady Minnie Paget to tell her how important the visit to 'my dear native land' had been for her. 'You cannot imagine how happy I was to go to the Coronation and to be again in the place where I spent the most beautiful years of my life.' She was delighted 'to find old acquaintances unchanged in spirit ... or in body.'[55]

Hélène arrived safely back in Italy but soon had to join the extended family at the Church of Gran Madre di Dio in Turin for the second family funeral within a fortnight. Queen Maria Pia of Portugal—Emanuele Filiberto's aunt and Amélie's mother-in-law—had been in a decline since the Lisbon assassinations of her son and grandson and the Lisbon revolution, when she returned to her native Italy. Since then, she had been showing signs of senility—such as watering the flowers on her carpets—and had been too ill to attend the funeral of sister

Princess Clothilde on 28 June.[56] Maria Pia herself died on 5 July. Amélie arrived for her mother-in-law's funeral, as did the King and Queen of Italy along with other members of the family including Laetitia, having just buried her own mother at Superga less than a fortnight earlier. Also attending the funeral was Emanuele Filiberto's younger half-brother, Umberto, the Count of Salemi, who had recently embarrassed himself and the family while a student at the naval academy in Leghorn, where he was constantly in debt and a number of charges—

including kleptomania—were made against him.

9

1911–1914

I take a very great pleasure in nursing.
I may say I am in my element. I am a born nurse,
and I thank God I was endowed with the strength
necessary to carry out the work.[1]

On the morning of 29 September 1911, Luigi, the Duke of the Abruzzi, now a vice admiral in the Italian Navy, was in command of two squadrons of destroyers near the port of Preveza in the Epirus, now part of north-west Greece but then still under Ottoman rule. Italy had issued Turkey an ultimatum stating that the 'general exigencies of civilisation' obliged Italy to occupy the North African provinces of Tripolitania, Fezzan, and Cyrenaica and had given 2.00 p.m. on this date as a deadline to comply.[2] The deadline came and went without any response, although Turkish patrol boats gathered at the entrance to the Gulf of Arta. Aboard his flagship, the *Vettor Pisani*, Luigi had received orders that in case of attack, he was to make a threat of force without actually firing on enemy vessels. At 2.45 p.m., the first shots were fired when two Turkish torpedo boats cleared the harbour and headed for the Italian destroyers. A skirmish ensued with one of the Turkish crafts disabled, a destroyer damaged, and a third ship captured. Luigi saw an opportunity to capture the rest of the Turkish fleet in port but received orders from the minister of the navy to pull back his ships. Luigi sailed to Taranto to discuss the issue directly with the admiral, but was ordered to simply continue patrolling the area and not to engage without receiving precise orders to do so.[3] This was the first action in what would become a year-long conflict to wrest the provinces from Ottoman rule in an attempt to create a new overseas Italian empire in the area now known as Libya.

Meanwhile, much of the Italian fleet grouped off the coast of Tripoli and began shelling that city on 3 October, and the city was easily captured by 1,500 sailors. A further embarkation of 20,000 Italian troops began a week later, and Tobruk, Derna and Khoms were also quickly taken, while Tobruk and the interior proved more difficult.

Italy's identity as a nation was still developing, with a hope of 'reclaiming' lands formerly held by its predecessor states, such as the Venetian Empire along the Adriatic, which the nationalists called 'Unredeemed Italy' (*Italia rendenta*) as well as establishing an empire in Africa to compete with the other European Great Powers. To accomplish these goals alongside consolidation of a national sense on the main peninsula itself was a concern of generations. As early as the days of Mazzini, he was proclaiming that 'Ideas ripen quickly when nourished by the blood of martyrs.' Francesco Crispi echoed those feelings, saying that Italy must have its 'baptism of blood' to prove its status as a 'great nation.' Later, that sanguinary theme would be taken up again by Gabriele d'Annunzio, the poet-journalist whose extravagant and excessive life-style captured the Italian imagination.[4]

With the outbreak of war, Hélène found a new focus for her energies away from court life. She had some practical medical experience during her African trips, and now she formally trained in nursing duties at the Gesù e Maria Hospital in Naples under the supervision of the nursing matron, Miss Grace Baxter, who had been born in Florence to British parents and studied at Johns Hopkins School of Nursing in the United States. Hélène began going to classes dressed in an ordinary nurse's uniform and at the same hours as the other trainees. She told a reporter: 'I take a very great pleasure in nursing. I may say I am in my element. I am a born nurse, and I thank God I was endowed with the strength necessary to carry out the work.'[5]

Hélène accompanied a number of aristocratic Italian ladies under the direction of the Marchesa Costanza Guiccioli, who left Naples for Tripoli aboard the Red Cross steamer *Memfi*. Some fifty volunteers from the Red Cross embarked aboard the hospital ship including 24 nurses, including 'Dama infermiera n. 3,' as Hélène was to be known. King Victor Emmanuel was not pleased about Hélène or any of the women going, and he telegraphed the prime minister, Giovanni Giolitti, to find some way to impede their departure. Giolitti in his turn was annoyed and embarrassed about being asked to do something which he felt should have been settled in the family.[6] Telegrams went back and forth, but in the end, neither the King, nor the Duke of Aosta, nor the President of the Council proved any hindrance to Hélène. As with her trips to Africa, Hélène did what Hélène wanted to do.

The arrival of the Red Cross ladies in Tripoli was announced on 30 October. The correspondent for *La Stampa* bemoaned the fact that Hélène had been limited to a brief tour of the harbour area with the Duchess of Belgioioso in a Lancia and otherwise had been instructed not to leave the ship because of security concerns. 'Wouldn't it have been marvelous,' the reporter asked his readers, 'if the Duchess, a well-known horsewoman, could have appeared on horseback at the top of a dune and mirrored against a brilliant sky to inspire the troops just like a modern Joan of Arc?'[7] That was not to be, particularly considering the volatile situation then current in the country.

At the end of October, there had been a military reversal, and Turkish officers sent local tribesmen against Italian forces in Sciara Sciat. Some 307 Italians were killed or wounded, 294 went missing, two companies captured and 250 massacred in a Muslim cemetery. Three days later, in a second battle, 250 more Italians were killed or wounded, and later 'it was discovered that Italian captives had been mutilated, blinded, eviscerated, crucified, buried alive or torn to pieces.'[8] Reacting to this in three days of rage and panic, the Italian army summarily executed any Arab found with a knife or gun. Some thousand 'rebel' prisoners were summarily executed for what was called treason, although they had been defending their homeland, and several thousand more were deported. The Italian press kept this concealed from the national public, but the international press lambasted this action, which did Italy's world-wide reputation no good at all. Annexation of all of Libya by royal decree was announced on 5 November even though less than one per cent of the country was actually under Italian control.[9]

Aboard the *Memfi*, Hélène worked long hours, visiting every ward on the ship, and not really resting until the ship reached Sicily to transfer its wounded passenger and return to Libya for more. She wore the same uniform as the other nurses and resisted any attempt to give her preferential treatment. When the doctors suggested that her own health might suffer as a result of her exertions, she replied 'saying that to undergo the hardships of life, when she was performing what she considers a sacred duty, always resulted in her feeling better.'[10] Hélène left Naples again aboard the hospital ship *Memfi* on 8 December 1911 surrounded by her new nursing sisters from the Red Cross. Emanuele accompanied her on board to take leave, but it was her Zulu servant Pedro who sailed with her for Tripoli. Hélène was back in Naples briefly later in the month when Emanuele Filiberto was there as they both visited the war wounded, lunched with the Prince de Trabia at the Butera Palace, and then Emanuele accompanied Hélène back to the *Memfi* for another crossing. By the end of December, Hélène was in Tripoli, pleased that she didn't suffer from seasickness, and saying that 'God knows how much longer this war will last' and 'hoping that she would be able to remain a nurse for the duration.'[11]

On the political front, in Rome, there was an overwhelming vote in the Chamber of Deputies to support the Tripoli Annexation bill, and the next day—24 February 1912—the Senate unanimously concurred. Emanuele and his cousin the Duke of Genoa made a rare appearance in the Senate to give their personal support to the bill, and the press noted that the 'intervention in debate of two members of the Royal Family added not a little both to the solemnity of the occasion and to the warmth of the patriotic demonstration made by the Upper House.'[12]

On the battlefront, the war dragged on and did not prove so easy to win when it was realized that the Senoussi and other Bedouin tribes of the interior were not simply against the Ottomans, but against anything other than independence. Italy was not able to control more than the coastal strip, and the struggle with the desert peoples would continue for another twenty years until Mussolini's invasion in 1931. Meanwhile, Italy also struck at Turkey in the Aegean occupying the Dodecanese Islands and Rhodes in May 1912.

Hélène's health was not strong enough to continually make the journeys back and forth aboard the *Memfi,* and in February, she gave way to 'gentle insistence' of the Marchesa Guiccioli that she must miss one of the crossings. It was, in fact, rather more serious than the simple tiredness that was originally broadcast by the newspapers. After washing one of the wounded soldiers, Hélène suffered from an attack of influenza but a bit later insisted on going to attend a gravely wounded man when she suffered a chill and then developed a high fever. Still, when the hospital ship reached Naples, she still wanted to assist in the disembarkation of the wounded. Finally she went to Capodimonte and saw a doctor who diagnosed bronchial catarrh and prescribed several days of bed rest. The King and Queen came to Hélène's bedside to visit and to hear her many stories about the care of the wounded—and most importantly about her desire to return to service as soon as possible.

Hélène's wartime nursing efforts were recognized by the press, which called her an 'admirable sister of charity' and of 'great piety' for her work. D'Annunzio would extol her in *La Canzone d'Elena di Francia,* and *La Stampa* thought it ingenious that d'Annunzio compared the efforts of Hélène and her ancestor St Louis, who crossed the same sea with cross and spear. The newspapers reported:

> The duchess is the idol of the army and daily reports of her condition are sent to the soldiers in Tripoli. Just before she was stricken, a wounded lieutenant found a nurse bending over him. He was told that two bullets had been extracted from his arm and expressed a desire to keep them as souvenirs. The nurse departed and returning a few minutes later presented him with a heart-shaped, jeweled case containing the bullets. Surprised at the value of the case, the lieutenant asked an attendant to tell him the nurse's name. 'It was the Duchess of Aosta, a cousin of the king' was the reply.[13]

Another report in the *New York Times* told:

> The moment she goes on board she became the head nurse, or Signora Ellena. Her title of 'Royal Highness' is dropped and she ranks no higher than any other of the devoted nurses, except that she is at the head. This is by her own express desire, and, to tell the truth, it has caused considerable embarrassment, as many of the nurses who are accustomed to meeting her in society are taking the liberty of putting themselves on an equality with her. The doctors are perhaps the most forgetful. If one makes a slip and calls her 'Your Royal Highness' before a

patient who is not supposed to know her rank, the glance which he gets makes him murmur, 'She is a Princess right enough,' but he never makes the mistake again. The patients are for the most part too racked with pain to know what is going on, but some from Naples have recognized her, and their greatest boast on getting well is that they owe their lives to her. They tell many tales of her kindness in writing to their families in somewhat bad Italian, she being French, as they delight to point out, while many a poor mother or wife has owed the knowledge that her loved one was lost to the kind hand of the Princess.[14]

In June, both Hélène and Emanuele joined the King and Queen when they came to Naples to visit the war wounded in the military hospital. Later, Hélène with some of the nuns from the Daughters of Charity visited with hospitalized refugees who had been forced out of Turkish territories. However, she was still not well herself, and in July, Hélène went to Vichy for the water cure; Emanuele joined her there in August. Later in the month, Queen Mother Margherita's mother, the elderly Dowager Duchess of Genoa, died and Hélène was back in Turin to join the rest of the family for the funeral service at the Church of the Gran Madre di Dio, followed by burial in the family vault at the nearby Basilica of Superga. A few months later, the whole city was distressed to learn that the new tomb had been desecrated by thieves in search of jewels.

At the end of August, with fighting continuing in North Africa, a report came about Captain Maurizio Piscicelli, Hélène's long-time travelling companion. While escorting a caravan of reinforcements, he was gravely wounded in his arm and leg when his cavalry unit was attacked on 30 August 1912. Piscicelli made good use of his convalescence and expanded an article he had written for the Royal Geographical Society into a book, *Nella regione dei laghi equatoriali* (*In the region of the equitorial lakes*).

On 8 September 1912, Emanuele and Hélène took twelve-year-old Aimone to Livorno, the great naval centre on the Gulf of Genoa, near Pisa, and home of the naval academy. They stayed the night in the Palace Hotel, and the next day the boy, took his oral and written exams in mathematics, and one day later, oral exams in geography, history, and French. Having successfully completed his exams, Aimone formally entered the academy on the 12th, and then prepared for his first voyage of instruction.[15] Hélène, Emanuele Filiberto, and Amedeo all went back to Livorno on the 17th to bid farewell to Aimone as he set out aboard the *Flavio Gioia* bound first for Gaeta, then on to Tripoli, and then along the Tripolitan coast, where the war had all but finished.

Although it is said that Amedeo had also wanted to enter the navy, Aosta family tradition determined that the firstborn should go into the artillery. Therefore, a year later, on 21 October 1913, Amedeo entered the Nunziatella (*Reale Collegio Militare della Nunziatella di Napoli*), the military college at Naples, his name indicated in special red ink in the matriculation book to distinguish him from the other cadets marked in simple black ink.[16]

The Libyan War officially ended with Treaty of Ouchy on 11 November 1912, after the Ottoman Empire needed its troops in the Balkans to counter major revolts there, although only a small strip of coastline was actually occupied. Libya, the island of Rhodes, and the Dodecanese Islands were all ceded to Italy, but in Libya, there would be some fifteen more years of fighting before the interior of the country was subdued, as the bedouin continued to fight for independence from the Italians, just as they had against the Turks. Still, the Italian press treated it as a great victory and proclaimed that 'Italy in one gigantic step has smashed the restrictions of international law, has broken treaties, defied the rest of Europe, and revived the traditions of Caesar Borgia and Machiavelli.'[17]

Italian casualties from the war totalled 3,380 dead—including 1,948 who died of cholera and other diseases—plus 4,250 wounded. Turkish casualties are said to have been as high as 10,000 dead and wounded and another 10,000 dead from reprisals and executions. As part of their war efforts, the Italians conducted not only the first aerial reconnaissance flights but also the first aerial bombardments in history.[18]

In late November 1912, Hélène and Amedeo went to visit her sister Isabelle in North Africa. Isabelle and her family had moved to Morocco in 1909, first to Tangiers, and then after the death of her father-in-law, the Duc de Chartres, to Larache in 1910, with the Duc de Guise using the incognito of Monsieur Orliac. In February 1913, Hélène returned to Naples from Morocco 'in perfect health,' but within weeks was back in Egypt, where she stayed at Shepherd's Hotel in Cairo for about a fortnight before returning once again to Naples. While there, Hélène was elected a member of the Royal Geographical Society in London on the strength of her African journeys and writings.[19]

In the spring, Hélène went to visit her ailing mother at Villamanrique and spent a fortnight with her. While there she learned of the engagement of her twenty-three-year-old nephew Manoel of Portugal to the German Princess Augusta Victoria of Hohenzollern-Sigmaringen, part of the Roman Catholic branch of the Kaiser's dynasty. Known in the family as 'Mimi,' Augusta Victoria was the granddaughter of a Portuguese infanta and niece of the King of Romania, but it was not exactly a brilliant dynastic marriage—even for a deposed monarch—although an earlier King of Portugal (Pedro V) had married an earlier Princess of Hohenzollern (Stephanie) in 1858. With an ailing mother and now with the first of the younger generation preparing to marry, the generations had begun to shift, and forty-one year-old Hélène sighed to Amélie—'How old we are getting, my dear.'[20]

On 4 September 1913, Hélène and Emanuele both attended the wedding at Sigmaringen, the home of the bride, Princess Augusta Victoria. Amélie was there, of course, and Prince August Wilhelm of Prussia arrived to represent his father, the Kaiser. The youngest Orléans sister Louise came with her husband Carlos of Bourbon-Sicily, and various German, Italian, Portuguese, and French relatives came as well, but the special guest of honour was the Prince of Wales who escorted Hélène in the wedding procession. It was also the occasion of a reconciliation between Hélène and her younger brother Ferdinand Montpensier.[21]

Apparently, the sibling rift came about when Montpensier was suggested as a candidate for the throne of the newly created state of Albania. At some point, the Duke of Aosta went to Rome expressly to help in the cause, but Montpensier failed to thank him for his efforts, and Hélène was miffed and refused to have lunch with him the next time she was in Paris. In any event, the Albanian proposal came to naught, when Ferdinand declined saying 'There is no crown in the world that could attract me if, to obtain it, I must put into question two titles of which I am rightly proud, that of French citizen and that of French prince. I am resolved to decline any candidacy to the throne of Albania.' Another version of the story is that the Duc d'Orléans vetoed the suggestion leaving his brother without a real choice in the matter. Emanuele Filiberto's brother Luigi, the Duke of the Abruzzi, was also mentioned as a candidate for this soon-to-be-created throne, but that likewise came to nothing.[22] Instead, the offer was eventually made to a nephew of Queen Elisabeth of Romania, the German Prince Wilhelm von Wied, who reigned briefly from March to September 1914.

It was this autumn that saw the publication of *Viaggi in Africa*, the story of Hélène's first three trips to Africa.[23] Editions were published in both Italian and French. The preface is a reproduction in Hélène's distinctive handwriting that says that her notes were not originally intended for publication but that her sons had pleaded:

> Mother, make us a book with pictures we can look at, and read, and re-read. We will keep it as something close to our hearts. We will learn there the names of the mysterious countries that you have known. We dream of caravans, of travels in piroques, of endless deserts, of hunts and of battles. When we are big it will be our turn to go there.

The book was filled with 487 photographs, many of which Hélène took herself, and is a detailed retelling of the poetry and beauty, challenges and charms that she found in Africa.

In October, the *New York Times* reported the publication of *Viaggi in Africa* and that Hélène had left Naples on 19 October for Cairo to begin another trip. The paper reported that the Duchess would be returning to Central Africa for four or five months 'accompanied by her negro servant, Pedro, whom she brought to Italy on her return from her first trip', and that she had 'been commissioned to collect material for another book for publication next Autumn.'[24] In fact, this new journey was going to completely new destinations.

From Naples to Port Said and onwards to Suez, in October 1913, Hélène was aboard the P&O steamer *Arabia* in the Red Sea heading for new adventures in places she had not yet visited. Once again, Susan Hicks Beach accompanied her and kept a parallel account to the one which the Duchess compiled for publication, although Susan kept her record for family eyes only. From aboard the *Arabia*, Susan wrote:

> The Duchess & Capt Piscicelli turned up all right at Port Said, & she is looking rather well. We shan't know any definite plans till we get to Bombay & hear from the Viceroy, but meantime a man on board called Rhys Williams tells me that he has heard from India that our names are down on the official list of guests at the Viceroy's shoot in Mysore, Nov 9–15, which sounds all right. So we hope that is the case, it means tiger & lion shooting & an elephant keddah, which would be very interesting, even if little shooting came our ways ... There seems to be quite a possibility of having the Duke of Montpensier's yacht between Saigon & Batavia, but I am glad to say the duchess says she won't go in it if he is there.[25]

So, it seems that the sibling reconciliation of the previous month was still not complete or successful.

Their first major port of call was Bombay. In her book concerning this trip, *Vers le soleil qui se lève* (*Towards the Rising Sun*), Hélène attempted a more historical and anthropological approach for her readers than in her previous book. She began with an historical description of the Parsis and then goes into a description of a Parsi cremation site—complete with a photograph of burning bodies. They were accompanied by Malcolm Hailey, General Commissioner of Delhi, whose wife was the Roman Countess Andreina Balzani. When they reached Elephanta Island, Hélène commented that porter-carried chaises, of which she was happy to take advantage, were the result of 'civilization, but most of all, I think, the invasion of Cook's tourists' even if it seemed that the walk resembled that of crabs on the beach.[26] Once there, they were able to explore the temple complex of caves sacred to Hinduism and best known for the twenty-foot high image of the god Shiva—its faces representing the deity's three aspects as creator, destroyer and preserver.

When they got to Bombay itself, the size and beauty of the city that struck Hélène; however, immediately it was the smell, an ambient smell never before sensed, impregnated with spices, the scents of sandalwood mixed with curry that stayed with her. They did not stay there long and continued their journey by rail, joining a special train headed for Delhi with a Royal Commission looking into the Indian Public Services, which included Sir Valentine Chirol, a War Office Reporter, 'a man who had travelled everywhere, knew everything, had seen everything, spoke every language,' but who had the strange characteristic that when he spoke, not a single muscle of his face moved and he gave the impression that someone else was actually doing the talking. Also travelling with Sir Valentine as members of the commission were Sir Murray Hammick, the chairman Lord Islington, Ramsay MacDonald (the future prime minister) and 'Sir Charles,' chief of the Indian police—'an enormous man of extreme ugliness *mais sympathique*.'[27]

Unlike her African trips, Hélène was at first happy to accept official hospitality, including the viceroy's train carriage complete with a kitchen, salon, and bathroom. However, the saloon carriage proved 'exceedingly shaky & noisy' and Hélène decided she 'doesn't want more trains than she can help.' Likewise, she quickly tired of the official residences and began to insist on hotels 'for the continual official society is not what she wants at all.'[28] Even the travels plans were in flux, as the planned shoot in Assam was given up because it would cost too much, and Rajputana was struck off the itinerary as it was out of the way and would require yet more train travel.

They did visit the Taj Mahal at Agra and Lucknow where the ruins of the Residence reminded her of the uprising; here, she strained to hear echoes of the bagpipes of the Scottish forces relieving the siege. Next, they went on to Benares to photograph the ritual bathings in the Ganges and a fakir on a bed of nails. Then, it was on to a hunting camp at Nuisapaure near Benares, where Hélène's hope to bag a tiger was realized. The beaters went into the woods, and the sound of their voices and the beating of the *tam-tam* began getting closer. Then, everything went silent; they knew that there was a tiger in the woods, and not far. Then, she saw the animal:

> It arrived softly, softly, without any noise, stealthily. It seemed to walk on velvet and advance with caution. What a beautiful animal! I had all the leisure to admire it, but then it stopped. It stopped, raised its head, looked straight at me; a fine branch of bamboo stood between his gaze and mine. I held my breath. The tiger kept his head upright, still, its eyes fixed toward me; one moment more which seemed like an eternity. Evidently it was unsettled, but it didn't see me. It took up its slow walk with silent steps. With infinite care, I put my carbine to my shoulder. I aim and follow its every movement, but I must wait until it passes me. Finally it reaches the spot: a roar, only one, responds to my rifle shot; my ball broke its spine. Tonight we follow one of our old customs of the hunt in Africa and we dine on tiger filet. The flesh is white and delicate, like a turkey, but better. We eat this excellent dish under the reproachful eyes of the Indian servants who, evidently, attach to it a superstitious idea that we do not grasp. The tiger is a sacred animal. Perhaps they think that we have eaten the reincarnation of an ancestor.[29]

The Maharajah of Benares offered her the use of his palace, but Hélène again preferred private accommodations, 'thoroughly happy being in a hotel again, without society, it is much more peace for her, with no need to make conversation, or do more sight-seeing than she wants.' However, she was happy to take advantage of the Maharajah's automobiles for the next leg of their journey until exchanging the cars for elephants. When they reached Calcutta, Hélène moaned about their stay at the Grand Hotel 'in frightful, dirty rooms, dark and smelly.'[30]

Then from Madras, it was on to the island of Ceylon and Colombo. Although Hélène found Ceylon enchanting, she also saw its 'wound'—endless illnesses, unknown to Europeans, which ravaged the population. They met Professor Dr Aldo Castellani, an Italian expert in tropical diseases, best known at this time for having isolated the cause of sleeping sickness in East Africa. Castellani, who was now director of the Bacteriological Institute in Colombo, showed them specimens of various illnesses. The cases of elephantitis that they saw inspired two photos by Hélène which she later used in her book. Later, Dr Castellani would become well known to the Aostas, both in Italy during the First World War and in London, where he ran a private clinic for many years.[31]

The Governor, Sir Robert Chalmers, reported that Hélène's party—which included Susan Hicks Beach, Maurizio Piscicelli, '& two Christian Zulu boys in fezzes'—stayed at the King's Pavilion in Kandy and then 'made a motor-tour to Anuradhapura, Trincomalee & other places of interest.' They had met Chalmers in Colombo, and Susan, for one, wasn't sure what to make of him, thinking him 'an odd mixture; he has the appearance, manners & phrases of a pompous family butler, with a prodigious memory.' However, 'if one can get him started on his pet hobby—Sanskrit & Pali & Buddhism—he becomes really interesting & some of the tiresome manner disappear.'[32]

From Colombo, it was on to Kandy, which despite the low-hanging clouds and mist appeared to Hélène like a dreamland with its sacred lake reflecting the golden robes of the passing monks, and a small island with a terrible history of rebellious queens being placed there by kings to die of hunger. The charms of Kandy with its Temple of the Tooth, housing the dental relic of the Buddha himself, gave way to a tour deeper into the jungle forest of the interior. They visited the cave temples at Dambulla and the great mountain-top fortress of Sigirya. Hélène found the presence of the Buddha everywhere in Ceylon, even in the jungle, which had reclaimed so much of the early civilisation of the island. In her published account of this part of the journey, Hélène gives a history lesson on the ruins she sees, and then when they stop at the Rest House at Polonuaruwa with its melancholy lake, she returns to her poetic mode: 'The sun sets; the waters of the lake become dark, reflecting like a mirror the white fluffy clouds gilded by the last rays of the setting sun.' She called the ruins of the ancient capital Polonuaruwa, 'this tragic museum of lost grandeur', and she felt that the experience left her with 'a sadness which is great, vast, powerful, and which would never leave.'[33]

Intertwined with the Buddhist presence was a Hindu one, centred around

Trincomalee and the temple of Isurumuniya, although it was the Buddha Tree there that seemed most venerated. There were many photographic opportunities for Hélène throughout the island, and it was with regret that she departed:

> We leave Ceylon with its azure waves, buried ruins and hidden treasures, and its superb and melancholy jungle, almost frightening in its all-powerful sovereignty. We leave its temples with the giant Buddhas whose enigmatic smiles continue to obsess.... We leave these silences full of the mystery of nature.[34]

While Hélène was touring the East, a better-known lady was touring Italy. The portrait of the Mona Lisa (*La Giocanda*) had disappeared from the Louvre in Paris in August 1911. As one of the greatest art thefts in history, the news made headlines around the world—'*Inimaginable!*' cried *Le Matin*—and 'Parisians displayed a sense of personal grief, as if a well-loved celebrity had died' while the Louvre's security 'was regularly lampooned in songs, postcards, cabarets and variety shows.' Rewards were offered and detectives dispatched, but nothing substantial happened in the case until December 1913, when an art dealer in Florence received a letter from Vincenzo Peruggia, a labourer who claimed he had the Mona Lisa in his possession and wanted to sell it for half a million lire 'for expenses' and on the understanding that it would be displayed at the Uffizi and never returned to Paris. In Peruggia's hotel room, a few hundred yards from where it was originally painted, the Mona Lisa emerged out of a small wooden trunk from underneath a pair of shoes, a shirt, and some woolen underwear. The thief, who had been a workman at the Louvre, thought that the large number of Italian paintings there had been stolen by Napoléon and he claimed that he wanted to repatriate at least one. When asked why he chose the Mona Lisa, Peruggia responded 'because it seemed to me the most beautiful.'

Once confirmed as the original, the recovery of the painting made international headlines once again before it was sent on a triumphant tour beginning at the Uffizi in Florence, then to Rome—where both the King and Queen were among the spectators—before two final days at the Brera in Milan, 'where sixty thousand half-hysterical Italians surged' for a last glimpse before the painting was returned to Paris. Peruggia was tried in Florence, found guilty, and sentenced to a year and fifteen days in prison. However, public sentiment was behind him, and the sentence was reduced to seven and a half months. As he had spent nearly that time on remand, he was released from custody almost immediately.[35] The Mona Lisa then returned to Paris where it was acclaimed as joyously as it had been in Italy.

On 3 January, Hélène, Susan, Piscicelli, and Pedro approached Singapore, and from there onwards to Siam aboard the Koh-Si-Chang, a small boat with three cabins for its nine passengers. The rain and wind made the boat 'dance like the devil', and Hélène and Susan woke to find their belongings swimming in a foot of water. Once they reached the Ménam River, the boat stabilised after five days 'of continual rolling and pitching', and they found much of Siamese life concentrated around the canals and the river, which was full of boats.[36] At the mouth of the river, they found that the banks were 'low, & covered with trees palms, etc., & the water of the dirtiest, & full of the refuse of the whole of Siam, & not much wider than the Thames at Westminster.'[37]

Two days later, after having the Italian minister to dinner, he took them 'to a gambling hall down an alley off a main street.' The big open building was 'full of people of all sorts all desperately busy in little group round a mat gambling for small coins with dice.' If not in the little groups, they were 'in large groups round a shiny octagonal mat where a chinaman dealt out cowries in piles of 4, & they betted in ticals (=1/8) & notes as to the number there would be over, & 3 croupiers with long bamboos raked about the money.' The larger group had 'mostly women in that circle & none of them looked wealthy.'[38]

Hélène found Bangkok retained its exotic feeling despite the number of automobiles driving at full speed somehow managing not to knock people over—at least none that Hélène saw. She remarked on the fact that the current king, Rama VI, King Maha Vajiravudh—who had been educated at Sandhurst in England—was thirty-three years old and unmarried in a country where the king was expected to marry early and often, usually with a princess of the blood royal, sometimes his own sister.[39] Hélène commented that these obligatory marriages between close relations denigrated the race, with many princes and princess being tubercular; five in the previous year alone had died and been cremated. They visited the royal palace which she found furnished in European style, and in a 'better taste than our own royal palaces, which wouldn't be difficult.' To Hélène's taste, less European were 'barbaric' public executions, but that didn't stop her from photographing a beheading.[40] They met the king and his brother Prince Chakrabongse (who had been educated at the Corps des Pages in St Petersburg and was married to a Russian), and conversation went along easily in English. Prince Chakrabongse had represented the king at the wedding of Crown Prince Wilhelm of Germany in 1883, at the funeral of King Umberto in 1900, and later at the coronation of King George and Queen Mary in 1911, and could have known Hélène from any of those occasions, although she does not mention any previous meeting. The brothers were both sons of Rama V, King Chulalongkorn, who over the years had thirty-two wives and about eighty children, a number of whom were sent to study in Europe. Among these other sons was the Prince Chira who had studied in Copenhagen with Hélène's brother-in-law, Jean de Guise. The father of all these princes remains best known to westerners as the young prince taught by Anna Leonowens and immortalized through the book, play, and films of 'Anna and the King of Siam.'

Later, they were joined by the Queen Mother who expressed a longing to see Europe but admitted to sea sickness which made a visit unlikely. Hélène wrote that 'they served us a European tea on little tables, but the tables, the plates, everything was brought by people on their knees.' She continued, 'I haven't seen this type of serving since my visit to Leo XIII in 1890. There, at the Vatican, it was people in soutanes from the Middle Ages; here it is by yellow faces and in blue pagnes.'[41]

From Siam, they went along the Mekong River reaching Phnom-Penh on the 24th. Once there, an expected meeting with King Sisowath was cancelled because the king was 'tired.' 'Poor man,' Hélène wrote, 'he is sixty-four years old, is a great smoker of opium ... and has four hundred women to content,' but she would see him upon their return from Angkor Wat. They spent a full day exploring and photographing at the splendour of the Khmer Empire at Anghkor, and then it was already evening. Then, the 'shadows invade the architectual mass. The red rays light up the towers like an apotheosis in the form of tiaras, these towers of grey stone fade into the darkness of the dying day.' With all these wonders to see, Hélène worried that 'we are going too fast.' There were other marvelous ruins to see at Angkor Thom and Bayon and Prah-Khan before returning to Phnom-Penh. There, the King entertained them in the dance hall of the palace, a room without walls, the orchestra playing a 'bizarre music' made through lamentations and metallic cries, a music of Asia, powerful and fascinating. Then, the music turned melancholy, and the room filled with young dancers, some as young as seven or eight. Hélène found the dancers' gestures of feet and arms and long tapered fingers so unnatural that the dancers seemed have come directly out of the bas-reliefs of Angkor Wat.[42]

The travellers then moved on to Java and Batavia, where they found the canals stagnate, obstructed by volcanic ash from recent eruptions; that made old Batavia unhealthy, and so most of the Dutch settlers had moved to Weltevreden, several kilometres south. Hélène was struck to see blond, pink-skinned Dutch women and children on foot, in cars, and on bicycles under the murderous sun. She decided that it must be the survival of the fittest after so many years of colonization. Hélène was particularly impressed by the orchids and water lily pads in the botanical garden, the thermal springs, and a visit to the palace of the old sultan at Djokjakarta. The 'kraton' of the sultan contained nearly 15,000 people, almost all of them women because—aside from the harem and the dancers—the sultan was always served by women in his private apartments. From Batavia, it was on to Borneo, where Hélène visited and photographed the Dayaks, the headhunters with their collection of skulls hanging from the rafters of their halls. Hélène noted that the local custom among the Dayaks was to gather together the bones of family members once the flesh had disappeared and place them in a family tomb—'a practice still followed in the Escorial and in Naples.'[43]

Sheltered under a big black umbrella with her white pith helmet draped with a trailing veil, Hélène and her party were taken by boat (*en pirogue*) across a seemingly endless flooded plain, where she was able to photograph a herd of

buffalo swimming towards a distant shore. Then it was on to Célèbes, Makassar.
To explore the interior, the party gathered provisions for two weeks to a month,
hired a saronged, betel-chewing cook, and minimised their baggage to a mere
three carloads. The waterfall at Bantimoeroeng and a visit to the Queen of
Makassar at Ténété were among the highlights. The Queen arrived, surrounded
by servants, and dressed in a long *jaquette* of green satin over a red silk sarong. The
Queen—indeed simply the queen of the village of Ténété—spoke of her desire
to visit Europe but knew it was unlikely as the Dutch government gave her only
500 florins a month, about 1,000 francs.[44]

By 3 April, the travellers were at Thursday Island, New Guinea, where Hélène
found the little town more Japanese than Australian, one quarter entirely dominated by Japanese pearl fishers and shops. In the interior of New Guinea, Hélène
visited the Papuas, and photographed their elaborate feathered dance headdresses,
extending twice their body length.[45]

From the Dutch East Indies, they travelled to New Zealand and Australia,
but before leaving Macassar, all of them had to be re-vaccinated.[46] The travellers
arrived in Sydney on 13 April during race week when all the hotels were already
bursting with guests. An Italian man whom they had met on the boat came to
their rescue:

> [He] eventually secured us room at a lodging house, turning others out to do
> it, & it is very comfortable & much nicer than a hotel. It is a private hotel really,
> though it is apparently an insult to call it so. He also carried us off at once to the
> show & to see jumping, etc. & again yesterday.

Susan complained that 'the reporters here seem as bad as America, it was apparently telegraphed from Thursday Island that we were coming, so we were
besieged at Brisbane & again here.' The reporters appeared at the hotel daily, 'but
the landlady defeats them, but there are also demands for patronage for various
shops & charities—Sydney seems fearful keen on royalty, not having seen many.'[47]

Indeed the *Sunday Times* of Sydney ran an article about 'A Royal Visitor',
describing Hélène as being 'a tall, slight woman, with a carriage and appearance
very much like the Princesses of England. She has large beautiful eyes and pretty
brown hair, which she dresses in the style of Queen Alexandra.' 'In the evening, she
favours exquisite gowns, chiefly black, and always wears a bunch of flowers at her
waist. In the day-time she wears perfectly-cut coats and skirts which she matches
to hats of contrast.' One night during the week, she entertained the local Italian
consul for dinner and was 'seen wearing an exquisite pearl dog-collar; the gown in
this case being black, with an entire corsage embroidered in small diamants, very
simple in make and beautifully cut.' To 'use her own words', Australia was 'the
first white country of the East I have visited.' The Australian journalist reported

that the 'entire suite is simple in their tastes, but keen on seeing everything of interest. They go sight-seeing all day, but remain home in the evening', complaining about the cold in Sydney compared with the recently visited topics. Along with Susan Hicks Beach ('a tall, clever Englishwoman, an excellent linguist, with that reserved manner that marks many of the British nation') and the Marchese Piscicelli ('good looking with perfect polished manners'), their party included two boys from Tripoli, a Chinese maid (who speaks only French and her own language, and sleeps outside the Duchess's door at night) and two parrots, which Hélène had carried from one of the eastern islands.[48]

In April, they arrived in Wellington, New Zealand, and then went onwards to Raratonga in the Cook Islands; finally, by May, they reached Tahiti. At Papeete, their ship raised anchor and 'slowly advanced into the sun.'[49]

Crossing the Pacific, they arrived at San Francisco on 14 May 1914 aboard the RMS *Moana* from Sydney, Wellington, Rarotonga, and Papeete; the ship manifest listed: Countess della Cisterna, a lady with twelve pieces of luggage; S. Hicks Beach, a lady with six pieces of luggage; and 'Marquis Maurizio Piscecella', a farmer with ten pieces of luggage, all travelling first class; while 'P. Gioachino,' aged seventeen, a servant born in Africa, was travelling third class. The last portion of *Vers le soleil qui se lève* is the least personal, written in the third person, as it continues their travels, charting the leg of the journey more as a geography book than a travel journal.

After a brief stay at the Fairmount Hotel in San Francisco, they boarded a train for New Orleans and spent the next three days and nights travelling across Arizona and Texas; Susan picked up that part of the story.

> The first part was all cornfields & fruit farms—big open rolling country—it must be wonderful soil when sufficiently watered but by the middle of next day we were in desert, white sand & low scrub, & yellowish hills which we climbed to descend to 270 feet below the sea, clouds of dust, & hardly a living thing anywhere, only a very occasional little wayside station, with a shanty & a tank. Further on over more hills there was some attempt at grass, with almost an appearance of green in the hollows, & a certain number of horses & cattle, all looking rather poor, & an occasional hut or house each with a water wind-mill attached... Part of the time we were along the Mexican border, & there were little camps of U. S. A. soldiers, rather useful looking people—ready for offense or defence.

However, they found the form-filling bureaucracy annoying. Susan wrote: 'We don't think we like America, there are more fusses & more rules & regulations as to what one must or must not do than anywhere else, the emigration officers at the ports are endless, they are always wanting to know our full names ages addresses destinations occupations etc. etc.'[50]

At New Orleans, they boarded the SS *Cartago*, one of the United Fruit

Company's vessels, and proceeded to Colon in Panama to see the canal, just recently finished and allowing cargo barges through but not ships yet. They spent two days in Panama City, 'all buying Panama hats, although knowing that they were made in Ecuador and just as expensive as back in London'; on the day scheduled for visiting the canal itself, Hélène was tired and Susan went to investigate on her own. After Panama, they sailed to Jamaica, then on to Cuba, but Susan complained that they were unable to land:

> … owing to foolish quarantine regulations at Colon. The Americans & their regulations annoy us a good deal—we have just been asked to fill up forms for the fourth time with our names, ages, addresses, height, colour, nearest relations & all sorts of other details; it certainly is the least free country in the world.[51]

They eventually arrived in New York on 5 June aboard the *Santa Maria*.

On the last leg of their journey home, Hélène and Susan made a side visit to Boston to see Mrs Alice Meyer, the wife of the former minister to Italy and Russia. Mrs Meyer and her daughter Julia went to the station where, 'after the smoke had cleared the train pulled out there we saw an extremely tall thin lady in black, accompanied by a tall young woman but not so thin!' Mrs Meyer was quite as royalty-struck as ever, but she was instructed that the visit was a secret one, with Hélène travelling incognito as the Countess of Cisterna, and no one was to be told.[52]

Susan returned to England, leaving New York aboard the White Star liner *Adriatic* and arriving at Liverpool, 19 June 1914. Hélène, Piscicelli, and Pedro returned from New York via Madeira, Gibraltar, and Genoa, where they arrived aboard the steamer *Sassonia* on the 25th, and Hélène was met there by her sons. However, since the beginning of June, Emanuele Filiberto had been ill with a form of typhoid fever, and Hélène and the boys departed for Capodimonte immediately to be with him.

10

1914–1918

The War killed my soul[1]

Hélène had been back in Italy only a few days when the news came from Sarajevo of the assassination of the Austrian Archduke Franz Ferdinand and his wife Sophie, which set off a chain of events that would soon affect the whole world. For Hélène, it was also the murder of someone who had once been suggested as a possible husband for her. Franz Ferdinand had been considered as a match for Hélène as early as 1893, and that was certainly encouraged by some courtiers as well as her own family. Franz Ferdinand was quite wealthy as the heir of Francis V, Duke of Modena, who had died in 1875, and then he had become heir to the whole Hapsburg empire when his own father renounced his succession rights following the suicide of Crown Prince Rudolph in 1889. It is said that Franz Ferdinand's father, Archduke Carl Ludwig died in 1896 from 'too much piety.' Having gone on a pilgrimage to the Holy Lands, Carl Ludwig insisted on drinking from the River Jordan, caught dysentery, and died the same spring.[2]

Hélène and Franz Ferdinand had met several times including when both attended a family luncheon at Marlborough House during the London summer social season of 1894, and then Hélène went to Vienna that autumn to visit Aunt Clémentine, and the newspaper rumours of an engagement escalated. 'Maybe' was the best result they could extract from the Archduke, but before any progress could be gained, he went to a ball in Prague and there met the Countess Sophie Chotek, a lady-in-waiting to the Archduchess Isabella. Although they were not allowed to marry until 1900—and then only morganatically—it seems that Franz Ferdinand never considered another bride after he met Sophie.

The Sarajevo killings were the work of the local 'Young Bosnians' backed by the Serb terrorist group The Black Hand, but they followed a string of similar royal assassinations staged by anarchists—those of the Empress Elizabeth in 1898,

King Umberto in 1900, and Grand Duke Serge of Russia in 1905—and others by nationalist assassins, King Alexander and Queen Draga of Serbia in 1903 and most recently Queen Alexandra's brother King George of the Hellenes in 1913.

As the Hapsburg court buried their heir and official Court mourning continued, the long term consequences of Franz Ferdinand's death were not yet evident, and most of Europe continued its usual summer routines. Meanwhile, Emanuele Filiberto's physical condition worsened; he suffered a relapse in mid-July. His temperature reached 103.6 F (39.8 C), his pulse varied between 112 and 120, plus there was abdominal pain, kidney trouble, and a heart weakness. At one point, Emanuele's condition was so severe that a rumour of his death swept through Naples, but that was quickly denied. The furniture was removed from his room and disinfected. Hélène spent the nights at his bedside. As always, she was at her most impressive in times of crisis. Hélène received visits from Giuseppe Cardinal Prisco and the Prefect of Naples; although thousands gathered to get some news, most visitors were kept at the gate for fear of infection—only the close family was allowed to visit. Amedeo and Aimone were assured by their father that he was doing better. The Duke of the Abruzzi and Count of Turin came to be with their brother. Their cousin, the Portuguese Duke of Oporto, who was living in the Royal Palace in Naples, was allowed a visit. The King phoned from Rome, made arrangements for half-hourly phone updates, and then drove to Capodimonte for a two-hour visit. Finally, Abbot Onorato Winspeare of the Monte Cassino Abbey came to offer a votive mass in the palace chapel. After that, the crisis passed, but the recovery was a slow one.

While Emanuele was recovering, the fever of war spread throughout Europe. On 23 July, Austria issued its ultimatum to Serbia, and five days later war was declared. As a member of the Triple Alliance with Austria and Germany, Italy began to prepare for deployment of its troops against France. However, the Italian government declared neutrality on 3 August without consulting either the King or the new Chief of Staff, General Count Luigi Cadorna, a man with no battlefield experience who had only taken up office on 27 July following the sudden death of the popular Alberto Pollio. Cadorna went to the Prime Minister, Antonio Salandra, who confirmed that war with France was no longer part of the plan. 'So what should I do?' he asked. Salandra said nothing. 'Prepare for war against Austria?' suggested the general. 'That's right,' the prime minister responded, and a massive yet surreptitious redeployment of troops to the northeast began.[3]

Germany declared war on Russia on 1 August, invaded France on the 2nd, and Belgium on the 3rd. On the 4th, Great Britain declared war against Germany, and then against Austria-Hungary on the 12th. The dominoes of Bismarck-inspired treaty pacts, which were originally intended to ensure peace, fell heavily across Europe, as the recent arms race throughout the continent eventuated in what would become the bloodiest war known to history.

As the early months of warfare began in western Europe, the devastation was horrendous, far worse than the most pessimistic had imagined. Tens of thousands were killed. On 22 August in the Battle of the Frontiers, fought in Alsace-Lorraine, the French Army alone lost 27,000 men killed plus wounded and missing—these casualty numbers exceeded those of any other nation in a single day throughout the entire war, worse even than the British on the first day of the Battle of the Somme. Among the dead were General Foch's only son and his son-in-law, both captains in the French Army. Civilians suffered terribly as the German and Austrian armies developed a paranoia about *franc-tireurs*, civilian snipers, and indiscriminately shot men, women and children, burning towns and villages to the ground in revenge for sniper attacks. Civilian deaths increased when Germany sent a Zeppelin to bomb the city of Liège, the first instance of a bombing raid on a European city, although the Italians themselves had pioneered that terror in Africa. During the course of the war, Serbia would suffer the highest proportional number of deaths, losing one in six of its entire population, some three-quarters of a million people. While both sides exaggerated atrocities for propaganda purposes, the case against German and Austrian troops is well documented, sometimes by their own armies, which would publish photographs of public civilian executions in a vain attempt to stop the resistance. Later in the year, when two members of the Garibaldi family were killed with the French army in December, their funeral drew more than 300,000 mourners in Rome.[4] During this first year of the fighting in Europe, France bled, Germany bled, Britain bled, Russia bled, Austria bled, Serbia bled, and Italy waited.

While the rest of Europe was fighting, the Aosta family was still at rest and recuperation following Emanuele's illness. During August and into September, they stayed at Ravello on the Amalfi coast. Robert Proctor, an artist from New Zealand, happened to be staying at the same hotel and regularly shared meals with the family over the course of three weeks. At their meals, Proctor reported that 'their table life was simple and unrestrained' although the two boys dressed in military dress, and they all enjoyed 'some pleasant conversations.' In his anglo-centric way, he considered it a great compliment that he thought the boys were 'more like young Englishmen than Italians' and Hélène herself was 'to all appearances an English lady.' Hélène sat for Proctor for a portrait on the balcony in the sunlight, and during the six 'free-and-easy sittings,' Hélène had the boys alternatively read aloud to her from Jerome K. Jerome's book *Three Men in a Boat*, and she regularly stopped the narrative to talk about the Thames side places mentioned in the book and which she remembered from her youth.[5]

During this period of neutrality, Hélène finished her work on *Towards the Rising Sun*, her trip around the world, signing off the preface in October and dedicating the new book to her travelling companions but asking them not to read it—'since your eyes have already seen the things of which I speak and words will spoil the images that they have retained.' It was published by Francesco Viassone in Ivrea, but unlike her earlier book on African travels, this one was published only in French, although it proved popular enough to achieve a second edition in 1918. *Towards the Rising Sun* told the story of her journey through the East and Far East, and was full of over five hundred illustrations, many of them from Hélène's own camera.

Meanwhile, the rest of the Hélène's family sought to identify with the Entente cause. Her older brother, Philippe, duc d'Orléans, had separated from his wife in 1911, and Mariska returned to her native Hungary, where she remained throughout the war, the one member of the close family living in a country of the Central Powers. Philippe sold his Wood Norton estate in 1912 and purchased a château at Woluwé-Saint-Pierre outside Brussels where he lived until returning to London during the German occupation of Belgium. He was anxious to join the fighting himself and was said to be 'looking forward to joining the campaign with the Italian army' in June 1915 when knocked over by a motorcar in London, injuring his hip. Later in the war, Philippe wrote directly to King George 'rely[ing] on the old and faithful friendship which unites us' to ask that Philippe be allowed to take up a place with his old regiment, the King's Royal Rifles, but this was politely declined 'for political reasons.'[6] Then, he offered himself for military service with the American government, but that suggestion was also politely declined.

Their younger brother, Ferdinand Montpensier, was travelling in Asia and found himself in the port of Yokohama when the war broke out. He went to the French consul there and made an offer of his services to France, which was not surprisingly turned down. However, Montpensier then offered the British Admiralty the use of his yacht, the *Mekong*, with a 1,500-mile range of wireless telegraphy plus four one-pounders and an automatic 7-mm gun, an offer which was 'gratefully accepted.' Ferdinand returned to Europe, vainly attempted to get into the British army, and eventually had to content himself with running a cinema for soldiers in the hospital his mother opened in the Château de Randan.[7]

Queen Amélie volunteered with the English Red Cross; through them, she did some hospital visiting in Paris in that first autumn of the war, and later back in England at the hospital in Wandsworth. Their sister Isabelle and her family moved from Morocco to live with the Comtesse de Paris at Randan, where the Duc de Guise volunteered with the Red Cross; he too had been declined for military service by both the French and British governments. Guise served first as an ambulance driver in Normandy and later as a simple stretcher-bearer in the trenches, for which he was eventually awarded the Croix de Guerre.[8]

Italy for the moment retained its neutral status as a political tool to barter between the Central Powers and the Entente to see which would offer it the most post-war territory. The Trentino (the Tyrol to the Austrians), the Alto Adige, Trieste, and the Dalmatian coast were all claimed by Italy as part of its territorial ambitions—*Italia irredenta*, 'unredeemed Italy,' as it was called. This political ideology, which grew into a full-blown theology under the Fascists, had been part of the motivation of the *risorgimento*, a first step in reclaiming the concept of Italian pre-eminence in the world, a new Roman Empire. The irredentists became among the loudest voices in any political debate, especially those surrounding foreign policy. The immediate goal became the Adriatic coastline, formerly part of the Venetian empire but now under Austrian control.

While the more established countries of Europe sought overseas territories, especially in Africa, this concept of historically inspired contiguous expansion was a theme also common to many of the newer nations which had sprung out of the decaying Ottoman Empire. Greece had successfully developed its own 'Great Idea' (*Megali Idea*) and doubled its territory after the First Balkan War in 1912 and would add more after the First World War. Romania and Bulgaria likewise fought for the 'greater' territories which they remembered nostalgically from the Middle Ages, while Yugoslavia would eventually develop as a unified Slav state under the aegis of Serbia. Diplomatic and expansionist considerations aside, Italy was simply not prepared for war in 1914. Its army was under-manned, under-armed, under-supplied, and still struggling in North Africa.[9]

The new year of 1915 began with the Allied offensive in Artois and Champagne, and the first German Zeppelin attacks on England. For Italy, nature once again took the upper hand, demonstrating its unique power in an earthquake which hit Avezzano on the morning of 13 January. This small town in the Abruzzi region, about a hundred kilometres east of Rome, was virtually destroyed and its population almost entirely wiped out in the one minute that the earth shook. Some 30,000 across the region were killed, and damage occurred as far away as Rome itself. It was one of the worst earthquakes ever to strike Italy. Hélène went immediately to the Red Cross Hospital at Sant'Egidio to visit the injured in hospital and, jointly with her husband and brothers-in-law, donated 15,000 lire to the Roman women's committee endeavoring to clothe those affected by the disaster. While she was visiting the *Cassa nazionale infortuni* in Via Cavour, Rome, four badly wounded people were brought in from Avezzano, and Hélène herself was among those offering immediate care before they could be relocated in nearby hospitals.

During the winter, Dr Aldo Castellani, recently returned from Ceylon, became a regular visitor at Capodimonte, as he and the whole country began to prepare for war. He described dining at the palace. 'One walked through a long sequence of spacious state apartments filled with masterpieces of painting and sculpture before reaching the drawing-room where the Duke and Duchess received their guests.' After that, 'one passed through another series of salons to the dining-room, which was brilliantly lit with Murano crystal candelabra and chandelier (the dim lighting of dining-rooms had not yet come into fashion).' At dinner, they were 'served by gigantic footmen in gorgeous uniforms and white perukes—but only on official occasions, as normally the duke and duchess lived a simple life.' An admirer of the Duchess, Castellani wrote that she 'was tall and slim, with refined features and a delicate profile; she had blonde hair, blue eyes, and a rosy complexion.' She was 'erect and regal in appearance' and 'had an indescribable grace of deportment.' For Castellani, 'to watch her walking was a pleasure to the eye: Virgil's verse came spontaneously to mind—*Vera incessu patuit dea*—the true goddess was revealed in her step.'[10] The whole Aosta family would mature to be quite tall—Hélène herself at 1.85 m, Aimone would reach 1.90 m, and Amedeo 1.99 m—while the King and Queen were 1.54 m and 1.74 m respectively.[11]

Although the rest of the world calls this conflict the First World War, the Great War, or the '14-'18 War, in Italy it is known as the '15-'18 War or more honestly, the Italo-Austrian War (Italy did not declare war against Germany until the 28 August 1916). It was only in 1915, after the bloodbaths of the western front that Italy finally decided that its territorial ambitions would best be served by offi- cially joining the Triple Entente of Britain, France, and Russia, which they did by having the Italian ambassador, Marchese Guglielmo Imperiali, sign the Treaty of London on 26 April on behalf of the government. This was done secretly, but the next day, the French press was already reporting it. However, it was not until 4 May that Italy finally repudiated the Triple Alliance treaty and so, technically, between those two dates 'Italy found herself simultaneously allied to both sides in the war, a circumstance that caused much embarrassment when it became generally known.' Foreign Minister Sidney Sonnino attributed that 'to the king's express wish.'[12]

While the King had extensive powers over both domestic and foreign issues, even to the point of being able to declare war without consulting Parliament, Victor Emmanuel was not the sort of man to attempt such forceful actions. During this time, it is said that the King more than once hinted at abdication in favour of Emanuele Filiberto 'who had none of his own disinclination for the business of monarchy.' Such rumours had existed for years and would continue for decades into the future, their substance waxing and waning over the years.

However, Prime Minister Antonio Salandra and foreign minister Sonnino were of a different character. It was the Prime Minister who committed Italy to fight. 'With the King's support, he had carried out a *coup d'état* in all but name.' The recall of Parliament was delayed from the 12th to the 20th, and then when Parliament did finally meet to vote for war, the deputies rose to their feet and joined with the spectators in the galleries to sing the National Anthem.[13]

Things changed very quickly in May. General mobilization of the army began on 22 May. On the 23rd, Italy declared war on Austria-Hungary. By royal decree, the King appointed his sixty-one-year-old uncle Tommaso, Duke of Genoa, as lieutenant general, or regent, of the kingdom while Victor Emmanuel himself went to the front line as commander-in-chief, which somewhat boosted his per- sonal popularity and from where he issued a proclamation that Italy would fight 'for the defence of civilisation and the liberation of oppressed peoples.'[14] Branding the war as one of Italian liberation increased the pro-war frenzy, at least among the political classes. Two days after the declaration of war, Emanuele Filiberto replaced General Luigi Zuccari and took command of the Third Army, having already left for the front on the 23rd. All the Aosta brothers went to war. The Count of Turin became inspector general of the cavalry, the Duke of the Abruzzi was named as chief of the joint naval forces in the Adriatic, and the young Count of Salemi was a captain in the infantry.

Among those assigned to the headquarters of the Third Army was the poet and increasingly popular public figure Gabriele d'Annunzio, who had returned from five years of debt-induced exile in France to whip up proactive fervour for the war through his speeches across the country. Now, he took the opportunity to revive his commission as lieutenant from his youth. Although at age fifty-two he must have been the oldest lieutenant in the army, a roving commission gave him access along the entire front, a role which eventually expanded to enable him to be an aviator, an infantryman, a sailor and an organizer of expeditions. He became the country's most prominent polemicist against anything which did not promote a bigger, stronger Italy in actions that later won for him the epithet of being John the Baptist to the Fascist movement. His image as a war hero only increased when he was co-piloting a flying boat which was attacked by Austrian fighter aircraft. They were forced to make an emergency landing in the sea, during which d'Annunzio sustained head injuries and lost the sight in his right eye. It was after one of his flying expedition that d'Annunzio coined a new battle cry for the Italian army, a cry he claimed was based upon those of the Roman empire. '*Eia! eia! eia! alalà*'. On the eve of the 11th Battle of the Isonzo, he sent a copy of it to Emanuele Filiberto, who returned his deep thanks saying it became particularly dear to the Brescia Brigade and signing off his response as 'E. F. di Savoia called "The Taciturn."'[15] The relationship that the poet and the soldier developed during the war was a warm one, which developed a new importance in the post-war period.

Along the northern border, the front of Italy's war with Austria stretched from the Piave River in the Veneto, through Friuli to the Carso Plateau approaching Trieste on the Adriatic. Although officially now part of the Entente, Italy's war was essentially a simultaneous war against Austria only with the goal of gaining supremacy in the Adriatic. War against Germany was not declared for another fourteen months.[16]

The first month of the war brought unexpectedly high casualties to Italy— between eleven and twenty thousand in the first weeks alone—and the army's medical service was desperately bad. Hélène and Emanuele Filiberto turned over the Palazzo della Cisterna in Turin to the Red Cross as a hospital, and Hélène turned her attention to nursing. She had already begun preparing for the eventuality of war back in April when she called her *Dama di Palazzo* Anna Torrigiani to the palace to start nursing and hospital planning and asked Anna to accompany her on the inspection tours which would be starting.[17]

Throughout the war, Hélène kept a diary, but unlike her travel books which were written for general consumption, the war diary was a more personal aide-memoire, and entries often consisted simply of the name of a hospital visited. However, it too was eventually published in 1930 as *Accanto Agli Eroi* (*Alongside the Heroes*), although the purpose of that publication was different as demonstrated by the preface which was written by Benito Mussolini. Though there was much foreshadowing of the Fascist era during the First World War, it still lay in the future and the immediate issues concerned the often very bloody warfare in which Italy now found itself. On 26 April 1915, Hélène was appointed as the Inspector General of the Volunteer Nurses of the Italian Red Cross—which gave her the rank of major general in the Italian army[18]—and as such was tireless in her visits to the front, to hospitals. From the beginning, she completely reorganized the nursing service and required practical training for the nurses. 'And this was very necessary,' Dr Castellani reported:

> For at the beginning of the First World War the Red Cross nurses in Italy were called *Dame* (Ladies), and practically all of them were of the nobility—a plethora of duchesses, marchionesses, countesses, and baronesses. They were beautifully attired, charming and glamorous in their becoming uniforms—sky blue in winter, white in summer, with a Red Cross on the blouse. Their intentions were of the best, but their practical knowledge rudimentary. Their routine ward work consisted chiefly of wiping the feverish brows of the patients, and patting their foreheads very soothingly.[19]

The first entry in Hélène's published diary dates from 4 May 1915 in the Celio Military Hospital in Rome. The initial words were prosaic:

> The nurses provide regular service in the two departments: surgery and medicine. They follow the doctor's view, take note of the requirements, running closely. Order—discipline—good teaching—well-made dressings. The practical exercises will last from November to June, the nurse can then between the Hospital and Dispensary, take the time to become a nurse not in name only, but in fact.[20]

Although her entries were extremely brief, mere notes—Mussolini would later call them 'telegraphic' in his preface to the published version—their staccato nature often emphasized order and discipline, and also track her extraordinary energy and rapid movements throughout the hospitals of the kingdom. The highest complement that she could pay to nurses was that they were calm and serene. In that first month alone, she went from Rome to Milan, Bergamo, Turin, Alessandria, Genoa, Spezia, Livorno, Pisa, Naples, Venice, Padua, Treviso, Belluno, and Udine. Fortunately, Anna Torrigiani also kept a diary which was also later published and which contains generally much fuller entries.[21] As Anna and her husband Carlo—known within the ducal family as Nannia and Carluccio—were with Hélène through much of the war, Anna's account fills out much of the outline provided by the Duchess.

On 23 May, the same day that full mobilization was declared, Hélène received a telegram from Emanuele Filiberto that he had been slightly injured in a car accident, having only left Naples the previous day for a 'destination unknown.' Although Hélène's first instinct was to go to him immediately, a second telegram from one of his colleagues calmed her; she and the Torrigianis left that night for Rome en route for Venice. From Bologna northwards, the trains were full of troops.[22]

The young princes caught up with them at Milan on 1 June. Amedeo, who had not yet reached his seventeenth birthday, had volunteered with the mounted battery of the artillery regiment, and sent to his father the pen with which he signed his act of enlistment, a memento which Emanuele Filiberto kept for the rest of his life.[23] When Amedeo arrived in uniform for the first time, Anna Torrigiani declared him 'splendido.' Hélène and the Torrigianis watched the regiment load their horses onto a train in preparation for departure for the front, Amedeo handling his own mount. When the train pulled out of the station at 8.00 p.m. that night, Amedeo was 'cheerful and serene.' Ten days later, fifteen-year-old Aimone left for Livorno and service as a midshipman in the Navy.[24]

From the very beginning of the war, Hélène saw the inadequacies of the health care system, which would be stretched even further as casualties poured in. In June, she made her first visit to Bologna since the declaration of war and found conditions inconsistent. Nursing students at the Ospedale Asilo Infantile were all on the crash course and animated by good will, but lacked discipline even in their uniforms. While the Red Cross Night Clinic was 'perfect and wonderful,' clean and with good food, at the Asilo De Amicis there were 400 patients crammed like sardines in boxes. Disinfectants were spread, but they forgot to clean. There were no bathrooms, little food, and missing linens and pillows. At the Ospedale Sanità Militare, she found beds stacked on top of each other, food and clothing scattered on the floor, and no chairs or tables.[25] Establishing higher standards and better conditions in the hospitals along Red Cross lines became one of Hélène's main aims in the coming years.

The wider Royal Family all became part of the war effort. The men were all in uniform, and the women concentrated on the relief aspects. A committee, including Queen Elena, Queen Mother Margherita, and Princess Jolanda, began organizing relief work to provide extra clothing and 'all other comforts' for the troops to take to the field of battle. Those efforts centred in the Pitti Palace in Florence. In Rome, the Queen Mother established a hospital in the Palazzo Margherita, while Queen Elena established a 200-bed hospital at the Quirinale under the Red Cross with the Princess di Paternò as inspector. When she visited, Hélène found it a wonderful environment and particularly commented on the fact that the recuperating soldiers could pass their days in the palace gardens.[26]

Right from the beginning of the war, General Cadorna ordered the Second and Third Army to the Isonzo River with the goal of capturing Monte Nero,

Sleme and Mrzli Vrh to the east, three objectives which the Italians would not reach until 1916 and which they would never exceed. Due to leaks in military intelligence and because the Austrian army was simply better prepared, when Italian armies reached the Isonzo, they found the Carso plateau overlooking the river already fully fortified with Austrian troops in trenches protected by three belts of barbed wire and a mine zone five metres wide.[27]

In the first Battle of the Isonzo in July, the Duke of Aosta commanded the Third Army, and all the Italian troops suffered heavy losses against the Austrian gun emplacements on Mount Cosich and the surrounding hills. The battle cry 'Savoia' sounded through the valleys, but the Austrian machine gun fire was the more effective. Of the 250,000 men who went into battle that day, there were 2,000 dead, 11,500 wounded, and 1,500 missing. Likewise, the second Battle of the Isonzo later in the same month gained little but increasing numbers of casualties—42,000 dead, wounded, and missing. As in the first battle, a response to Emanuele Filiberto's call for reinforcements came too late to be of any assistance. In addition, disease spread among the troops and around 21,000 contracted cholera; 4,300 of them died.[28] There would eventually be twelve battles of the Isonzo between the Italian and Austrian armies, starting in 1915 and culminating with the battle better known as Caporetto in October and November 1917. The Austrian army continued entrenched atop the Carso escarpment and firing down upon the Italian army below. From a tactical point of view, the situation seemed hopeless, but General Cadorna kept up the attacks.

In May 1915, d'Annunzio told a crowd in Rome that Italian soldiers would soon turn the Isonzo red with barbarian blood. The Austrian army did indeed suffer extraordinarily high losses during the first months of the war. In August 1914, their standing army had consisted of some 450,000 men. By 1915, the number of casualties nearly equaled that. As a result, the official history of the army says that the old professional army 'died in 1914' and was replaced by a 'conscript and militia army.' However, Italian total losses were even higher, and only some eight thousand of the five and a half million Italians who fought in the war were volunteers, while the rest were conscripts.[29]

Hélène's own nursing role was made very public in July, when the illustrated supplement of *Le Petit Journal* offered a full-page illustration of a battlefield incident. A wounded Austrian officer, laying on a stretcher, pulled out a dagger and attempted to stab Hélène, who was bending over him helping him onto a stretcher.[30] A later re-telling of the story said that it occurred when she bent over to offer him a drink of water. According to this version, the Austrian pulled the knife out of his tunic and raised his arm, which an Italian officer seized and then pulled out his revolver and executed the man.[31]

Until August 1915, women nurses were forbidden to serve at the front lines in Italy.[32] Once the ban was lifted, Hélène was among those moving into the war-zone. Among her visits that autumn, one that particularly impressed her was to the

British Red Cross hospital established at Villa Trento, between Udine and Gorizia. At this point, it was a fifty-bed hospital with plans to expand it to 200 beds, but already had twenty-six ambulances as part of their services. Hélène noted with her usual note of praise, 'everything was very well organized.'[33] However, just as Hélène was impressed with the work of the British Red Cross, the hospital's director (George Treveleyan) was impressed with her. He wrote about the 'important development' of trained nurses:

[This] took place under the fostering case of the Duchess of Aosta, the head of the Italian nurses. She was a frequent visitor at Villa Trento, a good friend to us English, and, as we are proud to remember, an admirer of our hospital. It has been a great good fortune for this difficult early period of female nursing in Italy, and for the sick and wounded during the war, that the Duchess of Aosta was a born leader. She established the position of female nurses at the front against all old-fashioned critics. Not only does she possess the distinctively 'royal' qualities in an attractive form, but she is a lady of great wisdom in management and of tireless energy and devotion. In difficult times, both in the Retreat and very notably during the equally rapid and longer advance in November 1918, when the excellent machinery of the Italian field hospitals was thrown out of gear by the pace, the Duchess was to the fore where things were worst, carrying with her a group of her best nurses to plant down where they were most shockingly needed, and herself going for an incredible number of hours without food or rest.[34]

Hélène continued her hospital work, and the western press began to take note of it. The *New York Times* and *Washington Post* both wrote of her 'competent and unwearying work as an inspector since the beginning of the war the satisfactory working of the Italian hospital system is in great measure attributed.' It also reported from Udine that Hélène, accompanied by Aimone, had gone to the front to visit Emanuele Filiberto and Amedeo had recently has been promoted to the rank of corporal 'for efficiency in work with the artillery.'[35]

An artillery officer's private letter, which was published in the international press, described Amedeo:

A simple soldier, following the regiments, sleeping on straw, as his comrades do, and eating their rations. In fact, he is treated without any preference. He has made himself much beloved by his high spirits and his manner toward the soldiers. On various occasions he has shown great courage. He is always first to volunteer for dangerous work, is tireless, and ever ready to help a comrade in distress.[36]

No day was routine or predictable on the front lines, with each bringing its own challenges and sorrows. On 19 November, Anna Torrigiani records that they left in the morning to go to Hospital 99 in Visco, where they knew that Alberto Ricasoli had died the day before, just one hour before his mother was able to reach him. There, they found his mother, the Baronessa Giuliana, still strong and resilient even in her great sorrow, and Hélène accompanied her to the church for the final absolution. From there, Hélène and Anna went on to Red Cross Hospital number four at Manzano to deliver clothing for soldiers returning from the front line. There, they found the officers and two amputees they visited earlier doing better. Next, they went on to the English Hospital at Villa Trento, where a new case of cholera had been isolated, and finally to Red Cross Hospital fourteen at Soleschiano to leave more clothing with the nurses, who seemed very tired with so much work.[37]

The Red Cross set up hospitals behind the lines wherever room was available, and Hélène visited as many as she could—a thirty-bed hospital in a private villa on the lakes at Garda, in a seminary at Verona, or in a school at Viareggio. By the end of December, she was back in Naples visiting wounded prisoners in the military hospital and then to Rome where she visited the Red Cross hospital in the Quirinale Palace with Queen Elena. In the New Year, Hélène attended a lecture by Professor Pascale at the Surgical Clinic in Naples on the theory and practice of frozen feet, and then attended the amputation of the right foot and the toes on the left foot of 'a poor sergeant.'[38]

Day after day, Hélène went from hospital to hospital around the country. It was not unusual for her to visit as many as five or six on a single day. In March, Hélène visited the Red Cross hospital in Porto Maurizio, and she recorded that among the many nurses there was Emily Tyler Carow, a sister-in-law of the American former President Theodore Roosevelt. Miss Carow had been living in Italy since about the turn of the century, and like many other society ladies, turned to nursing activities during the war.[39]

Hélène's long-time travelling companion Susan Hicks Beach and her sister Tora worked on a Red Cross coffee stall in Rouen during the war. Late in 1915, Tora left for Egypt with her sister-in-law so that Marjorie could spend Christmas with her husband Michael, Viscount Quenington, Susan and Tora's only brother. They remained in Egypt longer than expected as German U-boats were targeting passenger ships in the Mediterranean. So, Tora began running the British Empire Nurses' Club, and Marjorie worked in a canteen for soldiers until she contracted typhoid from which she died on 4 March 1916. Tora stayed on with her brother, but Viscount Quenington, serving with the Royal Gloucestershire Yeomanry, had to return to duty, and the next month he died as the result of wounds received in a battle at Ketia in Egypt, 23 April 1916. At home in England, just a week later, their father, Lord St Aldwyn, died in London.

Only occasionally did Hélène have the time or energy to write more expansively about conditions in any particular hospital, as she did about one on the banks of the Isonzo very near the front lines. On 15 May, Austria began a major offensive aimed at seizing Padua and surrounding the Italian armies along the Isonzo.[40] The day after, Hélène wrote from near Monfalcone:

> San Canziano, Sezione di Sanità, Villa Marcorin.
>
> After much searching, we find the hospital in a factory on the other side of the Ponte Michelis. Trucks arrived, full of wounded men. They improvised an operating room, where for 24 hours three surgeons worked without rest. It is a massacre, everything is full of blood, despite this everything is in perfect order and the doctors operate, cut, disinfect, do everything with quickness, calm and patience; I am in admiration. The rooms are cluttered with beds where the most serious wounded were, not able to be moved. In the granary which was reached by a separate narrow staircase, gathered together were the dead and the dying. The death rattle, blood, putrefaction: it is a horrific sight. Not a moan was heard, everyone was resigned. Among the moribund I saw a young sub-lieutenant whose lung had been hit by a bullet, who was not to be moved. Going back down to the ground floor, in a shed on the hay, there were many wounded, the less serious and the ill, leaning one on another ... And trucks continued to arrive non-stop for 24 hours, full of men and of blood! The drivers were exhausted. I return to the operating room and assist in an operation to extract grenade shrapnel from the shoulder of a soldier of the Cavalleria Guide regiment, Cesar Razzoli. He didn't even moan. The bombardment continues, the factory is almost in sight; the trucks leave again, the bombs whistle above our heads.[41]

There were still two more hospitals to visit that day—Hospital forty-seven in a monastery, and back to Hospital forty-five where she had visited wounded cavalry officers the previous day.

Later in May, Hélène was still close to the front, in the town of Porpetto—Red Cross Hospital 47. Amedeo was with her there, and together they went to see his former classmate Valfredo della Gherardesca who was suffering from '*uno* shock *nervoso*.' Hélène wrote that the visit did the patient much good, and that the hospital itself was an advanced one. Later the same evening, Amedeo left with his regiment for the Trentino.[42]

Days could be incredibly varied, especially so close to the front. Hélène spent the night of 30 May in Moggio Udinese, north of Udine. During the night there was a bombing raid. The next day she moved to Cormons and then to Manzano, ever closer to the battlefield. At the Lazzaretto 221, Hélène went to see the Missionary Sisters of Mary and attended a Benediction with a litany sung in a beautiful voice by the military chaplain. Later the same day, at Hospital 235 in Torre di Zuino, she found five who had been wounded in the bombing, four dead, one of whom had been decapitated. She complimented the nurses who were quiet and serene, comforting the patients from when the first bombs began to drop.

Hélène caught some of the tragic poetry of the moment. She could see the beauty of a villa now used as a field hospital, but she also saw it full of soldiers suffering from 'serious injuries, heartbreaking cases, severe suffering, admirable resignation. A lieutenant dying from a wound to his skull and calling out for his mother in his delirium.'[43]

On her forty-fifth birthday on 13 June, Hélène simply carried on her now usual routine but was cheered by the flowers that Amedeo sent to her. She was in Vicenza that day and visited two hospitals, first Ospedale 213 in the Scuola San Felice, where there were 200 gravely wounded soldiers, but Hélène was able to declare that everything was in order. Later, it was on to the Red Cross hospital on Colle Corbellini, where the premises were still being prepared. It was not until the end of June that the Austrian army was pushed back into a retreat, and the front line re-established. Italian losses during this one campaign amounted to 148,000 men as opposed to 80,000 Austrians. Nevertheless, the line held.[44]

The Sixth Battle of the Isonzo in August brought victories for the Italian army—first the capture of San Michele on the 7th, and then two days later, the major city of Gorizia fell. Emanuele Filiberto was in command of the Third Army at the capture of Gorizia, and 'patriots declared that a wholly Italian army had defeated a great foreign army for the first time since the fall of the Roman Empire.' Once again, the human cost was high, with 51,221 Italians dead, wounded, or missing and 37,458 Austrians suffering a similar fate.[45] Under Hapsburg rule since 1500, Gorizia had been a popular summer residence for the nobility, sometimes known as the Austrian Nice. It also became the home of the exiled last of the old Bourbon line, and the Monastery at Castagnevizza was the last resting place of King Charles X, his grandson, the Comte de Chambord, the old Duchesse d'Angoulême (daughter of Louis XVI and Marie Antoinette) and others of the family.

In September, Hélène and Aimone went to the front lines to visit Emanuele Filiberto and Amedeo at their various posts as well as to visit some of the field hospitals. Then came the seventh (14–16 September), eighth (10–12 October) and ninth (1–4 November) battles of the Isonzo, which saw Emanuele Filiberto and the Third Army advance into the western Carso, but at the cost of 125,000 dead and wounded.[46]

Many stories surfaced about Hélène both during and after the First World War. One of these supposedly took place during the Battle of Monfalcone (also known as the 8th Battle of the Isonzo). As the story goes, badly wounded soldiers had just been brought into an improvised field hospital in a tent. A young doctor worked with devotion but was not sufficient to the task without someone to assist him. Suddenly, a woman in a nurse's uniform entered the tent and right away, very simply, set about the task of helping him. Her skill, her experience, and her sangfroid struck the young surgeon deeply. He complimented her and asked her name. 'I am the Duchess of Aosta,' the Princess replied. 'Highness,' the doctor babbled. The Duchess interrupted with a smile. 'There is no Highness here; call me *Signora infermiera* [Madam Nurse], and pass me the vial of iodine.'[47] Hélène was never one to record such incidents in her war diary, but it may correspond to her clinical reference to the Army Ambulance 4 at the village of Gradisca on 11 October: 'It is bleak. A crowd of seriously injured men came directly from the front in a pitiful state. Many of the wounded died on the way, or from the ambulance to the bed, and some lived only a few hours. Groaning, shouting: a horrible spectacle! Others are resigned. Disorder reigns, pain, death.'[48]

Anna Torrigiani remembered 4 November, the Feast of San Carlo Borromeo, as a day of particular agony and pain, while the 'Princess, as always, has been the consoling angel.' They learned of the death of twenty-year-old Lieutenant Luigi Roberti, brother of Maria Roberti, one of their nurses. They went immediately to the barracks of the 4th Bersaglieri cycle troops at Scodovacca, where they found the body of the 'handsome young man lying on a stretcher, soaked in blood, and now dead.' His sister was kneeling beside the body; Hélène immediately went to comfort her and did not leave her side. The Bersaglieri made an impromptu coffin from zinc petrol tins, and the chaplain recited the prayers of the dead before the coffin was placed on a truck and taken for burial in the local cemetery with many of the regiment present. Anna wrote that it was a most poignant scene that evening with the moon appearing every now and then among the clouds, as they looked down into the grave to see the flag-covered coffin amid the tombs of so many other heroes. For her, it was 'something truly unforgettable.'[49]

During the Ninth Battle of the Isonzo, during that first week of November, the Third Army under the Duke of Aosta maintained its field position, but the arrival of Austrian re-enforcements forced Cadorna to end the fight. Discipline among the poorly prepared troops, however, became a growing problem. At the beginning of the battle, Emanuele had six men summarily executed for mutiny. Under Article 116 of the military penal code, whenever four or more soldiers refused an order or even complained—either verbally or in writing—they were considered mutineers if the 'offense' took place on the front line, and the penalty was death. The first executions for mutiny had taken place when two soldiers from the *brigata Ferrara* were shot on 11 December 1915. Nine days later, eight more soldiers from the *brigata Salerno* were similarly executed.[50]

Deserters had been regularly shot by the British and French armies ever since the first months of the war, but now the Italian army took the question of discipline much further. From the beginning of the war, General Cadorna had insisted on an 'iron discipline' and now he institutionalized decimation within mutinous units. Italian soldiers were shot by their own as object lessons. The first documented example of decimation occurred when several hundred soldiers fled from the Austrian army which was about to take the town of Arsiero. Their company commander, under orders, selected by lot a lieutenant, three sergeants and eight men and had them shot. Cadorna also decided that any Italian soldier taken prisoner should be counted as a deserter and should be shot 'using machine guns or artillery where necessary.' Multiple summary executions now took place. One judgement on Cadorna's 'directives on discipline' was that they had 'passed from severity to depravity.'[51]

Statistics show that during 1916, there was an average of 1,539,000 Italian soldiers in the field. Of those, between May and November—the heaviest fighting season—357,400 died or were wounded, around 1,670 each day. During the first six months of the year, forty per cent of the wounds were caused by machine guns and rifles while fifty-five per cent from artillery strikes.[52] This was in addition to the constant issues of disease—particularly cholera and the ever-present issue of venereal disease among the troops.

As fighting on the Italian front eased in late November, Hélène crossed into northern France, to Picardy, where she visited surgical ambulance stations at Bray-sur-Somme and Les Burcelar before going on to a transit station for soldiers in Amiens. All these operations were manned by French Red Cross personnel.[53] At the time, her two sons were both on leave in London, where they visited the King and Queen at Buckingham Palace on 29 November and then two days later joined King Manoel and Queen Augusta Victoria, along with Queen Amélie and the Duc d'Orléans, when they all went to Marlborough House to greet Queen Alexandra on her birthday.

On 25 January 1917, Hélène was with Emanuele Filiberto at the Red Cross Hospital in San Giorgio di Nogaro to award to Lieut. Paolucci the military gold medal of valour in the presence of his parents, his sister and his fiancée. He was suffering greatly, and there was little likelihood of saving him, but as Hélène said, there was always hope.[54]

What Hélène did not record in her diary was that the King had awarded her the Silver Medal for bravery earlier in the month for having nursed cholera patients and wounded soldiers under fire. Emanuele Filiberto presented the medal on behalf of the King on 16 March at San Giorgio di Nogaro. The citation read:

> H. R. H. Princess Elena di Savoia, Duchess of Aosta, Inspectress General of the Italian Red Cross volunteer nurses. Tireless in works of piety, self-sacrificing, a shining example of courage and cheerfulness to the Red Cross nurses, despite dangers of every kind, she stayed in cholera hospitals and in field hospitals in locations hit by enemy artillery, along the whole front from the Trentino to the Isonzo, always calm, without fear, kindly bringing comfort, bringing everywhere, even among crumbling buildings and under bombs from the foe's airplanes, a loving comfort to our ill and wounded soldiers, inspiring in everyone the highest virtue and faith.[55]

At the end of January, the King reorganized naval forces and appointed Paolo Thaon di Revel as Commander of the Mobilized Naval Force, effectively replacing the Duke of the Abruzzi who now became Thaon di Revel's subordinate. The French and British allies considered this a disgrace, and Abruzzi himself resigned his post 'for reasons of health.' He became a special aide to the King for the remainder of the war but played no further military role.[56]

In February, Hélène was in Rome and Naples, but returned to the front in March for another tour of hospitals around Udine and Cormons. In April, she was back in Naples to attend a conference on tuberculosis, a subject always close to her heart, and a demonstration of how ambrina might be used in the treatment of burn victims.[57] While there, she also sent a package of gold ornaments to the Director-General of the Bank of Naples in response to an appeal from some Neapolitan ladies who urged the women of Italy to offer gold to their country, an action which would be much more dramatically repeated in 1935.

This spring also brought the difficult news of revolution in Russia and the abdication of Tsar Nicholas—another one who was once suggested as a husband for Hélène. For the Italian war effort, prospects were dire when it was revealed that negotiations were underway for a separate peace between the new Bolshevik government and Germany, which was realized with the Treaty of Brest-Litovsk, which was signed in March 1918. By removing the threat to its eastern front, Germany was now able to concentrate more on the war on the western front, and more critically for Italy could join forces with Austria in the southern area.

In May 1917, Hélène's diary records visit after visit to medical units and hospitals at the front. She can usually manage only the name of the unit and perhaps some of the personnel.

May 21st: Cervignano, Field Hospital 237; Scodavacca, Field Hospital 054; Villa Vicentina, Field Hospital 58; Field Hospital 53; Quisca, Red Cross mobile surgical ambulance, number 1; San Giovanni di Manzano, Field Hospital 22.
May 22nd: Scodovacca, Field Hospital 54 revisited; La Fredda, Field Hospital 16; Perteole, Field Hospital 240; San Giovanni di Manzano, Field Hospital 22.
May 23rd: Scodovacca, Field Hospital 55; Field Hospital 54; Porpetto, Red Cross war hospital 47; Castello di Porpetto, Field Hospital 56; Vedrignano, field hospice (*ospedaletto*); San Giovanni di Manzano, Field Hospice 22.[58]

Day after day, hospital after hospital.

The desperate situation in the hospitals reflected the terrible consequences of the Tenth Battle of the Isonzo which had begun on 12 May. Emanuele Filiberto was once again leading the Third Army. Even though the Austrian army was tremendously outnumbered, the strategic heights ensured their superiority. Aosta threw sixty battalions into the fight from the reserves that he had managed to gain, but the losses were tremendous and by midday of the second day of action the Third Army had suffered losses of 25,000 men. On the 23rd, the Third Army batteries opened heavier fire than had yet been seen on the Carso. At the end of three weeks of fighting, the Italian army had more than 150,000 casualties, including 36,000 killed, while the Austrian dead numbered 7,300. The biggest single offensive by the Italians to date had been repulsed, and not a single strategic goal achieved.[59]

An analysis of Emanuele's role at this time is given by Mark Thompson in his study, *The White War*:

> The Duke of Aosta, leading the Third Army, cut an imposing figure. Tall, handsome, melancholy, he was not given to airing controversial views or large conceptions. The bright young things around Cadorna at the Supreme Command thought he was diffident and dull-witted. Colonel [Angelo] Gatti, the brightest of the bright, liked him but judged him 'uncultured' because his grammar was faulty.
>
> When the two men met on the evening of 26 May, Gatti was startled to hear the Duke say that, while the battle had gone well, at this rate it would take more than ten years to win the war. Final victory could only come by crushing the Central Powers, which would always recover from smaller defeats. But how could this be achieved? People had had enough of the war; at some point they would rebel. The Allies could not be expected to give more help. The army would press ahead, taking bits of territory here and there, until the people of the warring states cried 'Enough.' He is absolutely right, Gatti thought. There is no military solution. American intervention may make a difference, but who knows when?[60]

Even Frederic Henry, the fictional protagonist in Ernest Hemingway's *A Farewell to Arms*, had an opinion about the leadership:

> The Austrian army was created to give Napoleon victories; any Napoleon. I wished we had a Napoleon, but instead we had Il Generale Cardona, fat and prosperous, and Victor Emmanuel, the tiny man with the long thin neck and the goat beard. Over on the right they had the Duke of Aosta. Maybe he was too good-looking to be a great general but he looked like a man. Lots of them would have liked him to be king. He looked like a king.

When General William Robertson, the Chief of the Imperial General Staff, visited the front in March, he agreed. 'Of the 5 Army Commanders, the Duke of Aosta is generally regarded as being the best ... The remaining 4 Army commander gave me quite a contrary impression. White face and white hands and other indications shew that these officers spend far more time in their comfortable headquarters than they spend at the front.'[61]

When Hélène arrived in Gorizia in the middle of August, the city was under an intense bombardment. Just before she got to Hospital 129, a medium calibre shell had hit the hospital and killed a young medical student who was making the bed of a wounded soldier. Irene di Robilant was one of the nurses there; together, they evacuated the patients to the cellar of Hospital 129, which was more secure even though it too had been hit by enemy fire that morning. In spite of the horrors, Hélène was able to record her praise of the nurses who were calm and serene; the hospital itself was beautiful and very well kept.[62]

In August, the eleventh battle of the Isonzo saw 1,200,000 Italian troops launch an offensive attack against Austrian lines, the entire length of the front from Tolmino to the sea. Emanuele Filiberto's Third Army had artillery support withdrawn by General Cadorna who transferred it to the Bainsizza. Hidden machine-gun nests were responsible for mowing down yet more soldiers, and by the time fighting finally halted on 10 September, there were 143,334 Italian dead, wounded, and missing, with 110,000 Austrian losses, the worst for Italy since the beginning of the war.[63]

The Second Army awoke at 2 a.m. on 24 October to the heaviest bombardment they had yet suffered. Thick fog and sleet added to the misery of the day. The combined German and Austrian armies pummeled Italian lines, which broke into retreat, out of the village of Caporetto and across the River Isonzo. Among the German soldiers that day was the young lieutenant Erwin Rommel, who would make a bigger mark in warfare twenty-five years later. By the end of the 26th, the Central Powers had advanced through Caporetto and westwards. The next day, General Cadorna gave the Second and Third Armies orders to pull back to the River Tagliamento in twenty-four hours. By the 29th, the combined German-Austrian forces had reached Udine, where Cadorna had already abandoned his headquarters in the archbishop's palace. A million troops and some 400,000 refugees were now trying to escape. By 5 November, the Germans and Austrians had reached the Tagliamento, and moved to the River Piave. The last Italian troops to cross the Piave blew up the bridges on the afternoon of the 9th.[64] 'As the line broke Italian troops turned and streamed to the rear, throwing away their rifles as they went.' As they did, 'their officers, weeping or enraged, looked on helplessly, or did likewise,' and then 'for days on end the narrow roads through the mountains were clogged with exhausted men, who jettisoned their equipment, burnt their stores, blew up bridges behind them and pressed doggedly homewards.'[65] The shame that the leadership of the Italian army felt at the retreat is reflected in a dire proclamation issued by Emanuele Filiberto, who commanded the Third Army during the battle and the whole army 'after the debacle':

A PROCLAMATION

Some portions of the 149th Infantry (Regiment), and the 3rd Battalion of the 71st Infantry (Regiment) have shown themselves painfully lacking in their duty to the State, and have covered themselves with the blackest shame that can stain the honour of a soldier.

I denounce as worthy the execration of all soldiers and armies the troops

who have been capable of such an infamous betrayal, and I order the immediate disbanding of the 149th Regiment and the 30th Battalions of the 71st
Regiment, and I hereby decree that the colours of the 149th, for which other
soldiers have won glory with their life's blood, shall fly no longer over a regiment unworthy to follow them.

The names of the wretches who have covered themselves with imperishable
shame shall be published in their native villages, and the state aid which Italy
grants to the families of her defenders shall be withdrawn from the relatives of
these miscreants.

May the curse of all those soldiers who sublimely sacrificed their lives for
their country on the blood-stained heights of the Carso, and the scorn of those
who, ever ready to do their duty, are fighting and shall fight for the glory of Italy,
for ever rest on those who proved themselves no longer worthy to stand upon
the soil they sprang from.

EMANUELE FILIBERTO of SAVOY

This report was sent to the British War Cabinet and the dispatch also included a
bulletin issued at the time but which was withheld from the press:

WAR BULLETIN OF THE 27TH OCTOBER, 1917.

The Enemy, by the weight of his attack and through the cowardly defection
of the brigades from Rome, Pesaro, Foggia and Elba, has succeeded in setting
his foot upon the sacred soil of our country.

May the curse of God and of our Fatherland rest on them.[66]

In the battle and subsequent retreat which brought the Italians to the Piave,
their losses had been enormous with some 12,000 killed, 30,000 wounded, and
294,000 were taken prisoner. The Italian army retreated 150 kilometres, and fourteen thousand square kilometres with a population of 1,150,000 had been lost.
This was the worst disaster of the war for Italy, and one hundred years later the
name Caporetto still brings up images of a disastrous and ignominious rout. The
King himself was among those caught in the retreat, and once again he considered abdication to avoid the humiliation of surrender. Among the many dead was
Hélène's longtime travelling companion Maurizio Piscicelli, who was commanding the 147th Infantry Regiment, the last battalion which fought 'to the bitter
end' after being attacked from the front and the flank by the combined German-
Austrian forces, an action for which he was posthumously awarded the *medaglio
d'argento*. When war was declared, Piscicelli had rejoined the Aosta Cavalry with
the rank of lieutenant colonel, but later transferred to this infantry unit.[67] In 1916,
he had married Margherita Perrone di San Martino, sister of Ferdinando Perrone
di San Martino, Hélène's *gentiluomo di corte*. Their only son died young, and the
widowed Margherita entered a convent and joined the Sorelle Ausiliatrici del

Purgatorio at San Remo; a street in Naples was later named in his honour.

Hélène was on a round of hospital visits in Naples at the time of the Caporetto disaster, but she quickly returned to the front lines and on 1 November was at Portogruaro, between the Tagliamento and the Piave. Anna Torrigiani recorded a bombing attack from the air that night, bullets hitting the roof of Hélène's railway carriage like heavy hailstones. They moved on to San Giusto, where they found Prince Amedeo 'always so calm and serene, despite everything.'[68] As part of the retreat, Hélène and her Red Cross nurses crossed the Piave and went to Treviso, where she wrote:

> The vigil. The treacherous moon that illuminates and guides the fatal flight of birds of lead, carrying death, has disappeared, and the sun knows how to gild the darkest misery, has not yet appeared on the horizon. It is night, all is quiet, the air is cluttered by the pain of a long week of agony and sorrow to the hearts of all Italians.
>
> For many, for the heroes, the fighting was fierce. They did not want to abandon the land of heroism that the brothers had reconquered staining the blood out of stone, where the Carso had become vermilion. But the order came, and the retreat was accomplished, leaving the graves there and letting the souls go. The retreat was accomplished, the troops descended, flowing to the plain...
>
> It is night—all is silent—the air is icy cold. The soldiers silently camp out in the field at the fires, huddled in groups to warm the numb limbs. A small low room is dimly lit by a lamp, they cannot breathe because of the fog of smoke and air. There are gathered the officers, no longer human beings, but the ruins of life.
>
> Into the night they talked, they probably cried about the defeat, struggled against troublesome fatigue, as long as the will is surrendered to nature, and one after another, each bowed his head, his eyes are lifeless, the memories are disappeared.
>
> But standing alone among them, General impassive and silent vigil, his eyes are wide open, as if they could close in more than ever, reddened by vigils, rimmed with fatigue; in the eyes are engraved the recent visions of horror and two deep furrows dug perhaps the ravages of tears, mark my cheeks dried up.
>
> His head upright, arms crossed, proud of his sleeping ones, the General is watching, waiting, hoping.[69]

The government fell, as did, finally, General Cadorna. On 1 November, General Foch saw the Duke of Aosta, paid a visit to the King at Padua, and then proceeded to Rome with the new Italian Prime Minister Vittorio Orlando, who declared that he was ready to fight to the bitter end, and if it were necessary, even to retreat to Sicily. 'There is no question of retreating to Sicily,' replied General Foch. 'It is on the Piave that we must resist.'[70]

According to a British diplomatic report, 'The deposition of Cadorna is not due to the Italian Government, but is a concession to General Foch and General Wilson, who knew they could never over-rule Cadorna, nor take command of the Italian Front while he remained in office.' However, now that he was deposed it was 'France and England who are directing everything in Italy. May their genius prove equal to the task—one would feel more serene if either of the generals selected had taken a Gorizia.'

Victor Emmanuel accepted the need to replace Cadorna without hesitation; but there was disagreement about his successor. Generals Foch and Robertson wanted the Duke of Aosta, but he was regarded as unacceptable 'for dynastic reasons.' Mack Smith reports that the Cabinet also preferred the Duke of Aosta as the new commander, but the King's rejection of the idea was possibly 'jealousy of a more outgoing and colourful personality; possibly he feared another military defeat and abdication, in which case his cousin's reputation ought to be preserved to be available for the succession or for him to be regent to the young Prince Umberto.' In a report to the War Office on the conditions within the Italian Army, British Red Cross Director George Trevelyan likewise considered Aosta 'probably the best Italian general,' but Emanuele Filiberto was still a royal prince and as such 'his failure might bring down the dynasty.' The choice as Supreme Commander finally fell on Armando Diaz, despite the fact that he had only been a corps commander for about three months. General Pietro Badoglio was chosen as deputy to Diaz.[71]

At the very end of the year, Hélène suffered another personal loss on the night of 30 December with the death of Anna Torrigiani, her *dama di palazzo* since her marriage and companion—along with her husband Carlo—throughout the war. Hélène recorded that the Marchesa—or, as she titles her in the published diary entry, Volunteer Red Cross Nurse Anna Torrigiani—returned home to Florence after the defeat at Caporetto. Instead of taking a much-needed rest, she volunteered to tend wounded soldiers in the infectious diseases area, the *Sala Bianca*, and there contracted what proved a fatal disease herself.[72] Hélène visited the *Sala Bianca* a few days later to see for herself where '*la mia cara*' Anna, who had been so much part of her life since she arrived in Italy, had fallen victim to disease. She was buried in the chapel of family's Villa di Spicciano in Chianti.

In February 1918, both Amedeo and Hélène received medals. On the 16th, it was announced from Headquarters that Amedeo was awarded the Silver Medal for Valour on the Field. The *Times* report noting almost incidentally—'and also on General Diaz, the Commander-in-Chief of the Italian forces.' The report continues:

Last June, on the Carso, the Duke of Apulia commanded a battery almost in the enemy's full view, and, despite a heavy enemy bombardment, he maintained uninterrupted fire by his own pieces, and when wounded, helped to repair a destroyed telephone wire. The citation accompanying the award declares him to be a shining example of fortitude as a soldier and a prince.

On 28 February, Hélène went to Rome, where she was awarded the Regina Maria Cross by a representative of the King of Romania. And the next month, General Mestre awarded Hélène the French Croix de Guerre, of which she was particularly proud as it was given to those who fought to defend their country. Although Hélène hoped to get to Spain to visit her mother and sisters, 'la Grand bataille France' which she expected to continue on the Italian borders required her to return to the front lines.[73]

Toward the end of April, Hélène had a luncheon visit at her villa from the young Prince of Wales, who had been her escort at the wedding of King Manoel in 1913. He now proclaimed Hélène a 'divine woman in her own way & very kind though she is about 50 now, rather old perhaps?!!' Edward thought that it would be "a great thing to be able to go there occasionally and get back to civilisation, as she has asked me to do!!" He reported too that domestic arrangements were not all that could be hoped for. 'She seldom even sees her husband the Duke, who commands an Italian army though he has behaved very badly to her 'et il y a un tas d'histoires' [and there are a heap of stories]!!' Two days later, Hélène together with Amedeo paid a return visit to the prince at his villa, but as Hélène was constantly on the move there weren't any of the further visits that Edward thought might have been a 'great thing.'[74]

The handsome young English prince wasn't particularly taken with the rest of the Italian Royals, whom he deemed 'a dud family except for the 3rd girl "Giovanna," who is a little darling, aged 11, & great fun!!'[75] Edward thought the Queen 'looks like a big unattractive housemaid,' the Regent, the Duke of Genoa was 'old & gaga', and upon Edward's visit to the Vatican Pope Benedict XV fared even worse—'a dirty little priest with spectacles who hadn't shaved for several days, though he did talk French!!' Nonetheless, the press had Prince Edward engaged to Princess Jolanda, the king's oldest daughter, a rumour that persisted for months.

Another young relative, Princess Marie José of Belgium had a different impression of Hélène. She said that the Duchess would regularly visit her at school in Poggio, outside Florence, but that she found Hélène's tall and thin figure, her haughty manner and her white wig intimidating—and also wondered whether Hélène was checking out a potential bride for one of her sons. As an adult, Marie José said she had to know Hélène better to appreciate her great qualities of courage and heart.[76]

In the very early morning hours of 15 June, the Austrian army began an artillery barrage against the Italian entrenchments on the Piave. Later that morning 100,000 troops crossed the river. However on the 19th, Italian reinforcements arrived and counter-attacked. Soon, the new Austrian positions were overwhelmed, and the Emperor Karl, who had personally taken charge of the attack, ordered his troops to withdraw, a process that took another four days. Early in July, Emanuele Filberto's Third Army was able to consolidate the Italian victory by seizing the Piave delta, which the Austrians had held since Caporetto. This rebuffing of the Austrian attack achieved 'more than either they or their allies realised at the time' for Italy; in September, Austria-Hungary approached Italy for discussions about ending the war.[77]

This time, however, Hélène was not there to aid in the nursing effort. Accompanied by the recently widowed Carlo Torrigiani, the faithful Pedro, and her maid Rosso, she had left Genoa on 24 May aboard the *Città di Bengasi* bound for Gibraltar and a rest break. Their ship was part of a convoy of seventeen vessels of different types from the various allied nations, each with a different style of camouflage. Travelling through the Mediterranean risked German attacks, but they reached port safely on the 29th. The next day, they went by train into neutral Spain, hoping to visit Hélène's mother at Villamanrique but discovered that she had gone to Madrid, which became their next stop. Her sister Louise and her husband met them at the station, and even her younger brother Ferdinand 'made the effort to come and receive me' but 'the sight of him did not rejoice me.' She found Louise's children 'charming' but her mother was now 'weak—thin and aged.' King Alfonso came to visit, discussed the war in great detail with her, and invited Hélène to join the royal family later at Santander. Most of all, she enjoyed sitting alone with her mother, 'like the good old times' and raking through 'the ashes of the past.' When it was time to leave, the old Comtesse was more moved than usual, and Hélène wondered 'which of the two of us will disappear first?'

From Spain, Hélène went on to Larache in Morocco to visit Isabelle and her family, but she had not let them know of her trip and while she found the children delighted to see her, Isabelle was at their farm, some sixty kilometres away tending to the harvest. Hélène was impatient to see her sister and arranged with the governor general to get horses for them and the two older children, Isa and Françoise, for the five-hour journey. However, first they had to wait for their baggage, which had been loaded on the backs of asses which were 'slower than tortoises.' Once they arrived, Pedro discovered that he had forgotten the keys on board the ship and had to return to find them, which cost another hour, by which time it was too hot in the sun and they decided to wait until it cooled. Finally, they began their gallop across the immense plains—'no roads, no limits.' When they finally arrived, the sisters collapsed into each other's arms 'the emotion, the surprise, the joy was suffocating—she is so close to my heart ... I held her like I did when she was very small.' When they had last seen each other in 1916, Isabelle was recovering from a bad bout of typhus which left her 'like a skeleton,' but now she was as round as an apple.[78]

During her stay in Morocco, Hélène wandered from Larache to Tangiers, to Mogador, Mecknes and Fez enjoying the sun of desert life until it was time to return to Europe, where she was a guest of the Spanish royal family at Santander in northern Spain from the end of July through the end of August. She did not return to Italy until 16 September when she arrived in Genoa aboard the steamer *Città di Cagliari*. Within a week, Hélène was back visiting hospitals in Venice,

Vicenza, Crespano, and throughout the warzone.[79]

Emanuele's half-brother, twenty-nine-year-old Umberto, Count of Salemi, died on 19 October at Crespano Veneto. Serving as a lieutenant in charge of a battery of cannon, Umberto had some health problems and one day fainted on duty. He asked to go for some medical attention, but his condition grew worse, and his brothers, the Duke of Aosta and Count of Turin, were called to his bedside. The young soldier died in the arms of his brother Turin at 9.30 p.m., probably from influenza, the Spanish flu, which would soon devastate the world killing more people than the war itself did. Umberto's funeral took place on the 23rd, and was attended by the King, the Duke of Aosta and both his sons, Amedeo and Aimone, as well as the Count of Turin, General Diaz, and General Giardino under whom he was serving. He was buried with his comrades in the Cemetery of Crespano Veneto sul Grappa. The King ordered thirty days of Court mourning, and Hélène went off to Moncalieri to be with his mother, Laetitia.[80]

Later that same day, the 23rd, a great push by Italian troops bolstered by three British divisions, two French, and one of Czech volunteers began the Battle of Vittorio Veneto, starting with an attack on Monte Grappa. By the 27th, bridgeheads on the Piave had been secured, by the 30th the Italians had taken Vittorio Veneto, and in the first few days of November they captured Udine. The great victory at Vittorio Veneto—which General Diaz was proudly able to declare 'Caporetto in reverse'—was effectively the end of the war for Italy, and the defeat of Austria was also effectively the end of the Austro-Hungarian empire. The capitulation of Austria and the resulting armistice line of 4 November brought Gorizia back under Italian control, and even before the Armistice, the Allied Powers agreed that Italy should provisionally—and temporarily—occupy the eastern shore of the Adriatic which had been promised in the Treaty of London. Accordingly, Italian warships landed troops in Pola, Zara, and Cattaro, and an Italian admiral was appointed as 'Governor of Dalmatia.'[81]

Hélène continued her hospital visits, and on 3 November was at the Red Cross hospital in Thiene, then at Marostica, and on to Crespano where she visited another Red Cross hospital and also went to pray at the grave of her recently buried brother-in-law Umberto. Later that same day, she crossed the Piave and went to the abandoned hospital at Sacile, where they organized some care and some meals. She also made certain that she praised the work of others. In a letter to the British ambassador in Rome, she wrote of the marvellous work the British Red Cross did at the front:

> that wherever help was needed, there the British Red Cross Commissioner, Sir Courtauld Thomson, was to be found with cars full of ever kind of food and medicines to help the starving people on the other side of the line and the ravaged hospitals, left by the Austrians empty of everything except untended sick and dying, and the dead.[82]

The armistice between Italy and Austria was signed and came into effect on 4 November, and the fighting ceased. King Victor Emmanuel was in Padua, and his car was mobbed by the people, many of whom tried to kiss his hand. When the King triumphantly entered Trieste on 10 November, Hélène was there with Aimone. The next day, she went to Caporetto itself and Cividale before attending the 10.30 a.m. *Te Deum* at the cathedral in Udine, where the Bersaglieri and the Savoia Cavalleria were deployed on the piazza and the *Marcia Reale* was played while the banners of both regiments lay at the foot of the altar. A week later, Hélène found Amedeo at Farrè, and she was able to write from the *Zone de Guerre* to her sister Amélie. 'Pardon me if I have not written to you for some time. My thoughts were with you and our dear Philippe, but the days only have 24 hours and I say without presumption that my hours are truly full and correspondence was impossible for me.' The result was worth it. 'What a great—what a beautiful—what a brilliant victory. And we Italians can be proud. Because to us came all the honours of the war since because of our crushing of Austria came the final great break—and because of that, world peace.' Along with the elation of victory and peace came the realization that there was still much to do. 'It is necessary for everything to be re-organized—the invaded countries are devastated—the people are hungry and decimated by disease and misery. For my part I have much to do.' On Christmas Day, the whole family was together with Emanuele Filiberto for the Messa del Soldato at San Giusto.[83]

By the end of the war, monarchies in much of Europe had changed beyond recognition. Hélène's cousin Ferdinand had abdicated the throne of Bulgaria and gone into exile; Kaiser Wilhelm had been deposed and sent into exile, and soon all the lesser kings, grand dukes, and princes throughout Germany would lose their positions; Emperor Karl of Austria was also deposed and sent into exile while his formerly great empire was dissolved into many new states; and in Russia, Tsar Nicholas was deposed and murdered along with his family. Although Hélène personally knew many of those impacted by these changes, her abiding concern was for the Italian soldiers whom she had tended throughout the hard years.

After the war, when she had some time to reflect on the sacrifices made by the young men of Italy, Hélène wrote that even during their final agonies, the soldiers would not utter a single word of mutiny or even of regret at being cut down in the flower of their youth. The last words that came from almost every mouth

Hélène dressed in Egyptian native costume while visiting that country, 1892.

The Comtesse de Paris with her three younger daughters (*left–right*) Isabelle, Hélène, and Louise.

Hélène and Emanuele Filiberto at Stowe House at the time of their engagement, 1895.

Hélène with her firstborn Amedeo, known throughout his life as 'Bouby', 1898.

Hélène in court dress wearing the
Cisterna family emeralds, 1899.

Hélène at the wedding of her
sister Isabelle to their cousin
Jean, Duc de Guise, 1899. She
accompanies the Princess of Wales
(later Queen Alexandra) and her
daughter Princess Victoria.

Above: Hélène and Emanuele
Filiberto with their two sons, 1902.

Left: The Comtesse de Paris
with her grandsons Amedeo and
Aimone at Randan, 1902.

Right: Hélène on horseback.

Below: A visit to Mar Lodge, 1906. Left–right: The Prince of Wales (later King George V); Princess Victoria; The Princess of Wales (later Queen Mary); King Edward VII; (in front) Princess Maud of Fife; Queen Alexandra; Princess Alexandra (later Duchess of Fife); Hélène, Duchess of Aosta; Arthur, Duke of Connaught; and Prince Arthur of Connaught.

Hélène in a canoe on the Busi River, near Nova Lusitania, Mozambique, 1909.

Hélène with a water buffalo, shot near Neumann Camp, northeast of Mount Kenya, 1910.

Hélène meets King Mzinga of the Warundi, 1910. 'He was a head taller than his subjects who were already taller than us.'

Hélène in her study.

Hélène with her sons,
Amedeo and Aimone, 1911.

Hélène in 1911; this is the
photo she chose as the
frontispiece for her first travel
book, *Voyages en Afrique*.

Right: Amedeo and his father,
Emanuele Filiberto, at the
beginning of the war, 1915.

Below: Emanuele Filiberto
awarding Hélène the Silver
Medal for Bravery, 1917.

Hélène in uniform as Inspectress
General of the Italian Red
Cross Nurses, 1918.

Hélène with her sons.

Hélène in 1923.

The Aostas visit the Vatican following the Lateran Pact, 1929. Vittorio Emanuele, Count of Turin; Emanuele Filiberto, Duke of Aosta; Hélène, Duchess of Aosta; Aimone, Duke of Spoleto; and Luigi, Duke of the Abruzzi.

Above: The family—Emanuele Filiberto, Hélène, Aimone, and Amedeo.

Left: Hélène in her Red Cross uniform with Mussolini.

Aboard the yacht Amrita, 1933—Hélène with her granddaughter Margherita and one of the African children who lived at Capodimonte with Amedeo at the wheel.

Hélène with Aimone.

Hélène at Capodimonte with Amedeo
and his daughters, Margherita and Maria
Cristina, 1940.

Hélène at Capodimonte with her
sisters Isabelle and Amélie.

Hélène in formal court dress for an
audience with the Pope, 1941.

Hélène in hospital, 1943,
with Otto Campini (*right*).

July 1945 at Capodimonte: (*from left*) Irene, Anne (partially hidden), Aimone, Maria Cristina, Margherita, and Hélène at far right. In front (in white suit) Otto Campini.

Hélène with her grandson Amedeo, 1945.

11

1919–1922

I need to write to glorify the wandering life,
a free life in the great calm of peace.[1]

The new year began with the arrival of the American President Woodrow Wilson in Rome. Hélène was with the King and Queen and the Duke of Genoa on the platform to meet Wilson's train, along with all the ministers, General Diaz, representatives of the Senate and Chamber, as well as the City of Rome, the ambassadors and ministers of the Allies and neutral powers. Through the decorated streets, lined with troops and full of cheering crowds, they rode to the Quirinale Palace, with the King and President in the first carriage. The Queen and the Duke of Genoa accompanied Mrs Wilson in the second carriage, while Hélène and Ferdinando, the Prince of Udine (eldest son of the Duke of Genoa), were with Miss Wilson in the third.

The Wilsons—the President, his wife Edith, and their daughter Margaret—had arrived in France at Brest on 13 December 1918 and Paris the next morning. Even though the United States had entered the war so late, President Wilson was at this point seen as one of the great heroes of the time. His famous Fourteen Points, which he indeed hoped would make this a 'war to end all wars', promoted a way towards a lasting peace by requiring an end to secret treaties, ensuring national and minority rights, and the creation of an international organization to create a stability built upon the inclusion of all nations, both great and small. Wilson's presence in Europe—as the first American president ever to leave the country during his term of office—was viewed as that of a saviour, drawing great crowds everywhere—'his picture was placed in churches along with those of the saints and, on his railway journey from the port of Brest to Paris, people knelt by the tracks as he passed.'[2] After a ceremonial reception at the Elysée Palace and various meetings, they went on to London and then returned to Paris, where they boarded the Italian royal train for Rome. As Mrs Wilson recalled:

[Their] arrival in Rome will always be the most brilliant canvas in all the rich pictures in my memory. Before we left Paris it had been grey with constant rain, rain, rain. But here the sky was a dome of sapphire pouring golden sunshine over a radiant world... the long windows of every house along the way were open wide, and from each hung rare old brocades or velvets with arms embroidered on them. American and Italian flags were flying and the people crowding everywhere. Troops lined every street, wearing their picturesque uniforms and 'two-story' caps. And the flowers! From the roofs, the windows and balconies, poured a veritable shower of purple violets and golden mimosa. From baskets filled with them, from white arms laden with them, they fell about our stately coaches, a libation fit for the gods.

Their Majesties had welcomed us at the station, and after the formal greetings and speeches, and review of troops, we had entered the royal coaches to proceed to the Quirinale Palace. I rode with the lovely Queen, who looks in every way her part, and I never had a greater thrill.[3]

When they reached the Quirinale, the whole party appeared on the balcony of the palace to the rapturous applause of the crowds below. Luncheon was followed by the Wilsons paying a courtesy call on the Queen Mother at the Villa Margherita and then visited Hélène at her apartment in the Quirinale.

The American visit to Rome was a short one, and after a banquet at the American Embassy and a visit to the Pope in the Vatican, the Wilsons were at the station once again, seen on their way by the King and Queen, Hélène, the Duke of Genoa, Prince of Udine, and Vittorio Emanuele Orlando as president of the Council.

The Paris Peace Conference opened on 18 January, and many concerns were brought to the international table. Premier Georges Clemenceau is reported to have worried that although 'we have won the war: now we have to win the peace, and it may be more difficult.'[4] In the following weeks and months, many flocked to Paris, and among these was Hélène who travelled there in the company of Queen Elena and her daughters Jolanda and Mafalda. They arrived incognito at the Gare de Lyon in the morning of 16 February and were met by the Queen's sisters Xenia and Vera as well as the Italian ambassador, Conte Lelio Bonin-Longare, and his wife along with the French director of protocol and various military officials. They drove immediately to the Hotel Meurice, the home in exile of Queen Elena's parents, who never accepted the 1918 annexation of their tiny country of Montenegro by the new Yugoslavia. Essentially, King Nikola had been deposed by his own grandson, King Alexander of Serbia, who had now become monarch of the new country of Yugoslavia, first known as the Kingdom of the Serbs, Croats, and Slovenes.

Although this was technically a private visit for Queen Elena to meet with her family, especially her father who was not well at the time, the Italian royals all had luncheon at the Elysée Palace, the home of the president of the Republic, on the 20th. The newspapers also decided to resurrect the rumour that Princess Jolanda was to marry the Prince of Wales, who happened to also be in Paris at the time.[5] The Italian royals were in the French capital for about a week before Queen Elena and her daughters returned to Rome, while Hélène continued on to Brussels.

Just a few minutes before her departure from Paris on the evening of 25 February, Hélène was awarded the cross of the French Légion d'Honneur in recognition for her work with the Red Cross throughout the war. In Brussels, King Albert met Hélène at the station and took her to dine at the Royal Palace on the first of her few days in the Belgian capital. While there, she awarded the Italian decoration of '*Au Mérit*' to Queen Elisabeth, having given the same award to Madame Poincaré in Paris.

From Brussels, Hélène travelled to London on behalf of Queen Elena and the President of the Italian Red Cross, to award Queen Mary and Queen Alexandra the Cross of Merit for their war work. In London, Amélie met her sister at Victoria Station, along with the Italian ambassador and the Marchesa Imperiali and representatives of the Foreign Office and the Italian Red Cross in Great Britain. The ambassador wrote in his diary that day that 'Her Royal Highness [is] always kind and affable. A real type of an authentic *grande dame*.'[6] The day before the presentation, Hélène wrote to Queen Mary from Claridge's about the arrival of their delegation and asked when the Queen might receive them. Accompanying her were Lydia Tesio—'one of our best Red Cross sisters—acting as my Lady in waiting,' Colonel Doctor Badnel, principal inspector of the Italian Red Cross, and the ever faithful Carlo Torrigiani. The same afternoon, Hélène and Amélie went to tea with Queen Mary who thought 'Hélène very grey but looking well.' When Emanuele Filiberto visited London later Queen Mary thought him 'a good deal aged.' On 3 March, Hélène returned with the rest of the delegation for the award to Queen Mary at Buckingham Palace and, in the afternoon, to Queen Alexandra at Marlborough House. Over the next few days, there were visits at Claridge's from Philippe d'Orléans, Amélie, Manoel and Mimi, as well as the Italian ambassador Imperiali, a dinner at the Italian embassy, a visit to the Red Cross hospital, and a luncheon for Hélène and Amélie at Buckingham Palace with the King and Queen, before Hélène returned to the Continent.[7]

Hélène's own accomplishments were recognized later in the year when she was awarded the Insignia of a Dame Grand Cross of the Order of the British Empire. The recommendation, which was endorsed by King George personally, noted that the Duchess was 'of the greatest possible assistance to the British Red Cross and Order of St. John in facilitating their work for the British troops and was indefatigable in her efforts not only for the Italian sick and wounded soldiers but also for the British sick and wounded.' Hélène went to Rome for the ceremony on 11 October when the ambassador, Sir Rennell Rodd, awarded the order's insignia.[8] Later, Hélène would also be among the first to be awarded the Florence

Nightingale Medal by the International Red Cross Committee in Geneva.

The awarding of medals continued, and Hélène accompanied Emanuele Filiberto to Trieste, where on San Giusto Hill on 10 April 1919, he awarded 'Comandante d'Annunzio' the gold medal for military valor. Aimone, preparing for a mountaineering expedition, was in Venice and flew to Trieste to meet his parents there, but en route the plane 'fell into the sea,' as the newspapers phrased it. A steamer travelling between Trieste and Capo d'Istria was able to pick up the two aviators and get them to Trieste. As soon as Hélène and Emanuele Filiberto arrived and were officially received by the Governor General, they rushed to the hospital where they found Aimone injured but conscious and resting. The pilot, Lieutenant Pierotti, had suffered fatal head injuries and died within a few hours. After recovering, Aimone left for Batum with an Italian exploration mission, departing from Taranto aboard the *Memfi*, formerly the hospital ship on which his mother nursed during the Libyan war.[9]

Hélène was back in Naples for only a few days, before she received news of the serious illness of her mother at Villamanrique, and she left immediately for Spain as did her scattered siblings. Amélie came from England, Louise and Carlos from Madrid, Ferdinand from France. Isabelle and Jean de Guise also arrived in time for the last moments, and their son Henri remembered how the bells of Villamanrique tolled all day long to mourn the passing of the Comtesse on 23 April. After the death of Comte de Paris in 1894, the Comtesse had lived mostly at the Château de Randan but made frequent visits to her palace at Villamanrique, which she had inherited from her parents. It was at Villamanrique that the first funeral masses were said, and Amélie, Hélène, Isabelle, Louise and Ferdinand all gathered to attend. After the Spanish funeral, Hélène and Amedeo went to Casablanca, where they joined Isabelle de Guise staying at the Residency as guests of General Lyautey, the French Resident-General, and then for a longer stay with Isabelle at Larache until 29 May.[10]

Meanwhile, the men of the family had the responsibility of taking the Comtesse back to England one more time, to be buried alongside the Comte. The Spanish king offered the battleship *Alfonso XIII* to do the honours as far as Southampton, with the Duc de Guise and Duc de Montpensier accompanying the coffin. In England, the Spanish Ambassador, Señor Don Alfonso Merry del Val, and various officers met the ship. A brief service was held at Weybridge on the Friday evening, and then a full Requiem High Mass and burial service took place on the Saturday, 17 May. A French flag covered the coffin and other French flags were arranged over the entrance to the church and on either side of the coffin. The men in the family were the ones who attended the English burial service— her sons Philippe and Ferdinand were present, along with her grandson King Manoel; her son-in-law, the Duc de Guise, and also the Duc de Vendôme. King George sent his second son, Prince Albert, to represent him. At the end of the burial service, a procession brought the coffin into the crypt where it was placed alongside the Comte de Paris, inside the stone sarcophagus originally made for their grandparents, King Louis Philippe and Queen Marie Amélie, before their coffins were returned to Dreux in 1876.[11]

The Comtesse had written a new will at Randan on 6 July 1911—with several subsequent codicils—stating that after 'the sad events and the sorrow which have so cruelly afflicted my family for some years past, I have had to modify my last dispositions' but she hoped that 'a time will return in France as glorious as the time that has passed away.' In her will, the Comtesse 'directed that all papers or letters in the handwriting of the Comte de Paris should be burnt, as the papers and letters contain only entirely personal and intimate souvenirs which she desired to pass with her.' All other family papers were left to the Duc d'Orléans plus the sapphires to complete the set of those left to him by the Comte. The Duc de Montpensier was left other jewelry and lace to be retained as 'heirlooms' plus her effects at Randan. The Comtesse also left money to fund the salary of the doctor in charge at the Asilo San Felipe in Villamanrique in memory of the Comte, and other money to be distributed to the poor in the districts where she had residences. Various life annuities were granted, including to Camille Dupuy, 'the devoted and faithful friend in exile,' and to Nellie Watson, 'as a proof of affection and gratefulness for her devoted care of me and my children during many years.' All her other diamonds, pearls, and jewels that belonged to her personally, her lace, châles, furs and personal linen jointly to her daughters to divide among themselves. Then, stating that her sons were already comparatively well provided for, she left the residue of her estate to her four daughters: Queen Amelia of Portugal (bringing into account 1,283,004f.); the Infanta Louise (bringing into hotchpot 1,050,900f.); Hélène, Duchesse d'Aoste; and Isabelle, Duchesse de Guise.[12] Louise had earlier received the villa in Cannes as a wedding present and now also inherited the Spanish palace of Villamanrique, while Orléans, Montpensier, Hélène, and Isabelle were to share the Forest of Randan (2,350 hectares). Amélie was left out of this division, taking into consideration the money given to her as a dowry. The Comtesse ended her will by saying 'In leaving them, I bless them all, having loved them all with equal affection, and I pray God and the Holy Virgin to spare them cruel trials and to protect them. May they never forget that it is in our Holy Religion that they shall find their only true consolation as their father and I have always there found the same.' Smaller personal bequests were also made privately, and to Hélène the Comtesse left two particular rings, the little silver trumpet presented to her by the Wood Norton Harriers, and most poignantly a pair of Eddy's cufflinks and 'the little photograph of me with Eddy and Miss Stonor, which never leaves me (desk Randan or Villamanrique).'[13]

Transfers of property were happening in Italy as well. The King announced that he had decided to turn over many Crown estates to the nation as museums or for the use of disabled soldiers and soldiers' orphans. Moncalieri—the home of Princess Laetitia which she had established as a hospital and workshop for

disabled soldiers—was one of the transferred estates, along with the royal palace at Monza, Paggio a Caiano near Florence and its villa built for Lorenzo the
Magnificent, as well as the huge Reggia di Caserta, built in the 18th century for
Carlos III. Other crown properties were turned over for the use of museums,
including the Doge's palace in Venice, Capodimonte, and Caserta, the Sforza castle in Lombardy, and Stupinigi in Piedmont, the Pitti palace and Boboli Gardens
in Florence, the royal palace, and La Favorita in Palermo. Not mentioned in the
public reports was that King Victor Emmanuel agreed to these donations in order
to greatly reduce his own expenditures in maintaining them. So, although the
civil list was accordingly reduced by a quarter, it is nearly certain that the king
did not suffer financially from this transaction.[14] A number of apartments for royal
use were retained within the larger palaces, including the Pitti Palace in Florence,
Princess Laetitia's home in Moncalieri, and most importantly for the Aostas, their
apartment at Capodimonte.

In September, Hélène was back in London again, this time with her two sons,
but now the ambassador felt that she was in poor health and sad, a fact he attributed to several allusions she made to the recent dismissal of Emanuele Filiberto
from his army command. From Almonds Hotel on Clifford Street off Bond
Street, Hélène wrote to 'dearest Georgie' about her plans for another escape trip
to Africa. The King was away at the time, and Hélène hoped he was 'having a
rest in the good scottish air away from difficulties & troubles which are now the
plague of Europe.' She had been hoping to see him 'to facilitate my having paper
for British colonies—a sort of permanent letter—which can go all round—to tell
governors of sorts that i am "me"—& asking him or them to help me in anny
thing i need—& also giving me a special permit to carry my 303 rifle.' At that
point, she had not decided:

> which side of Africa i shall go—but the doctor says i must go to some tropical
> climate right away from this dreadful Europe—as four years of war work have
> finished ruining my health—& then it is difficult to know where are as yet
> the differant African frontiers! Sir Rennell Rodd your ex ambassador in Rome
> kindly promised to look up the matter for me—but i though i had better let
> you know myself", signing off with 'My very best love to May—Ever your
> devoted old friend, Hélène.[15]

The Duchess's penmanship was strikingly angular, and her spelling idiosyncratic
at times. Hélène's niece—the younger Isabelle, Comtesse de Paris—would later
comment that 'Aunt Hélène was a remarkable spirit in every way, but her spelling, like that of many members of the family, was rather deficient.' So, whenever
she had a telegram to send, she would give it to her Zulu servant Pedro, and
he would correct the mistakes.[16] Generally, however, Hélène's correspondence
shows a good command of Italian, English, and especially French, which was her

usual language for letters as well as her preferred language for reading material.

While in London, Hélène was able to see her dearest sister Isabelle again. Although seven years younger than Hélène, Isabelle held a special place in her heart, deepened by their mutual love of Africa where the Guise family had lived since 1909. When they parted this time, Hélène wrote that 'it seems to me that you have carried away something of mine—something that you will keep with the old things from the past, things that you preciously preserve—Keep this piece of my heart which is always yours.'[17]

Before Hélène was able to get off on her newest African adventure, there was a new European crisis, and the Aostas ended up in the middle of it. Earlier in the year, the Paris Peace Conference had not gone the way that Italy expected. Part of their dithering about entering the war in 1915 was the hopeful expectation of negotiating territorial gains at the end of the war, first deciding which would likely be the winning side. The 1915 secret Treaty of London with Britain and France had promised Italy the Trentino, the South Tyrol, Venezia Giulia, the Istrian peninsula, Dalmatia, and almost the whole of Albania.[18] However, that had been done before the entry of the United States into the war, and now they would have to contend with President Woodrow Wilson's determination to ignore any secret treaties, to uphold the rights of recognized nationalities and especially to ensure that the entire Dalmatian coast went to the new country of Yugoslavia. Italian ambitions were to the contrary, were branded as imperialistic by the peace conference, and their cause was not benefitted when the Prime Minister decided to absent himself from the negotiations on the pretext of returning to Rome to seek support from the legislature. The other three key leaders simply proceeded to negotiate to Italy's detriment. D'Annunzio, however, very much played up the imperial theme reminding Italians of the glories of both the Roman Empire and the Venetian Empire, calling it their true inheritance. While d'Annunzio built up public opinion against the Allies and the Italian government for its lack of support in establishing a new and vast empire, Benito Mussolini began to develop his first militia groups, combat bands which he called the *fasci di combattimento*. The Fascist movement had grown so rapidly that when it held its First National Congress of *Fasci di Combattimento* in Florence in October 1919, there were already some 40,000 members in 150 local branches.[19]

In a great symbolic act, the peace treaty between the Allies and the Central Powers was finally signed on 28 June 1919, the fifth anniversary of the assassination of Archduke Franz Ferdinand. The venue was the Hall of Mirrors at Versailles, where the German Empire had been proclaimed in 1871, just months before Hélène's birth.[20] By the end of the peace negotiations Italy had indeed gained vast amounts of new territory, chief among them the South Tyrol and the port of Trieste. Recognizing Italian defense needs, even President Wilson had done a volte-face from his usual policy of emphasizing ethnic rights for minorities when he accepted the award of the largely German-speaking South Tyrol to Italy to provide a more secure northern border. On the Adriatic, the city of Trieste which had been developed by the Austro-Hungarian Empire as their great outlet into the Mediterranean now became Italian. The nationalists still cried for more, and complained bitterly that they had suffered a 'mutilated victory', a theme that would resound throughout the coming decade. President Wilson had gone from saviour-hero to villain.

Then, against a background of postwar social agitation and national strikes throughout Italy, three times in 1919, there were rumours of possible *coups d'état*, and Emanuele Filiberto was implicated each time. In June 1919, there were reports of a possible coup involving a former war minister, General Gaetano Giardino, with support from both d'Annunzio and Mussolini as well as the nationalist Luigi Federzoni. The rumours including even deposing the king if he resisted and replacing him with Emanuele Filiberto. The British ambassador wrote to London about the growth of an 'extra-parliamentary movement to take things out of the hands of the professional politicians' and did not envy the king's task in dealing with it. The King reacted 'by saying that he was ready to take a gun and fight in the streets to defend law and order and the constitution.'[21]

Perhaps as a reaction to these potential military threats, or perhaps simply as part of the general demobilisation and downsizing of the army, Emanuele Filiberto's Third Army was dissolved on 22 July 1919, and he was relieved of his command, a decision he learned of by telegram rather than in person, which only added to the humiliation of being dismissed after four hard years of war.[22] He was relegated to the essentially honorary position of Inspector of the Infantry. Having earlier been denied the High Command of the Italian army 'for dynastic reasons' and now left without a substantive military role, this effective demotion for fifty-year-old Emanuele appears to be the turning point when he began to explore other options. A few years later, when the King promoted Emanuele—along with Generals Badoglio, Caviglia, Giardino, and Pecori-Giraldi—to the rank of marshal in honour of the eighth anniversary of the victory at Piave, it was simply another empty honour.

Soon, rumours of a military *coup d'état* in Rome were circulating among diplomatic circles. H. W. Kennard wrote to the British Foreign from the embassy in Rome that the names of General Enrico Caviglia and General Gaetano Giardino were mentioned in particular, and the army was said to be 'much incensed' by the recent abrupt dismissals of high-ranking officers by the new Prime Minister Francesco Nitti, who had come into office in June upon the fall of the Orlando government. 'It has even been suggested that the King may abdicate, and the Duke of Aosta, who is very popular with the army, may act as Regent.' Kennard closed by saying 'I only mention such rumours as indicating the sultriness of the political atmosphere.' In August, there had been newspaper rumours that Emanuele Filiberto would perhaps make a visit to the United States and then go on to China and Japan, but these rumours came to nothing as matters heated up at home.[23]

There were more formal plans for Emanuele Filiberto to visit the United States the following year, plans which were said to be supported by the king and prime minister. These plans likewise came to nothing even though they had been brought to the attention of President Wilson who suggested 'I think it highly desirable that the contemplated visit of the Duke D'Aosta should be postponed. I am sure the new administration will desire an opportunity for a splurge, and such a visit would afford it.'[24]

The port city of Fiume on the Adriatic was part of the Austro-Hungarian Empire and had an Italian majority population, which in October 1918 had elected a National Council which in turn declared its desire to join Italy. Fiume was indeed part of the Adriatic territory promised to Italy by the Treaty of London and which had been occupied by Italian troops on behalf of the Allied Powers as a temporary expediency until the final peace was determined. Nonetheless, internationally, Fiume was seen as integral to the new kingdom of Yugoslavia (officially the Kingdom of the Serbs, Croats and Slovenes until 1929 but informally known as Yugoslavia), and the Treaty of St-Germain-en-Laye, one of the last of the Paris Peace Conference treaties, signed 10 September 1919, formally disestablished the old Austro-Hungarian Empire and established the new borders. Dissatisfied with the idea that Fiume would pass to the newly formed Yugoslavia, Gabriele d'Annunzio took matters into his own hands and collected a ragtag band of followers calling themselves the Legion, which included some 2,500 men—'adventurers, disillusioned veterans, notably the tough *arditi*, Futurists, and schoolboys,' as well as the frontline detachment of Sardinian Grenadiers which had formerly occupied Fiume.[25] Together they marched to claim Fiume. They arrived at Fiume on the 12th, and the next day d'Annunzio was given military control over the city. Only four days later, a nationalist delegation arrived to attempt to persuade d'Annunzio to march on Rome and proclaim himself as dictator of all Italy. D'Annunzio wrote to Emanuele Filiberto to remind him of their last meeting together in Venice on 28 July—just days after the disbanding of the Third Army—when they stood hand-in-hand and the duke told the poet: 'I have overcome every hesitation. When the country needs me and calls me, I am ready.' To this, d'Annunzio added 'The hour has come ... The army is ready and awaits its head. The streets are open, and everything leads to Rome.'[26] In the end, Emanuele Filiberto declined this blatant invitation to treason and d'Annunzio declined to act on own on a national scale, but it was a strange foreshadowing of what Mussolini could and did accomplish just a few years later.[27] For some reason, the Allies decided to treat it as an Italian rebellion to be solved by the Italian government and ordered its other troops removed from Fiume.

Despite—or perhaps because of—Aosta's possible involvement in planning a coup, a different role for him was considered. Only a few days after Kennard's letter, the British Ambassador himself, Sir Rennell Rodd, wrote to London:

> I think it would be possible when the opportune moment comes to bring the
> army into line under the Duke of Aosta, who is immensely popular with them,
> and substitute him for d'Annunzio if the powers could put Fiume provisionally
> under Italian occupation.

A few days later, Emanuele Filiberto was called to Rome to meet with Prime
Minister Nitti and Foreign Minister Tommaso Tittoni to discuss a possible role
for him in the Fiume situation. Rodd telegraphed the Home Office following
his own meeting with Tittoni who had told him that he believed the position
'could be saved' if they could secure d'Annunzio's withdrawal and get the Great
Powers' approval of Italian troops remaining in Fiume 'under orders of a General
or a Prince,' mentioning Aosta by name. In a follow-up letter the same day,
Rodd wrote that the government had already approached Emanuele Filiberto
to ascertain whether he would be ready to step in.[28] At this point, Aosta was
definitely working with the government rather than against it, but this would all
change very quickly.

By the next day, there were American diplomatic rumours out of Washington—
which was itself was reeling from the news that President Wilson had suffered an
incapacitating stroke—that Emanuele Filiberto was going to be sent to Fiume as
Joint Allied Commissioner to take control of Fiume with d'Annunzio agreeing
to serve under him. Instead, he left Turin on 11 October for Paris, and then on to
Belgium. The newspapers reported that the King had sent him into exile because
of his attitude toward d'Annunzio's raid on Fiume, but in view of the recent government proposals this is unlikely. The next month, Emanuele was back in Rome
greeting the King upon his return from San Rossore.

In early November, Hélène visited the war cemeteries at Monfalcone and
Aquileia, praying at the grave of Giovanni Randaccio, a young soldier and close
colleague of d'Annunzio who was killed at the Isonzo and whose dying body
the poet had supported on the battlefield and pillowed with the national tricolour, the same flag he now held in Fiume. Hélène then inflamed the political
situation—intentionally or otherwise—by going into the city of Fiume in a Red
Cross division to inspect Hospital No. 107. According to a local newspaper report,
Hélène, 'having inspected all the wards, accompanied by all the Doctors and the
Medical Officer, Major Cav Pulle, and after stopping at the bedside of several
patients, remained for a long period in prayer near the bier' of Luigi Siviero.
Siviero, the first of d'Annunzio's legionnaires to die in the city, had been killed by
a government patrol when he attempted to cross the demarcation line to go to
a tavern for a drink.[29] Then, in the evening, while passing through Piazza Dante:

> [She was] recognised by some officers and loudly cheered. Immediately, a large
> crowd of citizens collected and improvised a lively demonstration of affection

and gratitude for the august lady. So great was the crowd of civilians and soldiers that the car was obliged to stop several times, and the Duchess bent forward smiling to thank the citizens for their spontaneous and hearty reception.

Hélène found the people now in Fiume 'electrified' by d'Annunzio, the whole population 'shaking with a holy enthusiasm.' 'The delirious crowd, spread out in the streets, roaming while singing with the strength of a storm. Everyone was united in a single aspiration, and from each chest came a single cry of beauty and of hope: "Italy or Death."' D'Annunzio—whom Hélène called *Maître* and the Warrior Poet—told her that she would bring back a new book from her upcoming trip to Africa. Hélène responded 'How could I write? The War killed my soul; I am nothing more than a shadow, and shadows don't know how to write, shadows are inert, shadows don't know how to feel.' Having seen so much death and suffering, she felt that something inside her had been broken.[30]

The next day, d'Annunzio made Hélène's visit a key point of his funeral oration for Siviero, and reaction in Rome was furious. Prime Minister Nitti 'with extreme anger' told Emanuele Filiberto in no uncertain terms that he was not to enter any of the former war zone without specific authorization and that the same applied to Hélène. When Nitti informed the king, Victor Emmanuel first asked Queen Elena to join them, and then told the prime minister to supervise the movements of the Aostas and to inform him of all their actions. Nitti complained that Hélène not only 'spoke too much' but also 'acted too much and too inconsiderately'. He felt that with her 'vain and scheming spirit' she was no friend to the king and 'above all an enemy to the queen,' who she ridiculed as 'my cousin the shepherdess.' Even more worrisome was Emanuele's connections with d'Annunzio and the army, a combination which might provide a possible trigger for a coup and deposing the king. Nitti telegrammed the foreign minister Tittoni that the best thing would be for the Duke and Duchess to leave Italy for some time.[31]

For over a year, d'Annunzio reigned as ruler of Fiume until the 11 November 1920 Treaty of Rapallo between Italy and Yugoslavia, which declared Fiume to be an independent state, and it was ordered that d'Annunzio be expelled from the city, which took place finally on 18 January 1921. As a recent biographer of d'Annunzio assessed his role in the development of fascism put it, 'though d'Annunzio was not a fascist, fascism was d'Annunzian.' Signs of this were evident in the 'black shirts, the straight-armed salute, the songs and war cries, the glorification of virility and youth and *patria* and blood sacrifice,' which were part of life in Fiume three years before Mussolini's March on Rome.[32]

At some point during this tumultuous year of 1919, Amedeo was diagnosed with bilateral apical pulmonary tuberculosis and was sent to various sanatoria to recover and after that a long holiday was ordered.[33] Serious illnesses would plague Amedeo for the rest of his life, although his strong constitution and healthy good looks usually belied the underlying problems. At this time, the official cover for this 'holiday' seems to have been a trip to Somalia with his uncle. On 19 October Hélène went to see off Amedeo and Luigi Abruzzi *en route* for Mogadisco on a 'scientific mission.' This was the second visit Luigi made to the banks of the Webi-Shebelle River in Somalia in search of a location for an agricultural colony which he proposed to establish. Eventually, he created the Società Agricola Italo-Somala, which leased land to local labour in return for a salary and a share in the harvest. Over the years, the settlement became the most productive area in Somalia, and in 1921, the visiting governor christened the new settlement Villaggio Duca degli Abruzzi.[34]

In early December 1919, Hélène herself embarked on another lengthy trip to Africa, which would eventually provide the basis for her third major travel book *La Vie Errante: Sensations d'Afrique.* The epigraph for that book reproduced in Hélène's handwriting spoke of her unfulfilled, perhaps unfulfillable, quest. She strove 'towards the ideal, always pursued, never attained, which throughout life leads us from dream to dream to the tomb.'[35]

This departure, however, did not bring the lightness of spirit that earlier trips had. Hélène recognized the toll that the war had taken on her, combined with the fact that at age forty-eight, she was now in the 'autumn of life.' She reflected on youth: 'As for me, I regret perhaps that which wasn't done, the hopes that weren't realized, more than that which I was given. I am not one of those who judge youth as the most beautiful time of life! Youth is a liar. Maturity seems to me more comfortable. My old age strikes me with its gentleness, as the evening of life, in descending, carries with it its own illumination.' For Hélène, that never erased that 'thirst for the unknown' which drove her to travel.[36]

She left Naples aboard the *Porto di Savona* on 4 December and, accompanied by Carlo Torrigiani, headed for the Suez Canal. Most of her fellow passengers were colonial officials who had come to Europe to fight in the war and were now returning to take up their posts once again, leaving many dead companions on the battlefields. After settling a sailors' strike at Catania by providing a sufficient ration of tobacco for them, the *Porto di Savona* steamed across the Mediterranean, through the Suez Canal and into the Red Sea. The suffocating heat and heavy humidity combined to make 'red nights, tropical nights, where the body left its damp imprint on the sheet and where one could never find the hoped-for rest.' At Massawa in Eritrea, Hélène wondered if she would stop there, in what place would she begin her *vie errante*—her wandering life.[37]

Hélène grew quite wistful at this point. 'Am I not an uprooted one who always goes where destiny pushes her, an uprooted one whose name is written in the sand?'[38] She wondered if she were not like one of the blue lotus flowers called 'Sans Patrie,' the homeless. Floating along lakes and rivers, their roots just brushing the banks, pushed along by the current.

The blue lotus was an image from theosophy, a philosophy which interested Hélène. Based in a more ancient form of esotericism, the modern movement was

founded in New York City in 1875. Through it, theosophists sought to understand the mysteries of the universe and the bonds that unite humanity with the
divine. They also believed in clairvoyance and reincarnation and became strongly
linked with eastern, specifically Indian, thought. Hélène herself had long been
drawn to such considerations, and she kept a number of books on theosophy in
her personal library at Capodimonte. While at Castellamare in April 1909, she
read *Le soi et ses enveloppes* by Annie Besant, one of the movements leaders and
later a key personality in the women's suffrage movement as well as promoting
home rule for India and Ireland. While she was in Benares, India, in 1913, Hélène
also read John Murdoch's debunking book *The theosophic craze; the great Mahatma
hoax; How Mrs Besant was befooled and deposed...*, which encouraged Hindus to
avoid 'what is virtually a godless philosophy' and remain true to the concept of
'the Fatherhood of God and Brotherhood of Man.'

Towards the beginning of the First World War, Hélène received from Luigi
Luzzatti a copy of his Italian translation of *Crescent Moon* by Rabindranath Tagore,
who had been the first non-European to win the Nobel Prize for literature which
he was awarded in 1913. She wrote to Luzzatti, who had been prime minister for
about a year in 1910–1911, to thank him for the book, saying that she appreciated his fine translation of the work she had originally read in English as well
as his introduction:

> But I must confess that the contrast between the character of the Hindu race
> and the cult of action which animates the poet of *Gitanjali* does not appear to
> me as sharp as it seems to you. This is perhaps because I always thought that the
> entire Hindu race constitute a mass of contradictions in itself. It almost seems to
> me as if the two ancient stocks, the Aryan and the Negroid, which contributed
> to its formation, have not found the way to reconcile their sharp ethnic charac-
> ters after so many centuries. For this reason it is so easy to find in India people
> for all tastes, theories for all scholars, and proselytes for all sects. Buddha, who
> preaches renunciation, is side by side with Kâlî, who advises satiety. And the
> philosopher of contemplation will be condemned to finding proselytes who
> will raise titanic monuments for every speck of his ashes, filling the Orient with
> their monstrous *dagoubes*.
>
> But who knows what will grow from the seed that one sows? Surely the
> Enlightened One did not foresee the fetichism that was to arise about his name.[39]

They kept in touch—mostly in the form of brief telegrams—until after the war,
and Hélène's interest in both Hinduism and Buddhism, which was sparked by her
visit to Ceylon where she saw the two religions constantly intermingled, continued to some degree for the rest of her life. Her granddaughters remember in the
1930s that there was a small room at Capodimonte between her bedroom and
dressing room which was always kept closed. One day, it was left ajar, and inside,

they saw a statue of Buddha with candles burning in front of it.

The travellers continued along the Eritrean coast to Assab, but mechanical troubles with the ship delayed the journey. On New Year's Day 1920, they were still aground, and Hélène grew melancholy. 'There is no happy life, there are only happy days, for each of us, to content oneself in the present time, which is no more than an instant: the rest of existence is nothing more, or is uncertain,' and then 'Every day moves towards death, the last one arrives there.' As always, when Hélène was not able to be active, she grew bored quickly. For some reason, she went off on a different tangent and decided:

> Cannibals who bravely eat their enemies are more respectable than Christians who cowardly tear apart their friends. As for Christian charity, much is spoken, little is practiced! Charity is to wish for another that which you wish for yourself, it's to give what you have, the rich, their gold; the poor, their heart; and me, my life. It is knowing how to accept the hardest renunciations, it is holding out one's hand to one who has fallen, it is to warm what is cold, to suffer with one in sadness. But only the eyes which have cried much know how to see the tears at the bottom of hearts in pain. Charity is to know how to 'love', to love again, to love always.[40]

Finally, they got underway again and passed into French Somaliland, stopping at Djibouti, before steaming across the Gulf of Aden to Aden itself, and then into the Indian Ocean, bound for Mogadiscio, the capital of Italian Somaliland. There, they were finally able to bid farewell to their ship and begin their land journey on 10 January. Even at times like saying good-bye to the steamer, Hélène grew melancholy. '*Adieu Porto di Savona adieu!* Again an *adieu* amongst so many *adieux*! Life is a long *adieu* renewed each day, where sometimes tears burst forth, where always new beginnings are born.'[41]

Once she left the ship, Hélène moved into the bush and at Afgoi, she recorded her first night ashore. 'It is my first night on the ground of Africa, ground so much desired, ground finally refound, ground again and always more loved.' At Lugh, Hélène grew rhapsodic about her tent:

> My tent, my beautiful tent, a flying house for a wandering soul, a nomad like me, me at last under your shelter, me at last at home, after a long absence, after an abandonment of too many years. Dear tent, how much I love you, I am happy to own nothing other than you. Property restricts the souls and makes it lose something of its lightness. Here they call me "The Bedouin princess."[42]

Generally, this trip evoked more sadness than pleasure for Hélène. 'I meditate on the beauty of my wandering life and on the sorrow of my other life, of my European life, which I flee as I plunge myself into the bush, further each hour as if I was sinking into oblivion.' For Hélène, it was far better 'to feel lost in fabulous Africa, one no longer thinks about the goal one is trying to reach but is swallowed up by each hour. Every minute fills the heart, as if it were the most beautiful and the most pure; after which there is only a small very sweet anxiety of not knowing when or where it will end.' They continued inland by mule and camels carrying 50-litre water tanks, pitching their tents in the desert and onward to the banks of the Giuba and then back into the bush in the heart of Somalia. The caravan returned to the banks of the Giuba at the end of February and continued by automobile and then by boat to Zanzibar.[43]

While Hélène was approaching Zanzibar in March, so was Amedeo who had recently spent two months with his uncle Luigi Abruzzi in Somalia. When she reached there she found Amedeo critically ill in hospital with an attack of amoebic dysentery.[44] Coming so soon after his treatment for tuberculosis, the situation was considered critical. Hélène wrote of that moment in the hospital in Zanzibar in a way that was all too prescient of what would later happen in 1942:

Oh! Mothers who lose your children, your pain is not comparable to any other pain!

Today I saw Death, and she was at the bedside of my son. My heart stopped beating and Death bent down. My eyes closed; when I opened them again, Death had vanished.

Now my son lays on his bed, all white, in the middle of a completely pure room. Two women, rigid and silent, watch over him, and through the big open windows comes the salty air, reviving and beneficial and, his eyes half-closed, he rests my little child, today a man, a giant, but for me, his mother, always my little child, tender and cajoling. The ebb and the flow of the sea rocks his consciousness, the waves come to beat against the fine sand and the bottom of the hospital walls.

Today I was afraid, afraid of losing my firstborn, and now the reaction makes me tremble. I am tired and I rest my drooping arms, my vacant eyes; my thoughts float round about me, grounding themselves on the deep sea, and resting on its infinite immensity, from an eternal and religious silence.[45]

Amedeo did indeed recover from this illness, and mother and son returned to Europe together. In early April, they returned by train from Mombasa to Nairobi and the Norfolk Hotel. As she prepared to leave, Hélène grew despondent about the prospect. 'In Africa my wandering soul could remain, live, enjoy each hour that passes.' When she was in Europe:

It seems to me that I am never really there, coming from another world which I carry everywhere with me. There I always need to take refuge somewhere out of time and the world, and the wings of my astral body always transport me to Africa.

My isolated soul is taken by the nostalgia of forever being lulled into infinity. But infinity, what is it? In infinity there is the sky because of the stars, the sea because of its innumerable drops of drop, and the heart because of its tears.[46]

Hélène and Amedeo left for Italy, arriving first in Turin, and then going to Naples on 19 July.

The postwar period in Italy—the *dopoguerra*—saw Italy riven by workplace strikes, and for nearly a month many feared an imminent revolution. In September 1920, some half a million workers occupied factories and shipyards, 'running up red (socialist) or black (anarchist) flags and demanding worker control.'[47] Prime Minister Giolitti was able to mediate terms which included higher pay, shorter hours, and better conditions for the workers and avoided more serious ramifications. Hélène herself was briefly caught up in the tail end of the problems in a minor way when a strike by the railwaymen's union in October stopped her train a mile and three-quarters from the station in Naples, forcing her to walk the rest of the way along the rails.

Count Carlo Sforza, who was Foreign Minister from 1920 to 1921 under the post-war Giolitti government, complained that during this same period the Duke of Aosta had 'contracted a bad attack of thronitis: for two years he did not leave me a moment's peace, trying to persuade me to have him appointed King of Poland, King of Hungary...When I mentioned it to the King he used to mutter: "If it were only that..."'[48] Neither the thought of placing Emanuele Filiberto (or any of the others Aostas) on a throne, nor the dislike between the cousins was a new issue. Emanuele had indeed been heir to the Spanish throne during his father's brief reign in Madrid. In January 1917, the *Washington Post* published a report from Rome that King Constantine of the Hellenes was to be deposed and 'the *entente* allies have offered the throne to the Duke of Aosta', and claimed that 'the duke has the proposal under consideration and that the entente's choice has the approval of the Venizelist party, which has revolted against Constantine and set up at Salonika an independent government which has been cherished by the entente.'[49] Both during and immediately after the war, there were plans to create separate monarchies in Hungary, Albania, Finland, Lithuania and Poland, and princes from the various surviving monarchies had been suggested including Emanuele Filiberto, his brothers, and Hélène's brother Ferdinand. Although there had been many monarchies (including all the minor German kingdoms, principalities, grand duchies and duchies) in 1914 and only a few remained, the concept of a royal head of state still appealed to many.

There was alleged friction between Aosta and his cousin King Victor Emmanuel from their boyhoods onwards, and Emanuele Filiberto's name was frequently mentioned in the coming decade as part of potential coups. In October, *The Times* in London published another story that the Duke of Aosta, this time in company with General Enrico Caviglia and Admiral Enrico Millo, was meeting with Prime Minister Giolitti in Rome as leaders of a 'rumoured militarist plot.'[50]

The next year Emanuele Filiberto found himself publicly named in newspaper accounts 'accusing him of inspiring and protecting the Fascisti' as well as continually striving to gain the throne, when Francesco Ciccotti, editor of *Il Paese*, considered the chief newspaper supporter of Francesco Nitti, published a 'violent attack' on Aosta.'[51] A libel action was filed against the paper, and the issue seems to have temporarily subsided, and Emanuele Filiberto remained popular around the country as '*il duca invitto*' (the unconquered duke) and he continued to play a prominent role on the national scene.

On 28 October 1921, the bodies of eleven nameless soldiers who had died on different battlefields were brought to the Cathedral in Aquileia. A woman who lost her son in the war entered the Cathedral and dropped a white flower on one of the biers to determine which would be honored as the country's unknown soldier. Emanuele Filiberto, representing the army, then stepped forward and replaced the flower with a bronze wreath. The other biers were left to rest permanently within the Cathedral, but the one with the bronze wreath was taken to the church of Santa Maria degli Angeli in Rome to be blessed by the leading army chaplain. There, Hélène and her sons attended a memorial service on 3 November, when Princess Laetitia laid a wreath as president of the National Association of Mothers and Widows of the Fallen. The next day—the third anniversary of Italy's victory—Hélène and Emanuele Filiberto joined the King and Queen and the rest of the royal family when the unknown soldier was finally laid to rest at the Altar of the Country, which stood above the main steps of the Vittoriano and immediately beneath the gigantic equestrian statue of King Victor Emmanuel II.[52] Rome was overflowing with people from all over the country as pilgrims and mourners, to join in the event. They had slept in the streets, in the National Stadium, in the Colosseum, wherever they could find a spot.

> Bitter differences were set aside for the day as Communists wearing their badges with hammer and scythe stood alongside Fascisti in black shirts embroidered with skull and crossbones, mothers proudly displaying the medals won by their dead sons, little school children dressed in white, clustered around bespectacled priests, maimed soldiers who were carried on stretchers, blinded soldiers who wanted the hear, though they could not see the ceremony.[53]

It was in March 1921 that Hélène stepped down from her position as Inspector General of the Italian Red Cross Nurses, a post she had held since its inception in 1915, and a grateful Red Cross now conferred upon her the title of Honorary Inspector General of Volunteer Nurses.[54]

Many members of Hélène's extended family were in London during the late spring of 1921. Isabelle de Guise went to tea at the Palace along with her daughters Isabelle and Françoise and brother Ferdy Montpensier. The next week, it was Aimone who went to luncheon with the King and Queen one day, and then with the Prince of Wales lunched with Queen Alexandra at Marlborough House the next day. King George pronounced him 'charming' and wrote to Hélène that 'both May & I fell in love with him, he is so like you & talks like you, so how could we do otherwise' and signing off 'with best love from May, Ever your old friend Georgie.'[55]

Hélène herself arrived from Paris a few days later; she and Bob were back at Marlborough House visiting Queen Alexandra a few days later, and Hélène accompanied Queen Alexandra and Princess Victoria to the grand annual event of Trooping the Colour on Horse Guards Parade. The next day, they all went to the Palace for luncheon joined by 'Bob.'[56] It was full social season, and the Aostas did the rounds. Hélène attended a concert at the home of the Duchess of Rutland with Prince Alexis Obolensky singing. It was a splashy affair with Queen Alexandra, Princess Victoria, Infanta Beatrice of Spain, and the Princess Royal in attendance, but also the Aga Khan, Mrs Ronald Grenville, Lady Diana Cooper, and Mrs Cornelius Vanderbilt. It was one social event after another— Aimone dined with Lady Cunard at Carlton House Terrace, Hélène went to the Richmond Royal Horse Show with Queen Alexandra and Princess Victoria, then to the opening day of an exhibition of paintings by Onorato Carlandi at the Walker's Gallery, New Bond Street, and visited the Italian Hospital in London, where she 'showed great interest in its organization and management.'[57]

Hélène went on to Biarritz with both of her sons, but left after a few days to attend the wedding of her youngest brother. Ferdinand Montpensier was nearly thirty-seven when he married a twenty-five-year-old Spanish noblewoman, Maria Isabel González de Ocampo, Marquesa de Valdeterrazo. It was not the sort of royal match that might have been anticipated, but the family was getting desperate to produce an heir in the next generation. The low-key wedding took place at the Château de Randan, which Ferdinand had inherited from their mother. Philippe d'Orléans had left England for a hunting expedition to East Africa earlier in the month as he was still barred from entering France, but he was represented as a witness by his brother-in-law the Duc de Guise, with Queen Amélie as Ferdinand's other witness.

In 1921, Hélène started a new guestbook at Capodimonte, although like many things she did, it was neither routine nor ordinary. Guests would indeed sign their name as normal and a photograph of the occasion would be included, but in addition Hélène installed a balance just outside her apartment and would weigh her luncheon guests after they finished their meal. Over the years few would be exempt from this little game. Hélène herself weighed in at 63 kg that first year, and Manolo at 85 kg, while Bob was 71.6 kg when he returned from a naval cruise to South America but later earned multiple exclamation points in his entry when he reached 99.2 kg in 1935, while Bouby weighed 85 kg, one of his heaviest, at his first entry in 1921. Even the King and Queen of Spain were duly weighed and recorded, while Hélène's sister, the rather portly Queen Amélie, seems to be one of the few who refused to participate in this ritual.[58]

The year 1921 also marked the publication of Hélène's third and final major travel book, *Vie errante: Sensations d'Afrique*. Published by Francesco Viassone in Ivrea, as were her two previous volumes, this edition was perhaps, the least successful as a travel book, as Hélène tried to be more poetic and more philosophical, influenced, no doubt, by d'Annunzio's style and his injunction that she return from Africa with a book manuscript. Whereas in her earlier books, she emphasized the people and the hunting, now it was more attempts at being poetic about the landscapes, sounds, and her own emotions.

> No imagination, if the eyes had not seen it, no description could render the miracle of colours that the Nigerian sky showed us this evening when the sun, passing from blue to pink, from ochre to bronze, bathing the water in coloured light, declined toward the horizon. The sky is marvelously clear, everywhere the stars sparkle like diamonds on velvet. But the moon, which is waning, has not risen yet … Nature is a mirror where everyone can find oneself, receiving from it the joy or the sorrow that one brings.[59]

Hélène wrote these words in January 1922 while aboard the *Gazelle*, a barge negotiating the Niger River in French West Africa. This new adventure, which was the basis of 'Souvenirs d'Afrique,' later published in *La Revue Universelle*, provided Hélène with the opportunity to share more of her African impressions. Among the early memories of that trip, Hélène recorded that the 'laptops'—the Senegalese in the service of France—rowed well and strongly, with the perfect movement of a clock.

At Sansanding, in present-day Mali, Hélène encountered 'des Maures' (the Moors) for the first time encamped in a corner of the village with their camels in search of millet, which they did not cultivate themselves. Hélène was enthralled. 'They are all handsome, with a captivating beauty; heads of Christ hardened by the rough life of the desert… If I were young and strong I would follow them, I would go with them. Where? I don't know.'

Their guide—who spoke excellent French '*sans accent*'—had lived at Toulouse but was a son of the last king, Bama-Mademba, who had been dead for several years but had been both loved and feared and had had at his disposal three thousand warriors armed with rifles. Now, this son was a school teacher and his brother operated the village store and represented an English merchant firm at Bamako. Hélène thought this a 'curious destiny for the descendants of an ancient line which had reigned for a long time over this region of the great placid river.' The guide decried the advent of western civilization, remembering the old days when prisoners taken in battle did the work, and there was plenty of food for everyone. Now, one had to pay for everything, people worked very little, and there was hunger.

Hélène visited the village mosque, which she found 'poor, primitive, ruined, burned by the hot sun and so touching!' The boatmen were all Muslims, and 'each morning, each midday, and each evening with the same noble and tranquil movement, all of Islam bowed toward Mecca to adore God and to praise Mohammed, his prophet.'[60]

Further along the river at Mopti, they went by automobile to the cliff of Saugha, a place where Hélène felt she had either had a beautiful dream or been transported to another planet. Climbing up the stairs to the top of the cliffs made Hélène think of the image of the angels on Jacob's ladder. The villages in the plain grew smaller and smaller as they climbed higher and higher. The sunshine sparkled. As they reached the large flat rocks of the summit, suddenly groups of 'devils'—'red devil, black devil'—their faces covered by fabulous masks began a 'demented' dance to wild music. Suddenly it stopped and the silence was replaced by a solemn sort of plain-chant. The party then re-grouped and carried on as if in a dream.

It was now early February as Hélène rejoined the *Gazelle* on the Niger proceeding to Arabébé, a tugboat now towing them, replacing the polemen as the water grew deeper and wider. Due to a fear of rampaging lions in the area, five cows were staked out in the brush as potential meals for the lions, as alternatives to the people. However, the cows were spared as the lions seemed to have migrated.

At their next stopping point, they were greeted by Touaregs—the nomadic Berber people of the Sahara—'with their herds, their tents, their women, their camels.' They exchanged some milk for sugar and tea. Hélène found them too a handsome people, 'all of them taller than me.' In her honour, they saddled a camel, upon which she hoisted herself to their great amusement. When she was leaving Hélène conveyed her good wishes through the interpreter to the village chief. The chief in return that she pleased them and that they loved her. They declared that she was a great 'fama,' a great woman king. But then the chief posed the question, 'In France, the whites have kings but they suppress ours. Why?' Although Hélène was well aware that the natives assumed all Europeans were from France and that some of them had kings, she didn't record her response.

As they progressed to Niafonki, Hélène wondered why French archaeologists had not yet investigated the remains in the many tumuli in the Niafonki and Godam circle. From these great burial mounds came ancient bronze items, wooden sarcophagi, glazed pottery and blue glass beads which she felt raised the possibility that these artifacts may have originally come from Egypt.[61]

In the early afternoon of 9 February, they reached Kabara, the port for the fabled city of Timbuktu. To prepare 'my soul to see the mysterious city' the next day, Hélène had her chaise longue placed on top of a sand dune, from where she pondered what she would soon see. Then, a cloud of dust caught her attention, growing larger and closer until it stopped in front of her. It was Colonel Mangeot, who galloped to her side from Timbuktu along with his escort. When she heard that Madame Mangeot was also on her way to greet her in the village, Hélène mounted the colonel's horse and rode off to meet her so that she could avoid meeting her at the dock where the tug and barge had moored. News of Hélène's arrival had quickly spread through the village of Kabara, and Chebboun, a Touareg chief, came to see her. This was the chief who with men of his tribe had recently killed the lieutenant of the vessel *Hubert*. After the customary compliments, Hélène examined his weapons. Chebboun then took off the dagger which customarily never left a Touareg's arm and presented it to Hélène, which she took as a great sign of friendship, a great homage, and an extraordinary sign of deference. 'My first step to the Touaregs of Timbuktu is a triumph.' Then in the pale yet sparkling moonlight, a troop of horsemen and Meharists—the camel troops—came off the dune with a magnificent camel larger than the others at its head. The camel noiselessly knelt down, and Madame Mangeot descended. For dinner that night, they enjoyed roast crocodile which one of her companions found nauseating to even think about but which Hélène found delicious, rather like very tender young veal.

> Timbuktu the mysterious
> Timbuktu, the veiled queen
> Timbuktu, the door to the Sahara
> Timbuktu finally! Timbuktu, you are one of my great African dreams! *Salut*!

When they arrived in Timbuktu, the colonel was astride a thoroughbred horse, but Hélène chose to ride a camel as she had always imagined that was how she would arrive. A detachment of French lancers rode escort, while Tourareg horsemen galloped around them and entoning a war chant. Two young warriors spurred their horses forward and clashed swords in a mock duel. But before they reached the city, there was a small detour into the bush to pay homage at the monument to the French soldiers killed in the taking of Timbuktu in December 1893. The colonel read the inscription aloud and finished by saying 'And here is one of those who, with his tribe, massacred our predecessors', indicating Chief Chebboun.[62]

Timbuktu did not disappoint Hélène as they toured both the European quarter and the wider city with its earthen buildings and their soft, almost shapeless contours. Particularly in the native quarters, Hélène was much taken with the antiquity and the calm, the calm of silence and meditation. But after dining with the Mangeots, they remounted—some on camels, some on horses—and returned to Kabara. All too soon, Hélène was back onboard the *Gazelle* travelling the Niger. Along this stretch of the river, hippopotamuses were the main amusement as they snorted, rose, and ducked, and seemed to taunt and mock the travellers.

The crocodiles along the same stretch were more of a concern. However amusing they might be, the hippos were still big game, and one morning five were spotted so Hélène grabbed her helmet and rifle and went ashore at the edge of a swamp. She waded into the river up to her knees, her skirt soaked and heavy. The black guide behind her whispered 'Crocodiles.' Finally, Hélène, with the water nearly up to her waist, fired and hit one of the hippos which rose up so that she could see its stomach before it floated away.[63]

When the tug *Ibis* blew its whistle outside the village of Gao, the whole population gathered at the quay as the *Gazelle* came to rest amid a bed of waterlilies in flower. Two days later at Komi, Hélène and the high chief Mohammet Lahami left before daybreak on horseback to explore the area even though the chief's only French words were 'Bonjour, merci' which he repeated regularly. On 22 February, they transferred from the *Gazelle* to some smaller barges on which they would negotiate the rapids. Through the skill of the helmsman, the passage among the high, sharp rocks was both easy and safe. At various points along the river, Hélène was able to bag a number of animals, most often gazelles and reed bucks.[64]

Hélène ended her published account on 19 March in the British territory of Nigeria, but she stayed in Africa for several months more, continuing her trip into the Congo. She returned to Dakar, where she met her younger son Aimone for more hunting trips into the bush. Aimone was part of an Italian mission which later continued on to conferences in Brazil and Argentina. Included in the mission was Professor Mario Mazzei, a well-known economist. In October, the mission returned to Africa, stopping again at Dakar, where Mazzei went ashore and never returned. His secretary gave out the story that the professor, who was an enthusiastic sportsman, had gone shooting. Two days later, Mazzei's body was found in the bush about twelve kilometres away, and his secretary was arrested for murder.

It was not until 8 July that Hélène was met by her sister Isabelle at Casablanca where she arrived from Dakar at the conclusion of her travels. When she returned to Europe, Hélène travelled with her sons in Spain; on 7 August, they met with Queen Victoria Eugenia, her two eldest sons, and the newly married Lord and Lady Louis Mountbatten at a fair in Santander. Hélène continued on from San Sebastian to the Miramar Palace at the invitation of the Queen Mother Maria Cristina before going to Paris. The Savoys returned to Italy, and Hélène spent the autumn with her usual mixture of public and private events—opening a fair in Rome with Emanuele Filiberto, visiting an art exhibition at the Pitti Palace in Florence, and travelling to Palermo before finally returning to Naples.

Aimone and Amedeo were now both continuing and extending their military careers alongside developing other interests including sports and the developing field of aeronautics for both of them, and for Amedeo a particular interest in Africa like his mother, while Aimone followed his uncle Luigi's passion for mountaineering. In 1921, Amedeo went to the Congo under the name of Della Cisterna and worked for thirteen months as a laborer in a soap factory. Hélène alone went to see him off at the pier.[65] It is said that she had arranged for Amedeo to work at 'Hulières du Congo Belge' in Stanleyville for an old friend of the Orléans family, Lord Leverhulme of the famous Lever Brothers. Speroni gives two versions of how this African adventure came about. One was that at a reception at the Quirinale, the King and Queen were uncharacteristically late to arrive. When they did, there was silence and bowing of heads and one voice—that of Amedeo—saying '*Ecco Curtatone e Montanara!*' This was a play on the name of the historic Battle of Curatone and Montanara fought on 29 May 1848 near Mantova, one of the most symbolic battles of the first war for independence, but more directly it was a jibe against the monarchs. 'Here's Shorty and the Mountain Woman!' Derogatory comments about the king's stature and the queen's rustic origins were commonplace. One nickname for the king was *sciaboletta* or 'little sabre' as he could not wear a full-length one, and cartoonists sometimes portrayed him dragging the scabbard behind him upon a little trolley.[66] The king thought that, while such comments might have to be borne from the press, princes of the royal houses were another matter. Emanuele Filiberto was called in and told that some things might be forgiven to boys but not to those over twenty. 'Your son must learn to curb his tongue and show some judgement. Some things you can forgive a child but not someone who has already reached twenty years. A bit of distance from Italy will mature him.' Amedeo was to go into exile abroad for at least a year, giving up the titles and prerogatives of his rank. The other explanation was that he wanted to see how he would have fared in life if he were not a prince. This was indeed the explanation he later gave to his old governess, Rina Piano, telling her that he worked in a factory for a year under an assumed name, and at the end of that period was offered the position of a director of the factory. However, then his identity became known, and he felt that he had to leave. Hélène later commented to her sister that his departure for the Congo cost Amedeo a lot but was good for him.[67]

By September 1922, Aimone was back in Britain, where he lighted briefly at Claridge's in London both before and after spending a few days in Scotland. Soon, Aimone, now a lieutenant commander in the Italian Navy, would leave for China to join his ship in Shanghai, sailing aboard the White Star liner *Majestic* from Cherbourg to New York, where he stayed at the Ritz Carlton Hotel and thence across America to sail the Pacific. As usual, he travelled officially incognito but not unrecognized by the press.

Meanwhile, Amedeo was finishing up his university studies in Palermo, where he spent a great deal of time with the exiled Greek royal family. Ex-King Constantine declared him to be 'a nice lad and very cheerful.'[68] Constantine's eldest daughter, Princess Helen of Romania, was among the many smitten by his good looks and charm. She wrote to her husband:

The Duke of Aosta's son is one of the most charming boys I have ever met …

very good-looking, one metre ninety-nine without shoes on and a wonderful figure. He... does all he can to cheer Mama up and is as kind as possible. He is on the go all day, has [military] service in the early morning, university in the afternoon and rides and bathes and comes to see us in his spare time. He has a motobicycle which he tears about on. We only saw him three days, then he left for a week... and has not yet returned. You would love him.[69]

One observer wondered 'Will they tame him? He certainly is most attractive, but now he should rein himself in, be more the Royal Prince. There is only one life between him and the throne, if throne there is to be!' Amedeo lived in the Palais d'Orleans along with his *aide-de-camp* Nino Medici di Marignano and his young wife Merina Gigliucci, who brought her friend Beatrice 'Boots' Whitaker into their social circle and what became Amedeo's most serious flirtation of the Sicilian season.[70] It was at the end of the year 1923 that Hélène spent both Christmas and New Year's Day in Palermo with her beloved 'Bouby.'

In November 1922, Hélène had gone to visit the Greek Royal Family at the Villa Igeia in Palermo, where King Constantine and Queen Sophie were living in exile with their younger daughters Irene and Catherine. They were old friends of Hélène, with that British connection that meant so much to her. Constantine was a nephew of Queen Alexandra, while Sophie was a niece of King Edward, and they were all part of the great Sandringham house party following the 1911 Coronation. Only two years earlier, in 1920, Constantine had been recalled to the throne following the death of their second son, Alexander, who had been king in his father's absence. They had received a tumultuous welcome from the people, but the Allies refused to recognize him; within months, a Greek offensive in Asia Minor led to a crushing defeat by the Turks, who exacted a terrible revenge in the massacre of Greeks living in Smyrna. Constantine was blamed for the disaster, and abdicated a second time, a broken man.

Princess Marie, sister of Constantine, had already been widowed by the Russian Revolution and was now living in exile again. She settled in Venice and recorded several visits from Hélène that August, including once when she brought her sister Isabelle and her daughters along too. The Greek family's presence in Italy was actually rather controversial; while some old friends greeted them warmly, other called them 'the Greek traitors.' For the most part, they found the Italians 'all perfectly charming.' One of them, Countess Morosini had them to a ball where they met Hélène again, once more with her sister the Duchesse de Guise.[71]

The home of the Greek royal family in Palermo was only temporary, and plans were underway for a move. On the afternoon of 10 January 1923, King Constantine hosted a tea party for some of the local nobility, and in the evening he attended a party in the hotel ballroom. He seemed in better spirits than usual and was looking forward to starting for Naples in two days with his family to stay at Capodimonte, at the invitation of the Aostas. Afterwards, they planned to take up residence in Florence.[72]

The next morning, Constantine was struck by a cerebral hemorrhage, lost consciousness, and died suddenly, aged only fifty-four. Hélène and Amedeo immediately went to Queen Sophie, and 'with the greatest kindness and sympathy, took charge of everything.'[73] They arranged for a funeral worthy of a king. The steamer *Italia* carried Constantine's coffin to Naples, where Emanuele Filiberto met them with military honours. The coffin was drawn on a gun carriage escorted by Municipal Guards and detachments of infantry, followed by Hélène accompanying Queen Sophie with her daughters, the Neapolitan officials, and military officers. The funeral took place in the city's Greek Orthodox Church, where the coffin was temporarily laid to rest.[74] After the funeral, Queen Sophie and her family stayed with the Aostas at Capodimonte before they moved to Florence.

12

1922–1928

A Wandring spirit is my marrow which forbids rest.[1]

It is uncertain when Hélène first became aware of Benito Mussolini politically, but by the early 1920s, he was already a household name throughout Italy. Beginning in March 1919 when he formed the *Fasci Italiani di Combattimento*, Mussolini, the sometime newspaper editor, made a concerted effort to gain political power for himself. The right-wing ultra-nationalists proved a ready body for the tactics of terrorism, reprisals, and squad violence which local fascist groups, the *squadristi*, developed to break the control of socialist town councils and provincial administrations. While his early tendencies were republican, Mussolini let it be known that he would support the monarchy if nothing was done to hinder the fascist movement, and leaving the alternative a hanging question. However, at the same time, other Fascist leaders such as General Emilio De Bono and Cesare De Vecchi were strong monarchists as were many of the army generals who were warming to the fascist ideology. At court, the pro-fascists included not only Hélène and Emanuele Filiberto but also Queen Mother Margherita, 'who was enchanted by Mussolini and had no scruples about encouraging fascist violence.'

On 24 October 1922, Mussolini reviewed thousands of his blackshirt supporters in Naples, and announced a march on Rome to 'take by the throat our miserable ruling class.' To enthusiastic applause, he addressed an enthusiastic audience in the San Carlo Theatre, while outside in the Piazza del Plebiscito the crowds were chanting '*Roma, Roma.*'[2] Some 16,000 *squadristi* from around the country—fewer than anticipated—eventually mustered at appointed spots around Rome. The great 'March on Rome' was actually less a march than a gathering around Rome, yet it gave a clear message that the fascists were pushing for change and had strength and power behind them.

The King did not return from his holiday at San Rossore until the night of the 27th, when he issued an order for martial law, which the cabinet unanimously supported, and it was felt that a forceful response by the army could have dissipated the fascist movement at that point. However, at the last minute the King declined to sign the order into effect. The unspoken threat that Victor Emmanuel might be forced to abdicate in favour of Emanuele Filiberto, who had gone to be with the fascists near Perugia, was very likely the motivating factor.[3]

The King had crumbled under pressure. Luigi Facta, who had been prime minister only since February, resigned; on the 29th, the king invited Mussolini, this leader of a private army, to form a government despite the fact that there were only thirty-two fascists out of 500 deputies in parliament. Nonetheless, the change proved immensely popular, with the Roman crowds cheering the king for taking this decision. Although the king requested that Mussolini disband his squadristi, the new prime minister said that was impossible. Instead, it was agreed that the blackshirts could hold a victory parade in Rome, and tens of thousands of fascists poured into Rome for this demonstration of power.[4] Over the next few years, the country and the monarchy fell into grips of Mussolini's fascist dictatorship, which grew deeper and deeper.

Some time later, the Rome correspondent for *The Times* of London attempted an analysis of the public image differences between the King and the Prime Minister.

A number of foreign journalists who have on previous occasions been privileged to accompany the Italian Duce on some of his scenically grandiose visits to the great towns of Italy were enabled this week to witness a soberer and a much rare type of celebration, in which King Victor Emmanuel III, unaccompanied by his formidable and overshadowing Premier, appeared a central figure in a great public rejoicing. It is impossible to imagine a greater contrast of personal types than that between the titular and the effecive monarch of Italy. The Duce is, after all, incomparably the greatest manipulator of crowds in Europe. Not one endearing or inspiring gesture for which the occasion is granted does he omit to perform and the publicity resources of the nation are immediately utilised to maximum potentiality for the communication to every corner of the earth of the resulting popular enthusiasm. King Victor Emmanuel is, on the contrary, the man among Europe's public men who most frankly disdains the artifices of the crowd-charmer. Amid tempests of applause he stands immobile, almost embarrassed. A rare wintry smile is the utmost response he can conjure up for the delight of his hot-hearted southerners.[5]

Hélène was impressed by strong-willed men, and now, her own public image was growing more identified with her support of the fascist movement. In the post-war disruptions, she was looking to Mussolini as 'a savior who would bring stability, order, and a brighter future', like many other Italians.[6] She had been out of town at the time of Mussolini's rally in October, but in December 1922, when she attended at performance of *Siegfried* at the San Carlo Theatre in Naples, Hélène was saluted between acts one and two with the playing of not only the royal anthem, but also the fascist anthem. Emanuele Filiberto himself became a focal point for the Fascist loyalty to the Savoy dynasty. He and his brother Turin were acclaimed by a squad of Fascists when they arrived at Porto Nuova Station in Turin at the end of October—'Long Live the Commander of the Third Army! Long Live the House of Savoy'—and a couple of days later, another Fascist march through the city stopped at the Palazzo Cisterna and cheered him there as well. In March 1923 in Ferrara, Mussolini presented Emanuele Filiberto with a black shirt for himself as a linking symbol.[7]

During 1925–1926, King Victor Emmanuel signed a series of laws issued by the fascist government which suspended free speech, free assembly, and a free press; no longer would citizens be equal before the law. Civil servants—including judges—could be dismissed when their views 'were incompatible with government policy.' The Grand Council had to be consulted on all treaties with foreign government, and was given a role in deciding which prerogatives were retained by the crown. However, the Fascist party directorate that 'could intervene in determining who would succeed if the throne became vacant' was difficult for the royal family. However, as Mack Smith points out, 'this last clause was more threat than reality because it was imprecisely drafted and Mussolini was obliged to admit that the king's son Umberto had an indefeasible right to the succession.'[8]

Queen Amélie came to Capodimonte at the beginning of March 1923 on what would become extended annual visits; during the winter in 1925, she would stay from February until June. She recorded in her diary that Manolo met her with flowers at the station in Rome, accompanied by Bouby, Maria Caffarelli, Carlo Torrigiani, and others before she headed to Naples where Hélène met her at the station. In the coming years, many of Amélie's visits would coincide with Hélène's travels to Africa, and Amélie would act as chatelaine in her sister's absence. Hélène told her sister that on these occasions she would be 'la maitraisse de maison' and so would decide, for example, where her son and daughter-in-law, Manoel and Mimi, would stay when they also came—either in Hélène's own rooms or in those of Aosta. It seems that there was another distancing between husband and wife, as Hélène now referred to him simply as 'Aosta' and Amélie wisely followed suit. Hélène wrote to Amélie: 'My dear! I understand that our modest installation is not worthy of you, but the place is so beautiful, and you know you are doing me a favour keeping my house open during my long months of absence—where everything rusts at home—faucets, baths, as well as the legs of my domestics.' When she was at home, Hélène is said to have been very strict with her servants, fining them when they did something wrong. She was particularly displeased on one occasion when she returned from Africa to discover that a servant had taken black boot polish to the stuffed elephant head.[9]

However, in March 1923, Hélène soon went to Rome to accompany Queen

Elena to Antibes, where her mother lay seriously ill.[10] Much has been made of the supposed antagonism between Elena and Hélène, but one does not invite an enemy to the sickbed of your mother, and with her nursing training, Hélène was always ready to assist in such circumstances. Queen Milena died at Antibes on March 16th, and was taken back to San Remo to be buried with King Nikola who had died two years earlier. Hélène had already returned back to Naples, but only for a short time, as she was soon off to Paris, where she lunched with Princess Victoria and the Duke of Connaught at the Hôtel Imperial. Then, in May, King George and Queen Mary came to Rome. Arriving in a landau with footmen and coachmen in the scarlet livery of the royal household, Hélène and Emanuele Filiberto were among the first dignitaries at the station to greet their arrival. Once the British royal train had arrived, the procession to the Quirinale formed with King George and King Victor Emmanuel in the first carriage; Queen Mary and Queen Elena in the second with Aosta and the Prince of Piedmont. Hélène rode in the third carriage with Lady Minto, Sir Ronald Graham (the British ambassador), and Sir Charles Madden. When they reached the palace, 'suddenly the windows above the balcony were flung open, and three footmen raised a red velvet canopy over the balustrade.' King George walked out smiling, followed by King Victor Emmanuel, the two Queens, the Prince of Piedmont, and the Duke and Duchess of Aosta. 'For a whole two minutes, the party stood bareheaded in the sunlight, gazing down at the tumultuous crowd and out over the tranquil city. However, this was not enough. On retiring, they were imperiously recalled, and once again the whole party came out to bow thanks for a truly Royal welcome.'[11]

The next day, after the British royals went through the formal wreath-layings at the tombs of King Victor Emmanuel II and King Umberto at the Pantheon, and then again at the Tomb of the Unknown Soldier, Hélène and her sister Amélie went to have tea with them quietly back at the palace.[12] The next night, the Aostas were both at a dinner at the British Embassy along with the Italian king and queen, the Prince of Piedmont, and Princess Mafalda.

In late April, Hélène and Emanuele received radio-telegrams from Shanghai that their younger son Aimone was in hospital, recovering from pneumonia, having been taken ill while on a training cruise aboard his gunboat, the *Caboto*. However, his condition worsened into broncopulmonary grippe of the left lung, with secondary lombar pneumonia on the right lung. At one point, he suffered heart failure, losing both pulse and breathing for two minutes.[13] At his worst, Aimone had, at his own request, received the sacraments of the church, and Hélène felt that it was indeed a miracle that he had survived.

Hélène made the decision to go alone to China to be with '*notre* Bob.' She sailed from Marseilles on 18 May. While she was *en route*, Aimone underwent major surgery on his right lung, to allieviate the accumulation of pus there. By mid-June, when Hélène reached Aimone in the General Hospital at Shanghai, he was already out of danger, 'but still very low.' She praised the doctors and nursing sisters, his naval comrades who maintained his good spirits, and most of all, his aide, Lieutenant Adalberto Mariano, 'who helped him like a brother—he never left him, day or night.' In the future, Hélène would refer to Mariano as 'my third son', calling him by the endearment 'Marianino.'[14]

Aimone required a further fortnight in hospital—a total of three months—but Hélène was soon making plans to bring him back to Europe in slow stages, which would include a lengthy stay in the mountains of Canada to help his recuperation. From Shanghai, they went to Yokohama and then made the Pacific crossing aboard the *Empress of Asia* in a fast time of eight days and twenty-one hours, arriving at Victoria on 29 July 1923, and Vancouver the next day. Hélène and Aimone spent nearly six weeks in Canada while he continued to recover. They also took a trip to Alaska—'the land of gold! Everywhere there are mines of gold or silver—of platinum'; Hélène remembered that it was in Alaska where her brother-in-law Luigino had climbed Mount Saint Elias in 1897.[15] Back in Canada, they stayed at the Banff Springs Hotel in the Canadian Rockies of Alberta, while Hélène worried about the medical bills accrued during Aimone's illness. She planned to spend a few days in London and Paris before returning to Italy and wrote to ask Emanuele Filiberto to send £1,500 to her in care of Coutts Bank to cover the expenses but, upon reflection, lowered that to £1,000. 'It's quite a sum—but Bob is saved, and there is nothing to do but thank God.'

Finally, in early September—travelling as the Countess de la Cisterna and Lieutenant A. de la Cisterna—they sailed from Montreal to Liverpool aboard the Canadian Pacific Liner *Montrose*. When they arrivided on 8 September, the newspapers reported that 'also travelling with them was "Sambo," a clever nine-year-old negro boy, who can speak English, French, and Italian. He was adopted by the Duchess at the age of six.'[16]

En route back to Italy, Hélène was able to attend the wedding of her eldest niece, Isabelle's daughter Isabelle to Count Bruno d'Harcourt. Their ceremony took place on the 15th at Chesnay, outside Paris, and the newspapers reported that although Hélène wore black it was along with a '*grande cape de satin garance*'.[17] Amélie hosted the reception at her Château de Bellevue.

When King Alfonso and Queen Ena of Spain came to visit Naples in November, Hélène, Emanuele and Aimone met them at the station before leading a procession into the city, where they were enthusiastically greeted when they appeared on the balcony of the Royal Palace. Then the King, accompanied by Aosta, reviewed the troops of the Regular Army and the National Militia, drawn up on the Via Partenope on the sea front, while a naval squadron lay anchored in the bay. Later, the Aostas hosted them at a lunch at Capodimonte and a banquet there in the evening, joined them in touring the various museums and churches of the city, attended a concert at the San Carlo, and visited Pompeii by automobile the next day.

After greeting the Spanish king and queen in Naples, Emanuele Filiberto returned to Turin, took to his bed, having developed a severe case of pneumonia. By early December, the inflammation in the left lung spread, and his temperature rose. Hélène and Aimone kept watch at his bedside. When the infection spread to the right lung, the medical bulletins reported that the situation was serious, the worst was feared, and Emanuele received the Last Sacrament.[18] Masses were said for his recovery at the Basilica of La Consolata, and some five thousand telegrams of concern arrived, many from veterans of the Third Army, while the newspapers pointed out that Emanuele was only fifty-four years old, yet his father had died of pneumonia at the age of forty-five in the same palace where he now lay ill. However, the crisis passed, and there was some hope for improvement. King Victor Emmanuel came to visit on the 11th, when Emanuele Filiberto's condition was considered grave, but the next day, medical bulletins indicated a slight improvement. Later, the British ambassador was able to report directly to King George that Emanuele Filiberto was showing 'real improvement' days after his 'life was practically despaired of, and he received extreme unction.' He had not been in good health for some time, 'suffering from a form of blood-poisoning causing ulcers and affecting the glands.' Although not well enough to meet King Alfonso at Naples, but 'but with the high sense of duty that has always inspired him, he ignored considerations of health and insisted on going through with the various ceremonies.' The result was double pneumonia 'of a very septic character', and although 'his condition is showing a steady improvement, the danger is not yet over, and in any case his convalescence must extend over a long period.'[19]

Emanuele's recovery was slow. To help his recuperation, on 14 January, he and Hélène left Turin for Naples, and on the 26th they sailed out of Naples for Egypt, where they planned to remain until the end of winter in the warmer climes, along with Aimone who was continuing his long convalescence. King Fuad ordered a special train to take them from Alexandria to Cairo, where they were met by Fuad, who had been a classmate of Emanuele Filiberto in their academy days at Turin and for whom he had maintained 'a fraternal affection.' After a few days in Cairo, they went to Aswan where they stayed at the Cataract Hotel for about twenty days, taking a long trip on the Nile visiting the cataracts and also excursions on camel back. They were back in Cairo for the greatest public event of twentieth-century Egyptology—the official opening of King Tutankhamen's tomb on 6 March. More than two hundred guests were invited, including the Aostas and Prince Friedrich Leopold of Prussia, along with the British High Commissioner and Lady Allenby, all the Egyptian ministers—with the noticeable exception of the nationalist premier—and most of the diplomatic corps. Aside from the prime minister, another notable absentee was Howard Carter, officially the discoverer of the tomb, who had only recently abandoned his suit against the

Egyptian government so that one from the Countess of Carnarvon, widow of the expedition's financial sponsor, could proceed. However, as the correspondent from *The Times* noted, the event was 'essentially a political function' as throughout the day 'long crowds stood before the Winter Palace Hotel and the dahabiyas in which the Ministers were accommodated yelling political war cries, while at intervals along the route to the Valley of the Kings other gatherings carried on the task of removing from the minds of the government's guests any doubt in regard to the political sentiments of the populace.'[20] The Aostas returned from Alexandria to Naples on 17 March.

While they were in Egypt, word came of the death of Hélène's younger brother, Ferdinand. Although his health had been 'precarious for some months,' his death at the Château de Randan at the age of thirty-nine was unexpected; it was rumoured to have been the result of a heart attack following a drug over-dose. Hélène and Ferdinand had never been close, and she did not return for the funeral. He was buried in the family chapel at Dreux on 10 February in a service attended by the widowed Duchess, Queen Amélie, the Duc de Guise (representing the Duc d'Orléans, who was still prevented from going to France by the Law of Exile and so attended a Requiem Mass in London), and others from the extended family and French nobility. Ferdinand's widow inherited the entire estate, including the Château de Randan, but that was destroyed by fire the next year, along with Ferdinand's sporting trophies, his collection of Oriental furniture, lacquer, enamels, silk, and hundreds of gold and silver Buddhas, as well as a great deal of the Orléans heritage including King Louis Philippe's library.

On 7 March, Alessio Cardinal Ascalesi was announced as the new Archbishop of Naples. Aged fifty-one, Ascalesi was returning home as he was a native of the Campagna, originally from Castelnuovo, which is within the province of Naples. He had worked as a priest in the Dicoese of Spoleto from the time of his ordination at the age of twenty-two until he was made a bishop in 1909, and then a cardinal in 1916. Over the coming years, Cardinal Ascalesi would attend so many public functions together with Hélène that she jokingly called him her 'dancing partner.'[21]

A great personality who left the scene that spring was Eleanora Duse, the Venetian actress who had a tempestuous relationship with d'Annunzio. She had retired from public performances in 1909 through ill health but returned to the stage in 1921, and died in Pittsburgh during an American tour in 1924. When the *Duilio* brought her body back to Italy, and reached Naples in the evening of 10 May, a large crowd gathered on the quay. As soon as the ship docked, Hélène went on board and laid a wreath of white roses upon the coffin. Wrapped in the Italian flag, the coffin was brought ashore, placed upon a bier, and covered with flowers, including a wreath sent by Queen Elena.

Ever since Hélène began her extensive travels to Africa in late 1907, she and

Emanuele Filiberto had been living increasingly separate lives. Although there would be some time together, particularly after the war, the Duke had lived more and more at the Palazzo Cisterna in his native Turin, while Hélène remained with Capodimonte as her base in Italy. Their relationship over the years had transformed from a close if tempestuous marriage into one of duty, perhaps even of friendship and some shared interests, but certainly no longer sharing the love that Hélène had written about in their earliest days together. Royal marriages at this time were usually established for dynastic rather than personal reasons and if love did develop that was considered a bonus. A nineteenth-century Duke of Parma explained his own marriage by saying that after many years there was no love but there was esteem, while deploring his son's empty marriage that contained neither love nor esteem.[22] Hélène and Emanuele Filiberto seem to have settled into the former model. On her twenty-ninth wedding anniversary, Hélène wrote from Capodimonte to Emanuele, addressing him as '*Mon Meilleur Ami*'—my best friend. 'If sometimes clouds passed in our springtime sky, never did they completely obscure our beautiful star. And the great sun, clear and warm with friendship shines on our autumn—it will illuminate us beyond the tomb.'[23]

About this same time Hélène began to sign her name as 'France-Savoia-Aosta' or more simply 'F-S-A,' no first name or title. She even did this in her correspondence with Emanuele Filiberto or when annotating the books she had read. She never gives an explanation for this, but did continue the practice well into the next decade.

After visiting hospitals in the Trento in August, Hélène was in London with Amedeo, staying at Claridge's later in the month and again in early September 1924. This would have been the last opportunity for Hélène to see her dear friend Queen Alexandra, who was now terribly frail with an ever deepening deafness. The one-time beauty would now say of herself time and time again—'Ugly old woman, nobody likes me any more.' A favourite comment of hers would become 'Remember me as I was, not as I am.' Hélène also took time to visit Lady St Alwyn, the mother of Susan Hicks Beach, at her home in Gloucestershire, and to meet up with Susan herself while Hélène was staying at her usual London hotel, Almond's. Mother and son passed a few more days in Paris on their return to Italy and were able to spend some time with Amélie and Jean, the duc de Guise, as well as to visit the Duchesse de Chartres, Guise's mother who was also Hélène's aunt and godmother; Hélène considered her to be 'a truly extraordinary woman.'[24]

Hélène's presence at public events was more and more seen as supporting the growing fascist feeling in the country. In October, she went to Udine to visit *kindergartens* associated with the '*Italia redenta*' movement and received a warm welcome there. Even when she joined the King and Queen in Florence on Saturday, 1 November to unveil a monument dedicated to the four hundred Italian army physicians who fell during the war, Hélène headed hundreds of uniformed nurses in a procession through the streets of Florence following a wagon decorated with laurel branches sent from Rome, bearing patriotic emblems and drawn by six white oxen. Symbols from the old Roman Empire were increasingly used to link past glory and future glory in the public imagination.

The next week, Hélène was in Rome to attend the luncheon at the Quirinale in honour of Austen Chamberlain, the British Foreign Minister, who was in Italy to meet with Mussolini. The luncheon was hosted by the King and Queen, and also attended by Prince Umberto and the British Ambassador, Sir Ronald Graham, and his wife Lady Sybil. Still later in the month, she was helping to promote Italian colonization of Africa when she again joined the King and Queen to attend a film about Somalia and the work of the Società Agricola italo-somala of which Luigi Abruzzi was president.

Even with all her association and support of the increasing nationalism within Italy, Hélène was, once again, ready to leave the constraints of Europe for the freedom of Africa. While preparing for this journey, Hélène received a letter from her old friend, Françoise, the Comtesse Costa de Beauregard, who had accompanied Hélène on her first trip to the East (to Egypt and Palestine in 1893–1894). The Comtesse wrote of her concern that Hélène was preparing to go to be with the savages again when she was so well where she was, and quoted a Victor Hugo poem:

> *Que sert de n'effleurer à peine ce que l'on tient*
> *Quand on a les mains pleines,*
> *Et de vivre essoufflé comme un enfant qui vient*
> *De courir par les plaines!* [25]

Hélène responded, 'my friend Françoise, don't you know that the double advantage of these trips is that they give more precision to our thoughts and more liberty to our dreams?' For herself, Hélène felt:

> If I find myself once again on the roads of Africa, it is no longer for the marvel of my eyes. This country is mine. I know the nuance of each of its hours. If I come back to it, it is to relive its life—to feel my soul closer to its—to relearn the freedom of the nomad—to gulp the wild air of the desert regions and, in crossing these lands without master, to know a bit of the pride of a conqueror.[26]

This would probably be one of her favourite trips ever, as she had her beloved son Bouby as her travelling companion along with brother-in-law Luigi Abruzzi and Count Constantine Radicati di Passerano (known as Zaki), Hélène's new 'gentiluomo di corte' who had formerly served Queen Margherita. Together, they sailed from Naples on 13 December aboard the *Roma* bound for Port Saïd where they met Aimone, who was in charge of his first ship, the torpedo boat *Cassiopea*. Bob jumped on a barque and was quickly aboard the *Roma* to embrace his mother whom he had not seen for six months. They spent a happy day together, chatting and visiting the *Cassiopea*, where Bob was delighted to have his uncle— Admiral Luigi di Savoia Aosta—compliment him on the perfect upkeep of the ship. Hélène, however, was the worried mother. 'The boat is small... the sea is immense.' 'My heart skips a beat,' she wrote 'to see how tiny this floating prison is. I imagine it disappearing completely between two waves, rolling, pitching when the sea wind pushes the man strapped to the mast, blinded by the foam.' At least for today, her tall son aboard his tiny boat was safe and sound.[27]

The *Roma* moved on to Eritrea, where the party spent Christmas Day. They met with the governor Jacopo Gasparini and saw the ruins of Massua, following an earthquake there. Then, it was on to Aden, Ras Afun, and on 4 January they arrived at Mogadiscio, where Hélène was full of admiration for all the Italian workers, the 'pioneers' whom Luigi Abruzzi had settled in his agricultural comunity. Hélène visited the local hospital, the barracks, the Sisters of la Consolata, and even the garage, where she was delighted to see the mechanic Boero, who five years earlier had made a famous trip from Lugh to Afgoi in a single day. After that she wandered into the marketplace, the suq, to stock up on her perfumes. 'My companions, most of all Luigino, did not appreciate these tours of the native streets.' However, as usual, Hélène did what she wanted rather than what others expected of her. For a few days, she was the guest of Cesare De Vecchi, known from the First World War as the leader of the *arditi*, the storm troopers at Mount Grapa, and more recently as one of the leaders of the Fascist *squadristi* in the Piedmont. Mussolini had appointed him as the Italian governor of Somalia in 1923. Soon, it was time to say farewell to Luigino and continue the onward journey with Amedeo and Radicati.[28]

Hélène's party continued on the *Roma* to Mombasa, then Zanzibar, and finally Dar es Salaam, where they joined the railroad for the trip inland to Kigoma on the banks of Lake Tanganika. Once they were aboard the *Duc de Brants* and away from the noise and bustle of towns, Hélène felt that she had once again found her Africa:

> Five o'clock in the morning. Why are the mountains black, severe as remorse? Dawn is born, in the sky a single star still shines. On board, a cock sings. The waters of the lake are calm. I go back to bed and close my eyes, but soon a softness like a very tender caress lightly touches my brow and forces me to open them again. The sun has climbed above the mountains, and its first ray places on my forehead a friendly kiss, like a seal of acquaintance upon my vagabond soul.[29]

The next day they moved into the bush, with Bouby leading the porters to Uvira, at 800 metres in temperatures up to 27°. The altitude and temperature both continued to climb for a week until they reached camp at Camagnola at 1,200 metres and temperatures topping 37°. Their next goal was Kibati, in the volcano country. When some of the young porters came down with malaria, Hélène tended to them with quinine tablets, injections, and aspirin. When they were better, Hélène said that she had cared for them to the best of her ability, although she found them repugnant—'the poor devils,' sweating out the fever and vomitting on her feet.[30]

As they moved deeper into the bush at Burrunga, they arrived at the Mission there, where Hélène met an American, a 'M. Beurbery', and his son, who were there to film and capture gorillas—two for the Belgian zoo at Anvers and two more for America. 'There are some curious chaps in the world' thought Hélène as she prepared to hunt rather than capture. In the meantime, Bouby went off to scale Mount Nyamuragira, an active volcano, with the local administrator, Monsieur Buduisson, while they waited for their porters to arrive for the hunt. They expected 160, but only 100 arrived, and the local chief could provide no more, so Hélène picked fifty out of the arrivals and sent them on to Radicati at Burnga.[31]

Once Bouby returned, the caravan moved out. Five men carried 'tam-tams' on their heads and pounded out the beat, which the porters echoed in perfect harmony. They camped at Bunagana near the volcano Sabinio and the village of Chief Muniada, but the next morning discovered that of their hundred porters, most had fled during the night and only thirty-six remained. They had to leave behind twenty-cases in the care of one porter and one of their two soldiers, as Hélène and her party moved into the bamboo forest. Once they reached the foot of Sabinio, Bouby took time to climb the volcano, and when he returned in time for dinner, his arms were full of flowers which he had gathered for his mother.[32]

When they reached Lake Rohonda at 2,200 metres, Hélène wrote that 'the beauty is so great that the spirit cannot begin to conceive it. Human language has no words to paint it. It seems to me to no longer touch earth, but to swim in the wonderous.' They moved from the bush to the savannah before returning to the bush. 'We had barely started when it began to rain, and rain as it only can in Africa, the thunders "seem to be mad" from one end of the horizon to the other, like artillery fire.' They continued along the flat plain, but with difficulty. 'The feet of the porters seem to be mad. They no longer had control over their extremities and fell like houses of cards. I gave up counting the number of times I sat down violently in the mud.' They finally found a place to stop, and Hélène sat on the ground cleaning and oiling her carbine, which she entrusted to no one else, when a great troup of natives arrived carrying a huge banner. It was the *Roi N'dezy*, the great chief, who had come to exchange compliments, which they did in Swahili. Hélène found the chief 'an accomplished black man. He types, is Christian, only has one wife (so they said), but a vast wardrobe, including a smoking jacket which he puts on with a night shirt embroidered in red on the collar and sleeves.' This paradox was to accompany the hunting party, but always at a distance.[33]

When the caravan finally began moving, Hélène complained that 'I hope my funeral convoy will be less slow and more gay. We advance like tortoises.'[34] However, once they got onto the plain of Kiguonze, Amedeo found himself surrounded by a galloping herd of buffalo, some of them quite close, and he managed to shoot his first buffalo of the hunt. Later in the day, Hélène and Bouby sat looking out over Lake Albert Edward and the Ishasha River, while they amused themselves watching a family of five hippopotamuses in the water.

Hélène read widely and always travelled with a stock of books. One day, while they were still camped near Lake Albert Edward, a rainy spell gave her the opportunity to begin *Beasts, Men and Gods* by the Polish writer, traveler, and explorer Ferdynand Ossendowski. She was especially taken by the passage on his time with the lamas, Mongols, and Tibetans. That night, 'I did not dream, no I saw, I touched, I spoke with my dear departed ones and they spoke to me. A sweet vision, a persistent vision which made a profound impression which stayed with me all day.' 'Without doubt,' Hélène wrote, 'I am a subject predisposed towards occultism!'[35]

One day, Bouby killed a python that was more than four metres long, and he and Hélène ate the meat, which she found 'pale and slightly insipid.' Soon, he was after bigger game; one morning, he left when it was barely light to follow the tracks of three lions. When Hélène heard only two gun shots, her heart stopped as she knew how dangerous it was to deal with wounded lions. But when he returned, it was having killed two of the lions and been on the trail of the third.

Amedeo decided to go to Ruindi to find out when they would be relieved, and he made the one hundred twenty kilometre round-trip on foot in two days. 'You have to be twenty-six years old, be built like Hercules as my Bouby is, and still, still, to be well trained.' Then, they made their way back through the mud and rain, Hélène 'skating' on her rubber-soled boots with Amedeo's fist through her leather belt keeping her upright. Eventually, they made it back through the forest of Semliké, and into the Belgian Congo. When they reached the town of Irumu on 7 April, Hélène became furious that people had been telegraphing from Italy through the ministers, the local authorities, and the vice governor of the province about her whereabouts—only because she hadn't been heard of since 17 January.[36] When Hélène was in Africa, she wanted to forget about Europe and wanted Europe to forget about her, but that would never be the case.

It was at Irumu that she met 'Le Raid Citroën,' the great motorised expedition that André Citroën had sent to travel through the Sahara and through the continent to publicise his automobiles and their utility in all terrains. Special hard tracks were fitted to get them through the most difficult situations although the lack of roads was not necessarily an overwhelming problem, as colonial administrators made special provisions for the expedition. To ease their last 400 miles to

Stanleyville, the capital of the Congo, Belgian officials ordered 40,000 natives to hack a path through the jungle trees, which they accomplished in forty-five days. It was, as one commentator phrased it, 'problem solving in true colonial style.'[37]

A one-armed hunter named Mathieu, who had been disabled in the war but was still a great sportsman, took Amedeo into the wild for one last hunt, and he bagged an elephant, sending its tail back to Hélène. Soon, they continued on through the eastern provinces, to the White Nile where they boarded the *Nasir* for the trip to Khartoum, where Hélène stayed at the famous Gordon Hotel. Then, it was on to Egypt—'the gold, the yellow, the ocre of its sands, the black of its rocks, the green water. It is the Egypt of the Ptolemies and the pharoahs. It is ancient Egypt, full of poetry, of mystery, of religion.'[38] She visited the massive rock temples at Abu Simbel with their colossal statues of Rameses II, and in Cairo, she went to the Sphinx and pyramids on camelback, before finally returning to Italy in June. At the end of this trip, Hélène totalled up that she had covered 17,158 kilometres—9,963 km by sea, 2,325 km on rivers and lakes, 3,288 km by railroad, and 1,582 km on foot.

Hélène was back in Rome for a function which could not have stood in greater contrast to her recent time in Africa. This was the Silver Jubilee of King Victor Emmanuel, set for 7 June, Constitution Day, rather than 9 August, the actual anniversary of King Umberto's assassination, which was expected to be too hot in Rome. Newspapers reported that bunting decorated the street in the national colours of red, white, and green, and many women in the crowd wore those colours too—but Hélène wore black, while Queen Mother Margherita wore grey. The two of them were together in the stands for the great parade along with the King and Queen, their son and daughters Mafalda and Giovanna. First came the two-hour-long military and police parade, then a 'monster procession of more than 100,000 people.' The most touching section was the fifty surviving Garibaldi veterans wearing their red shirts, led by Ezio, the leader's grandson. 'Emotional Italians on all sides broke down, sobbed; others raised thunderclaps of cheers; mothers lifted their babies to see the old men, not one of whom was less than a septuagenarian.'[39] Mussolini was also in the grandstand, although his black-shirts did not march as a separate group but filtered into different organizations.

While the mid-1920s were characterized in much of western Europe and the United States as the 'Roaring Twenties', with its exhuberence and decadence, in Italy, those years were marked with a tightening grip of Fascism, encompassing every aspect of life. From October 1922 to December 1923, membership in the Fascist party grew from 300,000 to more than 780,000, with the growth being most pronounced in the south.[40]

Between 27 December 1924 and 2 January 1925, Italy was convulsed when tens of thousands of blackshirts rampaged throughout the country's cities ransacking the homes of anti-fascists and breaking into prisons to release their compatriots. As one author has described it, 'this was nationalism—patriotism gone feral.' Many expected that the King would dismiss Mussolini and declare martial law, but Victor Emmanuel was not bold enough to attempt this. Then, on 3 January, Mussolini took the next step when he appeared before Parliament to declare that 'I, and I alone, assume political, moral and historical responsibility for all that has happened.' In this speech, he declared not only his power, but also his intentions of dictatorship and that he was prepared to grab power as brutally as he thought necessary. Later in the year, Mussolini tightened his grip further by announcing his new programme of totalitarianism. In the future, all opposition parties, unions, and associations would be banned. Italy now became a one-party, one mentality state. War memorials sprang up around the country to remind citizens to be worthy of the sacrifices made on their behalf.[41] Even a new national fascist calendar was established, with the new year beginning on 29 October and years numbered beginning with 1922 to honour the March on Rome. Mussolini also received the official rank of a 'cousin of the King' when he was awarded the Order of the Annunziata in 1924.

The introduction of the eight-hour work day in March 1923 had been followed by the question of what workers would now do with their leisure time after work (*dopolavoro*). Mario Giani, who had been the manager of the American firm Westinghouse Corporation's plant at Vado Ligure, proposed recreational facilities for workers similar to those created by various American companies, notably Ford. Giani's slant on the theme would make these facilities community ones rather than strictly tied to a particular firm, not disimilar from the traditional workingmen's clubs. The Naples Dopolavoro was established in 1925 under the sponsorship of Duke Andrea Carafa D'Andria, the general consul of the fascist militia, and links between the clubs and the fascists throughout the country were strong and the government established a National Agency on After-Work (*Opera Nazionale Dopolavoro*), under the Ministry of the National Economy. Mussolini appointed Emanuele Filiberto as the first president of this new organization, and the Duke declared his willingness to head this 'eminently moral and patriotic mission'. Mario Giani came onboard as executive officer. However, while Giani was intent on keeping the clubs tied to the workplace and the unions, Mussolini was intent on tightening the government's hold as with many other aspects of Italian life. He informed Emanuele Filiberto of the 'delicate situation' that he faced, and in early April 1927, the Duke resigned as president in order to ease the 'fascistication' of the *dopolavoros*. Within six weeks, Giani was forced from office.[42]

Critics said that Aosta 'was remunerated for his pro-Fascist activities' on 20 December 1925 when a new law was passed which raised his annuity as well as that of the elderly Duke of Genoa as Princes of the Royal House from 400,000 lire to one million.[43] One million lire was approximately $140,000 at the time.

In the summer 1925, Hélène and Amedeo did some touring around Europe. In June, they were in London, where they went to tea with King George and Queen

Mary at Buckingham Palace. Hélène stopped to visit Amélie in Paris on their return in July, and later went to Vichy for a cure. Then, she went to visit Amélie at her home, the Château de Bellevue, at Le Chesnay, near Versailles. There was time for visits from her sister Isabelle, her niece Isabelle along with her husband Bruno d'Harcourt, and her childhood friend Renée St Maur. When Amélie accompanied Hélène to the Gare de Lyons for the train to Turin, she saw her sister settled into the compartment, but left before the train departed because Hélène '*déteste les adieux*.'[44]

In early August, Hélène was travelling again, first to Sofia, Bulgaria, from Italy *en route* for Vienna. Nothing further is known of these journeys, but Hélène may well have been hunting again, this time for daughters-in-law. Later in the month, Hélène and Amedeo were in Biarritz for part of 'The Season.' One night saw them at '*Le gala de lundi*' at the Hôtel du Palais—others that evening included Princess Paley, the Maharaja of Baroda, Prince and Princess Fouad, Prince and Princess Halim, and the Duchess of Westminster. Hélène and Amedeo soon left Biarritz for Bilbao where they were received by the Queen of Spain. From there, aboard a yacht, they left for Santander. In August, they were joined by Emanuele Filiberto on a visit to Fascau, Romania, to see King Ferdinand and Queen Marie. The inevitable rumours of an engagement came out, linking twenty-six-year-old Amedeo with sixteen-year-old Princess Ileana, the youngest and only unmarried daughter of the Romanians. There seems to have been nothing to those rumours, but there was a royal wedding approaching. On 23 September, the whole royal family gathered together at Racconigi for the marriage of the King's second daughter Mafalda to Prince Philip of Hesse—son of that 'not regularly pretty' Princess Margarethe of Prussia, whom Queen Victoria had tried to get Prince Eddy interested in so many years before. The reporter from *La Stampa* singled out Hélène's style as 'marvelous' amid all the others, dressed in pearl grey and wearing a diamond diadem.[45]

In England, Hélène's old friend and supporter Queen Alexandra was fading. In September, her niece Princess Marie of Greece returned to Sandringham, the royal estate in Norfolk. Marie had spent much of the previous year tending the elderly Queen in the absence of Princess Victoria, who was in Italy recovering from pneumonia; now, after an absence of just a month, Marie found that Alexandra 'had become very thin and somehow had lost her interest in everything and continually fell asleep.' Her long-time deafness 'had considerably increased, and we had to write down anything we wished to tell her.' Still, Alexandra managed to continue her daily routine of lunch with her suite and an afternoon drive. The elderly queen suffered a heart attack on 19 November and died about 6 a.m. 'A short time after, all her wonderful beauty returned, and she lay on her death bed with a happy smile, the picture of peace and so beautiful.'[46]

The Italian Court declared two weeks of mourning, and the Italian ambassador,

Marchese della Torretta represented the king at the funeral itself. Hélène attended a memorial service for her old friend at the English church in Naples on the day of the funeral as the cortège moved through the London snow to Westminster Abbey. All the flags were flown at half mast that day in Naples, as the High and Royal Commissioners, the whole consular corps, and the resident English and Danish colonies gathered together to say farewell to one of Hélène's staunchest friends throughout the years.

Although Hélène's strongest English connection died with Queen Alexandra, others continued and yet others were literally born. On 7 December, the Italian ambassador stood proxy for Hélène as she became godmother at the christening of Christopher Emmet, the eldest grandson of Sir Rennell Rodd, who had served as British ambassador to Rome from 1908 until 1919.

The same year also brought Angelo Conti to Capodimonte as the director of the art collection. Conti already had established a reputation as a journalist and art historian, and was a great friend of d'Annunzio. Since 1904, he had been director of the art museum in Naples, and in 1925 now came to Capodimonte, where he and his wife Emilia lived at Villa Palasciano. For the next five years until his death in August 1930, Conti became closely attached to the royal family at Capodimonte, including Queen Amélie who would see him regularly and have him escort her to different museums and historical sites.

Hélène also saw Conti regularly, often inviting him to breakfast or lunch, to meet with her sons, to lend books to him from her personal library, to talk about literature and its effect on the soul. When she read *The Legend of St Francis of Assisi* and *The Life of St Claire of Assisi*, she wrote to Conti that she particularly loved the fact that the great patrician had become the humble servant of God. 'Naturally your thought didn't leave me—and I associated you with the emotions that these books caused me.'[47] Years later when Hélène donated a fountain to water the horses making the climb to Capodimonte in 1934, it was placed outside the Church of Santa Maria del Buon Consiglio at Capodimonte, and she chose a verse from Francis to be inscribed there—*Laudato si mio Signore per sora aqua la quale è molto utile et pretiosa et casta*—'Praised be the Lord through Sister Water who is very useful and precious and chaste,'[48] Conti continued writing for the newspapers and became a publicist for the Aosta family, writing about Amedeo and the Meharisti, and later about his wedding.

In January, the matriarch of the Savoy dynasty Queen Mother Margherita died at the age of seventy-four at her villa in Bordighera, and 180 days of court mourning were ordered. Hélène and Aimone went to Bordighera to pay their respects, and a few days later joined Amedeo in Rome for the funeral itself as the Queen Mother was laid to rest in the Pantheon to the strains of Beethoven's 'Funeral March.' Emanuele was prevented attending the funeral because of an attack of LaGrippe. Years later, Hélène would still remember in her journal the anniversary of the 'first queen of Italy'—'She was a real queen!'[49]

Amélie came to Naples in February for another extended visit which would last until June. On her first Sunday at Capodimonte, Amélie prepared for Mass as usual and had a 'belle surprise' when she found that Hélène had arranged a lovely oratory just behind the dining room for their prayers, which pleased and touched her very much. Two weeks later, Amélie recorded seeing Hélène on horseback—the first time since Stowe House. In March, they had a brief one-day visit from their brother Philippe on his return from Ethiopia, the Red Sea, and Somaliland. His private secretary commented that Philippe seemed to have regained his former gaiety and spoke of spending the following winter in Andalusia with their sister Louise at Villamanrique. He returned to the Palais d'Orléans in Palermo, but was quickly taken ill with what was first called pneumonia but was soon diagnosed as smallpox. When they received the news, Hélène was in Rome, but Amélie decided to go immediately to Palermo. As the situation was not seen as particularly serious, Hélène went first to preside at the meeting of one of her charities in Milan. When she received a telegram saying that Philippe's condition had deteriorated she left immediately for Sicily but arrived too late. Her arrival at the Palais d'Orléans was delayed by the local health service which feared contagion, and Philippe was already in a *Tricolour*-draped coffin by the time she finally got there. Hélène wrote to her husband that she was 'full of pain—because despite his faults I love Philippe.'[50]

Emanuele Filiberto met the Duc de Guise when the Rome Express arrived at the station in Turin and informed him of the death which now made him the head of the house of France. When they arrived in Palermo, the palace was under quarantine. In his will, Philippe asked that his body be buried at sea within sight of the coast of France if he could not be buried at Dreux. However, because of the fear of contagion, he was buried quickly and temporarily in the Cemetery of St Ursula in Palermo, and in May Isabelle de Guise represented the family at a requiem Mass at Notre Dame in Paris, presided over by the Cardinal-Archbishop Dubois.[51] It was not until five years later that his coffin was finally taken to Dreux to rest in the family chapel.

In the meantime, the family gathered at Capodimonte to discuss the future. Jean, the Duc de Guise—as the senior male heir of King Louis Philippe—now became head of the house and, as such, fell under the provisions of the Law of Exile which still prevented the head of the House and his immediate male heir from living in France. Although Guise was a brother-in-law of d'Orléans, it was not through that connection that he succeeded as head of the house but rather because he was the only surviving son of the Duc de Chartres, himself the only brother of the Comte de Paris. The family moved from their Moroccan home at Larache back to Europe and chose to live at the Manoir d'Anjou, outside Brussels, which Guise had inherited from his brother-in-law.

In his will, Philippe gave his natural history collection to the museum in Paris, and the bulk of his property and family jewels to the Duc de Guise as the new head of the family. After other individual bequests—including including annuities to the mother of his illegitimate son, as well as to his current mistress—Philippe left 'the platinum ring with a large emerald and diamonds given by Hélène' to the Duke of Aosta, and Philippe made his sister Amélie the univeral legatee instructing that she 'shall select and give a souvenir to each one of my sisters.'[52] Once again, Hélène found herself on the short end of a family will.

While all this was transpiring within the family, there was a bungled assassination attempt against Mussolini in Rome. After a 9.30 a.m. appointment with the Duke of Aosta on 26 April 1926, Mussolini left his office in Palazzo Chigi for the Capitoline and the Palazzo dei Conservatore, outside of which, while the crowd shouted 'Viva il Duce!' and a band of students sang the Giovinezza, Violet Gibson fired a pistol at Mussolini, wounding him on the bridge of his nose, with a second shot misfiring.[53] Violet, the daughter of Lord Ashbourne, a former Lord Chancellor of Ireland, was deemed to be mad and—at Mussolini's request—was released without charges and sent back to England, where she spent the rest of her life in an asylum.

In early May, Hélène was in Rome for a variety of events promoting French-Italian relations. There was an exhibition at the Villa Medici honoring French artists who had won the Prix de Rome, French cavalry officers at the horse show, and receptions at the Royal Geographical Society and Rome Automobile Club in honour of André Citroën and the members of the French Central Africa Automobile Mission. Hélène had met them in the Belgian Congo the previous year, and now she attended a special showing of the film '*La Crosière noire*' at the Royal Palace. The King, ministers, generals, and diplomats were all there to applaud the daring of the expedition, although Hélène herself would always prefer camels to cars when travelling through Africa.

Mussolini survived yet another assassination attempt in September—this time a bomb thrown at his car by anarchist Gino Lucetti—but the bomb bounced off the windscreen of the car and the chauffeur recognized the danger, stepped on the accelerator, and so was thirty metres away when it exploded. Hélène was in Rome at the time, and she was among the first to go to the Foreign Office at the Palazzo Chigi to congratulate the Duce on his narrow escape. She saw Ercole Boratto, the chauffeur, and went to congratulate him. However, Il Duce interruped to say 'It was nothing to worry about. Even if the grenade had entered the car I'd have been able to throw it out—after all I served with the Bersaglieri.'[54]

At the end of October, Princess Laetitia received members of a local musical society, which was celebrating its centenary at her home at Moncalieri. While the music festival was still underway, Laetitia retired to her apartments where she suffered a cerebral hemorrhage which proved fatal early the next morning. Hélène joined the rest of the family for the funeral at the Church of Gran Madre di Dio in Turin, where Emanuele Filiberto and his brother Vittorio Emanuele were the chief mourners for their step-mother along with Laetitia's brother Prince Louis Napoléon. After the church service, they took the coffin to be buried in the royal vaults at Superga next to their father. She was only fifty-nine years old, and had been a widow since she was twenty-three.

The family's relationship with Laetitia had always been a difficult one; this was complicated by the fact that after Amedeo's death, Laetitia was left dependent upon a small royal allowance as most of his fortune depended upon the Pozzo della Cisterna inheritance which went to the sons of the first marriage. As the French newspapers reporting her death were pleased to say, her personality was very much that of a Bonaparte rather than that of her saintly mother Princess Clothilde. Laetitia had always been more at home in Monte Carlo than in her mother's very religious home at Moncalieri.

From December 1926 until March 1927, Hélène, accompanied by Zaki Radicati, went on another hunting trip, this one based in Eritrea. She began the trip from Port Said, from where she wrote to her old friend Renée St Maur that 'the last days have been killing and unnerving—now I have the reaction.'[55] Unfortunately, she doesn't expand on what had made those days so terrible.

On 18 December at Suez, she met up with Susan Hicks Beach, 'my friend, my companion.' There was 'no effusion, no words. I love her; she loves me. Our friendship is proof of all. Happy to see each other, to leave together, we know it. So, why say it?' Two days later, when they were already at sea aboard the *Mazzini*, they were met by Luigi Abruzzi who drew up alongside on his boat. 'God! How thin and pale he is!' Hélène thought. 'He has recovered, he says from bronchitis. I think it must have been more a pleurisy.'[56] After chatting for a while, Luigino got back on his boat, and they all continued on their routes.

Hélène, Susan, and Radicati next arrived at Massua and had a nine-hour railway journey to Cheren. They were at the Mission at Cheren for Christmas morning Mass, delivered by one of the Capuchin fathers, 'a bearded, yellow man.' After that they enjoyed the plum pudding that Susan's mother had sent out from England— 'We had it hot, cold & fried, it appeared 5 times until completely finished'—as well as the sloe gin provided by an English friend. One of the reasons for chosing Eritrea for this trip was simply one of expense. Susan wrote to her mother that as it was an Italian colony, 'Madame does well to come & shoot here—she is given free tickets on the railway—free shooting, & is lent camels, mules & their attendants. So it is much cheaper than anywhere else. She is looking better already since she has been here.'[57]

They remained at Cheren for New Year at the Mission. Hélène said that her first thought was for those she loved now and for those who were no more, and while she attended Mass at the mission to begin the year, she was annoyed by the 'stupid New Year telegrams' which arrived for her. She was anxious 'to leave, to go into places that were free, far from every constraint.' The next day, she was able to do that as their automobile caravan left, and she was able to spend the night under the trees in her tent; in thanks, she kissed the discoloured fabric of her 'flying house.'[58]

The caravan next progressed by camel and mule. At Hasta, Susan shot a large ape, and the whole tribe gathered on the brow of the mountain shouting and gesticulating encouragement, but Hélène turned away from watching 'this type of man struggle against death', crashing from rock to rock to the ground. A few days later, the three hunters went in different directions to test their luck. Radicati found a band of kudu on top of the highest mountain and shot a 'beautiful example' of the breed. 'Susan, nothing; me, nothing!' Hélène complained to her journal.[59]

From Nacfa, Susan wrote home to her mother:

> We have been having the best of times, & it is magnificent country, really beautiful great hills, & such wonderful colours, very dry of course, in some spots it only rains about once in five years, but there seems to be always water in the river beds within a few feet of the surface & good water too.... I have only got two gazelle, & two baboons, whose fur will make collars for the children; the kudu take a lot of getting & this is very difficult country just here. Count Radicati has got two beauties—he is a very good shot. He is very nice, & is always looking after me as well as Madame, & I am having a very idle time.'[60]

They returned briefly to Cheren to restock and plan the next stage of their safari, which would proceed by cars for two days while the roads remained relatively decent, and then switching back to camels and mules. Susan, however, had her mind on other things as she had to return to Europe early and not complete the full trip which Hélène anticipated would continue through mid-March. She confided to her mother 'I simply can't bring myself to leave yet,' and so continued to enjoy the hunt. 'We had some great hunts after kudu, but nobody got one. They are mighty difficult, for they are normally on the mountains, & their wives keep a very sharp look out, so that unless one hits them in a mortal place at the first glimpse one seldom gets near them, & they are away over the mountain tops before one has climbed the first.' Meanwhile, she was also able to report that 'Madame is looking very well too, & has twice the appetite & twice the energy that she started with.'[61]

What Hélène really wanted on this trip was a giraffe, and she decided not to shoot at anything else. The very next day, she and Susan went hunting together, and before noon, there was 'one giraffe seen, one giraffe killed.' Radicati had left before four in the morning, and bagged another kudu and a number of birds. Even though Hélène had sworn four years earlier that she would never shot a guinea fowl, that oath came to an end because the cook told her that they had no more meat. The camp soon took on the look of a charnel-house, where 'the dead animals are skinned, cut, shaped; the dry skins, skulls boiled in a pot. Vast areas of smoked meat are on the ropes and sausages from a butcher.'[62]

On the first day of March, Susan left the camp:

> My friend is leaving, my friend has left. '*Au revoir*,' '*Adieu*,' always sad words. I love her, my friend, companion of past times, voyages from other days, sometimes difficult journeys, hard, sometimes dangerous. Always ready, strong as steel, firm character, equal, precious assistant, few words, practical, useful, obliging; always faithful, despite thirteen years of absence from the caravan, she took up this time, completely naturally, the place she occupied twenty years ago.

The car that took Susan to Kassala returned to take Hélène to Gului, where she then mounted a truck already loaded with her cases. From there, they returned to Cheren and Massua. On the 24th, Hélène was at sea aboard the steamer *Somalia*, and a week later was at Cairo, where 'at the feet of the eternal Sphinx, I gathered the flower of the forgotten.'[63] She stayed at the Continental-Savoy, where Baron Louis Rothschild and Count Münster were also staying after their shooting trip to the Sudan.

Hélène returned to Italy from Alexandria. She was met at Genoa by Emanuele Filiberto, Aimone, Luigi Abruzzi, and the Duke of Bergamo, and went on to Turin but did not stay long and the same evening left for Rome with Aimone. Hélène brought back with her two Eritrean lads. These were probably the boys known as Muftà and Murat, who would still be with Hélène when she made one of her last trips to Africa in 1936. A doctor who grew up at Capodimonte remembers playing with the boys on a rug where they slept outside of Hélène's bedroom. Years later, a young relative would remember that Hélène herself sometimes would sleep on the floor on a tiger skin. The boys are probably the children whom Queen Amélie is said to have secretly baptised.[64] Their later history is uncertain, although Muftà is said to have become a well-known football player.

When Hélène did return to Italy, one of the high profile appearances that she made was in June when she joined Mussolini at Ostia to greet the Marchese Francesco de Pinedo on the completion of his round-the-Atlantic flight. This occasion encompassed the love affair that Italy and much of the world was developing with aeronautics, but it also marked the fact that Hélène's public persona was increasingly becoming more closely aligned to the fascist government. However, she truly preferred being out of the limelight and wrote to Angelo Conti in July that 'I am deliciously alone in the paradise of Capodimonte.'[65]

During the First World War, when Princess Marie José of Belgium was only eleven, she had attended school at Poggio, outside Florence. Later, she noted that Hélène d'Aosta was her most diligent family visitor and wondered if she hoped for a marriage between Marie José and one of her sons, although it was apparent that Queen Elisabeth and Queen Elena had ideas of another match. However, as late as the summer of 1927, there were similar rumours when Amedeo went to stay with his uncle and aunt, the Duc and Duchesse de Guise at the Manoir d'Anjou, which is close to Brussels. As he was invited to the Belgian royal palace at Laeken several times, it was thought that a marriage between him and Marie José was in the offing; instead, he fell in love with his cousin, Anne de Guise.[66]

On 6 September, Hélène and Emanuele Filiberto, along with Amedeo, went to Pisa to join the Duc and Duchesse de Guise and their children Henri and Anne. As a group, they motored to San Rossore, where they had lunch with the King and Queen. After the lunch, the Guises returned to Florence, while the Aostas left for Milan and Amedeo for Turin, and it was rumoured that Amedeo and Anne were engaged. Then, on the 14th, the news became official and was announced by the Prime Minister through the Stefani News Agency that the King had 'gladly given his consent.'[67] They celebrated the betrothal at Queen Amélie's Château de Bellevue, Versailles, on 23 October.

About this same time, it seems that Emanuele Filiberto—perhaps caught up in the romance of his son—wished to rekindle his own connection with Hélène, but she would have none of it. 'My Friend'—as Hélène now generally addressed Emanuele Filiberto when it wasn't 'My Best Friend' or even 'My Glorious Friend'—'as I told you—as I telegraphed you. The past is past—let us not speak of it anymore—let us learn from our experience—to use to the best the true, the beautiful friendship which units us.' Friendship is all she was now willing to offer, as she repeated later the same year when she wrote to him as 'your best, your most sure, your most faithful friend.'[68] She would always be there in times of emergencies, especially for the medical crises, and then she would be the dutiful and attentive wife, but not otherwise.

It was at Capodimonte on 3 November that Hélène and Emanuele Filiberto, as parents of the groom, held a private luncheon for a few invited wedding guests arriving for the nuptials of Amedeo and Anne in Naples. Among Hélène's personal guests that day were Susan Hicks Beach and her sister Tora. Never one to mince her words, Susan wrote home to her mother that 'Madame looks dead beat already, & so do the boys, & the Princess; she looks quite a nice girl' and 'Some of the presents were there, a lot of them very vulgar we thought in the way of plate etc.' That evening, there was a banquet in the Royal Palace of Naples, followed by a reception for about two thousand guests. 'There seem to be great muddles about invitations, all the princes who are expected to dine at Capodimonte tonight, were found not to have been invited this afternoon, & it seems a good many unexpected ambassadors are turning up too, which adds to complications.'[69]

Sister Tora picked up the story from there.

We wandered from room to room with the crowd & finally found ourselves forced to pass with every other creature, one by one through a long narrow room of which the opposite side was occupied by one long line of royalties. I should think at least twenty of them! 'like onions on a shelf' as Princess Anne described it next day! They were too far off to be able to speak to anyone unless they absolutely threw a remark at them & all of us unfortunates could only make four or five vague curtsies into space & wonder how badly we were doing it—a most uncomfortable performance for all parties—When everybody had passed I think they went to supper, & we all streamed into the gallery where there was a huge long buffet. While we were eating a large scarlet footman appeared & demanded that Susan should follow him. I went too for fear of losing her, & people gaped to see us being steered through them like that. It was really only that one of the court men had orders from Madame to tell us to come to luncheon next day, but having received the message we found ourselves looking on at Prince Amedeo & his bride holding a sort of reception in a room by themselves. She spotted me, which was very clever of her, came up to greet me & made me introduce Susan & talked a little to us. Then they departed, & we went home soon after.'[70]

The next morning, while the Hicks Beach sisters were trying to improvise trains for their dresses for the wedding, they learned of a large luncheon party to take place at Capodimonte.

So we got into our best day clothes & up to Capodimonte in a taxi—found ourselves going upstairs behind a party who we suspected of being royal, & who sure enough were greeted by curtseying ladies-in-waiting—one of whom proceeded to curtsey to us & enquire tentatively what princesses we were! Having discovered that we weren't she kindly steered us into the room where the presents were—also more royalties & some attendants whom we knew, so we tried to efface ourselves till Queen Amélie appeared & we were all sent in to luncheon. All the women first in due order—then all the men after. There were about forty altogether—no Kings! but Queen Amélie of Portugal & at least fifteen HRHes or sorts—& only two other women besides ourselves who were not ladies-in-waiting. Each of us had a pleasant man meet us who spoke French, so we survived—& all came out in the same way. I fancy it was quite an informal family affair really! & waited on by a troop of huge footmen in scarlet liveries—all men from the Kings bodyguard we were told & more used to doing guard than footman. We all stood about drinking coffee & looking at presents, & S & I counted up afterwards that we had conversed affably with one Queen & ten Royal Highnesses! It was really most entertaining in a way. Madame herself was not there till quite the end, having been kept by some fuss over preparations for next day, but the Aosta princes & the Orleans princesses all greeted us & talked—& Queen Amélie & the Duchess of Guise & the

Duke of Turin (Aosta's brother) all had S. brought up to them & made much of her & made her produce me. I have been her sort of shadow all through & enjoyed it hugely. She says 'they are all so extraordinary kind to me.' they are & it seem to me that the all really like her & think her something rather out of the common which is as it should be. Also they certainly are all people with very charming manners—Madame turned up at last & took us off to her rooms with the other two women—Miss Capel Cure & an elderly half English half Italian Donna Bettina de la Casa Nuova—both of whom she is attached to & both are extremely nice—my ink is finished I will send this & write more tomorrow.[71]

On the morning of 5 November, the weather was perfect as the bridal party rode in open state carriages from Capodimonte through streets bedecked with flags and tapestries along with a flurry of flowers thrown from windows along the route. They drove through the enthusiastic crowds along the route to the Royal Palace where the civil ceremony was conducted in the Tapestry Hall by Signor Tittoni, president of the Senate, in the presence of the royal guests, the Knights of the Annuziata, and of members of the Government. 'Signor Mussolini had intended to be present but I understand that the police authorities said that to guard His Excellency and also the King of Spain would overtax their resources.'

After the civil ceremony, the wedding party processed from the palace across the courtyard to the Church. They walked along a red-carpeted wood platform some three hundred metres long. 'The road was lined with troops and a dense mass not only of the population of Naples but of visitors from every part of Italy occupied the square and a number of stands.'[72] The *Times* reporter wrote that the 'flowing robes of the ladies, in shimmering silk and cloth of gold, with long veils of splendid lace and superb jewels, and the brilliant uniforms and decorations of the men presented a gorgeous spectacle.'[73] Along with the parents of the bride and groom, the guests included the King of Italy, the King of Spain, and Queen Amélie of Portugal, royal guests from Denmark, Greece, Belgium, and Bulgaria, the extended family, the diplomatic corps and some British guests, including the Duchess of Sutherland.

The British ambassador described Princess Anne as 'tall and stately' and remarked that the newlyweds 'made an extremely fine looking couple.' The bride wore a gown of white satin with the veil of antique Chantilly lace which Hélène had worn at her own wedding in 1895 and with a tiara which was a gift from her new parents-in-law. The groom wore the white uniform of a lieutenant-colonel of Artillery.

Inside, the church was decorated with tapestries from some of the city's historic churches and had thrones for the kings of Italy and of Spain set on the tribunes with seating for all the guests of honour. Officiating at the service was Mgr. Beccaria, the Chaplain-General to the King, rather than Alessio Cardinal

Ascalesi, the Archbishop of Naples. Officially, Ascalesi was taken by a 'sudden indisposition.' Unofficially, it was said to be the result of a complaint by the French ambassador about the connection of the Duc de Guise and Princess Anne herself with the right-wing monarchist newspaper *L'Action française*, which had been placed on the Vatican's index of banned publications at the end of 1926, particularly in regard to a letter Anne had written to its editor, Charles Maurras.[74]

Sir Ronald Graham, the British ambassador, attended the wedding as the personal representative of King George, and he wrote two reports of the day—one for Austen Chamberlain via the Foreign Office and one personally to the King.[75] In the latter, Sir Ronald could not refrain from some royal gossip about the presence of Princess Marie José of Belgium and the rumours of an engagement with her and the Prince of Piedmont, but 'it was very noticeable that His Royal Highness paid no attention to the Princess at all, and indeed seemed to go out of his way to avoid her. His attitude appears to confirm the stories that His Royal Highness is by no means anxious to contract this marriage, although the King and Queen of Italy would like him to do so.' The Ambassador suggested that 'very possibly His Royal Highness is enjoying too thoroughly his newly found liberty at Turin to desire to marry anyone at present.'

However, the Hicks Beach sisters again provide a different perspective to the day's activities.

Inside the Church is a simple circle, with columns & small apses round the walls, a great altar at the far side & a bare white marble floor—straight in front of the altar were 2 prie-dieux for bride & bridegroom & facing towards them on either side several rows of seats for royalties & their suites on one side, for diplomats & big-wigs of sorts on the other side, & across from door to altar a path was kept for gendarmes, leaving space on either side of it—In those spaces were the guests, all the men on one side, all the women on the other, & only a few chairs in the recesses against the walls. The men's side seemed to be full, but there were comparatively few women, so that we had room to walk about freely, & even when close up to the Gendarmes were only about 4 deep. We got there about an hour before the ceremony, & you never saw such a pretty sight as the women made in that marble setting. they were dressed in every sort of colour except white or black—many in beautiful colours & stuffe & every one with a great veil of lace—shawls they mostly were, arranged to cover the head like a cap & fall over the shoulders & down behind often almost to the ground—every sort of beautiful lace & quite extraordinarily becoming, so that it looked as if every woman were beautiful. It reminded me of Mr Abbey's picture of the Castle of the Maidens. the Royalties I believe all assembled first in the Palace & processed, 2 by 2, across the Piazza & up the church to their places—the 2 Kings first—Italy & Spain—then the bride with her Father, the bridegroom with Queen Amélie of Portugal, & all the others following—the bride was the only creature in white—a very simple dignified gown with a great wide train. He in a white uniform with a wide blue ribbon of some order over one shoulder—such a magnificent couple they looked. All the royal men of course were in uniform of some sort, & all the women in the same sort of get-up as the rest of us only more gorgeous in jewels etc. there was a cardinal bishop officiating & an endless mummery of dressing & undressing him & playing about with incense & things, Scarcely an audible word in the whole service though we were within a few yards of it! We were so close that we could see everyone & everything perfectly over the heads of a few others, & it really was rather gorgeous to look at. Then they all processed out again, the two kings separately in front—then, after a slight pause the couple, & all the others behind followed by their suites. After them all we women were let out (no men till afterwards) & found ourselves also processing across the piazza to the palace, with our trains down, & saluting soldiers on either side, & the populace beyond, & a glaze of sunshine. While S & I were actually out in the muddle the couple appeared on the balcony of the palace immediately facing us, & of course were hailed with shouts & clapping—no one seems to cheer in this country. It is all clapping with occasional shouts & the fascist salute of raising the right arm straight in front of you, which is rather delightful & somehow suggests a blessing. Of course there was an absolutely perfect setting for a show of this kind, & the whole effect was extraordinarily beautiful—a thing one would not have missed for a great deal.

Having reached the palace we went through rather the same sort of proceeding as at the evening party, only this time there were not the 'onions on a shelf' but the couple in a room by themselves distributing favours to everyone who passed, & beyond that another room with the others arranged more in groups so that they could greet their own friends—but equally alarming to pass through! However we survived, & when everyone had passed the royalties processed to a sit down lunch—& soon after the long buffet in the gallery was thrown open to the rest of us hungry mortals, & we all fell to like hounds in a kennel. It must have been about 2.30 & we had started at 10. Having fed, a great many went away, but we learned from officials that if we stayed we should see them all leave. So we waiting in the gallery with perhaps fifty others & in due course out they came & down to the courtyard where they got into a series of open landaus, the king's state carriages apparently, very well horsed with bright blue furnishings & scarlet footmen etc. & so I believe they all drove slowly through the town & back to Capodimonte.[76]

The Duke and new Duchess of Apulia went very briefly on honeymoon to Capri, but then returned to Capodimonte; on the 17th, they left Naples aboard the battleship *Ancona*, escorted by four destroyers and bound for Tripoli, where

Amedeo was to resume his command of the Saharan troops.

After the wedding festivities, Hélène returned to Morocco with her sister Isabelle and her unmarried daughter Françoise, and accompanied by her new gentleman of court, Don Luigi Tosti, duca di Valminuta. He was Hélène's own age and had been a general in the cavalry and a gentleman of court for Queen Margherita before joining Hélène's household.

Hélène stayed with Isabelle at Larache in Spanish Morocco until early January, and then began journeying eastwards, through Spanish and French Morocco, Algeria, and Tunisia—Rabat, Casablanca, Marrakech, Meknes, Fez, Taza, Oran, Algiers, and Tunis, where she arrived on February 19th for a fortnight. Her niece—and new daughter-in-law—Anne drove over from Tripoli to spend some time with her. It was an unusual African trip for Hélène, as much of it was done by car or rail, until the last leg of the trip which would be by camel caravan in preparation for a longer trip that she planned to do, crossing the Sahara from north to south. Hélène next went by train to Tozeur, where Count Radicati had gathered a caravan of twenty camels for that part of the trip, which would take them through southern Tunisia and Algeria. As the caravan moved toward Donz, the Duchess went by car to Keyli and the great estate of the Duke of Clermont-

Tonnerre. On 11 April, Hélène arrived back in Naples from Tripoli.

13

1928–1932

Son ostentatoire salut fasciste[1]

In May 1928, there was a grand historical pageant in Turin which began on the 27th to commemorate the 400th anniversary of the birth of Duke Emanuele Filiberto of Savoy and the tenth anniversary of the end of the war. The King and Queen arrived with Princesses Giovanna and Maria to the National Anthem played by massed bands. Then, thirty mounted trumpeters in three teams representing the six-teenth, eighteenth, and nineteenth centuries galloped around the stadium sounding their silver trumpets. The first group of historical characters, all dressed in elabo-rate costume and aboard beautiful horses then rode into the stadium led by Prince Umberto and his sister Princess Jolanda—representing Duke Emanuele Filiberto and his wife Marguerite de France. They were followed by their suite represented by many of the local nobility. The second group was led by Amedeo and Anne—representing King Vittorio Amedeo II and, appropriately enough, his wife Anne de France, accompanied by the Duke of Bergamo representing Prince Eugene of Savoy. The final group was headed up by the Duke of Pistoia and his sister Princess Bona representing King Carlo Alberto and Queen Maria Theresa. The three groups galloped toward the royal box with unsheathed swords, the first group shouting 'Saint Maurice,' the battle cry of the original Emanuele Filiberto. The second group followed with the battle cry 'Bonne Nouvelle,' and finally, the third group with the battle cry of Savoy. Hélène and Emanuele Filiberto hosted a dinner for about forty guests in honour of the *Carosello* at the Palazzo Cisterna. One observer remembered the elegance of the surroundings as well as the oddity that Emanuele Filiberto had a bucket of ice in front of himself for his drinks, but none was available for any of the guests. He also recalled that the waiters were not dressed in livery but only in tails, and that the coffee was so dreadful that many tried to hide their cups.[2]

Throughout the year, Hélène continued her ongoing interest in matters relating to health and education. In August, she attended the departure of 'The White Train', bound for Lourdes with over 200 ill patients in hope of a cure. In September, both Hélène and Emanuele Filiberto attended the opening in Turin of the First Congress of the Italian Society of Colonial Medicine and Hygiene, headed by Dr Castellani, their longtime personal doctor, even when he operated out of a clinic in London. The same month, Hélène headed the delegation of ladies from the Red Cross when Mussolini opened the Sixth Conference of the International Union of work against tubercolosis in Rome. The crowd at the Piazza del Campodoglio at the top of the Capitoline Hill greeted Hélène warmly, and she returned their greeting with the 'Roman salute.' Later in the autumn, on behalf of the King, Hélène awarded the silver medal of the Public Health Service to Mother Catherine who had been Matron of the British Hospital of the Blue Nuns in Rome for thirty-five years. That same month, Hélène and Anne attended the opening of a creche named in honour of Anne and blessed by Cardinal Ascalesi, and the opening of the 'Elena d'Aosta' school in Naples. Hélène was becoming increasingly prominent at public events that supported 'Il Capo del Governo', more so than any other member of the Royal Family, and would regularly appear in Luce newsreels at the cinemas around the country. Her public support for Mussolini was an interesting counterpoint to the reluctance of the King; when public appearances brought them together, Hélène's presence was always readily noticed as she was over six foot tall (1.85m) in her prime, in the days when the average Italian woman measured about a foot shorter, while Mussolini himself was just 1.69 m, and King Victor Emanuel was a mere 1.54 m.

Sometimes the *bravura* of the public sphere collided with the personal, as it did in the summer of 1928, when Adalberto Mariano—the boon companion to Aimone during his illness in Far East—was himself in a life-threatening situation. Mariano and Filippo Zappi, both from the Royal Italian Navy, were among the expedition aboard the airship *Italia*, a semi-rigid dirigible under the command of Umberto Nobile on a polar expedition. On its third flight, on 25 May, the airship crashed, and the crew was stranded in the arctic cold. It was not until 12 July that the Russian icebreaker *Krassin* found Mariano and Zappi had ventured forth to find help along with their Swedish meteorologist Finn Malmgren, who did not make it. Within a day, the rest of the survivors were located and eventually they were returned to Europe. Both Hélène and Emanuele Filiberto had gone to Rivarolo in the days before the rescue to commiserate with Adalberto's parents, and the journalists who also visited the house reported seeing a photograph of the Duke there inscribed by him 'For Adalberto Mariano with the affection of a father,' and they caught the Duchess saying 'Poor lady, I suffer too. For me "Marianino" is a third son!'[3] Although Mariano would lose his right leg as a result of the injuries suffered in the Arctic, he remained in naval service and would later serve Aimone as an adjutant during the war. In December, he stayed with Hélène at Capodimonte, and was there to join her at the lunch she gave for American Admiral John Dayton and the officers of his flagship, the cruiser USS *Raleigh*.

That autumn, diplomatic whispers fanned into newspaper rumours that King Victor Emmanuel was again considering abdication—and not in favour of his son, the Prince of Piedmont, but rather Amedeo, the Duke of Apulia. That rumour was running parallel to another, which according to the British Foreign Office 'has extraordinary vitality and comes up at regular intervals' that Signor Mussolini or the Fascist Party desired to do away with the throne and the House of Savoy.[4] Complicating the issue yet further was yet another rumour, suggesting that the new constitution of the Fascist Grand Council would allow 'the Grand council the right of selecting the successor to the King of Italy, just as they are to select candidates for His Majesty to nominate as Successors to the Prime Minister.' However, the British Foreign Office blamed this interpretation on 'foreign newspapers, particularly in America, where people often seem to experience a difficulty in distinguishing between fact and the most fantastic fiction in European matters.' But they did admit Amedeo 'enjoys much popularity with the Fascist Party,' while the Prince of Piedmont 'is looked upon as being ill-disposed towards that Party, a belief that is said, I know not with what truth, to be founded, *inter alia,* on more than one occasion when His Royal Highness has refused to remain standing during the playing of the Fascist song, "Giovinezza," which is played at all official functions immediately after the Italian National Anthem.'[5]

The rousing chorus of 'La Giovinezza' rang out between the verses which set out the Fascist thoughts and plans:

> Youth, youth, spring of beauty
> In the hardship of life, your song rings and goes on!

> Hail, people of heroes. Hail immortal Fatherland
> Your sons were born again with the Faith and the Ideal

> Your warriors' valour, your pioneers' virtue
> Aligheri's vision today shines in every heart

> In the Italian borders, Italians have been remade
> Mussolini has remade them for tomorrow's war, for labour's glory

> For peace and for the Laurel
> for the shame of those who repudiated our Fatherland.

> The poets and the artisans, The Lords and the countrymen
> with an Italian's pride swear fealty to Mussolini.

No poor neighbourhood exists
that doesn't unfurl the flags of redeeming Fascism

In November, on the tenth anniversary of the end of the war, Hélène wrote a short note to Emanuele Filiberto as the 'Duce della Vittoria,' 'fondly recalling the glorious past of the commander of the unconquered III Army.' She closed, remembering 'yesterday—like today—like tomorrow. All for God—for the King—for the Country' and then signed off with her cryptic F. S. A.—France-Savoia-Aosta.[6]

In the new year, Hélène set about trying to negotiate a marriage between her niece Françoise and King Boris of Bulgaria, even to the point that, according to Italian diplomatic sources, she 'worked hard with the Vatican.'[7] In any event, nothing came of her efforts, and eventually Boris would marry Giovanna, the second daughter of Victor Emmanuel and Elena. Failing a powerful match for her niece, Hélène promoted a wealthy one.

The widowed Prince Christopher of Greece had first met Françoise at the wedding of Princess Mafalda and Philipp of Hesse and was smitten. Later, he saw her again in Naples, and according to his memoirs, it was then that Christopher decided:

> [He] could never be happy in life again without that particular person. Some time passed, however, before I had a chance to propose. All I could do was to hint to the Dowager Duchesse d'Aosta about the feelings I entertained for her niece. She gave me evasive answers, and told me to be patient as the lady in question was not inclined to marry anyone for the moment.

About a year later, Hélène telegraphed Christopher to go to Naples immediately as she had something important to tell him. 'I went ... I saw ... and was conquered. There was my dream lady, and very shortly afterwards we were engaged.'[8] Christopher was extremely wealthy by royal standards because of his first wife, an American some fifteen years his senior. Nonnie May Stewart, who later changed her name to Nancy and married tin magnate William B Leeds, was eventually created Princess Anastasia of Greece by a grateful Greek king—grateful, that is, for the financial support that she was able to offer the family while in exile.

At the end of January, the extended Orléans family began to gather at Capodimonte for the upcoming wedding before moving on to Palermo. Once in Sicily, the Duc and Duchesse de Guise laid a wreath on the tomb of her brother, Philippe, the Duc d'Orléans, in the Cemetery of St Ursula. When Françoise and Christopher married in Palermo in February 1929, Emanuele Filiberto and King Manoel acted as her witnesses, while King George of the Hellenes and the Prince of Piedmont stood up for the groom. Hélène was there to be part of the celebrations for which she was partly responsible. Amedeo and Anne also attended along with five queens—Queen Amélie and her daughter-in-law Queen Augusta Victoria, Queen Sophie of the Hellenes and her daughter-in-law Queen Elisabeth as well as most of the Greek royal family, plus Queen Marie of Romania and her still unmarried daughter Ileana.

On the same day—11 February—that Françoise and Christopher married, Italy signed the Lateran Pact with the Vatican, an official ending to the emnity between the kingdom and the papacy which had existed ever since the seizure of the papal states by the new country of Italy and the virtual imprisonment of successive popes with Vatican City, which now became a tiny but recognized sovereign state in exchange for its renunciation of claims on the old Papal Territories. Prince Christopher wrote that because of the coincidence of timing, 'the emotional Sicilian crowd assembled outside the church for our wedding was in a frenzy of excitement,' and they didn't know whom to cheer most, the Pope, the King, Mussolini, or the newly married couple.'[9]

The resolution to this long-term problem between church and state was accomplished largely through the personal efforts of Mussolini, who now controlled just about everything that the government thought, said or did. When the King opened the new session of the legislature on 20 April it was a Chamber almost exclusively appointed by Mussolini and representative of Fascist ideology. Hélène—perhaps for the first time—was there to attend along with Amedeo, Anne, and the Count of Turin. But it was Hélène alone of the whole royal family who was there to cheer Mussolini's speech of 13 May on the treaty with the Vatican. She herself was greeted with an ovation by those attending, and she returned the ovation with a Roman salute. When Mussolini entered the Chamber, the crowd was on its feet shouting 'Viva il Duce,' and Hélène was among those standing and applauding warmly.

A few days later, on 25 May after 'listening to another masterly speech by Signor Mussolini', as the *Times* correspondent put it, the Italian senate passed enacted the Lateran Treaty by 283 votes to 10. Four annexes to the treaty and also the Concordat were then signed between the Holy See and the Italian Government. 'A general Order of the Day approving the "happy solution of the Roman Questions," was previously voted by 316 votes to six, and was notable for the participation of the Royal Dukes of Pistoia and Apulia'.[10]

Although he was originally violently anti-clerical, Mussolini had been laying the groundwork for this rapprochement for years in anticipation of harnessing the power of the church in bolstering the state. Towards this end, Il Duce had already required crucifixes to be hung in all classrooms, court rooms and hospitals; he made it a crime to speak again the church or to insult a priest; he required that the Catholic faith be taught in elementary schools; put religious holidays on the civil calendar; and 'showered the Church with money.'[11]

The formal reconciliation between the Papacy and the House of Savoy came on 5 December when Pope Pius XI—who had succeeded to the Throne of St

Peter in 1922—received King Victor Emmanuel and Queen Elena. On the day after Christmas, it was the turn of the Aostas. Hélène and Emanuele Filiberto, along with Aimone and the Count of Turin and Duke of the Abruzzi, arrived in a five-car motorcade with the ladies and gentlemen of their court. They were received by the papal majordomo, who along with Count Cesare De Vecchi, the new Italian ambassador to the Holy See, presented them for a private audience with the Pope in the small throne room according to the same ceremonial prescribed for the visit of ambassadors. As a gift, Aosta gave the Pope a miniature eighteenth-century golden altar, adorned with precious stones and two paintings. The Pope, in turn, gave a golden rosary to Hélène, and a gold jubilee medal to each of the princes. The party then visited Pietro Cardinal Gasparri and worshipped in St Peter's. In an odd stroke of fate, this Pope, while still a forty-two-year-old priest called Achille Ratti, had been interviewed by the Duke of the Abruzzi for his polar expedition in 1899 but had been rejected as the duke was concerned about the effect that the presence of a priest might have on his rough crew.[12]

Hélène and Anne were among a great crowd in Constantinople on 6 June when, just after noon, a squadron of thirty-five Italian Savoia torpedo and bombing seaplanes arrived, under the command of General the Marchese di Pineo, and with Amedeo and Italo Balbo among those on board. 'All the seaplanes alighted in perfect formation on the dead calm water of the Bosphorus.' Afterwards Turkish civil, military, naval, and air authorities hosted a reception followed by a banquet given by the Italian Ambassador, Orsini Barone.[13]

The next month, it was Hélène and Anne themselves who made the newsreels when they donned flying helmets and climbed into a plane piloted by Amedeo from Turin to Milan. Amedeo and Anne were in London in late August when Amedeo was being treated at Dr Castellani's clinic for a liver problem.[14] Hélène was in London herself the following month and visited the Italian Hospital there, accompanied by the Italian Ambassador. She later sent a donation of £50.

Alongside his naval service, Aimone had been developing his skills as an explorer. On 12 May 1928, he had left Venice for Bombay to begin arrangements for the Italian expedition the following year to the Karakorum mountain range on the border between Indian, Tibet, and China. Accompanied by Commander Mario Cugia, he arrived on 5 June at Simla, the summer capital of India, and stayed with Lord Irwin at the Viceregal Lodge. The Viceroy (later better known as Lord Halifax, when he was Foreign Secretary, Secretary of War, and during the Second World War, Ambassador to Washington) wrote a personal letter to King George about his visitor, who unluckily 'got some slight blood poisoning in his arm before he came up here, which has been giving him a good deal of trouble, and on the ground of which I have persuaded him to stay here until he is thoroughly restored. I am afraid it may be a matter of a few days yet.' Aimone, he felt, was 'a delightful person', but rather unfortunate as 'In the course of his life—I suppose he is now somewhere about thirty—he seems to have met, in most parts of his body, with a variety of accidents.' There was political talk as well, and the Viceroy was much interested 'in hearing from him his impressions, which are no doubt those of official Italy, concerning Mussolini, and it is remarkable the implicit confidence that Mussolini seems to enjoy, even for policies that would seem in sharp conflict with normal current thought.'[15]

Aimone's uncle, the Duke of the Abruzzi, had climbed in the Karakorum Range in 1909, establishing various height records at the time, although he was not able to succeed in scaling K2—something that was not accomplished until 1954 when Italian climbers Lino Lacedelli and Achille Compagnoni reached the summit. For this preliminary expedition, Aimone and his companions formed a caravan of 240 ponies with 16 tons of supplies and left Srinagar on July 6, split into three sections; they then headed for Askoli, which they reached on 5 August and where they established a base camp. Later in the month, they returned to Srinagar, announcing their hopes to return in March to begin their attempt in April or May.

After the preliminary expedition, Aimone and the team of sixteen set out from Naples again on 2 February 1929, bound for Bombay. The expedition was financed by the City of Milan under the patronage of the Italian Royal Geographical Society, and was said to be the most elaborately equipped team that had ever gone out from Italy. Just before his departure from Naples, 'the Duke was non-committal as to whether the party would attempt to climb K-2.' Instead, he said that 'the chief object of the expedition was to conduct floral, faunal and geological explorations in the almost unknown valley beyond K-2, at the bottom of which runs the Shaksgam.'[16] The party arrived back in Naples on 24 October aboard the steamer *Genova*.

Ever since gaining the throne of Italy, the House of Savoy had moved its family celebrations around the country in order to involve as many regions as possible in the support of the national monarchy. However, the celebrations needed to be centred in Rome itself for the wedding of the heir, Umberto, the Prince of Piedmont, to Princess Marie José, the only daughter of the King and Queen of the Belgians.

Prince Albert, the Duke of York, as the representative of his father King George, arrived in the evening of 5 January aboard the same train that brought Marshal Pétain; he was met at the station by Aimone. The bride had arrived from Brussels that same morning, and the whole procession was enthusiastically greeted by the people of Rome. Due to his personal leadership of a beleaguered Belgian during the war, King Albert held a particular status as an international hero following the First World War, and King Victor Emanuel was able to share in the adulation, both 'cheered with that admiration that Fascist Italy has always bestowed upon these two "soldier kings,"' as *The Times* reported announced to London.[17]

Royalty poured into Rome from throughout Europe and further afield, although the ratio was higher for those from deposed dynasties, which caused

King Albert to quip 'There are many unemployed in our trade.' It also meant a great deal of trouble in the tricky business of precedence—who would sit where? As the British ambassador explained to the Foreign Office, Duke Giovanni Battista Borea d'Olmo, the Grand Master of Ceremonies, was 'nearly 100 years old and quite past his work.' He was, in fact, ninety-nine, and would not retire until he was 103, living two years more after that. His subordinates were 'full of goodwill but possess neither knowledge nor competence.' Not only had the Royal Court done little entertaining since the beginning of the War and thus 'fallen out of the habit of conducting functions with due ceremonial', but it was also known that Queen Elena 'had taken the direction of affairs into her own autocratic hands, and this led to great confusion.'[18]

This meant that there was chaos at the pre-wedding reception in the Quirinale. The Kings and Queens of Italy and Belgium led the procession, followed by Queen Amélie with Ferdinand, the former King of Bulgaria. After that, there was no proscribed order until Aimone took the initiative and suggested that the princes simply give their arms to the various princesses and follow along in the procession. The throngs mingled unhappily, and mutterings continued over the next few days about representatives of reigning houses being subordinated to those from deposed monarchies. The Duke of York was particularly frustrated at being ranked below the former King of Afghanistan and is said to have complained to his father afterwards: 'There's one thing, Papa, I'll never go to Rome again!' To this, King George V replied: 'And I don't expect you'll have to!' Having been forced to abdicate the previous year, King Amanullah, on the other hand, enjoyed the public aspects of the celebrations tremendously and, thinking all the cheering was for him, grabbed a nearby top hat and waved it about; when he placed the large hat on his small head, his jubilant face suddenly disappeared from view.[19]

At the wedding itself, protocol was rather more closely proscribed. The bride and her father led the procession, followed by her mother on the arm of the Italian king, then the bridegroom escorting his mother, until finally the four kings, four queens, and the rest of the sixty-three royal guests were seated. Hélène processed on the arm of Prince Georg of Bavaria, her husband, son Aimone and the other Italian princes coming a bit later in the order of precedence.[20] Emanuele Filiberto and his brother Turin were witnesses for the groom while the bride had her two brothers.

The bride remembered the beauty of the sparkling diadems and the grandeur of the uniforms and dresses which gave the chapel a worldly beauty, while not mentioning that the train of her dress came off three times and had to be stitched on by dressmakers, delaying the service about two hours. For Marie José, what really clashed with the sense of occasion was the ostentatious Fascist salute that Hélène made on the day.[21]

In the evening after the wedding, the Queen held a small dance for the younger princes and princesses at the Villa Savoia. At the same time, the Duke of York hosted a dinner at the British Embassy for forty, which included Hélène and Emanuele Filiberto, Luigi Abruzzi, various ministers and ambassadors, as well as the governors of Rome and Florence, along with leaders of Roman and provincial society. The dance which followed the dinner was intended to be a small affair, but as this was the only unofficial event of the week, eventually around 700 guests arrived.[22]

Amedeo missed the great events in Rome as he was away on military service in Libya. At the beginning of October 1925, he had been assigned to the Ministry of the Colonies and left later that month for Cirenaica and Tripolitana, the eastern and western sectors of Libya, where he would spend much of the next six years and develop his passions for aeronautics and for the Meharists, the camel troops.[23]

The quest for a new Italian empire began shortly after unification, but started with a disappointment in North Africa, where Italy hoped for annexation of Tunisia, where there was a large Italian community already established; however, the Treaty of Bardo had awarded that protectorate to France in 1881. However, in February 1886, Italy did annex the Eritrean port of Massawa and occupied territory south of the Horn which would become Italian Somaliland. As a result of the Italo-Turkish War in 1911, Italy gained Libya and the Dodecanese Islands from the Ottoman Empire; although the government hoped for overseas expansion through the Treaty of Versailles following the Armistice in 1918, they had to be satisfied with the northern expansion of its continental border from territories split off the Austro-Hungarian Empire. Britain ceded Jubaland in southern Somalia to Italy, in the expectation that the Dodecanese would in turn be ceded to Greece; however, Mussolini formalized Italian administration in both Libya and the Dodecanese Islands by the 1923 Treaty of Lausanne.

Although Italy claimed all of Libya, the tribesmen of the interior, the Senussi, began a struggle against these new colonizers that would last for years. In December 1929, Amedeo was in command of a detachment that raised the Italian flag at Brack, an important oasis in the Sahara, around 350 miles due south of Tripoli and *en route* to Fezzan province, the only part of Tripolitana not under Italian control. By the next month, Amedeo and his troops had driven the Arab forces further south and opened up the road to Murzuk, the capital of Fezzan and an important link on a caravan route between the Sudan and the Mediterranean. Fighting continued, and Amedeo's detachment moved toward the town of Ghat, 125 miles south of El Bari, the furthest point occupied to that point.

By January 1931, Amedeo and his squadron of airplanes had taken part in the campaign which occupied the oasis of Kufra, which was considered the last stronghold of the Senussi. The Tricolour was raised at El Tag in the middle of the oasis in the presence of Amedeo, Marshal Badoglio, and General Rodolfo Graziani; with that victory, Italy gained complete control over all of Libya.

Badoglio, as governor, told the troops that they must be 'ferocious and inexorable'; they rounded up over 100,000 civilians (women, children, and old men), marched them across the desert (in some cases over a thousand kilometres), and interned them in barbed-wire compounds near Benghazi. Over the next three years, over forty per cent of the internees died of disease or malnutrition; Libyans resisting the occupation were bombarded from the air with poison gas.[24]

Aimone gave a series of lectures on his Karakorum expedition including one at the Royal Geographical Society in London in February 1930, when he also visited the King and Queen at Buckingham Palace. 'In no other region of the world,' he said in his lecture, 'was there to be found in such a confined space so large a number of big mountains and glaciers.' A particular goal became the 'probable' saddle in the upper basin of the Baltoro Glacier mentioned in Sir Martin Conway's map of 1892, which they investigated and recommended be named in honour of Conway.[25] As leader of the Karakoram Expedition, Aimone later received the Society's Patron's Medal, specifically approved by the King.

Hélène accompanied Aimone to Madrid in April when he repeated his Karakorum lecture under the auspices of the Royal Geographical Society. They stayed at the Royal Palace in Madrid with King Alfonso and Queen Ena, and newspaper attention focused on a possible relationship between Aimone and the Infanta Beatriz, elder daughter in the family. The American papers in particular hinted at an engagement between the two. After a week, they travelled to Seville to celebrate Holy Week with the King and Queen, and their two daughters, along with the Queen's brother and sister-in-law, the Marquess and Marchioness of Carisbrooke. During that morning, Seville accorded them a tumultous greeting. '*Viva el Rey*' resounded through the streets and after delegations of Spain's fifty-two provinces filed for an hour and a half past the Alcazar Palace, where they are staying, the King expressed himself as 'greatly pleased.'[26]

Many of the royal families were very fond of silly practical jokes, and while in Seville, Aimone fell victim to one. In the gardens of the Alcazar Palace, King Alfonso had Aimone sit on a marble bench. His weight caused six concealed water jets to squirt and soak the young prince, to the laughter of the King, Infanta Beatriz, and Hélène. According to the newspapers, Aimone, 'brushing the water from his face and trying to wring out his waterlogged clothes, laughed as heartily as the others.' The playful incident was seen by some as a real intimacy between the two families and possibly another step closer to a union between Beatriz and Aimone, but nothing came of it.[27] Perhaps the shadow of possibly being carriers of hemophilia hung too heavily over the young Spanish infantas, as two of their brothers as well as other relatives would die as a result of the impact of the disease, a terrible heritage among the descendants of Queen Victoria.

Hélène became a grandmother for the first time, when Anne gave birth to a daughter at Capodimonte on 7 April. The child was entered into the special register for princes of the blood royal with the name of Margherita Isabella Elena Maria Emanuela Gennaro, but Hélène missed that ceremony, although her sisters Amélie and Isabelle were both there. However, Hélène was back in Naples in time for Margherita's christening which took place in the chapel at Capodimonte on 28 May. An orchestra played Schumann's *Giorni di festa* as the procession entered with the King standing as godfather, the Queen with her daughters Mafalda and Maria, and her son-in-law Philip of Hesse, along with Emanuele and Aimone, the Count of Turin, Prince of Udine, and Christopher and Françoise of Greece. While Cardinal Ascalesi administered the sacrament, Hélène held her grand-daughter at the baptismal font as proxy for her sister Isabelle de Guise, who was godmother but unable to attend because of illness.

Hélène's long interest in photography, one of the mainstays of her African trips, found a new audience in May 1930 when her work was included in an unusual exhibition of royal photographers. Some of the work was by the late Queen Alexandra, who had earlier published some personal photos in a charity book in 1908.[28] That publication included several showing Hélène at Balmoral. This new display, which was mounted on behalf of the King Edward's Hospital Fund and its associated Voluntary Hospitals, was simultaneously shown at the Royal Society of Painters in Water Colours in London, in various cities in England, the dominions, and abroad, and in an innovation aboard the *Berengaria* sailing from Southampton for New York, where the photographic show was to be made public. The Duke of York, Princess Mary, her old friend Princess Victoria, and the Queens of Denmark and Belgium were among the other contributors.[29] Hélène's entry, entitled 'African Hairdresser.' showed a native woman sitting on a tub attending to the hair of another woman who squats in front of her. It was among the photos distributed across the United States by the Bain News Service of New York.

On 30 June, Hélène made a trip to Pola, arriving by motor launch from Brioni. She was there to lay a bronze palm on the grave of Nazario Sauro, one of the irrendentist heroes, who had been hanged by the Austrians. A large crowd augmented by civil, military, and church authorities gave her an enthusiastic welcome.

Hélène had founded on 1 September 1919 the National Work for Assistance to Redeemed Italy (*l'Opera nazionale di assistenza all'Italia redenta*), and under her direction, the *Opera* grew to include by 1934, 274 kindergartens with 13,935 children, forty-three care institutions, 360 rural day schools, 767 classes evening, etc., and in 1927 she was awarded the Golden Medal for public service. However, Hélène's patronage here had an unforeseen and unfortunate long-term effect when she took on the patronage of the kindergarten system in the city of Trieste at a time when the government was compelling Yugoslav children in the city to join Fascist organisations. If parents refused to contribute subscriptions for the state-run kindergartens, they were threatened with prosecution for 'insulting a member of the royal family.'[30]

Vast areas of southern Italy were hit by a major earthquake—the Vulture Earthquake—on 23 July. *The Times* reported a loss of over 1,400 lives, while *La Stampa* claimed 2,142 dead and 4,551 injured. In Naples itself, there were only three dead and four injured. Hélène was one of the first on site to visit the injured in hospital; accompanied by Sister Carolina and her *dama di Corte* baronessa Isabella Compagna-Doria, Hélène went to the Pellegrini Hospital to personally take two wounded children into care.

The destruction in Villanova was far more serious, as around 500 were killed out of a population of 2,600, while between 400 and 500 were injured. The podesta and his entire family were killed, and the only major building left standing was the municipal *Dopolavoro* club. Hélène went to the town as one of her earliest visits to stricken areas. When the newsreel photographers filmed her entering the area, she did not forget to turn to the camera and issue the Fascist salute. Once there, 'Here and elsewhere she had words of sympathy and consolation for the homeless victims. All observers are agreed that it would have been impossible to praise too highly the tireless energy with which the Duchess has carried out her noble mission.' The newsreel went on to tell that 'In every place that she visited her presence has brought comfort and hope to the sufferers and she has been able to give the authorities precious advice in their relief work.'[31] Poor construction of buildings with river stones bound together with inferior mortar or simply river mud was blamed for the massive destruction, along with the fact that many of the buildings sat upon clay or sandy soil.

Aimone continued to bolster his playboy prince image by racing motorboats. In September, he was piloting a boat in Venice, but when he drew near to over-take his oponents at the buoy of San Nicholo near the Lido, the boat's propeller shaft broke, as did Aimone's leg. The race was immediately stopped and Aimone taken by first aid boat to the military hospital of St Anne. At least one newspaper reported that Hélène helped doctors dress the fractured leg.[32]

The young Aostas regularly broke bones in various sporting activities, but generally, they were relatively minor injuries. Still, they must have had the death of Isabelle's husband, Bruno d'Harcourt, on their minds. Harcourt crashed his Bugatti on an early morning practice run for the Moroccan Grand Prix d'Automobile in April, two days before the race was scheduled to begin. He misjudged a turn between Medronna and Casablanca and went off the road. He was only found hours later, pinned under the car with a fractured spine; he died two days later in hospital.[33]

Although Hélène had hoped to arrange a marriage between her niece Françoise and King Boris of Bulgaria, his proposal went to Victor Emmanuel's daughter third daughter Giovanna, thirteen years his junior, in 1930. The marriage negotiations were complicated by the interfaith issue between the Catholic and Orthodox churches, but the situation was resolved by the papal legate in Sofia, Giovanni Roncalli (later Pope John XXIII). The Pope granted a dispensation upon the strict condition that any children of the union should be raised as Catholic.

On 25 October, it poured with rain as the guests arrived at the great Basilica of St Francis in Assisi. Prince Christopher of Greece, who was attending with his wife Françoise, remembered that to get to the main entrance of the church the whole 'wedding procession had to climb up a steep slope strewn with laurel leaves and box plants, and skirt over a long strip of grass. By the time, we reached the doors we were wet through and splashed with mud up to our knees. To make matters worse, there was a strong wind blowing which caught the long skirts and veils of the ladies and whirled them about until they looked like limp rags.'

Hélène was highlighted by *La Stampa* as 'fascinatingly regal' in her old-gold-coloured dress. With her face encircled with a veil tied under her chin, she 'evoked an image of an eastern fresco or the mosaics of Ravenna.' Although the wedding was low-key for a reigning sovereign marrying the daughter of another, it still provided front-page news for the country. There was a grand procession out of the church, led by the newlyweds, who were followed by his father, the ex-King Ferdinand of Bulgaria, escorting Queen Elena; then King Victor Emmanuel with Queen Sophie of the Hellenes; and all the various guests with Hélène coming out on the arm of her son Amedeo; and next to last in the line, Mussolini with Princess Isabella of Parma. During the festivities, King Ferdinand—the son of Princess Clémentine—announced that he felt much more Orléans than Coburg. Hélène's niece Françoise acidly commented, 'So, my uncle, you have already forgotten the war?'; Ferdinand had brought Bulgaria into the First World War on the side of Germany in 1915, and in the final days of the war, abdicated in favour of Boris to retire to his Austrian estates.[34]

In November, Hélène travelled to London and was there for the ceremonies to commemorate the end of the war. First, there was a service at the Italian Church of St Peter in honour of those who had formerly lived in London and had fallen, as well as for the general Italian victory. She lunched with King George and Queen Mary the next day, and joined them for what had become the focus of British Armistice Day, the service at the Cenotaph on Whitehall. A few minutes before 11.00 a.m., the King came out of the Home Office in the field service uniform of a Field Marshal, accompanied by the Prince of Wales, the Duke of York, and the Duke of Connaught. Queen Mary watched the wreath laying ceremony from a window in the Home Office, accompanied by Hélène, Queen Ena of Spain and her daughters Beatriz and Maria Cristina, the Duchess of York, Princess Helena Victoria and Princess Marie Louise.

At the end of December, the Italian Red Cross published *Accanto agli eroi* (*Alongside the Heroes*), Hélène's war diary, with a preface by Mussolini, dated September 1930. A limited edition of 2,000 was printed, 500 of which were a luxury edition priced at 100 lire, while the ordinary edition sold for 25 lire, all for the benefit of the Red Cross. Earlier, in 1923 Carlo Torrigiani had published his late wife Anna's war diary, dedicating it to Hélène, that 'untiring angel of charity.' Extracts from his own diary and that of Duchess Maria Caffarelli—Anna's successor as Hélène's *dama di palazzo*—supplemented the account for the period following Anna's death.[35]

It was unusual for Hélène to spend Christmas at Capodimonte, but she did so on this year in the company of her husband, her son Bob, and her sister Amélie (who was in Naples on yet another extended visit, this time from December until March). Amélie noted in her diary the exchange of gifts and good wishes among the little group on Christmas Day; then the following day, they went to the San Carlo Theatre, where they were greeted by the playing of the Royal March and the Fascist song, *Giovinezza*, followed by a public ovation toward the Aostas. Then on New Year's Day, they attended Mass together, followed by another exchange of gifts. There were several visits during the next few weeks from Cardinal Ascalesi, during one of which Hélène had a long conversation with him on the Pope's recent encyclical on marriage.[36]

That March saw the serious illness of Sister Maria Landi, a local nun known for her devotion to Our Lady of Good Counsel (*Madonna del Buon Consiglio*). As a girl, she had painted an image of the saint in 1884 which was said to have stopped an outbreak of cholera in Naples that year. The painting was brought out in 1906 following the eruption of Vesuvius; it was said to have cleared the ash cloud away from the city. Over the years, the home of Suor Landi at Via Duomo 36 near the Cathedral had become a place of pilgrimage for many; in January 1920, the foundation stone was laid for the Tempio dell'Incoronata Madre del Buon Consiglio on top of the ancient catacombs of San Gennaro, on the side of the hill topped by the Capodimonte Palace. The basilica would not be finally completed until 1960, but it eventually became the burial place not only of Suor Landi, but also Hélène herself, her daughter-in-law Anne, and Cardinal Ascalesi.

Hélène, Sister Carolina, who was Hélène's frequent agent in matters of local charity, and Queen Amélie went together to visit Suor Landi's sickbed, where the nun was being administered oxygen. Her condition was such that Hélène summoned Cardinal Ascalesi who also came to visit that day.[37]

Two days later, Hélène was packed and ready to take the after-dinner train to Syracusa, then the boat to Tripoli for another African tour. Her baggage had already left when they received a phone call from Dr Castellani in Rome that Emanuele Filiberto was ill with suspected bronchitis. Hélène reconciled herself to the possibility that she might have to forego her African trip and left for Rome, where Aosta's illness had agravated into pleurisy.[38] Aosta's crisis passed, but Suor Landi's did not, and she died on 26 March. Hélène was still in Rome, but sent a laurel wreath in her memory.

Hélène did make her trip to North Africa during the months of April and May, missing a number of family events. Count Radicati was once again her travelling companion and trek organizer. 'R. is the perfect travel companion you could wish for; patient and thoughtful, his temperament always very even, always thinking of others, works like ten men, perfect for giving direction of the caravan, the men, animals and other things.' Together, they travelled this time by automobile through Tripolitania—from Tripoli, to Mizda, Brack, Sebha, Gat, Sebha, Hon, Musrata, and back to Tripoli. Among their first stops were the ruins at Leptis Magna, often considered the best surviving Roman buildings anywhere in the world. 'Of the imposing beauty of the ruins of Leptis Magna I will not say anything because it is beyond the capability of my pen and also because those wonders have been described so many times that I would risk plagarism.' Although Hélène would complain about the springs in the car as they bounced through the desert, she was able to admire the countryside from vantage point, different from her usual one on foot, horseback, or aboard a camel. 'The terrain varies and joins the endless plains covered with rhinestones, a smooth calm sea, follows the golden sand dunes with clusters of black rocks, a stormy sea, and then a long stretch of slabs of rocks.'[39]

They visited Brack, which had been seized by the Italians under Amedeo's command only sixteen months earlier. In the military camp there, Hélène enquires who the commander of the fort is and hears that it is Major Otto Campini: 'Oh! for me it is a beautiful surprise. I did not know that he had been transferred there'; she makes it clear that she is pleased to meet 'the beautiful and sympathetic figure of a soldier and a Saharian' again. It is not known when they first met, but Campini had obviously made a favourable impression upon Hélène. The travellers spent a few days at Brack before moving on to Sebha, where Hélène saw the room where Amedeo had spent nearly a year. Temperatures in that part of the desert were thirty-eight degrees with strong winds especially at night, so that Hélène at one point commented to her journal, 'How beautiful life is when no wind is blowing!'[40]

Meanwhile, April in Europe began brilliantly with the grand wedding of Hélène's nephew, Henri, comte de Paris, who married his cousin Isabelle from the Brazilian branch of the family and who had spent much of her youth at the Château d'Eu, as had Hélène herself. As son and heir to the Duc de Guise, Henri was still excluded from France, and it was decided to hold the wedding at the Palais d'Orléans in Palermo, that estate which many had assumed Hélène would inherit from her great-uncle and godfather, the Duc d'Aumale, but he had instead left it to the Duc d'Orléans who in turn bequeathed it to Guise. Amélie, who had been staying at Capodimonte since mid-December, left Naples on 31 March by train for Palermo for this great family event.[41] Hélène was the only one of the Orléans sisters not to attend the festivities, but her sons were both there, with Amedeo acting as one of the groom's witnesses.

Less than a week later, the Spanish monarchy toppled, and more of Hélène's family found themselves in exile. On 14 April 1931, King Alfonso left Spain upon the proclamation of the Republic, just twelve months after the visit from Hélène and Aimone. At the Royal Palace in Madrid, Alfonso gathered the family together for a final farewell. There, the household guard offered him a final salute, shouting out 'Viva el Rey.' Alfonso turned at the lift door and responded 'Viva España' while outside the shouts were 'Viva la República.' The Queen, the Prince of Asturias, Infantes Jaime and Gonzalo, and the Infantas Beatriz and Maria Christina spent a final night in the palace while the republican flag flew overhead. The next morning, they motored to El Escorial where they caught a train out of the country. After he was away, the king issued a manifesto in which he acknowledged that the recent elections showed that he no longer held 'the love of my people', but he felt certain that it would be regained. In the meantime, he left the country without renouncing any rights and avoiding any effort to resist 'which might array my fellow-countrymen against one another in civil and patricidal strife.' On the 17th, Infante Juan left Gibraltar for Italy; the same night, Hélène's sister Louise, her husband Carlos, and their family arrived at Gibraltar aboard a Spanish ship from Seville, where rioting had broken out. They had been living in Seville since 1921, when Carlos was appointed captain general in Andalusia and Louise played a prominent part in promoting the work of the Red Cross there, but now they sailed for Marseilles and thence went by road to Cannes to stay with Carlos's father, the Count of Caserta. Meanwhile, the last member of the family to leave Spain was the seventy-nine-year-old Infanta Isabel, eldest daughter of Queen Isabel. She had earlier suffered a stroke and the Republic gave permission for her to stay in Madrid, but she considered this insolent and refused to remain in the country. She was taken by train to Paris, then by ambulance to the Convent of the Assumption at Auteuil. Arriving there on Monday, the 20th, she died on the Thursday. At the end of May, Hélène planned to visit Paris 'to make an act of homage' to the exiled Spanish royal family, 'who were always good, friendly, welcoming to me. I want them to know that I am not ungrateful and that I am faithful to them.'[42] However, events at home would prevent that visit.

A number of members of the Italian royal family—including Amedeo and Aimone as well as the Prince and Princess of Piedmont—gathered in Turin at the beginning of May for the exposure of the Holy Shroud, the relic said to be the burial cloth of Jesus that bore his image. It was only rarely exposed to view; the previous time was in 1898. The princes, dressed in evening clothes with decorations, and princesses in black and veiled, processed from the Royal Palace to the nearby Cathedral where the veneration took place. Since 1453, the relic had been in the possession of the Savoy family who brought it to Turin a century later. The cathedral chapel where it was preserved has been a place of pilgrimage ever since. For generations, it had been a privilege among the princesses of the House of Savoy to mend the Shroud, which they would do gowned in white, armed with golden needles and special thread. Hélène was among those who had taken part in this special ceremony.[43]

Later that month, much of the French side of the family gathered at Dreux, for the burial service of Hélène's brother, Philippe, the duc d'Orléans, who had died in 1926 and had been buried provisionally in Palermo. All three of Hélène's sisters were there with many members of the extended family, but none of the Aostas. The newspapers reported that Hélène was unable to attend as she was '*souffrante*'; her absence from several important functions that year was partly due to her trip to North Africa, but latterly may have been because she was the not one who was ill.

A private British diplomatic letter directed to King George reported that Emanuele Filiberto suffered a 'serious illness in the Spring' and 'great secrecy was maintained by His family over the illness.' The same letter reported 'another attack' from which 'there was little hope of saving His life.' However, once again, it was only 'when matters were practically desperate and The King and Queen of Italy had been summoned to the bedside that any publicity was given to it.'

It was at the end of June that medical reports began to be issued from the Palazzo della Cisterna after the King and Queen had motored over from San Rossore to visit the Duke, whose condition was 'still very grave.' Emanuele's condition grew worse, and he lost consciousness. Hélène, their two sons, and his two brothers waited in a vigil at the bedside. D'Annunzio sent a telegram expressing his hope for the recovery of 'his great chief'.

On the afternoon of 4 July, Emanuele Filiberto died aged sixty-two with Hélène, their sons and his brothers at the bedside. Soon afterwards, an airplane flew to San Rossore with a sealed document for the King expressing Emanuele Filiberto's wish to be buried 'among my soldiers' in the Carso at the Sacrario Militare di Redipuglia, the largest war cemetery in Italy. Amedeo and Aimone dressed their father in the uniform that he had worn at the Battle of the Piave. A helmet, a stick with an iron point, and a gas mask were laid at his left side. At his feet, three banners were spread, one with the colours of Italy, another with the Arms of Gorizia, and a third with the Arms of Trieste.

The British ambassador reported to King George that a 'remarkable wave of feeling and sympathy throughout Italy' arose at the Duke's death. Mussolini sent a telegram to Hélène stating that 'The combatants of the army of Vittorio Veneto and particularly those who had the honour of belonging to the Third Army raise high the torn flags to salute the body of the wise and brave commander who led them during eleven bloody and glorious battles on the rugged stone masses of the Carso and to the triumphant victory of the Piave.'[44]

Newspapers around the world reported on the death. *The Times* of London wrote:

> Both the Duke and the Duchess were much beloved at Naples, where their charity was generous and their interest in all that concerned the well-being of the city constantly displayed. The duke was a competent critic of art and an

enlightened patron of a good many sculptors and painters. Like his younger brothers, the Count of Turin and the Duke of the Abruzzi, he was a Senator since he attained the age of twenty-one, but his appearances in the Senate were rare, and, apart from military matters, he took little part in public life. On such occasion as he did speak in public—generally military ceremonies and celebrations—he showed no small gift of oratory. His keen interest in all matters affecting the Army and his services and merits were no more than adequately recognized by his promotion to the rank of marshal and by his nomination as a member of the Army Council.[45]

On the day after the death, the doors of the Palazzo della Cisterna were open for the public to pay their respects from 9 a.m. until 7 p.m. On the Monday, newspapers around the country published the following:

SPIRITUAL TESTAMENT OF HRH Emanuele Filiberto di Savoia, Duke of Aosta

Evening falls on my hard working day, and while darkness floods and submerges my earthly life and I feel the end approaching, I lift up my gratitude with infinite thanks to God for giving me life, but above all for being able to serve the country and my king with honour and humility.

It was my great fortune to have been able to see before closing my eyes to earthly light my youthful dream of the complete redemption of Italy and having been able, thanks to the valour of my soldiers, to contribute to the victory that crowned with laurel the sacrifices made: I die so serenely confident that a wonderful future will unfold for our country under the enlightened guidance of the King and the wise government of Il Duce.

To my august sovereign whom I have always served with loyalty, with ardour and faith, I address the dearest expression of my grateful heart for the affection that he has always had for me; to my dear nephew Umberto, promise and hope of Italy, my most affectionate and most fervent wishes. To Her Majesty the Queen, to my wife Hélène, to my sons Amedeo and Aimone, to my brothers, Vittorio and Luigi, to all my relatives my gratitude for the good that they desired for me and which I reciprocated with equal tenderness.

In this hour of my sad demise I particularly express my gratitude to Hélène for the care that she has always provided me and I pray my two sons will continue in the way that I outlined to them and that is summed up in the motto 'for the Country and for the King'.

My farewell goes out to all my colleagues and dear comrades of the Carso and the Piave, and again I express my gratitude for what they did under my orders to the glory of the Third Army and the greatness of the Fatherland. I desire that my grave, if possible, will be in the Cemetery of Redipuglia among the heroes of the Third Army.

I will be vigilant and safe with them, sentinels at the frontiers of Italy, in the presence of the Carso which saw epic deeds and innumerable sacrifices, close to the sea that received the bodies of the sailors of Italy.

Emanuele Filiberto of Savoy[46]

On the Wednesday, the coffin was taken to the church of The Gran Madre di Dio, an elegant but small church, on the banks of the Po, based on the design of the Pantheon in Rome. From the riverside, one can see the Basilica rising on the hill at Superga, the traditional burial place of the Savoy dynasty. All the shops and factories of Turin were closed as a sign of mourning as the funeral procession marched through the streets. Headed by detachments from the Army and the Navy, the clergy procession came next followed by the gun carriage—the same one which had been used to bear his father's coffin—carrying the coffin covered with the Italian flag. Then came the King, with all the Princes of his House, and the foreign representatives, among whom were Lord Cavan, head of the British Army on the Italian front during the war representing King George; General Guillaumat and Major Keller, representing France; and Prince Nicholas of Romania, brother of King Carol.

It was essentially a military rather than a royal funeral, and the Romanian prince was the only royal there who was not a close member of the family. None of Hélène's family attended. General De Bono, who represented Mussolini, walked alone in the middle of the procession; then came the Knights of the Annunziata, three Ministers—General Gazzera, Senator Sirianni, and General Balbo—and the representatives of the Senate, of the Chamber of Deputies, and of the Fascist Party. After the service in the church of the Gran Madre di Dio, the procession dissolved and the coffin left in a special train for Redipuglia, where it would arrive the next morning.

About 8 a.m., the special train with the King, the Prince of Piedmont, Lord Cavan, and all the officers, ministers, and representatives who took part in the funeral procession at Turin arrived at Redipuglia; soon after came the train in which were Hélène covered from head to toe in a long black veil and her two sons. The coffin was carried to the grave by four ex-officers, and after a short service, it was laid in the tomb, while guns fired, aeroplanes flew overhead, and bands played the *Hymn of the Piave*.

Italy's largest war memorial rises from the western face of the Mont Sei Busi at Redipuglia, just inland from the Gulf of Trieste. Though it is not very high, Sei Busi allows outstanding views from its summit, up to the first slopes of the Carso plateau, where so much blood was shed during the war. On the monumental terraces are buried the remains of 100,187 fallen (39,857 known and 60,330 unknown). Emanuele Filiberto's grave would eventually be at the main monument's lowest level, covered by a 75-ton monolith of porphyra.

A week after the funeral, Hélène and Aimone were in London staying at Almond's Hotel, where she was able to have long talks with her sister Amélie and Princess Victoria. She spoke of the 'admirable' death of Aosta, 'a great Christian, a great Soldier.'[47] In early August, Hélène, Bob, and Luigi Abruzzi returned for a memorial Mass at the cemetery in Redipuglia, but soon Hélène left again, this time to return to Normandy, where she had spent much of her childhood.[48] Later in the year, Hélène received news that upon Il Duce's recommendation, Parliament had granted her an annual allowance of 400,000 lire, the equivalent of the grant to the most senior princes of the House of Savoy.[49] This was probably the first regular source of income that she ever enjoyed.

On 4 November 1931, 'sadness had called' Hélène to the cemetery of Redipuglia for the anniversary commemorations of the armistice which ended the First World War for Italy. It was the same day that Umberto and Marie José made their official entry into Naples where they would be making their new home in the Royal Palace. While in the northeast, Hélène opened a new day nursery for children in Gorizio and a tuberculosis hospital at Idria. When she returned to Naples, she began a connection with the Prince and Princess of Piedmont that grew deeper over the years, especially with Marie José; they would regularly appear at functions together. One example, which Luce was able to show the nation through its newsreels, was in December when the three of them together opened a new Red Cross preventorium, an isolation hospital at Pozzuoli for those infected with tuberculosis but not yet active with the disease.[50]

Amedeo and Anne were also on the move. Shortly before his father's death, Amedeo assumed command of the 23rd regiment of artillery, based in Trieste; on 11 April, they had made their official entry into the city. On 2 May 1932, with the King's permission, Amedeo transferred from the Artillery to the Aviation Branch, retaining his rank as colonel.[51] The new Duke of Aosta moved his family to the Castello di Miramare, where his second daughter, Maria Cristina Giusta Elena Giovanna, was born 12 September 1933 and where she was christened the next day with Hélène as godmother and Jean de Guise as godfather. All the sirens in the harbour sounded in celebration of the new little princess.

Miramare was built on a seaside cliff in a 22-hectare (54-acre) park overlooking the Adriatic. When he became commander in chief of Austrian Imperial Navy, Archduke Maximilian had ordered the construction, which began in 1856 but was still unfinished when he sailed off to become briefly and tragically the Emperor of Mexico in 1864. It was to Miramare that the Empress Charlotte, suffering from a nervous breakdown, returned until repatriated to her native Belgium. Later, the Crown Princess Stephanie—widow of Rudolf—chose the chapel at Miramare for her second marriage to a Hungarian count. In 1914, Archduke Franz Ferdinand and his family lived there for a few months directly before his assassination in Sarajevo. At the end of the war, Trieste—along with

Miramare—was transferred to the nation of Italy, and was briefly the headquarters of Emanuele Filiberto immediately after victory was declared.[52] While the main body of the palace remained a monument to Maximilian and Charlotte, the guest wing was renovated for the Aostas in the contemporary 1930s style. Portraits of Emanuele Filiberto in uniform and Hélène standing between two dogs by Carlo Siviero are in the apartment today.[53]

Hélène spent New Year's with Amedeo and his family in Trieste, returning to Naples on 2 January. Her sister Amélie was already staying at Capodimonte and briefly considered meeting Hélène at the station; however, knowing how much Hélène disliked those public greetings and farewells, she waited to greet her at the palace. Two days later—on the six-month anniversary of Emanuele's death—a fire broke out mysteriously in his closed-up bedroom. The fire, discovered by Rosso, one of the servants, was put out by Hélène herself and her valet Muftà, using buckets of water before either the police or the fire brigade arrived.[54] A short circuit in the wiring was determined to be the cause, and although no one was injured, various paintings and pieces of furniture were destroyed by the flames.

Later in January, Queen Sophie of the Hellenes died in Frankfurt after a long struggle with cancer; her coffin was brought to the church of St Nicholas in Florence to rest beside that of her husband King Constantine and his mother Queen Olga. Attending the burial services were around fifty members of Sophie's family, together with Queen Elena, Hélène, Amedeo, and Anne. All of the women wore the long black mourning veils that reached all the way to the ground. The cortège entered the church following the coffin bearing Sophie's crown on a cushion. The service itself was short and simple; at its close, the mourners went into the side chapel to pray at the tomb of King Constantine.

In early February 1932, Hélène was in bed with a cough, fever, and a bad head cold; Amélie felt she should stay there, but Hélène had already scheduled her departure for North Africa, and on the 15th, she did indeed leave, as Amélie noted in her diary, with 'Radicati one *femme et le Nègre*.'[55] This time, Hélène travelled from Tunis to Alger, and then down to stay at the Hotel Transat in Beni-Ounif on the Algerian side of the border with Morocco. There, she was able to sit and read novels and travel books before heading back to Italy via Oran, thence to Alger and Tunis again.

On the very same day that Hélène left Europe, a month-long auction began of Emanuele Filiberto's private art collection of furniture, sculpture, paintings, musical instruments, porcelain, clocks, antique arms, and tapestries—some 3,017 pieces sold at his own request.[56] After the war, he had renewed his favourite hobby of collecting antique furniture, old silver, and pictures, and most mornings of the week he could be seen strolling around Turin or Naples hunting for bargains. Whenever he found something he liked better than something he had already, he would visit the antique dealers to sell. Emanuele would drive his own bargains, and 'many are the anecdotes of his good-humoured shrewdness and his frank pleasure when he got the price he asked.'[57]

Hélène was back in Italy by April and entertained the officers of the French battleship *Lorraine* when they visited Naples in June 1932. However, later that month she wrote to Amélie:

> My weakness increased, so much that I had to call a doctor who, being in Naples, can follow my health and be called from one moment to another. I was forbidden to go to Redipuglia on the 4th [for a memorial Mass], which is very painful, and if I do not strengthen, I can not budge from Capodimonte.[58]

Amedeo and Aimone were now beginning to take on more official roles, often representing the King at functions abroad. In May, Amedeo went to France to represent the King at the funeral of President Paul Doumer, who had been shot by a mentally unstable Russian emigré while opening a book fair in Paris. The funeral procession formed up at the Elysée Palace, and the Tricolour-covered coffin was followed to Notre Dame by the late president's nurses, the male members of his family along with close personal friends and members of his household. Then came the official representatives: the newly elected French president Albert Lebrun walking alone; followed by King Albert of the Belgians, likewise on his own; then walking abreast came Amedeo, the Prince of Wales, Prince Paul of Yugoslavia, and the eighteen-year-old Emperor Bao Dai of Annam. The services, according to the *Guardian* correspondent, contained 'all the funereal pomp and ceremony that appeal so strongly to the French taste' and concluded with the burial itself in the Pantheon.[59]

The next month, another tragic and unexpected death occurred, this time within the family. Hélène's nephew Manoel, the ex-king of Portugal, was only forty-two years old and apparently very fit. On the Friday, he attended the tennis matches at Wimbledon. In fact, on the Saturday, he himself was scheduled to play at the All-England Tennis Club at Wimbledon, where he played regularly. However, he complained of a sore throat on the Saturday morning, and his doctor advised simple bed rest, but in the early afternoon, an attack of breathlessness culminated in death from acute œdema of the glottis.

Unlike so many of his relatives, Manoel had been quite content in the role of retired royalty from a young age. As one newspaper put it: 'Dom Manoel was fitted by nature for the part of leisured "*roi en exil*" rather than an active pretender.' At his home at Fulwell Park in Twickenham 'he was able to satisfy his tastes for bridge and tennis and the opera and his passionate love of ancient books.'[60]

Queen Amélie made the journey from her home at the Château de Bellevue in Versailles to London, and Mass was said each morning in the salon of Fulwell Park, where the King's body lay in state watched over by the Sisters of de la Miséricorde. On 14 July, a High Requiem Mass was sung at Westminster Cathedral. The two queens Amélie and Mimi were present, along with King

Alfonso of Spain and King George of the Hellenes. The Duke of Gloucester represented the British king, while Amedeo and Anne, plus Louise and Carlos of Bourbon-Sicily represented the family. After the service, Manoel's coffin was taken to the family crypt at Weybridge to rest near his grandparents, the Comte and Comtesse de Paris, until the 29th when it was transferred to the H. M. S. *Concord*, a British warship, which carried it to Portugal where he was finally buried along with his murdered father and brother.

Hélène herself was not well at this time, restricted to her chaise-longue at Capodimonte, not able to go to Vichy with her niece Françoise in July as anticipated. When she was able to travel, she went first to Switzerland to be with her son Bouby, who was continuing his recuperation from an attack of amoebic hepatitis and abscess—'he is better but he is so thin.' Then Hélène dashed to England to embrace Amélie in her great distress, but when she took a car out to Fulwell Park Hélène discovered that Amélie had already left for France and so just met with the recently widowed Mimi. It was only now that Hélène revealed to Amélie that she had herself been close to death; although the doctors 'condemned' her, they could not say what the cause was. While in London, Hélène decided to stay for a few days for treatments with Dr Castellani, and also took the opportunity to visit with Susan Hicks Beach. In early September, Hélène returned to Italy aboard the S.S. *Otranto*, poignantly sailing right past Amélie's old home at Pena. With a fellow passenger on that journey, Lady Algernon Gordon Lennox, Hélène reminisced about so many friends who had disappeared over the years—Aunt Alix, Oliver Montague, Soveral, '*mon pauvre* Eddy,' and so many others.[61]

Aimone had also been in London with Hélène but then went to Salso Maggiore to try to work on improving his arm after his most recent accident. However, the next month he was sent to Belgrade to represent the country at the funeral of King Alexander of Yugoslavia who was assassinated in Marseilles, while on a state visit to France.

Hélène now did what she often did when faced with physical or emotional problems—she escaped to Africa. In September, she left Amedeo's home in Trieste to go to Genoa and thence to Morocco. Hélène went from Tripoli to Homs by automobile, then to revisit Leptis Magna, some of the most spectacular Roman ruins still in existence. She returned from Cyrenaica and Tripolitana via Tunis, Marseilles, and Gibraltar; she arrived in Genoa aboard the ocean liner *Conte Grade* on the night of 25 October.

She was back in Naples in November when she, Anne, and the Prince of Piedmont attended a service when Cardinal Ascalesi blessed a memorial tablet to Emanuele in the votive chapel of the Church of Santa Chiara. The text contained the wording of Emanuele Filiberto's 'Spiritual Testament.' Later that month, Cardinal Ascalesi also officiated at the consecration of the ancient Basilica of San Gennaro extra Moenia, near Capodimonte, the nexus of a great complex system of catacombs. Hélène attended this service too, along with Umberto and Marie

José, and the crowds loudly cheered the princes, the Duce, and Fascism.

Within days, Hélène was back in Africa yet again. In preparing to leave Capodimonte, she performed her usual ritual, passing from room to room, 'having contact one more time with my silent friends, the witnesses of my life.' Part of the routine was to speak to the black stone cat, representing the goddess Bastet, protectress of joy, love, and motherhood. It had been a gift from King Fuad of Egypt and was now a totem for the household. 'To the cat of the Pharoahs, to the household gods of my home ... I make the customary salute, confiding to him everything here and the distant future afar.' Zaki Radicati, as always, had everything prepared. Muftà was ready to depart, the palace staff stood in the courtyard prepared to bid her farewell, and finally Hélène rode to the quay to board the steamer S.S. *Duchessa d'Aosta*, seen off by the Prince and Princess of Piedmont. The last cable was sent; a last Fascist salute was given; and the boat slowly moved away, as did the official automobiles.[62]

The ship stopped first at Genoa, where her brother-in-law Luigi arrived with armsful of flowers. He spoke about his own woes, his suffering, the cures that he was forced to submit to. Hélène told him that if he returned to Somalia, he would only have to send her a telegram, and she would join him there. Luigi also spoke of Bob's departure the following day for America on the maiden voyage of the Italian liner *Conte di Savoia*, a new state-of-the-art gyro-stabilized ship.[63]

Bob himself arrived the next morning at 10 a.m. to say farewell to his mother, who warned him about the reporters in America—'the American press is the worst in the world—never treat the reporters badly but never see one alone but only ten at a time—or twenty—so they will not go around inventing tall tales.' She also charged him with reporting something 'very delicate' to an American lady— presumably Katherine Elkins and presumably about the ill health of the Duke of the Abruzzi. When it was time to leave, Aimone 'hugged me strongly, very strongly' as they said to each other (in English) 'My Mother!' 'Bless You, my Bob!'[64]

In New York, Aimone was feted by the Princess Guido Pignatelli di Montecalvo, the former Constance Wilcox of Madison, Conn. Later in the month, Aimone went on to Palm Beach, where he was a guest of John Sanford—a millionaire carpet manufacturer and race horse owner and son of a former American minister to Belgium—and his daughter Sarah at Villa Marina; there, they were joined by Mr Sanford's son-in-law and daughter, Sidney and Gertrude Legendre of New Orleans—a couple with similar adventuresome interests to Aimone as they met on an expedition to Abyssinia and later explored together in Southwest Africa, Iran, and Indo-China. Sanford's son Stephen, a polo player, joined the house party later.

Hélène, travelling aboard the S. S. *Duchessa d'Aosta,* made a stopover at Marseilles where Susan Hicks Beach joined the party direct from London. 'She is always the same, a bit thinner, a bit greyer, but solid in body, in spirit, and in mind.' It was also an opportunity for Amélie to visit with Hélène, the first time they had seen each other since Manoel's death. 'She seemed like Sadness itself walking! Poor Mother, poor Wife, poor Queen! Everything has been taken from her, ripped away, broken, destroyed!' Despite the rain, they descended from the ship and went through the streets of Marseilles as Amélie recounted her sufferings and agonies. They lunched together in town, but when it was time for Hélène to re-board the ship, she watched her sister leaving in her car, her eyes full of tears.[65]

Their next stop was for a single day at Tangiers, and as they approached the port they saw a motorboat flying the Italian flag. Even before she could distinguish the faces aboard, Hélène knew that 'my heart tells me that my sister, the sister I love, my double [*mon sosie*], my second self, was coming towards me.' As the motorboat drew alongside, Hélène had an anxious moment when a large wave required Isabelle to jump for the ladder platform: '*mon* Isa, my dear sister is not agile, with her very little feet.' Soon, they were together, with Isabelle 'radiant with youth and charm.' She arrived with her 'little court' plus the Italian minister Chigi and members of the consulate staff, but they were all ignored as Hélène and Isabelle went off, hand in hand, happy to be together—even though Hélène had just been there in October—as they 'admired one in the other, having the same views, the same thoughts, the same ideas.'[66]

It was just a brief visit; later that day, Hélène and her party sailed on toward Las Palmas, before they arrived at Douala in French Cameroon, where they were greeted by the 'local Governor—a fat little man with little black eyes just like a guinea pig—the company's agent & the Italian Consul General for most of Africa'—while their 190 pieces of luggage were transferred from their ship to land. Susan wrote:

> [They] were promptly put into a car, & brought to a sort of guest house close above the river, with immense rooms (each with bathroom with running water). There is a sort of little park round it full of palms of all sorts, mangoes bananas, bamboos, frangipani, crotons & various others, with beautifully kept green grass flats, awfully pretty altogether…The boat was really awfully nice, it might just as well have been a private yacht, as none of the other passengers were allowed in our part of the deck, only the captain & 1st officer came & made conversation occasionally…. Madame is well, but she has occasionally goes of asthma for no obvious cause, which pulls her about a lot.[67]

From Douala, they went by rail to the capital Yaoundé by rail, some 150 miles. From there, they went into the forest and by Christmas Eve reached the village of Kan. That night, she dreamed of Amedeo standing by her bedside with sad eyes. She reached out her arms to him crying 'My Bouby', fearing that some misfortune was going to befall him. 'My God, protect him!'[68]

The journal that Hélène kept on this journey bounces from Italian to French, unlike her others where she wrote solely in French. This one also stands out as she marked it 'private property for me alone and for whom it concerns.' It records the beginning of a new chapter in her life.

14

1933–1939

Movement is life. Travelling is necessary food for the body and the spirit.[1]

The town of Yaoundé had been founded by Germany in the interior of Cameroon in 1888 as a centre for the ivory trade, but following the First World War, the whole colony became part of the French African empire. When they left and Hélène bade farewell, it was to the French Governor Bonnecarrère and his wife, who was 'dressed to perfection for a very elegant reception in a Parisian salon.' Hélène and Susan, on the other hand, 'made poor figures, dressed in our traveling clothes,' but Hélène felt that she 'would not have been more in character with the Kamerun in a dress of satin and lace.'[2]

Hélène had her own definite thoughts about African life and travel, and satin and lace were not part of them. 'Movement is life. Travelling is necessary food for the body and the spirit. To change surroundings, countryside and climate, that is the gymnastic which keeps us flexible, ready for any event, never taken by surprise, nor startled by any circumstance, whatever might happen.' Rather it was 'the slavery to needs that civilization has created, is a sadness, a stone at the foot of real liberty.' In fact, 'the boxes, trunks, food, all that hinders those who dream of freeing themselves from obligations to live free in direct contact with nature. The packaging poisons the joy of my travels. But, what is there to do?'[3]

Their party moved out, and eventually camped at Dumbè on the night of 31 December when a cough kept Hélène awake so that she could 'see the old year die and the new one be born,' she wrote: 'To God I commended the souls of those whom I loved, who have departed before me on the great voyage without return; absent, but always present in my memory.' To those who were still alive 'From the bed where I suffer at this moment, I called, naming them, my two sons, support and consolation of my life, to bless them from afar. May the new year be sweet for them.'[4]

They moved into the monotonous bush, a dry and stony land, with trees dotted about amidst the high yellow plants. The travellers crossed the Bingué River in a small boat, and there were met by Monsieur LeFèvre, 'le Chef de Cercle,' who arrived by auto and who, Hélène felt, had 'just and clear ideas on the colony and on the way of treating the blacks!' A second automobile stopped, and a tall man dressed in sumptuous clothing in silk and satin descended. It was the chief of the Garone, the Hamido. Hélène was taken aback when he greeted her in fluent French, but Monsieur LeFèvre explained that the Hamido not only spoke French, but had been 'in France, to Paris, to the colonial exhibition and was taken everywhere, *hélas*, even to the Folies Bergères!' Hélène commented (at least to her journal) that the blacks should seldom see Europeans, and never where they live, or they would lose all respect for the whites.

When the Hamido continued to speak of his adventures and sightseeing in France, Hélène explained that many of the historic buildings that he saw were the work of her ancestors, although she was now Italian. 'Rome, the Pope,' he said, 'that's where the Missions come from.' Hélène told him that 'The Pope has a great village in Rome, but the King has all of Italy. The King and I are of the same family,' and she then went on to say that her older son was even taller than he was. 'If the King is of the same family as you, then your son is the Dauphin of Italy.' Again, Hélène confided to her journal—'I pray to God that the prediction of this black chief is not realized!'

The beat of the tom-toms and the singing which had never ceased grew even more beautiful as they continued their visit. LeFèvre took Hélène and Susan to meet his wife and then into town to purchase a few supplies at the 'Nigerian Co.,' where the director, an Englishman named Bird, told Hélène 'I know your son well! He is a good tennis player. Yes, while I was at the garrison in Palermo, I was an employee of the Whitakers, and we played almost every day with your son who beat me regularly.' 'How small the world is!'[5]

From there, they travelled by truck back into the bush, where the hunt began with some success, before they reached camp at N'ingingmi on the shore of Lake Chad in present-day Niger. Susan wrote home saying: 'We have at length arrived here, after many struggles with the lorries containing our luggage, but Madame was determined not to be beaten, but to show the owner of the car that it could be done.' Susan admitted being 'a little sorry for him' as the trucks 'have had some vy. hard wear & the price he contracted for—3 francs a kilometre seems very cheap, considering that big lorries eat a lot of petrol, & it costs nearly 4 a gallon.' Now, they were at the edge of the desert at the northern point of Lake Chad '& as soon as the camels arrive we start off almost due north to Tripoli, which will be some 40 days camel before we have to take to cars again.' Hélène, she felt, was 'wonderfully well really, & can always do anything she has set her heart upon.'[6] At N'ingingmi, they transferred to camels and began to trek across the Sahara. At the beginning of the segment of her travel journal which would eventually be published in the *Nuova Antologia* in 1935, Hélène quoted an old Spanish proverb: 'Whoever has not seen Seville, has not seen wonders. Whoever has not seen Granada, has seen nothing.' In the context of this adventure, on the edge of the Sahara, she added another line to the proverb: 'Whoever has not seen the desert wind, has not seen the devil.'

Hélène, Susan, and Count Radicati set out on camels in a caravan, with Hélène likening her saddle to sitting on the edge of the Tower of Pisa. In earlier years, Hélène had seldom let her European life intrude upon her African one, but now she remembered her Christmas Eve dream and wrote longingly: 'If my Bouby were here, I would be happy.'[7] Little more than a year earlier, Amedeo had still been serving with the Camel Corps in Libya on the other side of the Sahara.

They journeyed from well to well across the desert. 'The sand is white. The sun—pale—is white. The sky white.' At the well at Dibella, Hélène said that the long hours gave her time to think and she recalled her first journey to Egypt, 'oh! so many years ago.' Then, seeing temples and other places she could not even have imagined for the first time, she still felt that these things were not unknown to her but that once, a long time ago, she had lived there, in another life, a beautiful and superior life that her current modern spirit could not comprehend. Now in the centre of Africa, in the immensity of the Sahara, she felt a pull back into this primitive and nomadic life, lived in the middle of simple people, of tribes who always go further, seeking the sun, fleeing those closest to them.[8]

At Dibella, where the sand reflected like rose petals and where the sand sings ('It's true'), they were met by a caravan of forty camels which would take them from Bilma to Toummo.[9] They travelled through the desert, and at 'Séguédine of a thousand colours', Hélène found 'blue, white, pink, mauve, grey, black, brown—every imaginable colour—and the sun which lights them.'

In the middle of the desert, they received a telegram from Governor Badoglio asking whether they would want camels or autos for the next leg of their journey. Although Hélène would have prefered camels, she bowed to Radicati's recommendation and responded 'auto transport.' Ten days later, Major Guerini, commander of *Gruppo Meharista di* Murzuck, arrived with the convoys of autos; finally, five days after that, they reached the oasis at Murzuck.[10]

A few days later, they were at the oasis of Brack, where they stayed for a week.[11] Susan wrote to her mother about Hélène's concern for the Duke of the Abruzzi '& it is a question of whether she hurries off to see him if a ship can be produced, or whether he is so bad that it will be too late.' However, up to that point, they had had 'a most marvellous time, the Sahara is perfectly beautiful, & we have all loved the forty days we had on camels as far as the frontier.' The transfer to a car had not been 'at all a pleasant means of travelling—700 miles or so—bumping over enormous rocks skidding in sand, & getting frequently stuck, not to speak of the bruises to ones ribs, in spite of being a very tight fit in the car.' Up until the point that they got into the car, Hélène had been 'extremely well' as 'she flour-

ishes on eight hours a day on a bad camel, but is now tired, partly from the car, &
also from talking to officer & men at the six different posts we have stopped at in
seven days—besides two that have been with us since the frontier.'[12]

On 15 March, Hélène had received a telegram from Maria Caffarelli about
the increasingly serious illness of her brother-in-law the Duke of the Abruzzi
in Mogadiscio. 'Cannot sleep tonight,' she wrote in her journal, 'I think about
the grave state of Luigino, and about the most rapid way to arrive at Magadisco.'
While she was awaiting further news, another telegram arrived—this one from
Bob in Europe: 'I am fine despite contusions.'[13] During a storm near Pola when
their motorboat capsized, the Duke of Spoleto was thrown into the sea with
another naval officer and two men. After swimming ashore, Aimone and the
two sailors heard the officer hail them from the sea. They immediately plunged
in again and brought him ashore, where, by means of artificial respiration, they
revived him. The front of *La Domenica del Corriere* (12 March 1933) led with an
imaginative drawing of Aimone swimming through the waves supporting the
officer on his shoulder. The next issue of *Il Mattino Illustrato* also featured on its
cover a heroic drawing of Aimone lifting the other officer out of the waves.

However, Hélène's hopes of reaching Somalia in time to see her brother-in-
law were cut short by yet another telegram, this one announcing his death which
had occurred on the 18th. Luigi was the one member of the Savoy family with
whom Hélène had a particularly close connection based upon their shared interests in Africa and exploring in general. In Rome, the news was received on the
same day, but not publicly announced until the 21st so that the required period of
Court mourning would not interfere with the planned visit of the British prime
minister, Ramsay MacDonald. London's Foreign Office commented that the 'last
three years of the Duke's life were largely spent in the house of his family at Turin,
and for a time he accepted the post of President of the Navigazione Generale
Italiana.' 'The progress of his disease rendered him, however, increasingly incapable of work, and some two months ago, to the general astonishment and dismay,
he accounted his intention of returning to Somalia.' Shortly afterwards, he arrived
in 'the land that he had reclaimed and made fruitful', and he died there. The
report also noted that Luigi's private life 'was somewhat embittered by his inability to induce the Royal family to consent to his marriage with Miss Elkins, an
American heiress.'[14] Back in Rome, the King and Queen, Amedeo and Aimone
with Luigi's only surviving brother, the Count of Turin, attended a Mass in his
memory at the Church of Santa Maria degli Angeli on 29 March. According to
his wishes, he was buried in Somalia.

Meanwhile, while Hélène was still at the oasis of Brack just one day after receiving the news about Luigino; there, she encountered Otto Campini of the Meharist
troops again. Hélène wrote of that day in her journal, writing in the third person,
never mentioning him by name, although two photographs of the young man
appear; she made it clear that this was a real *coup de foudre*—not 'love at first sight' as

they had met before, but nonetheless a very real and life-changing meeting:

It is almost a fable: Today, someone said to me: 'Do you know? I have seen a miracle! I have just met a happy woman. She was going along, and her feet did not touch the ground.

She was going along as if hallucinating, her eyes enlarged, fixing her gaze. She was going along, intoxicated by the space and the expiring light which, here, is so clear.

She was loving ... who? Everything around her, everything was falling under the charm of this hour, made for latent desires or soothing sensual delights.

She was loving, she was loving the present minute and catching it as it went by. Thus she could dream of advancing minute by minute, ever further away, indefinably further away.'

There are in life, rare perfect moments when one wishes for nothing because one has everything, and she felt a shudder against her chest, "living happiness".

Under a spell from the first instance where the eyes of the young pagan god met her own, these eyes where so many dreams passed underneath the eyelids, an ardent and pure look, a dawn freshness where all the poetry of the East is reflected.

He always has a way of looking at things that the others don't see because solitude makes things simple. With his eyes bathed in space, he looks at you, perceives you, judges you, classifies you.

Eyes that seem like velvet, merciful eyes. His look quiets him, half closed as in a dream. But the human mouth, very human, at the bottom of voluptuous nostrils, had, in rare moments, a smile of love with moist lips, as if touched by a kiss.

She, she was happy; there where she went, she could go without fear. He gave out all around him strength and courage, as sure as the sun, his light.

When he was there, everything seemed light, serene, full of joy and sensual delight. He was one of these men whom one loves in life or in death.

He carries his conquering youth on his shoulders; he has the authority of a gesture accustomed to commanding.

One loves in him the bravery, the generosity, the disdain for all human power, the indifference which hides his stoicism, and the true heroism.

A manly face, burnt by the breeze and the implacable desert sun; a high forehead which declares an intelligence which is precise and visionary at the same time, an intelligence broadened with the horizons, and constant, tenacious and concentrated work.

His brown head, a proud and peaceful head, where the smile softens the pride of his allures; this rare smile, with a captivating charm and full of grace, is corrected by a certain terrible energy which sleeps deep within his eyes.

A fine face which enlightens the somber eyes like a summer night, luminous as a spring dawn.

And deep within those eyes, there is something that they have seen. The look is of a sparkling spirit which gives it fire, there where it meets its soul sister.

In the desert solitude, he has learned, with the art of command, the silent will of the look, a light and powerful look, a calm and soft look which looks deep within the sould; reflective, reserved, meditative, it seems to follow and endless interior dream. And moreover, these eyes which seem to glide, observe everything, register everything, see everything.

Reflective, reserved, meditative, patient and silent, preferring to keep himself away from things.[15]

As the surviving copy of Hélène's journal—like those of other trips—is type-written with photos included, it is not possible to say whether this outpouring was immediate or reflective at a later date and inserted into the notes for typing. Although several copies of that journal were produced, only the one now in the Fondo Campini in Turin, which remained among Hélène's private papers until her death, contains this particular episode. Whatever the case, Hélène was defi-nitely smitten by the young camel soldier, some twenty years her junior.

Otto Campini was a trim soldier, permanently tanned, prematurely grey, and slightly taller than Hélène. He had been born at Brusasco in Torino province in 1891, the son of a Piemontese general, and his two brothers were also colonels in the army. He had been a cadet at the Scuola Militare, became a lieutenant in 1912, and joined the *Nizza Cavalleria*, then later the Sahara Service with the camel troops.[16]

After the momentous break in Brack, Hélène and her party continued their journey, moving on to Fezzan and eventually to Tripoli, which they reached on 2 April. Before the end of the month, Hélène was back at Capodimonte, acting in her role as a princess of the Royal House, receiving delegations, visiting hospi-tals, and attending concerts. Increasingly, Hélène was performing these functions along with Umberto and Marie José, the Prince and Princess of Piedmont, who had moved from the Royal Palace at Turin to the one in Naples in 1931. Over the coming years, Hélène would grow truly fond of Marie José in particular.

The great event of the summer in Rome was the arrival of Italo Balbo's air fleet on 12 August, which had made the round trip across the Atlantic to visit the Chicago World's Fair, the Century of Progress. Twenty-five planes began the journey, with two wrecked *en route* (one in Amsterdam and the other in the Azores); now, twenty-three planes triumphantly set down on the River Tiber outside Rome to the cheers of around 100,000 spectators, which included the American ambassador and Guglielmo Marconi. Hélène had flown in from Naples with Umberto aboard a hydroplane to be part of the celebration, and Amedeo arrived in full uniform of the Aeronautical Division. The Duce greeted Balbo with the Fascist salute, which he had announced in 1932 would thereafter replace the 'bourgeois' handshake with the much more virile straight-armed Roman salute.[17] Balbo immediately returned the greeting in kind.

Italo Balbo was often held up by government publicists as the model of the fascist generation. In the opinion of his biographer Claudio Segrè, 'of all the major Italian fascist leaders, Balbo was virtually the only one to live the ideal fascist life—heroic, adventurous, self-sacrificing, patriotic.'[18] Already Minister of Aviation, Balbo was now made Italy's first Air Marshal as a reward.

In March, word came from Africa that Anne d'Aosta was seriously ill at Luxor with typhoid fever. Her mother Isabelle went to be at her bedside, as did Hélène who arrived in Alexandria on the 13th and left immediately for Luxor. Anne eventually recovered, and by April, Hélène was back in Rome, where she put in a very rare appearance at the opening of Parliament on 28 April, sitting with the other royal ladies, Queen Elena, with her youngest daughter Maria, and the Duchess of Pistoia. The King was surrounded by the princes of the House of Savoy—the Prince of Piedmont, Dukes of Aosta and Spoleto, Count of Turin, and the Dukes of Genoa, Pistoia, Bergamo, and Ancona. Signor Mussolini was also present to hear the King's speech to the deputies, all arrayed in their black shirts. It was a speech which emphasized 'the indissoluable ties binding together the House of Savoy and the whole Italian people with the Fascist régime.'[19]

As she so often did, Hélène left Italy in the autumn and returned once again to Africa. This time, she was accompanied by Otto Campini, who would seldom leave her side in the future. He was apparently living at Capodimonte from the spring of 1933, when he regularly begin to appear in Hélène's photo albums, but although he also appears in various photos for this trip, she only mentions him by name once in her journal and then only when referring to another man who had been a meharist like him.

Before leaving, Hélène spent some time with her sons near Bolzano in the South Tyrol. There she began her journal with the dedication: 'At my departure, I leave my blessing to my two sons, the pride of my maternal love. I have never received from them the least deception. May God grant to the one, strength and health; to the other, happiness.'[20] They sailed out of Genoa on 3 October, going first to Gibraltar, and then back along the coast of North Africa. There was a two-day stop at Larache, then to Rabat, Fez, and Mecknes, before returning to Gibraltar, then heading down the west coast to Dakar. There, they spent a few days at the Hôtel Atlantique before going on to Lagos, and from there, aboard the *Touareg* to Douala before returning to Nigeria and entering the interior.

In the capital of Ogun State, Hélène was particularly impressed by her meeting with the Alaké of Abeokuta, 'His Highness' Oba Aloiyeluwa. The Alaké came majestically down the stairs of his palace, the royal crown on his head, the pastoral cane in one hand, and the sceptre in the other. His hands and wrists were covered with rings and bracelets of pure gold. He extended his hand to Hélène and welcomed her in impeccable English. She found him amiable and jovial with an easy laugh. 'How is Mr Mussolini? That is a very great man. And Marconi?' Hélène told him that there were new discoveries in short wave technology, and that when he went from Lagos to London aboard ship, he would be able to telephone without wires.'Wonderful, that is magic.'[21]

When they arrived at Kano, Hélène was amazed at the changes since her last visit twelve years earlier—'roads, house, potable water, electric light, cleanliness and order where I knew an impractical quagmire.' Now, to prepare herself mentally and physically for the next stage of the journey, Hélène moved into her tent at Kano for the remainder of their stay, a bit more than a fortnight altogether. Then, on 26 November, the camel caravan began as they moved further up into French West Africa, 'French Nigeria' (today's Niger), and into the Sahara; their progress was slow but steady. Zinder, Daladi, Hera, Baboulé, Maya, Tanout. On Christmas Day, they were between Takukut and the wells of Eliki. Hélène poignantly wished 'from afar, Bon Noël to you who think of me today.'[22] The New Year was welcomed in their tents at the wells of Eliki, then they pushed on to the cliffs of Tiguedi. Next to Agadez, the Touareg stronghold, where they spent most of January. The once grand capital of the area with its grand mosque and sultan's palace had been the southernmost point of the old Ottoman Empire and now was part of France's vast colonial territories in West Africa.

A push across the Sahara sands brought them into southern Algeria, to Tamanrasset on 2 March 1935. There Hélène found the whole town garlanded, with flags at the windows, Tricolours everywhere. At first they discussed whether the decorations were for a fair, perhaps an Arab festival, perhaps to celebrate 'Dimanche Gras' at the beginning of carnival. But then Hélène discovered that the decorations were indeed done in her honour. 'It is sad never becoming accustomed to obligations and ... to duties that one's position from birth imposes. I escape from Europe to flee from the functions, the receptions, to no longer know or listen to those who are like me.' When she arrived at Hogdar, Hélène found 'its soul full of the memories of Father deFoucauld, its spirit full of the legends of the Touaregs' but there she sought 'silence, solitude, I would like to be alone to meditate, to think, to dream,' but instead had to 'submit to the "very gracious banalities" of an official reception!'

Hélène did make a little pilgrimage to the hermitage of Father Charles deFoucauld, a French Cistercian monk who had made his home among the Touaregs until he was killed by marauding Bedouin in 1916. His spirituality had become widely known in Europe through the 1921 biography by René Bazin, which Hélène had read in 1923; he would eventually be beatified in 2005. However, the moment of her 'mystic urge' was ruined by the indifference of the young captain and doctor who accompanied her. Still, in her last journal entry from this trip, Hélène wrote that: 'It seems to me that the troubled soul of Father deFoucauld finally found peace from his torments after his martyrdom. His mortal remains rest alone, as he lived, buried in the sand which he loved, facing the desert which attracted him irresistably, and which he conquered.'[23]

Springtime of 1935 brought the French naval squadron to Naples on an official visit to the Italian Fleet. Three cruisers and six destroyers entered the port, and its lead cruiser, the *Algérie*, fired a salute of twenty-one guns, which was answered by the shore batteries, and then a second salute in honour of Hélène, who was then in residence at Capodimonte. Public demonstrations peaked later that month in Rome, with a huge Fascist parade to honour the twentieth anniversary of Italy's entry into the First World War. King Victor Emanuel and the Prince of Piedmont were there alongside King Alfonso of Spain, who was living in exile in Rome, and visiting Prince Ibn Saud as well as Aimone.

Back in Naples, Hélène once again visited the Duomo on the occasion of the feast day of San Gennaro and the liquidification of his blood. The newspapers reported that she approached the high altar, kissed the relic, and spent a long time in prayer.

Beginning in February 1935, Italian troop build-up had progressed in Eritrea with an eye towards an invasion of Ethiopia. Troops were deployed from Libya, from ranks at home, from abroad, blackshirts, university students. Air Force personnel were particularly conspicuous—two of Mussolini's sons, Bruno and Vittorio, as well as his son-in-law Galeazzo Ciano flew Caproni bombers in *La Disperata* squadron. From the royal house, the Duke of Pistoia commanded the Blackshirts of the '23rd March' Division and the Duke of Bergamo was second in command to the regular Division 'Gran Sasso.' The military build-up continued throughout the summer; on 2 October, back in Rome, Mussolini roused the crowds in Piazza Venezia, warning them of the international conspiracy since the Treaty of Versailles that intended 'to rob them of a place in the sun.' The roar of the crowd finished off his speech—'With Ethiopia we have been patient for 40 years. Now, enough!'[24] In the early morning of 3 October, 100,000 Italian troops crossed into Ethiopia.

The League of Nations, in protest of the blatant aggression in Africa, imposed economic sanctions upon Italy on 18 November. The next day was proclaimed a Black Day in Italy. While the sanctions involved prevented importation of some items, coal, and crude oil were not included, and thus the sanctions proved more of a domestic propaganda victory for the Italian rather than an active means towards ending the war in Ethiopia. On the contrary, oil sanctions were scheduled to be debated at Geneva on 12 December, and Mussolini determined to capture as much territory as possible before then.[25]

As both a practical and public relations response to the impending League of Nations sanctions, an appeal was made to the nation to donate gold to the state. Amedeo's name was at the head of published list on 14 November when he gave a gold ingot weighing 1,340 g plus 20 kilograms of silver, said to be from family objects melted down for the purpose, along with 30,000 lire and 400 packages of clothes for winter relief. In January, Hélène went to the Casa del Fascio and presented another ingot of gold as a gift from her sister Amélie, who was then visiting at Capodimonte.

However, the event which provided the emotional pull for this effort was the

'Wedding Ring Day' on 18 December. Queen Elena frontlined the programme in Rome. Instructions were issued that the entire country should be beflagged from sunrise until sunset. That morning, despite rain squalls, a large crowd, mostly of women, gathered at Piazza Venezia. Achille Starace, as Fascist party secretary, greeted Elena at the foot of the steps which led up to three smoking urns guarded by young Fascists. After climbing the stairs, which were lined with the mothers and widows of those who had fallen for the fatherland in the First World War, the Queen opened her handbag and placed her wedding ring—as well as the King's—into the middle urn. She then went to the altar, where Monsignor Bartolomasi blessed boxes full of steel rings which were to be exchanged for the gold. Each inscribed: 'Gold to the country, 18 December XIV.' Then, holding a burning taper, she broadcast a short address to the nations:

> In ascending to the Sacrarium of the Altar of the Fatherland, together with the proud mothers and wives of our dear Italy, to lay on the Altar of the Unknown Warrior the wedding ring, symbol of our first joys, and of the greatest renunciations, as the purest offering of devotion to the Fatherland, bowing ourselves down to the earth as if to commune in spirit with our glorious sons who fell in the Great War, we invoke together with them before God, 'Victory.'
>
> Young sons of Italy, who are defending her sacred rights and are opening new paths for the brilliant march of the Fatherland, we wish that you may bring about the triumph of Roman civilization in the Africa which you have redeemed. Our greeting goes to the glorious flags, to the officers and soldiers of the land, sea, and air forces, to the Blackshirts, to the workmen, to the faithful Askaris.
>
> A happy Christmas.[26]

The Queen's message was then read throughout the country by members of the royal family. Anne d'Aosta did the honours in Trieste; Princess Jolanda in Turin; Princess Maria in Florence; and the Duchess of Pistoia in Bolzano. In Naples, Princess Marie José read the message, and Hélène was there to contribute her ring to the cause. For hours, women of all social classes streamed by the urns, often accompanied by husbands or fiancés who contributed their own rings. By noon, some 50,000 wedding rings were said to have been offered in Rome alone.

As winter approached, it was announced that in Naples, both Hélène and Marie José would be organizing and supervising the collection and packing of parcels of food and clothing for the children of men who had been called up or volunteered to serve in East Africa. Between 15 December and 31 March, Hélène and Marie José distributed food daily from Capodimonte and the Royal Palace.

Aimone was among those who left in December to serve in Africa, as was Vito Mussolini, nephew of the Duce and editor of the *Popolo d'Italia*, who volunteered for service with the Air Force. On the day before they left Italy, some 2,500

Blackshirts from the Tevere Division had sailed from Naples for Abyssinia. The Dukes of Pistoia and Bergamo were already there. A few months later, Princess Marie José left with the nursing corps to serve as a Red Cross volunteer working the military hospitals at Asmara and Mogadishu. Hélène was at the port in her Red Cross uniform to greet Queen Elena and Umberto when they arrived to bid farewell to Marie José. Together, they stood at the quayside in a heavy downpour of rain as the hospital ship *Cesarea* sailed under away an escort of three submarines, with the crowds cheering, the bands playing the Royal March and the Giovinezza, and a squadron of seaplanes circling overhead. Marie José stood on board in her crisp white Red Cross uniform and gave the Fascist salute.

As Christmas approached, the Fascist government issued an order banning Christmas trees in Italy. When that command was praised by the Vatican's newspaper, the *Osservatore Romano*, diplomats abroad, especially in the British Foreign Office, expressed their growing concern that 'there is little doubt that clerical circles in Italy tend to dance increasingly to Sig. Mussolini's tune.' While the Pope said nothing about the invasion of Abyssinia, Italian prelates across the land supported and endorsed the move, and London began to fear that 'the Vatican, without perhaps being fully aware of the fact, is beginning to appear in the light of an ally of Italian imperialist and expansionist ideas.'[27]

In the New Year, an Ethiopian counter-attack was quickly thwarted through the use of the Air Force—and of mustard gas. The Fascist battle cry, coined by d'Annunzio, rang out '*Eia eia eia alalà.*' '*Per il Re, per il Duce, eia eia eia alalà!*'[28] A decisive battle held at Mai Ceu on 31 March 1936 pitted the Ethiopian army directed by the Emperor Haile Selassie himself against the Italian army under their commander-in-chief Marshal Pietro Badoglio and ended in defeat for the Ethiopians. The retreating army, led by Haile Selassie astride a white horse and in uniform and pith helmet, was mercilessly bombed by Italian planes. In two days, the Ethiopian army lost more men than they did in the actual battle. 'The rivers were full of corpses.' The Emperor fled abroad; on 5 May, Badoglio entered Addis Ababa with 25,000 troops and 2,000 vehicles. The city which they entered had suffered burning and pillaging by the local population, and Badoglio used this to emphasize the need for the Italian 'civilizing mission.' 'If any doubts had still remained as to the state of barbarism of these people,' Badoglio reported, 'the condition in which we found Addis, destroyed and sacked by the express order of the Negus before he left, was quite enough to dispel them.'[29]

A few days later, on 9 May, King Victor Emanuel was declared Emperor of Ethiopia. On the 14th, the Chamber of Deputies was full of black-shirted deputies for the official proclamation. The visitors' gallery was likewise full of dignitaries—the German, American, and Japanese ambassadors—and Anne, the young Duchess d'Aosta, whom Mussolini saluted when he entered the Chamber to present the proposed declarations to his son-in-law, Count Ciano, as president of the Chamber. On 1 June, Italian Somaliland, Eritrea, and Ethiopia were legally combined into Africa Orientale Italiana (A. O. I), and Badoglio appointed the first Viceroy, although he resigned within a fortnight to be replaced by Gen. Graziani, hastily promoted to Marshal.[30] Aimone returned home to Naples on the evening of 10 July. Hélène and Umberto were there to greet him and Dr Aldo Castellani, who headed the group of 800 veterans aboard the *Cesare Battista*.

Earlier in the summer of 1936, Hélène finally visited Greece for the first time, something that her father had urged in 1894 when she travelled to the Holy Land with her brother, but Philippe had declined that extension to their journey. Now, Hélène and Campini accompanied Amedeo and his two young daughters aboard their yacht *Amrita* for a voyage around the Adriatic, visiting the Ionian Islands, the Corinth Canal, and Athens among other sights.[31] It was while docked in the port of Piraeus that Hélène was alone with her granddaughters when the yacht was boarded by thieves. As always, Hélène coped well with emergencies and sent the girls below decks while she picked up a club and saw the would-be thieves off. Dressed in trousers with her hair bound up in a kerchief, Hélène at age sixty-five was still a formidable opponent.[32]

Although warfare in East Africa became quieter and some troops were withdrawn to the homeland, tensions were high throughout Europe after Hitler occupied the Rhineland in the spring of 1936. Then, on 17 July, a military rebellion broke out in Spanish North Africa and within twenty-four hours spread to garrisons in mainland Spain. Although Republican forces initially defeated the rebellion in Madrid and Barcelona, elsewhere the Nationalists were bolstered by the independent decisions of Mussolini and Hitler to militarily aid the rebels starting with planes to airlift the Army of Africa, commanded by General Francisco Franco, to Seville.

It had been five years since Hélène's cousin King Alfonso had been forced from the throne, and Spain was now a different country than the one Hélène had known as a child visiting her grandparents and later her mother. During the next three years, thousands were killed both on the Republican and on the Nationalist sides, and horrific atrocities were committed by both. Over the course of the Spanish Civil War, and concentrated in the summer of 1936, a vicious anti-clericalism resulted in a terrible slaughter of the country's Catholic religious leaders—thirteen bishops, more than 4,000 priests, nearly 300 nuns, and over 2,000 others in religious orders. Shopkeepers, landowners, and professionals also became prime targets as Republican Spain went into a killing frenzy. Madrid and Catalonia saw the majority of deaths—some 38,000—during 'Red Terror' during the summer and autumn of 1936. Meanwhile, the 'White Terror' of the Nationalists rampaged with executions and mass killings primarily in the south but wherever they gained territory. A press *attaché* of General Franco told an American journalist that they had 'to kill, to kill, and to kill' all the reds 'to exterminate a third of the masculine population and cleanse the country of the proletariat.' Accurate statistics are available for only half of Spain and that totals over 80,000 victims, while recent studies suggest a figure of 200,000 Nationalist victims throughout the country.[33]

The war also claimed family casualties. Hélène's nephew, Louise's only son, Carlos of Bourbon-Sicily, known in the family as Carlito, was killed in action on 27 September fighting with the Nationalists at Eibar in the Basque country.[34] He had left the family home at Mandelieu, near Cannes, at the end of July, and hoping to serve in any army capacity that might be found, went to Spain against the wishes of his family. His sister Esperanza also served during the civil war, working as a nurse in Spain from 1936 to 1939. The next month, some more distant relations were killed—descendants of King Francisco de Paula's brother, the Duke of Seville, the same man who had been killed in a duel by Hélène's grandfather, the Duc de Montpensier, in 1870. The Marqués de Squilache, his brother the Marqués de Balboa, and the latter's son Don Jaime were all executed during one of the purges by Republican forces in the Modelo Prison in Madrid, where they had been held hostage. Two months later, their cousin Alonso of Bourbon-Orléans—grandson of Hélène's Uncle Antonio and the Infanta Eulalia—was killed near Madrid in an airplane accident, just a month after joining the insurgents. He had been educated privately in England and then at a polytechnic in Switzerland, before working as a draughtsman and engineer at a factory in Coventry. Alonso joined the Coventry Aero Club in June 1935 and qualified as a pilot in August 1936, leaving for Spain via Lisbon in October, dying on 18 November. His brother Ataulfo was meanwhile serving with the Luftwaffe's Condor Legion which Hitler sent to Spain the same month.

While the suffering and losses within the country was horrendous, and Hélène's family losses were personally tragic, the most long-lasting international implications were not so much with the renowned International Brigade but with the German and Italian military interventions. Mussolini and Hitler were both anxious to have another fascist state in Europe to swing the balance of power, and towards that end, both contributed manpower and weaponry to the struggle. Italy sent bombers, fighter planes, and transport planes along with the personnel to man them, along with tanks, field guns, and eventually sent the Corps of Volunteer Troops to fight in Spain. This unit, under the command of General Mario Roatta, initially consisted mainly of men drawn from the fascist militias and eventually reached 50,000 troops, although that number would include many Spanish serving under Italian officers. Germany also sent tens of thousands of fighters along with armaments; its most infamous contribution was the Condor Legion, which developed the technique of carpet bombing in their attacks against Republican positions around Oviedo. It was used most decisively in the destruction of the Basque capital of Guernica in April 1937, an act which swayed international public opinion in favour of the Republicans.[35]

The Spanish Civil War was at its beginning when Hélène spent some time at Crans in Switzerland and in August 1936 was able to visit her Amélie at Evian.[36] In October that year, it seems that Hélène made a major commitment in her private life. She spent much of that month at the Clinica Quisisana in Rome, although the reason for that stay is unknown.[37] Perhaps following an illness and wanting a regularisation of their relationship, there was said to have been a secret marriage between Hélène and Otto Campini at Capodimonte in October blessed by Cardinal Ascalesi, the Archbishop of Naples, although no documentary evidence has ever been found.

Over the following years, Otto Campini was always a discrete presence, often mistaken as Hélène's *aide-de-camp*. With her family, he was always strictly formal, addressing them as 'Your Royal Highness' rather than as a member of the family himself.[38] It was in September 1948 that the Milanese magazine *Tempo* published a cover story on '*Il marito segreto*'—the secret husband—about the marriage of Hélène and Campini. This was the first public acknowledgment of the probable union between the two.[39] When Hélène died fifteen years later, newspapers internationally noted this secret marriage as a standard and accepted part of her obituary.[40]

Two years earlier, there had been a rumour that a morganatic marriage had taken place between Hélène and her court gentleman-in-waiting Don Luigi Tosti, duca di Valminuta. Newspapers and magazines in France, and as far afield as Algeria, confidently announced that the wedding had taken place in Naples on 23 February 1934, but when she was asked about this directly, Hélène simply laughed heartily.[41]

Throughout the previous century, there had been many examples of morganatic second marriages among both Hélène's own family and the Savoys. Her great-grandmother, Queen Maria Cristina of Spain, the widowed Queen Regent, secretly remarried only three months after the death of her husband King Ferdinand VII (who was not only twenty-two years older than her but also her uncle). Eventually, she and her guardsman husband had four sons and three daughters together. Despite recurring pregnancies, they were able to keep the marriage secret from 1833 until 1840, but when the news did become public, Maria Cristina was forced out of the regency and before long left to spend the rest of her life in exile in France. Her daughter Queen Isabel II was married only once, but her husband was probably father to only two or three of her twelve children, and the army is generally considered to have provided fathers for the others.[42]

In Italy, morganatic marriages also took place, including King Victor Emmanuel II who married his longtime mistress 'La Rosina', hoping to get a papal remission of excommunication by legitimizing their relationship when upon what he thought was his deathbed. It was rather late for a wedding as their own daughter had herself married the year before. Queen Margherita's mother, the Duchess of Genoa, remarried little more than a year after the Duke's death and chose a simple lieutenant for her second husband. In Naples itself, King Ferdinando IV had morganatically married the Duchess of Floridiana as his second wife in 1814, and his widowed daughter-in-law Queen Maria Isabella took a mere count as her second husband twenty-five years later. Hélène's own sister Amélie was said to have intended marrying a French nobleman in 1913 shortly before her son's wedding, but Manoel forbade it on the grounds that a king's mother could only remarry into a reigning house.[43]

However uncertain the legal or religious relationship was, what was certain is that Otto Campini remained devoted to Hélène, and a respected member of the household, for the rest of her life.

Internationally, the Berlin-Rome Axis was established on 23 October. On 7 December, Amedeo, as a general in the Italian Air Force, arrived in Berlin at the invitation of General Hermann Göring, the Air Minister and Commander-in-chief of the German Air force, for a visit to inspect the various branches of the German air arm. While in Germany, Amedeo met with Hitler himself, and described the meeting in a letter to a friend:

> Small, modestly dressed, I would say shy. He greeted me, shook my hand, had me sit down, then sat down on the edge of the chair. He slid back slowly, then began the game and finally started talking. He is undoubtedly an intelligent man, but is verbose and talks a lot. He is a man who needs Göring, who is not intelligent but who is tenacious. He said to me that to intervene in Spain would require the consent of England. After Franco's victory, he added, Spain will become fascist or nazi. The answer was that fascism and Nazism are not goods for export.[44]

While this was transpiring in Europe, Hélène was once again in North Africa. In late November, she and Campini went for eighteen days of rest at an isolated seaside villa at Busetta, near Tripoli as guests of Air Marshal Balbo. Each morning, they would go for walks and then long gallops on tireless horses over the supple sands and through the palms and olive groves. It was, Hélène thought, a truly delicious stay.[45]

When they moved on to Gadames, Hélène was delighted to see a photograph of Campini posed as the model of the 'morally and physicially most pure and most handsome Meharist' on the wall of one of the bedrooms. As they continued into the desert and stopped at Derg, Hélène wrote: 'The sweet illusion of thinking that one travels in Africa to find heat! When at five o'clock I left my tent to wake up my two blacks, the obscure sky was invisible, and from the ground rose a thick fog, humid and cold, and it was raining.' Indeed, 'It is cold, cold! I went back to bed so as not to feel the fold. Only 5° above zero; you could see your own breath rise as mist in the semi-obscurity of the night.'[46]

Once again, Hélène found herself in Africa at Christmas; in Campini's company, her spirits were higher than usual. On Christmas Eve at the Uadi Awal of

Bir-ed-Decour, shw wrote of the sparkling stars in the cold and clear night as she looked 'for the shepherd's star, in this night, which guided the Magi kings to Bethlehem where they adored the Son of God, born in a stable, where the Virgin had laid him in a manger. Christmas, Christmas! A cry of hope!' Being 'close to nature in this day of redemption, and not in the middle of conventional parties which destroy true religion and poison life' was something for which she cried 'God be praised! There are still hidden corners of the earth where one can pray, to praise the Creator, to think and to dream in peace: to be happy!' The next morning, Hélène's thoughts were less charitable, and she admitted being ashamed that her first act on 'this very holy day' was to be angry with her two Eritrean servants—Mufta and Murat—for staying in bed out of the 4° cold instead of preparing their *café au lait*. Two days later, the servants were in disgrace again when Mufta broke not one but both of Hélène's mirrors in her toiletry set.[47]

On New Year's Eve, travelling from Hammada de Tinghert to the Wadi Nahia Hasinka, for the first time in ten days, they saw other people and animals as a caravan from Fezzan passed carrying dates to Derg. That night, after a dinner where the champagne was naturally cooled in the outdoor temperature, Hélène wrote:

The blessing of God be upon those whom I love!
A happy end of a year.
A happy beginning to a new year.
In the face of Creation, in direct contact with virgin nature, free and in peace with men who are far away, close to God from which nothing can distract me.[48]

Hélène's spirits remained upbeat as they arrived at the wells of Hassi Dembabba while worrying that 'it's so beautiful, too beautiful to last. So few perfect things are long in this world. And yet, and yet, do not curse fate, and thank God for the good things that He gives to us.' 'Sometimes on the path of life, we encounter such happiness, so beautiful, so pure, so perfect in the union of two souls who have only one thought, one is so happy to go hand in hand, at a rate equal to two hearts that beat as one, that one must stop, praise God, and admire with gratitude.' When they reached Brack later in the month, it was 'sweet Brack' with memories from four years earlier when she had fallen in love with Campini. 'Like then, we climbed the golden dune to make a pilgrimage of gratitude.' While at Serir El Gattusa, Hélène recorded a 'Curious impression! The air is soft, the sun is setting.' Inside her tent she 'sat in front of my table where all my familiar objects are arranged, and I proceed with my toilette, just as at Capodimonte; I do my hair quietly, my spirit vague and distant. To dream better, I lift up my eyes. What do I see? Camels at rest; and beyond that, infinity.'[49]

About 3 p.m. of 13 February, Hélène and Campini were at the oasis of Serir El Gattusa awaiting the arrival of the rest of the caravan. It was baking hot. Their quiet was disturbed by the rumbling of an airplane engine, and they said to each other 'What now!' When the plane landed, Otto went to investigate. He and the pilot walked back, and Campini shouted out '*Bonne nouvelle*'—Good news!—and then to clarify 'A motto of the House of Savoy.' '*Bonne nouvelle*,' he repeated, and the pilot made the announcement 'A son is born. The Princess of Piedmont has given birth to an heir to the throne.' Hélène recorded the moment in her journal:

> My emotion was so great that I closed my eyes over the tears of happiness which flowed. Above all I thank God for grace received, and I add: '*Viva il Re!*' I am happy. Happy for Marie José whom I love and who so much merits this great joy; happy for our blood of the House of Savoy which sees the succession to the throne ensured; happy, finally, for my beautiful country which I love more than anything else in the world.[50]

Marie José had previously given birth to a girl, Princess Maria Pia, and would later have two other daughters, but the birth of a son was particularly important as succession to the throne was through the male line only. The arrival of the Prince of Naples was celebrated in Ethiopia by the Viceroy giving alms to the poor, but the ceremony turned into an assassination attempt against Graziani, who was hit by a hand grenade which inflicted 365 wounds to his body. General Liotta, the commander of the Air Force, required a leg amputation, and over thirty others were wounded. There was a vicious retaliation by the Blackshirts and Italian civilian laborers, with killings and burnings rampaging throughout Addis Ababa; probably some 3,000 were killed. The viceroy ordered that all Amhara notables and ex-officers, eventually totalling 1,469, were shot by the end of March. Then, in May, Graziani, suspecting that the monks of the famous monastery of Debra Libanos were implicated in the assassination plot, ordered the execution of 297 monks and 129 deacons. With the exception of about thirty schoolboys, the entire population of the country's most famous religious centre was wiped out.[51]

Hélène and Otto Campini continued their journey through the desert, and on 2 March reached Uau el-Kebir, where Hélène wrote that the air pressure caused by the great gusts of winds affected her as did too much champagne. She remembered her childhood days when she would run into a storm, defying the elements, 'and like the day of our arrival four years ago at Tummo, I started to sing, the song of the sovereign storm.' However, the charm soon wore thin. 'Enough is enough. The plain, the sand, the wind, the infinite plain, the infinite wind, the infinite sand!' Travelling for hours at a time battling the sands and the winds, they eventually reached Tazerbo, where they spent Palm Sunday amid the palm trees, although the temperature was a suffocating 45°.

The next major push was to reach Koufra in the Libyan Desert:

> In the vague memories of my first African dreams, the names of 'Tombouctou, Koufra' sang in my ears the sweet harmony of the distant and mysterious

unknown which vibrated on the cord of the Eolien harp, and carried me across space on the wings of the pure and hot desert wind which no contact could defile. In the echo of my nomad heart, like one of the tales of the Arabian Nights, I could hear the echo repeat 'Tombouctou, Koufra.' I have seen Tombouctou, I am at Koufra.[52]

They then spent twenty-five days at Koufra—a sweet and calm life, the true '*dolce far niente*.' When it was time to move on, they exchanged their camels for cars and, in two and a half days, covered 680 km of flat desert sand, reaching Bengasi on 28 April. At Cyrene, they visited the Roman ruins and the 'Luigi di Savoia Agricultural Colony.' Once again, Hélène was reminded of her son Bouby's saying—'*la Mamma è molto ripanduta*'—a personal bastardised French/Italian way of saying 'Mamma is widespread' or 'Mother knows everyone'! This time, the saying referred to Captain Sommers, the engineer directing the excavations of the Cyrene ruins, who was the grandson of the Neapolitan merchant from whom Hélène had purchased a Kodak 9 × 9 more than thirty years earlier. 'Since then, it has never left me, and has taken photographs of my numerous trips and expeditions.' They went on to Derna, where Hélène had last visited as a nurse aboard the *Memfi* twenty-five years earlier, and then finally to Tripoli.[53]

While Hélène was still in North Africa, celebrations were being held for what was grandly called 'The First Year of the New Roman Empire' in Italy, with Victor Emmanuel as the new emperor (albeit of Ethiopia) and Mussolini as the founder of the empire. Half a million people were said to have gathered around Rome's Palazzo Venezia for the great review of troops led by Marshals De Bono and Badoglio; it was watched by much of the royal family. The Duchess of Sermoneta was in the Royal Stand on 9 May and believed it was the first time that Mussolini and the King appeared together in public, 'there must have been an agreement between them not to attend the same ceremonies.' The King and Queen stood in front, while 'Mussolini took his place so markedly behind that he was practically on the same line with the Court ladies.' However, the Duchess noticed that he spoke more with the Duke of Aosta than anyone else. The review itself was 'a picturesque sight as the native troops with their camels, mules and African equipment swept down the Via del Impero, and the dubats came leaping and pirouetting past with their white draperies flying.'[54]

In July, the Royal Family gathered in Turin to dedicate the city-centre monument to Emanuele Filiberto. Set in the Piazza Castello, in front of the old castle, the 27-foot-high monument surmounted a 90-foot long base representing an entrenchment, with the statue of Aosta standing in the centre with soldiers at the corners. Hélène and her sons were there for the ceremony along with most of the House of Savoy when King Victor Emmanuel unveiled the monument. Later in the month, Amedeo and Aimone again accompanied the King for the launching of the new battleship *Vittorio Veneto* at Trieste.[55]

In this season of grand Fascist occasions, the only distraction came when six chimpanzees—five females and 'one powerful male'—escaped from an experimental laboratory in Naples and made their way to the tall trees of the royal park at Capodimonte. A keeper shot the male, but the females escaped into the countryside, then attacked a young shepherd boy but were driven off by his dogs and his brother, and the chimps disappeared. Hélène, as well as the Prince of Piedmont, took particular interest in the case and asked the carabinieri and the game keepers to attempt to return the females to the laboratory alive so that the proprietor of the clinic would not suffer further financial loss.

Hélène and Amedeo went on a private visit to England in late September. As commander of the Aquila Air Force division, Amedeo contacted the Air Ministry in order to visit some RAF bases and see something of the activities of the British Air Force. While he dined at the Italian embassy with the Duke and Duchess of Kent, Prime Minister Neville Chamberlain, Anthony Eden, and Lady Diana Cooper, Hélène went to visit the widowed Queen Mary at Marlborough House, which had for many years been the home of her dear friend, the late Queen Alexandra. Amedeo soon left London, but Hélène stayed on at Almond's Hotel for a three-week visit accompanied by her seven-year-old granddaughter Margherita. They sailed from the Port of London, bound for Naples aboard *Orcades* of the Orient Line on 9 September, accompanied by 'Count' Otto Campini, according to the ship manifest.

This was probably the last visit Hélène made to England, and almost certainly the last to Almond's Hotel, which would be sold in 1941. The hotel on Clifford Street in Mayfair had for years been a favourite place to stay in London for Hélène's parents, as well as her sister Amélie and her sons, as well as 'the more exclusive French aristocracy.'

Although his visit to England had been ostensibly a private one, upon his return, Amedeo reported to Count Ciano, the Foreign Minister. Ciano, one reporter thought, was 'good-looking, spoke perfect English, and was an animated and amusing conversationalist. But he had an air of unbelievable arrogance; you felt all the time that he was trying to imitate his father-in-law, even to the way he threw out his chest and strutted as he walked.'[56] On 4 October, Ciano noted in his diary a meeting with Amedeo, 'who gave me an account of his trip to England. According to him the agreement should be possible. But, if forced to do so, England can make war and make it well. He repeated the words used by [the Italian ambassador in London, Count [Dino] Grandi.'[57]

A month later, on 15 November Amedeo was called to a meeting with Mussolini and Alessandro Lessona, the minister for Africa Orientale Italiana, at the Palazzo Venezia. At that meeting, Mussolini appointed Amedeo as the new viceroy of Ethiopia, and a week later, Mussolini nominally took upon himself the role of minister for the A. O. I.[58]

Earlier in the year Mussolini, along with sending military supplies and four divisions of troops into the Spanish Civil War, had proposed Amedeo to Franco as a possible candidate for the empty Spanish throne. That rumour arose again the following year, but the French *chargé d'affaires* wrote that this news was met with scepticism in Rome, as it ignored potentially both French and British opposition and, more probably, even stronger opposition from the Spanish people themselves, not forgetting the bad precedence of his grandfather, the previous Amedeo d'Aosta, who had gone to Madrid as king.[59]

However, for the present time, Amedeo's role would be in Ethiopia. Count Ciano, the foreign minister, met with Amedeo in early December and confided to his diary that 'He feels the great burden of responsibility. And this is a good sign. But he still seems to be a little disoriented. He is a nice man, to whom I sincerely wish success.' Even King Carol of Romania spoke highly of the appointment and pronounced Amedeo 'quite a remarkable man.'[60]

As Amedeo prepared to depart for Ethiopia, he could not help but contrast this grand state occasion of a departure with that of when he had first gone to the Congo when only his mother went to see him off. This time, when he left from Naples aboard the cruiser *Zara*, there was a twenty-one-gun salute, enthusiastic crowds in the flag bedecked streets and on the quayside, uniforms and black shirts everywhere. Hélène, Anne, Aimone, Uncle Toio, Umberto, and Marie José were all there to bid him farewell. As the final farewells took place, Hélène embraced and kissed her son who then respectfully kissed her hand. 'As the cruiser steamed out of the port the crowds on shore and the crews of the ships lying in the harbour cheered the Duke.'[61] The British Pathé newsreel set the tone:

> Down the Red Sea and into the Eritrean port of Massawa and there the duke's arrival is like the coming of a conquering hero. The young duke steps into the country over which he is to rule, the country which it will be his job to civilize in the Italian manner, to subdue dark-skinned chieftains who have spent all their lives fighting, to open up a country which is one of the wildest and has one of the worst climates in the world. The young man has a tough job.[62]

Once in Africa, Amedeo made the journey to Addis Ababa by air, piloting his own plane at the head of a squadron of bombers, escorted by two squadrons of pursuit planes. Marshal Graziani, the retiring Viceroy, and the chief civil, military, and ecclesiastical dignitaries of the city met him at the airport.

> He was greeted by a picturesque gathering of Ethiopian chieftains, notables, and prelates, while farther on had been assembled a crowd of 8,000 Moslems, many of whom, besides their coloured standards bearing verses from the Koran,

carried large posters eulogizing the greatness of the House of Savoy, exalting the generosity of the Duce as the protector of Islam, and expressing devotion to Italy. The day ended with a torchlight procession of Fascists through the city, followed by an enthusiastic demonstration outside the residence of the Duke.[63]

The immediate impact was evaluated by Anthony Mockler who considered that 'As soon as Graziani left office and Amedeo arrived, there was a palpable change in attitude in Ethiopia. A thousand detainees at Danane were liberated. A "better class of administrator" appeared. Serfdom was abolished and 400,000 *gebars* were given their own land in Galla-Sidamo.'[64] Although Amedeo became Viceroy, the military command was still held by General Ugo Cavallero for the time being.

Hélène left Naples for Egypt once again in January 1938, seen off by Aimone, only to return to Africa a few months later. Early in April, Amedeo suffered a severe bout of appendicitis and required surgery. Although his condition was said to be satisfactory, Hélène and Aimone decided to go to Addis Ababa to be with him. Along with Campini, they sailed from Brindisi on the 9th; upon arriving in Addis Ababa, they went directly to Amedeo's bedside in the Princess de Piedmont Hospital. Hélène was still there at the end of May when she was able to tell her friend Renée St-Maur that '*mon Bouby*' was better and she hoped to be back in Naples on the 13 June 'if I don't leave my carcass en route' and uncharacteristically confessed that she was afraid of this journey, asking Renée to pray for them.[65]

Amedeo left Addis on 7 June and returned to Italy with Hélène aboard the steamer *Conte Biancamano*, with a stop in Suez. Count Ciano saw Amedeo at the beach towards the end of the month and reported that he 'looks well but the wound has still not healed. Three months after the operation is a bad sign. He intends to return to East Africa and is very dedicated in his plans and projects. On the whole he is optimistic about the situation in the Empire. He believes that expenses can be reduced and obtain equally good results if we do not rush them. He speaks badly of the colonial functionaries: 50 per cent incompetent, 25 per cent thieves.' The next day, Mussolini received him to hear a report on conditions in Italian East Africa, and Amedeo eventually returned to Abyssinia from Venice on 4 August.

On the whole, Ciano seemed to regard Amedeo rather highly, but the same can not be said of his opinion of Aimone. When the King mooted his desire to send a royal mission to the upcoming wedding of King Zog of Albania in 1938 and suggested Aimone, Ciano worried because 'it was unforeseen and because Tirana is not London and to straighten out that drunken beanpole of Spoleto is not easy.'[66] In the event, it was the Duke of Bergamo who was sent off to the nuptials, along with Ciano himself who acted as one of the groom's witnesses.

The rise of Hitler and National Socialism in Germany had been every bit as quick and decisive as the rise of Mussolini and Fascism had been in Italy. The totalitarian states which developed through these political changes had much in common, not the least of which was the cult of personality with their leaders. When Mussolini was invited on a five-day visit to Berlin in September 1937, Hitler proclaimed him as 'one of those rare solitary geniuses who are not created by history but who make history themselves' but, nonetheless, used the occasion to display the new power of the Nazi regime and Germany's devotion to their Führer.[67] Mussolini was unhappy with the annexation of Austria in March 1938, but hosted Hitler on a state visit to Italy in early May. Hélène was in Addis when Hitler visited Rome, Naples, and Florence, and so missed the huge and enthusiastic processions through the cities of Italy which did indeed impress the Führer. The growing attachment of the two countries saw Germany leading, Italy following—first with their withdrawal from the League of Nations in December 1937, and then the implementation of racial laws that began a couple of months after the Duce's return from Germany.

Although until this point Jews had not been seen as any kind of threat or problem in Italy—either by the state or by the church—they now became a target; being 'Italian' had always been a matter of accepting the Italian way of life and law, rather than a racial issue. However, German modelling of Aryan racial superiority now led to a similar practice in Italy, and in July 1938 'The Manifesto of Racial Scientists' was published declaring that 'a pure Italian race exists.' Exclusionary laws were established, beginning the next month when all foreign-born Jews were forbidden from attending Italian schools. In September, foreign-born Jews who had been naturalised after 1919 had their citizenship stripped, and all Jews who were not citizens were ordered to leave the country within six months. The very next day, all Jewish teachers in the country were ejected from their posts, and all these new racial laws were aimed at anyone born to parents 'of the Jewish race', no matter what their own religious status was. Over the months more racial laws were added. Jews were no longer allowed in the military, they were removed from Fascist Party membership, and their membership in professional or scientific organisations was revoked. In November 1938, new Italian laws forbade mixed marriage with Jews, following German legislation forbidding marriage between Germans and non-Aryans in September 1935 as part of the Nuremberg laws, which also stripped Jews of their German citizenship.[68] Each of these new laws was taken by Mussolini to his twice-weekly visits to the Quirinale where King Victor Emmanuel signed them. His ineffectiveness in standing up against his prime minister would eventually be a major factor in destroying the monarchy.

Hélène's own thoughts on the racial laws are largely unknown, but it is said that she commented to her Jewish dentist, Dr Paolo Wigodcih, that 'It is a black page for the history of Italy. It seems to me a ridiculous measure, but will make many families weep.' Although her personal physician at this time was Dr Aldo

Castellani, it was a Jewish doctor, Prof. Bellom Pescarolo, who had nursed her through the near fatal illness in 1905, a connection which the *Jewish Chronicle* felt important enough to publicly record at the time. The King still had a Jewish physician in the late 1930s and attempted to get an exemption from the racial laws for him via the intermediaries of his son-in-law Prince Philipp of Hesse and Count Ciano, but that came to naught. Hélène's teenage years and connection with the Marlborough House set in London brought her into social contact with some of the great British Jewish families, notably the Rothschilds. Also, in her early married life, she was said to have been a pro-Dreyfus supporter during the vicious campaign in which her own brother, Philippe, the Duc d'Orléans, was to prove himself an increasingly virulent anti-Semite.[69] Her many trips into Africa proved time after time that Hélène found racial difference interesting rather than threatening, although the concept of racial equality would have been entirely foreign to her understanding.

Still, Hélène remained a prominent public supporter of the Fascist regime. She was present in Rome for the grand parade welcoming the Italian legionnaires back from service in Spain in October 1938, and again, the next month, for the great gathering for the twentieth anniversary of the end of the war. Earlier, at the end of August, Hélène had gone to Flims in the Swiss Alps, but complained her head was tired and weak. She then moved on to Lausanne, where she was able to spend a couple of days with Amélie and to consult with a physician, because she did 'not know what was happening with my old body.' The Swiss doctor diagnosed heart trouble.[70]

In December, another flurry of rumours drifted around Rome about the possibility that King Victor Emmanuel was seriously considering abdication in favour of his son Umberto, but that Fascist party members preferred Amedeo as a candidate. However, the British ambassador thought it unlikely that Mussolini would provoke a constitutional crisis by allowing such an action. He also pointed out that a law had been passed some two years earlier which made the succession to the throne subject to the approval of the Fascist Grand Council mandatory; it was no longer automatically through primogeniture.[71] In any event, it seemed that Il Duce's opinion of Amedeo would not make him king.

In Ethiopia, fighting broke out again; according to Ciano, Mussolini was very displeased with Amedeo's military leadership.[72] The British evaluation, however, was much more positive. It was reported to the Foreign Office that Amedeo had been indefatigable in visiting almost every corner of Italian East Africa and had 'probably not spent a single complete week in the capital'. His attack of appendicitis and the long recuperative leave in Italy had ended in the middle of August, when he returned to Ethiopia; then, the arrival of Anne in late September 'has helped to create a greater feeling of normality and the frequent visits which His Royal Highness has paid to hospitals, maternity and welfare centres, etc., have done something to reconcile the Italians to their exile.' In summary, 'The first year of the Duke's Viceroyalty must, from the purely personal point of view, be regarded as an unqualified success.'[73]

In January 1939, Hélène and Campini returned to Africa one more time. This would be her last trip to the continent that she loved so deeply and also her last trip outside of Italy. The entire tone of Hélène's last travel journal is mournful, almost as if she were convincing herself to end her travelling and hunting. From the beginning at Agfoi, she wrote 'Oh, you that have a heart, never go back over your footsteps! Your eyes today no longer reflect the past, and to see again loved places from earlier times, your heart will tear and an agony will descend into the deepest part of your soul.' They were joined by Amedeo for a pilgrimage to the tomb of her brother-in-law Luigi Abruzzi which made 'everything here sad.' Even the presence of Bouby could not raise her spirits, which sank even lower when he left. Then news came that Pope Pius XI had died in Rome. 'The world seems suspended in a moment of universal silence, of respect and of stupor,' Hélène wrote, 'The Pope is not supposed to die.'[74]

Nonetheless, Hélène and Campini carried on, venturing into Kenya and the hunting camp of Donald Kerr, who acted as their hunter, guide, and driver. At first, the pattern seemed the same as that of earlier days, and Otto quickly bagged a lion. However, the old thrill of the hunt was replaced by a deep poignancy in the sixty-seven-year-old Duchess. Virtually the last entry in the journal reads:

> In the great green plain, a zebra cries. His female, wounded by a shot from a carbine, has come out of the wood, perhaps seeking some air; slowly she moves towards the setting sun, with her companion close to her. When the unavoidable death forces her down on her haunches, he doesn't understand the wickedness of man; he approaches her, seems to push her to rise again because danger is approaching in the form of humans. We advance. Forced to leave the body, he goes off and starts to gallop around; finishing the circle, he stops, comes straight at us, bows his head a bit and starts to yelp: he is calling his female. The cry is soft; he yelps each time with a more mournful note that can truly be said to be damp with tears, coming from a broken heart. And we suffer from having caused this pain, and to hear such mournful sadness, almost human, which comes from the heart of this animal which cries for his dead companion.

Then, it was time for Hélène to say farewell to her wandering life:

> *Adieu la tente*
> *Adieu la vie libre*
> *Adieu la nature vierge.*[75]

Hélène and Campini then returned to Nairobi to prepare for the journey to Europe. As they did not want to hurry back home, they did not travel by the Red Sea and Suez, but rather by the Cape of Good Hope, stopping at every port along the way, eventually reaching Gibraltar and then on to Genoa.

On 9 March, the same day that his mother set sail for Italy, Amedeo flew out of Africa, travelling to Rome. Although the British Foreign Office said that he was travelling 'in strictest incognito,' the newspapers tracked his return via Khartoum, Cairo, and Benghazi where he was met by Marshal Balbo.[76] Count Ciano recorded that at the meeting in Rome, 'The Duke of Aosta spoke with considerable optimism about the condition of the Ethiopian Empire. I must, however, add that among the many people who have come from there he is the only optimist.' Despite this optimism, the Duke was well aware that the Italian position in Ethiopia would be seriously endangered should Italy became involved in world war. The entry thus continues to say that the Duke of Aosta 'urges us to avoid a conflict with France which would bring on the high seas the task of pacifying our empire and would jeopardise the conquest itself. I do not quite understand whether he was speaking as Viceroy of Ethiopia or as the son of a French princess.'[77]

During Amedeo's fortnight in Rome, Hitler invaded Czechoslovakia. His journey back to Ethiopia emphasized the strong relationship with Britain. A stop in Cairo included a meeting with the proconsul Sir Miles Lampson—the son-in-law of Dr Castellani—described Amedeo as 'tall, good-looking, athletic and very affable and friendly' with 'never a fault in his sense of humour.' At a dinner with Mr Bateman, a High Commission official, on 28 March Amedeo said 'Thank God that idiotic Spanish venture is over. I don't see perpetual peace in the offing yet. But don't take too literally all that Mr Brown [i.e., Mussolini] says.' On Ethiopia: 'Supposing you had shoved all the scum of London's East End into Ethiopia and let them run wild, you can imagine the sort of thing that would have happened. That's just what we did and I have to clean it up somehow.' The next day, he flew to the Sudan, spending two nights in Khartoum as the guest of Sir Stewart Symes, the governor general. He returned to Addis Ababa on 1 April, and a fortnight later General Cavallero was recalled to Italy, and Amedeo himself took command of the armed forces.[78]

On Good Friday, 7 April 1939, Italy invaded Albania, with only a weak and sporadic resistance; on the 16th, Victor Emmanuel was declared King of Albania. Although Mussolini personally disliked Hitler, he admired the German leader's dynamism and aggressive foreign policy, and their co-operation in supporting the fascists during the Spanish Civil War was augmented by joining together in the Anti-Comintern pact in 1937 along with the Empire of Japan. Following Hitler's annexation of Austria in March 1938 and occupation of Czechoslovakia's Sudetenland in October of the same year, Mussolini was prompted into 'a blatant act of emulation.'[79] A Member of Parliament in London commented that 'War seems nearer now that the Dictators are drawing together. Their methods show brutal similarity.'[80]

While the Albanian invasion was still very fresh, Aimone was sent to Teheran to represent Italy at the lavish wedding celebrations of the Crown Prince of Iran with Princess Fawzia, sister of King Farouk of Egypt. On 23 April, Aimone was one of the principal guests, along with Queen Mary's brother, the Earl of Athlone, and his wife, Princess Alice, representing Great Britain. The Shah, the Queen Mother of Egypt, and the Crown Prince himself received each delegation separately. Then, the festivities began with a brilliant banquet at the Gulistan Palace followed by a great reception in the Hall of Brilliants, complete with the legendary peacock throne; the evening ended with a display of fireworks in the gardens. Two days later, Iran displayed its military might with a grand review. Seventy airplanes began with a show of 'aerobatics,' followed by a cavalry display. Then for four hours, infantry and motorized troops marched past complete with Egyptian cavalry and infantry, Turkish infantry, and French, British, and Russian sailors. In the evening, Queen Nazli, the Egyptian Queen Mother, gave a banquet for all the guests at the Gulistan Palace with yet more fireworks at midnight, after which The Shah, Queen Mother, and other members of the royal families accompanied the new bride and groom 'along an illuminated route lined with soldiers and an enthusiastic crowd.' The next afternoon, Aimone hosted a reception at the Italian legation for the couple.

Aimone remained in Iran for a month; on 26 May, he flew to Athens, where his own engagement was announced to Princess Irene, the sister of King George. Aimone's name had earlier been linked with Infanta Beatriz of Spain and Princess Eudoxia of Bulgaria as possible brides, but nothing had come of either of those options, and his betrothal now was rather a surprise. Diplomatic tongues wagged in London, saying that the Italian government was in favour of the match in order to increase Italian influence in Greece, and that the engagement 'is likely to cause certain hearts to ache in Italy, for he was thought very attractive.' However, another diplomat added his own note to the report saying 'Prince Aimone is not nearly such a sound fellow as his brother the Duke of Aosta &, if recent rumours I have heard are true, Princess Irene wont have an easy time with him.'[80]

Aimone and Irene were both rather old to marry by standards of the day— Aimone was already thirty-nine and Irene, thirty-five. In 1923, she had been briefly and unofficially engaged to Prince Nicolas of Romania, and then four years later formally engaged to a cousin, Prince Christian of Schaumburg-Lippe, but that match too was later broken off. Later, Princess Victoria in England had wanted to match Irene with the Duke of Kent, even after he was linked with her cousin Princess Marina. Irene had trained as a nurse, qualifying after a three-year programme.[82] She worked voluntarily as a nurse during her time in Florence, living with her brother Paul and sister Katherine in the Villa Sparta until 1936 when the monarchy was once again restored and the family returned to Greece, taking with them the coffins of their parents, King Constantine and Queen Sophie, and their grandmother, Queen Olga, for burial in the family cemetery at Tatoi. Once back in Greece, she became the head of Girl Guides there.

The engagement was officially announced in Rome on 25 May; just three days later, Irene joined Hélène and Marie José for a march in the capital of 70,000 Fascist women, some in uniform and some bearing rifles, while others wore their traditional regional costumes.

The wedding was set for the beginning of July, and royal guests came into Florence from across Europe. The pink, green, and white marble facade of Florence's Duomo—under Brunelleschi's magnificent dome and alongside Giotto's belltower and the legendary baptisery—provided the backdrop for an event that would unite the Royal Houses of Italy and Greece. Each of the many guests arrived with their own histories—often a reminder of King Albert's quip at the wedding of his daughter Marie José to Umberto—'There are many unemployed in our trade.'[83] King Alfonso of Spain and King Ferdinand of Bulgaria were both already deposed and exiled from their own countries; Queen Giovanna of Bulgaria and the Crown Prince of Romania were both to be exiled in the coming decade, while Irene's own family were in and out of power for decades. The Duchess of Brunswick came from Germany; she was the only daughter of the deposed Kaiser and first cousin to the bride, along with her husband, the Duke, and their sons Ernst August and Georg Wilhelm. Also attending was their daughter Frederika, who had married Irene's youngest brother, Crown Prince Paul, the previous year. Another first cousin of Irene's was also there, the Grand Duke Dmitri Pavlovich of Russia, one of Rasputin's assassins during the First World War, then the lover of Coco Chanel in 1920s Paris and more recently wed to an American heiress. The glamourous Duke and Duchess of Kent, at whose wedding Irene had served as a bridesmaid, came from England. Amedeo met them at Peretola airport along with the British Ambassador Sir Percy Loraine and Lady Loraine, the British consul, other members of the British community, and General Vespignano. There had been some concern in the Foreign Office in London that the Duke might have to propose a toast during the festivities recognizing Victor Emmanuel as the King of Albania and Emperor of Ethiopia, thus tacitly acknowledging his right to those titles, but since he was going as a private guest rather than as a representative of the King, the Duke assured them that 'he did not think there was any risk' of this happening.[84] From the airport, the Kents drove to the Hotel Excelsior, where Aimone and other wedding guests were also staying, and that evening, a family dinner was held at the Pitti Palace.

The day of the wedding—1 July—was one of radiant sunshine, with flag-bedecked streets and throngs of cheering people, as the wedding party made its way to the Cathedral of Santa Maria del Fiore. Hélène—tall and still slender, gowned in gold lamé, and wearing a sautoir of pearls and a black hat adorned with black ostrich feathers—stood on the steps of the cathedral with Aimone before they went into the service. Then, the bride arrived with her brother King

George, who presented her in marriage. Irene's witnesses were her other brother, Crown Prince Paul, and her uncle Prince George of Greece; and Aimone's witnesses were his brother Amedeo, the Duke of Aosta, and Umberto, the Prince of Piedmont. Count Ciano was to have been present but excused himself, due to mourning for his father. Achille Starace, the Secretary-General of the Fascist Party, was there in his capacity as Crown Notary, but otherwise Piers Dixon, a British diplomat, reported that Fascist signs were 'noticeably absent from the ceremonies, and amid the blazing uniforms of Kings and Princes the eye sought in vain for the black shirts which in their thousands form nowadays the almost unrelieved feature of numerous parades and ceremonies in the Italian capital.' The Party's representative, Achille Starace, made a rather 'pompous entry somewhat late' and that 'seemed to cause some amusement as he took his place among the high dignitaries of the Crown.'[85]

After the service, the bride and groom left in a car given as a wedding gift from King Victor Emmanuel and Queen Elena; they drove to the nearby Church of the Santissima Annunziata, where the new duchess followed the tradition of Florentine brides and laid flowers at the Shrine of the Madonna. While waiting for the other guests to leave the cathedral steps, Hélène greeted other guests, in particular Princess Nicholas of Greece, mother of the popular Duchess of Kent, in a tender moment caught by the newsreel photographers.[86]

The King of the Hellenes gave a post-wedding luncheon for guests and their suites at the Excelsior Hotel, where most of the guests were staying. Then, in the evening, an informal dinner party for the royals was held at Villa Sparta. The next day, the bride and groom—Irene in black and wearing a glittering Greek tiara, and Aimone in the white dress uniform of the Navy—went to the Vatican for a papal blessing from Pius XII.[87]

As Irene had been raised as a member of the Greek Orthodox Church, she had been required to go through the humiliating service of *abjura*, a renunciation of her faith, in order to become a member of the Roman Catholic Church before her marriage to Aimone according to the rules of the House of Savoy. Queen Elena had faced the same situation when she married Victor Emmanuel. However difficult Irene found this ceremony, she did embrace the Catholic Church and developed a particular devotion to the Dominican Order, eventually becoming a

Third Order Dominican herself.[88]

15

1939–1942

The war has spread like oil on water[1]

The glitter and glamour of the wedding in Florence provided a temporary and very thin mask over the political troubles already closing in over Europe. Ever since the springtime invasion of Albania, there had been increasing diplomatic concerns about a similar Italian invasion of Greece, with Corfu a particular worry.[2] Now, a German threat against Poland was in the foreground. Among the many guests at Aimone and Irene's wedding was another of the bride's innumerable first cousins, the German Prince Philipp of Hesse, who was also the son-in-law of King Victor Emmanuel and later claimed to be the 'official personal courier between Hitler and Mussolini for the conveyance of written and verbal messages.' In his conversations with the Duke of Kent during the wedding festivities, Hesse was told that Britain would consider a German attack on Poland as a cause of war. Although Kent was not acting as an official spokesman for the government in London, Philipp took the warning seriously and when he returned to Germany, he—in his own words—'told Hitler everything.' Any German 'attack on Poland would be the beginning of a world war. England would enter this war. Such a war would end in catastrophe for Germany and Europe.'[3] Hitler, who had just negotiated a non-aggression pact with Russia, did not take the message seriously, and on 1 September, Germany invaded Poland. Among the thousands fleeing was Hélène's niece Dolores (daughter of her sister Louise), who had married Prince August Czartoryski in 1937 and was now pregnant with their first child. The young couple had been living in Cracow, where August—who was also a descendant of King Louis Philippe through the Duc de Nemours—ran a family museum; they fled when the bombings began. The Gestapo arrested them, and it was only through the intervention of the Spanish ambassador in Berlin that they were released and were able to continue to Paris and eventually to her family in neutral Spain.

Two days after the invasion of Poland, Britain and France both declared war on

Germany, while Mussolini announced on the 3rd that Italy remained officially neutral. The Pact of Steel—signed between Germany and Italy—on 22 May had established a mutual defense agreement, although Mussolini emphasized that due to the costs and efforts of their recent military forays into Spain and Africa, Italy would need three years to prepare for another conflict. As Italy was so publicly allied to Germany, Rome's declaration of neutrality was viewed skeptically. Recalling Italian actions at the beginning of the First World War, the British Foreign Office considered that 'Italian neutrality will have to be regarded with suspicion and that Italian promises are worth nothing at all; but it is not so certain that Italy's neutrality is really part of a cunning Axis plot ...The balance of advantage lies in having Italy neutral.'[4]

But during this period of official neutrality, war preparations began throughout Italy and its overseas territories. In October, Princess Marie José took on the role of National Inspector of the Red Cross. Hélène, who had held the same position during the First World War, attended the ceremony in Rome. Both princesses wore the Red Cross uniform and saluted with outstretched arm as they walked past the military honour guard and then through the ranks of nursing sisters. Hélène embraced her successor and kissed her warmly on both cheeks before Marie José signed her acceptance and gave a brief speech. Earlier in the year, the two had had a conversation about the need of a simple and practical course on hygiene and first aid to give to nurses headed for the colonies. This sent Hélène rummaging among her books; soon, she sent Marie José her copy of *Manuel du Voyageur & du Resident au Congo*. Although recognising that the text was forty years old and more recent innovations had developed, Hélène had carried it on all her African trips and found it both simple and helpful in caring for those around her.[5]

With Amedeo and Anne both in Ethiopia, Hélène's two granddaughters— Margherita, aged nine, and Cristina, aged six—came to stay with her. During the warm weather, their favourite moments were at the seaside. Hélène brought her horses and Irish wolfhounds with her to Torre di Patria, and swam with the girls, helping Margherita to get over her fright as a beginner. Together, they watched the two fishermen, whom Hélène named Cain and Abel, walk out into the water among their nets on stilts and then enjoy the 'telline' they gathered with spaghetti for lunch. Sometimes, they would lunch next to the fireplace and then sit on the floor and play dominoes. Life was at its most relaxed at Torre di Patria; it was one place that Hélène never invited her sister Amélie who was considered too formal. Hélène rode her horses sidesaddle as she had done since her youth, except when she would don her bathing costume and ride bareback into the sea, something she continued doing into 1942 when she was over seventy.

Hélène made Christmas 1939 special for the girls with an enormous Christmas tree in the Salone della Culla at Capodimonte. Margherita and Cristina stayed in Queen Amélie's apartment and in the small oratory there, Hélène had placed a *presepio*, the traditional Italian crib scene with many small figures carved in wood. On Christmas day itself, shepherds arrived from the Abruzzi with their sheep and played bagpipes under their windows. Among the gifts, the girls received a Sicilian cart complete with donkey. Poor Turiddu, though, was scared by the noises and brayed desperately when the fireworks were set off.

Barbar books and *A Thousand and One Nights* were favourites sitting on the bookshelves, and on the tables were large glass vases full of stones which Hélène had brought back from Africa. She would set the girls at one of those tables to compose letters to their parents in Ethiopia, and if they showed little enthusiasm for that would quote Kipling to them—'the camel's hump is an ugly lump which well you can see at the zoo, but uglier yet is the hump you get when you have too little to do... too little to do!'[6]

Amedeo was called to Rome as a strategy for war in East Africa was developed. Ciano recorded in his diary on 6 April 1940:

> The military action plan is: defensive action on all fronts and offensive action toward Djibouti; air and naval offensive all around. But the Duke of Aosta, whom I saw this morning, said that it is not only extremely problematical that we can maintain present positions, because the French and English are already equipped and ready for action, but the population, among whom rebellion is still alive, would revolt as soon as they got any inkling of our difficulties. I talked about this with the Duce and, for whatever it was worth, repeated that Italy unanimously hates the Germans.[7]

During Amedeo's three-week stay in Italy, Germany invaded and occupied Denmark and Norway on 9 April, and the move on the western front accelerated the following month. Hitler's invasion of the Low Countries and France began on 10 May, and culminated in the occupation of Paris with Germans marching down the Champs Elysées on 14 June. Thus it had been months before Hélène's birth in 1871, and thus it was again.

Virginia Cowles, a young American journalist for the Hearst newspapers, was in Rome at the beginning of May, and reported on the atmosphere in the capital:

> You could already feel the tension. Gone was the lazy indifference of the previous August; now everyone pored over the newspapers, clung to the radio, talked, gesticulated, remonstrated, argued, and moaned. You could feel the Nazi grip tightening. Germans were everywhere: the Embassy staff had swollen to over eighty; there were Nazi officials, military experts, all manner of technicians, and an endless flow of tourists.... Superimposed on the apprehensive atmosphere was an artificial gaiety. It was the big season in Rome; there was a round of feverish entertaining that reminded me of the hectic days in London the

summer before the war. I found to my surprise that the idle gentlemen and the elegant ladies of Roman society, usually dismissed as decadent, were standing up fiercely (if inconsequentially) to the pro-German current. They refused to have anything to do with the Germans. It was their proudest boast that not a single German had ever crossed the threshold of the ultra-smart Golf Club. They went out of their way to entertain members of the British and French Embassies and professed anti-Nazi views with dangerous frankness.[8]

On 10 June, Italy entered the war on the side of the Axis when Mussolini formally declared war on Britain and France from the balcony of the Palazzo Venezia. The next day, Allied bombings began over Turin and Genoa. The Fascist government suffered a major public relations blow, when on the 28th, the national hero Italo Balbo was accidentally shot down by his own men over Tobruk. He was replaced as Governor General of Libya by Marshal Graziani, who had so recently been summarily dismissed from Ethiopia.

On 3 August, the Italian invasion of British Somaliland began with relatively little British opposition, and within a fortnight Somaliland was in Italian hands. Amedeo had opposed the invasion and complained that many valuable resources of men and supplies had been wasted on a useless stretch of sand, and Il Duce was not pleased with his attitude.[9] Ciano reported to his diary on 13 August that 'Mussolini is very resentful towards the Duke of Aosta because of the delay of operations in Somaliland. He repeats the formula: "Princes ought to be enlisted as civilians."'[10] Nonetheless, the country was exultant at the results. The Italian army had beaten the British army. For the first time in the war the British had lost a colony to the enemy, and A. O. I. now had a coastline which stretched from the Red Sea into the Gulf of Aden.

Later that same month, Hélène's brother-in-law and head of the House of Orléans since 1926, Jean, the Duc de Guise, died at Larache in Spanish Morocco, a month before his sixty-sixth birthday. His funeral was attended by the Duchesse, her daughters Isabelle and Françoise, various Spanish officials, and minor French and Arab functionaries. Henri, the Comte de Paris, new head of the house and serving anonymously in the French Foreign Legion, flew in from France by way of Rabat. When they met at a lunch in March 1938, Ciano had dismissed Isabelle, duchesse de Guise as 'a repainted and insignificant old woman. She bombarded me with banal questions to which I could only offer banal answers.'[11]

Isabelle was the sibling with whom Hélène felt the closest, due to their shared love of Africa. After the death of her father, Hélène was never particularly close to any of her relatives, except for Isabelle; their connection became even closer when their two children married. However, at this point, their countries were officially at war with each other, and the Italian state in 1940 confiscated the Palazzo Orléans in Palermo as 'enemy property.' The same year, the Aosta family sold the Palazzo della Cisterna in Turin to the local government, and it became the seat of the provincial administration.

In the Balkans, Romania officially allied itself with the Axis on 5 July. King Carol abdicated on 6 September in favour of his young son Michael, but in reality left the country in the hands of the fascists led by Marshal Antonescu. On 4 October, Hitler and Mussolini met at the Brenner Pass to discuss strategy, although most of the talking was done by Hitler and most of the conversation centred on Britain, France, Spain, and Russia; the fact that Germany was already deploying to invade Romania was not mentioned. Then, on the 7th, German troops entered Romania seizing the oil fields and refinery at Ploeşta, and Romania was stripped of most of the territory gained at the end of the First World War. Mussolini was furious at being kept in the dark, and just a week later he 'astonished the chief of the General Staff, Marshal Pietro Badoglio, and his deputy, Mario Roatta, by demanding the occupation of Greece.' When Hitler arrived in Florence on 28 October, Mussolini met him at the train declaring 'Führer, we are marching! This morning a victorious Italian army has crossed the Greek border!'[12]

Ever since the invasion of Albania, it had been widely believed that Greece would be Italy's next target. One assessment of the invasion was that it was 'essentially the culmination of Mussolini's ego and frustrated aspirations of Italian grandeur.'[13] For the first few days, the Italian army encountered little to no resistance as they expected. However, on 1 November, the Greek army began a devastating counter-offensive. Within days they drove back some of the invaders across the Albanian border. Italian dreams of expansion had been beaten by Greek defense of the homeland.

While this was transpiring, Britain's Royal Air Force struck Italian targets both on the mainland and in Albania. The most important of these was the hit against the naval base at Taranto between 11 and 12 November when Italy's navy was crippled with the loss of three battleships—two sunk and the other critically damaged.

Bombs were falling in Naples too. Anne and her daughters were staying with Hélène at Capodimonte, and they remember her walking in the courtyard during the nighttime bombings over the city, wearing a djellabah and invoking the bombs to fall on Capodimonte rather than the city. In the morning, Hélène and Anne would go into the city to help in the hospitals.[14] However, 'after repeated nocturnal visits of aeroplanes over Naples,' Hélène sent them on 4 November 1940 to Florence, where they stayed throughout the winter. Irene was already living at Fiesole in the hills north of Florence at the Villa Cisterna, near to her sister Queen Helen, who had left Florence to return to Romania on 13 September. Two days after Anna and the girls left Naples, more bombs were dropped around the gardens and park at Capodimonte, and then another round on 3 December, this time dropping on the orchard and near the gates. After that, there was a long silence from the nighttime bombings.[15]

Meanwhile, Irene accompanied her sister on a visit to Hitler at Berchtesgaden, arriving there on 10 December. Queen Helen later recalled:

The whole place was hidden in a thick mist, which never lifted for a moment, and so we could get no impression of the outside of the famous Eyrie. Before we were offered tea, I spoke to Hitler for half an hour in his study. His manner was courteous, though rather than of a man used to being pressed for time. He made his attitude to Rumania, and to Michael, quite clear. He had no intention of permitting anarchy, but I felt that he considered our country to be his to command. About Michael, he said, 'A man is not fit to rule over a country until he is at least forty. Your son has a long time to develop himself, and it is your task to see he is prepared in the right way!' He rapped this out like a machine-gun. 'Until then,' he continued, 'he must be guided by Antonesco.' And that was that! …As soon as we joined the others for tea, he seemed shy and rather ill-at-ease.[16]

Throughout a bitterly cold winter, Greek troops held their own again Italian forces, and Mussolini's hope for an easy victory had turned into a disaster for Italy—not only with its military defeats and losses but also diplomatically in its relations with Germany. Eventually, on 16 March, Mussolini called off the offensive as it had failed to make any progress, yet at the cost of 51,190 dead or missing and 64,476 seriously wounded—compared with 13,408 Greek dead and 42,485 wounded—with many others suffering amputations following severe frostbite in the winter cold.[17] Irene continued serving as a Red Cross sister; as such, when went into one hospital and realized that the wounded were all Greeks, she went back to the first bed to sit down and cry.[18]

Hélène was occasionally back and forth to Rome in early 1941. In February, she went to the Grand Hotel, to enquire about the failing health of her cousin, the former King Alfonso XIII of Spain, who died on the 28th at the age of fifty-four after a series of heart attacks; Hélène did not return for the funeral but sent a memorial wreath to the service which took place in the Church of Santa Maria degli Angeli. She was back in Rome again in March when she was received by Pope Pius XII. It was a formal visit with Maria Caffarelli and the other ladies and gentlemen of her court with her and an escort of Swiss Guards. Hélène, dressed entirely in black as was the custom for women being received by the pope, wore her high diamond tiara to hold the black veil in place, counterbalanced by the court train of her dress. She still presented a strikingly regal image.[19] There was also time for a long private conversation between Hélène and the Holy Father.

In April, Hélène wrote to Erminia Piano of her 'unwavering faith' and that she knew her sons were in God's hands. While Amedeo and Aimone were both fighting for Italy, their in-laws and extended family were likewise doing so for their native or adopted countries. Among others, Irene's young cousin Prince Philip of Greece was serving in the British Navy and took part in the March battle at Cape Matapan, where three Italian heavy cruisers were lost.[20] In mid-April 1941, the ineffectual Italian invasion of Greece of the previous autumn was followed by German attacks which resulted in the occupation of the country and the fall of Athens on 27 April. After the fall of Crete, all of Greece was in German hands. Although two elderly aunts—Prince Philip's mother Alice and the Duchess of Kent's mother Helen—remained in Athens throughout the war, the rest of Irene's family fled from mainland Greece to Crete and thence to Cairo. King George and Crown Prince Paul went to London with the Greek government in exile, while Crown Princess Frederika, her young children, and other members of the family continued on to South Africa for the duration of the war.

Amedeo had been appointed as a general in the Air Force in February, and according to the report of radio in Rome, he sent his acceptance to the Duce in the following words:

> The announcement of my promotion and your words deepen my faith and increase my iron determination. We will last somehow, at any cost, thanks to my enthusiastic collaborators of the Air Force and thanks to the general people, who are ready for any sacrifice for the achievement of the Fascist Italian victory.

On the ground in Ethiopia, things were looking distinctly different than they had just the previous summer when Somaliland had been seized by the Italians. While the British had supported the return of Haile Selassie and his efforts to rally support among the tribesmen, the Chiefs of Staff in London 'circulated a paper in which they hinted that we might support the Duke of Aosta as a rallying point against Mussolini.' Sir Archie Sinclair of the Air Ministry wrote on Christmas Day, 1940, that he 'should have no objection to supporting the Duke of Aosta against Mussolini if it does not involve betraying Abyssinia, of which he is the Italian Governor, for the second time. I am sure that any such proposal would be hotly condemned by a vociferous and not uninfluential body of public opinion in this country.'[21]

The British campaign to retake Somaliland and liberate Ethiopia began in late January 1941. General Sir William Platt led his forces from the Sudan, while four brigades of mostly African troops under General Alan Cunningham moved up from Kenya. Platt has been characterised as 'a martinet and a distinctly crusty martinet', but also 'a very good soldier.' The first British victory at the watering hole of El Waq, on the border between Kenya and Somalia, took the Italians by surprise. Amedeo heard the news over the BBC News and demanded an immediate inquiry. When General Gustavo Pesenti claimed he knew nothing of the situation, Amedeo flew there with his *aide-de-camp* General Giovambattista Volpini. When Amedeo confronted Pesenti in person and received an account of the incident, Pesenti concluded that a struggle was hopeless and that Amedeo, as Viceroy, should seek a separate peace between AOI and Great Britain. 'Though he was immediately ordered by the duke to be silent, he insisted on speaking, pointing out the political and psychological repercussions that such an audacious move could have in Italy.' Amedeo commanded him to stop talking, saying that Pesenti ought to be shot for making such treasonable remarks, and he himself for listening to them.[22]

The British continued their campaign into Somaliland and captured Mogadishu on 25 February. They reached Harar a month later. In the face of advancing British troops—which in six weeks had already captured nearly 50,000 Italian prisoners, nearly three times their own number—Amedeo on 3 April retreated to the mountain stronghold of Amba Alàgi with General Volpini, General Pietro Pinna, the commander of the nearly completely depleted air force, and his chief of staff General Claudio Trezzani and some 3,850 men.[23] Two days later, the British forces liberated Addis Ababa, and on 5 May—five years to the day after Marshal Badoglio had taken the city—the Emperor Haile Selassie returned to his capital. British forces under Platt and Cunningham converged on the plain of Amba Alàgi, and Amedeo and his remaining troops were besieged in their mountain hideaway.

Throughout the siege, Amedeo continued his usual practice of keeping a diary. On 6 May, he wrote:

> The one thing that really pains me and I cannot endure is boredom. Like Mama, just the same. If I have a life I do not like or have to be with people who annoy me, I'm there; but then it hurts. It gives me nervous colitis. I can no longer eat and perish. Here, however, with the guns, the fresh air, the taste of the fight I do well and I feel like a lion.[24]

Hélène wrote to Amedeo encouragingly: 'You are the pillar without which the Empire would collapse like a house of cards, your reputation alone gives courage to your own people, keeps unity among the heads and also demands respect from the internal enemy.' However, 'the English are doing everything to get rid of you. Alvaro's Mother has arrived in Rome with a message from the British Ambassador in Madrid for our King, asking him to recall you immediately—so that they would have their hands more free. Aunt B ... always was an intrigant.'[25] Elsewhere, 'Serbia is done for—but Greece is still resisting. Churchill—furious—is threatening to bomb Rome if we bomb Athens or Cairo. General de Gaulle has left for Athens.'[26]

Indeed, there had been reports of Amedeo being anti-British; apparently, these originated from Irene's brother, the King of the Hellenes. Sir Michael Palairet, the British minister to Athens, reported back to the Foreign Office a talk he had had with King George. The Greek king said that he knew the British government regarded Amedeo as pro-British, 'but he had for some time past had reliable information which strongly contradicted this view.' Personally, he 'believed that the Duke of Aosta's association with Mussolini was close and according to his reports the duke was bitterly anti-British whatever he might pretend. He thought he ought to give us this warning for what it might be worth.'[27]

Hélène wrote again to Amedeo on 27 April:

I know many of the faults of the English, but up to now—at least as regards the officers—I have found them men of honour. The way in which the enemy general blackmailed you is, on the contrary, a mean action. he did you a great service, for if before this you had been raised to the stars, your fine reply exalted you above the sun! Your contemptuous answer is worthy of you and of the name you bear. But I understand anxiety. However you took the right course without hesitation ... Just think. Our country needed for its defence that firebrand, that damned fool Pedana, and I had to put the administration into the hands of Berardi who is still more of a blockhead. And then, when I had hardly given him the difficult explanations and made things over to him when he was 'called up', not 're-called' because he had never done his military service. Cosenzia too has been re-called. On the other hand Boccelli, who went through the whole of the great war, is at home and Campini in spite of his numerous applications, is still available.[28]

Hard pressed by the lack of supplies and especially potable water, Amedeo made the difficult decision to surrender. Early on the morning of 16 May, he sent his *aide-de-camp*, General Volpini, to open negotiations. However, Volpini never made it to the British camp; he was killed on the way by 'free-lance Abyssinians.' Later that day, a truce was established between Italian and British forces, even though rogue Abyssinian elements, intent upon murder and looting, continued to harass the Italian troops until the next morning when Colonel Dudley Russell arrived with the terms of surrender. After some negotiations, Amedeo agreed to a 'Surrender with Honour,' a custom that had largely fallen out of use after the Napoleonic wars, in which the vanquished army would march out of its fortifications with their arms, and once clear of their fortress, would surrender their weapons with an exchange of salutes. General Moseley Mayne, commander of the Fifth Indian Infantry Division, took the salute on the morning of 19 May with the pipes of the Transvaal Scottish playing 'The Flowers of the Forest.' The Italian officers saluted, but the sombre dignity of the occasion was lost with the rank-and-file 'too busy coping with tier luggage, which varied from bulging suitcases to cabin trunks, which all too often caused them to stumble on the steep descent.' The next morning, Amedeo paid his respects at the Italian cemetery and inspected a guard of honour from the Worcestershire Regiment, the senior regiment present, and then surrendered himself as well as his army.[29]

On 25 March, Yugoslavia—under the regency of Prince Paul—had crumbled under German pressure and signed a pact of loyalty with the Axis. Reaction against the move resulted in a military coup which overthrew the regency and established seventeen-year-old King Peter as the ruler. Although the new leaders did not renounce the Pact with Germany, they clearly distanced themselves from Berlin, and Hitler was said to be speechless with anger. Anti-Axis sentiment was the major impetus for the coup, but underlying that was resentment of the pro-Croatian policies of the previous government.[30]

In the early morning of Sunday, 6 April, Germany moved across the borders of both Yugoslavia and Greece and a heavy bombardment of Belgrade began. On the 10th, Croatia declared its independence from the rest of Yugoslavia. Ciano had met with Ribbentrop in Vienna and with Ante Pavelic´, the Croatian fascist leader of the Ustasha, in Ljubljana, and a plan was crafted to break Croatia away from Yugoslavia and establish it as a monarchy under a prince of the Savoy dynasty. King Victor Emmanuel was delighted with the suggestion. Ciano felt that the King would have designated Amedeo if he had been in the country. In fact, the previous year, Amedeo's name had been suggested for the crown of Hungary, which was still officially a monarchy under the regency of Admiral Horthy. Count Ciano as Foreign Minister wrote in his diary: 'We again discuss the crown of Hungary with Villani: union under one head, or else coronation of the Duke of Aosta. Doesn't matter which, so long as we proceed faster, because the question of Croatia is quickly coming to a head.'

However, those thoughts came to naught; with Amedeo now engaged in Africa, the only likely candidates for Croatia were Aimone or Prince Filiberto, Duke of Pistoia, the forty-five-year-old second son of the King's maternal uncle, the late Duke of Genoa. A career army man who had reached the rank of general, Pistoia had volunteered to fight in Abyssinia, where he commanded the Blackshirts of the '23d of March' Division which captured Amba Aradam. Despite his closeness to his mother's family, the Genoas, and his problematic relationship with the Aostas, the King decided in favour of Aimone 'because of his physical appearance and also, up to a certain point, because of his intellectual capacities.' This was despite Mussolini calling Aimone a 'complete mental defective.'[31]

In fact, as Denis Mack Smith has written:

> [The king] had little respect for his various cousins whom the regime sometimes tried to exploit. He had no great opinion of Amedeo. He positively disliked the Count of Turin who had the good sense to be alarmed by the invasion of Ethiopia. The Duke of Bergamo, who publicly lectured the School of Fascist Mysticism about Mussolini's being 'a man sent by divine providence,' was referred to by the king as an imbecile; and the same word was used of the Duke of Pistoia who in 1937 wrote a pro-fascist article for the Duce's personal newspaper. Nor can the palace have approved when the Duke of Genoa sent an unreservedly pro-Nazi statement for publication by the journal of Dr Goebbels in Berlin.[32]

So, it was to be Aimone.

On 7 May, Mussolini, Ciano, and Pavelić met at Monfalcone and confirmed their plan, but it was only the next day that Aimone was informed of the intentions. 'When we looked for him, to give him the news, we managed to find him, only after twenty-four hours, in a Milan hotel, where he was hiding in the company of a young girl.' The start was not particularly promising as Aimone's first reaction was not to take it seriously; he laughed when he heard that his proposed regnal name was Tomislav II because in its Italian form of Tomislao, it sounded like 'the name of a ruler in an operetta or that of a music-hall comedian.'[33] Only when the King announced that it was Aimone's duty and that it was already too late to reject the offer did Aimone accept—and then perhaps only because of the promise of an increased income. However, Aimone did demand to be kept fully informed of developments in the independent state of Croatia (*Nezavisna Država Hrvatska*) and to be allowed a personal cabinet to begin collecting information.

King Victor Emmanuel left almost immediately to visit his own relatively new kingdom of Albania and was now on his way to Tirana. Aimone, who was staying at the Quirinale Palace, telephoned his friend Colonel Agenore Bertocchi, who served under him at La Spezia, and said 'Come here quickly; I'm in a mess.' Aimone then asked him to act as unofficial secretary to his 'Croatian office,' and eventually to accompany him as *aide-de-camp* to Croatia. When Ciano returned from Tirana, he met with Aimone for a political briefing:

> A long conversation with Spoleto. He is proud of having been chosen as King of Croatia, but has no exact idea of what he is supposed to do and is vaguely uneasy about it. I emphasize that he will be a lieutenant-general with a crown at the service of the Fascist Empire. In any case, it will be necessary to keep the reins tightly in our grasp.[34]

Matters moved quickly, and a Croatian delegation proceeded to Rome. Pope Pius XII granted private audiences both to Aimone—who was specifically received as a Prince of Savoy and nothing grander—and to the Croatians, who promoted the symbolism of the Crown of King Zvonimir, who had been crowned with a crown sent by the Pope in 1075. Aimone, on the other hand, told the Pope that he had prepared a memorandum for the King to express 'his doubts about the wisdom of proceeding so quickly to the designation of a monarch.'[35]

The next day, Mussolini and Ciano processed in court carriages through the streets of Rome with the Croatian delegation, some in uniform, some in national costume. At the Quirinale the Croatians made a formal offer of the crown, and Victor Emmanuel 'designated' Aimone in that position. This was the first time that the Croatians had laid eyes upon their potential king, and Ciano recorded that 'there was a murmur of approval among them' but cynically added 'Let us hope that it will be the same when they hear him speak.'[36] When the party left the throne room of the Quirinale, Crown Prince Umberto deferred and gave precedence to his cousin Aimone in his new role; all the press commented upon this. Mussolini and Pavelić then proceeded to the Palazzo Venezia where they signed the Rome Agreement formalizing a new relationship, and appeared on a balcony before an enthusiastic crowd.

Due to his new role as king-designate of Croatia, Aimone resigned his military commission. The news was published in the papers on 23 May through a letter in which Aimone stressed that his duties as a prince of the House of Savoy required him to take up other responsibilities. A naval friend, Admiral Duke Denti di Piraino, suggested that Aimone contact Baron Guariglia, the ambassador in Paris until 1940, for advice. Ciano recorded another visit from Spoleto and that he 'wishes to take Guariglia with him to Zagreb, and this seems to me an excellent choice. He said nothing of any particular importance, but the tone of his conversation was distinctly anti-German.'[37]

Even in the middle of the war, Hélène remained aware of her public image and did what she could to manipulate that. When Amedeo sent her a cash gift, she wrote back:

> Bouby dear, thank you for your generosity. I have made myself popular with your present by buying fresh Treasury Bonds—a patriotic act which will be published and will make a good impression. Then—in a little while—I will sell the Treasury Bonds and spend the money on other more useful Charities.

Throughout her life in Naples, Hélène responded to the needs of the poor of the city and surrounding areas. This made the headlines in times of disasters—as in the earthquakes and volcanic eruptions which shook the city from time to time—but most often her actions were done quietly and secretly. Often, Sister Carolina acted as her charity agent, particularly in regard to the Cottolengo and the work of the Don Orione fathers. In July 1942, Hélène would donate a house in Naples—la Casa Ravaschieri on the via Donnalbina—for the work of the Don Orione fathers with its special emphasis on the poor and orphans. Don Orione himself, who died in 1940, was especially remembered for his work following the 1908 earthquakes at Messina and Reggio Calabria and later in Marsica. In March 1943, this house would officially become known as the 'Piccolo Cottolengo Don Orione.'[38]

After nine months of no bombings over Naples, Hélène sent for her daughter-in-law Anne and grandchildren to return from Florence. It was hot in Florence, so Hélène insisted that they return to Capodimonte. But she wrote to Amedeo that 'I wish I had never done so. The night of their return, while they were on their way, between Florence and Rome, there was a pandemonium in my City. The railway with trains loaded with explosives, etc.—you can imagine my emotion. I thought only of sending them back to a safe place.'[39] They went instead a bit further south, to Sorrento.

Hélène herself spent at least part of the war living in one of her properties, the Torre di Patria, a fifteenth-century watchtower at Castel Volturno, about thirty-five kilometres northwest of Naples. This was part of the royal estate of Licola, a place that the family frequented as a seaside retreat where they could also enjoy cross-country riding. From the early 1930's Hélène would regularly stay there throughout the year. She was at the Torre in September 1941 when she wrote a short series of letters to Amedeo which have survived because they went through British censors and copies ended up among the Foreign Office papers in London. Hélène also continued her regular reading during the tensions of the war; among her choices, she found Isabelle Eberhardt's novel *Trimardeur* 'too boring' to read, while others, including Paul Bourget's *Un Divorce* (which she had last read during her serious illness in 1904), Ignace Legrand's *A Sa Lumière*, and A. J. Cronin's *The Keys of the Kingdom* (which she read in French) were all engaging enough to read aloud when she was back at Capodimonte.[40]

The Croatian situation was still far from settled, and Aimone remained in Italy. Hélène wrote to Amedeo in September:

Bob is very kind. In spite of his hard work in Rome he spends one day a week with me, it also does him good because he can relax. Just imagine, he is learning the language of the Country to which they want to send him. It appears that it is very difficult—but it is certainly not more complicated than the characters of the natives. Bob in the meanwhile, as his future Country doesn't want him, has applied to his uncle [King Victor Emmanuel] to return to the Army with a Command at the Front.[41]

Later in the month, she wrote that that 'You must be surprised that Bob is still here. We hope that he will always stay here.' Nobody wanted him in his new country, and the whole affair 'was all arranged in a hurry, badly organised,' and 'this whole kingdom is a quite incomprehensible put up show because the trade of the country, the mines and industries of this new kingdom without a King—are in the hands of the Germans.' So, his mother wondered, 'what should Bob do there?' Hélène reported to Amedeo that: 'The war has spread like oil on water. Terrific suicidal fire going in all directions a dantesque drama with, in the background, the tortures of hunger, cold and poverty and the tremendous apetites of the persons in powers.' The household staffs of both Hélène and Anne grew smaller as men were called up to military services, and little luxuries like coffee were a thing of the past.[42]

The British Foreign Office twice refused to transmit messages from Hélène to Amedeo, recalling her reputation as 'the only pro-fascist member of the Royal family.' By October, Hélène was unable to get messages through to Amedeo by means of the 'proper channel,' the Brazilian Embassy, and she resorted to contacts with the Vatican, and asked them to convey the simple message 'Received five of your letters June July, we are all well. Mamma.'[43]

There was also still great concern among British officials as to Amedeo's true leanings. The Governor of Kenya, Sir Henry Moore, wrote to the Secretary of State for the colonies, 20 September 1941, that one of his own conversations with Amedeo gave him the impression 'that he would not have returned to Abyssinia after his last visit to Rome had Mussolini not led him to believe that Italy's entry into the war was not repeat not imminent.' However, both Irene's brothers, Prince Paul and King George of the Hellenes, continued to 'regard him as in fact a supporter of the Fascist Regime and have independently issued warnings against being misled by his engaging English manners.' Moore wrote that he did not know what their distrust was based upon, but he had heard contrary opinion from those who had known him well over a long period. Moore also reported that Amedeo regularly received the *East African Standard*, but had no wireless set, and could not discuss the course of events with Italians other than his own personal staff 'as he expressly wished to be separated from his own Italian general officers when taken prisoner.' He was free to write letters, so long as they were passed to the Officer of the Guard and then passed through ordinary censorship channels.[44]

Amedeo was interned about seventy kilometres away from Nairobi at Dònyo Sàbouk, a hunting lodge belonging to Lady McMillan which had formerly been used to house convalescing South African soldiers but was said to have been abandoned because of its unhealthy malarial surroundings. The late Sir Northrup McMillan and his wife Lucie were American by birth, British by naturalisation, and Kenyan by preference. According to Amedeo's family, it was through the intervention of Queen Mary that arrangements for his internment at the McMillan home were made. Among his visitors were Sir Henry Moore and seventy-three-year-old Lady McMillan who balanced on her walking stick to drop a curtsey as if she were being received at court.[45]

It appears that letters flowed from Africa to Italy but not back again. However, in early December the family managed to get two telegrams transmitted to Amedeo through Vatican channels, although Sir Henry Moore wrote back that 'Use of this unauthorised route is a matter of concern to local censorship and I should be grateful if Vatican may be requested to confine any messages to recognised channels.'[46]

Hélène's efforts to keep in touch with Amedeo were not helped by an interview that the British Foreign Office had with Anna Laetitia, Countess Pecci-Blunt, the Italian-born wife of an American citizen who was taking her daughter to New York. The Countess was a niece of Pope Leo XIII who granted them the title when she and her husband married. The husband was born Cecil Blumenthal in New York but changed his name to Blunt after his widowed mother became the Duchesse de Montmorency through a second husband. Due to the Jewish connection, the Countess was taking her child to the safety of America.

The Countess made no secret of the strongly pro-British feeling of the Roman aristocracy as a whole, particularly of the 'Black Aristocracy'—those who had sided with the Pope rather than the Savoys after the 1870 taking of Rome—to which she belonged. She stated that in early August she had seen the Duke of Spoleto who had told her that he bitterly resented his appointment as King of Croatia and that he had been forced into this against his will by Mussolini and intended to delay his departure as long as possible. This did not surprise the Countess as she had known him to be extremely British in outlook. She also knew the Dowager Duchess of Aosta and said that she was the only pro-Fascist member of the Royal Family, as she had, for motives of personal ambition, supported the Fascists from the beginning with a view to securing the Italian throne for her son instead of the Crown Prince. At one time she had very nearly succeeded in securing her aim in view of the Crown Prince's bad relations with the Government. In general the Dowager Duchess of Aosta is considered an intriguer in Rome.[47]

A minute on the Foreign Office report notes that it is 'Interesting but contains nothing new. The Dowager Duchess of Aosta is mentioned as the only Fascist member of the Royal family—an additional reason for not assisting her in sending special messages to her son.'

Aimone, in the meanwhile, however kind he was to his mother, continued to make a fool of himself. Ciano, who was never one of his supporters, wrote in November that the King wanted Aimone out of Rome:

> In fact, the behaviour of this young man is quite absurd. He is living with the Pignataro girl and brings her to his private railroad car. He frequents restaurants and taverns and gets drunk. A few nights ago, in a restaurant near Piazza Colonna, he put a twisted towel around his head in imitation of a crown, amid the applause of the waiters and of the owner, a certain Ascensio, who divides his time between the kitchen and jail. Ascensio happens to be the Duke's best friend. He is a fine man to be a king!

The same theme continued into the New Year, and in January 1943, Ciano wrote in his diary that 'Acquarone talks to me about the Duke of Spoleto. The Duke doesn't give a damn about Croatia, and wants only money, money, and more money. On the whole, it is in our interest to give him at least a little. I shall propose to the Duce that we give him a hundred thousand lire a month.'[48]

Aimone's affair with Olga Pignatari was one of long-standing; it began within a few months of his marriage to Irene and lasted until they lost contact during the war.[49] Irene herself was not naive about these things and is said to have commented: 'I am not worried about his lovers, real or imagined, rather I am jealous of the Navy.'[50]

Amedeo fell ill with malaria on 28 December, and a month later was still recovering at Nairobi General Hospital, until the authorities transferred him to the Maya Carbery Nursing Home in Nairobi at the beginning of February. The malaria brought on an acute attack of the tuberculosis from which he had been suffering for over twenty years, and his condition deteriorated quickly.

Despite being a strapping young man, Amedeo had suffered through a long series of serious illnesses, which was detailed by the British Director of Medical Services as follows:

1919–20: Bilateral apical pulmonary T. B. Treated in Sanatoria and followed by long holiday.

1920: Amoebic dysentery.

1922: Severe S. T. malaria and blackwater fever.

1932: Amoebic hepatitis and abscess.

1933: Left pleural effusion.

1935: Acute mastoiditis followed by radical mastoid operation.

1937: Ruptured acute appendix with peritonitis. Was ill in bed for seven weeks with pyrexia and cough. Initially a post operative basal congestion but sputum became positive for B. Tuberculosis later.

1939: Influenza. sputum again showed B. Tuberculosis but dried up rapidly.

Dec. 1941: Tick typhus. Has had several attacks of malaria apart from illnesses shown.

29.1.42: Patient was admitted to this hospital on the 4th day of his illness. He had had smears taken prior to admission, and a scanty infection of P. falciparum demonstrated. He had received Quinine grV Q. I. D.[51]

The British War Cabinet met at Downing Street in the early evening of 19 February 1942, with Winston Churchill chairing the meeting. Anthony Eden, as Secretary of State for Foreign Affairs, reported a telegram from the Minister of State stating that the Duke of Aosta was suffering from acute tuberculosis and recommending an offer of repatriation. Under the Prisoners of War Convention, prisoners who were seriously ill could be repatriated and, indeed, negotiations with the Italian government were proceeding along those lines. However, no prisoners had yet been exchanged, and so the Cabinet decided that repatriating Amedeo at once would show 'undue discrimination in his favour on account of his position', but should only be done as part of some general arrangement concerning other prisoners. However, they also recognized the potential propaganda value for the Italians if he died as a prisoner without any previous indication of his illness, and so arranged for a 'suitable announcement.'[52] A follow-up memo from the War Office recommended that, if army medical advisers could certify that he was fit for the journey and if he were able to agree in writing to the risks of the journey, he could be transferred to Cairo for treatment there.[53]

At 2 p.m. on 1 March, Giuglio Verin, Administrator of Amedeo's household, was called to his bedside to record his last will. Amedeo's first concern was for the education of his daughters, which he entrusted to Anne according to general principles that they had 'agreed upon some time ago, hearing and taking into consideration the advice of my mother and, thereafter, also that of my brother.' From his government bonds, Amedeo left 300,000 lire 'To the Leader, for work in assistance of the Regime,' then 200,000 to the care of orphans of airmen, and then other monetary bequests to his staff, and then the balance to the orphans of those who had fallen in Italian East Africa. He left the balance of his estate to his legal heirs according to the usual pattern, except for his personal effects which were to 'be divided in an amicable manner between my mother, my wife and my brother, according to the well-known "1, 2, 3," method; with the exception of my diary, which I leave to my brother.'[54] That same day, Ciano recorded in his diary 'Very bad news on the duke of Aosta's state of health. He has miliary tuberculosis, and hence his fate is sealed. Mussolini is not interested, and even the royal house does not seem to be very much moved by it.'[55]

At 3.45 a.m. on 3 March at the Maya Carbery Nursing Home in Nairobi, POW 1190, Amedeo di Savoia, died, having received the last rites of the church.[56] The family learned the news through Reuters news broadcasts on the radio. In Florence, Irene heard the reports first, and telephoned the Pitti Palace, where Anne and her daughters were staying, asking the staff to cut the electricity, so that the family would not hear the news in the same way, and Irene would be able to inform them in person. Aimone received the news through the office of the Royal House, which likewise had learned through Radio Reuters. The next day, he went to Capodimonte to break the news to Hélène. As he recorded in his diary, 'I gave the tragic news to Mama. What torment, what pain, but what courage, what strength of spirit. May God give her the strength to endure this blow.'[57] In 1920, while visiting Amedeo who was suffering from an attack of amoebic dysentery in a hospital in Zanzibar, she had had a premonition of this happening and wrote about it movingly in *La Vie Errante*. Although written more than twenty years earlier, the words are hauntingly close to the reality of March 1942; the passage is quoted in chapter 11.

Rome learned about Amedeo's death on the same day, and Ciano wrote in his diary:

> The Duke of Aosta is dead. With him disappears a noble figure of a Prince and an Italian, simple in his ways, broad in his outlook, human in his spirit. He did not want this war. He was convinced that the empire could hold out for only a few months, and, besides, he hated the Germans. In this conflict, which drenches the world in blood, he feared a German more than an English victory. When he left for Ethiopia in May 1940, he had a premonition of his fate. He was determined to face it, but was filled with sadness. I communicated the information to the Duce, who expressed his regret laconically.

In the afternoon, Prince Otto von Bismarck, the German envoy to Rome, telephoned to say that his government was preparing to launch a campaign against the English Secret Service because of the duke's death. 'He added that he personally thought that the plan was in "bad taste." He is right. There is nothing to support this accusation; on the contrary, it's quite absurd. I brought this to the Duce's attention, and he expressed himself against it.'[58] When asked by the Propaganda Minister to announce that her son died through privations inflicted upon him by the British, Hélène refused. 'I detest untruthfulness,' she replied. 'My son was well looked after, and I am grateful to the British for their consideration.'[59]

The next day, Ciano wrote that 'the death of the Duke of Aosta made a great impression on the country. There was sincere sorrow shared by all. A young working-class boy, whose brother is a prisoner, said to me, "Today my mother cried. All the mothers of prisoners are weeping today."'[60]

The family gathered around Hélène at Capodimonte—Aimone arrived at 3.30 a.m., Anne came from Florence in the afternoon, and shortly after that, the King and the Prince of Piedmont arrived by car from Rome. The whole city mourned Amedeo as a son of Naples; flags were at half-mast everywhere.

Amedeo's funeral took place in Kenya on the 7th with military honours. The senior Roman Catholic chaplain to the forces officiated at a Requiem Mass at the Church of the Holy Family in Nairobi, with Amedeo's personal chaplain, Father Boratte assisting. The Bishop of Zanzibar gave the absolution. The pallbearers included General Guglielmo Nasi, General Scala Martini, and General Sabatini, who served under Amedeo in the East African command, as well as General Doadiace, former Vice-Governor of Ethiopia, and the 'Blackshirt General' Torre. General Cesare Nam, who had served as Emanuele Filiberto's *aide-de-camp* and Amedeo's personal physician, Dr Edoardo Borra, were also present. At the grave-side service in the military cemetery at Nyeri, General Nasi gave the 'Call to the Dead', to which all the Italians responded. Lieutenant-General Sir William Platt (to whom Amedeo had surrendered) and General Nasi stood side by side at the head of the grave and saluted.

In Rome, a requiem mass was held for Amedeo at the Church of Sudario in the morning of 11 March, and Ciano reported in his diary that only members of the Royal Court were invited, including of course members of the Order of the Annunziata who were officially 'cousins of the King.' The Royal Family itself was seated in a pew hidden from the view of the others. When the ceremony has just begun, a 'bent and aged' woman in mourning entered, took the first seat she could find, and wept throughout the service; it was the Duce's wife Rachele, and when Ciano later told Mussolini, the Duce was very much surprised as he did not think his wife would go to an intimate ceremony of the royal house. 'But,' as Ciano confided to his diary, 'that old woman who was weeping in the Church of the Sudario today was not the wife of a great leader. She was simply the mother of a twenty-year-old lieutenant killed in his airplane.'[61] Bruno Mussolini had died in an air crash in August 1941.

The Duchess of Sermoneta recalled that another memorial service for Amedeo was held the next day at the Church of Santa Maria degli Angeli, this time by order of Mussolini. It was to be a purely military ceremony with only men present, but as the Queen was going to attend, her ladies-in-waiting (including the duchess) would also be there. She recorded that the King and Queen sat on one side of the altar with the court behind them while Mussolini sat opposite, 'so that I was able to watch him carefully throughout the long service. He looked much older, and his expression was more ferocious than ever. His whole head was shaved, in a futile attempt to disguise the fact that he was quite bald...This was the last time I saw him.'[62]

The widowed Duchess Anne wrote to Amedeo's *aide-de-camp* Captain Aldo Tait:

> If you and the others go to his tomb, think of me, pray and place, if you can, some flowers for me and the little ones. God bless you who loved him, admired him, for what you were to him, for what you did for him. My deeply grateful heart will never forget it. To all of you, I think of you, and I say to you with much affection—courage. I offer my pain to God.[63]

Later the same month, on the 19 March, Aimone saw his wife off from the Santa Maria Novella station in Florence, as she headed a Red Cross hospital train going to Russia to repatriate wounded Italian soldiers. At Lvov, Irene confronted the blatant anti-Semitism of Nazism for the first time through a sign in a park which starkly stated: 'Entry forbidden to dogs and Jews'; that level of racism had not yet seeped into Italy. There were trains of dirty, wounded, and demoralized Romanian troops, and German wounded picking at insects. When they reached Dniepropetrowsk, they stopped at the hospital where Red Cross sisters were working in near-impossible circumstances—the old building, formerly a school, was 'gray, sad and in poor condition', with missing windowpanes replaced by paper, toilets in a terrible state. The sisters and patients had a great party, delighted that a princess had come to repatriate them. The frozen wastes looked like a white sea, according to Irene's lady-in-waiting, Mathilde de Bellegarde. However, the worst of the cold had already passed, such as days when the Capuchin priest told of the Communion wine freezing and having to break it with his teeth in order to swallow it. 'This was war, very different from the mythology of the propaganda machine.' The train finally arrived back in Florence on 30 April and was met by Aimone and Princess Marie José. However, the privations of the trip proved too much for Irene, and she miscarried the child she was expecting.[64]

Later in the summer of 1942, in August, Prince George (the Duke of Kent, brother to the King of Great Britain, and son of Queen Mary) was killed on active service in a flying accident while he was going to inspect troops in Iceland.

Hélène wrote to Queen Mary through an intermediary; she wrote simply as one grieving mother to another: 'Your good friendship has always been dear to me from distant youth up to current events—the expression of my affectionate sympathy and deepest condolences at this painful event which wounds the heart of a mother.'[65] Hélène wrote this short note in Italian, rather than English which she normally used with the British royal family. Perhaps, this was a symbol of her strident nationalism, perhaps simply a recollection of that mutual 'distant youth', knowing that Queen Mary had spent some of that time living in Florence.

In December, an unexpected connection with Great Britain was being sought by Aimone. Through the Italian Consul General at Geneva, he attempted to establish a channel of communication with the British government to discuss the possibility of leading 'an armed uprising against Mussolini and the Fascist regime', a plan that he said he had discussed with the Prince of Piedmont. Aimone admitted from the first that he could only rely on support from the Italian Navy and perhaps some of the Bersaglieri, but not the Army and definitely not the Air Force. Nonetheless, he set out five requirements for moving ahead: RAF support to deal with the German and Italian air forces; an agreed landing by British and American troops to assist in the overthrow, but not to treat Italy as a conquered country; the Italian fleet should not be handed over to the Allies; the monarchy should be preserved; and these guarantees be given in the name of all the Allied countries. The thoughts were forwarded along to the U. S. Secretary of State, but the British government felt that King Victor Emmanuel was already completely discredited as a leader and London remained 'extremely doubtful of the willingness or ability of any of the royal family to lead a revolt against Fascism.' Like most of Aimone's plans, these came to naught.[66]

La Stampa Sera reported that Hélène was back in the Vatican at the end of January 1943 for a 'long and friendly conversation' with Pope Pius in his private library, although the subject of that conversation is not known. By the springtime, Irene was once again expecting a child; Hélène, along with Irene's sister Helen of Romania, and Marie José individually made brief visits to her in Florence, although the air raids warning sirens were increasing in frequency there.[67]

16

1943–1945

The War killed my soul [again][1]

The Allied invasion of Sicily began on 10 July, and on the 19th, Rome was bombed for the first time with its rail stations and outlying airfields as the principal targets. That same day, Mussolini met with Hitler at Feltre in the Veneto. Hitler spoke for two hours about the inadequacy of Italian defenses, particularly of its airfields. Mussolini was supposed to put forth the case that Italy was no longer in a position to continue the war but instead he remained virtually speechless. As a result, 'his failure to put Italy's case convinced even the more extreme fascists that he was a broken man, resourceless, perhaps inwardly reconciled to defeat.' On the night of the 24–25th, the Grand Fascist Council met with Mussolini for the first time since the war, and this meeting would prove to be its last. Under the leadership of Dino Grandi, the council argued and debated Mussolini's role, and by 3 a.m., a majority—including Count Ciano—voted to restore military command to the king.[2]

That afternoon, Mussolini went for his regular meeting with the King, who now told him that he had become 'the most hated man in Italy', and therefore Marshal Badoglio must take over as head of government.[3] After years of dithering and acquiescing to Mussolini's constant centralisation of power in his own person, King Victor Emmanuel finally acted. The initiative for the action came indirectly from several fronts—particularly through Princess Marie José working through Duca Pietro d'Acquarone, minister of the Royal Household, and from the Vatican, which was in direct communication with Washington about the future of Italy. Mussolini was placed under arrest, and Italian national radio broadcast the news that night at 10.48 p.m. 'Seldom in the history of any country has the news of a politician's fall been immediately greeted with more overwhelming scenes of public delight, and some people were bound to see this as proof that the king should have acted earlier, perhaps much earlier,' as Mack Smith has commented on the Duce's downfall, 'but a vast majority in the country was overjoyed to think, overoptimistically, that the collapse of dictatorship meant the war was over.' Many, including Badoglio, felt that the king should also abdicate at this time and pass the throne to his son who was less tainted by years of association with fascism. However, Victor Emmanuel refused to consider this.[4]

Instead, the war not only continued but increased in ferocity for the Italian people. Naples had been a major target for Allied bombing raids since the beginning of the war, and that now escalated. In June 1940, French planes had bombed the city four times, but between November 1940 and September 1943, some 111 bombings raids by British and American planes took place.[5] Many of the city's landmarks were also hit, including the historic church of Santa Chiara which suffered a direct hit on 1 August 1943. This place was the burial site for the early Angevin monarchs, and more recently for the Bourbon-Sicily line, Hélène's own ancestors, including the parents of Queen Marie Amélie. In 1922, Hélène had requested the restoration of the Bourbon royal crypt with thirty-seven members of the family there. The church was badly damaged by fire after the bombing, and the Poor Clare nuns gathered together the remains of the royal family and placed them in wooden coffins, which were transferred in 1944 to the Church of San Francisco di Paola, where they remained until 1958, when they were returned to a refurbished chapel in Santa Chiara.

Two days later, heavy bombing raids left over a thousand dead and wounded. Although she already had a fever herself, Hélène went out to visit the victims at the Little Cottolengo and Pellegrini. While passing through the lanes, there was another wave of bombers; by the time she got back to Capodimonte, she had developed breathing problems. Hélène herself recognized the seriousness of her situation and asked for and received the last rites of the Church. Her doctor, Prof. Aldo Castellani, ordered emergency hospitalization in a clinic in Rome, where double pneumonia was diagnosed. Her condition gave rise to enough rumours that *La Stampa* asked her permission to publish the facts for all those who had 'particular affection and devotion' for the Princess. However, because of the condition of the Post Office and telegrams being directed to the armed forces, it was recommended that letters and telegrams requesting further news on the Duchess should not be made. Hélène remained at the Clinica Quisisana in Rome for three weeks, until 2 September with Campini at her side.[6]

By the end of the month, the city's principal water main had been hit and Naples was without water.[7] In the heat of the summer, the city reeked of sewerage and garbage. The glass-vaulted ceilings of the Galleria Umberto were shattered and lay on the floor in shards, yet just across the Via San Carlo, the opera house was barely touched and, after some minor repair, would be re-opened within three weeks following the liberation.

The Allied invasion of Italy progressed, and Marshal Badoglio signed an unconditional but secret armistice with the Allies on 3 September, which was not publicly announced until the 8th, when the invasion at Salerno was scheduled. The Italian fleet, including the cruiser *Emanuele Filiberto Duke of Aosta*, surrendered. Aimone was at La Spezia when he heard the news over the radio for the first time. Although ordered to Rome, he soon joined the King who with his immediate family and the government fled Rome for Brindisi in southern Italy, in the early morning hours of the 9th.[8] Meanwhile, Mussolini was freed on the 12th by a combined force of paratroopers and a Nazi S. S. Commando Unit, as Germany took control over most of Italy, setting up a puppet regime known as the Salò Republic.

Hélène remained in Naples, while Anne and her two daughters—Margherita, now thirteen, and Maria Cristina, ten—were at the Pitti Palace in Florence, and Irene stayed at the Villa Cisterna in nearby Fiesole. Irene's lady-in-waiting, Countess Matilde de Bellegarde recorded in her diary:

> At 8 p.m. Badoglio's proclamation was transmitted on the radio: 'Before the overwhelming strength of the enemy, Italy has asked for an armistice.' I was dining with Her Royal Highness, immediately we heard cheers and hurrahs coming from the city ... in all the hills around people lit up fireworks with joy ...These poor people that rejoice so much, do not understand anything really? ...What will become of our Duke? I tried to call and call La Spezia to learn something of him but no answer.

Aimone had, by this time, been able to flee La Spezia and was among those heading south. Irene phoned her sister, Queen Helen, when she heard the news of the capitulation on the radio. It was to be the last time that they would speak in three years.[9]

The reaction of Germany to Italy's desertion of the Axis was swift and harsh. Italian soldiers were disarmed and sent to Germany as workers, while those who had been serving alongside German troops in Greece were now summarily executed. They also ordered the arrest and deportation of the royal family, and during the next few weeks, the Germans began to take their revenge on the Savoys. The King's youngest daughter Maria, her husband Prince Louis of Bourbon-Parma, and their children were arrested by the Nazis on the 14th and sequestered at Oldenburg for the duration of the war. Princess Giovanna's husband, King Boris of Bulgaria, died suddenly and under mysterious circumstances on 28 August after a trip to Berlin; there is a strong supposition that he was assassinated by the Nazis, worried that he too would capitulate to the Allies. A week after Princess Maria's arrest, her sister Mafalda returned to Rome from the funeral services for King Boris, and she took refuge in the Vatican, where she entrusted her children to the care of Cardinal Montini—later Pope Paul VI. Mafalda herself left the security of the Holy See, thinking that she was to meet her husband at the German embassy, but instead, she was arrested the next day and was sent to Buchenwald on 20 October.[10]

Having left Rome so quickly, the Royal Family in Brindisi lacked many of its possessions, including essential clothing. As Queen Elena was in deep mourning for her son-in-law Boris, there was particular concern about getting a black dress made for her. Unexpectedly, a large box arrived from Capodimonte. Hélène had taken a large selection of clothing and coats from her own wardrobe to help. As the Queen was about the same height and size, this was a particular help at a time of particular need.[11]

Meanwhile, Irene, aged thirty-nine, was heavily pregnant and suffered because of the frequent bombing raids. Then, on 25 September, 'Thirty-five American (or English) planes passed north of the town, towards the west' as Irene's lady-in-waiting Countess de Bellegarde recorded in her diary:

> Then they came back and came straight towards us, ducking, flying over the villa, and we heard the thundering noise of the bombs. Gigi, Her Royal Highness's steward, shouted, 'Down!' A useless warning for the Princess in her state. Whilst we tried to get down to the shelter the bombs exploded in Via Bolognese: everything shook as in an earthquake. Her Highness, who was extremely calm as always in such situations, comforted a child in tears close to her. After the bombing she retired to her room where she was taken ill. She asked me to call the doctor, Lapiccirella, but the phone line was always busy... We tried to contact Rome. Impossible—long distance communications do not work anymore. I rang the Duchess Anna up in the Pitti Palace to warn her that the Princess had a prelabour rupture of her waters and she told me that she would come immediately. I thought of calling Doctor Bacialli in Bologna. I tried to call but it was impossible.

The baby was born eighteen days prematurely on 27 September, and because of his weak state, was given an emergency baptism. He was given the grand name of Amedeo Umberto Constantino Giorgio Paolo Elena Maria Florenzio, covering both the Italian and Greek families. Many reference sources add the name Zvonimir at the end of the list of names; although this was intended to be included as a complement to his father's regnal name of Tomislav in Croatia, it was never actually part of his registered name. A day or two later, the Royal Chaplain arrived to formally administer the sacrament of baptism, but before the water was applied or the blessing given, another air raid commenced and the chaplain unceremoniously leapt out of the room. It was not until little Amedeo was six years old and could hold his own candle and make his own baptismal promises that he would finally be officially baptised.[12]

In Naples, occupied by the Wermacht since the capitulation, the Germans went on a spree of destruction. Instructions not to leave anything that might of use to the approaching Anglo-American forces were far exceeded as the Germans began to destroy the city's cultural heritage as well. On 26 September, they dowsed the shelves of the university library in kerosene and set it on fire. Those fifty-thou-sand volumes were still burning two days later when other troops discovered some eighty-thousand books and manuscripts at Nola, which had been gathered together for safety from archives across southern Italy. Those too were consigned to the flames, as were the contents of the Civic Museum.[13]

As the Allies drew nearer following the landings at Salerno, spontaneous anti-German uprisings broke out in Naples—*Le Quattro giornate napoletane*—The Four Neapolitan Days (27–30 September). The breaking point came when col-umns of young men from the city were rounded up, with some still in their pyjamas, having been yanked out of bed and away from their families; they were marched in the pouring rain through the streets and up to the woods of the Royal Park at Capodimonte, to be boarded onto black trucks destined for the labour camps of Germany. The German garrison had withdrawn and retrenched to the forests of Capodimonte; from there, they would bombard the city over the coming days. Despite warnings that for every German soldier killed or wounded, the citizens of Naples would pay this back a hundred times, guerrilla-style fight-ing rampaged throughout the city. Barricades were erected in the streets, and an estimated two-thousand citizens took up arms and captured German rifles, pistols and machineguns and submachineguns, along with bottles filled with ben-zine to use as bombs. By the end of the street fighting, official figures put the Neapolitan partisan casualties at 178 men and women dead, 162 wounded, seven-ty-five maimed or rendered invalid, and nineteen missing.[14]

It was probably around this time that a German soldier was shot on the road to Capodimonte by a sniper in the park. A German patrol rounded up all Hélène's staff against the wall of the palace, and finally Hélène and Campini too, with the intention of shooting everybody. Hélène stepped forward and said to the Wehrmacht officer 'I am the only one responsible for this household, so you can shoot me. And that's all.' The officer called off the execution.[15]

On the morning of 1 October, a solitary bicyclist rode across the streets of the city announcing the arrival of the Allies. As the culmination of all this vio-lence from all sides, when the British troops arrived, followed immediately by the Americans, they found Naples a ruin, while Vesuvius smouldered on the skyline. The city was a shambles. Rubble filled the streets, and dead bodies lay on the pavement. Almost half of the population had fled the city. A hundred barrage balloons hung over the port to protect it from low-flying airplanes, while some two-hundred ships lay wrecked in the harbour, including the remains of the munitions ship, the *Caterina Costa*, which had exploded in May. Both typhoid and cholera broke out, and many suffered from increasing starvation. The sewerage system had been destroyed by the Germans, and water was in short supply. By the end of September, electricity was cut off.[16]

Gen. Mark Clark of the US Fifth Army knew that it was an important victory, as the first major continental city to be wrested from the Axis, but acknowledged that 'it was a hard-won victory, but there was little that was triumphant about our journey.' A German air raid had taken place shortly before their arrival and the harbour was badly hit. 'The port area could be described only as a mess. There was utter destruction of ships, docks, and warehouses, such as not even ancient Pompeii, through which we had passed earlier in the day, had ever seen.' Indeed, as another witness described it:

> The Germans had blown up the sewage and water systems, and left booby traps and delayed-action mines. There was typhus in the overcrowded back streets, and black marketing was rampant. It was reckoned that forty per cent of the women had taken to prostitution. As you drove into the city there were placards warning Allied troops that this was a particularly dangerous area for venereal disease.[17]

Norman Lewis, a Welsh writer who had married into the Sicilian noble family of Corvaja and was serving as a British intelligence officer, left some of the most graphic descriptions of wretched, ravaged Naples. The city smelled 'of charred wood, with ruins everywhere, sometimes completely blocking the streets, bomb craters and abandoned trams. The main problem is water. Two tremendous air-raids on August 4 and September 6 smashed up all the services, and there has been no proper water supply since the first of these.' On top of the damage previously inflicted by Allied bombing, 'German demolition squads have gone round blowing up anything of value to the city that still worked.'[18]

On the first Sunday, British and American troops joined together for a service of thanksgiving in the cathedral, but immediately after the service, the first German time-bomb exploded in the artillery barracks occupied by the Engineer Battalion of the 82nd Airborne division in the heart of the city. It was to be the first of a number of similar incidents during the coming weeks, including when, on the 7th, the central post office was destroyed by a German bomb, with more than a hundred killed. On 10 October, Lewis wrote about complaints that Allied troops were looting in the city, and that officers were more effective in that than the other ranks.

> The charge has been made that officers of the King's Dragoon Guards, to whom fell the honour of being the first British unit to enter Naples, have cut the paintings from the frames in the Princess's Palace, and made off with the collection of Capodimonte china. The OSS have cleaned out Achille Lauro's sumptuous house. Some of the bulkier items of booty are stated to have been crated up for return to England with the connivance of the Navy.[19]

The same day, a detachment from the American Army's 307th Combat Engineers (Airborne Division) was sent to Capodimonte to check the palace and grounds for any booby traps or other explosive devices to ready it as headquarters for General Clark and the US 5th Army. They explored the palace, its cellars, the tunnel leading into the bay, and the outbuildings. The last building inspected was a carriage shed. The Germans had used its roof for artillery spotting, and the gun emplacements of the 88's were clearly visible on the lawn. While standing there, another explosion shook the city, and the unit quickly went off to explore that. While at Capodimonte, Clark stayed in the apartment of the Duchess Anne.[20]

At the university, it was reported that Allied soldiers 'ransacked the laboratories, hopelessly mixing up collections of shells and stones which had taken decades to assemble.' Soon, troops 'were to be seen driving about the city in jeeps decorated with hundreds of fabulously colored stuffed toucans, parrots, eagles, and even ostriches from the zoological collection.' A combination of British, French, and American personnel were billeted in Capodimonte and at the Royal Palace, 'where, with the delighted help of Neapolitan ladies of the night, they stripped brocades from the walls, presumably to be converted into garments of one kind or another.' The National Museum became a hospital-supply warehouse.[21]

Later in the month, Lewis wrote graphically about 'the struggles of this city so shattered, so starved, so deprived of all those things that justify a city's existence, to adapt itself to a collapse into conditions which must resemble life in the Dark Ages.' Throughout Naples, 'people camp out like Bedouins in deserts of brick. There is little food, little water, no salt, no soap.' As so many Neapolitans had lost everything in the bombings, including most of their clothes, Lewis reported 'some strange combinations of garments about the streets, including a man in an old dinner-jacket, knickerbockers and army boots, and several women in lacy confections that might have been made up from curtains.' As for traffic, there were 'no cars but carts by the hundred, and a few antique coaches such as barouches and phaetons drawn by lean horses.' A lack of food led to a desperation that emptied even the local aquarium of its tropical fish. There was a story that General Clark himself was served a delicacy from there—manitee with garlic sauce. The level of prostitution in Naples was said to be the worst in the country, with the result that more hospital beds in the city were occupied by those suffering from syphilis than from wounds and all other sicknesses put together.[22] There was a thriving trade in black market goods, most often stolen Allied Army supplies; they were the mainstay of the local economy.

Mortimer Wheeler, an archaeologist by training and sometime keeper of the London Museum but now a brigadier in the British Army, drove up to Capodimonte on his first day in Naples, expecting to mark it out as his brigade headquarters. As he entered the grounds, he remarked:

The old Dowager Duchess of Aosta, erect as a guardsman and lightly supported by a tall ivory-topped stick, was walking back across the lawn in the rain. She had been to the burial of five neighbouring townsfolk, for whom my advance party had just dug graves a hundred yards away, and as we entered the palace together she told me the story, to the following effect.

The Hermann Goering armoured division, she said, had been there the previous day and, shortly before it pulled out, two of its Panzer Grenadiers had been shot—their new graves were likewise on the lawn. They had probably been picked off by American snipers at the head of our advance, but the German commander accused the Italian populace, sent a squad to the nearest house by the palace gates, pulled out the first five civilians, lined them up on the lawn and shot them, leaving them for us to bury. He then said that he would show those … Italians what his tanks could do. He brought a tank up to the front of the palace (the tracks were still there) and fired a round at the palace itself. It made, however, almost no impression on the thick walls, so he swung his gun round and blew the inside out of the house from which the unhappy hostages had been collected. He then moved out—and we moved in.

The old duchess was utterly charming and bravely sad. Had I seen her younger son, the admiral? He had been in command of the little ships of the Italian fleet and had written to her two or three weeks earlier to ask her whether she thought that he ought to surrender or right on. 'I am only a woman', she had replied, 'and I know nothing of these matters. You must write to the King and ask him.' Since then, she had heard nothing. Had he surrendered? Where was he? I could not tell her, but ten days later her son himself answered her questions by walking into the palace. He and his fleet had participated in that disciplined and dignified surrender at Malta of which the rearmost units of my brigade had been admiring witnesses en route for Salerno.

The duchess took me round her palace, showed me her excellent French tapestries, her indifferent pictures (the best, including the Goyas, had gone), and her great armoury of muskets, of which she was particularly proud, though the Germans had abstracted the choicest—together with her own treasured rifles, for she had been a great game-shooter in her day. Her rooms were full of the dismembered heads of her victims, and she knew the saga of each one of them.[23]

Then, on 21 October, the bombings began again. This time it was the Germans bombing Naples. There were long raids, but they were 'stoutly met by the Anglo-American defences,' so the general damage was slight despite some casualties.[24] However, Allied efforts began to restore services although food supplies remained critically low for the rest of the year. Immediately after the liberation, one witness felt that there was a complete 'moral collapse' of the people due to the lack of food and their willingness to do or sell anything toward relieving their hunger. 'Six-year-old boys were pressed into the business of selling obscene postcards; of selling their sisters, themselves, anything.' Health concerns included the rampart incidents of venereal disease, which could be somewhat eased through the recent development of penicillin. Another newly developed aid was DDT; hundreds of thousands of Neapolitans were sprayed with the white power to kill the lice which caused skin typhus, and for months people wandered around the city looking as if they had been dipped in flour.[25]

British diplomats were already looking toward the future and their 'desire to see a more liberal and broad-based Italian government.' Harold Macmillan, then serving with Cabinet authority as a roving minister with a remit for the Mediterranean, wrote that while some refused to serve in a government under Badoglio, others refused to serve under the king, and others demanded a civilian prime minister or even a republic—or 'at least an abdication by the King, a renunciation of his rights by the prince of Piedmont, and a succession by the young Prince of Naples (six or eight years old and in Switzerland) with a regency.' However, a further complication was 'that under the Italian constitution the Regent ought to be the next-of-kin. This means the new Duca d'Aosta, who is regarded as quite impossible.' Count Sforza was seen to be 'running an intrigue to force the abdication of the King, to get Badoglio to act as Regent (in spite of the strict law) and to become Prime Minister himself.' On the other hand, General Badoglio was seen as 'too loyal, as a soldier, to the person of the King to take the lead in such a scheme', although Macmillan surmised that 'he might accept it if somebody else produced the crisis, and I am not sure how far he is working a *combinazione* with Sforza with this in view.'[26]

While these various plans were being considered, Allied bombings continued to move up the country. On 1 November 1943, Ancona on the Adriatic was hit by bombers—three groups of about twenty-four each—targeting the port district which virtually disappeared within a few minutes and with thousands of casualties, including some three hundred within one makeshift shelter. The next day, Rome Radio declared Ancona 'completely dead—a cemetery of smoking ruins.'[27]

In early December, an adjutant to the German commandant announced that he was going to requisition Villa Sparta, the Florentine home of Queen Mother Helen of Romania, as accommodation for his general and staff. As Romania was still part of the Axis, that was not possible without an invitation. As Helen was absent from Florence, the young adjutant approached Irene, who lived in the neighbouring Villa della Cisterna, to convince her to allow them to occupy the villa. She simply referred the officer to the Romanian Embassy in Rome.

Gerhard Wolf, the German consul at Florence, had been helpful throughout the difficulties, and within a few days, his services were called upon again. This time it was because Irene had been approached by Professor Karl Gebhard, a well-known orthopaedist who was also a lieutenant-general in the S.S. and a close associate of Himmler. He told Irene that the German government had 'little satisfaction' with the post-Mussolini government, and then expressed his regrets at Aimone's absence—'otherwise, instead of liberating Mussolini, reliance could have been placed on *apparently* trustworthy members of the Royal family'—even though Roberto Farinacci, a former fascist party secretary, had dismissed Aimone as a 'frondeur [political rebel] sick with ambition.' Irene made no response, but Gebhard continued on, saying that the Germans felt the most able Italian general was Count Carlo Calvi di Bergolo, the King's son-in-law, 'whom the present government apparently seeks to assassinate, but who is under S.S. protection.' That is, under arrest. Calvi di Bergolo, who had been nominated as the commander of the 'Open City' of Rome on 8 September 1943, had been arrested there on the 23rd of that month along with his officers and deported to Germany, where he remained until liberated by the Allies in June 1944. Gebhard offered to place Irene and her son under similar 'protection' as he told her that Mussolini's government was preparing to arrest all members of the royal family. The next day, he returned with General Wilhelm Harster, the head of the Gestapo in Italy, who wanted to know her plans in the event of an Allied move into Florence. She responded that she would go to Stresa, but Harster objected and instead offered to place a plane at her disposal to take her to Germany. However, Irene insisted that she had become an Italian by marriage and wished to remain in Florence 'under all circumstances' or if all else failed, to go to a family estate at Sartirana Lomellina in the province of Pavia, which had been bequeathed to Duke Amedeo in 1934 upon the death of Margherita di Gattinara.[28]

Bernard Berenson, the American art historian who lived in nearby Settignano, summarised the situation in his diary on 25 February 1944:

> It seems that the Nazi authorities have ordered the present Duchess of Aosta to quit Florence and to go where she wished, provided it was safe from the Allied occupation. She protested that she did not want to leave. They have allowed her to remain for the present, warning her, however, that at the next summons she might have no more than one hour to get ready in. Why? The only explanation that occurs to me—the explanation offers by the person who reported this piece of news—is that the Nazis want to keep firm hold on the baby the Duchess had some months ago. Consequently, in case of victory they would not countenance the resurrected regime of Mussolini and his republic, but restore the monarchy in the person of this infant of the Aosta branch. They could then rule Italy through men of straw who acted as regents. In that case the dowager Duchess of Aosta—author, I believe, of many of our woes—would at last be able to sing *Nunc Dimittis*. She would have seen the ambitions of a lifetime, the plotting of many decades, brought safe to port and crowned with success.[29]

Meanwhile, the surviving Fascists were cannibalising themselves. In particular, Count Ciano—the former darling of his father-in-law Mussolini—had been arrested in October; on 11 January 1944, he was executed with four other Fascist chiefs for betraying Mussolini, who did not raise a hand to save him.

In Naples, German bombings continued, and on 19 March nature added its voice when Vesuvius erupted. Norman Lewis described the day:

> It was the most majestic and terrible sight I have ever seen, or ever expect to see. The smoke from the crater slowly built up into a great bulging shape having

all the appearance of solidity. It swelled and expanded so slowly that there was no sign of movement in the cloud which, by evening, must have risen thirty or forty thousand feet into the sky, and measured many miles across ... At night the lava streams began to trickle down the mountain's slopes. By day the spectacle was calm but now the eruption showed a terrible vivacity. Fiery symbols were scrawled across the water of the bay, and periodically the crater discharged mines of serpents into a sky which was the deepest of blood reds and pulsating everywhere with lightning reflections.[30]

Over the next few days, the eruptions grew more violent, rivers of lava flowed and grey ash settled everywhere, but eventually, the tremors abated. The villages of San Sebastiano al Vesuvio, Massa di Somma, Ottaviano, and part of San Giorgio a Cremano were destroyed, as were a number of American aircraft stationed at Pompeii Airfield near the base of the volcano. Still, the loss and damage was not as bad as it had been in 1906.

In May 1944, there was another British visitor to Capodimonte—Edward Croft-Murray, formerly curator of prints and drawings at the British Museum, but now of the Allied Military Government's Subcommission for Monuments, Fine Arts, and Archives. His purpose was to check the condition of the museum collection. Most of the paintings, including the great Titians from Capodimonte, plus the best examples from the Roman jewellery collection and Pompeian bronzes from the National Archaeological Museum in Naples, had been moved to Monte Cassino in September, 1943, just days before the capitulation when the abbey fell to the Germans. Fortuitously, before that building was bombed into oblivion by the Allies, much of the art was secretly moved to the vaults of the Vatican where the hoard was still being safely kept. However, some fifteen cases of art were found to be missing from the Vatican consignment and were said to have been taken north as part of an intended birthday present for Hermann Göring.

Back at Capodimonte, Croft-Murray wandered through rooms of ancient armour and weaponry, much of it covered in surface rust as the windows had been blown out and the resultant damp had done its job. Croft-Murray wrote to a friend that 'we have protested very strongly about this, but unfortunately I rather gather that the old duchess of Aosta, who lives there, has been one of the difficulties as she bullied the Italian authorities into letting her have the prior claim of having her own windows put in before the Museum could be dealt with.'[31]

As part of an agreement with the Allies to keep the monarchy in place—at least until the Italian people could decide their own government—King Victor Emmanuel agreed that upon the liberation of Rome, he would essentially retire and appoint Umberto as regent with the title of *Luogotenente* (Lieutenant General) of the Kingdom. The Allies entered Rome on 4 June. The next day, Umberto was sworn in as Lieutenant General, and on the 8th, he flew to Rome, where he was given a warm welcome as a symbol of liberation and the return to normality.[32]

However, the Germans still held half the country, and they now continued their scorched earth policy of destruction in their retreat northward. Eight days after the Allied liberation of Rome, the duchesses and their children, accompanied by Admiral Angelo Longanesi Cattani, fled to Pavia province under heavy bombardment. Originally the S. S. planned to take Irene and the baby to Germany as hostages, but through Anne's intervention, the family was allowed to remain together and move north. Under German military escort, they left the Villa Cisterna together at 5 a.m. on the morning of 13 June aboard Irene's eight-cylinder Lancia Astura, carrying the diadem that Irene had worn at her wedding with them for security. Their group included Irene's lady-in-waiting, Countess Bellegarde, and little Amedeo's nurse. During the trip, the party was subjected to air attacks several times, and the women had then to take the baby and the two girls to the shelter of nearby farms or sheds until the danger was over. They stayed on the family estate at Sartirana Lomellina under reasonable conditions for some weeks, and hoped that they might be allowed to remain there, but that was not to be.[33]

On 7 July 1944, Aimone was received by Pope Pius XII in a private audience which lasted for forty minutes, followed by a forty-five minute conference with Cardinal Maglione, the Papal Secretary of State. The *New York Times* reported that normally there would not be a story on such an event, but 'these are not normal times and Roman political circles are buzzing with comments.' One of the issues was that even though 'he has never dared go to Zagreb to be crowned and indeed has no interest in his supposed throne,' Aimone had never renounced his supposed throne and the latest *Almanach de Gotha* still listed him as King in Croatia. 'Nevertheless, it is considered significant that he keeps the title for the House of Savoy just as Victor Emmanuel has such titles as the "King of Jerusalem." Royal houses never know when such things may come in handy.'[34]

On 26 July, while having lunch at Sartirana celebrating the Feast of Santa Anna, Anne, Irene, and the children were interrupted by two SS men in plain clothes asking to speak to Anne saying that they were all to leave in one hour's time. Anne asked to see a written warrant to that effect which they did not have thus gaining a few hours more. The baby, Amedeo, who was unwell, had to be wakened from his cot and prepared for travelling. The party—the two Duchesses, the two young princesses and the baby prince resting on a cushion on the knees of his nurse Countess Angelica Lodron—left the castle in a Lancia Astura driven by Comandante Angelo Longanesi-Cattani, who was responsible for their security. Four cars made up the motorcade, machine-guns projecting from the windows in case of an attempted rescue by Partisans. They were driven to the Hotel Regina in Milan—known as a waiting station for those destined for Nazi prisons or concentration camps—and waited in the car for about forty to sixty minutes. Then, they were driven to Innsbruck, where they were placed in a hotel adjoining the railway station—a frequent bombing target—and kept under close S. S. guard.

Fortunately, no bombing occurred while they were there, but the building collapsed shortly after they left. A couple of days later they were taken as 'diplomatic internees' to the Hotel Ifen in Hirschegg, Austrian Bavaria, about fifty miles from Lake Constance. Their place of interment was a mountain hotel, formerly a sports resorts and nearly 4,000 feet about sea-level. Here, as their companions, they found thirty-five other high-profile internees, Italians and Frenchmen, Belgians, Serbs, and others.[35]

From the first days, Anne renewed her acquaintance with a fellow internee André François-Poncet, the former French ambassador to Berlin, and through him met the larger French community at Hirschegg which included the dean of the Sorbonne, the president of the Bank of Algeria, and Albert Sarraut, a former prime minister. François-Poncet was enchanted and declared that Anne showed herself to be 'natural, very simple, nice, humane, very much a woman of the world.' The Italian detainees—who included Carmine Senise, former head of the Italian police; and Francesco Nitti, the former prime minister—proved less welcoming. In particular, Nitti's antagonism toward the Aosta family had not abated since their clash during the Fiume affair and now carried on to the next generation. At Hirschegg, he continued to make caustic and scornful remarks about the family and ignored their presence; they likewise ignored him. Senise, on the other hand, was much more gracious and in his memoirs of the time wrote that 'I would need a whole book to tell you of the acts of kindness and compassion performed by these Duchesses towards all people.' He then recounted a particular incident when he had been made to understand that he would stand trial before a special court which would most likely lead to execution. 'Duchess Anna then called me and spoke to me with such noble words I felt that I could face death in peace. I asked of her only that when she returned to Italy, to comfort those whom I had loved so much.' That same night, 'with great emotion, I found in my room a gold medallion of the Virgin of Pompeii and a sheet of paper on which was a prayer written in her own hand.'[36]

When they first arrived, the royal party had only a minimum of things with them; in particular, it was noted that Princess Margherita lacked shoes and stockings. Substitutes for the former were provided by Father Beda Feser, a Cistercian monk who was the local parish priest, who gave his own pair of shoes, while three pairs of white stockings were loaned by Ambassador François-Poncet. After they had been at Hirschegg about a fortnight, a large truck arrived carrying 'trunks, suitcases, boxes, bags of all sorts' which the German soldiers had filled 'pêle-mêle' at Satirana with the royal belongings. Bags of flour and jars of oil were brought along with clothes and smaller items, like the soaps, chocolates, and handkerchiefs which Duchess Anne distributed as gifts to her French compatriots.[37]

Accompanying the truck was Irene's faithful lady-in-waiting, Matilde de Bellegarde, as well as a maid. Life at Hirschegg was restrictive with movement limited to walks in the compound, and lack of heating in the winter proved difficult as did the quality of the food. Compared with the concentration camps where slave labour and extermination reigned, it was a privileged existence for the diplomatic internees, but an uncertain future and possible execution brought constant fear. Irene and her infant son remained a particular focus in case they were needed in the event of a regime change. According to a Swiss report quoted by Reuter, 'a new monarchist party has been founded in German-occupied Italy by Piero Narini, former Governor of Milan Province. This party does not support the Savoy–Carignano line, of which Victor Emmanuel is the head, but the Savoy–Aosta line.'[38]

One day, Irene was walking the baby in his carriage and chatting with Ambassador François-Poncet who recalled their mutual acquaintances among the House of Hohenzollern from his time in Berlin. Irene said that her mother detested her brother, the Kaiser, and in turn had been detested by him, while she was always very closely attached to her English mother, the Empress Frederick.[39] Therefore, it came as a surprise when Irene was called into the hotel office to take a phone call from her first cousin, the former Crown Prince of Germany, who was then living nearby. The commandant sat with his feet on the desk listening. 'Are you here for long?' Irene's cousin asked. 'For a while,' she responded. 'Are you here for the skiing?' 'I don't feel well enough to ski.' There was little more that she could say with the commandant listening. There was no further contact until Irene was released, and then a small pin with an 'F' for Friedrich was sent to her. Essentially, the Crown Prince was apologising by saying 'I didn't realize what was going on.'[40]

In the South Tyrol, Prince Philipp of Hesse—Mafalda's husband (and yet another of Irene's many first cousins)—was at a different prison for high-profile individuals. In April 1943 Philipp had been placed under house arrest at Berchtesgadener Hof, from where he was released twice to visit family in Italy, in June and July 1943. In September, he was taken to Flossenburg, where he remained until 15 April 1945, then to Dachau for ten days, and finally to Niederdorf in the South Tyrol until liberated by the American Army, on 4 May, but then incarcerated by the Allied forces.[41] Among the others in the camp was Prince Frederick Leopold of Prussia, the same German prince who had joined the Aostas at the opening of King Tutankamen's tomb in 1924. He had been arrested by the Nazis 'because he listened to the Allies' broadcasts,' and was first interned at Dachau, then moved to the Tyrol shortly before the US Army liberated Dachau, 30 April 1945. When finally liberated by the US Army on 7 May 1945, his fellow prisoners included Prince Xavier of Bourbon-Parma, Stalin's son Jacob, Austria's former chancellor Kurt Schuschnigg and his wife, France's former premier Léon Blum, and Hungary's former premier Nicholas von Kallay.

As Allied troops progressed further northward, Florence fell on 11 August, but the German army followed a course of destruction. With the exception of the Ponte Vecchio, all the bridges across the Arno were blown up, including

Michelangelo's classic Trinity Bridge. Irene's home in nearby Fiesole, the Villa Cisterna was also destroyed in the fighting following the liberation.[42]

Meanwhile, the day-to-day situation in Naples continued grim. Countess Ranfurly, who was working as a secretary to the Allied Forces, noted in her diary of one trip through the city:

> We drove slowly through the slums of Naples because the streets were so crowded with workers waiting for a hopelessly inadequate supply of trams. The poverty and squalor are heartbreaking. People live in garages and alleys and ghastly houses. The only bright things to be seen are the onions and red vegetables and little birds in cages that hang from the walls. Children, with bare bottoms and no shoes, play in the sickening filth of the streets, building, with their good imaginations, castles of manure. Men walk along bent nearly double under the bundles of faggots and vegetables they carry. Donkey carts creak by festooned with scarecrow human beings, their limbs and faces bony with undernourishment. Despite it all the people in these slums seem gay and kind. Here a smiling father leads his tiny grubby child across the cobbled street—there some women sit laughing in a doorway as they patiently delouse each other's heads.[43]

In March 1945, Aimone disgraced himself again, this time through poor judgement that cost him his position. It was during a dinner party he held aboard a cruiser in Taranto harbor that Aimone foolishly said he thought that all the high court judges who had recently been passing sentences on fascisti—especially at the trial of Gen. Mario Roatta, Fascist chief of staff, and Fulvio Suvich, Fascist Ambassador to the United States—should be shot. Unfortunately for him, the comments were heard by another guest, Sylvia Sprigge, correspondent for the *Manchester Guardian*. A few days later, she repeated the story in confidence at another party and from there the news leaked to *Avanti* and *Unita*. After that, the news spread. Sprigge wrote to *Avanti*, annoyed that her private comments to friends had been made public but essentially corroborating the story. The left-wing press—Socialist, Communist, Actionist, and Republican papers—then took up the cause.

A letter to the Prime Minister Ivanoe Bonomi from the Lorenzo Maroni, President of the High Court, was followed by a further complaint by Mario Berlinguer, public prosecutor at General Roatta's trial, combined with the press campaign brought a recommendation by the Minister of Marine for some decisive action. After the premier met with various senior officials, he responded to the court saying that 'Although the duke has declared that the sentence uttered by him has been misunderstood and that he did not mean to express the feelings that have been construed from his words in connection with the High Court, it is nevertheless safe to conclude that his attitude was not in conformity with the obligations of his position.' Umberto, as Lieutenant of the Realm, then dismissed Aimone from his post as admiral. Initial reports in *Il Popolo*, the Christian Democratic paper, had Aimone sentenced to six months in a fortress, but in fact on the morning of 10 April Aimone simply left Rome slid away quietly for an undisclosed destination in the south. News of this reached Irene at Hirschegg, and it naturally left her deeply concerned about the future.[44]

However, worse news for the Italian Royal Family was just days away. On 14 April 1945, the Italian newspapers published the fact that Princess Mafalda had died at Buchenwald the previous 27 August. Her son Heinrich learned the news from an Allied radio broadcast on the 20th. Mafalda had been arrested by the S.S. on 24 September 1943 after having brought her children to safety in the Vatican. She naively thought that as the wife of a German prince and daughter of the Italian king, she would be safe. During her incarceration in Buchenwald, an Allied bombing raid sent the prisoners into the trenches for safety, but Mafalda was hit so badly that her arm required amputation. The operation was done hurriedly and badly, resulting in her death. She was temporarily buried at Buchenwald, and later in the cemetery at Weimar.[45]

Failing to make his escape into Switzerland, Mussolini was captured near Lake Como, and then taken to Milan where he was executed by partisans on 28 April. His body, along with those of his mistress Clara Petacci and twelve other Fascists, were taken to a gasoline station at the Piazzale Loreto in Milan. There, the corpses were beaten and spit upon before being hung by the feet, a public display which became an internationally notorious photograph.

The news of Mafalda's death naturally raised concerns about the Aosta women and children, who had not been heard of for months. Irene's brother, King George of the Hellenes, who himself was in exile in London, sent requests in April for information through the Greek Embassy to the Supreme Headquarters for the Allied Expeditionary Forces. The last reports they had received through German and neutral sources had been in February.[46] In early May, there was an inaccurate rumour that Irene might be in Vienna. In fact, the two duchesses with their children were still at Hirschegg.

The quick collapse of Germany brought its own problems, and the duchesses feared that the retreating German troops would shoot all the prisoners. Irene 'spent agonised hours wondering how best to hold her child when the time came, so that he should be instantly killed.' But 'the risk was averted by Austrian Partisans, who declared that they would shoot fifty German fugitives for every internee executed.' The camp was liberated by Austrian partisans who shot the commandant, known by the title of 'Kriminal Direktor.' Shortly afterwards, on 2 May, the French troops of General Maurice Durosoy arrived in jeeps, armored cars, and trucks arrived; they made a special detour after having spoken to the Duchess Anne on the telephone. Anne, who had spent part of her youth in Morocco, spoke to Durosoy, whom she knew well, in Arabic, so as not to be understood by the Kriminal Direktor. After the liberation, an order to shoot all the hostages at Hirschegg was found delayed in the nearby town of Kempten.[47]

The same day, all the Italian contingent left the camp, with Princess Irene herself driving the car containing the whole family. They were able to cross into Switzerland on the 6th, and stayed in Lausanne with Uncle Toio, the Count of Turin, who Benedetto Croce described as 'the only one who behaved with dignity and kept away from Fascism. But he is old, deaf and mentally incapable, so much so that he used to say he was "the imbecile of the family."'[48]

VE Day came on 8 May; celebrations ensued, and on the 14th, King George of the Hellenes was able to cable their sister Queen Helen of Romania that Irene and her son Amedeo had reached Switzerland the previous week and were safe at the Hotel de la Paix, pending arrangements for travelling to Italy. In the meantime, British diplomats visited Hélène at Capodimonte and were able to report back to the Foreign Office that she was 'found in good health.'

It was not until 7 July that the young Duchesses and the children were finally able to enter Italy along with Uncle Toio. At Chiasso, they were driven by American forces to Milan, whence an American plane flew them to Naples, from where Hélène and Aimone were finally able to meet them at Capodichino Airport at 5 p.m.; it was the first time that Aimone met his little son. They returned to Capodimonte, and over the next few days, relaxed photographs were taken of their reunion—except for little Amedeo. The only photograph ever taken of him with his father shows a tearful boy struggling to get away from the stranger. However, even on the momentous day of their return, Hélène kept to her practice of weighing her houseguests and recording the totals in her guest book: Anna, 60 kg; Margherita, 56.1 kg; Cristina, 43.1 kg; Irene, 65.2 kg; Amedeo, 12.8 kg; and Toio, 66.4 kg.[49]

The family spent the summer together in Naples with Hélène, and then in October, the younger members returned to Florence. Anne and her daughters went to their apartment in the Pitti Palace, while Irene and Amedeo returned to the Villa Cisterna, which was still only partly restored.[50] Capodimonte seemed very quiet and empty, as Hélène wrote to Irene on 29 November 1945:

> I no longer hear the door of the inside stairs slam—nor the pattering of our treasure's tiny feet, agile and already strong—nor do I see your sweet smile or your sparkling eyes that light up my horizon. But I know your thoughts are with me and that is such a consolation. For my part, I have given you all the tenderness of a mother's heart, I understand and know you—and I love you, I sincerely appreciate you and am grateful for your devotion to Bouby [presumably Hélène meant Bob] and ... for having given me the most wonderful and adorable grandson on this earth. Give me patience—and hope—I automatically look for Amedeo at the time he used to come to me and, in the evening or at lunch, I always look at my chair that he used to push outside on the lawn. Our

Amedeo is still little but he has taken a great place in everyone's heart. May God bless him and bless you as well.[51]

17

1946–1951

How ugly old age is.—je suis une putrefaction[1]

About midday on 9 May 1946, King Victor Emmanuel and Queen Elena were in their Villa Maria Pia at Posillipo on the Bay of Naples with their grandson, Prince Henry of Hesse, Mafalda's eighteen-year-old son, who was preparing to return to Germany at the end of his Italian vacation. Umberto—who had only visited his father twice in the previous two years—suddenly appeared unannounced, looking pale and serious.[2] Henry left the room, but when he returned ten minutes later, his grandmother Queen Elena told him with tears in her eyes that she and the King would be leaving for Egypt that afternoon at 6 p.m. Henry and his uncle Umberto would return to Rome by plane at 5 p.m. Ellery Stone—the American admiral who was Allied Chief Commissioner for Italy—also arrived to speak with King Victor Emmanuel, and an official Abdication Act was signed. That afternoon saw a series of cars arriving from Rome, carrying with them Princess Jolanda, the Queen's sister the Grand Duchess Militza, the Duca Pietro d'Acquarone, minister of the Royal Household, and others, while frantic packing took place in the villa, all co-ordinated by their son-in-law Count Calvi.

Hélène and her daughter-in-law Anne arrived from Capodimonte for their farewells at 5.30 p.m., and the King received them immediately. By 6 p.m., they were all waiting for the arrival of the *Duca degli Abruzzi*, one of the few Italian warships still afloat, which arrived half an hour later. Slowly, the party descended the steps from the villa down to the sea for their final farewells. Queen Elena embraced her grandson Henry and told him to greet his father, and the King kissed him good-bye. Hélène kissed the hand of the King and embraced Queen Elena. Umberto embraced his mother and offered his father a military salute. The former king, now travelling as the Count of Pollenzo, 'departed with no word of thanks to his servants, timid, taciturn, impenetrable as ever; and, equally in character, he took with him dozens of crates containing family documents and state papers.'[3]

Having missed their airplane, Umberto—accompanied by his nephew Henry—returned to Rome by car, his first entry into the capital as king; that evening, Rome Radio broadcast a short statement from the Royal Household:

> King Victor Emmanuel II has signed his Abdication Act in Naples at noon to-day and, in accordance with the traditional custom, has left the country. As soon as the new King returns to Rome an official communication to the Prime Minister will be made.[4]

A date was set for the national plebiscite that would have two immediate goals—first, a popular referendum to choose between the monarchy and a republic, and secondly, to elect a constituent assembly to put that choice into practice. These simultaneous elections would be by universal suffrage; women would be voting for the first time. At the end of May, Hélène's daughters-in-law and grandchildren returned from Florence to Capodimonte, from where all the Aosta family took part in the referendum.[5]

King Victor Emmanuel's surprise abdication unfortunately came much too late for it to do any good. On 2 June, the national referendum voted in favour of a republic. The final count was 12,700,000 in favour of a republic; 10,700,000 for continuing the monarchy; and 1,500,000 non-valid votes. There was a sharp north-south divide in the country with all the southern provinces supporting the monarchy, while all the north went for the republic. Naples voted overwhelmingly (80 per cent) in favour of continuing the monarchy—the highest figure for anywhere in the country. One analysis suggests that this might be the legacy of the patronage system which had been established when Naples was still the capital of the kingdom under the Bourbons and when the King's favour symbolised their way of life. 'It signified quite simply that the electorate could not conceive of a way of life without a monarchy.'[6]

With the abolition of the monarchy came legislation exiling the royal family. Although the new regulations officially exiled only the head of the House of Savoy and his immediate male heir—similar to the laws which had exiled Hélène's father and brother from France so many years earlier—Umberto wanted all of the Royal Family to leave the country.

In the afternoon of 5 June 1946, Aimone was in Rome at the Quirinale with King Umberto, as Queen Marie José and the children prepared to go into exile in Portugal. Marie José—accompanied by her lady, Countess Guandeline Spalletti Crivelli, and Dr Aldo Castellani—was driven to Ciampino Airport, with the children following in a second car. When they landed in Naples after a brief flight, the Queen, Countess, and Doctor drove to Capodimonte where the three

Duchesses of Aosta were waiting. Castellani commented: 'What a noble figure is the Dowager Duchess, tall, slim, and erect, the silvery whiteness of her hair enhanced by her deep mourning.' Hélène took Marie José into another room for a long private conversation, while the others waited in the small salon. Marie José had been sent by Umberto to convince Hélène that she must join them in leaving for Portugal, but when she got to Capodimonte, she found Hélène unshakeable. 'You must leave Italy. These are the orders of the King!' '*Je m'en fiche!*' ('I do not care') was the answer. 'I will not budge from here even if they want to try to make me by force.' Hélène did indeed stay at Capodimonte, the only member of the Royal Family to remain in Italy. During their wait, Irene sadly commented to Dr Castellani 'This is my third experience of sudden enforced departure—twice in Greece and now in Italy.' Some consolation would come for Irene at the end of the summer, when a Greek plebiscite restored that monarchy, and her brother George II could return to the throne.

A sad farewell followed as Marie José and her party went to Villa Maria Pia, where the children had already gone; from there, they left for exile at 4 a.m. the next morning aboard the cruiser *Duca degli Abruzzi*, the same ship that had taken her in-laws into exile less than a fortnight earlier. Dr Castellani and Countess Spalletti accompanied 'the May Queen' into exile, along with her children, the Duke and Duchess of Genoa and the Duke and Duchess of Ancona.[7]

Umberto left the Quirinale for the last time on 13 June, and the Savoy dynasty scattered across three continents. With Marie José and their children Umberto went initially to Cascais in Portugal, although the next year Queen moved to Switzerland with her son while the daughters remained with their father.[8] Victor Emmanuel and Elena remained in Egypt, together with their eldest daughter, her family, and some of Elena's Russian relatives. Queen Giovanna and her children joined them at Alexandria when they in turn were exiled from Bulgaria following a plebiscite there in September 1946. The Duke and Duchess of Ancona eventually went to Brazil; the Duke and Duchess of Genoa and the Bulgarian royal family to Portugal; and the Duke and Duchess of Pistoia and the Duke of Bergamo to Switzerland.

Anne and her daughters drove from Capodimonte to Rome's military airport where a special Italy military plane flew them to Brussels along with Uncle Toio. Hélène's brother-in-law, the Count of Turin, had lived in Switzerland during the Salò republic, sadly said 'I will never see Italy again.' In Brussels, he went into hospital, where he was visited by Queen Elisabeth of the Belgians, but died within a few months. After over a year in Belgium, Anne and her daughters went to Switzerland.[9]

Aimone and Irene were less fortunate when they also attempted to settle in Belgium. The Belgian Cabinet discussed the issue on the morning of 6 June and agreed that the Italian Royal Family could go to Belgium 'for the time being at all events.' Later that day, Irene arrived at Evere aerodrome from Rome; it was thought that the King and Queen might arrive later in the day. However, by the end of August, it was clear that the Aostas in particular were not welcome. Queen Elisabeth and the Prince Regent Charles 'will have nothing whatever to do with the Aostas'; the British Foreign Office got involved when Doreen, Lady Brabourne, a friend of Aimone and Irene, contacted her cousin Sir Hugh Knatchbull-Hugessen, then British ambassador to Brussels, to see if he could—or would—intervene on their behalf. Sir Hugh in turn wrote to London to Sir Orme Sargent, the permanent undersecretary of state, stressing that the Aostas were friendly with the British king and queen as well as Queen Mary and were often invited for private meals together. Irene was indeed in London at that time as a guest of her brother, King George of the Hellenes, who was at that point still in exile himself. However, the advice that Sir Hugh got back was while Irene was 'beautiful and apparently quite harmless', Aimone was 'an altogether bad lot.' Due to the circumstances and 'particularly because the Court of Brussels will have nothing to do with the present duke of Aosta', Sir Hugh and his staff 'would be well advised to continue to give him a wide berth.'[10]

In the end, Irene also moved to Switzerland with her son, while Aimone went to South America, first to Brazil and then on to Argentina, where he arrived on 8 December 1946.[11] He had first visited that country while in the navy and had celebrated his twentieth birthday there.[12] His stated hopes were to establish an agricultural colony for Italians in Patagonia, emulating the model that his uncle Luigi Abruzzi had created in Somalia. In September 1947, he took direction of the company that he hoped would bring workers from the Piedmont and the Veneto to start a new life.

Also in December 1946, Hélène applied to the British Foreign Office through an old acquaintance, Sir D'Arcy Osborne, minister to the Holy See, for permission to live in Kenya if she were forced to leave Italy because of the law of exile. Hélène said that she was 'not directly approaching the King nor any member of the Royal family as she does not want to embarrass His Majesty.' She wanted to go to Kenya because she had been there before and had found the climate very beneficial to her health. 'Also her son is buried there.' The British recommendations were favourable, but in the event, permission was not required as Hélène was allowed to stay in Italy.[13]

Although Hélène was probably never aware of it, her sister Queen Amélie made her will on 25 October 1946—strangely, five years to the day before she would die. In that will, as well as a few individual bequests, Amélie left her entire estate to be divided among her three sisters—Hélène, Isabelle, and Louise, or their heirs. Amélie wrote 'I pray God and the Most Holy Virgin to protect them always in everything, they will remember that it is in our Holy Religion that they will find strength, courage and real consolation, as I have always found in my misfortunes.' She also left individual items to each of the sisters. The portrait by of their great-grandmother, Queen Marie Amélie, Harry Scheffer was to go to Hélène; 'it will recall so many memories to her of our childhood and adolescence. Whenever she looks at it, I ask her to think of a sister who loved her with the deepest affection and whose heart was full of tender gratitude.'[14]

The winter of 1947 brought influenza to Capodimonte; Hélène fell victim and was in bed for about ten days, coughing, sneezing, wiping her nose, and feeling 'inundated with the shabbiest sufferings, griefs and humiliations.' With the exception of the faithful Otto Campini, Hélène was alone in Italy. Her son Aimone was in South America, her daughters-in-law and grandchildren in Switzerland.[15]

In the spring of 1947, Irene was still living in Geneva and finally had a visit from her sister Queen Helen, who was at last allowed to leave Romania. It was the first time that the sisters had met since the war. They spoke of plans for the future, especially where Irene might live if she were granted permission to return to republican Italy. Although Helen's Villa Sparta in Florence had been spared, Irene's Villa Cisterna had been virtually destroyed during the fighting for the hills north of Florence. They also spoke of their brothers—King George and Crown Prince Paul—whom Irene had seen in London after her escape but Helen had not seen in seven years. However, on 1 April, just two weeks into Helen's visit, they received a telegram from Athens announcing that King George had died of a stroke. Helen was allowed only a three-day visit by the Russians, and she and Irene made the five-hour flight from Geneva to Athens. The state funeral took place in Athens Cathedral, and then was followed by the private burial in the family cemetery at Tatoi. Permission for Queen Helen to remain in Athens longer was refused by Bucharest, and two days after the funeral, she flew back to Geneva with Irene and then the next day on to Romania.[16]

In November 1947, Irene was invited to London to attend the glittering wedding of Princess Elizabeth with her cousin Prince Philip of Greece. Although Philip's sisters who had all married in German princely families were not invited, it was otherwise a great reknitting of family ties for the royal families of the Allied Powers. Queen Helen and King Michael picked Irene up at Lausanne, with King Michael co-piloting the plane. After one of the post-wedding parties, Sir Henry 'Chips' Channon, who referred to Irene as her sister's 'devoted shadow,' commented that 'I have always loved this pair of Greek swans who have been so buffeted about dynastically and matrimonially.'[17]

On the day of the wedding itself, Hélène telegraphed her sister Amélie in France for news—'have you received letter unsettled ask for news.' Amélie wasn't certain what disturbed Hélène—our dear 'Terrible No. I'—whether it was reports in the newspapers or the strikes, but took this as proof that her sister had finally resumed some active interest in life and also some of her old strength and interest in life.[18] Just a month after the grand London wedding, Michael and Helen were themselves exiled from Romania and joined Irene at the Hotel Beau Rivage in Lausanne.

Soon, some of the new strength which Hélène had found would now be needed because of a political development. The new Italian Constitution (dated 27 December 1947, to come into effect on 1 January 1948) made provisions that no member of the House of Savoy could vote or hold public or elected office in the new republic.[19] All ex-kings of the dynasty, their spouses and male descendants were forbidden entry into Italian territory. Most importantly for Hélène, the assets, existing on national territory, of the former kings of the House of Savoy, their spouses, and their male descendants shall be transferred to the State. Transfers and the establishment of royal rights on said properties which took place after 2 June 1946 shall be null and void.[20]

Although this meant that Hélène could legally remain in Italy, she would lose her home at Capodimonte. For years, she had occupied an apartment within the palace, which also included not only the famous art gallery, but since the war had also housed the officers of the Academy of Aeronautics, which transferred from Caserta to Naples. As a token of respect, it is said that Hélène was offered the opportunity to retain her apartment for life as a guest of the republic, but that she wanted no favours from the new government. In place of the royal arms, Hélène's personal standard featuring a porcupine with the motto 'Cominus et eminus'—'From close and from far'—which had adorned her bookplates for years was raised over the palace.[21]

In December 1947, Hélène moved from the palace at Capodimonte, which had been her residence since 1905, to Castellammare and a first-floor hotel apartment of seven rooms, plus a small private terrace from where she could contemplate the sea.[22] There were also accommodation for her two maids, Emma and Giuseppina, and her driver Angelo Chirico. Otto Campini, as always, was discretely in the background.

The Royal Hotel di Quisisana at Castellammare di Stabia, about thirty kilometres south of Naples on the road to Sorrento, was itself originally a royal palace, with parts dating back to the time of Charles d'Anjou in 1268, and it had been the home of monarchs through the various Neapolitan dynasties, including Joseph Bonaparte and Joachim Murat. With the unification of Italy, the palace passed as a Crown Asset to the Savoys; in 1879, it was signed over to the local municipality and was made into a hotel. During its heyday, an artistic community centred itself at the Royal. Crispi, Hindenburg, Matilde Serao, Victoria Aganoor Pompili, the Countess of Noailles along with the painters Morelli and Palizzi were among its earlier residents. Now, it became Hélène's final home.

Over the years, Hélène had developed a strong connection with Dr Guerriera Guerrieri, the woman who had catalogued the library at Capodimonte for Hélène and who had been largely responsible for safeguarding the national library collection and sending large parts of it away for security during the dark days of the war.[23] It was now to Dr Guerrieri that Hélène entrusted some of the things that were most precious to her as she began to disestablish her old life and move into a new one. While most of the furnishings and artwork remained at the nationalized palace, Hélène's personal belongings were crated into two separate lots. The first would become the Fondo Aosta at the national library in the old royal palace and occupies the rooms which were originally the private office of King Ferdinand I of the Two Sicilies, Hélène's own great-great-grandfather. The second lot of material—including her working library, as well as some of her own manuscripts and personal belongings—would follow her to Castellamare.

Hélène donated her collection of some 11,000 books, her photographic collection, her hunting trophies and other objects collected during her African journeys, along with the bookcases and furnishings to the Biblioteca Nazionale di Napoli. It was an immense collection which had filled her own private apartment at Capodimonte and would eventually occupy five rooms in the library located in the old Royal Palace in the centre of Naples. The books, which also included Amedeo's personal library, covered a wide variety of subjects, history and travel, children's books, music, French novels, and about 1,000 books on Africa alone, mostly in English or French. There were also some 9,800 photographs, mostly dating from about 1890 to 1930 and mostly about her travels and humanitarian work. Hélène's hunting trophies of stuffed animals were more eclectic, plus the various collections she had accumulated over the years of indigenous art, idols, gongs, axes, daggers, lances, and guns from the old Sala Africa at Capodimonte. There was a collection of minerals, an inscribed stone slab from the Algerian Sahara, and prehistoric remains from the Incan people which had been presented to Hélène by the Consul of Bolivia.

Temperamentally, Hélène was probably the one member of the family most suited for exile. For years, she had given up her way of life by choice and chosen the preferred 'wandering life' (*la vie errante*), as she titled one of her travel books, without the luxuries that come with living in a palace. There had been so many examples of this throughout her life of giving up one life style and being forced into another. However, now that she was approaching eighty, and the choices became forced rather than by choice, it must have been difficult.

Three days before the new constitution took effect, King Victor Emmanuel died in his Egyptian exile. On a practical level, this meant that the former king's personal fortune was retained. As he officially died under the old constitution, the changes in property ownership had not yet taken place, and his personal assets were safeguarded. His assets in England alone totalled over £1.5 million when the estate was administered.[24]

Victor Emmanuel's funeral took place on the last day of the year at the Cathedral of Saint Catherine in Alexandria, the mourning members of his family, all now deposed, included Queen Mother Elena, King Umberto, Queen Mother Giovanna of Bulgaria and her son King Simeon, the late king's daughter Jolanda and her family, plus two of the sons of Princess Mafalda. King Zog and Queen Geraldine of Albania, likewise in exile in Egypt, also attended.

Within weeks, a final tragedy came to Hélène on 29 January 1948, when Aimone died in room 320 of the Plaza Hotel in Buenos Aires, where he had been staying 'in the company of a friend.' At first, the death was reported to be the result of a violent attack of asthma, which had kept him in bed for three weeks. Later, the cause of death was given as a myocardial infarction following a bout of tuberculosis, although the family said that it was following a gall bladder operation. He had undergone surgery at São Paolo and was recovering at Rio de Janeiro on 4 December 1947, according to the annotation on the last photograph that he sent to his mother before going to Argentina. Irene was still in Switzerland, at this time on vacation in Davos with her sister Queen Helen, King Michael, and his fiancée Princess Anne of Bourbon-Parma. King Michael's *aide-de-camp* was the first to hear the radio news, which he relayed to Countess Lodron who in turn had to inform Irene.[25] Gandhi was assassinated in India the next day and that naturally drew the major newspaper headlines away, but there was still notable coverage of Aimone's death in the Italian press.

Just before noon on 31 January, Aimone was taken from the home of Gen. Maurizio Masengo, where a *chapelle ardente* had been created for him, to the Church of Nuestra Señora del Pilar in Buenos Aires. A cortège of twenty-five accompanied him there, including personal friends and Irene's first cousin the Grand Duchess Marie of Russia, who was living in Buenos Aires at the time. A large number of the local Italian community attended the requiem mass. Crowns of flowers from Irene, their son Amedeo, and President Peron were placed on top the coffin, and at the foot, a large arrangement with the simple words '*La tua mamma*' on the ribbon. Following the funeral, the coffin was taken to the city's Northern Cemetery and placed in the private tomb of the Counts of Campello.

Upon learning of Aimone's death, Queen Mary wrote to Hélène, sending her condolences from England. Queen Mary, who had also lost two sons—her two youngest children: Prince John in 1919 and Prince George, the Duke of Kent, on active service during the war in 1942—and would later lose a third when King George died in 1952, shared in the type of loss that only a mother could know.[26] Hélène's note to Queen Mary in 1942 when the Duke of Kent died and this exchange show that there remained at least a tenuous, positive connection between Hélène and the British royal family of which she herself was nearly a part. Queen Mary once commented that she had learned about each son's death through a telephone call. That forced distancing was something that Hélène experienced too, as both of her sons died on different continents.

Suddenly, the family seemed very small and distant. All three of her Aosta brothers-in-law had died unmarried and childless. In her own family, Hélène's two brothers were both dead, and by 1949 all three of her sisters would be widows. Three of her four nephews had died young. Henri, the Comte de Paris, was the only son of that generation to survive, and his three sisters were all widowed at a young age. Assassination, warfare, accident, and illness had all taken their toll.

During the growth of the Fascist movement and particularly during the war itself, a vast gulf developed between Hélène and her French family, particularly with her nephew, Henri, Comte de Paris. Amélie had no word of her throughout the war; even relations with her favourite niece, Françoise, simply no longer existed. When Françoise went to Naples in 1948, she found a city devastated, and her aunt secluded at Torre di Patria. It was a bitter reunion. 'Why have you come? Why have you come?' Hélène kept repeating. Françoise reported back that 'the disappointments, then the bereavements, had frozen Aunt Hélène in her bitterness.'[27]

However, in June, Anne, Irene and the children were allowed to return from their Swiss exile to live in Italy when Prime Minister Alcide de Gasperi decided that 'widows and children do not represent a danger to anyone.' Irene moved to Villa Sparta in Fiesole outside of Florence, the home of her sister Helen, now exiled from Romania, until the Villa Cisterna could be adequately repaired. Anne and her daughters would live between Florence and Sorrento.[28]

Hélène became very ill again at the end of 1948, and her daughter-in-law Anne arrived from Florence to care for her. A slight ray of consolation came to them through a letter from Sir Percy Loraine, who had been British Ambassador to Italy from 1939 until he left Rome in 1940 when diplomatic relations were broken. He had long been a friend of the family, and his wife, Louise, Lady Loraine, and her sister Béthine, Lady Abington, were among the few pre-war friends who continued to visit the Aostas. Now, Sir Percy was able to report that he had been in touch with British officials to ensure that Amedeo's grave in Kenya would be properly tended. Anne wrote back, acknowledging 'all we have lost with Bouby' but that they were grateful to know that 'his grave is well kept yet maintaining a character of great simplicity—just as Bouby would have wished— A soldier's grave.'[29]

During her last few years, Hélène began to call her little grandson Bouby, the same diminutive she gave to his uncle half a century before. Perhaps this was intentional, perhaps not. She was visited by her granddaughters Margherita and Maria Cristina, who took her little bouquets of broom, in memory of happier days. Now after a lifetime of voracious reading, Hélène read little except the *Osservatore romano*. However, she continued to write, answering begging letters for subsidies from her estates in the Campania, as well as to old friends until she could no longer hold a pen. She wrote to her oldest friend, Renée St Maur, about 'how much I love you—and how much I think about you but I cannot write. How ugly old age is.—*je suis une putrefaction*—I offer everything to the Lord but am so humbled. I love you.'[30]

Hélène and Renée had known each other since childhood, as Renée's father had been private secretary to the Comte and Comtesse de Paris. Their friendship lasted for decades 'without a cloud' as Hélène phrased it.[31] In their correspond-ence, Renée was always known as 'Chiffon,' the name of the heroine in novels by the society author Gyp, which Hélène read copiously in her young days, and she became '*Tante* Chiffon' to the younger generations.

Now, Hélène did not go out often, but would occasionally take drives in the scenic countryside and every Friday afternoon would visit some close friends at the Excelsior Hotel in Naples. Most often, however, she would pray, visited by Cardinal Ascalesi and other clergy especially by local monks in a tradition started by her first confessor, Don Salvatore DeMartino. In her final years, the Franciscan mysticism, which she had first begun to discover in the 1920s with Angelo Conti, held a special importance in her spiritual life. The last book Hélène is known to have read took her back to the Christian mysticism of the Africa desert with *Sur les traces de Charles deFoucauld*.[32]

During the summer of 1950, Hélène's sister Isabelle visited and found her '*très très diminuée, affaiblie*'—very, very diminished, weakened. However, Hélène was well enough to visit Pompeii with Isabelle, and join the family at Sorrento for meals during Isabelle's visit which lasted into July.[33] Then, on Thursday, 18 January 1951, at about four in the afternoon, Hélène suffered a cerebral throm-bosis. Campini phoned for emergency assistance from Dr Bartolo Quartuccio and also contacted the priests of Frati Minimi at the Church of San Francesco di Paola, in the nearby village of Pozzano, where Hélène regularly attended Mass. At 7.30 in the evening, she received the last sacraments, and the family was notified. Two telegrams were sent to Queen Elena. King Umberto phoned twice for news and Queen Marie José three times. Over the next two days, Quartuccio visited every two hours with injections of morphine to ease the pain.

Hélène's former household gathered at the Royal—Duchessa Elena di Serracapriola, Marchese Gioachino, and Marchesa Isabella Caracciolo di Borchiarolo along with Admiral Castracane. Irene arrived from Fiesole with Countess Morelli on the Friday, and Anne came from Switzerland with Duchess Caffarelli on the Saturday. Later that evening, Anne phoned her daughters in Switzerland to pray for their grandmother.

Although the apartment was filled with books, ceramics, bronzes, ancient weapons, and other mementoes from Capodimonte, Hélène's bedroom was fur-nished with simple hotel pieces. The end came there at 11.15 p.m. on Saturday, 20 January. Her closest friend, the Duchess of Serracapriola, was at the bed-side at Hélène's last breath, while the others were in the adjoining room. Two large candlestands were brought in, placed on either side of the bed, and the candles were lit.

At the end of the First World War, Hélène reflected on lost time and that as life approached its end, one wished to return back to the past. 'It is so short, life, and one wastes so many days!'[34]

Hélène's death made front-page news in Italy, including *La Stampa*, while in

England *The Times* ran a simple small notice on an inside page: 'We also announce with regret the deaths of Princess Hélène of France, widow of Prince Emmanuel Philibert, duke of Aosta, who died in 1931' sandwiched between similarly brief notices about the death of a lady palaeontologist, a former high sheriff, and a chaplain from the First World War. London's *Daily Telegraph*, however, had a brief leader on the front page with a couple of inside paragraphs that remembered Hélène as 'one of the closest friends of Queen Alexandra', as well as her early life in England, her frequent hunts with the Grafton, and that she 'later made a considerable reputation as an explorer and big-game hunter in Central Africa.'[35]

On the 24th came the funeral which Hélène had planned herself, as well as insisting that the civil death record would be in the name by which she signed herself as 'Hélène de France.' At her request, her face was covered with a veil. The coffin was simple, made of dark walnut, and was wrapped in a flag with the ducal crown. Atop was the Italian tricolour which had been draped on Amedeo's coffin in Kenya and had been preserved by an English officer, as well as a small cushion bearing the decorations which Hélène valued the most—the two silver medals, two war crosses and campaign medals she had been awarded as a Red Cross nurse—rather than those she received simply as a member of the Royal Family.[36]

Avoiding any pomp, the coffin was brought to Naples in a simple black hearse. The procession travelled from the hotel along the Pompeii highway, where it temporarily broke down. Women along the route silently crossed themselves and threw flowers. A large crowd packed the square in front of the Cathedral in Naples, warmly and respectfully applauding the arrival of the coffin.

Seven-year-old Amedeo was appointed the representative for King Umberto and as such led his heavily veiled mother and aunt and cousins Margherita and Maria Cristina into the church. The only other members of the family were the Duke of Bergamo and his two sisters, Bona Margherita and Adelaide. Otto Campini was there too but, as usual, discretely in the background.

The coffin was carried into the cathedral by Duca Giovanni Maresca di Serracapriola, Duca Antonio Riario Sforza, Barone Mario Gallotti (at whose villa in Posillipo the Duchess and her sons often visited) and five fishermen from Mergellina. A honour guard of sisters from the Red Cross in their black cloaks lined the entry. Archbishop Alfonso Gastaldi officiated at the Mass, assisted by Cardinal Ascalesi and Monsignore Massacappellano from the military shrine at Redipuglia. The Pope sent his condolences in a telegram.

At the end of the service, the family left the Cathedral, and the crowd lifted young Amedeo to their shoulders and carried him some two kilometres, with his mother holding his hand the whole time and telling him not to cry. By the end, Amedeo had lost his tie, along with his shoes and socks, and his face was covered with the spittle from many attempted kissses by the masses of people.[37] The crowd even briefly picked up the car and, as *La Stampa* phrased it, carried it 'like a black shiny dolphin on the waves.'

After the service, Hélène's coffin was taken to the chapel of the small convent of the Suore Ancelle della Chiesa, next to the fountain that she had donated years earlier, facing the Basilica of Santa Maria Incoronata, which was still under construction.[38] Eventually, Hélène would be buried in a chapel inside the basilica, which is on the hill at Capodimonte, where she had spent the greatest part of her life. Her marble tomb there bears the shield of the House of Savoy on the left, and the shield of the House of Bourbon on the right, with the simple inscription:

Endnotes

Preface:

1. Hélène d'Aosta, *La Vie Errante* (1921), p. 43.

Chapter 1:

1. Queen Victoria to Comte de Paris, 26 June 1871. RA VIC/MAIN/J/92/8.
2. *The* Times, 31 Jan. 1871; Horne, *Seven Ages of Paris* (2002), pp. 290–291, 293, 295, 296.
3. Horne, *Seven Ages of Paris* (2002), pp. 298, 300, 306-307, 311-312; *The Times*, 2 Feb. 1871.
4. Irvine, *Boulanger Affair Reconsidered* (1989), p. 21; Barrière, *Les princes d'Orleans* (1933), p. 111.
5. *The Times*, 12 June 1871, 5a.
6. Osgood, *French Royalism* (1960), pp. 2, 7.
7. Comte de Paris to Queen Victoria, telegram, 13 June 1871. RA VIC/ MAIN/Y/51/134. The civil registration of her birth gives her name as 'Hélène Françoise Henriette.' However, most sources, including her marriage registration, give the name as 'Hélène Louise Henriette.'
8. Van Kerrebrouck, *La maison de Bourbon* (2004), 4, pt 2:551, note 38.
9. Comte de Paris to Queen Victoria, 16 June 1871. RA VIC/MAIN/J/92/5.
10. Queen Victoria to Comte de Paris, 26 June 1871. RA VIC/MAIN/J/92/8. Auguste of Mecklenburg-Schwerin (1776-1871) was the stepmother of the Comte's mother and widow of the Hereditary Grand Duke Friedrich.
11. RA VIC/MAIN/QVJ (W) 10 June 1846 (Princess Beatrice's copies). Retrieved 29 July 2016.
12. Barrière, *Les princes d'Orléans* (1933), p. 11; Asquith, *Autobiography* (1920-1922); Adrien Dansette, *Le Boulangisme* (1946), 165, quoted in Osgood, *French Royalism*

(1960), p. 38.

13. *The Times*, 1 June 1883.

14. RAVIC/MAIN/QVJ (W), 8 July 1864 (Princess Beatrice's copies). Retrieved 29 July 2016.

15. Van der Kiste, *A Divided Kingdom* (2007), pp. 52-71.

16. Cashmore, *The Orléans Family in Twickenham* (1982).

17. Poisson, *Les Orléans* (1999), p. 302.

18. Comte de Paris to Queen Victoria, Twickenham, 21 July 1871. RAVIC/ MAIN/J/92/13; Comte de Paris to Queen Victoria. Twickenham, 30 July 1871. RAVIC/MAIN/J/92/15; *The Times*, 5 Aug. 1871; Catinot-Crost, *Amélie de Portugal* (2000), p. 20.

19. Poisson, *Les Orléans* (1999), p. 304; Catinot-Crost, *Amélie de Portugal* (2000), p. 22.

20. Osgood, *French Royalism* (1960), p. 23.

21. RAVIC/MAIN/QVJ (W) 19 Feb. 1874 (Princess Beatrice's copies). Retrieved 29 July 2016.

22. Comtesse de Paris to Marthe, vicomtesse Vigier, 7 May 1875. Archives du Château de Chantilly. Fonds Orléans (1 PA 2).

23. *The Times*, 10 June 1876.

24. Comte de Paris to Queen Victoria, 15 June 1876. RAVIC/MAIN/J/92/35.

25. Queen Victoria to Crown Princess of Prussia, 4 July 1877 in Queen Victoria, *Darling Child* (1976), p. 54.

26. Van der Kiste, *A Divided Kingdom* (2007), p. 84; Maria de la Paz, Infanta of Spain, *Through Four Revolution* (1933), p. 76.

27. Priestley, *The Story of a Lifetime* (1908), pp. 156-160.

28. Hélène d'Aosta to Amélie du Portugal, 29 June 1932. AnP 300 AP III 954/219; Corpechot, *Memories of Queen Amélie of Portugal* (1915), pp. 43-44; Hélène d'Aosta, *La Vie Errante* (1921), pp. 124-125.

29. Monniot, *Le journal de Marguerite*, 2 vols. Fondo Aosta, D 16.93; Comte to Paris to Hélène d'Orléans, Montbozon, 9 Sept. 1878; Private family collection; Comte de Paris to Hélène d'Orléans, Seville, 18 April 1879. Private family collection.

30. Telegram from the Comte de Paris to Queen Victoria, 23 Jan. 1881. RAVIC/ MAIN/Y/51/190; Duchesse de Chartres to Amelia Bliss, Villa des Fayères, 22 Jan. 1881. Amelia Sprigings (later Bliss) of Claremont, Esher: Letters from Members of the French Royal Family and Household (Surrey History Centre, Woking), 7223/3/44.

31. Corpechot, *Memories of Queen Amélie of Portugal* (1915), pp. 33-34.

32. Catinot-Crost, *Amélie de Portugal* (2000), p. 38.

33. Poisson, *Les Orléans* (1999), p. 315; Comtesse de Paris to Marthe, vicomtesse Vigier, 15 Feb. 1883. Archives du Château de Chantilly. Fonds Orléans (1 PA 2).

34. Chambord, *Journal* (2009), p. 779.

35. Chambord, *Journal* (2009), pp. 783-784.

36. Corpechot, *Memories of Queen Amélie of Portugal* (1915), pp. 42-43; Van Kerrebrouck,

La Maison de Bourbon (2004), 2:552 n. 68. Note that Catinot-Crost, *Amélie de Portugal* (2000), p. 44, says it was Amélie.

37. RA GV/PRIV/GVD/1885: 21, 23 Oct.; Van Kerrebrouck, *La Maison de Bourbon* (2004), vol. 4, pt. 2:555, 556n.14.

38. RA GV/PRIV/GVD/1886: 1 March.

39. Pailler, *Charles Ier, Roi de Portugal* (2000), p. 50; Telegram from Comte de Paris to Queen Victoria, 7 Feb 1886. RA VIC/MAIN/J/65/110.

40. Catinot-Crost, *Amélie de Portugal* (2000), p. 59; *The Times*, 17 May 1886.

41. Pailler, *Charles Ier, Roi de Portugal* (2000), p. 55; Catinot-Crost, *Amélie de Portugal* (2000), p. 64.

42. RA GV/PRIV/GVD/1886: 24, 25, 26, 27 May.

43. Poisson, *Les Orléans* (1999), p. 317; Law of Exile quoted in Osgood, *French Royalism* (1960), p. 41. The law of exile was not abrogated until 24 June 1950.

Chapter 2:

1. Comte de Paris to Queen Victoria, telegram, Lord Warden Hotel, Dover, 25 June 1886. RA VIC/MAIN/J/88/13.

2. Salagnac, *Quatre règnes en exil (1820-1940)* (1947); Laugel, "Expulsion des Princes", 332, quoted in Osgood, *French Royalism* (1960), p. 42.

3. Comte de Paris to Queen Victoria, telegram, Lord Warden Hotel, Dover, 25 June 1886. RA VIC/MAIN/J/88/13; Queen Victoria to Comte de Paris, telegram, 25 June 1886. RA VIC/MAIN/J/88/14.

4. Comte de Paris to Queen Victoria, 31 July 1886. RA VIC/MAIN/J/88/16.

5. Barrière, *Les princes d'Orléans* (1933), pp. 8, 55; Waddington, *Letters of a Diplomat's Wife* (1903), p. 274.

6. Lewis, *Queen of Cooks* (1925), p. 7.

7. *The Times*, 27 Oct 1886.

8. Francis Knollys to Ponsonby, 12 Nov. 1886. RA VIC/PP 1/22/58.

9. Quoted in Catinot-Crost, *Amélie de Portugal* (2000), p. 24.

10. Barrière, *Les princes d'Orléans* (1933), p. 59; Aronson, *Queen Victoria and the Bonapartes* (1972), p. 202.

11. Queen Victoria to Lord Granville, 5 June 1880. RA VIC/MAIN/J/92/41; Aronson, *Queen Victoria and the Bonapartes* (1972), p. 49.

12. RA VIC/MAIN/QVJ (W) 9, 10 Jan. 1887 (Princess Beatrice's copies). Retrieved 29 July 2016.

13. Pailler, *Charles Ier, Roi de Portugal* (2000), p. 59, states that the Comte de Paris and Queen Maria Pia were godparents, but the Comtesse de Paris gives herself and the King of Portugal in her letter. Comtesse de Paris to Queen Victoria, 15 April 1887. RA VIC/MAIN/J/66/2.

14. Comtesse de Paris to Comte de Paris, 4 July 1887. AnP 300 AP III 375.

15. RA GV/PRIV/GVD/1887: 17 June; Prince Albert Victor to Hélène d'Orleans, 17 June 1887, quoted in Michael of Greece, *Eddy & Hélène* (2013), 6.

16. *The Times*, 18 July 1887; RA GV/PRIV/GVD/1887: 16, 20 July.

17. Comtesse de Paris to Comte de Paris, 4 July 1887. AnP 300 AP 375; Blunt, *My Diaries* (1919-1920), 1:68-69.

18. Comtesse de Paris to Comte de Paris, 8, 9, 17, 22 June 1888 and Hélène de France to Comte de Paris, 17 June 1888. AnP 300 AP 375; Transcript of extracts from Queen Victoria's Letter to the Princess Royal, 14 May 1888. RA VIC/ADDU/32/1888: 14 May; *The Times*, 16 May 1888; *Le Figaro*, 6 June 1888.

19. Hélène de France to Comte de Paris, 14 June 1888. AnP 300 AP 375.

20. Comtesse de Paris to Comte de Paris, 15, 22 June, 6, 8 July 1888. AnP 300 AP 375.

21. RA GV/PRIV/GVD/1888: 27 Nov.; Comtesse de Paris to Prince George of Wales, 24 Dec. 1888. RA GV/PRIV/AA/43/21.

22. Pailler, *Charles Ier, Roi de Portugal* (2000), pp. 62-63; Comte de Paris to Prince of Wales, April 1889. RA VIC/MAIN/J/92/80a; Hélène de France to Comte de Paris, 8, 21 Feb. 1889 and Amélie de Portugal to Comte de Paris, 10 March 1889. AnP 300 AP 375.

23. Amélie de Portugal to Comte de Paris, 10 March 1889 and Hélène de France to Comte de Paris, 21 Feb. 1889. AnP 300 AP 375.

24. RA GV/PRIV/GVD/1889: 4 May.

25. Prince of Wales to Crown Princess of Prussia, 8 May 1889. Telegram. RA Addl MSS A/4 (8); *The Times* 31 May 1889.

26. Barrière, *Les princes d'Orléans* (1933), p. 10; Osgood, *French Royalism* (1960), pp. 46, 47, 48, 50.

27. Hélène de France to Comte de Paris, 30 July, 4, 8, 16, 22 Aug. 1889. AnP 300 AP 375.

28. RA GV/PRIV/GVD/1889: 2,4, 5,6, 7 Dec.

29. Michael of Greece, *Eddy & Hélène* (2013), p. 9. This wedding of the Crown Prince and Crown Princess of Greece—both first cousins to Prince Eddy—did not require a conversion by the bride, but when she did that later of her own conviction it created a break with the bride's brother, the Kaiser. Another first cousin to Eddy, Princess Elisabeth of Hesse converted to Russian Orthodoxy in 1884 to marry Grand Duke Serge, as did her sister Alix when she married Tsar Nicholas II in 1894.

30. Pope-Hennessy, *Queen Mary* (1959), p. 134.

Chapter 3:

1. Lord Salisbury to A. J. Balfour, 16 Sept 1890, in *Salisbury-Balfour Correspondence* (1988), 330.

2. Comtesse de Paris to Queen Victoria, 7 Feb. 1890 (telegram). RA VIC/MAIN/Y/52/77; Hélène de France to Comte de Paris, 8 Feb. 1890. AnP 300 AP 376.

3. Barrière, *Les princes d'Orléans* (1933), pp. 17, 24.

4. Hélène de France to Comte de Paris, 20 Feb. 1890. AnP 300 AP 376; Barrière, *Les princes d'Orléans* (1933), p. 27, 33.

5. Comtesse de Paris to Comte de Paris, 23 March 1890; Hélène de France to Comte de Paris, 25 March 1890. AnP 300 AP 376.

6. Barrière, *Les princes d'Orléans* (1933), p. 39.

7. Barrière, *Les princes d'Orléans* (1933), pp. 37, 40, 41, 43, 52, 76, 77.

8. Prince Albert Victor to Hélène d'Orleans, 27 May 1890, quoted in Michael of Greece, *Eddy & Hélène* (2013), pp. 9-10.

9. Prince Albert Victor to Prince George, 13 Sept. 1890. RA GV/PRIV/AA39/62.

10. RA VIC/ADDA12/1684, VIC/MAIN/Z/475/2.

11. Queen Victoria to Prince Albert Victor, 19 May 1890. RA VIC/MAIN/Z/475/3.

12. Sir Henry Ponsonby to Sir Francis Knollys, 28 Oct 1890. RA VIC/ADDC07/1.

13. Cardinal Manning to Comte de Paris, 22 June 1890, quoted in Michael of Greece, *Eddy & Hélène* 2013), pp. 11-12.

14. Comte to Paris to "My dear General", [undated, but after 22 June 1890], quoted in Michael of Greece, *Eddy & Hélène* (2013), pp. 13-15.

15. Even the Princess of Wales acknowledged that the marriage of a prince with a Roman Catholic commoner—even one closely attached to the Royal Family—would be unacceptable. 'There it is and, alas, rather a sad case I think for you both, my two poor children. I only wish you could marry and be happy, but, alas, I fear that cannot be.' Quoted in Battiscombe, *Queen Alexandra* (1969), p. 172.

16. *The Times,* 1 Sept 1890.

17. Prince Albert Victor to Prince George, 13 Sept 1890. RA GV/PRIV/AA39/62.

18. Memorandum of Queen Victoria, 29 Aug. 1890. In *Salisbury-Balfour Correspondence* (1988), pp. 319-320.

19. *The Times,* 1 Sept 1890. The Court Circular reports the visit taking place on 30 Aug., but it was actually on the 29th when the Queen wrote to the Prime Minister, and as recorded in Queen Victoria's journal.

20. Prince Albert Victor to Prince George, 13 Sept 1890. RA GV/PRIV/AA39/62.

21. Balfour to Salisbury, 30 Aug. 1890, in *Salisbury-Balfour Correspondence* (1988), p. 318; Prince Albert Victor to Hélène de France, 5 Feb. 1891, quoted in Michael of Greece, *Eddy & Hélène* (2013), p. 53.

22. Salisbury to Balfour, telegram, 30 Aug. 1890, and Balfour to Salisbury, 30 Aug. 1890, quoted in *Salisbury-Balfour Correspondence* (1988), pp. 319-321.

23. Balfour to Salisbury, 30 Aug. 1890, in *Salisbury-Balfour Correspondence* (1988), p. 321.

24. Princess of Wales to Queen Victoria, [30 Aug 1890], extract in Arthur James Balfour to Lord Salisbury, 30 Aug 1890, in Harcourt Williams, ed., *Salisbury-Balfour Correspondence* (1988), p. 322.

25. Queen Victoria to the Princess of Wales, 30 Aug. 1890. Copy in the Papers of the 3rd Marquess of Salisbury, Hatfield. Quoted in Wilson, *Victoria* (2014), pp. 489-490.

26. Queen Victoria to the Prince of Wales, 7 Sept 1890. RA VIC/PRIV/L/3/27a.

27. Balfour to Salisbury, 30 Aug. 1890, in *Salisbury-Balfour Correspondence* (1988), p. 322.

28. Balfour to Salisbury, 31 Aug. 1890 and Prince Eddy to Queen Victoria, quoted in Balfour to Salisbury, 31 Aug. 1890, in *Salisbury-Balfour Correspondence* (1988), pp. 324-325.

29. Prince Albert Victor to Hélène de France, 31 Aug. 1890, Comtesse de Paris to Princess of Wales, 31 Aug. 1890, quoted in Michael of Greece, *Eddy & Hélène* (2013), pp. 18-19.

30. Prince Albert Victor to Prince George, 13 Sept 1890. RA GV/PRIV/AA39/62; Sir Henry Ponsonby to Queen Victoria, 2 Oct 1890. RA VIC/MAIN/D/10/187.

31. Prince Albert Victor to Hélène de France, 2 Sept. 1890 and Princess of Wales to Comtesse de Paris, 5 Sept. 1890, quoted in Michael of Greece, *Eddy & Hélène* (2013), pp. 20-21.

32. Balfour to Salisbury, 30 & 31 Aug. 1890, Lord Salisbury to Queen Victoria, 9 Sept 1890, in *Salisbury-Balfour Correspondence* (1988), pp. 323, 325-329.

33. Infanta Eulalia to Princess Ludwig Ferdinand, 5, 11 Sept. 1890, in Maria de la Paz, Infanta of Spain, *Through Four Revolutions* (1933), p. 206.

34. Comtesse de Paris to Comte de Paris, 17 Sept. 1890. AnP 300 AP 656; Prince Albert Victor to Prince George, 13 Sept 1890. RA GV/PRIV/AA39/62.

35. Barrière, *Les princes d'Orléans* (1933), p. 104-105.

36. This new style of handwriting distinctively begins with her 28 Sept 1890 letter to her father from Loch Kennard Lodge.

37. Hélène de France to Comte de Paris, 28 Sept. 1890. AnP 300 AP 656.

38. Hélène de France to Prince Albert Victor, 27 Oct 1890, quoted in Michael of Greece, *Eddy & Hélène* (2013), p. 37.

39. Memorandum by the Comte de Paris of a conversation with Queen Victoria, 1 July 1891, quoted in Michael of Greece, *Eddy & Hélène* (2013), p. 66.

40. Memorandum by Lord Cadogan, 12 Sept 1890. Parliamentary Archives, CAD/RC/48.

41. Queen Victoria to Lord Cadogan, 12 Sept 1890. Parliamentary Archives, CAD/RC/51.

42. Lord Salisbury to Queen Victoria, 16 Sept 1890 (copy). RA VIC/ADDC07/1.

43. Sir Henry Ponsonby to the Prince of Wales, 17 Sept 1890. RA VIC/ADDC07/1.

44. Sir Henry Ponsonby to Sir Francis Knollys, 15 Oct 1890. RA VIC/ADDC07/1.

45. Lord Halsbury to Queen Victoria (undated copy, but before 1 Oct 1890). RA VIC/ADDC07/1. Copy of the replies in the Cadogan Papers, Parliamentary Archives (RC/60/2) annotated 'sent to the Queen Septr 22/90.'

46. Comtesse de Paris to Comte de Paris, 15 Oct 1890. AnP 300 AP III 657/6.

47. Sir Henry Ponsonby to Sir Francis Knollys, 15, 30 Oct 1890. RA VIC/ADDC07/1.

48. Brun, *Descendance inédite du Duc de Berry* (1998), pp. 27-28.

49. Hélène de France to Pope Leo XIII, 1 Nov. 1890, quoted in Michael of Greece, *Eddy & Hélène* (2013), p. 38.

50. Prince Albert Victor to Prince George, 10 Feb 1891. RA GV/PRIV/AA39/63.

51. Memorandum by Gen. de Charette, 5 Nov. 1890, quoted in Michael of Greece, *Eddy & Hélène* (2013), pp. 39-41.

52. Kertzer, *Prisoner of the Vatican* (2004).

53. Comtesse de Paris to Comte de Paris, 6 Nov. 1890. AnP 300 AP III 657/10.

54. Prince Albert Victor to Hélène de France, 7 Nov., 9 Dec. 1890, quoted in Michael of Greece, *Eddy & Hélène* (2013), pp. 42-43, 45-46.

55. Professor Michael McCarthy quoted in Bevington, *Stowe House* (2002), p. 8.

55. Bevington, *Stowe House* (2002), pp. 8, 10, 20, 50-51.

56. *The Times*, 11 Nov 1890.

57. Barrière, *Les Princes d'Orléans* (1933), pp. 139-140.

58. *The Times*, 21 Oct. 1891

59. Memorandum by Gen. de Charette, 5 Nov. 1890, quoted in Michael of Greece, *Eddy & Hélène* (2013), p. 40.

60. *Le Figaro*, 17 Nov. 1890.

61. *The Standard*, 3 Dec. 1890; *The Huddersfield Daily Chronicle*, 4 Dec. 1890, which titled their reportage of the events 'An Odd Story from Paris'; Prince of Wales to Comte de Paris, 5 Dec. 1890. AnP 300 AP III 656/25.

62. Pope Leo XIII to Comte de Paris, 14 Dec. 1890. AnP 300 AP III 657/65.

63. Comte de Paris to Queen Victoria, 27 Dec 1890. RA VIC/MAIN/Y/52/82; Prince Albert Victor to Prince George, 1 Jan 1891. RA GV/PRIV/AA39/63; Princess Hélène to Queen Victoria, 30 Jan 1891. RA VIC/MAIN/Y/52/86.

64. Prince Albert Victor to Prince George, 10 Feb 1891. RA GV/PRIV/AA39/63. The next surviving letter from Eddy to George was from Dublin, 16 Oct. 1891, and contains no mention of Hélène.

65. Princess of Wales to Prince George, 3 June 1891. RA GV/PRIV/AA31/18; Prince Albert Victor to Hélène de France, 15 Jan. 1891, quoted in Michael of Greece, *Eddy & Hélène* (2013), p. 52.

66. Empress Frederick to Queen Victoria, 28 March 1891. RA VIC/MAIN/Z/50/28; Prince Albert Victor to Hélène de France, 23 March 1891, quoted in Michael of Greece, *Eddy & Hélène* (2013), p. 55; Comte de Paris to Hélène de France, 30 March 1891. Private Family Collection.

67. Hélène de France to Prince Albert Victor, 1 May 1891, quoted in Michael of Greece, *Eddy & Hélène* (2013), p. 60. Date of Hélène's departure is from Catinot-Crost, *Amélie de Portugal* (2000), p. 98. *The Times*, 4 May 1891, had mistakenly published that Hélène would be returning with her mother.

68. Comtesse de Paris to Hélène de France, 18 May 1891, quoted in Michael of Greece, *Eddy & Hélène* (2013), p. 61; Comte de Paris to Hélène de France, 18 May 1891. Private family collection.

69. Comtesse de Paris to Hélène de France, 31 May 1891, quoted in Michael of Greece, *Eddy & Hélène* (2013), p. 62.

70. Prince Albert Victor to Hélène de France, 2 June 1891, quoted in Michael of Greece, *Eddy & Hélène* (2013), p. 64.

71. Princess of Wales to Prince George, 3 June 1891. RA GV/PRIV/AA31/18.

72. Memorandum by the Comte de Paris of a conversation with Queen Victoria,

1 July 1891, quoted in Michael of Greece, *Eddy & Hélène* (2013), p. 65.

73. Lord Salisbury to Queen Victoria, (21?) June 1891. RA VIC/MAIN/A/68/40a.

74. *The Times*, 1 Oct. 1891.

75. Queen Victoria to the Comtesse de Paris, 5 Dec. 1891. RA VIC/MAIN/Z/475/26.; Queen Victoria to the Princess of Wales, 5 Dec. 1891. RA VIC/MAIN/Z/475/27; Comte de Paris to Queen Victoria, 7 Dec 1891. RA VIC/Z 475/80; Comtesse de Paris to Queen Victoria, 8 Dec 1891. RA VIC/Z 475/112.

76. Princess Maud of Wales to Hélène de France, 21 Jan. 1892, Princess Victoria of Wales to Hélène de France, 22 Jan. 1892, quoted in Michael of Greece, *Eddy & Hélène* (2013), pp. 79–80; RA GV/PRIV/GVD/1892: 14 Jan.

77. Princess Maud of Wales to Hélène de France, 21 Jan. 1892; Princess Victoria of Wales to Hélène de France, 22 Jan. 1892, quoted in Michael of Greece, *Eddy & Hélène* (2013), pp. 79–80.

78. Princess Victoria of Wales to Hélène de France, 22 Jan. 1892, quoted in Michael of Greece, *Eddy & Hélène* (2013), p. 80; Princess Louise, Duchess of Fife to Hélène de France, 22 Jan. 1892; Princess of Wales to Hélène de France, [undated], quoted in Michael of Greece, *Eddy & Hélène* (2013), pp. 82, 85.

79. Hélène de France to Queen Victoria, [undated], Princess Beatrice of Battenberg to Hélène de France, 1 Dec. 1892, quoted in Michael of Greece, *Eddy & Hélène* 2013), pp. 84, 87. The wreath remained there at least into the 1950s. Pope-Hennessy, *Queen Mary* (1959), p. 199.

Chapter 4:

1. Empress Frederick to Queen Victoria, 19 Nov. 1892. RA VIC/MAIN/Z 54; Memorandum by the Comte de Paris of a conversaation with Queen Victoria, 1 July 1891, quoted in Michael of Greece, *Eddy & Hélène*, 65; Pasteur, Chargé d'Affaires de France à Copenhague à M. Develle, Ministre des Affaires étrangères. Copenhague, 8 Oct. 1893. In *Documents diplomatiques français (1871–1914)*. 1re ser [1871–1914], 10:557.

2. Comte de StPriest to an unidentified general, Bayonne, 10 Oct. [10 8bre] 1893. RA VIC/MAIN/I /88/7; Unidentified general to Queen Victoria, 15 Oct. 1893. RA VIC/MAIN/I/88/8.

3. Friedrich von Holstein to Philipp zu Eulenburg, Berlin, 2 Dec. 1893, in Eulenburg, *Korrespondenz* (1983), p. 1151; Nicholas II, Diary, 29 Jan. 1894, quoted in Maylunas & Mironenko, *A Lifelong Passion* (1996), p. 22.

4. Massie, *Nicholas and Alexandra* (1967), p. 26; *The Times*, 9 Jan 1891.

5. *Le Matin*, 3 Nov. 1894; Hulst, *A Royal and Christian Soul* (1895), pp. 48–49.

6. Amélie de Portugal to Comte de Paris, 7 Jan. 1892, Carlos of Portugal to Comte de Paris, [without specific date] Jan. 1892. AnP 300 AP 376.

7. Barrière, *Princes d'Orléans* (1933); see also Van Kerrebrouck, *La Maison de Bourbon* (2004), 4:554, n.16.

8. Lewis, *Queen of Cooks* (1925), pp. 8–9.

9. Queen Victoria to the Empress Frederick, 19 Nov 1892 (transcript of extracts). RA VIC/ADDU/32/1892: 19 Nov.

10. Hélène de France to Queen Victoria, [undated, probably spring 1893], quoted in Michael of Greece, *Eddy & Hélène* (2013), 88; and 24 May 1893 (RA VIC/MAIN/Y/52/93); 19 Dec 1893 (RA VIC/MAIN/Y/52/94).

11. Van der Kiste, *Edward VII's Children* (2004), p. 36.

12. Carlos of Portugal to Comte de Paris, 24 March 1892. AnP 300 AP 376; Comte de Paris to Carlos of Portugal, 28 March 1892. Private family collection

13. Amélie de Portugal to Comte de Paris, [no specific date] Jan. 1892, Hélène de France to Comte de Paris, 3, 22 March 1892. AnP 300 AP 376.

14. Hélène de France to Comte de Paris, 27 April, 10 May 1892. AnP 300 AP 376.

15. Hélène de France to Comte de Paris, 16 July, 13, 20, 27 Aug., 8 Sept. 1892. AnP 300 AP 376; RA VIC/MAIN/QVJ (W) 19 Nov. 1892 (Princess Beatrice's copies). Retrieved 29 July 2016.

16. RA GV/PRIV/GVD/1893: 23 June; Philippe, Comte de Flandres, to Queen Victoria, 27 March 1892. RA VIC/Q7/8. On 7 Sept. 1893, Article 85 of the Belgian constitution had two sections added which required royal consent for the marriage of princes; Bilteryst, *Le prince Baudoin* (2013), p. 254; Paoli, *Fortune & Infortunes des princes d'Orléans* (2006), pp. 326–327.

17. RA VIC/MAIN/QVJ (W) 5 July 1893 (Princess Beatrice's copies). Retrieved 29 July 2016.

18. McKinstry, *Rosebery* (2005), p. 352, quoting John Morley's diary, 13 Nov. 1893.

19. Hélène d'Orléans to Queen Victoria, 19 Dec. 1893 [19 X^bre 1893]. RA VIC/MAIN/Y/52/94; Blunt, *My Diaries* (1919–1920), 1:69, 148; Hélène d'Aosta, *Voyages en Afrique* (1913), p. 6.

20. Comte de Paris to Hélène de France, 17 Jan., 7, 21 Feb. 1894. Private family collection; Hélène d'Aosta, *Voyages en Afrique* (1913), pp. 7–8; Hélène d'Aosta, *Attraverso il Sahara*, p. 19.

21. Comte de Paris to Hélène de France, 8, 15 March 1894. Private family collection.

22. Eulenburg, *Korrespondenz* (1983), 1287. The horse was sent back to Spain for Hélène, arriving there in April. Comte de Paris to Hélène de France, 2 April 1894. Private family collection.

23. Röhl, *Wilhelm II* (2004), pp. 654–655.

24. Empress Frederick to Queen Victoria, 2 May 1894. RA VIC/MAIN/Z/56.

25. Queen Victoria to Empress Frederick, 14 May 1894. RA VIC/ADDU/32/1894: 14 May.

26. Queen Victoria to Empress Frederick, 4 July 1894. RA VIC/ADDU32/1894: 4 July.

27. Gen. Gardiner to Queen Victoria, 22 Aug 1894. RA VIC/MAIN/J/92/83; Duc de Nemours to Queen Victoria, 4 Sept. 1894. RA VIC/MAIN/J/92/86.

28. In her journal, dated 9 Sept. 1894, Queen Victoria recorded that 'On getting up

received a telegram from Philippe Orléans, announcing the death of his excellent father, which took place at two this morning.' Most sources give 8 September as the deathdate. RA /MAIN/QVJ/1894: 9 Sept.; 'Illness of Prominent Persons' (1994), p. 926, quoting JAMA 23(1894):443.

29. Prince of Wales to Queen Victoria, St James's, 14 Sept. 1894 [telegram]. RA VIC/ MAIN/J/92/97; François, Prince de Joinville to Queen Victoria, 9 Sept 1894. RA VIC/MAIN/Y/52/109; Hélène d'Aosta, *Voyages en Afrique* (1913), p. 235.

30. Lord Carrington to Sir Henry Ponsonby, 12 Sept. 1894. RA VIC/MAIN/Y/52/J92/95.

31. VanKerrebrouck, *Maison de Bourbon* (2004), 4:871–872; Langham–Carter, *The Royal French Tombs at Weybridge* (1975).

32. *The Times*, 31 Oct 1894.

33. Gramont, *Ami du prince* (2011), pp. 39, 41, 42, 49, 52.

34. Henri, Duc d'Aumale, Draft Memorandum [perhaps a draft letter to the Comtesse de Paris], 21 Oct. 1894. Archives du Château de Chantilly. Fonds Orléans (1 PA 2).

35. *The Times*, 21 Feb 1893, 5d; Oliva, *Duchi d'Aosta* (2003), suggests there was a meeting with Hélène in Jan. 1893, this cannot be confirmed; RA VIC/MAIN/ QVJ/1893: 22 Feb, 23, 25 March.

36. Queen Victoria to the Empress Frederick, 20 Oct. 1892. Transcript of extracts. RA VIC/ADDU/32/1892: 20 Oct.; Duchess of Saxe-Coburg to Marie, Crown Princess of Romania, 24 July 1893, 21 June 1897, in Mandache, ed., *Dearest Missy*, 130, 303.

37. Farini, *Diario* (1961–1962), pp. 174, 662.

38. Henri, Duc d'Aumale, draft letter to the Comtesse de Paris], 5 Nov. 1894; Duc d'Aumale, draft memorandum, 14 Dec. 1894; Auguste Laugel to Duc d'Aumale, 11 Feb. 1895. Archives du Château de Chantilly. Fonds Orléans (1 PA 2).

39. RA VIC/MAIN/QVJ (W) 9 March 1895 (Princess Beatrice's copies). Retrieved 29 July 2016.

40. Cazelles, *Le Duc d'Aumale* (1984), p. 458.

41. Comtesse de Paris to Queen Victoria, 19 March 1895 [telegram]. RA VIC/ MAIN/J/42/49; Empress Frederick to Queen Victoria, 22 March 1895. RA VIC/ MAIN/Z/57; Queen Victoria to Empress Frederick, 27 March 1895. RA VIC/ ADDU/32/1895: 27 March; Victoria, Empress Frederick of Germany, *The Empress Frederick Writes to Sophie* (1955), p. 193.

42. Cazelles, *Le duc d'Aumale* (1984), pp. 9–28.

43. Farini, *Diario* (1961–1962), p. 662.

44. Hélène d'Orléans to Queen Victoria, 24 March 1895. RA VIC/MAIN/Y/52/127.

45. RA GV/PRIV/GVD/1895: 5 & 6 April.

46. Comtesse de Paris to Queen Victoria, 22 April 1895. RA VIC/MAIN/Y/52/128.

47. Asquith, *An Autobiography* (1920–1922), 2:262–264.

48. Hélène de France to Duke of Aosta, 13 June 1895. Collezione Duca d'Aosta, Nunziatella.

49. RA VIC/MAIN/QVJ (W) 23 June 1895 (Princess Beatrice's copies). Retrieved 29 July 2016.

50. Hélène de France to Queen Victoria, 24 June 1895. RA VIC/MAIN/Y/52/133; Queen Victoria to Hélène de France, 24 June 1895, quoted in Michael of Greece, *Eddy & Hélène*, 92–93; *The Graphic*, 29 June 1895.

51. Blunt, *My Diaries* (1919–1920), 1:210; *The Times*, 26 June 1895; Gramont, *Ami du prince* (2011), p. 56.

52. *The Illustrated London News*, 22 and 29 June 1895 both provided lengthy articles on the wedding.

53. Gramont, *Ami du prince* (2011), p. 56.

54. Blunt, *My Diaries* (1919–1920), 1:210–211; *The Manchester Guardian*, 26 June 1895; *The Graphic*, 29 June 1895. The Aumale necklace at some point after World War I was in the collection of Sybil Sassoon, Lady Chomondeley. It was sold at Christie's London in 1990; and again at Christie's Geneva, 10 Nov. 2015, this time for $2,632,492. A second emerald necklace came from the Pozzo della Cisterna family, and it was inherited by Archduchess Margherita of Austria who gave it to her daughter-in-law Princess Astrid of Belgium.

Chapter 5:

1. Attributed to Massimo d'Azeglio (1798–1866), quoted in Putnam, *Making Democracy Work* (1993), p. 18.

2. Farini, *Diario* (1961–1962), p. 725; Castellani, *Microbes, Men and Monarchs* (1960), 238.

3. Farini, *Diario* (1961–1962), pp. 725, 729.

4. Piano, *Memorie* (1956), p. 9; Thompson, *The White War* (2008), pp. 257–258.

5. Putnam, *Making Democracy Work* (1993), pp. 18, 121.

6. Mack Smith, *Italy and its Monarchy* (1989), p. 25.

7. Duggan, *Fascist Voices* (2012), p. 11; Mack Smith, *Italy and its Monarchy* (1989), p. 112; Putnam, *Making Democracy Work* (1993), p. 107; Thompson, *The White War* (2008), pp. 137–138.

8. Gary Boyd Roberts, "Notable Kin—SurprisingConnections, #5: James Edward Oglethorpe, Henry Sampson of the Mayflower, other Colonial Immigrants, and Kings of Italy" www.americanancestors.org/james-edward-oglethorpe-henry-sampson-of-the-mayflower/. Accessed 18 June 2012.

9. The title Duke of Aosta had earlier been used in the Savoy family for several generations, including Vittorio Amedeo Teodoro (1723–1735), the oldest son of Carlo Emanuele III of Sardinia, and later by his younger sons Giuseppe Carlo *Emanuele Filiberto* Augusto (1731–1735) and Carlo Francesco Maria Augusto (1738–1745); then by the youngest son King Vittorio Amedeo III, Giuseppe Benedetto Maria Placido (1766–1802).

10. Farini, *Diario* (1961–1962), p. 1362.

11. On the controversy surrounding this marriage, see Mellano, *I prinicipi Maria Clotilde e Amedeo di Savoia e il Vaticano* (2000), chapter 6, esp. p. 157.

12. *Colorado Springs Gazette* (Colorado Springs, Colorado), 8 Sept 1894.

13. Quoted in Chamberlain, *Nietzsche in Turin* (1996), p. 23.

14. Hélène d'Aosta to Queen Victoria, 23 Dec. 1895. RA VIC/MAIN/Y/52/138. The letter is actually dated "23 Xbre 95" as Hélène sometimes employed the old-fashioned usage of numbering the months after their Latin derivatives, e.g. September as the seventh month, October as the eighth, etc.

15. 1871 census for Stonyhurst, Aighton, Lancashire.

16. Hélène d'Aosta to Queen Victoria, 23 Dec. 1895. RA VIC/MAIN/Y/52/138.

17. *Boston Daily Advertiser* (Boston, Mass.), 18 Feb. 1896.

18. Mockler, *Haile Selassie's War* (1984), pp. xxxix, xxxxi; Cervi, *Il Duca Invitto* (1987), p. 66; Gooch, *The Italian Army* (2014), p. 28. Gooch gives alternative casualty figures—5000 Italians and 1000 ascaris; another 1500 wounded; and 2700 taken prisoner.

19. Mack Smith, *Italy and Its Monarchy* (1989), p. 122.

20. RA QM/PRIV/QMD/1896: 7 Sept.; Duchess of York to Duchess of Teck, 9 Sept. 1896, quoted in Pope-Hennessy, *Queen Mary* (1959), p. 332.

21. Hélène d'Aosta to Queen Victoria, 8 Sept. 1896. RA VIC/MAIN/Y/52/153.

22. 'Woolston v. Woolston, Louis Philippe, duc d'Orléans, and Peters,' *The Times*, 29 Oct. 1895; Defrance, *La Médicis des Cobourg* (2007), p. 330; Hélène d'Aosta to Queen Victoria, 8 Sept. 1896. RA VIC/MAIN/Y/52/153.

23. Regolo, *Jelena* (2002), p. 195.

24. Hanson, 'Connubial Equality' (2010), pp. 1–3.

25. Regolo, *Jelena* (2002), p. 215.

26. see Regolo, *Jelena* (2002), p. 225 et seq.

27. *Calendario d'Oro* (1897), 13–77.

28. *The Times*, 6 Nov 1896; *Vogue*, 10 Dec. 1896.

29. Stancioff, *Recollections of a Bulgarian Diplomatist's wife* (1931), p. 129.

30. Hélène d'Aosta to Queen Victoria, 27 Dec. 1896. RA VIC/MAIN/Y/52/159.

31. Gramont, *Ami du prince* (2011), p. 79.

32. Christopher of Greece, *Memoirs* (1938), p. 248; Cazelles, *Le Duc d'Aumale* (1984), p. 467.

33. *Le Figaro*, 8 May 1897.

34. O. Lichtscheidl, M. Wohlfart, 'Biographies of Elisabeth's Siblings,' www .hofburg-wien.at.

35. Cazelles, *Duc d'Aumale* (1984), p. 467; RA VIC/MAIN/QVJ (W) 7 May 1897 (Princess Beatrice's copies). Retrieved 29 July 2016.

36. *Le Figaro*, 8 May 1897; *Echo de Paris*, 19 May 1897; Cazelles, *Duc d'Aumale* (1984), p. 465; Barrière, *Les princes d'Orléans* (1933), p. 115.

37. Jacques, duc d'Orléans, *Les chasses des princes d'Orléans* (1999), p. 34.

38. Regolo, *Jelena* (2000), pp. 299–300. Another report from one of Turin's

contemporaries states that he went to Canada on a sporting tour, having 'been sent out of Europe by the King, consequent to his successful duel' (*The Times*, 28 Sept. 1935, a letter by Cecil B. Levita, who was assigned to the Count's staff by Lord Aberdeen, the Governor General of Canada). Telegram, Hélène d'Aosta to Count of Turin. Fondo Aosta, Naples.

39. Jacques, duc d'Orléans, *Les chasses des princes d'Orléans* (1999), p. 35.

40. *The Boston [Mass.] Advertiser*, 20 Sept. 1897.

41. Farini, *Diario* (1961–1962), p. 1365; Comtesse de Paris to Queen Victoria, [telegram] 25 Oct. 1898. RA VIC/MAIN/J/42/74a.

42. Farini, *Diario* (1961–1962), pp. 673, 1366; Hélène d'Aosta to Duc d'Orléans, 21 Jan. 1900, 3 Jan. 1901. AnP 300 AP III 815/83, 86.

43. Victoria, Empress Frederick of Germany, *Empress Frederick Writes to Sophie* (1955), p. 287.

44. Trevelyan, *Princes under the Volcano* (1972), p. 299.

45. Gustavo Mola di Nomaglio, "Per la giustizia, la carità, l'assistenza: Casa Savoia dalla 'Mendicità sbandita' alla Croce Rossa Italiana," in Cipolla, *Storia della Croce Rossa in Piemonte* (2015), 157; Hélène d'Aosta to Duc d'Orléans, 17 March 1899. AnP 300 III 815.

46. RA VIC/MAIN/QVJ (W) 10 April 1899 (Princess Beatrice's copies). Retrieved 29 July 2016.

47. Queen Victoria to the Empress Frederick, 9 Sept. 1899, in *Beloved and Darling Child* (1990), p. 235.

48. Jean, duc de Guise, *Sous le Danebrog* (1901), pp. 3, 4, 6, 11, 25.

Chapter 6:

1. Hélène d'Aosta, "Da Tripoli a Gat," 21 April 1931.

2. Bracalini, *Casa Savoia* (2001), pp. 72–73; *The Manchester Guardian*, 31 July 1900.

3. Mack Smith, *Italy and its Monarchy* (1989), p. 138.

4. Mack Smith, *Italy and its Monarchy* (1989), p. 147, citing Antonio Salandra. *Il diario*, ed. G.B. Gifuni, Milan, 1868, 31; Puntoni, *Parla Vittorio Emanuel III* (1993), p. 221.

5. Tenderini and Shandrick, *The Duke of the Abruzzi* (1997), pp. 25, 40.

6. Abruzzi, *On the "Polar Star"* (1903), 1:48; Tenderini and Shandrick, *The Duke of the Abruzzi* (1997), pp. 54, 57, 58, 66. The latter account also states that Hélène and Emanuele Filiberto went to Norway to see Luigi on his way, but this statement is not confirmed by *La Stampa*, which has the Duke and Duchess at the races in Turin on the 20th having just returned from Milan. See 15 May 1899, which indicates there was an unfounded rumour that Emanuele Filiberto would go to Norway.

7. Hélène d'Aosta to Philippe, duc d'Orléans, 27 Jan. 1901. AnP 300 AP III 815/84. *La Stampa* reported on 30 Jan. that the Aostas would be leaving the next day, but on the 31st recorded the departure of only the Duke. *Le Figaro* (1 Feb.) announced that Hélène joined Emanuele on the 9.00am train from Paris to Calais on the

morning of 31 Jan., but this seems to be inaccurate.

8. Gramont, *Ami du prince* (2011), p. 110.

9. *Revue d'Action Française*, 15 July 1901, quoted in Osgood, *French Royalism* (1960), p. 72; Gramont, *Ami du prince* (2011), pp. 175, 181–182.

10. George von Lengerke Meyer Papers, Massachusetts Historical Society, Boston, Mass. (hereafter MHS).

11. Meyer Papers, MHS.

12. Pope-Hennessy, *Queen Mary* (1959), pp. 370–371.

13. Battiscombe, *Queen Alexandra* (1969), pp. 246–248.

14. RA GV/PRIV/GVD/1902: 26 June.

15. Sermoneta, *Things Past* (1929), p. 56.

16. RA GV/PRIV/GVD/1902: 2 July.

17. *The Sunday Times*, 6 July 1902; RA GV/PRIV/GVD/1902: 10, 11 July.

18. Catinot-Crost, Amélie de Portugal (2000), pp. 138, 145.

19. Alice Meyer, 7 June 1903. Meyer Papers, MHS.

20. Meyer Papers, MHS; Lami, *Le passioni del Dragone* (2009), p. 84.

21. Blunt, *My Diaries* (1919–1920), 2:99, 101.

22. Piano, *Memorie* (1956), pp. 11, 15.

23. Piano, *Memorie* (1956), p. 16.

24. Howe, *George von Lengerke Meyer* (1920), pp. 101.104.

25. Piano, *Memorie* (1956), pp. 16–17; Howe, *George von Lengerke Meyer* (1920), p. 107.

26. Catinot-Crost, *Amélie de Portugal* (2000), p. 157; *The Times*, 11 Dec. 1904; Piano, *Memorie* (1956), p. 18.

27. Reproduced in Casale, 'L'opera di Elena D'Aosta per la Croce Rossa' (2011), p. 44.

28. Piano, *Memorie* (1956), pp. 19–20.

29. Queen Alexandra to King George V, 8 April 1905. RA GV/PRIV/AA33/4, quoted in Battiscombe, *Queen Alexandra* (1969), p. 257, but mistakenly identifying 'dear Granny Isabel' as 'Dowager Queen Isabel'; *The Times*, 27 March 1905, 3d.

30. Howe, *George vonL. Meyer* (1920), p. 135; Hélène d'Aosta to Alice Meyer, 25 May 1906; and to George vonL. Meyer, 22 June 1906. Meyer Papers, MHS.

31. Baedeker, *Southern Italy and Sicily* (1912), p. 97; Lewis, *Naples '44*, 178–179.

32. Susan Hicks Beach, Journal, 23, 24 May 1908. Hicks Beach Papers, Gloucestershire Record Office, D2455/F3/11/2/4.

33. Piano, *Memorie* (1956), pp. 24, 28–29.

34. Viktoria Luise, Duchess of Hanover, *Bilder der Kaiserzeit* (1969), pp. 132–135; *The Manchester Guardian*, 7 June 1905; *Daisy, Princess of Pless, by Herself* (1928), p. 110.

35. Piano, *Memorie* (1956), p. 35; Mack Smith, *Italy and its Monarchy* (1989), pp. 7–8.

36. *Washington Post*, 12 April 1906.

37. Piano, *Memorie* (1956), pp. 38–39.

38. Hélène d'Aosta to Alice Meyer, 25 May 1906. Meyer Paper, MHS; Piano, *Memorie* (1956), p. 54.

39. *The Times*, 9 April 1906.

40. 'The Hero of Vesuvius,' Chapter 8: The Eruption—Part I. www.vesvius.tomgidwitz. com/html/8__the_eruption_-_phase_i.html, downloaded 11 Oct 2008.

41. *The Times*, 9, 13 April 1906.

42. Quoted in Scarth, *Vesuvius: A Biography* (2009), p. 264.

43. *The Times*, 11 April 1906; Morris, *The San Francisco Calamity*.

44. Piano, *Memorie* (1956), p. 62.

45. Hélène d'Aosta to Duc d'Orléans, 27 Sept 1906. AnP 300 AP III 815/218; RA GV/PRIV/GVD/1906: 28 Sept. The photograph album is in the Fondo Aosta, Biblioteca di Napoli.

46. Hélène d'Aosta to Duca d'Aosta, 21 Oct. 1906. Collezione Duca d'Aosta, Nunziatella.

47. Piano, *Memorie* (1956), p. 65.

48. *Queen Alexandra's Christmas book: Photographs from my Camera* (1908).

49. Hélène d'Aosta to Duc d'Orléans, 8 Feb. 1907. AnP 300 AP III 815/140.

50. Ella Douglas Pennant to Lady St Aldwyn, 30 Dec 1907. GRO:D2455/ F3/7/1/3/12; Amélie, journal intime, 11 Nov. 1929; Eustace, 'Britannia,' 332. Susan thus became 'the Honourable Miss Hicks Beach' in 1906, and then when her father was created Earl St Aldwyn in 1915, 'Lady Susan Hicks Beach.'

51. Susan Hicks Beach to Lady St Aldwyn, 30 Aug. 1907. Hicks Beach Papers, Gloucestershire Record Office. GRO: D2455/F3/7/1/3/12.

51. Piano, *Memorie* (1956), p. 81.

52. RA GV/PRIV/GVD/1907: 17 Nov.

Chapter 7:

1. Hélène d'Aosta, *Souvenirs d'Afrique* (1929), 257.

2. 'Will Aosta be exiled?,' *Chicago Tribune*, 11 Dec.1907.

3. *La Stampa*, 14 Dec 1907.

4. Farini, *Diario* (1961–1962), p. 673.

5. Asquith, *An Autobiography* (1920–1922), 2:262–264.

6. Jacques, duc d'Orléans, *Les chasses des princes d'Orléans* (1999), p. 35.

7. Ferdinand, duc de Montpensier, *Ma première croisière* (1907).

8. TNA FO 371/469/40596.

9. *New York Times*, 7 November 1909, pt 3, 3:6. Nothing of the sort was recorded by the British diplomatic reports of the time (TNA FO 371/469).

10. Caroline Moorehead, *Martha* Gellhorn, chap. 13 ('The Capital of My Soul').

11. Hélène d'Aosta, *Voyages en Afrique* (1913), pp. 3–4.

12. Hélène d'Aosta, *Voyages en Afrique* (1913), pp. 4, 6.

13. Susan Hicks Beach's photo album from this first journey is now in the collections at Northwestern University.

14. Susan Hicks Beach, Journal, 5 Dec. 1907. GRO: D2455/F3/11/2/4.

15. Susan Hicks Beach to Lord St Aldwyn, 5 Dec. 1907. GRO: D2455/F3/7/1/3/12

16. Granville to Sir Edward Grey, Bart., 15 Oct. 1909. TNA: FO 367/.137 f 38376.

17. Susan Hicks Beach to Victoria Hicks Beach, 8 Dec. [1907]. GRO: D2455/F3/11/1/3

18. Hélène d'Aosta to Emanuele Filiberto d'Aosta, telegram, 11 Dec 1907. Collezione Duca d'Aosta, Nunziatella.

19. Susan Hicks Beach, Journal, 8 Dec. 1907. GRO: D2455/F3/11/2/4.

20. Susan Hicks Beach, Journal, 9 Dec. 1907. GRO: D2455/F3/11/2/4.

21. Susan Hicks Beach to Lady St Aldwyn, 15 Dec. 1907. GRO: D2455/F3/7/1/3/12.

22. Susan Hicks Beach, Journal, 10, 11 Dec. 1907. GRO: D2455/F3/11/2/4.

23. Hélène d'Aosta, *Voyages en Afrique* (1913), pp. 8, 10.

24. Hélène d'Aosta, *Voyages en Afrique* (1913), pp. 11–12; Susan Hicks Beach, Journal, 24 Dec. 1907. GRO: D2455/F3/11/2/4.

25. Churchill, *My African Journey* (1909), pp. 209 et seq.

26. Susan Hicks Beach, Journal, 25 Dec. 1907. GRO: D2455/F3/11/2/4; Susan Hicks Beach to Lady St Aldwyn, 26 Dec. 1907. GRO: D2455/F3/7/1/3/12; Hélène d'Aosta, *Voyages en Afrique* (1913), p. 13.

27. Susan Hicks Beach, Journal, 19, 23 Dec. 1907. GRO: D2455/F3/11/2/4.

28. Susan Hick Beach to Victoria Hicks Beach, 31 Dec 1907. GRO: D2455/F3/11/1/3

29. *The Times*, 2, 29 Jan. 1908.

30. Report of Lt-Col Delmé-Radcliffe, 12 Feb 1908, on a conversation with the King of Italy, 10 Feb. TNA: FO 371/469/6961)

31. Hélène d'Aosta, *Voyages en Afrique* (1913), pp. 15, 17.

32. Hélène d'Aosta, *Voyages en Afrique* (1913), pp. 18–20; Churchill, *My African Journey* (1909), p. 111.

33. Susan Hicks Beach to Victoria Hicks Beach, 8 Jan 1908. GRO: D2455/F3/11/1/3

34. Hélène d'Aosta, *Voyages en Afrique* (1913), pp. 23, 27.

35. Hélène d'Aosta to Duc d'Orléans, 22 Jan. 1908. AnP 300 III 815/151.

36. Susan Hicks Beach to Lady St Aldwyn, 22 Jan 1908. GRO: D2455/F3/7/1/3/12.

37. Hélène d'Aosta, *Voyages en Afrique* (1913), p. 29.

38. Hélène d'Aosta, *Voyages en Afrique* (1913), pp. 38, 46.

39. Hélène d'Aosta, *Voyages en Afrique* (1913), p. 52.

40. Susan Hicks Beach, Journal, 2 March 1908. GRO: D2455/F3/11/1/3.

41. Gribble, *The Royal House of Portugal* (1915), p. 291.

42. Susan Hicks Beach, Journal, 9 March 1908. GRO: D2455/F3/11/1/3.

43. Bell, *Glimpses of a Governor's Life* (1946), p. 177.

44. Susan Hicks Beach, Journal, 24 March 1908. GRO: D2455/F3/11/1/3.

45. Bell, *Glimpses of a Governor's Life* (1946), pp. 98, 114, 178.

46. Susan Hicks Beach, Journal, 17 March 1908. GRO: D2455/F3/11/2/4.

47. Susan Hicks Beach, Journal, 20, 24 March 1908. GRO: D2455/F3/11/2/4.

48. Susan Hicks Beach to Lady St Aldwyn, 26 March 1908. GRO: D2455/ F3/7/1/3/12.

49. Bell, *Glimpses of a Governor's Life* (1946), p. 104.

50. Susan Hicks Beach, Journal, 28 March 1908. GRO: D2455/F3/11/2/4

51. Hélène d'Aosta, *Voyages en Afrique* (1913), p. 73.

52. Susan Hick Beach, Journal, 31 March 1908. GRO: D2455/F3/11/2/4.

53. Nicholls, *Red Strangers* (2005), p. 65.

54. Hélène d'Aosta, *Voyages en Afrique* (1913), p. 78.

55. Hélène d'Aosta, *Voyages en Afrique* (1913), pp. 73–74, 76, 78, 82–83, 85–86; Susan Hicks Beach, Journal, 28 March 1908. GRO: D2455/F3/11/2/4.

56. Hélène d'Aosta to Duca d'Aosta, 4 May 1908. Collezione Duca d'Aosta, Nunziatella.

57. Susan Hicks Beach, Journal, 17, 23 May 1908. GRO: D2455/F3/11/2/4; Susan Hicks Beach to Lady St Aldwyn, 25 May 1908. GRO: D2455/F3/7/1/3/12

58. Susan Hicks Beach, Journal, 24, 25 May 1908. GRO: D2455/F3/11/2/4.

59. Hélène d'Aosta to Duc d'Orléans, 25, 28 June 1908. AnP 300 AP III 815/161, 162.

60. Blunt, *My Diaries* (1919–1920), 2:220.

61. *Le Matin*, 22 Aug. 1908. "Est-ce mal physique? Est-ce mal moral?"

62. *New York Times*, 18 Oct. 1908.

63. Tenderini and Shandrick, *The Duke of the Abruzzi* (1997), p. 94.

64. Bell, *Glimpses of a Governor's Life* (1946), pp. 117–119.

65. Tenderini and Shandrick, *The Duke of the Abruzzi* (1997), p. 118.

66. Mack Smith, *Italy and Its Monarchy* (1989), p. 181; *Manchester Guardian*, 1 Jan. 1909; Tavormina, 'Le Infermiere Volontarie CRI' (2015), pp. 210–211.

67. Henry Cabot Lodge to Theodore Roosevelt, 8 May 1905, in Roosevelt, *Selections from the Correspondence* (1925), 2:118.

68. Theodore Roosevelt to Anna Roosevelt Cowles, 13 April 1909, in Roosevelt, *The Letters of Theodore Roosevelt* (1951–1954), 7:5–6.

69. Rodd, *Social and Diplomatic Memories* (1925), chapter V: Rome, 1908–1910

70. Empress Marie to Tsar Nicholas II, 29 April/12 May 1909, in Coryne Hall, *Little Mother of Russia*, 229, quoting Bing, ed., *Letters*, 241.

71. *The Times*, 3 May 1909; Bell, *Glimpses of a Governor Life* (1946), p. 211.

72. Hélène d'Aosta, *Voyages en Afrique* (1913), p. 97.

73. Hélène d'Aosta to Lady St Aldwyn, 13 Sept. 1909, 17 Sept. 1909 (telegram). GRO: D2455/F3/7/1/3/14.

74. Hélène d'Aosta to Duc d'Orléans, 11 Sept 1909. AnP 300 AP III 815/168.

75. Hélène d'Aosta to Duc d'Orleans, 23 Sept 1909. AnP 300 AP III 815/169.

76. The boys' college was mis-identified as Saint Andrew's College in DeVecchi di Val Cismon's 1942 biography of Amedeo, and that mistake has been repeated in all subsequent published biographies of Amedeo and books on the Aosta family, some

extrapolating the mistake to call the school 'Saint Andrew di Eton,' while Bosworth, *Mussolini* (2002), p. 495, makes it a 'Scottish school,' presumably based solely upon the mistaken name. The name and location of the college were presumably not public knowledge, as *The Times*, 2 June 1915, 6f, says : 'Both their Royal Highnesses were educated at Westgate' rather than Reigate, and the *Manchester Guardian*, 11 Sept. 1915, also reported that they had been educated at Westgate-on-Sea. However, Hélène clearly states in her letter to her brother Philippe that it was St David's Reigate, and in 1936 both Amedeo and Aimone—along with the Duke of Westminster and the Duke of Northumberland—were among those who sent 'Messages of good wishes to the School and regrets of absence' to the Old St David's Association when the annual football match was held at St David's, Reigate (*The Times*, 16 Nov 1936, 15e). At the Fondo Aosta, Biblioteca Nazionale di Napoli, is a novel, *Captain Black*, by Max Pemberton, which is inscribed 'A Souvenir of Many Happy Days at St Davids, Reigate from Edward Rose, August 1911, to Aimone.' Rose, an American from Denver, was a fellow pupil at the college. The family photograph albums also contains a number of shots of St David's.

77. *The Times*, 20 Sept. 1946.
78. *The Sunday Times*, 28 Jan. 1951 (writing as 'Atticus').
79. TNA: RG14 PN3214 (St David's School, Wray Park Road, Reigate).
80. Hélène d'Aosta, *Voyages en Afrique* (1913), pp. 97, 98.
81. Susan Hicks Beach to Lady St Aldwyn, 25 Oct 1909. GRO: D2455/F3/7/1/3/14.
82. Hélène d'Aosta, *Voyages en Afrique* (1913), p, 101.
83. Rodriques, 'Prince Dom Luis Filipe of Portugal and the Regicide of 1908' (2008), 1:40.
84. Hélène d'Aosta, *Voyages en Afrique* (1913), pp. 123–124, 127.

Chapter 8:

1. Hélène d'Aosta, *Voyages en Afrique* (1913), p. 159.
2. Hélène d'Aosta, 'Diana in Africa,' *Harper's* Weekly, 12 March 1910 (part 1). A slightly different version of this episode appears in *Voyages en Afrique* (1913), p. 147, under the date 9 Dec. and place given as Lusitania.
3. Hélène d'Aosta, *Voyages en Afrique* (1913), pp. 148, 151.
4. 'Diana in Africa,' *Harper's Weekly*, serially in vol. 54 (1910): March 12, pp. 14–17; April 30, pp. 11–12; May 7, pp. 9–10; Aug. 6, pp. 8–9; Aug. 20, pp. 12–13.
5. Hélène d'Aosta, *Voyages en Afrique* (1913), p. 153.
6. Hélène d'Aosta, *Voyages en Afrique* (1913), p. 159.
7. Amedeo di Savoia-Aosta to Duc d'Orléans, 27 Jan 1910 (AnP 300 AP III 815/172; Aimone di Savoia-Aosta, same, 815/173.
8. Hélène d'Aosta, *Voyages en Afrique* (1913), pp. 159, 161.
9. Based on the age of 16 given in 1914 on the passenger lists during the round the world journey. Hélène noted that Pedro's mother came to greet him in Dec.

1909, after they left camp at Ghindu-Guenge before getting on a boat to Lusitania. Hélène d'Aosta, *Voyages en Afrique* [1913], p. 154.

10. Regolo, *Jelena* (2002), p. 476.

11. Hélène d'Aosta, *Voyages en Afrique* (1913), pp. 164–165.

12. Hélène d'Aosta, *Voyages en Afrique* (1913), pp. 165, 167, 172, 221.

13. Hélène d'Aosta, *Voyages en Afrique*, 172. See Formiche raccolte duranti i viaggi di S.A.R. la Duchessa Elena d'Aosta nella regione dei grandi laghi dell'Africa equatoriale. *Annuario del Museo Zoologico della R. Universitadi Napoli* (N.S.) 3 (No. 26), 2 pp.

14. Hélène d'Aosta, *Voyages en Afrique* (1913), pp. 185, 188, 190–191.

15. Hélène d'Aosta, *Voyages en Afrique* (1913), pp. 192, 196, 197, 199.

16. Hélène d'Aosta, *Voyages en Afrique* (1913), pp. 216–217.

17. Hélène d'Aosta, *Voyages en Afrique* (1913), pp. 217, 220.

18. Hélène d'Aosta, *Voyages en Afrique* (1913), pp. 223, 227–228, 233.

19. Susan Hicks Beach to Lady St Aldwyn, 30 April 1910. GRO: D2455/F3/7/1/3/14.

20. *Washington Post*, 3 April 1910.

21. Susan Hicks Beach to Lady St Aldwyn, 25 Oct 1909. GRO: D2455/F3/7/1/3/14.

22. Hélène d'Aosta, *Voyages en Afrique* (1913), pp. 231–232.

23. Susan Hicks Beach to Lady St Aldwyn, 30 April 1910. GRO: D2455/F3/7/1/3/14.

24. Susan Hicks Beach, Journal, 4 May 1910. GRO: D2455/F3/7/1/3/12.

25. Hélène d'Aosta, *Voyages en Afrique* (1913), pp. 234, 235.

26. Susan Hicks Beach, Journal, 4 May 1910. GRO: D2455/F3/7/1/3/12.

27. Hélène d'Aosta, *Voyages en Afrique* (1913), p. 242.

28. Hélène d'Aosta, *Voyages en Afrique* (1913), pp. 244–245.

29. Hélène d'Aosta, *Voyages en Afrique* (1913), pp. 246–247; Susan Hicks Beach, Journal, 1 Dec. 1909. GRO: D2455/F3/11/1/2.

30. Hélène d'Aosta, *Voyages en Afrique* (1913), pp. 248, 250, 251.

31. Hélène d'Aosta, *Voyages en Afrique* (1913), pp. 254, 256, 258.

32. Hélène d'Aosta, *Voyages en Afrique* (1913), p. 263.

33. Hélène d'Aosta, *Voyages en Afrique* (1913), pp. 269–271.

34. Tenderini and Shandrick, *The Duke of the Abruzzi* (1997), pp. 101, 143.

35. Eulalia of Spain, *Court Life from Within* (1915).

36. Amedeo di Savoia-Aosta, "Diario di Amba Alàgi", 6 May 1941. Reproduced in Berretta, *Amedeo d'Aosta* (1955), p. 307.

37. Hélène d'Aosta, *Souvenirs d'Afrique* (1929), 257; Sir Robert Chalmers to King George V, 4 March 1914. RA PS/PSO/GV/C/P/655/1.

38. Hélène d'Aosta, *Voyages en Afrique* (1913), p. 278; Hélène d'Aosta to Duc d'Orléans, 21 Dec. 1910. AnP 300 AP III 8115/178.

39. Hélène d'Aosta, *Voyages en Afrique* (1913), p. 279; Susan Hicks Beach to Lady St Aldwyn, 12 Oct. 1910. GRO: D2455/F3/7/1/3/15.

40. Hélène d'Aosta, *Voyages en Afrique* (1913), p. 280.

41. Susan Hicks Beach to Lady St Aldwyn, 5 Nov 1910, Victoria Hicks Beach to Lady St Aldwyn, 24 Oct. 1910. GRO: D2455/F3/7/1/3/16.

42. Hélène d'Aosta, *Voyages en Afrique* (1913), p. 290.

43. Susan Hicks Beach to Victoria Hicks Beach, 16 Nov 1911. GRO: D2455/F3/11/1/2.

44. Hélène d'Aosta, *Voyages en Afrique* (1913),289, pp. 293–294; Susan Hicks Beach to Victoria Hicks Beach, 2 Dec 1910. GRO: D2455/F3/11/1/2

45. Hélène d'Aosta, *Voyages en Afrique* (1913), pp. 300, 301, 306; plates CLXX, CLXXVI.

46. Susan Hicks Beach to Lady St Aldwyn, [8?] Dec 1910. GRO: D2455/F3/7/1/3/15

47. Hélène d'Aosta, *Voyages en Afrique* (1913), pp. 308, 313; Susan Hicks Beach, Journal, 5, 6 Jan. 1911. GRO: D2455/F3/11/1/2.

48. Susan Hicks Beach, Journal, 28 Jan., 2 Feb. 1911. GRO: D2455/F3/7/1/3/15.

49. Hélène d'Aosta, *Voyages en Afrique* (1913), pp. 314, 319, 344; Susan Hicks Beach, Journal, 15, 20 Feb. 1911. GRO: D2455/F3/7/1/3/15.

50. Hélène d'Aosta, *Voyages en Afrique* (1913), pp. 343, 352.

51. Susan Hicks Beach to Lady St Aldwyn, 4 March 1911. GRO: D2455/F3/7/1/3/15.

52. Susan Hicks Beach to Victoria Hicks Beach, 14 April [1911]. GRO: D2455/F3/11/1/2

53. Susan Hicks Beach to Lady St Aldwyn, 1 May 1911. GRO: D2455/F3/7/1/3/15; Hélène d'Aosta to Lady St Aldwyn, 22 May 1911 (telegram). GRO: D2455/F3/7/1/3/15.

54. Hélène d'Aosta to Duc d'Orléans, 31 May 1911. AnP 300 AP III 815/181; *La Stampa*, 5 June 1911.

55. Hélène d'Aosta to Lady Mary Paget, 13 July 1911. British Library. Add MSS. (Paget Papers).

56. Catinot-Crost, *Amélie de Portugal* (2000), p. 22

Chapter 9:

1. *The Sunday Times*, 19 Nov. 1911.

2. Thompson, *The White War* (2008), p. 14.

3. Tenderini and Shandrick, *The Duke of the Abruzzi* (1997), pp. 124–127.

4. Hughes-Hallet, *The Pike* (2013), pp. 183, 334.

5. *American Journal of Nursing* 12 (1911):223; *The Sunday Times*, 19 Nov. 1911.

6. Tavormina, 'Le Infermiere Volontarie CRI.' (2015), 222; Malgeri, *La Guerra Libica* (1970).

7. *La Stampa*, 12 Nov. 1911.

8. Gooch, *The Italian Army* (2014), 44.

9. Mack Smith, *Italy and its Monarchy* (1989), pp. 187–188.

10. *The Sunday Times*, 5 Nov. 1911.

11 Hélène d'Aosta to Duc d'Orléans, 29 Dec 1911. AnP 300 AP III 815/188.

12. *The Times*, 26 Feb 1912.

13. *La Stampa*, 7 Nov 1911, 22 Jan. 1912; *The Alaska Citizen* (Fairbanks, Alaska), 29 April 1912. The full text of d'Annunzio's 'La Canzone d'Elena di Francia' is printed in Gabriele D'Annunzio, *Laudi del Cielo del Mare della Terra e degli Eroi. Libro IV: Merope* (Milan: Fratelli Treves Editori, 1912), pp. 93–105.

14. *New York Times*, 4 Aug. 1912.

15. Sanfelice di Monteforte, *I Savoia e il Mare* (2009), p. 244.

16. Catenacci, *Amedeo d'Aosta e la Nunziatella* (1993), p. 33; College records of the Nunziatella, Naples.

17. *Pro e contro la guerra di Tripoli* (Naples, 1912), 115, quoted in Mack Smith, *Italy and Its Monarchy* (1989), p. 190; Thompson, *The White War* (2008), p. 14.

18. Choate, *Emigrant Nation* (2008), p. 176.

19. Hélène d'Aosta to Wilfred Blunt, 20 Dec. 1912. Letters to W.S. Blunt, 2nd series. Blunt/Box 62/Aosta. West Sussex Record Office; Henri, comte de Paris, *Mémoires d'exil et de Combats* (1979), p. 11; Poisson, *Les Orléans* (1999), p. 339; *The Geographical Journal*, 41(1913):399; *The Times*, 14 March 1913.

20. Hélène d'Aosta to Amélie de Portugal, 21 April 1913. AnP 300 AP 954/210.

21. Gramont, *Ami du prince* (2011), pp. 556, 559–60.

22. Gramont, *Ami du prince* (2011), pp. 556, 560, 561. See also *Documents diplomatiques français (1871–1914)*. 3rd series (1911–1914), vol. 5, doc. 382; 25 April 1913. *Archives Diplomatique*, vol. 127, p. 96; Tenderini and Shandrick, *The Duke of the Abruzzi* (1997), p. 96.

23. Milano, 1913. French edition published as *Voyages en Afrique*. Extracts had been published in the Italian newspapers as early as as 1910, and more detailed extracts from the French edition ('Sur le fleuve Luapula' and 'Le retour de troupeau') were published in *Moukanda: Choix de lectures sur le Congo et quelques régions voisines* (Bruxelles: J. Lebègue & Cie., 1914).

24. *New York Times*, October 20, 1913.

25. Susan Hicks Beach to Lady St Aldwyn, 25 Oct. 1913. GRO: D2455/F3/7/1/3/17.

26. Hélène d'Aosta, *Vers le soleil qui se lève* (1918), pp. 5–7, 8.

27. Hélène d'Aosta, *Vers le soleil qui se lève* (1918), pp. 11, 15.

28. Hélène d'Aosta, *Vers le soleil qui se lève* (1918), p. 16; Susan Hicks Beach to Lady St Aldwyn, 6 Nov 1913. GRO: D2455/F3/7/1/3/17

29. Hélène d'Aosta, *Vers le soleil qui se lève* (1918), pp. 79, 98–99.

30. Susan Hicks Beach to Lady St Aldwyn, 13 Nov. 1913. GRO: D2455/F3/7/1/3/17; Hélène d'Aosta, *Vers le soleil qui se lève* (1918), pp. 102, 116.

31. Hélène d'Aosta, *Vers le soleil qui se lève* (1918), p. 139; Castellani, *Microbes, Men and Monarchs* (1960), pp. 81 et seq.

32. Sir Robert Chalmers to King George V, 14 March 1914. RA PS/PSO/GV/C/P/655/1; Susan Hicks Beach to her sister Victoria, 24 Dec. [1913]. GRO: D2455/F3/11/1/2.

33. Hélène d'Aosta, *Vers le soleil qui se lève* (1918), pp. 140, 151, 162, 168, 174.

34. Hélène d'Aosta, *Vers le soleil qui se lève* (1918), pp. 190–192.

35. Sassoon, *Mona Lisa* (2001), pp. 178, 180; McMullen, *Mona Lisa* (1976), chapter XIV: Journey to Italy.

36. Hélène d'Aosta, *Vers le Soleil qui se lève* (1918), pp. 197, 200.

37. Susan Hicks Beach, Journal, 8 Jan. 1914. GRO: D2455/F3/11/1/2.

38. Susan Hicks Beach, Journal, 10 Jan. 1914. GRO: D2455/F3/11/1/2.

39. He did not marry for the first time until 1921.

40. Hélène d'Aosta, *Vers le Soleil qui se lève* (1918), pp. 209, 218–219.

41. Hélène d'Aosta, *Vers le Soleil qui se lève* (1918), pp. 220–222.

42. Hélène d'Aosta, *Vers le Soleil qui se lève* (1918), pp.250, 277, 294.

43. Hélène d'Aosta, *Vers le soleil qui se lève* (1918), pp. 304, 345, 357, 358.

44. Hélène d'Aosta, *Vers le soleil qui se lève* (1918), pp. 376, 388, 405, 408.

45. Hélène d'Aosta, *Vers le soleil qui se lève* (1918), pp. 413, 422.

46. Susan Hicks Beach to Lady St Aldwyn, March 28, 1914. GRO: D2455/F3/7/1/3/17

47. Susan Hicks Beach to Lady St Aldwyn, 15 April 1914. GRO: D2455/F3/7/1/3/17.

48. *The Sunday Times* (Sydney, Australia), 19 April 1914.

49. Hélène d'Aosta, *Vers le soleil qui se lève* (1918), p. 448.

50. Susan Hicks Beach to sister Victoria, 21 May 1914. GRO: D2455/F3/11/1/2.

51. Susan Hicks Beach to Lady St Aldwyn, 30 May 1914. GRO: D2455/F3/7/1/3/17

52. Draft letter from Mrs Alice Meyer, 6 June 1914. Meyer Papers, MHS.

Chapter 10:

1. *La Guerre a tué mon âme* from Hélène d'Aosta, *Vie errante* (1921), p. 1.

2. Remak, *Sarajevo* (1959), p. 8.

3. Thompson, *The White War* (2008), p. 23.

4. Hastings, *Catastrophe* (2013), pp. 148, 158, 159, 161, 181, 192; Thompson, *The White War* (2008), p. 36.

5. *Otago Daily Times* [New Zealand], 28 Feb. 1917.

6. Poisson, *Les Orléans* (1999), p. 340; Van Kerrebrouck, *La Maison de Bourbon* (2004), 553–554; Duke d'Orléans to King George V, 3 March 1917. Copy in TNA: WO 339/100805.

7. TNA: ADM 137/111/2, f.85, 87, 101; Catinot-Crost, *Amélie de Portugal* (2000), pp. 253–254, 258.

8. Henri, comte de Paris, *Mémoires d'exil et de Combats* (1979), pp. 22–23; Christopher of Greece, *Memoirs* (1938), pp. 251–252.

9. Gooch, *The Italian Army* (2014), pp. 50–52.

10. Castellani, *Microbes, Men and Monarchs* (1960), pp. 80–81.

11. Satta and Savoia, *Cifra Reale* (2014), pp. 72, 73.

12. Mack Smith, *Italy and Its Monarchy* (1989), p. 210.

13. Mack Smith, *Italy and its Monarchy* (1989), pp. 210–211, 213; Thompson, *The White War* (2008), pp. 26, 18.

14. Thompson, *The White War* (2008), p. 62; Mack Smith, *Italy and its Monarchy* (1989), p. 217.

15. Woodhouse, *Gabriele D'Annunzio* (1998), pp. 294–295, 296, 299; Salierno, *D'Annunzio e i Savoia* (2006), p. 66.

16. Mack Smith, *Italy and its Monarchy* (1989), p. 217.

17. Thompson, *The White War* (2008), pp. 73–74; Torrigiani, *Diario di Guerra* (1923), p. 3.

18. FO372.1296 f 107880

19. Castellani, *Microbes, Men and Monarchs* (1960), p. 81.

20. Hélène d'Aosta, *Accanto agli eroi* (1930), p. 21.

21. Torrigiani, *Diario di Guerra* (1923). Anna's own entries which end with her death are continued through 1919 from her husband's own diary, and later by Duchess Maria Caffarelli.

22. Torrigiani, *Diario di Guerra* (1923), pp. 5–6.

23. Catenacci, *Amedeo d'Aosta e La Nunziatella* (1993), p. 42. The pen is now in the Aosta Museum at the Nunziatella.

24. Torrigiani, *Diario di Guerra* (1923), pp. 7, 9.

25. Hélène d'Aosta, *Accanto Agli Eroi* (1930), pp. 31–32.

26. Hélène d'Aosta, *Accanto agli Eroi* (1930), pp. 49.

27. Gooch, *The Italian Army* (2014), pp. 95–96.

28. Thompson, *The White War* (2008), pp. 106–107; Gooch, *The Italian Army* (2014), p. 112, 198.

29. Thompson, *The White War* (2008), pp. 186, 77; Hughes-Hallett, *The Pike* (2013), p. 428.

30. *Le Petit Journal, supplément illustré*, no. 1280 (4 July 1915).

31. *Le Gaulois*, 17 Feb. 1919.

32. Trevelyan, *Scenes from Italy's War* (1919), p. 104.

33. Hélène d'Aosta, *Accanto agli Eroi* (1930), p. 75.

34. Trevelyan, *Scenes from Italy's War* (1919), pp. 104–105.

35. *New York Times*, 11 Sept. 1915; *Washington Post*, 11 Sept. 1915.

36. *New York Times*, 23 June 1915.

37. Torrigiani, *Diario di Guerra* (1923), p. 39.

38. Hélène d'Aosta, *Accanto agli Eroi* (1930), pp. 97–98, 101.

39. Hélène d'Aosta, *Accanto agli Eroi* (1930), p. 116, which mistakenly calls the lady 'Miss Karol.'

40. Gooch, *The Italian Army* (2014), pp. 155–156.

41. Hélène d'Aosta, *Accanto agli Eroi* (1930), p. 126.

42. Torrigiani, *Diario di Guerra* (1923), p. 128; Hélène d'Aosta, *Accanto agli Eroi* (1930), p. 130.

43. Hélène d'Aosta, *Accanto agli Eroi* (1930), pp. 132–133, 137.

44. Torrigiani, *Diario di Guerra* (1923), p. 68; Hélène d'Aosta, *Accanto agli Eroi* (1930), p. 139; Gooch, *The Italian Army* (2014), p. 160.

45. Thompson, *The White War* (2014), p. 176; Gooch, *The Italian Army* (2014), p. 185.

46. Gooch, *The Italian Army* (2014), pp. 185–186.

47. *Le Gaulois*, 17 Feb. 1919.

48. Hélène d'Aosta, *Accanto agli Eroi* (1930), p. 158.

49. Torrigiani, *Diario di Guerra* (1923), p. 88.

50. Gooch, *The Italian Army* (2014), pp. 140, 167.

51. Hastings, *Catastrophe* (2013), pp. 307, 322; Thompson, *The White War* (2008), pp. 222–223, 225; Gooch, *The Italian Army* (2014), p. 168; Hughes-Hallett, *The Pike* (2013), 427; Thompson, *The White War* (2008), p. 262.

52. Gooch, *The Italian Army* (2014), p. 163.

53. Hélène d'Aosta, *Accanto agli Eroi* (1930), p. 141.

54. Hélène d'Aosta, *Accanto agli Eroi* (1930), p. 178.

55. *La Stampa*, 11 Jan. 1917.

56. Tenderini and Shandrick, *The Duke of the Abruzzi* (1997), p. 137.

57. Hélène d'Aosta, *Accanto agli Eroi* (1930), p.183.

58. Hélène d'Aosta, *Accanto agli Eroi* (1930), p. 188–189.

59. Thompson, *The White War* (2008), pp. 250–257.

60. Thompson, *The White War* (2008), pp. 257–258.

61. W. R. Robertson, Note by C.I.G.S. on his visit to Italian Headquarters, 22–24 March, 1917. TNA: CAB 24/9/9.

62. Hélène d'Aosta, *Accanto agli Eroi* (1930), p. 201.

63. Gooch, *The Italian Army* (2014), pp. 224–226.

64. Gooch, *The Italian Army* (2014), pp. 242, 244.

65. Hughes-Hallett, *The Pike* (2013), p. 434.

66. TNA: CAB 24/35/28.

67. Thompson, *The White War* (2008), p. 324; Mack Smith, *Italy and its Monarchy* (1989), p. 228; Gooch, *The Italian Army* (2014), pp. 235–236; Albanese, *Principessa beduina* (2007), pp. 62–63.

68. Torrigiani, *Diario di Guerra* (1923), pp. 119–120.

69. Hélène d'Aosta, *Accanto agli Eroi* (1930), pp. 218–219

70. Foch, *The Memoirs of Marshal Foch* (1931), p. 262.

71. 'Extract from letter received from Rome,' 13 Nov. 1917 [not otherwise identified but among the papers of Earl Balfour]. TNA: FO 800/213 f. 342; Mack Smith, *Italy and its Monarchy* (1989), p. 230; G. M. Trevelyan, 'The conditions of the Italian Army, 1915–1917.' TNA: WO 106/807; Roskill, *Hankey* (1970), pp. 454–455. Count Sforza places this plan earlier in the war, at the end of the spring of 1915. Sforza, *L'Italia dal 1914 al 1944* (1946), p. 52.

72. Hélène d'Aosta, *Accanto agli Eroi* (1930), p. 226.

73. Hélène d'Aosta, *Accanto agli Eroi* (1930), p. 233; Diario, 238–239; Hélène d'Aosta to Duc de Guise, 1 May 1918 (AnP 300 AP III 932/3.

74. Edward, Prince of Wales, to Freda Dudley Ward, 29 April 1918, in *Letters from a Prince* (1980), p. 25; Torrigiani, *Diario di Guerra* (1923), p. 139.

75. Edward, Prince of Wales, to Freda Dudley Ward, 30 May 1918, in *Letters from a Prince* (1980), p. 37.

76. Marie José, Queen of Italy, *Albert et Elisabeth de Belgique* (1971), p. 267.

77. Thompson, *The White War* (2008), pp. 344–347; Gooch, *The Italian Army* (2014), pp. 282, 287.

78. Cahier, 'Entre ciel et eau, Genes, 24 mai 1918—9 juin.' Private family collection.

79. Cahier, "commençant, Tanger, 27 juin 1918—15 septembre, en vue de Gênes". Private family collection; Hélène d'Aosta, *Accanto agli Eroi* (1930), pp. 249–250.

80. Hélène d'Aosta, *Accanto agli Eroi* (1930), p. 253. Umberto was later reburied in the Tempio Ossario di Bassno del Grappa with more than 5,000 of his comrades. *Calendario Reale, 1943*, p. 86.

81. Thompson, *The White War* (2008), p. 361. Hughes-Hallett, *The Pike* (2013), p. 454.

82. Torrigiani, *Diario di Guerra* (1923), p. 149; *The Times*, 2 Dec. 1918.

83. Gooch, *The Italian Army* (2014), p. 301; Hélène d'Aosta, *Accanto agli Eroi* (1930), p. 265, photos opp. p. 240, 244; Torrigiani, *Diario di Guerra* (1923), p. 152; Hélène d'Aosta to Amélie de Portugal, 17 Nov. 1918. AnP 300 AP 954/211.

84. Hélène d'Aosta, *La Vie Errante* (1921), p. 12.

Chapter 11:

1. Hélène d'Aosta, *Vie errante* (1921), p. 1.

2. Goldstein, *The First World War Peace Settlement* (2002), p. 5.

3. Wilson, *Memoirs* (1939), pp. 229, 253, 260–261; *La Stampa*, 5 Jan. 1919.

4. Clemenceau to Gen. Mordacq, quoted in Watson, *Georges Clemenceau* (1974), p. 327.

5. Torrigiani, *Diario di Guerra* (1923), p. 157; Edward, Prince of Wales, to Freda Dudley Ward, 19 Feb. 1919, in *Letters from a Prince* (1980), 141.

6. Imperiali, *Diario* (2006), p. 641.

7. Hélène d'Aosta to Queen Mary, 2 March 1919. RA QM/PRIV/CC/45/567; RA QM/PRIV/QMD/1919: 2 March; Queen Mary to King George V, 29 July 1921. RA QM/PRIV/CC8/249; Imperiali, *Diario* (2006), p. 642.

8. TNA: FO372.1296 f 107880; FO372/1298 f 143383.

9. Speroni, *I Savoia Scomodi* (1999), p. 320; *The Times*, 30 April 1919.

10. Henri, Comte de Paris, *Mémoires d'exil et de combats* (1979), p. 44; Hélène d'Aosta to Jean, duc de Guise, 28 May 1919. AnP 300 AP III 932/5.

11. The coffins of the Comte and Comtesse de Paris remained at Weybridge until they were reburied in the family chapel at Dreux in 1958. TNA: HO282/13.

12. AnP 300 AP III 712/3

13. *The Times*, 5 April 1923; 'Extrait des dernières volontés de Madame La Comtesse de Paris.' Private family collection.

14. Mack Smith, *Italy and its Monarchy* (1989), p. 243.

15. Imperiali, *Diario* (2006), p. 682; Hélène d'Aosta to King George V, 14 Sept 1919. RA GV/PRIV/AA43/302.

16. Isabelle, comtesse de Paris, *Tout m'est bonheur* (1978), p. 172.

17. Hélène d'Aosta to Duchesse de Guise, 8 March 1919. AnP 300 III AP 954/204.

18. Woodhouse, *Gabriele D'Annunzio* (1998), p. 316.

19. Hughes-Hallett, *The Pike* (2013), p. 517.

20. Goldstein, *The First World War Peace Settlements* (2002), p. 19.

21 Salierno, *D'Annunzio e i Savoia* (2006), pp. 10–11; Mack Smith, *Italy and its Monarchy* (1989), pp. 238–239; Barbagallo, *Francesco S. Nitti* (1984), p. 297.

22. Imperiali, *Diario* (2006), p. 682.

23. H.W. Kennard, to Earl Curzon, 26 Sept 1919. no. 413 [135270/123/3. pp 80/801, *Documents on British Foreign Policy* (1952), first series, vol. 4 (1919), 80–81. London, 1952]; *New York Times*, 14 Aug. 1919; rumour repeated in *Le Figaro*, 14 Aug. 1919. There were more formal plans for Emanuele Filiberto to visit the United States the following year, plans which were said to be supported by the king and prime minister. These plans likewise came to nothing even though they had been brought to the attention of President Wilson who suggested 'I think it highly desirable that the contemplated visit of the Duke D'Aosta should be postponed. I am sure the new administration will desire an opportunity for a splurge, and such a visit would afford it' (Norman Hezekiah Davis to President Woodrow Wilson, 23 Dec. 1920; Wilson to Davis, 27 Dec. 1920; printed in *The Papers of Woodrow Wilson* (1966–), 66:543–544, 67:8]

24. Norman Hezekiah Davis to President Woodrow Wilson, 23 Dec. 1920; Wilson to Davis, 27 Dec. 1920; printed in *The Papers of Woodrow Wilson* (1966–), 66:543–544, 67:8.

25. Woodhouse, *Gabriele D'Annunzio* (1998), pp. 320, 332.

26. Quoted in Salierno, *D'Annunzio e i Savoia* (2006), p. 11.

27. Hughes-Hallett, *The Pike* (2013), p. 501.

28. Sir R. Rodd (Rome) to Earl Curzon, 2, 6 Oct 1919. *Documents on British Foreign Policy, 1919–1939*. First series, vol. 4 (1919), 90, 103.

29. Hughes-Hallett, *The Pike* (2013), pp. 425–426; Salierno, *D'Annunzio e i Savoia* (2006), p. 103; *Era Nuova*, 6 Nov. 1919, quoted in Diary of the British Military Mission, Fiume, 6 Nov. 1919, as submitted by Lt. Col. S. C. Peck, Commanding Officer. TNA: W.O. 106/853; Speroni, *I Savoia Scomodi* (1999), p. 328.

30. Hélène d'Aosta, *La Vie Errante* (1921), pp. 9, 11. The sentiment about the war having killed her soul was one which she repeated at the end of the Second World War (Prinvate family information).

31. Salierno, *D'Annunzio e i Savoia* (2006), pp. 104–106.

32. Woodhouse, *Gabriele D'Annunzio* (1998), p. 349; Hughes-Hallett, *The Pike* (2013), p. 6.

33. The chronology is confused as Amedeo's medical report during his final illness report stated that following the diagnosis of Bilateral apical pulmonary T.B, he was treated in Sanatoria and followed by long holiday. This "long holiday" is presumably the trip that

he made to Somalia with his uncle. Maj. L.S. Harington and Lt Col J. Wakeford to the Director of Medical Services, East Africa command. General Hospital, Nairobi, 8 Feb. 1942. Reproduced in Speroni, *Amedeo duca d'Aosta* (1984), p. 188.

34. *Le Figaro*, 20 Oct. 1919; *La Stampa*, 19 Oct. 1919; Tenderini and Shandrick, *The Duke of the Abruzzi* (1997), pp. 141–144.

35. 'A l'idéal toujours poursuivi—jamais attaint—qui à travers la vie nous mène de rêve en rêve jusqu'au tombeau.'

36. Hélène d'Aosta, *La Vie Errante* (1921), pp. 11, 24–25.

37. Hélène d'Aosta, *La Vie Errante* (1921), pp. 21, 37, 38.

38. Hélène d'Aosta, *La Vie Errante* (1921), p. 38.

39. Hélène d'Aosta to Luigi Luzzatti, 10 Jan. 1916, quoted in Luzzatti, *God in Freedom* (1930), p. 291.

40. Hélène d'Aosta, *La Vie Errante* (1921), pp. 52, 53.

41. Hélène d'Aosta, *La Vie Errante* (1921), p. 59.

42. Hélène d'Aosta, *La Vie Errante* (1921), pp. 63, 71.

43. Hélène d'Aosta, *La Vie Errante* (1921), pp. 80, 98, 105, 118.

44. Maj. L.S. Harington and Lt Col J. Wakeford to the Director of Medical Services, East Africa command. General Hospital, Nairobi, 8 Feb. 1942. Reproduced in Speroni, *Amedeo duca d'Aosta* (1984), p. 188.

45. Hélène d'Aosta, *La Vie Errante* (1921), p. 131.

46. Hélène d'Aosta, *La Vie Errante* (1921), p. 143.

47. Hughes-Hallett, *The Pike* (2013), p. 569.

48. Sforza, *Contemporary Italy* (1944), p. 313.

49. *Washington Post*, 21 Jan. 1917. The same newspaper had reported on 21 Aug. 1910 that the Duke of the Abruzzi was likely to replace King George at that time. Abruzzi was also suggested as a possible king for Albania in 1914.

50. *The Times*, 29 Oct. 1920.

51. Barbagallo, *Francesco S. Nitti* (1984), p. 425.

52. Bolton, *Roman Century* (1970), p. 197.

53. *New York Times*, 2–3 Nov. 1921, quoted in Hanson, *Unknown Soldiers* (2006), p. 330.

54. DePaola, 'La fascistizzazione della professione infermieristica' (2012), p. 135.

55. RA QM/PRIV/QMD/1921: 19, 25 May; King George V to Hélène d'Aosta, 26 May 1921. From auction catalogue (www.sophiedupre.com, accessed 27 April 2015). Aimone had also been in London in Nov. 1919, when he likewise had visited the King and Queen at Buckingham Palace, staying to luncheon . At that time Queen Mary proclaimed him 'very nice' and noted that he 'talks English well.' [RA QM/PRIV/QMD/1919: 1 Nov.].

56. RA QM/PRIV/QMD/1921: 5 June.

57. *The Times*, 15, 27 June 1921

58. Capodimonte Guestbooks, 1921–1926, 1929–1936, 1937–1945. Private family collection.

59. Hélène d'Aosta, *Souvenirs d'Afrique* (1929), p. 258. A draft version of this appears as 'Sénégal—Niger—Tchad—Chari—Congo, 1921–1922,' among Hélène's unpublished travel journals in the Fondo Campini (Torino).

60. Hélène d'Aosta, *Souvenirs d'Afrique* (1929), p.259–260, 272.

61. Hélène d'Aosta, *Souvenirs d'Afrique* (1929), pp. 264–268.

62. Hélène d'Aosta, *Souvenirs d'Afrique* (1929), pp. 269–270.

63. Hélène d'Aosta, *Souvenirs d'Afrique* (1929), pp. 270–271, 385, 386.

64. Hélène d'Aosta, *Souvenirs d'Afrique* (1929), pp. 388, 392, 398.

65. Bertoldi, *Aosta* (1987), p. 204.

66. Thompson, *The White War* (2008), p. 19.

67. Speroni, *Amedeo duca d'Aosta* (1984), pp. 48–49; Albanese, *Principessa beduina* (2007), pp. 82–83, calls this a false episode but then goes on to repeat the story, adding that 'lord Lewer' was someone that Hélène knew from one of her trips; Piano, *Memorie* (1956), p. 110; Amélie du Portugal, Journal intime, 28 March 1923. AnP 300 AP III 718.

68. Constantine of Greece to Paola von Saxe-Weimar, 9 Nov. 1922, in Saxe-Weimar, *Lettere di Costantino re di Grecia* (1928), p. 202.

69. Lambrino, *King Carol II: A life of my grandfather* (1988), p. 82, speaks of a potential flirtation between Helen and Amedeo. King Ferdinand writes to Queen Marie, 26 Aug 1926, nearly four years later] Carol had confided 'something very painful, making allusion at an affection which he believes Sitta has for the Aosta boy. He did not accuse her of having gone too far but he said there had been a change in her since she came back from Palermo.' Prince Nicolas in his diaries wrote that 'Duke Amadeo delle Puglie, son of the Duke of Aosta, was a charming man, tall, handsome and very likeable... As things between Carol and were already deteriorating quite seriously, it was very possible that these young people were attracted to each other, that they should even have fallen in love and planned a separation from Carol at Helen's initiative.' Nicolas claimed to have heard this story both from his mother and from the Queen of Spain [p. 83].

70. Trevelyan, *Princes under the Volcano* (1972), 280, 376–377, 386, 400.

71. Marie of Greece, *A Romanov Diary* (1988), pp. 244–245.

72. Van der Kiste, *Kings of the Hellenes* (1994), p. 141.

73. Christopher, Prince of Greece, *Memoirs* (1938), p. 199

74. A year later, when Queen Sophie moved to Florence, the coffin was moved to the Russian Orthodox Church there. In 1936, it was moved again—along with the coffins of his mother, Queen Olga, and wife, Queen Sophie—to the Greek Royal Family's burial ground at Tatoi, outside Athens.

Chapter 12:

1. Quoted in English, Hélène d'Aosta, "Eritrea, decembre 1926—mars 1927", 14 Dec. 1926. Sir Samuel White Baker (1821–1923), quoted in Edward Gilliat, *Heroes of Modern Africa*.

2. Mack Smith, *Italy and its Monarchy* (1989), pp. 246, 248, 249; Duggan, *Fascist Voices* (2012), p. 58.

3. Duggan, *Fascist Voices* (2012), p. 59; Salvemini, *The Fascist Dictatorship in Italy* (1928), pp. 109, 154, saw Emanuele Filiberto as 'the pivot of the military conspiracy' and indeed 'behind all the seditious movements which followed the war.'

4. Mack Smith, *Italy and its Monarchy* (1989), p. 252; Duggan, *Fascist Voices* (2012), p. 60.

5. *The Times*, 25 May 1927.

6. Kertzer, *The Pope and Mussolini* (2014), p. 62.

7. Now in the Collezione Duca d'Aosta, Nunziatella.

8. Mack Smith, *Italy and its Monarchy* (1989), pp. 263, 265.

9. Amélie du Portugal, Journal intime, 2 March 1923. AnP 300 AP III 718; Hélène d'Aosta to Amélie du Portugal, 16, 26 Nov. 1924. AnP 300 AP III 954/213, 214; Hélène d'Aosta to Amélie du Portugal, 16, 26 Nov. 1924. AnP 300 AP III 954/214; Private family information.

10. Amélie du Portugal, Journal intime, 7 March 1923. AnP 300 AP III 718.

11. *The Times*, 10 May 1923, includes a photo of this scene, Hélène chatting with King George.

12. RA QM/PRIV/QMD/1923: 8 May.

13. Hélène d'Aosta to Duke of Aosta, 27 April 1923 (Collezione Duca d'Aosta, Nunziatella, Naples); *La Stampa*, 2 May 1923; Ufficio Storico della Marina Militare, Rome. cart. P.P. S12, quoted in Sanfelice di Monteforte, *I Savoia e il mare* (2009), p. 258.

14. Hélène d'Aosta to Duke of Aosta, 17 May, 24 June 1923 (Collezione Duca d'Aosta, Nunziatella, Naples); Ufficio Storico della Marina Militare, Rome. cart. P.P. S12, quoted in Sanfelice di Monteforte, *I Savoia e il mare* (2009), p. 258; *La Stampa*, 13 July 1928.

15. Hélène d'Aosta to Jean, duc de Guise, 17 July 1923. AnP: 300 AP III 392/11; Hélène d'Aosta to Duke of Aosta, 19 July, 7, 20, 23 Aug. 1923. Collezione Duca d'Aosta, Nunziatella, Naples.

16. *The Sunday Times*, 9 Sept. 1923.

17. *Le Gaulois*, 16 Sept 1923.

18. Amélie du Portugal, Journal intime, 10 Dec. 1923. AnP 300 AP III 718.

19. Sir Ronald Graham to King George V, [Dec. 1923]. RA GV/PSO/C/P/780/30.

20. *The Times*, 7 March 1924.

21. Conversation with Silvana Casale, Fondo Aosta, Biblioteca Nazionale di Napoli, 18 Oct. 2011.

22. Charles-Louis, Duke of Parma, to Thomas Ward, 11 Dec. 1853, quoted in Balansó, *Les Bourbons de Parme* (1996), p. 111.

23. Hélène d'Aosta to Duke of Aosta, 25 June 1924. Collezione Duca d'Aosta, Nunziatella.

24. Battiscombe, *Queen Alexandra* (1969), p. 296; Hélène d'Aosta to Lady St Aldwyn, 1 Sept. 1924. GRO: D2455/F3/7/1/6/6; Hélène d'Aosta to Jean, duc de Guise, 22 Sept 1924. AnP 300 AP III 932/13.

25. 'Dans l'Église de ★★★'

26. Hélène d'Aosta, 'De l'Océan indien au Nil blanc,' introduction.

27. Hélène d'Aosta, 'De l'Océan indien au Nil blanc,' 19 Dec. 1924.

28. Hélène d'Aosta, 'De l'Océan indien au Nil blanc,' 6 Jan. 1925.

29. Hélène d'Aosta, 'De l'Océan indien au Nil blanc,' 16 Jan. 1925.

30. Hélène d'Aosta, 'De l'Océan indien au Nil blanc,' 6 Feb. 1925.

31. Hélène d'Aosta, 'De l'Océan indien au Nil blanc,' 7, 9, 11 Feb. 1925.

32. Hélène d'Aosta, 'De l'Océan indien au Nil blanc,' 15, 17 Feb. 1925.

33. Hélène d'Aosta, 'De l'Océan indien au Nil blanc,' 19, 27 Feb. 1925.

34. Hélène d'Aosta, 'De l'Océan indien au Nil blanc,' 28 Feb. 1925.

35. Hélène d'Aosta, 'De l'Océan indien au Nil blanc,' 7 March 1925.

36. Hélène d'Aosta, 'De l'Océan indien au Nil blanc,' 21 March, 7 April 1925.

37. 'Citroen / Croisere Noire' on www.youtube.com/watch?v=FSzGkWtrQik, accessed 27 July 2013.

38. Hélène d'Aosta, 'De l'Océan indien au Nil blanc,' 21 May 1925.

39. *Time Magazine*, 15 June 1925.

40. Bosworth, *Mussolini* (2002), p. 175.

41. Morris, *Trieste and the Meaning of Nowhere* (2001), p. 114; Hughes-Hallett, *The Pike* (2013), pp. 614, 619, 626.

42. de Grazia, *The Culture of Consent* (1981), pp. 24–38.

43. Salvemini, *Fascist Dictatorship in Italy*, 109; *La Stampa*, 24 Dec. 1925.

44. RA QM/PRIV/QMD/1925: 29 June; Amélie du Portugal, Journal intime, 12 July 1925. AnP 300 AP III 718.

45. *La Stampa*, 24 Sept. 1925.

46. Marie of Greece, *A Romanov Diary* (1988), pp. 259–260.

47. Hélène d'Aosta to Angelo Conti, 13 Oct. 1925. Fondo Conti.

48. She later donated a second fountain at Capodichino in Naples (1943) and for that chose a verse from the Gospel of Matthew (11.28): Come unto me ye that are thirsty and I will give you life.

49. Hélène d'Aosta, 'De Gadames à Koufra, Decembre 1936—juin 1937,' 4 Jan. 1937. Fondo Campini.

50. Amélie du Portugal, Journal intime, 14, 27 Feb., 14, 27 March 1926. AnP 300 AP III 718; Poisson, *Les Orléans* (1999), p. 344; Récamier, *L'âme de l'Exilé* (1927), pp. 363; Amélie du Portugal, Journal intime, 14, 27 Feb., 14 March 1926. AnP 300 AP III 718; Poisson, *Les Orléans* (1999), p. 344; Amélie du Portugal, Journal intime, 14, 27 Feb., 14 March 1926. AnP 300 AP III 718; Poisson, *Les Orléans* (1999), p. 344; Hélène d'Aosta to Duca d'Aosta, 28 March 1926. Collezione Duca d'Aosta, Nunziatella, Naples.

51. Henri, Comte de Paris, *Memoires d'exil et de combats* (1979), p. 68

52. Hanson, 'The Last Word' (2012), pp. 41–43.

53. Saunders, *The Woman Who Shot Mussolini* (2010), pp. 8, 12–13

54. Olla, *Il Duce and his women* (2011), p. 304.

55. Hélène d'Aosta to Renée St Maur, 17 Dec. 1926. Author's Collection, UK.

56. Hélène d'Aosta, 'Eritrea,' 18, 20 Dec. 1926.

57. Susan Hicks Beach to Lady St Aldwyn, 24, 29 Dec. 1926. GRO: D2455/F3/7/1/3/25; Hélène d'Aosta, 'Eritrea,' 25 Dec. 1926.

58. Hélène d'Aosta, 'Eritrea,' 13 Dec. 1926, 1, 2 Jan. 1927.

59. Hélène d'Aosta, 'Eritrea,' 12, 16 Jan. 1927.

60. Susan Hicks Beach to Lady St Aldwyn, 20 Jan [1927]. GRO: D2455/F3/7/1/3/25,

61. Susan Hicks Beach to Lady St Aldwyn, 28 Jan., 25 Feb [1927]. GRO: D2455/F3/7/1/3/25.

62. Hélène d'Aosta, 'Eritrea,' 9, 10 Feb. 1927.

63. Hélène d'Aosta, 'Eritrea,' 1, 31 March 1927.

64. Conversation with Silvana Casale, Fondo Aosta; Marie Amélie von Heller (daughter of Princess Clémentine of Saxe-Coburg-Gotha), quoted in Defrance, 'Between Egypt and Europe' (2013), 7; Jullian, *D'Annunzio* (1971), p. 175.

65. Hélène d'Aosta to Angelo Conti, 11 July 1927 (postcard). Fondo Conti.

66. Marie José, *Albert et Elisabeth de Belgique* (1971), p. 267; George Graham to Lord Stamfordham, 11 Nov. 1927. RA PS/PSO/GV/C/P/1673/72.

67. Charles Winfield to Austen Chamberlain: 14 Sept 1927. TNA: FO372/2406 f11234.

68. Hélène d'Aosta to Emanuele Filiberto d'Aosta, 3 Aug., 24 Dec. 1927. Collezione Duca d'Aosta, Nunziatella.

69. Susan Hicks Beach to Lady St Aldwyn, 3 Nov. 1927. GRO: D2455/F3/7/1/3/26.

70. Victoria Hicks Beach to Lady St Aldwyn, 6 Nov. 1927. GRO: D2455/F3/7/1/3/26.

71. Victoria Hicks Beach to Lady St Aldwyn, 6 Nov. 1927. GRO: D2455/F3/7/1/3/26.

72. Sir Ronald Graham to Austen Chamberlain, 10 Nov 1927. TNA: FO 372/2406 f11234

73. *The Times*, 7 Nov 1927.

74. Sir Ronald Graham to King George V, 11 Nov. 1927. RA PS/PSO/GV/C/P/780/48. The same story is repeated by Queen Amélie, Journal intime, 5 Nov. 1927. The decree of Pius XI placing *L'Action française* on the Index was issued on 29 Dec. 1926, although not published until 6 Jan. 1927. The ban would eventually be lifted by Pius XII on 5 July 1939. Osgood, *French Royalism* (1960), pp. 111, 156.

75. Sir Ronald Graham to Austen Chamberlain, 10 Nov 1927. TNA: FO 372/2406 f11234; Sir Ronald. Graham to King George V, 11 Nov. 1927. RA PS/PSO/GV/C/P/780/48.

76. Susan Hicks Beach to Lady St Aldwyn, 9 Nov. 1927. GRO: D2455/F3/7/1/3/26.

Chapter 13:

1. Marie José, *Albert et Elisabeth de Belgique* (1971), p. 379.
2. 'Il Carosello Storico di Torino (1928)' at www.araldicasardegna.org/tra_pubblico_ privato/carosello_storico.htm, accessed 2 Nov. 2011.
3. *La Stampa*, 13 July 1928.
4. Minute by C. Howard Smith, 17.10.28. TNA: FO 371/12950/7698
5. Rome, 9 Oct 1928. Charles Wingfield to Lord Cushendun. TNA: FO 371/12950/7698.
6. Hélène d'Aosta to Emanuele Filiberto d'Aosta, 4 Nov. 1928. Collezione Duca d'Aosta, Nunziatella.
7. Piacentini, Italian minister to Sofia, to Benito Mussolini, 19 Jan. 1928, 12 Sept 1928, in *I documenti Diplomatici Italiani*, 7th ser. (1922–1935), 6:31–33, 564–565/
8. Christopher of Greece, *Memoirs* (1938), p. 246
9. Christopher of Greece, *Memoirs* (1938), p. 247.
10. *The Times*, 27 May 1929.
11. Kertzer, *The Pope and Mussolini* (2014), pp. 50, 63.
12. Archivio Luce: January 1930: Titolo assegnato: I duchi d'Aosta visitano il Papa; Tenderini and Shandrick, *Duke of the Abruzzi* (1997), pp. 51–52.
13. *The Times*, 7 June 1929.
14. Archivio Luce (www.archivioluce.com) AO381: July 1929: 'La duchessa d'Aosta, il duca e la duchessa delle Puglie si preparano al volo da Torino a Milano'; Jean, duc de Guise, to Amélie of Portugal, 11 Aug. 1929. AnP 300 III 954:71
15. Lord Irwin to King George V, 11 June 1928. RA PS/PSO/GV/C/P/522/246.
16. *New York Times*, 24 Feb 1929.
17. *The Times*, 6 Jan. 1930.
18. *The Daily Telegraph*, 29 Jan 2001; Castellani, *Microbes, Men and Monarchs* (1960), p. 117; Sir Ronald Graham to the Foreign Office, 12 Jan. 1930. TNA: FO 372/2684 (Royal Matters, 1930), fT614.
19. Christopher of Greece, *Memoirs* (1938), p. 259.
20. Papásogli, *La Regina Elena* (1965); Maria Gabriella di Savoia, *Vita di corte in Casa Savoia* (2006), p. 153.
21. Marie José, *Albert et Elisabeth de Belgique* (1971), p. 379; Christopher of Greece, *Memoirs* (1938), p. 258.
22. Sir Ronald Graham to the Foreign Office, 12 Jan. 1930. FO372/2684 (Royal Matters, 1930), fT614.
23. Berretta, *Amedeo d'Aosta* (1955), pp. 82, 334–335.
24. Hughes-Hallett, *The Pike* (2013), pp. 629–630.
25. *The Times*, 25 Feb. 1930.
26. *The Times*, 16 April 1930.
27. *New York Times*, 16 April 1930; *Time Magazine*, 28 April 1930.

28. *Queen Alexandra's Christmas Book: Photographs from my Camera* was published by *The Daily Telegraph*.

29. *Kodak Exhibition* (1930).

30. Gordon-Smith, G., 'Treatment of the Yugoslav Minority in Trieste and Istria,' p. 443.

31. Giornale Luce A0626, 00/07/1930. Archivio Luce; *The Times*, 25 July 1930.

32. *The Times*, 19 Sept 1930; *Charleston Daily Mail* [Charleston, West Virginia], 24 Sept. 1930.

33. Seymour, *Bugatti Queen* (2004), p. 108.

34. Christopher of Greece, *Memoirs* (1938), pp. 259–260; *La Stampa*, 26 Oct. 1930; Dimitroff, *Boris III of Bulgaria* (1986), p. 103.

35. *Libro d'Oro*, v 7 (1926–1932).

36. Catinot-Crost, *Amélie de Portugal (*2000), p. 305; Amélie du Portugal, Journal intime, 25–26 Dec. 1930, 1, 14 Jan. 1931. AnP 300 AP III 718.

37. Amélie du Portugal, Journal intime, 14 March 1931. AnP 300 AP III 718.

38. Amélie du Portugal, Journal intime, 16, 18 March 1931. AnP 300 AP III 718.

39. Hélène d'Aosta, 'Da Tripoli a Gat,' 6, 14, 30 April 1931.

40. Hélène d'Aosta, 'Da Tripoli a Gat,' 14, 19, 21 April 1931.

41. Catinot-Crost, *Amélie de Portugal* (2000), p. 305.

42. Van der Kiste, *A Divided Kingdom* (2007), p. 172; Hélène d'Aosta to Renée StMaur, 29 May 1931. Author's Collection (UK).

43. Private family information.

44. Sir Ronald Graham to King George V, 10 July 1931. RA PS/PSO/ GV/C/P/780/71; Mussolini's telegram and Hélène's response, as well as d'Annunzio's telegram, are reproduced in Albanese, *Principessa beduina* (2007), pp. 229–231.

45. *The Times*, 6 July 1931.

46. *La Stampa*, 6 July 1931.

47. Amélie du Portugal, Journal intime, 15 July 1931. AnP 300 AP III 718.

48. *Le Figaro*, 6 Aug 1931; Hélène d'Aosta to Camille Dupuy, 29 Sept. 1931 (postcard). Author's collection (UK).

49. 1090. Capo del Governo, primo ministro segretario di Stato, Mussolini, ministro delle finanze, Mosconi 'Conversione in legge del R.D.L. 24 agosto 1931, n. 1092, concernente l'appannaggio di annue L. 400.000 in favore di S.A.R. la Principessa Elena di Francia, Duchessa d'Aosta madre' [approved] *16.10.1931*. (archivio. camera.it/patrimonio/archivio_della_camera_regia_1848_1943/are01o/chiavi/ persone/Elena+di+Francia,+duchessa+d'Aosta). Accessed 1 June 2015.

50. *La Stampa*, 5 Nov. 1931; www.asso4stormo.it\web\ago\ago13.htm; Archivio Luce: 25 December 1931. Durata: 00:02:19. Titolo proprio: Pozzuoli. Le LL. AA. RR. i Principi di Piemonte e S.A.R. la duchessa d'Aosta Madre inaugura il preventorio della croce rossa.

51. Berretta, *Amedeo d'Aosta* (1955), p.113.

52. Salierno, *D'Annunzio e i* Savoia (2006), p. 73–74.

53. Miramare was occupied by German troops in 1943; and between 1945 and 1954 was the headquarters of allied military governments. It opened as a museum, 2 June 1955.

54. Amélie de Portugal, Journal intime, 2, 4 Jan. 1932. AnP 300 AP III 718.

55. Amélie de Portugal, Journal intime, 14, 15 Feb. 1932. AnP 300 AP III 718.

56. *Catalogo delle collezioni private d'arte appartenute a S. A. R. Emanuele Filiberto di Savoia, Duca d'Aosta, che saranno poste in vendita, in ossequio al desiderio espresso dal defunto augusto principe. Galleria Dante Giacomini, Casa di Vendita All'Asta S.A., Via San Pantaleo, Roma. L'esposizione ad invito acrà luogo dal giorno 8 al 14 febbraio 1932. Le vendite all'asta si effetveranno a principiare dal giorno 15 febbraio, alle ore 15,30.* pp. 145. pl. CXVI. Milano, Roma, [1932.] 4o [Galleria Dante Giocomini no illus.; 3017 works]. Accompanying photos show the interior of the Palazzo della Cisterna.

57. *The Observer,* 5 July 1931.

58. Hélène d'Aosta to Amélie du Portugal, 29 June 1932. AnP 300 AP III 954/219. Newspapers reported that Hélène was at Redipuglia for the anniversary Mass along with her sons and brothers-in-law, but apparently this was not correct.

59. *The Manchester Guardian,* 13 May 1932.

60. *The Manchester Guardian,* 4 July 1932.

61. *Le Figaro,* 6 July 1932, announced that they had arrived at Vichy, but the 11 July issue notes that the Dowager Duchess is currently suffering at Naples and not able to go to Vichy; Hélène d'Aosta to Amélie of Portugal, 8, 22, 28 Aug., 6 Sept. 1932. AnP 300 III 954/222, 223, 224.

62. Private family information; Hélène d'Aosta, 'Da Napoli a Duala,' 26 Nov. 1932.

63. Hélène d'Aosta, 'Da Napoli a Duala,' 29 Nov. 1932.

64. Hélène d'Aosta, 'Da Napoli a Duala,' 30 Nov. 1932.

65. Hélène d'Aosta, 'Da Napoli a Duala,' 1 Dec. 1932.

66. Hélène d'Aosta, 'Da Napoli a Duala,' 4 Dec. 1932.

67. Susan Hicks Beach to Lady St Aldwyn, 18 Dec. 1932. GRO: D2455/F3/7/1/4/3

68. Hélène d'Aosta, 'Da Napoli a Duala,' 24 Dec 1932. Probably from this trip: Salvatori, T., 'Birds Collected by the Duchess of Aosta in Equitorial Africa,' *Ann. Mus. Zool. K. Univ. Napoli,* IV, no 10 (1933?). List of 190 species.

Chapter 14:

1. Hélène d'Aosta, 'Da Napoli a Duala,' 30 Dec. 1932.

2. Hélène d'Aosta, 'Da Napoli a Duala,' 30 Dec. 1932.

3. Hélène d'Aosta, 'Da Napoli a Duala,' 30 Dec. 1932.

4. Hélène d'Aosta, 'Da Napoli a Duala,' 31 Dec 1932–1 Jan. 1933.

5. Hélène d'Aosta, 'Da Napoli a Duala,' 5 Jan. 1933.

6. Susan Hicks Beach to Lady St Aldwyn, 24 Jan. 1933. GRO: D2455/F3/7/1/4/3.

7. Hélène d'Aosta, *Attraverso il Sahara*, 5, 7, 8.

8. Hélène d'Aosta, *Attraverso il Sahara*, 18; Hélène d'Aosta, 'Da Napoli a Duala,' 13 Feb. 1933.

9. Hélène d'Aosta, 'Da Napoli a Duala,' 14 Feb. 1933.

10. Hélène d'Aosta, 'Da Napoli a Duala,' 27 Feb., 9, 14 March 1933.

11. Hélène d'Aosta, 'Da Napoli a Duala,' 17–23 March 1933.

12. Susan Hicks Beach to Lady St Aldwyn, 17 March 1933. D2455/F3/7/1/4/3.

13. Hélène d'Aosta, *Attraverso il Sahara*, 45; Hélène d'Aosta, 'Da Napoli a Duala,' 16 March 1933.

14. TNA: F.O. 372/2977.

15. Hélène d'Aosta, 'Da Napoli a Duala,' 19 March 1933.

16. Bertoldi, *Aosta* (1987), pp. 146–147; Albanese, *Principessa beduina* (2007), p. 253 n.79. Campini died in his native Brusasco in 1974. A funeral notice appeared in *La Stampa* (8 July 1974), and he was buried in the local cemetery with his two nephews, both holders of the 'medaglia d'oro.' His funeral was attended by his nieces and their families, as well as Hélène's granddaughter Margherita with her husband, Archduke Robert of Austria-Este and Gr.Uff. [Grand'Ufficiale] Filippo Venza, a naval officer attached to Hélène's son Aimone (Private family information).

17. Kertzer, *The Pope and Mussolini* (2014), p. 180.

18. Segrè, *Italo Balbo* (1987), p. xii.

19. *The Times*, 30 April 1934.

20. Hélène d'Aosta, 'De Lagos à Alger,' 25–25 Sept 1934.

21. Hélène d'Aosta, 'De Lagos à Alger,' 8 Nov. 1934.

22. Hélène d'Aosta, 'De Lagos à Alger,' 9–11 Nov., 25 Dec. 1934.

23. Hélène d'Aosta, 'De Lagos à Alger,' 2 March 1935.

24. Mockler, *Haile Selassie's War* (1984), p. 55; *The Times*, 3 Oct. 1935.

25. Mockler, *Haile Selassie's War* (1984), pp. 67, 68.

26. *The Times*, 19 Dec. 1935.

27. Chadwick, *Britain and the Vatican* (1986), p. 9.

28. Mockler, *Haile Selassie's War* (1984), pp. 81, 102. Woodhouse, *Gabriele D'Annunzio* (1998), p. 307.

29. Mockler, *Haile Selassie's War* (1984), pp. 121, 142.

30. Mockler, *Haile Selassie's War* (1984), p. 150.

31. Photograph album 67 (Luglio 1936—Agosto 1937). Private family collection.

32. Private family information.

33. Beevor, *The Battle for Spain* (2006), 82, 87, 88, 94.

34. Amélie du Portugal, Journal intime, 28 Sept. 1936. AnP 300 AP III 718.

35. Beevor, *The Battle for Spain* (2006), 81, 135–136, 199, 232.

36. Amélie de Portugal, Journal intime, 19 Aug 1936. AnP 300 AP III 718.

37. Hélène's whereabouts during certain periods of her life can only be traced through the annotations she made in her reading material where she noted the month and

place where various books were read. Information on many annotations provided by Silvana Casale, Fondo Aosta, Biblioteca nazionale di Napoli.

38. Private family information.

39. *Tempo*, 18–25 Sept. 1948, pp 15–17.

40. *Gazzetta del Popolo, Daily Telegraph*.

41. *Le Temps*, 5 March 1934; *L'Ouest-Éclair* (Rennes), 10 June 1934; *Nouvelliste Valaisan* (Saint Maurice, Switzerland), 6 March 1934; *La Femme de France*, 8 April 1934; Albanese, *Principessa beduina* (2007), p. 95.

42. Addington, *The Royal House of Stuart* (1969–1976), 2:124–125, 142; Van der Kiste, *A Divided Kingdom* (2007), p. 34.

43. Catinot-Crost, *Amélie de Portugal* (2000), p. 232.

44. Bertoldi, *Aosta* (1987), p. 189.

45. Hélène d'Aosta, 'De Gadames à Koufra,' 5 Dec. 1936.

46. Hélène d'Aosta, 'De Gadames à Koufra,' 10, 19 Dec. 1936.

47. Hélène d'Aosta, 'De Gadames à Koufra,' 24, 25, 27 Dec. 1936.

48. Hélène d'Aosta, 'De Gadames à Koufra,' 31 Dec. 1936–1 Jan. 1937.

49. Hélène d'Aosta, 'De Gadames à Koufra,' 2, 22 Jan., 11 Feb. 1937.

50. Hélène d'Aosta, 'De Gadames à Koufra,' 13 Feb. 1937.

51. Mockler, *Haile Selassie's War* (1984), pp. 174–181.

52. Hélène d'Aosta, 'De Gadames à Koufra,' 2, 21 March 1937.

53. Hélène d'Aosta, 'De Gadames à Koufra,' 20–22, 28 April, 8, 13, 17 May 1937.

54. Sermoneta, *Sparkle Distant Worlds* (1947), p. 138.

55. Archivio Luce: 7 July 1937.

56. Cowles, *Looking for Trouble* (1941), p. 260.

57. Ciano, *Diary* (2002), p. 12.

58. Mockler, *Haile Selassie's War* (1984), pp. 186–187.

59. Thomas, *The Spanish Civil War* (1961), p. 383, citing Cantalupo, 85–6, 147ff.; Jules Blondel, Chargé d'affaires de France à Rome, to Georges Bonnet, Ministres des Affaires étrangères, Rome, 20 May 1938, in *Documents Diplomatiques français, 1932–1939*, 2e series (1936–1939), 9:813–814.

60. Ciano, *Diary* (2002), p. 32; Yvon Delbos, French minister of Foreign Affairs, 'Visite en Roumanie, 8 et 9 decembre 1937,' in *Documents Diplomatiques français, 1932–1939*, 2e series (1936–1939), 7:649.

61. Bertoldi, *Aosta* (1987), p. 204; Giornale Luce B1220 (22/12/1937, Napoli): La partenza del Vicerè Amedeo d'Aosta dal porto di Napoli); *The Times*, 16 Dec 1937.

62. 'The Duke of Aosta arrives at Port Said' (Jan 1938) : British Pathe (Film ID 951.20)

63. *The Times*, 29 Dec. 1937.

64. Mockler, *Haile Selassie's War* (1984), p. 187.

65. Hélène d'Aosta to Renée St-Maur, 29 May 1938. Author's collection (UK).

66. Ciano, *Diary* (2002), p. 78, 103.

67. Quoted in Kertzer, *The Pope and Mussolini* (2014), p. 267.

68. Kertzer, *The Pope and Mussolini* (2014), pp. 100, 116, 209.

69. Albanese, *Principessa beduina* (2007), p. 94 (which does not reference the quotation); *The Jewish Chronicle*, 3 Feb. 1905; Kertzer, *The Pope and Mussolini* (2014), p. 321; Gramont, *Ami du prince* (2011), pp. 175, 181–182.

70. Photograph album, no. 70. Private family collection; Hélène d'Aosta to Renée St Maur, 26 Aug. 1938 (Author's Collection [UK]); Amélie de Portugal, Journal intime, 1, 4 Sept. 1938. AnP 300 III 718; Hélène d'Aosta to Renée St Maur, 3 Sept. 1938 (Author's Collection [UK]).

71. Perth to Viscount Halifax, 23 Nov. 1938. TNA: FO 371/22441/206.

72. See Ciano's *Diary*, 1 Jan. 1939.

73. TNA: FO 371/23376. Addis Ababa, 8 Dec 1938.

74. Hélène d'Aosta, 'Voyage du 13 janvier 1939 au 13 mai 1939,' 27 Jan. 10 Feb. 1939.

75. Hélène d'Aosta, 'Voyage du 13 janvier 1939 au 13 mai 1939,' 16, 25 March 1939.

76. TNA: FO 371/23376.

77. Ciano, *Diary* (2002), p. 200.

78. Mockler, *Haile Selassie's War* (1984), pp. 194–195, 197.

79. Willingham, *Perilous Commitments* (2005), p. 7.

80. Channon, *Chips* (1970), p. 239.

81. TNA: FO 371/23780, ff. 70–71.

82. John Wimbles, 'Elisabeta of the Hellenes: Passionate Woman-Reluctant Queen,' *Royalty Digest* (2002), 172; *The Times*, 14 Oct. 1927; Duke of Kent to Prince Paul of Yugoslavia, 26 Sept. 1934, quoted in Balfour, *Paul of Yugoslavia* (1980), p. 94; Lee, *Helen Queen Mother of Rumania* (1956), p.170.

83. *The Daily Telegraph*, 29 Jan 2001.

84. TNA: FO 371/23780 f.82.

85. Michael of Greece, *Mémoires insolites* (2004), p. 78; Report by Pierson Dixon. TNA: FO371/23827.

86. Giornale Luce B1542 (05/05/1939). Archivio Storico Istituto Luce.

87. Satta and Savoia, *Cifra Reale* (2014), p. 20.

88. Private family information.

Chapter 15:

1. Hélène d'Aosta to Amedeo d'Aosta, 15 Sept 1941, Torre di Patria. TNA: FO371/29963, f3599

2. e.g., TNA: FO 371/23780 f. 32, 52.

3. Petropoulos, *Royals and the Reich* (2006), pp. 189–196.

4. Willingham, *Perilous Commitments* (2005), p. 10; F.O. Memorandum, 1.9.39. F.O. 371/23818, quoted in Waterfield, *Professional Diplomat* (1973), p. 248.

5. Archivio Luce: 4 October 1939. Giornale Luce B1597; Hélène d'Aosta to Marie José di Savoia, 20 Jan. 1939. Fondo Campini (tucked inside the cited text).

6. Private family information.

7. Ciano, *Diary* (2002), pp. 338–339.

8. Cowles, *Looking for Trouble* (1941), p. 355.

9. Mockler, *Haile Selassie's War* (1984), p. 250.

10. Ciano, *Diary* (2002), p. 376.

11. Ciano, *Diary* (2002), p. 68.

12. Quoted in Willingham, *Perilous Commitments* (2005), p. 13.

13. Willingham, *Perilous Commitments* (2005), pp. 4, 7.

14. Private family information.

15. Hélène d'Aosta to Amedeo d'Aosta, 15 Sept 1941. TNA: FO371/29963, f3599

16. Lee, *Helen Queen Mother of Rumania* (1956), pp. 198–199.

17. Willingham, *Perilous Commitments* (2005), pp. 38–39.

18. Private family information.

19. Van der Kiste, *Divided Kingdom* (2007), pp. 187–188; Photo album, no. 73. Private family collection.

20. Piano, *Memorie* (1956), p. 121; Eade, *Young Prince Philip* (2011), pp. 136–138.

21. *The Times*, 19 Feb 1941; TNA: FO 954/6A: Extract of letter from Sir A. Sinclair [Air Ministry], dated 25/12/40.

22. Mockler, *Haile Selassie's War* (1984), pp. 195, 305.

23. Mockler, *Haile Selassie's War* (1984), pp. 367, 369–70.

24. Amedeo di Savoia-Aosta, 'Diario di Amba Alàgi,' reproduced in Berretta, *Amedeo d'Aosta* (1955), pp. 297–330.

25. Aunt B. (Alvaro's mother) was Princess Beatrice of Saxe-Coburg-Gotha, a granddaughter of Queen Victoria and wife of Infante Alfonso of Spain (the son of Hélène's cousin, the Infanta Eulalia, and of her uncle, Antonio d'Orléans). Amedeo had served as a witness at Alvaro's Roman wedding in 1937.

26. Hélène d'Aosta to Amedeo d'Aosta, 20 April 1941. TNA: FO371/29963, f3599

27. Sir M. Palairet, Secretary of State (Athens) to Foreign Office, 4 April 1941. TNA: FO371/29963. R3599/7 April 1941

28. Hélène d'Aosta to Amedeo d'Aosta, 27 April 1941. TNA: FO371/29963, f3599.

29. Glover, *An Improvised War* (1987), *pp.* 168–169.

30. Willingham, *Perilous Commitments* (2005), pp. 69–70.

31. Pavlowitch, 'King Who Never Was' (1978), pp. 465–466; Ciano, *Diary* (2002), pp. 311, 420; Macartney, *October Fifteenth* (1961), 1:361; Bosworth, *Mussolini* (2002), p. 380.

32. Mack Smith, *Italy and Its Monarchy* (1989), p. 272.

33. Ciano, *Diary* (2002), p. 422; Pavlowitch, 'King Who Never Was' (1978), pp. 466, 468.

34. Pavlowitch, 'The King Who Never Was' (1978), p. 468, quoting the diary of Col. Bertocchi, 3–4, in the papers of the Duke of Aosta; Ciano, *Diary* (2000), p. 425.

35. Pavlowitch, 'The King Who Never Was' (1978), p. 468, quoting Bertocchi, Diary, 3–4 (Aosta Papers).

36. Ciano, *Diary* (2002), p. 426.

37. Ciano, *Diary* (2002), p. 430.

38. Hélène d'Aosta to Amedeo d'Aosta, 2 Sept 1941. TNA: FO371/29963, f3599.; www.campania.donorione.it/napoli.htm

39. Hélène d'Aosta to Amedeo d'Aosta, 15 Sept 1941. TNA: FO371/29963, f3599

40. Lett. Amena E 12(1bis (Torre di Patria, March 1943), L 51(Capodimonte, Aug. 1944), B 1(37 (Capodimonte, Sept. 1945). Fondo Aosta. [Cronin], Fondo Campini (Cominciato a alta voce il 7–IX–1943. Capodimonte. Terminato il 20 settembre 1943).

41. Hélène d'Aosta to Amedeo d'Aosta, 2 Sept 1941. TNA: FO371/29963, f3599.

42. Hélène d'Aosta to Amedeo d'Aosta, 15 Sept 1941. TNA: FO371/29963, f3599

43. TNA: FO371/29963. R9421/3599/22; C.O. 323/1857/18, R8910.

44. Sir H. Moore to Secretary of State for the Colonies, 20 Sept 1941. TNA: FO 371/29963/R8638.

45. Berretta, *Amedeo d'Aosta* (1955), p. 261; Aldrick, *Northrup* (2012);.Private family information; Berretta, *Amedeo d'Aosta* (1955), p. 272.

46. Sir H. Moore to Secretary of State for the Colonies, 2 Dec. 1941. TNA: CO 323/1857/18, f 47.

47. TNA: FO371/29930, R9350, 24 Oct 1941.

48. Ciano, *Diary* (2002), pp. 466, 483.

49. Satta and Savoia, *Cifra Reale* (2014), pp. 98–101. Olga Pignatari died early in 1945, just two days after her thirtieth birthday. Her brother Francesco was better known as 'Baby Pignatari,' a well-known playboy of the 1960's and sometime husband of Princess Ira von Furstenberg.

50. Satta and Savoia, *Cifra Reale* (2014), p. 83.

51. Maj. L.S. Harington and Lt Col J. Wakeford to the Director of Medical Services, East Africa command. General Hospital, Nairobi, 8 Feb. 1942. Reproduced in Speroni, *Amedeo duca d'Aosta* (1984), p. 188.

52. War Cabinet, 19 Feb. 1942. TNA: CAB 65/25/22.

53. War Office to GOG-in-charge, 21 Feb. 1942. TNA: CO 323/1857/18 f. 23.

54. Filed with The Principal Probate Registry, London, 15 Aug 1953. The remaining value of Amedeo's estate in England at that time was £35,639 (*The Times*, 21 Aug 1953).

55. Ciano, *Diary* (2000), p. 498.

56. TNA: WO 32/9886.

57. Satta and Savoia, *Cifra Reale* (2014), pp. 31–32, 89.

58. Ciano, *Diary* (2002), p. 499.

59. Castellani, *Microbes, Men and Monarchs* (1960), p. 82.

60. Ciano, *Diary* (2002), p. 500.

61. Ciano, *Diary* (2002), p. 502.

62. Sermoneta, *Sparkle Distant Worlds* (1947), p. 191.

63. Bertoldi, *Aosta* (1987), p. 224; Speroni, *I Savoia Scomodi* (1984), p. 421.

64. Amedeo d'Aosta, *In Nome del Re* (1986), pp. 73–75; Satta and Savoia, *Cifra Reale* (2014), pp. 33–34.

65. Hélène d'Aosta to Queen Mary, Aug. 1942, Capodimonte. RA QM/PRIV/ CC45/1331.

66. Joseph Gilbert Winant (U.S. Ambassador to the Court of St James's to Cordell Hull (U.S. Secretary of State), 18 Dec. 1942, in *Foreign Relations of the United States of America* (1943), 2:315–316.

67. *La Stampa Sera*, 1 Feb. 1943; Satta and Savoia, *Cifra Reale* (2014), p. 36.

Chapter 16:

1. *La Guerre a tué mon âme* from Hélène d'Aosta, *Vie errante* (1921), p. 1. This phrase that Hélène used after the First World War, she again used in relation to the Second World War.

2. Mack Smith, *Italy and its Monarchy* (1989), p. 305; Bosworth, *Mussolini* (2002), p. 400.

3. Bosworth, *Mussolini* (2002), p. 401.

4. Mack Smith, *Italy and its Monarchy* (1989), pp. 303, 306; Badoglio, *Italy in the Second World War* (1948), pp. 46–47.

5. Artieri, *Le Quattro Giornate* (2007), p. 23.

6. Photograph album, no. 75. Private family collection.

7. Croce, *The King and the Allies* (1950), p. 13.

8. Satta and Savoia, *Cifra Reale* (2014), pp. 91–92.

9. Quoted in Rodrigues, 'Captives' (2013), p. 14; Lee, *Helen, Queen Mother of Rumania* (1956), p. 218.

10. van Kerrebrouck, *Maison de Bourbon* (2004), vol. 4, pt 1, pp 483, 485n.3; Regolo, *Marie José de Savoie* (2001), p. 261; Petropolous, *Royals and the Reich* (2006), p. 299.

11. Regolo, *Jelena* (2002), p. 661.

12. Spiegelfeld-Lodron, 'Ricordi della mia vita' (n.d.), p. 1; Lee, *Royal House of Greece* (1948), p. 132; Private family information.

13. Nicholas, *The Rape of Europa* (1994), p. 323.

14. Artieri, *Le Quattro giornate* (2007), pp. 34–35, 45–46, 48.

15. Years later in 1951, following one of Hélène's last wishes Father Beda Feser located the Wehrmacht officer and presented him with a gold watch as a token of her gratitude (Private family information).

16. Artieri, *Le Quattro giornate* (2007), p. 65; Brey, *The Venus Fixers* (2009), pp. 75–76.

17. Clark, *Calculated Risk* (1951), p. 207; Trevelyan, *Rome '44* (1981), pp. 36–37.

18. Lewis, *I Came, I Saw* (1996), chapter 7; Lewis, *Naples '44* (1978), p. 26.

19. Clark, *Calculated Risk* (1951), p. 211; Lewis, *Naples '44* (1978), p. 33.

20. Miale, *Stragedy* (2005), p. 86. Googlebooks accessed 23 April 2011; Private family information.

21. Nicholas, *The Rape of Europa* (1994), p. 233.

22. Lewis, *Naples '44* (1978), pp. 46, 55, 88.

23. Wheeler, *Still Digging* (1958), pp. 148–149. A very different, and much less convincing version was given in Villari, *The Liberation of Italy, 1943–1947* (1959),

p. 130, 'The aged Duchess of Aosta had refused to receive British generals at her villa at Capodimonte on the outskirts of Naples, regarding them as representatives of a Government which had treated her son, the heroic defender of Italian East Africa, so harshly while, as a prisoner of war, he lay dying in a Kenya hospital. The retort to this motherly gesture was that the Capodimonte park was turned into a bivouac for colored troops. At the same time, the magnificent Royal Palace in Naples was turned into a combination of a club and a brothel for the troops, and when finally evacuated was found reduced to the conditions of a huge pigsty.'

24. Croce, *The King and the Allies* (1950), p. 29.

25. Moorehead, *Eclipse* (1945), p. 63; Brey, *Venus Fixers* (2009), pp. 77–78.

26. Macmillan, *War Diary* (1984), 26 Oct. 1943.

27. *Manchester Guardian*, 3 Nov 1943

28. Enrico d'Assia, *Il Lampadario di Cristallo* (1992), p. 139; Satta and Savoia, *Cifra Reale* (2014), p. 43; Tutaev, *The Consul of Florence* (1966), pp. 101–105; Nigra, *Il Borgo di Sartirana Lomellina et il suo Castello* (1986), 21.

29. Quoted in Tutaev, *Consul of Florence* (1966), p. 279.

30. Lewis, *Naples '44*, 93.

31. Brey, *Venus Fixers* (2009), pp. 28–30, 96.

32. Mack Smith, *Italy and its Monarchy* (1989), p. 329.

33. Rodrigues, 'Captives' (2013), p. 15; TNA: FO 954/14A: Italy: Rome tel. no. 220; From Rome (High Commissioner) to Foreign Office. 17 July 1944; Satta and Savoia, *Cifra Reale* (2014), p. 50; Lee, *Royal House of Greece* (1948), p. 133.

34. *New York Times*, 8 July 1944.

35. Private family information and Spiegelfeld-Lodron, '*Ricordi della mia vita*' (n.d.), p. 4.

36. François-Poncet, *Carnets d'un captif* (1952), pp. 188–190; Carmine Senise, *Quando ero capo della polizia: Diario, 1940–1943* (Milano: Ugo Murzia editore, 2012), 162, quoted in Rodriques, 'Captives' (2013), p. 17.

37. Rodriques, 'Captives' (2013), p. 16; François-Poncet, *Carnets d'un captif* (1952), pp. 193, 197.

38. Quoted in Tutaev, *Consul of Florence* (1966), p. 279.

39. François-Poncet, *Carnets d'un captif* (1952), p. 193.

40. Private family information. Jonas, *The Life of Crown Prince William* (1961), pp. 211–212, gives an alternative version, which the current Duke of Aosta says is incorrect.

41. Petropoulos, *Royals and the Reich* (2006), p. 299.

42. Tutaev, *Consul of Florence* (1966), p. 106.

43. Ranfurly, *To War with Whitaker* (1995), p. 274.

44. Domenico, *Italian Fascists on Trial* (1991), p. 124; TNA: FO371/49769 (1945, Italy, file no. 3 pp 1708–2312), f2174, f2001; *New York Times*, 9, 11 April 1945; François-Poncet, *Carnets d'un captif* (1952), p. 394.

45. In 1951 her husband and children reburied Mafalda in the family cemetery at Kronberg. Barneschi, *Frau von Weber* (1983), p. 145; Petropoulos, *Royals & the Reich* (2006), p. 303.

46. TNA: FO371/48415 f7697.

47. Lee, *Royal House of Greece* (1948), p. 135; Private family information.

48. Croce, *The King and the Allies* (1950), p. 59.

49. TNA: FO371/48415 f7697; C E King to W G Hayter, Foreign Office, 18 June 1945. TNA: FO371/48415 f7697; Albanese, *Principessa beduina* (2007), pp. 111–112; Rodrigues, 'Captives' (2013), p. 19; Lee, *Royal House of Greece* (1948), p. 135; Satta and Savoia, *Cifra Reale* (2014), p. 71; Capodimonte Guest Books. Private family collection.

50. Satta and Savoia, *Cifra Reale* (2014), p. 77.

51. Albanese, *Principessa beduina* (2007), pp. 114–115.

Chapter 17:

1. Hélène de France to Renée St Maur, Castellamare, 2 Oct 1948. Author's Collection (UK).

2. Mack Smith, *Italy and its Monarchy* (1989), p. 336. Marie José had not seen her in-laws since returning to Italy Regolo, *Marie José* (2001), p. 267. FO371/60536 (Italy 1946, file 1, pp 1869–2000) f 1877. : From Rome to Cairo, Sir N. Charles, 22 May 1946.

3. Puntoni, *Parla Vittorio Emauele III* (1993), p. 338; Enrico d'Assia, *Il Lampadario di Cristallo* (1992), pp. 213–214; Regolo, *Jelena* (2002), p. 683; Mack Smith, *Italy and its Monarchy* (1989), p. 338.

4. *The Times*, 10 May 1946. The 'traditional custom' referred to the 1849 abdication of Victor Emmanuel's great-grandfather, King Carlo Alberto of Sardinia, who went to live in exile in Portugal.

5. Mack Smith, *Italy and its Monarchy* (1989), p. 337; Satta and Savoia, *Cifra Reale* (2014), pp. 79–80.

6. Mack Smith, *Italy and its Monarchy* (1989), p. 340; Allum, *Politics and Society in Post-War Naples* (1973), p. 96.

7. Castellani, *Microbes, Men and Monarchs* (1960), pp. 193–195; Regolo, *Marie José* (2001), p. 288.

8. Regolo, *Marie José de Savoie* (2001), p. 310.

9. Private family information.

10. TNA: FO371/60536, f1988, FO371/60540.

11. Piano, *Memorie* (1956), pp. 126–127.

12. Satta and Savoia, *Cifra Reale* (2014), p. 86.

13. Sir D. Osborne to the Foreign Office, 20 Dec 1946; Sir N. Charles to Foreign Office, 24 Dec. 1946. TNA: FO 371/60543.

14. Principal Court of Probate, London.

15. Hélène de France to Renée St Maur, 23 March 1947. Author's Collection (UK).

16. Lee, *Helen, Queen Mother of Rumania* (1956), pp. 266–267.

17. Lee, *Helen, Queen Mother of Rumania* (1956), p. 276; Channon, *Chips* (1970), p. 511.

18. Amélie de Portugal to Renée St Maur, 20 Nov. 1947. Author's Collection (UK).

19. Constitution of the Italian Republic. Online publication by the Senato della Republica (accessed 30 Nov 2008, www.senato.it/documenti/repository/istituzione/costituzione_inglese.pdf)

20. Constitutional law no. 1 of 23 Oct. 2002 has established that the first and second paragraphs of the 13th transitional and final provision of the Constitution cease to be applicable as of the date of the entry into force of said Constitutional law (10 Nov. 2002).

21. Private family information. The porcupine had become an emblem with the Orléans family when Louis, duc d'Orléans, founded the Order of the Porcupine in 1394, although it was terminated by King Louis XII.

22. Satta and Savoia, *Cifra Reale* (2014), p. 106.

23. Guerrieri, Il fondo Aosta della B. N. di Napoli (1959), 3:639–45.

24. When Queen Elena died in 1952, her estate still in England amounted to nearly £350,000. National Probate Index (England & Wales).

25. Photograph album, no. 76. Private family collection; Spiegelfeld-Lodron, 'Ricordi della mia vita' (n.d.), p. 13.

26. Unfortunately, neither Queen Mary's condolences nor Hélène's reply survive, as the latter was culled from the Foreign Office papers when transferred to the Public Record Office. However, they were recorded in the index as T3385/T55211/186/379. It is interesting to note that Hélène's response went through the Foreign Office and thus did not end up in the Royal Archives.

27. Isabelle, Comtesse de Paris, *Tout m'est bonheur* (1978), p. 172.; Catinot-Crost, *Amélie de Portugal* (2000), p. 335; Michael of Greece, *Mémoires insolites* (2004), pp. 76, 78. The date of this meeting is from a conversation with Prince Michael of Greece, 5 April 2012.

28. Satta and Savoia, *Cifra Reale* (2014), p. 106.

29. Anne d'Aosta to Sir Percy Loraine, Dec. 1948. TNA: FO 1011/214 (Papers of Sir Percy Loraine)

30. Amedeo d'Aosta, *In Nome del Re* (1986), p. 132; Private family information; Hélène de France to Renée St Maur, 2 Oct 1948. Author's Collection (UK). Bertoldi, *Aosta* (1987), p. 148.

31. Hélène d'Aosta, Cahier XI (1926–1941). Private family collection.

32. Hélène's copy, marked simply 'H. 1950' is in the Fondo Campini.

33. Catinot-Crost, Laurence. *Amélie de Portugal* (2000), p. 357; Private family information.

34. Hélène d'Aosta, *La Vie Errante* (1921), p. 43.

35. *The Times*, 23 Jan. 1951; *Daily Telegraph*, 22 Jan. 1951.

36. Bertoldi, *Aosta* (1987), p. 148.

37. Private family information.

38. Private family information.

Bibliography

Manuscript Collections

Abbreviations

AnP = Archives nationales, Paris
GRO = Gloucestershire Record Office
MHS = Massachusetts Historical Society, Boston
RA = Royal Archives, Windsor Castle
TNA = The National Archives, Kew, United Kingdom (formerly Public Record Office)

France

Archives nationales, Paris [AnP]
    Fonds de la Maison de France (branche d'Orléans) 300 AP
Archives du Château de Chantilly
    Fonds Orléans. 1 PA

Italy

Private family collection.
Fondo Angelo Contri, Archivio Contemporaneo "Alessandro Bonsanti". Gabinetto G. P. Vieusseux, Florence
Fondo Aosta, Biblioteca Nazionale, Naples.
Fondo Campini, Biblioteca Giuseppe Grosso, Palazzo Cisterno, Torino.
    Unpublished travel journals of Hélène d'Aosta:
1. Sénégal—Niger—Tchad—Chari—Congo, 1921–1922

2. De l'Océan indien au Nil blanc à travers les lacs equatoriaux et la région des volcans. Janvier–mai 1925

3. Eritrea, decembre 1926–mars 1927

4. Da Tripoli a Gat, 11 April–11 Maggio 1931

5. Da Napoli a Duala (Amerounlago—Tchad—Sahara—Fezzan –Tripoli), 26 Nov 1932–2 April 1933

6. De Lagos a Alger à travers le Sahara. 7 novembre 1934–19 mars 1935

7. De Gadames à Koufra, Decembre 1936–juin 1937

8. Voyage du 13 janvier 1939 au 13 mai 1939

Collezione Duca d'Aosta, Musei nazionale di S. Martino, Scuola Militare 'Nunziatella', Naples.

United Kingdom

British Library, London
    Paget Papers
Gloucestershire Record Office, Gloucester [GRO]
    Hicks Beach Papers
The National Archives, Kew (formerly Public Record Office) [TNA]
    Colonial Office Papers
    Foreign Office Papers
    Home Office Papers
Parliamentary Archives, London
    Cadogan Papers
Principal Probate Registry, London
Royal Archives, Windsor Castle [RA]
Surrey History Centre, Woking, Surrey
    Papers of Amelia Sprigings (later Bliss) of Claremont, Esher
Author's Collection (UK)
    Correspondence of Hélène d'Aosta with Renée St Maur and others.

United States

Massachusetts Historical Society, Boston
    George vonL. Meyer Papers

Published Sources

Abruzzi, L., duca degli, *On the "Polar Star" in the Arctic Sea*. 2 vols. (London: Hutchinson & Co., 1903)

Addington, A. C., *The Royal House of Stuart*. 3 vols. (London: Charles Skilton, Ltd., 1969–1976)

Albanese, C., *La Principessa beduina: L'avventurosa vita di Elena di Francia duchessa d'Aosta* (Milano: Mursia, 2007)

Aldrick, J., *Northrup: The Life of Sir William Northrup McMillan, 1872–1925* (Kijabe, Kenya: Old Africa Books, 2012)

Alexandra, Queen of Great Britain. *Queen Alexandra's Christmas book: Photographs from my Camera*. London: The Daily Telegraph, 1908.

Allum, P. A., *Politics and Society in Post-War Naples* (Cambridge: Cambridge University Press, 1973)

Aosta, Aimone, duca d' (duca di Spoleto), and Ardito Desio. 'The Italian Expedition to the Karakoram' and, 'Geological Work of the Italian Expedition....' in *The Geographical Journal*, Vol LXXV/5, May 1930. London: Royal Geographical Society, 1930.

Aosta, Amedeo, duca d' (1898–1942). 'Diario di Amba Alàgi,' in A. Berretta, *Amedeo d'Aosta: Il prigioniero del Kenya* (Milano: Edizioni librarie italiane, 1955)

—. *Studi Africani*. Bologna: Nicola Zanichelli editore, 1942

Aosta, Amedeo, duca d' (b 1943), *In Nome del Re: Conversazione con Gigi Speroni*. Milan: Rusconi, 1986.

—. (see also, Satta, Danila, *below*)

Aosta, Hélène de France, duchessa d', *Accanto agli eroi: diario di guerra di sua altezza reale la duchessa d'Aosta ispettrice generale delle infermiere volontarie della Croce rossa italiana*. Prefazione di B. Mussolini (Roma: Croce rossa italiana, 1930)

—. 'Attraverso il Sahara.' Published in *Nuova Antologia* (1935), pp. 3–48.

—. 'Diana in Africa', *Harper's Weekly*, 54 (1910), March 12 (pp. 14–17); April 30 (pp. 11–12); May 7 (pp. 9–10); Aug. 6 (pp. 8–9); Aug. 20 (pp. 12–13).

—. *Souvenirs d'Afrique*, in *La Revue universelle*, 1 mai 1929 (pp. 257–272), 15 mai 1929 (pp. 385–401)

—. *Vers le Soleil qu se lève* (Ivrea: Francesco Viassone, 1918)

—. *Vie Errante: Sensations d'Afrique* (Ivrea: Ditta Francesco Viassone, 1921)

—. *Voyages en Afrique* (Milan: Fratelli Treves & Paris, Librairie Nilsson, 1913)

Aronson, T., *Queen Victoria and the Bonapartes* (London: Cassell, 1972)

Artieri, G., *Le Quattro Giornate: Breve storia di un'epopea* (Firenze: Casa Editrice Le Lettere, 2007)

Asquith, M., *An Autobiography*. 2 vols. (London: T. Butterworth, 1920–1922)

Assia, H. d' [Prince Heinrich of Hesse], *Il Lampadario di Cristallo* (Milano: Longanesi & C., 1992)

Badoglio, P., *Italy in the Second World War: Memories and Documents* (London: Oxford University Press, 1948)

Balansó, J., *Les Bourbons de Parme* (Biarritz: J&D Éditions, 1996)

Balfour, N., and S. MacKay, *Paul of Yugoslavia: Britain's Maligned Friend* (London: Hamish Hamilton, 1980)

Barbagallo, F., *Francesco S. Nitti* (Torino: Unione Tipografico-Edittrice Torinese, 1984)

Barneschi, R., *Frau von Weber: Vita e morte di Mafalda di Savoia a Buchenwald* (Milano: Rusconi, 1983)

Barrière, M., *Les princes d'Orléans* (Paris: Gallimard, 1933)

Battiscombe, G., *Queen Alexandra* (London: Constable, 1969)

Beevor, A., *The Battle for Spain* (London: Weidenfeld & Nicolson, 2006)

Bell, H., *Glimpses of a Governor's Life: From Diaries, Letters, and Memoranda* (London: Sampson Low, Marston & Co., Ltd., 1946)

Berretta, A., *Amedeo d'Aosta: Il prigioniero del Kenya* (Milano: Edizioni librarie italiane, 1955)

—, *Con Amedeo d'Aosta in Africa Orientale Italiana in pace e in guerra* (Milano: Casa Editrice Ceschina, 1952)

Bertoldi, S., *Aosta: Gli Altri Savoia* (Milano: Rizzoli, 1987)

Bevington, M., *Stowe House*. 2nd edition (London: Paul Holberton Publishing, 2002)

Bilteryst, D., *Le prince Baudoin: Frère du Roi-Chevalier* (Bruxelles: Racine, 2013)

Blunt, W. S., *My Diaries: Being a personal narrative of events, 1888–1914*. 2 vols. (London: Martin Secker, 1919–1920)

Bolton, G., *Roman Century, 1870–1970* (London: Hamish Hamilton, 1970)

Bosworth, R. J. B., *Mussolini* (London: Arnold, 2002)

Bracalini, R. with Maria Gabriella di Savoia, *Casa Savoia: Diario di una Monarchia* (Milano: Mondadori, 2001)

Brey, I. D., *The Venus Fixers: The Remarkable Story of the Allied Soldiers Who Saved Italy's Art During World War II* (London: Picador, 2009)

Brun, C., *Descendance inédite du Duc de Berry* (Paris: L'intermediaire des chercheurs et curieux, 1998)

Casale, S., 'L'opera di Elena D'Aosta per la Croce Rossa', in *La Campania e la Grande Guerra: I Monumenti ai Caduti di Napoli e Provincia*, ed. M. R. Nappi (Rome: Gangemi Editore spa, 2011), 41–55.

Cashmore, T. H. R., *The Orléans Family in Twickenham, 1800–1932* (Twickenham: Borough of Twickenham Local History Society, 1982)

Castellani, A., *Microbes, Men and Monarchs: A Doctor's Life in Many Lands* (London: Gollancz, 1960)

Catenacci, G., *Amedeo d'Aosta e la Nunziatella* (Naples: Associazione Nazionale Nunziatella, 1993)

Catinot-Crost, L., *Amélie de Portugal, princesse de France* (Biarritz: Atlantica, 2000)

Cazelles, R., *Le duc d'Aumale* (Paris: Éditions Tallandier, 1984)

Cervi, M., *Il Duca Invitto: La vita di Emanuele Filiberto di Savoia Aosta principe e condottiero* (Novara: Istituto Geografico de Agostini, 1987)

Chadwick, O., *Britain and the Vatican during the Second World War* (Cambridge: Cambridge University Press, 1986)

Chamberlain, Lesley, *Nietzsche in Turin: The End of the Future* (London: Quartet Books, 1996)

Chambord, Henri, comte de, *Journal (1846–1883), Carnets inédits*. Edited by Philippe Delorme (Paris: François-Xavier de Guibert, 2009)

Channon, H., *Chips: The Diaries of Sir Henry Channon* (London: Penguin Books, 1970)

Choate, M. I., *Emigrant Nation: The Making of Italy Abroad* (Cambridge, Mass.: Harvard University Press, 2008)

Christopher, Prince of Greece. *Memoirs of H. R. H. Prince Christopher of Greece* (London: The Right Book Club, 1938)

Churchill, W., *My African Journey* (Toronto: William Briggs, 1909)

Ciano, G., *Ciano's Diary, 1937–1943: the Complete, Unabridged Diaries of Count Galeazzo Ciano, Italian Minister for Foreign Affairs, 1936–1943* (London: Phoenix Press, 2002)

Cipolla, C., A. Ardissone and F. A. Fava, eds., *Storia della Croce Rossa in Piemonte dalla nascita al 1914* (Milano: Franco Angeli, 2015)

Clark, M., *Calculated Risk: His Personal Story of the War in North Africa and Italy* (London: George G. Harrap & Co., Ltd., 1951)

Cook, A., *Prince Eddy: The King Britain Never Had* (Stroud, Glos.: Tempus, 2006)

Corpechot, L., *Memories of Queen Amelie of Portugal* (London: Eveleigh Nash, 1915)

Cowles, V., *Looking for Trouble* (London: Harper & Brothers, 1941)

Croce, B., *The King and the Allies: Extracts from a Diary by Benedetto Croce, July 1943–June 1944.* Translated by Sylvia Sprigge (London: George Allen & Unwin Ltd, 1950)

Defrance, O., 'Between Egypt and Europe: The curious fate of Clémentine of Saxe-Coburg and Gotha', *Royalty Digest Quarterly* 2013 (4), 1–13.

—. *La Médicis des Cobourg: Clémentine d'Orléans* (Bruxelles: Éditions Racine, 2007)

de Grazia, V., *The Culture of Consent: Mass Organization of Leisure in Fascist Italy* (Cambridge: Cambridge University Press, 1981)

Defrance, O., 'Between Egypt and Europe: The curious fate of Clémentine of Saxe-Coburg and Gotha,' *Royalty Digest Quarterly* 2013 (4)

DePaola, T., 'La fascistizzazione della professione infermieristica,' in I. Pascucci and C. Tavormina, *La professione infermieristica in Italia: Un viaggio tra storia e società dal 1800 a oggi* (Milan: McGraw-Hill, 2012)

De Vecchi di Val Cismon, C. M., *Amedeo di Savoia, Viceré di Etiopia* (Rome: Instituto per l'Enciclopedia de Carlo, 1942)

Dimitroff, P., *Boris III of Bulgaria (1894–1943): Toiler, Citizen, King* (Lewes, Sussex: Book Guild, 1986)

Documents on British Foreign Policy, 1919–1939, ed. by E. L. Woodward and Rohan Butler (London, 1952)

Domenico, R. P., *Italian Fascists on Trial, 1943–1948* (Chapel Hill, N. C., 1991)

Duggan, C., *Fascist Voices: An Intimate History of Mussolini's Italy* (London: The Bodley Head, 2012)

Eade, P., *Young Prince Philip: His Turbulent Early Life* (London: Harper Press, 2011)

Edward VIII, King of Great Britain (Duke of Windsor). *Letters from a Prince*, ed. by Rupert Godfrey (London: Little, Brown & Co., 1980)

Eulalia, Infanta of Spain, *Court Life from Within* (New York: Dodd, Mead & Co., 1915)

Eulenburg, P. *Philipp Eulenburgs Politische Korrespondenz*, ed. Röhl, John C. G., 3 vols. (Boppard am Rhein: H. Boldt, 1983)

Eustace, K., 'Britannia: Some High Points in the History of Iconography on British Coinage,' in *British Numismatic Journal* 76 (2006).

Farini, D., *Diario di fine secolo*, edited by Emilia Morelli. 2 vols. (Rome: Bardi Editore in Roma, 1961–1962)

Foch, F., *The Memoirs of Marshal Foch* (London: William Heinemann, 1931)

France. Ministère des Affaires étrangères. Documents diplomatiques français, 1871–1914. 1re ser. 1932–1939, 2e ser.

François-Poncet, A., Carnets d'un captif (Paris: Librairie Arthème Fayard, 1952)

Glover, M., *An Improvised War: The Ethiopian Campaign, 1940–1941* (London: Leo Cooper, 1987)

Goldstein, E., *The First World War Peace Settlements, 1919–1925* (London: Longman, 2002)

Gooch, J., *The Italian Army and the First World War* (Cambridge: Cambridge University Press, 2014)

Gordon-Smith, G., 'Treatment of the Yugoslav Minority in Trieste and Istria a danger to the peace of Europe,' *Advocate of Peace through Justice* (World Affairs Institute), 90 (1928): 443.

Gramont, A. de, *L'ami du prince: Journal inédit d'Alfred de Gramont (1892–1915)*, ed. Éric Mension-Rigau (Paris: Fayard, 2011)

Gribble, F., *The Royal House of Portugal* (London: Eveleigh Nash, 1915)

Guerrieri, G., ''Il fondo Aosta' della B. N. di Napoli', in *Studi in onore di Riccardo Filangieri* (Napoli: L'Arte tipografica, 1959)

Hanson, E. W., ''Connubial Equality': Russia & Montenegro,' *Royalty Digest Quarterly* (Falköping, Sweden), 2010 (1):1–3.

—. 'The Last Word: 2. Philippe, Duc d'Orléans. *Royalty Digest Quarterly* (Falköping, Sweden), 2012 (4): 41–43.

Hanson, N., *Unknown Soldiers: The Story of the Missing of the First World War* (New York: Alfred A. Knopf, 2006)

Harcourt Williams, R., ed., *Salisbury-Balfour Correspondence: Letters exchanged between the Third Marquess of Salisbury and his nephew Arthur James Balfour 1869–1892* (Hertford: Hertfordshire Record Society, 1988)

Hastings, M., *Catastrophe: Europe goes to War, 1914* (London: William Collins, 2013)

Hulst d'Hauteroche d', M., *A Royal and Christian Soul: A Sketch of the Life and Death of the Comte de Paris* (London: R. Washbourne, 1895)

Horne, A., *Seven Ages of Paris* (London: Macmillan, 2002)

Howe, M. A. D., *George von Lengerke Meyer: His Life and Public Services* (New York: Dodd, Mead and Co., 1920)

Hughes-Hallett, L., *The Pike: Gabriele D'Annunzio, poet, seducer and preacher of war* (London: Fourth Estate, 2013)

'Illness of Prominent Persons' *JAMA: Journal of the American Medical Association*, 28 Sept. 1994, vol. 272, p. 926.

Imperiali, G., *Diario (1915–1919)* (Soveria Mannelli [Catanzaro]: Rubbettino, 2006)

Irvine, W. D., *The Boulanger Affair Reconsidered: Royalism, Boulangism, and the Origins of the Radical Right in France* (Oxford: Oxford University Press, 1989)

Italy. Ministero degli Affari Esteri. *I Documenti Diplomatici Italiani*. 7th series (1922–1935) (Rome: Libreria dello Stato, 1967)

Jonas, Klaus W., *The Life of Crown Prince William* (London: Routledge & Pegan Paul, 1961)

Jullian, P., *d'Annunzio* (London: The Pall Mall Press, 1971).

Kertzer, D. I., *The Pope and Mussolini: The Secret History of Pius XI and the Rise of Fascism in Europe* (Oxford: Oxford University Press, 2014)

—, *Prisoner of the Vatican: The Popes' Secret Plot to Capture Rome from the New Italian State* (Boston: Houghton Mifflin Co., 2004)

Kodak Exhibition—Royal Photographers On behalf of King Edward's Hospital Fund for London and the Voluntary Hospitals. This volume commemorates the Exhibition of Royal Photographers which started on a World Tour on behalf of the Hospitals on May 23rd 1930 (Bristol & London: Vandyck Printers Ltd., 1930)

Lambrino, P., *King Carol II: A life of my grandfather* (London: Methuen, 1988),

Lami, L., *Le Passioni del Dragone: Cavalli e donne: Caprilli campione della Belle Époque* (Milano: Ugo Mursia Editore, 2009)

Langham-Carter, R. R. *The Royal French Tombs at Weybridge*. Monograph 24 (Walton & Weybridge Local History Society, 1975)

Lee, A. G., *Helen, Queen Mother of Rumania, Princess of Greece and Denmark* (London, Faber and Faber, 1956)

—. *The Royal House of Greece* (London: Ward, Lock & Co., 1948)

Lewis, N., *I Came, I Saw: An Autobiography* (London: Picador, 1966)

—. *Naples '44* (London: Collins, 1978)

Lewis, R., *The queen of cooks—and some kings. (The Story of Rosa Lewis)*. Recorded by Mary Lawton (New York: Boni & Liveright, 1925)

Luzzatti, L. *God in Freedom: Studies in the Relations between Church and State* (New York: Macmillan Co., 1930)

Macartney, C. A. *October Fifteenth: A History of Modern Hungary, 1929–1945*. 2 vols. (Edinburgh: University Press, 1961)

McKinstry, L., *Rosebery: Statesman in Turmoil* (London: John Murray, 2005)

Mack Smith, D., *Italy and Its Monarchy* (New Haven & London: Yale University Press, 1989)

Macmillan, H., *War Diaries: Politics and War in the Mediterranean, January 1943–May 1945* (London: Macmillan, 1984)

McMullen, R., *Mona Lisa: The Picture and the Myth* (London: Macmillan, 1976)

Malgeri, F., *La Guerra Libica (1911–1912)* (Rome: Edizioni di Storia e Letteratura, 1970)

Manach, D., *La Descendance de Louis-Philippe I, Roi des Français* (Paris: Éditions Christian, 1988)

Mandache, D., ed., *Dearest Missy: The Correspondence between Marie, Grand Duchess of Russia, Duchess of Edinburgh and of Saxe-Coburg and Gotha and her daughter, Marie,*

Crown Princess of Romania, 1879–1900 (Falköping, Sweden: Rosvall, 2011).

Maria de la Paz, Infanta of Spain, Princess Ludwig Ferdinand of Bavaria, *Through Four Revolutions, 1862–1933* (London: John Murray, 1933)

Maria Gabriella di Savoia and Stefano Papi, *Vita di corte in Casa Savoia* (Verona: Mondadori Electa Spa, 2006)

Marie of Greece, Grand Duchess George of Russia, *A Romanov Diary* (New York: Atlantic International Publications, 1988)

Marie José, Queen of Italy, *Albert et Elisabeth de Belgique: Mes Parents* (Paris: Librarie Plon, 1971)

Massie, R. K., *Nicholas and Alexandra* (New York: Atheneum, 1967)

Maylunas, A., and S. Mironenko, *A Lifelong Passion: Nicholas and Alexandra, Their Own Story* (London: Weidenfeld & Nicolson, 1996)

Miale, F., *Stragedy,* (Victoria, B.C., Canada, 2005. Googlebooks accessed 23 April 2011)

Mellano, M. F., *I prinicipi Maria Clotilde e Amedeo di Savoia e il Vaticano (1870–1890): Attraverso la corrispondenza diplomatica della santa Sede ed altri documenti* (Torino: Centro Studi Piemontesi, 2000).

Michael, Prince of Greece, *Bourbon-Orléans: A Family Album* (Falköping: Rosvall, 2009)

—, *Eddy & Hélène ... an impossible match* (Falköping: Rosvall, 2013)

—, *Mémoires insolites* (Paris: XO Éditions, 2004)

Mockler, A., *Haile Selassie's War: The Italian-Ethiopian Campaign, 1935–1941* (New York: Random House, 1984)

Mola di Nomaglio, G., 'Per la giustizia, la carità, l'assistenza: Casa Savoia dalla 'Mendicità sbandita' alla Croce Rossa Italiana,' in *Storia della Croce Rossa in Piemonte dalla nascita al 1914*, eds. C. Cipolla, A. Ardissone, and F. A. Fava (Milan: FrancoAngeli, 2015)

Moorehead, A., *Eclipse* (London: Hamish Hamilton Ltd., 1945)

Morris, C., ed. *The San Francisco Calamity: By Earthquake and Fire* (Gutenberg Project, EBook 1560)

Morris, J., *Trieste and the Meaning of Nowhere* (London: Faber and Faber, 2001)

Nicholas, L. H., *The Rape of Europa: The Fate of Europe's Treasures in the Third Reich and the Second World War* (London: Macmillan, 1994)

Nicholls, C. S., *Red Strangers: The White Tribe of Kenya* (London: Timewell Press, 2005)

Nigra, C., *Il borgo di Sartirana Lomellina ed il suo Castello* (Novara : Stab. Tip. E. Cattaneo, 1941)

Nitti, F., *Meditazioni dell'esilio.* 2nd edition (Naples: Edizioni Scientifiche Italiane, 1947)

Oliva, G., *Duchi d'Aosta: I Savoia che non diventarono re d'Italia* (Milano: Editions Mondadori, 2003)

Olla, R., *Il Duce and his women* (Richmond, Surrey: Alma Books, 2011)

Orléans, H. d', comte de Paris. *Mémoires d'exil et de combats.* Atelier Marcel Jullian, 1979.

—. *Mon Album de famille.* Text by Prince Michael of Greece. Paris: France Loisirs, 1996.

Orléans, I. d', comtesse de Paris. *Tout m'est bonheur.* Paris: Éditions Robert Laffont, 1978.

Orléans, J. d', duc d'Orléans. *Les chasses des princes d'Orléans.* éditions Gerfaut. 1999

Orléans, J. d', duc de Guise, *Sous le Danebrog.* Paris, 1901.

Osgood, S. M., *French Royalism under the Third and Fourth Republics* (The Hague: Martinus Nijhoff, 1960)

Pailler, J., *Charles Ier, Roi de Portugal* (Biarritz: Atlantica, 2000)

Paoli, D., *Fortunes & Infortunes des princes d'Orléans (1848–1918)* (Paris: Éditions Artena, 2006)

Papásogli, G., *La Regina Elena* (Milano: Massimo, 1965)

Pavlowitch, S. K., 'The King Who Never Was: An Instance of Italian Involvement in Croatia, 1941–3,' *European Studies Review*, 8 (1978): 465–487.

Petropolous, J., *Royals and the Reich: The Princes von Hessen in Nazi Germany* (Oxford: Oxford University Press, 2006)

Piano, E., *Memorie di una Istitutrice di Casa Savoia* (Torino: Editrice Superga, 1956)

Pless, Daisy, Princess of. *Daisy, Princess of Pless, by Herself* (London: John Murray, 1928)

Poisson, G., *Les Orléans: Une famille en quête d'un trône* (Paris: Perrin, 1999)

Pope-Hennessy, J., *Queen Mary, 1867–1953* (London: George Allen and Unwin, Ltd., 1959)

Priestley, E., *The Story of a Lifetime* (London: Kegan Paul, Trench, Trübner & Co., Ltd., 1908)

Puntoni, P., *Parla Vittorio Emanuele III* (Bologna: Società editrice il Mulino, 1993)

Putnam, R. D., *Making Democracy Work: Civic Traditions in Modern Italy* (Princeton, N.J., 1993)

Radziwill, C., *Nicholas II: The Last of the Tsars* (London: Cassell, 1931)

Ranfurly, H., *To War with Whitaker: The Wartime Diaries of the Countess of Ranfurly, 1939–45* (London: Heinemann, 1994)

Récamier, J., *L'âme de l'Exilé: Souvenirs des Voyages de Monseigneur le Duc d'Orléans* (Paris: Librarie Plon, 1927)

Regolo, L., *Jelena: Tutto il racconto della vita della regina Elena di Savoia* (Milano: Simonelli Editore, 2002)

—, *Marie-José de Savoie, La reine de mai* (Bruxelles: Éditions Racine, 2001)

Remak, J., *Sarajevo: The Story of a Political Murder* (London: Weidenfeld and Nicolson, 1959)

Rodd, R., *Social and Diplomatic Memories, 1902–1919* (London: Edward Arnold, 1925)

Rodriques, A. P., 'Captives—The Duchesses of Aosta and the Nazis', *Royalty Digest Quarterly*, 2 (2013): 13–19.

—. 'Prince Dom Luis Filipe of Portugal and the Regicide of 1908,' *Royalty Digest Quarterly*, (2008).

Röhl, J. C. G., *Wilhelm II: The Kaiser's Personal Monarchy, 1888–1900* (Cambridge: Cambridge University Press, 2004)

Roosevelt, T., *Selections from the Correspondence of Theodore Roosevelt and Henry Cabot Lodge, 1884–1918*. 2 vols. (New York: Scribner, 1925)

—. *The Letters of Theodore Roosevelt*, ed. by E. E. Morison et al., 8 vols. (Cambridge, Mass.: Harvard University Press, 1951–1954)

Roskill, S., *Hankey: Man of Secrets*. Volume I: 1877–1918 (London: Collins, 1970)

Salagnac, G. C., *Quatre règnes en exil ou d'Henri V à Jean III (1820–1940)* (Paris: Editions France-Empire, 1947)

Salierno, V., D'Annunzio e i Savoia (Rome: Salerno Editrice, 2006)

Salvemini, G., *The Fascist Dictatorship in Italy* (London: Jonathan Cape, 1928)

SanFelice di Monteforte, F., *I Savoia e il Mare* (Soveria Mannelli [Catanzaro]: Rubbettino, 2009.

Sassoon, D., *Mona Lisa: The History of the World's Most Famous Painting* (London: Harper Collins Publishers, 2001)

Satta, D., and Amedeo di Savoia, duca d'Aosta, *Cifra Reale* (Nove: La Compagnia del Libro, 2014)

Saunders, F. S., *The Woman Who Shot Mussolini* (London: Faber and Faber, 2010)

Saxe-Weimar, P., *Lettere di Costantino re di Grecia seguite da la mia vita sino ad oggi* (Milano: A. Mondadori, 1928)

Scarth, A., *Vesuvius: A Biography* (Harpenden, Herts: Terra Pub., 2009)

Segrè, C. G., *Italo Balbo: A Fascist Life* (Berkeley: University of California Press, 1987)

Sermoneta, V., Duchess of, *Sparkle Distant Worlds* (London: Hutchinson, & Co., 1947)

—, *Things Past* (London: Hutchinson & Co., 1929)

Seymour, M., *The Bugatti Queen: In Search of a Motor-racing Legend* (London: Simon & Schuster, 2004)

Sforza, C., *Contemporary Italy: Its intellectual and moral origins* (New York: E. P. Dutton & Co., Inc., 1944)

—, *L'Italia dal 1914 al 1944 quale io la vidi*, 3rd edition (Rome: Arnoldo Mondadori editore, 1946)

Smith, D. J., *One Morning in Sarajevo: 28 June 1914* (London: Weidenfeld & Nicolson, 2008)

Speroni, G., *Amedeo d'Aosta* (Milano: Fabbri Editori, 2001)

—, *Amedeo duca d'Aosta: La resa dell'Amba Alagi e la morte in prigionia nei documenti segreti inglesi* (Milano: Rusconi, 1984)

—, *I Savoia scomodi: La Saga degli Aosta* (Rimini: Santarangelo di Romagna, 1999)

Spiegelfeld-Lodron, Angélique, 'Ricordi della mia vita alla corte della famiglia reale' (unpublished typescript. Private family collection).

Stancioff, A., *Recollections of a Bulgarian Diplomatist's wife* (London: Hutchinson & Co., 1931)

Tavormina, C., 'Le Infermiere Volontarie CRI durante il terremoto calabro-siculo e nalla guerra di Libia,' in *La storia del nursing in Italia e nel contesto internazionale*, ed. G. Rocco, C. Cipolla and A. Stievano (Milano: Franco Angeli, 2015)

Tenderini, M. and M. Shandrick, *The Duke of the Abruzzi: An Explorer's Life* (Seattle, Wash.: The Mountaineers, 1997)

Thomas, H., *The Spanish Civil War* (New York: Harper & Brothers, 1961)

Thompson, M., *The White War: Life and Death on the Italian Front, 1915–1919* (London: Faber & Faber, 2008)

Torrigiani, A. di, *Diario di Guerra, MCMXV–MCMVIX* (Firenze, l'Arte della Stampa,

1923)

Trevelyan, G. M., *Scenes from Italy's War* (London: T.C. & E.C. Jack, Ltd., 1919)

Trevelyan, R., *Rome '44: The Battle for the Eternal City* (London: Secker & Warbury, 1981)

—, *Princes under the Volcano* (London: Macmillan, 1972)

Tutaev, D., *The Consul of Florence* (London: Secker & Warburg, 1966)

Van der Kiste, J., *A Divided Kingdom: The Spanish Monarchy from Isabel to Juan Carlos* (Stroud, Glos: Sutton Publishing, 2007)

—, *Edward VII's Children* (Stroud, Glos.: Sutton Publishing, 2004)

—. *Kings of the Hellenes: The Greek Kings 1863–1974* (Dover, N.H.: Alan Sutton, 1994)

Van Kerrebrouck, P., *La Maison de Bourbon, 1256–2004*. 2ème ed. (Villeneuve d'Ascq: P. Van Kerrebrouck, 2004)

Victoria, Queen of Great Britain, *Beloved and Darling Child: Last Letters Between Queen Victoria and Her Eldest Daughter, 1886–1901*, edited by A. Ramm (Stroud, Glos.: Sutton, 1990)

—, *Darling Child: Private Correspondence of Queen Victoria and the Crown Princess of Prussia, 1871–1878*, edited by R. Fulford (London: Evans Brothers, 1976)

Victoria, Empress Frederick of Germany, *The Empress Frederick Writes to Sophie, Crown Princess and later Queen of the Hellenes*, edited by A. G. Lee (London: Faber and Faber, 1955)

Viktoria Luise, Duchess of Hanover, *Bilder der Kaiserzeit* (Göttingen-Hannover: Göttinger Verlagsanstalt, 1969)

Villari, L., *The Liberation of Italy, 1943–1947* (Appleton, Wisc.: C.C. Nelson, 1959)

Waddington, M. K., *Letters of a Diplomat's Wife, 1883–1900* (London: Smith, Elder & Co., 1903)

Watson, D. R., *Georges Clemenceau: A Political Biography* (London: Eyre Methuen, 1974)

Waterfield, G., *Professional Diplomat: Sir Percy Loraine of Kirkharle Bt., 1880–1961* (London: John Murray, 1973)

Wheeler, M., *Still Digging: Adventures in Archaeology* (London: Pan Books Ltd., 1958)

Willingham, M., *Perilous Commitments: The Battle for Greece and Crete, 1940–1941* (Staplehurst, Kent: Spellmount, Ltd, 2005)

Wilson, A. N., *Victoria: A Life* (London: Atlantic Books, 2014)

Wilson, E. B., *Memoris of Mrs. Woodrow Wilson* (London: Putnam, 1939)

Wilson, W., *The Papers of Woodrow Wilson*, ed. Arthur S. Link et al. (Princeton, N. J.: Princeton University Press, 1966).

Woodhouse, J., *Gabriele D'Annunzio: Defiant Archangel* (Oxford: Clarendon Press, 1998)

Young, K., *Arthur John Balfour* (London: Bell, 1963)

Newspapers & Periodicals

Australia: *The Sunday Times* (Sydney)

Italy: *La Stampa, Giornale Luce, Domenica del Corriere*

France: *Le Figaro, Le Matin, Le Gaulois, Le Temps*

Great Britain: *Illustrated London News, Daily Telegraph, The Manchester Guardian, The Times, The London Gazette, The Observer; The Dundee Courier & Argus; British Pathe Films, The Graphic*

United States: *New York Times, Washington Post, Time Magazine; Colorado Springs Gazette.*

Spain: ABC (*Photo Archive*)

Websites

www.archivioluce.com

www.nuffield.ox.ac.uk/economics/history/paper14/14paper.pdf

www.campania.donorione.it/napoli.htm

www.hofburg-wien.at

www.senato.it/documenti/repository/istituzione/costituzione_inglese.pdf

Index

Members of royal families are indexed by first name and ranked by their highest title; nobles are indexed by title, and others by surname.

Friedrich III, Emperor of Germany, 44

Friedrich Leopold, Prince of Prussia, 225, 363

Fuad, King of Egypt, 255, 300

Gallotti, Barone Mario, 377

Gambetta, Léon, 15

Gandolfi, Marchese Ralph, 154

Gasparini, Jacobo, 259

Gasparri, Pietro Cardinal, 282

Gastaldi, Archbishop Alfonso, 377

Gattinara, Margherita di, 359

Gazzera, Gen. Pietro, 295

Gebhard, Prof. Karl, 358-359

Georg, Prince of Bavaria, 284

George V, King of Great Britain, 31-34, 41-42, 44-45, 47, 70, 74, 79, 81, 87-88, 123-125, 136-137, 140, 180-181, 202, 214, 227, 230, 241-242, 253, 263, 274, 282, 286, 289, 297

George VI, King of Great Britain, 283-284, 287, 289

George I, King of the Hellenes, 41, 200

George II, King of the Hellenes, 280, 298, 328, 336-337, 343, 365-366, 370-371

George, Prince of Greece, 85, 329

George, Duke of Cambridge, 36, 43, 96

George, Duke of Kent, 320, 327-328, 330, 348, 374

Geraldine, Queen of Albania, 373

Gherardesca, Valfredo della, 211

Giani, Mario, 263

Giardino, Gen. Gaetano, 223, 232

Gibson, Violet, 267

Giolitti, Giovanni, 184, 240

Giovanna di Savoia, Queen of Bulgaria, 221, 262, 277, 280, 328, 369, 373

Girouard, Sir Percy, 176

Goebbels, Joseph, 339

Gonzalo, Infante of Spain, 292

Gordon-Lennox, Lady Algernon, 299

Göring, Hermann, 316, 360

Gounod, Charles, 26, 96

Graham, Sir Ronald, 253, 258, 274

Gramont, Comte Alfred de, 88-89, 108, 121

Grandi, Count Dino, 320, 350

Graziani, Gen. Rodolfo, 285, 313, 318, 321-322, 333

Guerini, Maj., 304

Guerrieri, Guerriera, 372

Guiccioli, Marchesa Costanza, 184, 186

Guiche, Duchesse de, 159

Guillaumat, Gen. Adolphe, 295

'Gyp', 376

Haile Selassie, Emperor of Ethiopia, 312, 336-337

Hailey, Countess Andreina Balzani, 190

Hailey, Malcolm, 190

Halifax, Lord, 282

Hammick, Sir Murray, 191

Harcourt, Comte Bruno d', 254, 264, 288

Helen, Princess Nicholas of Greece, 329, 336

Helena, Princess Christian of Schleswig-Holstein, 18-19, 24, 45

Hélène de France, Duchess of Aosta, birth and childhood, 18-19, 27-33; exile and life in England, 35, 37-48; romance with Prince Eddy, 41, 47, 50-75, 79; health problems, 45-46, 79-80, 128-129, 141, 157, 186, 299, 315, 351, 371, 375-376; potential suitors, 76-78, 81-82, 84-85, 88-89; travel to Egypt and Palestine, 83-84; engagement and wedding with Duke of Aosta, 89-97; marital problems, 112, 137, 141-142, 155-157, 221, 256-257, 271;